D1737106

THE FATE OF CITIES

THE FATE OF CITIES
Urban America and the Federal Government, 1945–2000

ROGER BILES

UNIVERSITY PRESS OF KANSAS

© 2011 by the University Press of Kansas

All rights reserved

Published by the University Press of Kansas (Lawrence, Kansas 66045),
which was organized by the Kansas Board of Regents and is operated and funded by
Emporia State University, Fort Hays State University, Kansas State University,
Pittsburg State University, the University of Kansas, and Wichita State University

Library of Congress Cataloging-in-Publication Data

Biles, Roger, 1950–

The fate of cities : urban America and the federal government, 1945–2000 /
Roger Biles.

p. cm.

Includes bibliographical references and index.

ISBN 978-0-7006-1768-5 (cloth : alk. paper)

1. Urban policy—United States—History—20th century.

2. City planning—United States—History—20th century.   I. Title.

HT123.B49 2011

307.76097309'04—dc22

2010038987

British Library Cataloguing-in-Publication Data is available.

Printed in the United States of America

10 9 8 7 6 5 4 3 2 1

The paper used in this publication is recycled and contains 30 percent
postconsumer waste. It is acid free and meets the minimum requirements of the
American National Standard for Permanence of Paper for Printed Library Materials
Z39.48-1992.

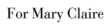

For Mary Claire

CONTENTS

PREFACE

In his landmark book, *A Nation of Cities: The Federal Government and Urban America, 1933–1965*, the historian Mark I. Gelfand traced the growing involvement of the federal government in the cities from the 1920s through the mid-1960s. By the 1960s, degenerating infrastructures, rising crime rates, the flight of the middle class to the suburbs, and recurring racial violence gave rise to widespread talk of an urban crisis in America. Reflecting the increased attention to urban problems during that tumultuous decade, government officials in Washington, D.C., involved themselves more in local affairs and appropriated greater sums of money for use in urban areas than ever before. Recognizing that a series of policies initiated earlier in the century had frequently damaged aging inner cities and promulgated rapid suburban growth, policy makers on Capitol Hill and in the White House attempted in limited fashion to make amends. According to Gelfand, the creation of the Department of Housing and Urban Development in 1965 constructed a much improved framework for addressing the problems of the cities and at the same time represented the symbolic recognition of urban America's importance. The birth of the Department of Housing and Urban Development reflected the urban flavor of President Lyndon Johnson's Great Society reform program, which sought especially to confront the challenges of poverty and race relations in the nation's declining Rust Belt cities.[1]

The Fate of Cities examines the federal government's relationship with urban America in the second half of the twentieth century. As in *A Nation of Cities*, this book considers primarily the impact of policies conceived in Washington, D.C., on the older central cities of large metropolitan areas. To be sure, federal policies inevitably affected small towns, medium-sized cities, and suburbs along with urban cores, and policy makers increasingly considered the impact of new legislation and policies on entire metropolitan regions. For much of the twentieth century, however, the impact of federal policies could be seen most emphatically in the aging cities of the nation's old Industrial Belt. Moreover, the political leadership of those cities and others active in what came to be known as the urban lobby labored strenuously to create and sustain links between the nation's capital and the embattled city halls striving to arrest inner-city decline. *The Fate of Cities* assesses the federal government's role in one of the most important developments in the post–World War II era—the abandonment and continuing deterioration of the nation's inner cities.

The story told here deals with the interplay between the ten presidents who occupied the White House between 1945 and 2000 and the members of Congress who passed the legislation that affected urban America during those years. The policies fashioned in Washington, D.C., affected welfare allocations, crime and law enforcement, education, public health, employment rates, and other important factors determining the nature of urban life, but this book deals mostly with housing and transportation policy as the most significant influences on the physical form and development of metropolitan America. The presidents varied in their commitment to the nation's communities—their actions often determined as much by partisan interests as by changing conditions in neighborhoods and central business districts in metropolises scattered across the land. Their concerns with the health of municipal budgets, the quality of middle-income and working-class housing, and the effectiveness of transportation for commuters, workers, and shoppers waxed and waned according to other domestic and foreign policy issues that intervened. Initiatives to improve the quality of urban life typically proved to be transitory, ad hoc proposals seldom receiving consistent attention and adequate funding across administrations. Some presidents announced their intentions to devise a comprehensive urban policy, but only one—Jimmy Carter—actually made a sustained effort to do so; by all accounts, he failed. Legislation passed during the Johnson years, building upon a liberal foundation constructed by Franklin D. Roosevelt's New Deal, Harry Truman's Fair Deal, and John F. Kennedy's New Frontier, constituted the high-water mark of the federal government's efforts to revive the ailing cities—followed during roughly the last third of the twentieth century by a growing interest among national policy makers in decentralization and devolution.[2]

The federal government's abandonment of the cities in the last decades of the twentieth century, manifested in both Republican and Democratic presidential administrations, owed to several factors. Hewing to their party's ideological foundations, Republican presidents from Richard Nixon to George H. W. Bush excoriated the federal government's growth, endorsed the return of authority to state and local officials, and pledged to curtail spending on costly social programs. Democrats Jimmy Carter and Bill Clinton, elected during a time of conservative reaction against Great Society liberalism, also espoused the virtues of decentralization and promised a fiscal responsibility that reduced domestic spending. Republican administrations successfully cultivated voters in the burgeoning suburbs and the Sunbelt, consigning the remaining inhabitants and elected officials of the distressed inner cities to a struggle against deterioration and economic decline; mindful of the same demographic changes and recent shifts in electoral behavior, Democratic presidents propounded a politics of moderation that closely resembled Republican nostrums and confounded the liberal members of their party who had celebrated Great Society advances. Faced with the need to arrange priorities for the allocation of scarce and often dwindling resources in an age when Americans and their elected representatives expressed concern about an expanding federal budget that seemed to defy all attempts at cost-cutting, these presidents found the cities convenient targets for economies. Downtown revitalization and neighborhood gentrification preserved pockets of affluence but fell short of reversing the loss of population, industry, and retail that fueled urban decline. Decaying inner cities continued to lose ground despite the repeated efforts of local officials and the people and organizations in Washington, D.C., fighting an uphill battle against more powerful constituencies. By the end of the twentieth century, the federal government's investment in urban revitalization seemed a romantic memory of the activist 1960s.[3]

ACKNOWLEDGMENTS

I am pleased to thank the many people who helped me during the long life of this project. It has been a great pleasure to work with the editors and staff at the University Press of Kansas—especially with Jennifer Dropkin and Monica Phillips. Fred Woodward, the esteemed director of the press, proved to be both patient and encouraging as he awaited delivery of the final draft. I was very fortunate that the press selected two distinguished historians—Carl Abbott and Jon Teaford—to review the manuscript. They both provided useful recommendations for revision, and I have tried to incorporate their suggestions in ways that would make the book more accessible to specialists and general readers alike. The finished product, I believe, is better for their careful reading of an earlier version of the manuscript.

The Fate of Cities, which is the product of many years spent studying urban policy in the post–World War II years, benefited enormously from conversations I have had with scholars interested in the development of urban America. Many of those discussions occurred during and after sessions at the biennial meetings of the Urban History Association and the Society for American City and Regional Planning History, while others occurred in less formal settings. I would especially like to thank Mark Rose and Ray Mohl, who shared their ideas about the subject during long walks and lively dinners in a host of American cities. Mark read the Nixon chapter in draft form and discussed with me at length the changing role of the federal government in urban affairs; Ray shared his encyclopedic knowledge of urban transportation history and discussed how my book would fit into the historiography. Thanks also to Kristin Szylvian and Jack Bauman, who have collaborated with me on two books, for their wisdom and passionate commitment to scholarship. Mark, Ray, Kristin, and Jack are dear friends as well. My department chairs at Illinois State University, Diane Zosky and Tony Crubaugh, have furnished travel money and moral support. Craig Fairbanks and Mary Tinney provided lodging and good company during my research visit to the San Francisco Bay area; Norm and Katie Warpinski did the same when I visited the Bush Library.

Personnel at several libraries and archives guided me through research collections; they were unfailingly helpful and friendly. At Illinois State University's Milner Library, Vanette Schwartz and Angela Bonnell went the extra mile to make my research easier. Many thanks to the staffs at the Harry S. Truman Presidential Library, the Dwight D. Eisenhower Presidential Library, the John F. Kennedy Presidential Library, the Lyndon B. Johnson Presidential Library, the National Archives II, the Gerald R. Ford Presidential Library, the Jimmy Carter Presidential Library, the Ronald Reagan Presidential Library, the George H. W. Bush Presidential Library, the William J. Clinton Presidential Library, the Library of Congress, the Chicago History Museum, the Minnesota Historical Society, the Hoover Institution at Stanford University, the Bentley Historical Library at the University of Michigan, and the Edmund S. Muskie Archives and Special Collections Library at Bates College. I was able to defray the cost of travel to research collections by receiving a Moody Grant from the Lyndon B. Johnson Foundation, a Travel Grant from the Gerald R. Ford Foundation, and an O'Donnell Grant from the Scowcroft Institute of International Affairs at the George H. W. Bush Presidential Library.

During the many research trips and countless hours pecking away at the word processor, I have been sustained in this crazy enterprise by the love and support of my family. My children, Brian, Jeanne, and Grant, remain in my thoughts daily even though they have scattered throughout the country. A good friend once told me that parents are only as happy as their unhappiest child. He was right. My wife, Mary Claire, cheerfully tolerates my idiosyncrasies and compulsive work habits. This book is dedicated to her with all my love.

THE FATE OF CITIES

INTRODUCTION

In the absence of systematic planning or government control, American cities grew rapidly and haphazardly in the nineteenth century. After the Civil War, an industrial explosion and the arrival of millions of rural Americans and European immigrants led to unprecedented urban expansion. As economic hothouses, the cities fueled the triumph of American capitalism, nurtured a favorable environment for risk-taking entrepreneurs, and provided jobs for a massive and diverse labor force. Yet the unchecked growth of the cities created serious problems. Jammed into hastily constructed dwellings, bereft of adequate sanitary facilities, and sometimes even denied potable drinking water, the working classes endured severe overcrowding in squalid tenements. The absence of environmental safeguards, inattention to public health, and the inability of municipal governments to deliver reliable services made cities inhospitable places for many residents. As trade unions struggled to improve conditions on the shop floor and government denied any role in social welfare provision, profit-minded capitalists found it easy to exploit their workers freely. City halls and state governments struggled to manage the political, economic, and social affairs of communities steeped in a privatest ethic that favored opportunity over regulation. Crusading reformers representing a variety of religious and secular social agencies battled heroically against municipal corruption, vice, crime, and disease; they fought for better housing, public transportation, education, parks and playgrounds, clean air and water, and safer workplaces. In the late nineteenth and early twentieth centuries, neither the state and local government officials responsible for urban governance nor the progressives engaged in various reform activities looked to the federal government for help with city problems.[1]

American entry into the First World War forced the federal government into the role of housing developer. Under the auspices of the Department of Labor's U.S. Housing Corporation and the U.S. Shipping Board's Emergency

Fleet Corporation, the federal government built approximately 16,000 houses as part of the effort to move workers more expeditiously into factories and shipyards. Believing that labor productivity could be increased through the improvement of working-class life, architects, urban planners, and housing reformers strove to create model communities. Looking beyond the wartime emergency, reform-minded housing professionals hoped to create working-class communities that would serve as models for future housing developments. Rather than hastily throwing together temporary domiciles that would be destroyed after the war, they convinced the officials in Woodrow Wilson's administration and the members of Congress to build permanent housing of high quality. In addition, the U.S. Housing Corporation and Emergency Fleet Corporation planners outfitted war-labor communities with schools, libraries, churches, and recreational facilities. Because construction began only five months before the armistice in November 1918, the government built few residences and completed most of the projects after the war. Despite the hopes of reformers that the model communities would be transferred to tenants as housing cooperatives, Congress ordered the wartime units sold at public auctions. A postwar investigation launched in 1919 found the U.S. Housing Corporation guilty of spending too much money on excessively elaborate housing designs and needlessly expensive amenities. Widely considered to have been an unfortunate expedient of the emergency mobilization effort, the wartime experiment in government-constructed housing ended in controversy.[2]

In the 1920s, with the exception of sponsoring the occasional conference to extol the virtues of homeownership, the federal government returned the business of housing to the marketplace. Secretary of Commerce Herbert Hoover endorsed the suburban ideal through his hardy support of the "Own Your Own Home" campaign, the Home Modernizing Bureau, the better homes in America movement, and the Architects' Small House Service Bureau, but his hortatory efforts stopped well short of countenancing outright government intervention in housing. Private construction boomed during the decade, completing an average of 883,000 new homes annually between 1922 and 1929. Residential developments mushroomed across the landscape on the outskirts of cities, and hundreds of new suburbs sprang up around the nation's metropolitan areas. Unlike the residents of the earlier streetcar suburbs who needed to reside within close proximity of fixed trolley and railroad lines, commuters living in the automobile suburbs that appeared in the 1920s could buy homes anywhere served by the expanding road network. Rather than investing in urban mass transit, state and federal governments enhanced suburbanization by subsidizing automobility at every turn. The Federal Road

Act of 1916, the first legislation to involve the federal government in highway improvement, authorized grants to states that created highway departments. The Federal Highway Act of 1921 provided aid to state roads as part of a planned nationwide system of interconnected highways and created the Bureau of Public Roads (BPR), which by 1923 was designing a national network of highways linking all cities with at least 50,000 residents. Ignoring the consequences for metropolitan development, government officials explained federal support for highway construction as simply a means of improving the nation's expanding transportation system.[3]

The cataclysmic shocks of the Great Depression sharply curtailed suburban expansion and ravaged American cities. Residential construction ground to a halt, and the shortage of money for routine housing maintenance accelerated the rate of deterioration in existing structures. Rising unemployment rates and mounting business failures led to mortgage foreclosures, evictions, and homelessness. In city after city, hundreds of idle workers stood in breadlines and queued up in front of soup kitchens and unemployment offices. With no money to feed themselves and their families, the dispossessed combed through garbage cans and congregated outside restaurants and hospitals hoping to find scraps and partially spoiled food. They erected ramshackle quarters out of undressed lumber, scrap iron, corrugated tin, wooden crates, and rusting automobile chasses on the outskirts of cities. These desolate settlements, caustically dubbed "Hoovervilles" after Herbert Hoover, the remote and aloof president who seemed indifferent to the suffering of the masses, lighted cityscapes at night as their inhabitants warmed themselves in front of makeshift fires in oil drums. With fewer and fewer people receiving paychecks, the taxes paid to city governments decreased accordingly. As city coffers emptied, local officials laid off policemen, firemen, public school-teachers, and other civil servants. Municipalities lacked the cash to meet payrolls and pay their bills, defaulted on bond issues, and teetered on the edge of insolvency. Turned away from state capitols where governors and legislators faced the same acute financial problems, desperate mayors frequently avoided bankruptcy by going hat-in-hand to banks asking for loans. In some cities, powerful financiers not only demanded additional cuts in municipal budgets as prerequisites for loans but even stipulated which positions be eliminated and whose salaries be pared.[4]

As the Depression lingered and the fiscal situation worsened in urban America, many city residents and local officials questioned whether the federal government should serve as the financial benefactor of last resort. Harold S. Buttenheim, the editor of the influential trade journal *American City*, feared that too much activity by the federal government would turn "Uncle Sam" into "Boss Sam." Other experts on municipal affairs disagreed strongly, however, urging increased expenditures for relief and inviting more federal government activity. Such urban chief executives as Mayor Fiorello H. LaGuardia of New York City and City Manager C. A. Dykstra of Cincinnati pursued federal largesse early and often in the 1930s. As Depression conditions plumbed new depths, an increasing number of embattled mayors clamored for aid from Washington, D.C. Concerned that worsening conditions in his city might lead to violence, Chicago Mayor Anton Cermak advised the Banking and Commerce Committee of the U.S. House of Representatives that "it would be cheaper for Congress to provide a loan . . . to the City of Chicago, than to pay for the services of Federal troops at a future date."[5]

Mayor Frank Murphy of Detroit took the lead in pleading the case of urban America to the federal government. Murphy's efforts to help his constituents won him national acclaim as he advocated massive government spending as the only means of saving the cities. He argued that budget balancing was "only an objective. It isn't a god, a sacred thing that is to be accomplished at all costs. It is not right to shatter living conditions and bring human beings to want and misery to achieve such an objective. . . . To sacrifice everything to balance the budget is fanaticism." At Murphy's invitation, twenty-six big-city mayors met in 1932 and decided to ask the federal government to fund a $5 billion public works program. Although unsuccessful in this venture, the petitioners cooperated to form the U.S. Conference of Mayors as a permanent urban lobby in the nation's capital. For the first time, a vehicle existed for the administrators of large cities (membership was limited to mayors of cities with populations of 50,000 or more) to present their shared concerns to the president and Congress. In the 1930s the U.S. Conference of Mayors fought many losing battles for new programs and increased funding but achieved some notable successes as well. As former city manager and New Dealer Louis Brownlow observed in the wake of this activism, "It has been said that the Federal Government has discovered the cities; it is equally true that the cities have discovered the Federal Government."[6]

Although President Hoover resisted the call for increased federal activism, he relented in authorizing some modest government activity in the housing industry that laid the foundations for later New Deal departures. Recognizing the importance of home building to economic recovery, he convened the President's National Conference on Home Building and Home Ownership in 1931 to stimulate the ailing real-estate industry. The conference issued a series of recommendations that highlighted the necessity of both private and public activity to spark housing construction, acknowledging the need for expanded government involvement to forestall a crisis that would lead to an even greater federal presence in the marketplace. Anticipating New Deal ventures, the conference called for government action to create lower interest rates, amortized mortgages, and more low-income housing. In 1932 the president signed the Federal Home Loan Bank Act, which created a credit pool for mortgage lenders to make more capital available for home purchases. The Federal Home Loan Bank Board scrupulously avoided risk, however, by denying more than 41,000 loan applications and granting only 3. By 1933 home mortgage foreclosures averaged 1,000 per day. Hoover also signed the Emergency Relief and Reconstruction Act of 1932, which authorized the Reconstruction Finance Corporation to make loans to banks, building and loan associations, and insurance companies. As with the Federal Home Loan Bank Board, the Reconstruction Finance Corporation (RFC) insisted upon high interest rates and consequently made few loans to builders. A provision of the law to encourage the building of low-income housing by limited-divided corporations produced only one project, Knickerbocker Village in New York City. Hoover's constrained efforts at federal intervention, which critics dismissed as "too little, too late," failed to improve conditions in the cities.[7]

The mayors found only a marginally sympathetic ear in the White House after the election of Franklin D. Roosevelt in 1932. Roosevelt recognized the necessity of concentrating federal funds in densely populated metropolitan areas, but he neither liked cities nor envisioned an urban renaissance generated by the New Deal. Rexford Tugwell, a key member of Roosevelt's Brains Trust and head of the Resettlement Administration, characterized the president as a "child of the country" who saw cities as nothing "other than a perhaps necessary nuisance." During the Hundred Days of intense legislative activity at the beginning of his administration, Roosevelt refused the U.S. Conference of Mayors' request that the Reconstruction Finance Corporation purchase tax delinquency and tax anticipation warrants in cities to expand short-term credit. He explained that "the less the Federal Government has to do with running a municipality in this country the better off we are going to be in the days to come." Sounding an additional warning, Roosevelt argued, "If the Federal Government started to finance cities, it would give us some kind of obligation to see that they were run right."[8]

His beliefs shaped by an idyllic childhood on a large estate in Dutchess County, New York, an abiding attachment to rural life, an interest in natural resource conservation, and a self-professed expertise in agriculture, Roosevelt favored back-to-the-land schemes as the solutions for urban problems. He took special interest in such New Deal programs as the Civilian Conservation Corps and various initiatives to resettle the cities' unemployed masses in nearby bucolic settings, heeding auto magnate Henry Ford's famous remark, "We shall solve the problems of cities by leaving the city." To implement these designs, Roosevelt chose Tugwell, who carefully outlined his goals: "My idea is to go just outside centers of population, pick up cheap land, build a whole community and entice people into it. Then back to the city and tear down whole slums and make parks of them."[9]

Tugwell foresaw a need for 3,000 such "Green Belt towns," but money existed for the completion of only 3—Greenbelt, Maryland, outside Washington, D.C.; Greenhills, Ohio, outside Cincinnati; and Greendale, Wisconsin, outside Milwaukee. The National Industrial Recovery Act authorized the creation of 100 subsistence homesteads near major cities, but the tiny communities that were built contributed little to the decentralization effort. Sprawling cities eventually absorbed many of the subsistence homesteads, and inhabitants of the others returned to the cities when economic recovery ensued. Regulated depopulation of the cities never occurred on a large scale, in great measure because of hardening congressional opposition by the late 1930s to what became known as Tugwell's "Communist towns." Moreover, as the historian Paul K. Conkin noted, "The time and expense required in developing successful communities proved to be much above earlier expectations. In a period when quick results were demanded, the community idea soon appeared to be very impractical."[10]

Although resettlement proved unwieldy, the New Deal aided cities through myriad programs that supplied financial aid for relief and public works. Federal funds made possible significant improvements in the infrastructures of hundreds of towns and cities, both through the construction of new facilities and the refurbishment of existing structures. Public works programs not only provided emergency employment for the cities' jobless, but also left a legacy in bricks and mortar that served communities for decades thereafter. The Works Progress Administration (WPA) built 500,000 miles of streets, 500,000 sewerage connections, 110,000 public buildings, 100,000 bridges and viaducts, and 600 airports in American cities. In its most expensive project, the WPA built New York City's LaGuardia International Airport, spending over $40 million and employing at one time 23,000 workers. In Chicago the WPA completed the seventeen-mile Outer Drive alongside Lake Michigan, including the Outer Drive Bridge over the Chicago River, and landscaped adjacent Lincoln Park. The agency provided Cleveland a lakefront highway, Boston the Huntington Avenue Subway, and Kansas City the better part of its downtown skyline.[11]

The Public Works Administration (PWA) employed fewer workers, operated with a smaller budget, and spent much less money than the WPA, but also left its mark on urban America. The list of its contributions included New York City's Lincoln Tunnel and Triborough Bridge, Chicago's State Street Subway, Philadelphia's Thirtieth Street Railroad Station, a remodeled state capitol and new Tennessee Supreme Court Building in Nashville, a new water supply system in Denver, and Oklahoma City's new civic center. Moreover, the PWA built hospitals, municipal buildings, port facilities, sewage systems, and 70 percent of the new public schools erected between 1933 and 1939. The federal government allowed Baltimore to combine WPA and PWA grants (the only city so favored), which made possible a massive overhaul of the city's streets, bridges, sewers, and harbor. Despite complaints about loafing at construction sites and the inefficiency of the agency's "semi-colon" boys in Washington, D.C., the PWA and WPA provided jobs to millions of idle workers and gave many downtowns a major face-lift.[12]

The New Deal also enhanced the nation's automobility. Despite harsh economic conditions, the number of motor registrations increased in seven of the ten years during the 1930s; overall, from 1929 to 1940 the number of registered automobiles increased by 4.5 million nationally. Many emergency work projects entailed highway construction, initially speeding the flow of traffic in and out of the cities' central business districts but also enhancing the accessibility of the suburbs. As a result of federal expenditures, civil engineers and local officials introduced several new innovations in automobile transit, including limited-access highways, divided expressways, and cloverleaf exchanges. Bridges designed to connect central cities with a sprawling hinterland, such as the eight-mile San Francisco Oakland Bay Bridge, became economically practical with subventions of federal funds to complement state and local dollars. Mass transit experienced a brief increase in ridership during the Depression years because of relatively cheap fares, but the New Deal's subsidization of expressway construction paved the way for the automobiles' growing importance after the return of prosperity.[13]

For the one-third of the American people "ill-housed, ill-clad, ill-nourished," whose circumstances kept them from finding suitable lodging in the private housing market, the New Deal provided a limited amount of public housing. In 1932 famed housing reformer Lawrence Veiller claimed that U.S. cities "have the worst slums in the civilized world." Nevertheless, spirited resistance to government-funded low-income housing came from the National Association of Real Estate Boards, the United States Chamber of Commerce, and banks and other lending institutions concerned about government competing with the private building industry. Section 202(d) of the National Industrial Recovery Act provided for a housing division in the PWA and encouraged the formation of local housing authorities to apply for federal grants-in-aid. Within four years the PWA had launched construction of 21,800 units in fifty-one public housing projects nationwide. Attractively designed and solidly built, PWA projects such as the Carl Mackley Houses in Philadelphia and the Harlem River Houses in New York City won lavish praise from architects, planners, and local officials—and from big-city residents who eagerly moved into unoccupied units as soon as they became available. The PWA's provision of subsidized housing stalled, however, when a U.S. district court ruled in *U.S. v. Certain Lands in the City of Louisville* that the federal government could not condemn private property under the auspices of eminent domain. A court decision issued years later overturned the *Louisville Lands* precedent, but in the meantime direct federal construction of low-income housing ceased in favor of grants-in-aid or loans to municipalities.[14]

Undaunted by the *Louisville Lands* ruling, housing reformers worked closely with Senator Robert F. Wagner (Democrat, New York) and his aide, Leon F. Keyserling, to draft legislation for a permanent public housing agency in the federal government. In 1935 and 1936 their efforts failed in Congress, largely due to the paucity of support from the White House. Admitting his lack of interest in public housing, Roosevelt flippantly told a visiting delegation from the International Housing Study Commission his solution for clearing slums from New York City's Lower East Side: "You don't need money and laws; just burn it down." According to housing expert Ernest Bohn, "the President could not get interested in tearing down a few slums in a few cities. If FDR wanted to lend his support to public housing a bill could have been passed in 1935." In 1937 the president finally provided a tepid endorsement, emphasizing the benefits to the moribund construction industry, and the Wagner-Steagall Act creating the U.S. Housing Authority became law. Congress empowered the U.S. Housing Authority to extend sixty-year loans at 3 percent interest to local housing authorities for up to 90 percent of a public housing project's cost and to underwrite the cost of construction and maintenance. Such generous conditions quickened the tempo of activity; within a year 221 communities had established local housing authorities, and by 1941 the U.S. Housing Authority had sponsored 130,000 new units in more than 300 projects nationwide. Yet the Wagner-Steagall Act represented at best a limited commitment to low-income housing. The law authorized $500 million in loans and $60 million in subsidies at a time when experts estimated the need for at least $2.5 billion just to demolish tenements in New York City alone. Housing reformers saw the 1937 law as a modest beginning.[15]

Never interested in providing federal subsidies for public housing, Roosevelt developed a New Deal housing policy designed to encourage homeownership for the working and middle classes in America. Formulated at a perilous time of unprecedented home mortgage foreclosure rates, the policy favored the residents struggling to hang onto their homes and the vulnerable workers who found purchasing a house so imposing because of high down payments and interest rates. The Home Owners Loan Corporation (HOLC), created in 1933 to refinance loans at low interest with long-term notes, assumed one-sixth of urban mortgages and halved the number of foreclosures from 1933 to 1937. The HOLC stemmed the foreclosure crisis but stopped short of fully restoring the crippled real-estate market to health. To resuscitate the homebuilding industry, what Roosevelt believed to be "the wheel within the wheel to move the whole economic engine," the New Deal created the Federal Housing Administration (FHA) in 1934. The FHA mortgage program insured loans made by private institutions, extended the length of the loans from eight to ten years to twenty to thirty years, and reduced both the amount of down payments from approximately 50 percent of the loan to 10–20 percent and the subsequent amount of monthly payments. The Federal Savings and Loan Insurance Corporation, created along with the FHA in 1934, insured savings up to $5,000 in savings-and-loan and building-and-loan associations. Having generally eliminated the need for second mortgages and having made first mortgages more accessible for potential home buyers, these New Deal agencies extended the possibility of homeownership to many more people. From 1934 to 1972, owing to the availability of FHA and Veterans Administration loans, the percentage of home owners in the American populace increased from 44 to 63.[16]

Roosevelt saw homeownership as a cherished American ideal, and his New Deal programs aided the private construction industry by subsidizing low-density, single-family housing units. With the FHA unwilling to approve loans for virtually any other type of dwelling and limiting stipends for repair of existing structures, the agency encouraged new construction on the metropolitan periphery where cheap land existed in the suburbs. The ability of homeowners to deduct the interest on their mortgage payments and local property taxes from their federal income taxes, a provision established by the inaugural federal tax code in 1913, offered another considerable incentive for Americans to buy rather than rent. Such policies offered few benefits to the urban core, where high-density multifamily dwellings predominated; the indigent and families with insufficient income to take advantage of more generous mortgage rates remained trapped in deteriorating inner-city neighborhoods. Thus, New Deal innovations hastened the movement of the middle class to the suburbs and the decay of the inner cities.[17]

New Deal housing programs also closely adhered to the principle of racial separation that had long operated in the North as well as the South. The few subsistence homesteads completed in the 1930s barred African Americans, but more significantly the HOLC and the FHA established policies of segregation that affected millions of homeowners. The HOLC refinanced mortgages based upon a uniform system of appraisal designed to predict neighborhood change. HOLC appraisers categorized neighborhoods in all cities according to the quality of housing stock as well as the occupation, income level, race, and ethnicity of the population. Large residential security maps divided each city into four types of neighborhoods by color—green, blue, yellow, and red—in descending order of preferability. By designating neighborhoods inhabited wholly by African Americans as least desirable, the HOLC created the policy of redlining. The agency maintained that its classification system did not promote segregation, and, indeed, the HOLC awarded some mortgages to homeowners in redlined neighborhoods. By making their maps available to private lending institutions, however, HOLC officials provided the means for segregationists to defend existing racial exclusionary practices. More significant in the long run, the FHA adopted HOLC appraisal techniques without emulating its egalitarian values. In short, the federal government reinforced the confinement of poor African Americans and Latinos in inner-city ghettos and barrios.[18]

Prior to guaranteeing a loan for a prospective home buyer, the FHA required an "unbiased professional estimate" that included an evaluation of the neighborhood as well as the property itself and the credit worthiness of the borrower. Expressing concern with "inharmonious racial or nationality groups," the FHA refused to recommend loans in redlined neighborhoods and urged property owners to adopt restrictive racial covenants. (Subsequent to the U.S. Supreme Court's 1948 decision in *Shelley v. Kraemer*, which ruled such covenants unenforceable, the FHA disavowed their use in 1950 but continued to redline predominantly black living areas.) Obviously, neither the HOLC nor the FHA broke new ground in reducing the value of real-estate on the basis of racial occupancy; private interests had been making such judgments for decades. But as the urban historian Kenneth T. Jackson noted: "For perhaps the first time, the federal government embraced the discriminatory attitudes of the marketplace. Previously, prejudices were personalized and individualized; FHA exhorted segregation and enshrined it as public policy."[19]

By the end of the Depression decade, the New Deal had created a two-tiered housing policy. The top tier, managed principally by the FHA but also by such federal agencies as the HOLC, the Federal National Mortgage Association (Fannie Mae), and the Home Loan Bank Board, generously provided mortgage insurance and other emoluments to financial institutions for the subsidization of home builders and developers. The lower tier underwrote on a much smaller scale the operation of a public housing program for the low-income families unable to compete in the private housing market. The policy enhanced suburban growth and severely limited the flow of government benefits to core cities. New Deal policies that underwrote the division of metropolitan America by social class likewise reinforced racial divisions by limiting federal support of areas whose investment value might be jeopardized by the influx of "inharmonious racial or nationality groups." Continued federal aid for road building made it easier for families to move to the suburbs. The increased federal presence in the cities during the 1930s, while providing assistance during a period of sustained economic crisis, also established precedents of seminal importance for the remainder of the twentieth century.

Mobilization for World War II ended the Great Depression and brought millions of African Americans, women, southern whites, Mexican Americans, and Mexicans into the nation's cities to work in munitions factories, shipyards, and military bases. In the century's second Great Migration, an estimated 1.6 million African Americans sought jobs in booming industrial cities outside the South. The abrupt arrival of large numbers of black workers resulted in competition for jobs and scarce living space, heightened racial tension, and riots in Harlem, Detroit, and Los Angeles. Firming up ties with cities in the South and Southwest established after the First World War, the federal government built new naval bases, air stations, and military training posts in a number of Sunbelt locations. As the historian Roger W. Lotchin has shown, the location of military bases and aircraft factories in and around Los Angeles, San Diego, and San Francisco created a series of metropolitan-military complexes in California communities. Defense workers arrived in communities that sorely lacked adequate housing, public transportation, schools, day care centers, medical clinics, sanitation facilities, and other municipal services. In the face of the wartime emergency, the federal government poured money into the cities to meet the urgent need for housing and social services. Wartime agencies in Washington, D.C., such as the Office of Civilian Defense and the Office of Community War Services established links with municipal governments and channeled federal largesse into empty local coffers; the National Housing Agency and the Division of Defense Housing Coordination similarly supervised the effort to provide lodging for defense workers.[20]

The housing shortage continued to nettle policy makers in Washington, D.C., from the prewar years of mobilization until Japan's surrender in August 1945. As early as June 1940, Roosevelt authorized the U.S. Housing Authority to build public housing for defense contractors and civilians employed by the armed forces. Named defense housing coordinator by the president in July 1940, Charles F. Palmer worked with the Defense Homes Corporation and other wartime federal agencies to help private industry meet the nation's wartime housing needs. The best efforts of Palmer and the Division of Defense Housing Coordination notwithstanding, the private housing industry proved incapable of supplying an adequate amount of affordable housing for defense workers, and U.S. Representative Fritz G. Lanham (Democrat, Texas) introduced legislation in Congress authorizing the federal government to build additional public housing. His bill stipulated that such housing could be constructed only in communities demonstrably suffering from shortages and prohibited any postwar conversion of defense housing into low-income units without the explicit approval of Congress. Roosevelt signed the National Defense Housing Act (known as the Lanham Act) on October 14, 1940, which authorized the federal government to construct temporary and permanent defense housing for civilians, noncommissioned officers, and their families. By the end of the war, a succession of housing agencies in Washington, D.C., spent over $2 billion in building 700,000 units of housing for the men and women laboring in defense industries.[21]

The disposition of wartime public housing, as mandated by the Lanham Act, proceeded haltingly. The lingering postwar housing shortage, public outrage at the government's attempts to evict veterans and their families from wartime housing projects, and disputes involving government agencies, veterans' organizations, and real-estate associations disrupted the process. The federal government also suspended disposition in 1950 due to the outbreak of the Korean War. Ten years after the conclusion of the Second World War, federal agencies had disposed of 87 percent of all wartime housing. Temporary units met a variety of fates, having been torn down, sold to private investors, rented on a short-term basis to veterans, and moved to college campuses to serve as dormitories for the rising number of postwar under-graduates matriculating under the G.I. Bill. The federal government sold most permanent units to veterans and private investors, and Congress allowed local housing authorities to assume control of approximately 2 percent of the permanent units for use as low-income public housing projects. With very few exceptions, policy makers in Washington, D.C., insisted on the eradication of wartime housing initiatives and the return to predominance of the private market.[22]

The federal government's hasty retreat from the housing field at the end of the war occurred despite the best efforts of the National Resources Planning Board (NRPB). The product of a merger between the National Planning Board and the National Resources Board in 1939, the NRPB became the principal New Deal agency dedicated to urban planning during World War II. Invoking the National Resources Board's 1937 report, *Our Cities: Their Role in the National Economy*, the NRPB proposed sweeping changes in housing and transportation, metropolitan consolidation, and unprecedented levels of cooperation among federal, state, and local governments. In 1942 the agency's Urbanism Committee offered a detailed plan for urban redevelopment and recommended the creation of a cabinet-level Department of Urbanism after the war to ensure a fair hearing for urban concerns in the federal government. Congressional conservatives bridled at the NRPB's plans for enhanced government attention to the cities after the war, imputing the agency's plans to socialist origins, and severely reduced its budget in 1942. The following year, Congress terminated the NRPB altogether. A certain amount of centralized planning may have been required to win the war, conservatives reasoned, but the return of peacetime would obviate the need for such dubious activity. Unlike in Great Britain, where the national government established firm control of postwar urban policy and created a number of new communities outside major metropolises, private interests in the United States successfully resisted the scattered and unorganized attempts to initiate comprehensive urban planning after the war.[23]

The wartime demise of the NRPB, an ambitious federal agency that conducted far-ranging studies into all areas of American urban life and advanced a daring agenda for postwar planning, reflected the rising level of concern about the growth of federal influence in the cities. Emergency conditions spawned by two world wars and a cataclysmic economic depression enhanced the role of federal agencies in local affairs, but at the same time raised determined opposition to future government involvement in metropolitan development. The business community's jeremiads against New Deal and wartime initiatives in urban America belied the fact that the federal government by 1945 had intervened more to bolster existing institutions and to continue ongoing changes than to undermine those forces. In helping to create a two-tiered housing policy, federal bureaucracies directed tiny sums of money to low-income housing while bestowing upon the private housing market a cornucopia of grants, loans, mortgage assistance, tax incentives, and other forms of capital guaranteed to nurture the real-estate industry as never before. Far from mandating public policies that forced decentralization upon a resistant American populace, the benefits showered upon suburbs rather than cities by the federal government underwrote well-worn paths of metropolitan development established in previous decades. Federal agencies parceled out dollars to inner cities via means-tested programs administered by visible public entities while funneling much greater—but less visible—subsidies to private institutions for the use of the suburban middle class. What would the federal government do in the second half of the twentieth century as the gap continued to widen between the declining inner cities and the comparatively affluent suburbs? Having played a significant role in the worsening fate of the cities, how would federal officials respond to cries for more equity in the decades following the Second World War?[24]

1

THE FAIR DEAL AND THE CITIES

After Franklin D. Roosevelt's death on April 12, 1945, Harry Truman assumed the presidency without a coherent urban policy but with a broad commitment to continue his predecessor's liberal domestic agenda. President Truman promised to craft his Fair Deal program according to the existing New Deal model, which he had faithfully supported before entering the White House. As a U.S. senator from Missouri, Truman explained, he had consistently voted for New Deal legislation both out of party loyalty and out of a conviction that such progressive measures truly benefited the American people. In 1937 he had supported the landmark Wagner-Steagall Housing Act, despite heated opposition from real-estate and banking interests. As the influential chairman of the Senate Committee to Investigate the National Defense Program, Truman led the crusade to curtail profiteering in defense-related business activity and thereby acquired a greater appreciation of housing shortages in the nation's cities. During his 1944 campaign for the vice presidency, he repeatedly predicted that the problem of inadequate housing and the need for urban redevelopment would confront the United States in the postwar era. "The heart of a community is its housing," he asserted in November 1944, and only a commitment to housing by the federal government could "secure the greater welfare of the individual citizen."[1]

As part of his pledge to sustain New Deal reform, Truman's interest in progressive policies that favored urban populations reflected his awareness of the political importance of the nation's largest cities. Much of the support for Franklin D. Roosevelt's initiatives emanated from the cities hardest hit by the Great Depression, a reflection of the fact that many of the New Deal's relief, recovery, and reform programs focused on those localities. In short, the elevation of the Democratic Party to majority status rested largely on an urban base. The shift of the urban electorate to the Democratic Party, which began with Al Smith's candidacy in 1928 and accelerated during the years of the Roosevelt presidency, revolutionized American presidential politics in the twentieth century. Having tallied the voting results of the nation's twelve largest cities from 1920 to 1948, the political scientist Samuel J. Eldersveld concluded that Democratic triumphs in the electoral college depended upon their margins of victory in those metropolises. In fact, Eldersveld noted, the Democrats would have lost the presidency in 1940, 1944, and 1948 without the substantial pluralities won in those dozen cities. Although he articulated no systematic approach to the solution of urban problems during his presidency, Truman at least understood the political importance of attending to the concerns of the voters residing in America's largest cities.[2]

On September 6, 1945, Truman sent to Congress his 16,000-word Message on Reconversion, which included a detailed list of twenty-one proposals outlining the fundamentals of his Fair Deal reform program. (Underscoring the continuity between the New Deal and the Fair Deal, Truman chose Franklin Roosevelt's principal speechwriter, Samuel H. Rosenman, to draft the message.) Although his design for reconversion included no explicit policy to deal comprehensively with the problems of America's cities, the eleventh proposal dealt with the critical postwar necessity of federal support for housing, slum clearance, and other forms of urban reclamation. Yielding to private enterprise the primary role in saving the cities, Truman nevertheless asserted the need for significant federal aid to stimulate redevelopment. He announced as his program's principal goal a decent home for every American family. "The people of the United States, so far ahead in wealth and productive capacity, deserve to be the best housed in the world," he intoned. "We must begin to meet that challenge at once."[3]

As Truman sought to keep the New Deal alive after the war, federal policy toward the cities developed at the outset of the Cold War when the numbing fear of nuclear warfare figured in the calculus of federal policy makers. Not long after the United States had leveled much of Hiroshima and Nagasaki, military and civilian officials in Washington feared that the downtowns of large U.S. cities offered the best targets to Soviet bombers. Metropolitan decentralization, a process already begun throughout the country earlier in the century and certain to continue after the war, seemed to dovetail with national security interests. The War Production Board built large defense factories on the outskirts of U.S. cities during the Second World War, locating the Kaiser Steel plant thirty-five miles outside of Los Angeles, for example, and the Willow Run bomber facility seventeen miles outside of Detroit. "We cannot afford *not* to disperse our cities," warned Tracy B. Augur, past president of the American Institute of Planners, in 1948. "If we delay too long, we may wake up some morning and find out that we haven't any country, that is, if we wake up at all that morning."[4]

At a time when war between the United States and its communist foes dominated public discourse, metropolitan decentralization meant not only the opportunity to save lives but also to preserve strategically vital industrial and research facilities crucial to the expanding military-industrial complex. Research laboratories and factories needed to be scattered and situated far from central business districts, military and civilian officials cautioned. Accordingly, the federal government built generous incentives into policies that encouraged businessmen to select suburban locations over urban ones and awarded tax breaks to contractors who built factories on the urban periphery. The military awarded defense contracts to firms that operated a long way from "nuclear ground zeros," thereby identifying themselves as good risks to survive atomic strikes launched by the nation's enemies. The federal government sent a clear message to potential clients in search of lucrative contracts when its publications asked, "Is your plant a target?" Skyrocketing federal expenditures on scientific research and technology promised huge rewards to corporations that heeded the call for metropolitan dispersal.[5]

The federal government's underwriting of manufacturing decentralization had important consequences in a number of areas of American life. The attraction of high-paying, defense-related jobs to the suburbs contributed to the segregation of metropolitan regions by class and race. Losing industrial jobs and failing to compete successfully for military contracts, inner cities found themselves saddled with growing numbers of unemployed blue-collar workers. While encouraging suburbanization, policies in Washington also redounded to the benefit of some cities and the detriment of others. As defense dollars streamed into the rapidly growing Sunbelt, the Pacific Northwest, and New England, metropolitan areas surrounding San Diego, Seattle, and Boston prospered especially. Such Sunbelt communities as Phoenix, Houston, San Diego, Dallas/Ft. Worth, and San Antonio enjoyed unprecedented growth and prosperity as members of the postwar "Gunbelt." In the Midwest, by contrast, the flight of industry after the war leached the economic vitality from Detroit, Milwaukee, Cleveland, Pittsburgh, and other Rust Belt cities whose factories had earlier fueled the nation's rise to industrial preeminence. According to some observers, the tilt from Rust Belt to Sunbelt can perhaps best be seen in Los Angeles surpassing Chicago as the nation's "second city." Demographic and economic shifts had political consequences as well, for the increase in the number of congressional seats in the Sunbelt meant a corresponding rise in the number of Republicans and conservative

Democrats in Congress—legislators whose predispositions favored suburban interests at the expense of inner cities.[6]

While national security concerns assumed great importance for Truman at the close of the Second World War, a number of insistent domestic issues also demanded his immediate attention—none more so than the severe housing shortage that had plagued the American people for years. The collapse of the construction industry during the Great Depression and the inattention to homebuilding and maintenance during the war left the nation's housing stock depleted by 1945. Returning servicemen vied for scarce housing with workers who had left their rural origins in search of wartime employment and remained in crowded metropolises after V-J Day. Big-city newspapers recounted a series of horror stories in which discharged soldiers and sailors, as well as workers and their families, struggled to find affordable housing— or in many instances, any housing at all. An advertisement in an Omaha newspaper listed as real estate an oversized ice box, seven by seventeen feet, that could be fixed up for habitation. In Chicago, where officials estimated the number of homeless veterans at 100,000, the local government sold old streetcars for conversion into makeshift homes, and a newlywed couple in New York City lived in the display window of a downtown department store before finding an apartment. San Francisco residents unable to find suitable lodging lived in cars parked on city streets and used the restrooms in the public library. Such sensational stories, many of which involved the shabby treatment of veterans, quickly made housing a combustible political issue that Truman could ill afford to ignore.[7]

On October 15, 1945, John W. Snyder, director of the Office of War Mobilization and Reconversion (OWMR), announced the removal of wartime restrictions on building materials as the administration's initiative to spark home construction. A wealthy St. Louis banker and longtime friend of the president who preached the virtues of free enterprise, Snyder eagerly terminated government regulation of the housing industry. The cessation of wartime controls proved a disaster, however, as investors promptly built retail outlets, bars, bowling alleys, and luxury homes but very little affordable housing. Bowing to the pressure from veterans' organizations, a chastened Snyder called for a resumption of price controls. On December 12 Truman mandated the use of no less than 50 percent of all construction materials for residential housing, limited the cost of all new homes to $10,000, and formed within OWMR the Office of Housing Expediter (OHE) to address the many facets of the housing crisis immediately. The OHE also assumed the responsibility for the rent control program that had been administered during the war by the Office of Price Administration (OPA), which ceased operation completely in 1947.[8]

Truman chose as housing expediter Wilson W. Wyatt, who had gained national acclaim as the mayor of Louisville, Kentucky (1941–1945), for his pioneering work in city planning and slum clearance. Turning down a lucrative position at a corporate law firm, Wyatt accepted the job when Truman pledged his unqualified support and guaranteed the housing expediter extraordinary powers to demolish administrative bottlenecks, unravel red tape, and bypass unresponsive bureaucracies. Quoting famed Chicago architect and planner Daniel H. Burnham, Truman exhorted Wyatt to "make no little plans" and assured him that he would be empowered to "use every agency and every resource of the Government." A few weeks later, the president underscored his support for Wyatt when he named him successor to John B. Blandford Jr. as administrator of the National Housing Agency (NHA).[9]

Wyatt spent several weeks studying the problem and formulating a plan for jump-starting the moribund housing industry. "It will take a dynamic program to achieve this goal," Wyatt warned the president. "Neither business-as-usual, labor-as-usual, building-as-usual, nor government-as-usual will suffice." The housing expediter recognized the intense pressure on the government to surrender wartime controls, yet he argued that private business would only build homes beyond the reach of most veterans; government intrusion on behalf of consumers seemed necessary. On February 8, 1946, Truman pledged his wholehearted support to Wyatt's Veterans' Emergency Housing Program, which set as its goal the completion of 2.7 million homes in the next two years—1.2 million units in 1946 and 1.5 million units in 1947. (The completion of 1.2 million new homes in 1946 would equal six times the average output for 1944 and 1945.) The legislation endorsed by the president also included sales and rental preferences for veterans, a continuation of wartime rent control, government subsidies to encourage the production of scarce building materials, and RFC loans for the manufacture of prefabricated housing.[10]

The opposition to the veterans' emergency housing bill, which was introduced by Congressman Wright Patman (Democrat, Texas), foreshadowed the arguments made repeatedly in the post–World War II era by conservative critics fearful of an expanded role for the federal government in urban affairs. Calling for an end to wartime controls, they characterized the legislation as inimical to the country's free enterprise system. Such Republican congressmen as Jesse Wolcott of Michigan and Frederick C. Smith of Ohio railed against government subsidies and predicted inefficiency, waste, and cronyism

as the natural consequences of an expanded federal bureaucracy; they likewise contended that private industry would be more than capable of fulfilling
the nation's pressing need for more housing if left alone. Republican Senator
John Bricker of Ohio commented caustically on Wyatt's appointment as
"housing czar," saying: "The very name is repulsive to the American public
and yet is typical of the bureaucratic approach toward the people of America—that they must be pushed around, directed, restricted and regulated."
President Truman closely followed the bill's progress in Congress, urging senators and representatives to pass the legislation with minimal amendments.
The final measure passed by Congress on May 13 contained few changes, and
the president signed the bill into law on May 22. An exultant Wilson Wyatt
noted that passage of the Veterans' Emergency Housing Act of 1946 shifted
his program into "high gear."[11]

At the same time that Congress approved emergency measures for
veterans' housing, the Truman administration also sought comprehensive
housing legislation in keeping with the goals articulated in the president's
Fair Deal manifesto of September 1945. In November of that year, Senators
Robert F. Wagner (Democrat, New York), Allen J. Ellender (Democrat,
Louisiana), and Robert A. Taft (Republican, Ohio) introduced a housing bill
encompassing virtually all of Truman's stated objectives. The Wagner-
Ellender-Taft (W-E-T) bill enhanced the lending capabilities of home loan
banks, liberalized Federal Housing Administration (FHA) terms for home
insurance, provided unprecedented levels of federal aid for urban redevelopment, and authorized the construction of 500,000 units of public housing in
four years. The bipartisan sponsorship of the bill by three noted experts on
housing gave reformers hope that passage of such sweeping legislation might
be politically feasible. As the driving force behind the 1937 Wagner-Steagall
Act and principal legislative draftsman of much of the New Deal, Robert
Wagner had more experience in housing legislation than anyone else on Capitol Hill. Allan Ellender passionately believed in the necessity of public housing to aid poor people in the growing slums of the urban South, and his advocacy guaranteed considerable support among southern legislators. A vocal
critic of the New Deal and the recognized leader of conservative Republicans
in Congress, Robert A. Taft vehemently rejected much of Truman's Fair Deal
but embraced the need for public housing as a necessity for America's troubled cities. Convinced that public housing would be administered by local
authorities, that the federal government's role would be limited to providing
funding, and that the private housing industry would continue to predomi-
nate, Taft lent his name to the path-breaking bill. When the Senate passed

the W-E-T measure on April 15, 1946, by a simple voice vote, liberals hoped that real housing reform might be possible in the heady days following the war.[12]

The W-E-T bill foundered in the House of Representatives, however, where conservative Republicans wielded more power than their counterparts in the Senate. The influential business groups arrayed against the legislation included the National Association of Real Estate Boards (NAREB), the National Association of Home Builders (NAHB), the United States Chamber of Commerce, and the Home Building Industry Committee. Jesse Wolcott of Michigan, a consistent opponent of public housing with close ties to the real-estate lobby, led a two-month filibuster in the House Banking and Currency Committee that prevented formal hearings on the bill. A canny parliamentarian, Wolcott employed a series of delaying tactics that kept the bill bottled up in the committee and off the House floor, where it may well have garnered enough votes for passage. At one point, a Republican member of the House Banking and Currency Committee invoked an arcane rule that kept an infuriated Senator Taft from testifying on behalf of the bill. Truman's attempts to intercede failed, and on July 31 the committee voted 12 to 10 not to report the W-E-T bill to the House floor. At a time when public opinion polls demonstrated considerable acceptance of an expanded role for government in the provision of affordable housing, the Seventy-ninth Congress adjourned in 1946 without passing substantive housing legislation.[13]

Meanwhile, the initial optimism regarding the Veterans Emergency Housing Program dissipated as conservative forces again gained the upper hand. Wyatt had immediately demanded an end to "nonessential" construction so that scarce materials would be available for veterans' housing, but for a variety of reasons very few units became available in the summer and autumn months of 1946. The housing industry suffered horribly because of the rash of strikes that swept the nation in the postwar months, with the resultant work stoppages in the lumber and steel industries especially damaging to builders; shortages of such materials as electrical wiring, gypsum board, brass pipe, and nails also slowed construction schedules. As idle workers leaned on their shovels, empty foundations and partially completed structures reminded the public that the impressive numbers of housing "starts" periodically reported by Wyatt were not translating into available lodging for an impatient public. By the end of summer, the construction industry had completed only 190,000 new dwellings. The disappointing performance of the Veterans Emergency Housing Program lent credibility to the charges of inefficiency and incompetence in the Truman administration leveled by the

Republicans in the 1946 election campaign—as evidenced in their slogan, "Had Enough?"[14]

From the outset, Wyatt hoped that breakthroughs in the infant prefabricated housing industry would offset the slowdowns at construction sites, over which he could exercise little control. Accordingly, he applied for $90 million in loans from the RFC, the government-owned corporation charged with providing capital to American businesses in the form of investments that would benefit the economy. George E. Allen, the director of the RFC and a conservative Mississippi banker who took seriously his responsibility to safeguard the taxpayers' money, refused to approve the loans because he deemed them questionable investments. Citing "insufficient equity" offered by the industrial house manufacturers seeking the loans, Allen also noted that these new businesses lacked the successful track records that would justify such speculation—despite the fact that the First National Bank of Chicago had agreed to lend the Lustron Corporation, which specialized in the large-scale production of prefabricated homes, $20 million if the government would provide a 90 percent guarantee. President Truman met for forty-five minutes with Wyatt and Allen, allowing both men to plead their cases, and then promised to evaluate the potential contribution of the prefabricated housing industry. Weeks went by without Truman making a decision, in large measure no doubt because continued technical problems in the industry limited output and called into question the feasibility of Wyatt's prediction that 750,000 prefabricated homes could be completed by the end of 1947. On November 28, 1946, long after the critical summer months for housing construction, Allen approved loans totaling $38 million for ten industrial housing firms (excluding Lustron).[15]

The Veterans Emergency Housing Program's troubles led to a decline in public confidence and a resultant rise in the influence of critics who questioned government's presence in the housing market. Not surprisingly, real-estate interests and private builders deplored the continuation of wartime controls and argued that major breakthroughs in the number of housing starts would come only with the restoration of free enterprise. The lobbying effort against the Veterans Emergency Housing Program, which Franklin D. Roosevelt Jr. characterized as "one of the highest-powered, most selfish lobbies known in the annals of our country," portrayed government bureaucracy as the primary impediment to the provision of housing for the American people. Even the leadership of the most influential veterans' groups in the United States sided with the real-estate lobby in blaming the government for their constituents' difficulties. Ignoring considerable support for Wilson

Wyatt's program among the rank and file of their organizations, the leaders of the Veterans of Foreign Wars, the American Legion, and AMVETS declared their fealty to private enterprise, and the American Legion called for the liquidation of the NHA.[16]

The final blow for the Veterans Emergency Housing Program came on November 9, 1946, when Truman announced the end to all price controls except on rents, sugar, and rice. Interpreting the impressive Republican successes in the congressional elections that month as a repudiation of wartime controls, the president acknowledged that ending price controls on building materials would fatally undermine Wilson Wyatt's program. Fourteen months after the end of the war, Truman argued that he had maintained price ceilings much longer than he had anticipated in the summer of 1945, and he likely expected the new Republican Congress to terminate government controls when it convened in January 1947. Unfortunately, while the case for ending price controls in the economy generally appeared undeniable, the damaging impact on the veterans' housing seemed equally certain. On November 27 Wyatt presented Truman with his program for 1947, which called for the resumption of price controls and generous RFC loans to the prefabricated housing companies, and threatened to resign if it did not receive presidential approval. In a December 3 meeting between the two men, Truman rejected the plan and accepted Wyatt's resignation. The next day, the president publicly announced the end of Wyatt's tenure, noted the staggering difficulties confronting the housing expediter at the end of the war, and formally thanked him for his service to the nation.[17]

The Veterans Emergency Housing Program built 1,003,600 nonfarm housing units in 1946, short of the goal of 1.2 million set by Wilson Wyatt at the beginning of his tenure as housing expediter. "There are really only two choices," Wyatt had told Truman in November of that year. "The country must adopt and carry through an all-out veterans' housing program—a real emergency program—or return to building as usual." The president's decision to return to building as usual, which arguably reflected the realities of the postwar political climate, left Wyatt convinced that he had not received the unqualified support the president had promised just a few months before. Housing reformers praised Wyatt's heroic efforts and attributed the failure of the veterans housing program to the regrettable impact of the real-estate and building lobbies and to the influence of conservatives in the Truman administration such as John Snyder and George Allen. Truman's desertion of Wyatt, liberals feared, called into question not only the president's commitment to housing reform but also his avowed dedication to New Deal principles. In the face of sizable Republican gains in the 1946 elections, these liberals asked pointedly whether Truman's fledgling Fair Deal would in fact include measures designed to address the nation's serious housing problems.[18]

The demise of the Veterans Emergency Housing Program and the OPA, the government agencies that administered rent control in the immediate postwar period, left the president with the problem of how to deal with the soaring costs of lodging during the critical housing shortage. Conservative critics of the veterans housing program attacked rent control with equal venom, again charging government with harmful interference in the free market and condemning the liberal assault on property rights. For his continued insistence that rent control remained necessary to offset exorbitant rents and wholesale evictions, the president earned the condemnation of real-estate interests and many landlords; on the other hand, he received the support of organized labor, the United States Conference of Mayors, the National Association for the Advancement of Colored People (NAACP), and many veterans' organizations. Recognizing the groundswell of support for an extension of rent control in some form, the Republican Congress passed a bill that provided for a "voluntary" 15 percent increase in rent but withdrew from Frank Creedon, Wyatt's successor as housing expediter, most of his enforcement powers. Calling the bill "plainly inadequate" but fearing that no better measure would be passed by Congress, Truman signed the Housing and Rent Act of 1947 on June 29. In a message to Congress the following day, the president said: "It is clear that, insofar as the Congress is concerned, it is this bill or no rent control at all. I have chosen the lesser of two evils." For the duration of the Truman administration, Congress passed and the president signed legislation annually that extended some form of rent control.[19]

With the charter of the NHA due to expire at the end of 1947, Truman signaled his continued commitment to housing reform by announcing a reorganization plan that would permanently maintain all of the federal government's varied programs in a single agency. Created by Franklin D. Roosevelt's executive order in 1942 and justified as a wartime necessity, the NHA had combined in one bureaucracy the FHA, Federal Home Loan Bank Board (FHLBB), Federal Works Agency (FWA), and several other government agencies involved in housing. Reformers praised Truman's initiative as what they hoped would be the first step toward creating a cabinet-level "department of urbanism." Predictably, NAREB and its allies saw the creation of the NHA as a greater concentration of power in Washington, D.C., and a concomitant loss of influence by private firms at the local level. Further, they saw the linking of the FHA's homebuilding programs for the middle class with the FWA's construction of public housing as an unhealthy marriage that would inevitably redound to the detriment of private real-estate interests. To deflect charges that the consolidated agency would centralize control further, Truman changed the name of the NHA to the Housing and Home Finance Agency (HHFA).[20]

According to a 1945 law, the reorganization plan that Truman submitted to the Eightieth Congress in 1947 could be defeated only by negative votes in both the House and the Senate. Powerful conservative forces in the House easily killed the measure and, prodded by Jesse Wolcott's Banking and Currency Committee, passed a resolution counseling the Senate to do so as well. Harry Cain (Republican, Washington) and Harry Byrd (Democrat, Virginia) spearheaded the forces opposed to the reorganization plan in the Senate, but a bipartisan coalition led by Republicans Robert Taft, Charles Tobey (New Hampshire), and Ralph Flanders (Vermont) effectively countered the real-estate lobby's dire warnings of excessive centralization. So did the fact that Raymond M. Foley, Wilson Wyatt's successor as administrator of the NHA, would likely be in charge of the new agency. A colorless bureaucrat who had served capably as administrator of the FHA before being promoted to head the NHA, Foley believed that government should work cooperatively with private enterprise and cultivated excellent relations with the real-estate and building industries during his years in Washington, D.C. He acknowledged the need for public housing construction but never in competition with the private housing industry. The reorganization plan carried by a vote of 47 to 38 in the Senate, and the HHFA became a permanent federal agency on July 27, 1947.[21]

The bipartisan cooperation reflected in the creation of the HHFA raised reformers' hopes that the comprehensive housing legislation defeated in 1946 could be passed by the Eightieth Congress in 1947. The Taft-Ellender-Wagner (T-E-W) Act (the order of the bill's sponsors changed after Taft became Senate majority leader) met no better fate than its predecessor, however, as congressional Republicans refused to support any legislation that included provisions for public housing. Despite the fact that the Senate Banking and Currency Committee passed T-E-W by a 7-to-6 margin, Taft recognized the unlikelihood that the bill would escape Jesse Wolcott's Banking and Currency Committee in the House and declined to call for its consideration on the Senate floor in 1947. In response to the public clamor for housing legislation, Wolcott called for the creation of a fourteen-member, joint congressional committee to examine the housing situation in its entirety and to determine if any merit existed in the call for government intervention.

Amid cries from Senator Wagner and his allies that the need for action had long since been established and that the committee's investigation merely constituted another frustrating delay, Wolcott's resolution passed overwhelmingly in both the Senate and the House. The creation of the investigating committee forestalled any action on housing until the legislators issued their findings on March 15, 1948.[22]

The joint congressional committee's deliberations contributed little to the national discourse on housing policy but produced two notable results: first, the time wasted and expense incurred provided Harry Truman with more ammunition with which to attack the Eightieth Congress in the 1948 presidential election and, second, the committee hearings brought national attention for the first time to the freshman senator from Wisconsin, Joseph R. McCarthy. As vice chairman of the joint committee, McCarthy exhibited the reckless behavior he would later perfect in his tainted crusade to uncover Communists in government; in 1947–1948 he badgered witnesses and cut ethical corners in the fight to protect Americans from the threat of public housing. Raking in financial contributions from the Lustron Corporation and other private housing interests, McCarthy fought a solitary campaign to keep public housing from being listed among the joint committee's recommendations. The joint committee's final report, signed by the other thirteen members, urged an increase in FHA loans, slum clearance, public housing, and the creation of a national housing policy—measures already forwarded in essentially the same form by the T-E-W bill. In his minority report, McCarthy ratified most of the joint committee's findings but objected to the inclusion of public housing.[23]

In his 1948 reelection campaign Truman hammered away repeatedly at the Republicans' obstruction of housing legislation in the preceding years. Joking that the Republicans had changed their 1928 campaign slogan of "two cars in every garage" to "two families in every garage," he characterized decent, affordable housing as a fundamental right of all Americans and affirmed that goal as a central feature of the Fair Deal. In a special housing message to Congress on February 23, 1948, he identified five housing goals for his administration—reduced building costs, enhanced rental housing construction, slum clearance, a continuation of rent controls, and the construction of 500,000 units of public housing. He pledged his unqualified support for the latest incarnation of the T-E-W bill, which its sponsors had introduced following the issuance of the joint congressional committee report on March 15, and challenged the House leadership to break the logjam in Jesse Wolcott's Banking and Currency Committee after the Senate passed the measure by acclamation on April 22. When the members of the House Banking and Currency Committee surprisingly voted 14 to 13 to recommend T-E-W, Wolcott took the fight to the House Rules Committee, where he testified against the measure. Responding to Wolcott's warning that public housing would "fashion the key to open the door to socialism in America," the conservative Rules Committee barred consideration of the bill on the House floor by a vote of 6 to 2. The conservatives opposed to public housing denied the House membership the opportunity to vote on comprehensive housing legislation for the third straight year.[24]

In June 1948, on the eve of the Republican Nominating Convention in Philadelphia, Congress hastily passed a modest housing bill offered by conservative Senator William Jenner (Republican, Indiana). The "teeny-weeny" housing bill, as Truman called it, allowed the RFC to purchase second mortgages on veterans' homes and allocated a small sum of money for veterans' cooperative housing developments. Lambasting the "slipshod legislation" for failing to address any of the five objectives he had announced in his February 23 special address to Congress, Truman nevertheless signed the bill on July 1. As the legislative session concluded and Republicans departed for Philadelphia, Truman said of the nation's housing situation: "This is one of the many jobs left unfinished by the Eightieth Congress."[25]

At the Democratic Nominating Convention later that month, Truman mocked the Republican platform drafted a few weeks earlier for enumerating a series of platitudes that bore no resemblance to the party's actual beliefs. The "do nothing" Eightieth Congress had had every opportunity to pass laws encompassing the principles espoused by the Republicans, Truman charged, and had failed to do so—as in the case of public housing and slum clearance, which the party suddenly embraced at the convention after years of staunch opposition. The president announced that he was calling Congress into a special session so that the Republican leadership could prove that their platform amounted to more than empty campaign rhetoric. Addressing the special session two weeks later, he specifically called for passage of the T-E-W bill and emergency legislation on inflation as two urgent matters that could not wait until 1949. Knowing full well that Jesse Wolcott and his minions in the House made the passage of T-E-W virtually impossible, Truman intended to highlight for the voters the gap between Republican campaign promises and the party's legislative record. The Republican leadership resolved to forestall consideration of the T-E-W bill in both chambers of Congress during the special session, while Taft agreed for the sake of party unity not to introduce the measure until 1949.[26]

Still, public pressure for housing legislation kept the issue alive in the special session. Two liberal Republican senators, Ralph Flanders of Vermont and Charles Tobey of New Hampshire, challenged Taft's leadership by championing a bill that included provisions for public housing and slum clearance. Joseph McCarthy introduced an amendment to the Flanders-Tobey bill that deleted public housing and slum clearance while adding incentives for the construction of inexpensive houses and apartments. With Taft's imprimatur, the bill with the McCarthy amendments passed the Senate by a vote of 48 to 36 and, at the urging of Jesse Wolcott, passed in the House by a whopping margin of 352 to 9. On August 10 Truman signed the Housing Act of 1948, which he called "an emasculated housing bill," because it would provide some help in meeting the housing shortage. At the same time, he noted that the Republicans had "deliberately neglected" the urban poor by eliminating public housing and slum clearance. Throughout the rest of the presidential campaign, Truman pointed to the Housing Act of 1948 as a prime example of how the Republicans had shirked their responsibilities in the special legislative session—and specifically of how the party's failure to support meaningful housing reform that aided the poor and working class as well as the middle class revealed its indifference to the plight of ordinary Americans. Truman won reelection by slightly more than 2 million votes, and the nation's twelve largest cities contributed 1.4 million of the victory margin. Clearly, housing reform served as an important issue in the populist campaign that returned Truman to the White House in 1948.[27]

Truman claimed that his reelection constituted a mandate for real housing reform and immediately declared his unwavering support for the latest version of T-E-W. The bill proposed in 1949, which proclaimed as its goal "a decent home and suitable living environment" for every American family, provided in Title III for the building of 810,000 units of low-income housing over the next six years, an impressive rate of 135,000 units per year that dwarfed the earlier public housing appropriations of the 1930s and 1940s. Title I of the law offered generous subsidies for urban redevelopment whereby slum clearance would elevate depressed property values, boost property tax revenues, and encourage private investment in beleaguered central business districts. Local Public Agencies (LPAs) could use federal funds to purchase and clear slum property, a process that would inevitably raise the sale price above the market value of the land. The federal government would pay two-thirds of the difference, known as the "write down," with the LPAs being responsible for the remaining one-third. The benefits of the "write down" would accrue to real-estate moguls and developers who would otherwise not be inclined to take a chance on revitalizing anemic central business districts, and the cities would recoup their investment through the collection of higher tax revenues generated by the property improvements. The bill contained something for everyone—unprecedented amounts of public housing for liberals and, under the rubric of urban redevelopment, vast money-making opportunities for downtown developers—all in the name of alleviating the housing shortage while simultaneously saving America's cities.[28]

After T-E-W quickly passed the Senate Banking and Currency Committee, Paul H. Douglas (Democrat, Illinois) led the liberal forces in support of the bill with its unprecedented budget for public housing and slum clearance. Assigned the job of floor manager for Title I, the former professor of economics at the University of Chicago lectured his colleagues about slums as a "moral cancer, a health hazard and an economic loss" and hung enlarged photographs of some of the nation's worst slums throughout the Senate chamber. To dramatize further the intolerable conditions prevalent in slum areas, Douglas guided six senators on a highly publicized tour of some of the District of Columbia's most blighted neighborhoods, including the infamous "Schott's Alley" area located within one hundred yards of the Senate Office Building. Title I carried without significant amendment.[29]

The bill's commitment to public housing generated the usual opposition, however, as conservatives railed that "socialized housing" meant yet another step in the erosion of local control and the insidious expansion of federal power in Washington. The attack on public housing in the Senate came indirectly in the form of an amendment offered by two Republicans, John Bricker of Ohio and Harry Cain of Washington. The Bricker-Cain Amendment, introduced by two steadfast opponents of civil rights, prohibited any racial or ethnic discrimination in any of the housing units constructed under the bill's auspices. The Republicans knew that such a proviso would be unacceptable to southern Democrats, many of whom had originally allied with northern liberals in support of the measure. To the charge that the bill could not pass saddled with his amendment, Bricker smugly responded: "If it does not pass, there is something wrong with the bill, something wrong with the Constitution of the United States, or something wrong with the platforms of the Democratic and Republican parties, both of which parties came out frankly and without any equivocation in favor of civil rights."[30]

Douglas and other liberals agonized over whether to vote for the amendment, thereby affirming their commitment to racial equality and almost surely defeating the housing bill, or to increase the possibility of attaining meaningful housing legislation by rejecting a measure that articulated principles they

held dear. Just before the vote on the Senate floor, Douglas spoke against the
Bricker-Cain Amendment. He excoriated the cynicism underlying the
amendment, noting indignantly Bricker's avowed intention of voting against
T-E-W even if his amendment carried. "As for me," Douglas concluded, "the
choice is clear. I want slum clearance and housing for four million people. I
want it for all groups, regardless of race, creed, or color." Southern Democrats and northern liberals followed Douglas's lead, defeating the Bricker-
Cain Amendment 49–31; the next day, T-E-W passed in the Senate by a 57 to
13 margin.[31]

In the House, the perennial graveyard of comprehensive housing legislation, the reconstitution of committees after the 1948 election gave housing
advocates hope that the outcome might be different than in past years. When
the House Banking and Currency Committee approved T-E-W by a straight
party vote, 15 to 7, and the Rules Committee reported the bill to the House
floor by a vote of 8 to 4, the real-estate lobby intensified its ongoing campaign against legislation that contained public housing. *Headlines*, the news-
letter of NAREB, condemned the supporters of T-E-W as "fellow travelers"
and urged legislators to vote against "the most dangerous piece of legislation
of our generation"; the organization's president termed the bill "pure socialism." Truman vigorously condemned the real-estate lobby in a letter to
Speaker of the House Sam Rayburn (Democrat, Texas) that was subsequently released to the press, calling its members "shortsighted" and "utterly
selfish" and saying that he had never seen "a more deliberate campaign of
misrepresentation and distortion." The heated debate on the House floor
lapsed into comical violence when eighty-three-year-old Adolph Sabath
(Democrat, Illinois) and sixty-nine-year-old E. E. Cox (Democrat, Georgia)
exchanged punches before being separated. After the defeat of an amendment to eliminate public housing, the bill passed by a vote of 227 to 186; Truman signed the Housing Act of 1949 on July 15.[32]

According to Richard O. Davies, the most careful student of housing policy in the Truman administration, the passage of the Taft-Ellender-Wagner
Housing Act constituted the high-water mark of Truman's Fair Deal. Despite
the fact that the Democratic Party controlled both houses of Congress after
the 1948 election, the president proved unable to obtain the other major goals
in his reform agenda—including a national health program, a permanent
Fair Employment Practices Commission, a full employment bill, increased
federal aid to education, agricultural reform, expanded federal control of
public power, and repeal of the antiunion Taft-Hartley Act. The 1949 housing law's significance also stemmed from having established, in Truman's

words, "the necessity for appropriate Federal aid to supplement the resources of communities." The measure set the nation along a path of slum
clearance and urban redevelopment, with the federal government as a key
facilitator for private investment, and expanded Washington's commitment
to the construction of low-income housing. The potential sweep of these initiatives, especially the possibility that the federal government would authorize the construction of significant amounts of public housing, explained the
vigor with which private real-estate and housing interests battled against
comprehensive housing reform during the Truman years.[33]

As soon as Congress passed the law, several cities applied for Title I
and—to a much lesser degree—Title III funds. Indeed, for years preceding
the adoption of the legislation, these municipalities had been preparing
local ordinances, arranging the necessary support within state governments,
drawing up redevelopment blueprints, and marshaling their resources in the
expectation of a dramatic increase of available capital for slum clearance.
As historian Robert M. Fogelson noted, T-E-W "provided the money for
urban redevelopment without which the state enabling acts were worth-
less." In New York City, Robert Moses, chairman of the city's postwar public works program, assembled political coalitions during the postwar years
that allowed him to reconfigure the cityscape dramatically after 1949.
Redevelopment-minded developers and businessmen in Chicago secured
passage in the Illinois General Assembly of the Blighted Area Redevelopment
Act of 1947 and the Relocation Act of 1947 that not only laid the groundwork
for massive slum clearance but, according to historian Arnold R. Hirsch,
served as models for Title I of the federal law passed two years later. In
St. Louis, famed planner Harland Bartholomew worked with Mayor Aloys
Kaufmann, the editors of the *St. Louis Post-Dispatch*, labor leaders, church
groups, downtown businessmen, and the local chapter of the League of
Women Voters to identify funding sources in anticipation of national legislation. Immediately following passage of T-E-W, the Detroit Housing Commission identified four sites in the urban core for slum clearance projects
(three in predominantly African American neighborhoods) and eight tracts
on vacant land in white neighborhoods.[34]

The speed with which these municipalities responded demonstrated a
greater interest in slum clearance than in low-income housing construction,
to be sure, and underscored how the primary rationale for an expanded federal presence in the cities rested upon an uneasy coalition between developers and reformers. The former sought to elevate depressed property values
and encourage private investment in declining central business districts,

while the latter savored the promise of 810,000 units of public housing. Housing reformers, planners, big-city mayors, bankers, and builders all supported the bill, leading Catherine Bauer, the influential author of *Modern Housing*, to observe wryly: "Seldom has such a variegated crew of would-be angels tried to sit on the same pin at the same time." The law mandated that redevelopment be "predominantly residential," in that at least 50 percent of either the buildings cleared or the new construction had to be residential—a requirement that proved elastic in the coming years. Seduced by the prospect of a low-income housing bonanza, reformers supported what ultimately turned out to be largely a vehicle for constructing office buildings, parking garages, swank apartment complexes, and shopping centers. Despite the benefits of the write down, the cost of construction, taxes, and other expenses drove the affordability of the new housing beyond the reach of the working and middle classes. The quest for the "slumless city," observed New Haven Mayor Richard Lee, proved to be much more important to big-city officials than the provision of low-income housing.[35]

The record on public housing construction during the Truman years turned out to be disappointing to hopeful reformers. Concerned about the availability of materials as the United States assumed control of the United Nations army in Korea, the president stipulated in July 1950 that only 30,000 low-income housing units be completed by the end of the year and that the FHA reduce its insurance outlay for new home construction by half. The private housing industry, which had faltered immediately after World War II, set construction records in 1950–1951, and its spokesmen argued that low-income housing was no longer necessary. Congress cut allocations for public housing to 50,000 units in fiscal year 1951 and 35,000 units in fiscal year 1952. By December 1951, more than two years after the passage of T-E-W, construction had commenced on just 84,600 public housing units—a far cry from the 135,000 units per year authorized by the law. By the time that Truman left the White House in 1953, local housing authorities had started or completed a paltry total of 156,000 units and contracted for just 53,000 more.[36]

Liberals suffered another setback when they attempted to secure legislation for cooperative housing. Intended for the "forgotten third" of Americans whose modest earnings fell short of the amount needed to purchase a home in the private real-estate market but exceeded the eligibility standard for low-income housing, cooperatives gained a following during the 1930s in such New Deal agencies as the Resettlement Administration and the Farm Security Administration. After World War II, their appeal increased among organized labor, women's groups, and such veterans' organizations as the American Legion and the Veterans of Foreign Wars. Housing reformers commissioned architects such as Frank Lloyd Wright and Garett Eckbo to design "consumer cooperatives" that embodied the principles of community planning. Although the participation of left-wing planners and architects drove away some supporters, the potential of cooperative housing for the working class proved strong enough that two southern Democrats (Representative Wright Patman of Texas and John Sparkman of Alabama) introduced bills in 1949 for federal aid to cooperative societies. President Truman endorsed the legislation, which failed in congressional committees.[37]

With the president's continued support, the legislative struggle for cooperative housing resumed the following year. Title III of the Housing Act of 1950 created the National Mortgage Corporation for Housing Cooperatives, an independent agency empowered to grant fifty-year low-interest loans to cooperatives. As they had done in 1949 over the issue of public housing, the powerful real-estate, homebuilding, and banking lobbies again combined forces in opposition. Spokespersons for such organizations as NAREB, the National Association of Home Builders, the American Bankers Association, and the United States Savings and Loan League variously assailed cooperatives as communistic, socialistic, and un-American; further, they raised a series of questions about which families would be categorized as middle income in order to be qualified for the purchase of cooperatives. When the chairman of the Federal Reserve Board opposed creation of the National Mortgage Corporation for Housing Cooperatives because of the threat he argued it might pose to the operation of the FHA and the Veterans Administration (VA), Senator Paul Douglas rejoined that perhaps such federal agencies had outlived the purposes for which they had been created in the Depression era—a suggestion that mortified the banking and building industries that had become enamored of the federal government's progrowth policies embodied in the FHA and VA. Senator John Bricker successfully introduced an amendment that eliminated Title III, and the Housing Act of 1950 became law without any mention of federal aid to cooperatives.[38]

Nor was it clear to reformers that the slum clearance and urban redevelopment provisions of T-E-W would effectively address the growing problem of racial segregation in America's cities. Beginning in the 1930s, federal policies had underwritten the rapid decentralization of metropolitan America and simultaneously bolstered residential racial segregation. Federal mortgage and taxation policies opened up for the first time the possibility of home ownership for millions of city dwellers, accelerating the migration of middle- and working-class whites to the suburbs. Meanwhile, discriminatory property appraisal policies ("redlining") pioneered first by the HOLC and then widely utilized by the FHA and the VA upheld racial zoning, the use of racially restrictive covenants, and other local practices that augmented the decay of aging downtowns. As Washington increased its aid to cities after the Second World War, would local governments and private businesses be able to use enhanced federal resources to preserve racial segregation as a component of their slum clearance efforts?[39]

The task of protecting the interests of African Americans fell principally to the Race Relations Service (RRS), an agency within the federal government that originated with the attempt by Harold L. Ickes of the PWA to promote equity in New Deal programs. In 1938 Ickes's top adviser on "Negro Affairs," African American economist Robert C. Weaver, established the RRS in the USHA to safeguard against racial discrimination in the national housing program. Weaver argued forcefully in a 1940 memorandum that "public housing should not be used to extend residential segregation," but he failed to muster support within the government for such a policy and left the USHA. In 1947 the RRS moved to the HHFA, where Weaver's successor, Frank S. Horne, presided over a reduced budget and staff. Under Horne's aggressive leadership, the RRS routinely encountered indifference—and sometimes outright hostility—in its repeated demands for racial equality in the administration of the government's private and public housing programs.[40]

After the U.S. Supreme Court ruled racially restrictive covenants unenforceable in the landmark 1948 case *Shelley v. Kraemer*, FHA Commissioner Franklin D. Richards affirmed that the decision would have no impact on the agency's lending practices. He denied that it was the "policy of the Government to require private individuals to give up their right to dispose of their property as they [saw] fit as a condition of receiving the benefits of the National Housing Act." Horne vigorously disagreed, writing HHFA administrator Raymond Foley that *Shelley* raised "not only strict legal questions but also considerations of public policy and of what Mr. Justice Frankfurter in his concurring opinion termed 'good conscience' which are not adequately covered by the FHA response." Only after persistent prodding from the White House did the FHA announce in December 1949 that it would cease after February 1950 to insure property bound by racially restrictive covenants—an announcement that granted developers three months to have their applications for covenant-bound property approved before the new policy became operational. Even after the February 1950 deadline passed, the FHA dragged its feet on compliance and allowed local developers to make new homes available only to whites. At the same time, Truman stopped short of preventing federal assistance to segregated housing developments.[41]

Opponents of racially segregated housing suffered another major setback on June 3, 1950, when the U.S. Supreme Court declined to hear *Dorsey v. Stuyvesant Town*, a case originating in New York City that dealt with the right of landlords to refuse to rent to African Americans. In 1943 the Metropolitan Life Insurance Company had signed a contract with the city of New York to build Stuyvesant Town, a complex of housing units for 8,759 families, while the municipality had agreed under the 1938 state constitution to cede public streets, condemn private property, and provide tax exemptions valued at $25 million. As one of the first urban redevelopment partnerships between private industry and state and local governments, the agreement between Met Life and New York City foreshadowed the kind of cooperative action authorized by the T-E-W law in 1949. On June 26, 1947, as the first occupants prepared to move into Stuyvesant Town, Met Life refused to rent to African American veterans and denied that acceptance of government aid in any way limited the freedom of private business to practice discrimination in the marketplace. Proclaiming that "housing is not a civil right," State Supreme Court Justice Felix C. Benvenga ruled in favor of Met Life in July 1947; the New York State Court of Appeals affirmed his decision in July 1949. The U.S. Supreme Court's refusal to consider the *Dorsey* case sealed the fate of Stuyvesant Town and, according to Frank S. Horne, signaled private developers that they need not "play ball on a mixed basis." The Met Life imbroglio led directly to the founding of the National Committee Against Discrimination in Housing.[42]

The Housing Act of 1949 offered the promise of slum clearance and the construction of low-income housing, but wary opponents of racial discriminations saw potential pitfalls in the law. A major concern, according to Frank S. Horne, involved whether the Title I redevelopment program would ignore the relocation needs of the large minority populations uprooted in slum clearance efforts. As well, he hoped that the housing constructed on redevelopment sites would be available without racial restriction. In short, Horne summarized, "the central issue is whether racial discrimination of any type is to be sanctioned in a program of city rebuilding which depends on *public* funds and powers as well as on private investment." The defeat of the Bricker-Cain Amendment as a precursor to the legislation's passage raised concerns that local officials and federal agencies would point to Congress's unwillingness to guarantee nondiscrimination as a defense for maintaining the current practices that maintained racial segregation. Indeed, much of the political support for Title I stemmed from the expectation that the federal government's role would be limited to the provision of resources and that local control would remain paramount.[43]

Events soon justified the concerns of Frank S. Horne and others in the RRS. In Nashville, Tennessee; Aiken, South Carolina; Savannah, Georgia; Baltimore, Maryland; and several other southern communities, federal authorities supported local plans for slum clearance that razed houses occupied by African Americans and built public housing for whites. According to George B. Nesbitt, a race relations adviser in HHFA's Division of Slum Clearance and Urban Redevelopment (DSCUR), the two redevelopment projects in Baltimore highlighted the type of "Negro clearance" that Title I made likely absent the federal government's oversight. The Housing Authority of Baltimore worked in conjunction with local FHA market analysts to funnel white population to the suburbs and confine construction of new housing for African Americans within the inner city. When the NAACP challenged the HHFA's approval of the Baltimore proposals, Raymond Foley's narrowly legalistic defense argued that the agency's position on restrictive covenants met the requirements of the Housing Act of 1949. Citing the limits of government power, the HHFA administrator said: "This agency does not have the authority to compel any local public agency to establish requirements governing the racial characteristics of the families to be rehoused in redevelopment projects."[44]

The drive to enlist the federal government to bolster racial segregation proceeded in northern cities as well, no more assiduously than in Chicago, where enterprising developers and politicians had laid the legal groundwork earlier for urban redevelopment and immediately took action when Congress passed enabling legislation in 1949. A Title I project for the New York Life Insurance Company's Lake Meadows housing development on the city's South Side displaced 3,600 African American families, 2,700 of which were ineligible for public housing and had to seek lodging in the already overcrowded private market; Title III assistance for the construction of 11,550 to 15,050 public housing units on mostly inner-city sites preserved racial segregation and dumped another 6,000 African Americans into the same inhospitable private housing market. RRS members charged that Chicago officials, with the backing of NAREB, the Chicago Title and Trust Company, and the Taxpayers Referendum Council, explicitly designed the Title I and III proposals to preserve racial segregation. Robert C. Weaver, then serving as temporary chairman of the National Committee against Discrimination in Housing

(NCADH), concurred that local prejudice rather than sound planning offered the only explanation for the Chicago plans. Weaver warned against approval of the highly publicized Chicago initiatives because of the doleful precedent the HHFA would be setting.[45]

In July 1951, while HHFA administrators were considering the proposals, racial rioting erupted in Chicago's western suburb of Cicero. When an African American veteran and his family moved into an apartment in the gritty industrial community populated largely by eastern European immigrants, thousands of whites took to the streets to maintain the homogeneity of their neighborhood. The arson and vandalism continued for several days and nights before hundreds of National Guardsmen, Cicero policemen, and Cook County sheriff's deputies restored order. Horne and Nesbitt explained the outburst in Cicero as a byproduct of Chicago's notorious history of racial violence and residential segregation. Further, they explicitly linked the turmoil in the suburb to the city's redevelopment proposal by noting that slum clearance in Chicago pushed African Americans out of their homes and sent them into hostile environments like Cicero in search of housing. If the HHFA approved Chicago's plans, Walter White, executive secretary of the NAACP argued, the federal government would be using the Housing Act of 1949 as a tool for the perpetuation of racial segregation and laying the groundwork for continued interracial clashes nationwide in the future.[46]

In an October 15, 1951, meeting in HHFA headquarters in Washington, Raymond Foley conferred with Chicago officials to finalize a plan for the city's redevelopment efforts. The HHFA approved the public housing sites as well as the Lake Meadows development while warning the city that such proposals would not be countenanced in the future; the federal agency also urged the city to seek vacant sites for African American residential housing and promised to utilize the FHA more extensively in the future to locate private housing for minority families. Nesbitt doubtless spoke for others in the RRS when he observed that Chicago officials had no reason to adhere to the HHFA's nonbinding recommendations. Foley made clear that, although the HHFA sought to improve the living conditions of African Americans, the federal government would not use force against local authorities to achieve that goal. "It seems to me that under our system of government," he concluded, "non-segregation by governmental compulsion is just as obnoxious as segregation by governmental compulsion."[47]

Railing against "Negro clearance" in southern and northern cities alike, members of the RRS acted as the conscience of the federal government but failed to alter the practices of the HHFA during the Truman administration.

The NAACP likewise protested the HHFA's complicity in defending and enhancing racial segregation, charging in a January 11, 1952, memorandum to Raymond Foley that "the chief force now contributing to the maintenance and extension of Negro ghettos comes from the Federal Government itself through the operations of the federal housing agencies." Noting that more than 55 percent of new construction of private and public housing in the nation was being financed by the FHA, VA, and HHFA, Robert C. Weaver charged in 1952 that "federal housing policies, more than any single factor, determine the racial patterns of the cities of tomorrow." Philleo Nash, a special assistant to the president for minority affairs, observed in a June 23, 1952, memorandum to Truman that the actions of the federal government were helping to create African American central cities surrounded by white suburbs—a far cry from the rosy picture of future housing conditions sketched by the president when he signed the Housing Act of 1949 a scant three years earlier.[48]

While the slum clearance provisions of Title I accelerated the remarkable growth of white suburbs in the postwar years, so too did the operation of the FHA. Denying that metropolitan segregation resulted from any design in Washington, FHA officials and real-estate interests contended that federal mortgage programs merely facilitated latent centrifugal forces in urban areas. Ignoring the crucial importance of expanded credit provided by the federal government, the champions of suburban growth repeatedly explained metropolitan demographic changes in terms of the free market's benevolent operation. Working in tandem with bankers, Realtors, mortgage lenders, and builders, FHA officials revised policies and rewrote guidelines to aid the homebuilding industry. FHA Administrator Raymond Foley set the tone in August 1945 by appointing a committee to explore ways the agency could "be of help to private enterprise in all broad phases of the post-war housing market" and to suggest "what further authorities may be necessary and desirable to put us fully in [that] market."[49]

In similar fashion, the Federal National Mortgage Association (FNMA) spurred suburbanization and excluded minorities from the federally subsidized mortgage market. Created in 1938 to create a secondary market for government-insured loans, the FNMA ("Fannie Mae") purchased FHA- and VA-approved mortgages and quickly became one of the leading sources of funds in the postwar housing construction industry. Builders, brokers, and developers followed FHA appraisal guidelines, which discriminated on the basis of race, in order to qualify for loans from Fannie Mae, FHA, and VA. Confronted with the same discriminatory policies at each government lending agency, minorities encountered great difficulty obtaining mortgages, paid more for their loans, and frequently resorted to building their own houses.[50]

With FHA, VA, and FNMA guarantees minimizing the risk for banks and other lending institutions, suburban developers in postwar America operated on a much grander scale than previously feasible. Builders nationwide followed the example of William Levitt, who had perfected mass-building techniques during the war while erecting large quantities of defense housing. Levitt built three massive communities ("Levittowns") after 1945—in Pennsylvania, New Jersey, and New York—with mortgage guarantees from the FHA and VA. Utilizing assembly-line techniques, buying directly from manufacturers, and installing standardized components, Levitt's armies of carpenters, electricians, plumbers, roofers, and landscapers were completing 150 houses a week by the summer of 1948. Levitt and other builders tailored the suburbs they developed to the standards outlined in the FHA *Underwriting Manual*, spurning multi-unit, rental housing for single-family dwellings, strictly separating land uses, and emphasizing homogeneity rather than diversity. The *Underwriting Manual* cautioned against "invasion" by minorities or low-income interlopers. Clearly, federal agencies shaped the emerging suburban landscape as much as they underwrote it.[51]

The rapid growth of suburbs and the changing contours of inner cities after 1945 also owed to decisions about transportation policies crafted in Washington. Government officials began thinking during the war about issues involving the allocation of federal dollars for transportation, anticipating that the close of hostilities would allow for increased spending on projects that would affect metropolitan America, but planning commenced years earlier. In the early decades of the twentieth century, support for federal funds being used for transportation improvements had grown slowly as most Americans continued to consider such issues the province of state and local governments. The inhabitants of large cities traditionally had balked at good roads movements designed to pull farmers out of the mud, particularly when so many urbanites could get around fine on foot, omnibuses, streetcars, or subways. With urban mass transit declining precipitously by the 1930s, concerns about accommodating the growing volume of automobile traffic in urban areas increased the discussion of the federal government's role. In 1939 the Bureau of Public Roads (BPR), which had been created by the Federal Road Act of 1921, laid out a detailed plan for a national network of highways that linked the nation's large cities and included express highways within metropolitan areas; the plan, *Toll Roads and Free Roads*, referred specifically

to the need for slum clearance and urban redevelopment as part of the effort
to unclog city traffic. The Defense Highway Act of 1941 authorized states to
begin planning for postwar highway construction and encouraged cities to
work cooperatively with state highway departments to prepare these blueprints immediately.[52]

In 1944, with the end of the war appearing imminent, federal involvement in transportation increased on several fronts. The National Interregional Highway Committee, which had been appointed by President Franklin D. Roosevelt with the BPR's Thomas H. MacDonald as chairman, issued
its final report, *Interregional Highways.* The report called for a 40,000-mile
interstate highway system that included provisions for urban beltways and
multilane expressways and alluded to the need for slum clearance in larger
cities. The metropolitan highway network would improve access to the city
core for those living in outlying areas, retard decentralization, and fight
inner-city decay. Also that year, the House of Representatives' Committee on
Roads held hearings on postwar spending for highways. A steady stream of
big-city mayors, planners, and civil engineers testified that a massive postwar highway construction effort would be necessary to accommodate the expected surge in automobile traffic and that such an enormous project could
happen only with financial assistance from Washington. In a rare moment of
prescience, Detroit Mayor Edward J. Jeffries allowed that a more extensive
network of expressways would not only make the central business district
more accessible to the periphery but also would make the periphery more accessible to the central business district. A policy designed to bolster downtowns would ultimately do more to enhance suburbanization, Jeffries predicted, so that potentially "there is nothing left [in Detroit] but industry."
Such clear-eyed realism was rare in midcentury, however, and Congress
readily passed the Federal Aid Highway Act of 1944. The law allocated $1.5
billion for highway construction during the three years immediately following the war, with one-fourth of all federal funds designated for urban primary roads.[53]

The government's commitment to build more urban highways elicited a
warm response from the American population, which by the end of the 1930s
saw the nation's future dominated by the automobile. Even as the Great Depression lingered and rising tensions in Europe made the nation's future uncertain, the highway lobby worked overtime to shape public opinion. According to the historian Mark I. Foster, the influential General Motors Futurama
exhibit at the 1939 New York World's Fair "stimulated public thinking in
favor of massive urban freeway building." General Motors executives

Charles Wilson and Alfred Sloan sought to create in Futurama a vision of the American landscape in 1960 in which sleek new automobiles and capacious highways represented the full promise of modernity. The centerpiece of the exhibit, which had been seen by an estimated 25 million visitors, contained a seven-lane superhighway designed to allow motorists to drive at speeds of 100 miles per hour. Awestruck fairgoers left Futurama with lapel pins that said "I have seen the future." A companion exhibit at the World's Fair, "Democracity," presented an idealized community of the future. In a sparsely populated metropolitan region of 11,000 square miles, the over-whelming majority of the 1.5 million inhabitants commuted from suburbs on high-speed expressways to work in the central city; the scale model of the fu-turistic metropolis contained no mass transit.[54]

At the same time that throngs of people marveled at the Futurama and Democracity exhibits, a number of interest groups in Washington began lob-bying elected officials to increase spending on roads in the nation's popula-tion centers. The United States Conference of Mayors urged the federal gov-ernment to allocate increasing sums of money for urban rather than rural road building, and groups such as the American Road Builders' Association (ARBA) and the American Concrete Institute (ACI) naturally called for heightened spending that would benefit their constituents. The Automotive Safety Foundation predicted fewer traffic fatalities as well as higher land values with high-speed expressways, promises echoed by the American Asso-ciation of State Highway Officials (AASHO), the American Automobile As-sociation (AAA), and the American Trucking Association. The Urban Land Institute (ULI), the most active lobby representing downtown business inter-ests and partial author of the T-E-W bill, produced a series of pamphlets, newsletters, and other written materials trumpeting urban expressways as the "salvation" of central cities.[55]

Urban planners also joined the consensus proclaiming the necessity of expressways for the future well-being of the cities. Like their counterparts in the business community, planners saw the resurrection of the central busi-ness district as the linchpin of urban revitalization and believed that salvag-ing property values downtown remained essential for maintaining the viabil-ity of other neighborhoods across the cityscape. Further, the judicious location of expressways would resuscitate the city center both by increasing accessibility from the periphery and funneling shoppers within the city to the center by discouraging cross-town trips; as an added benefit, massive ex-pressways would serve as impenetrable barriers between neighborhoods as a means of preserving residential segregation. Harland Bartholomew, the most renowned urban planner of the era, told a University of Pittsburgh audience in 1949 that haphazard suburban growth caused "economic strangulation" to central cities, and the revival of the urban cores depended upon the creation of extensive freeway networks. Some urban planners dissented and warned that more freeways would simply accelerate decentralization, but the vast majority of planners lent their voices to the swelling chorus extolling superhighway construction as a key element in urban revitalization.[56]

Despite the avid backing of many interest groups, extensive wartime planning, and the widespread recognition of the need for quick action as the number of automobiles in the nation rose dramatically, highway construction proceeded slowly in the years immediately following the war. Between 1945 and 1949, as domestic auto firms ceased production of tanks and airplanes and returned to the manufacture of sedans and coupes, the number of automobile registrations increased from 31 million to 44.7 million. Road builders completed only 5,057 miles in 1946 as President Truman initially assigned priority to housing and then curtailed all public works spending to curb inflation; not until 1948 did the annual miles of road completed rise to the modest outputs of the 1930s. That year, Congress passed a bill extending the Federal-Aid Highway Act of 1944 with urban roads receiving one-sixth of the amount allocated for the next two years. Because of the rising cost of fighting the Cold War, increased by the dispatch of U.S. troops to Korea beginning in 1950, Truman recommended limited federal funding for highways. The rationing of steel during the Korean War, exacerbated by a two-month strike by steelworkers in 1952, further curtailed road building. The Federal-Aid Highway Act of 1950, which established spending levels for the next two years, raised the percentage of funds allotted for urban highways to one-fourth of the total but authorized $260 million less than the AASHO had requested in its testimony before Congress that year.[57]

While federal outlays for highways increased only gradually, the pattern of road building in the postwar years indicated that the new emphasis upon urban expressways championed by the BPR and endorsed by the National Interregional Highway Committee had triumphed. Thomas H. MacDonald, who served as BPR commissioner from its founding in 1921 until his retirement in 1953, tirelessly preached the gospel of urban expressways as the panacea for a host of city problems, including inefficient transportation, downtown deterioration, and inadequate housing. As McDonald told the National Chamber of Commerce in 1947, "The time when highway needs of the cities might be regarded as of lesser concern than rural needs is past, and too long past." He blithely dismissed the concerns of those officials like Mayor Jeffries who feared the long-term effects of high-speed expressways on the urban core, claiming that those roadways would allow displaced inner-city residents to relocate in the suburbs and commute comfortably to their downtown jobs. MacDonald acknowledged that road builders had an obligation to help uprooted families when they lost their homes to highway construction sites and insisted that suitable new housing be located before slum clearance proceeded, but he unfailingly touted the necessity of urban expressways for the survival of the nation's cities.[58]

At least in the 1940s, MacDonald managed to implement his ideas about merging housing and highways by having the BPR's Urban Roads Division cooperate with municipal planning agencies in some of the nation's largest cities. Believing that local bureaucracies frequently overlooked the impact of slum clearance and relocation on city populations, he sought to use the power of his agency to cultivate a keener awareness of the effects of government power on homeowners. He spoke out publicly, for example, when he found municipalities remiss in their use of funds provided by the BPR. In Chicago, he noted, city officials had made no preparations to aid the displaced families of 8,100 housing units scheduled to be razed as part of an expressway construction program. In New York City, BPR officials worked with the local planning commission to determine the routes for expressways that would have the least impact on existing neighborhoods. The Urban Roads Division distributed a manual on the relocation of uprooted tenants to city and state highway officials as part of an effort to raise awareness of the problem.[59]

MacDonald continued throughout the late 1940s and early 1950s to campaign for urban expressways but decreasingly mentioned the government's obligation to find suitable lodging for uprooted families. He stopped calling for road building with a social conscience at the same time that the powerful push for more highways drowned out dissenters urging caution. In 1949, citing scarce resources and political opposition, Truman declined to couple housing and highway programs for the benefit of slum clearance efforts. Fully engaged in the struggle to get the T-E-W Act through Congress, the president shied away from attaching a highway component to the legislation that might erode political support for his primary objective. Having been moved in 1949 from the Federal Works Agency to the U.S. Department of Commerce and finding itself isolated from the urban programs managed by the HHFA, the BPR increasingly devised plans to move automobiles and trucks more efficiently through urban spaces and neglected the broader social implications of rearranging cityscapes to provide more roadways. The professionals who built highways thought only about the logistics that concerned them: how to provide new and better roads to relieve worsening traffic congestion. As the historian Mark Rose described it, "In the day-to-day routines of road engineers, as they made decisions about route locations and geometric standards, they focused on budgets and road building, not urban matters."[60]

The single-minded drive to solve urban problems by building highways dismissed mass transit as an outmoded technology that had served a useful purpose in the growth of cities in decades past and had played a necessary role during the Second World War, when the government rationed gasoline and rubber, but had no future in the modern world of automobility. Automobile registrations increased 75 percent between 1946 and 1954 as Americans reaped the benefits of a sustained postwar prosperity and the miles of roadways increased exponentially throughout the nation. At the same time, mass transit ridership correspondingly declined; from 1946 to 1956 the number of mass transit passengers fell from 23.4 billion to 11 billion. The BPR made virtually no mention of urban mass transit in its postwar deliberations, reports the historian Bruce Seely, and in 1948 it explicitly identified expressways as the sole viable solution for urban transportation shortcomings. Until he left the BPR in 1953, MacDonald stumped exclusively for expressways and ignored mass transit as an important part of the solution to the cities' transportation problems. Just as few planners objected to the consensus urging the mass construction of urban expressways, only a few dissidents (principally downtown merchants and urban planners) called for the provision of additional public transit along with more highways as the only means of satisfying the huge and growing transportation needs of the large cities. As the historian Mark I. Gelfand observed of these dissenters, "Their words were lost to most in the din of blaring horns."[61]

The expressways built with federal dollars connected central business districts not only with the burgeoning suburbs but also with airports built on the metropolitan peripheries that likewise received substantial financial aid from Washington. As commercial aviation served clienteles other than the U.S. Post Office and the military after World War I, local officials and planners began to contemplate the important future role of airports for urban growth. In 1928 urban planner John Nolan argued that "in large cities the airplane calls for improved motorways of the superhighway type" and that the growth of aviation would require an improved infrastructure for the automobile and motorbus. Significant amounts of financial aid began flowing to municipal airports in the 1930s through such New Deal relief agencies as the Federal Emergency Relief Administration (FERA), the Civil Works Administration (CWA), and the WPA. In fact, federal public works programs accounted for 77 percent of funding for municipal airport construction from 1933 to 1938. In passing the Civil Aeronautics Act of 1938, which called for a six-year program of airport improvements, Congress broke new ground in allocating funds for that purpose. After the Second World War, congressmen in Washington, mayors, chambers of commerce, and military representatives acknowledged that the growth of aviation would be an important part of urban development as cities adapted to changes in the nation's modernizing transportation system. The federal government needed a network of high-quality municipal airports to support the growing aeronautics industry, and cities recognized the potential for economic growth in their partnership with commercial aviation.[62]

Both federal bureaucrats and local officials adduced that airport expansion and construction could be accomplished in myriad ways beneficial to cities. In effect, airport construction could play a role in large-scale urban redevelopment schemes that historian Paul Barrett has termed the "'two-birds-with-one-stone' approach of urban renewal." As early as 1930, for example, the Harvard School of City Planning proposed that "in some cases a blighted district might be so low in value and so much of a public menace . . . that public money might legitimately be used to acquire it as part of a municipal airport." By the end of World War II, Civilian Aeronautics Administration (CAA) officials were advising municipal governments to purchase slum land as sites for commercial airfields. The Federal Airport Act of 1946, which allocated $500 million in federal aid directly to larger cities and to smaller communities indirectly through state aviation agencies over the next seven years, provided up to 50 percent of the costs for airport construction. In subsequent years, although some big-city mayors complained that Congress never fully funded the law, the infusion of federal dollars made possible the construction of sprawling airports on the outskirts of cities throughout the country.[63]

The subsidization of airport construction, along with the provision of additional resources for highways and housing, reflected an expanding federal presence in the cities immediately after the Second World War. Having crafted no comprehensive plan for urban development, President Truman supported such programs piecemeal because the nation's municipalities desperately demanded attention after the years of neglect caused by the Great Depression and global war. Moreover, he recognized the centrality of the urban vote in Franklin Roosevelt's electoral successes as well as the potential importance of that support for his political prospects. The postwar housing situation, characterized as a "national calamity" by one observer, assumed primacy on Capitol Hill as well as in the White House. The result of the bipartisan determination to address the critical housing problem—the T-E-W Act—produced a mixed legacy. On the one hand, the promise of Title III remained largely unfulfilled in the Truman years as the construction of low-income housing lagged far behind the ambitious goals announced in 1949; the powerful coalition of business interests opposed to public housing remained a formidable opponent and remained so for the rest of the twentieth century. On the other hand, Title I launched a new era of urban redevelopment and urban renewal with profound implications for urban America in the 1950s and beyond. During the Truman administration federal agencies such as the FHA, VA, FNMA, and HHFA also exerted a powerful influence on metropolitan development through the perpetuation of racial segregation and the corresponding growth of suburbia. The federal government's presence in the housing market, enhanced during the New Deal era, expanded further in the Truman years.[64]

In order to preserve political capital and scarce resources for the vexing housing problem, Truman advanced proposals for the completion of ambitious urban highway networks more cautiously and requested fewer dollars from Congress for road construction. The idea of extensive expressway networks in large metropolitan areas connected to a massive national grid of highways, which had been discussed in Washington as far back as 1939, remained alive in the BPR pending the availability of funding. In the late 1940s and early 1950s, urban residents could only marshal local resources through the approval of bond issues for limited highway construction; the big breakthrough awaited the passage of federal legislation creating an interstate highway system. In transportation as well as housing policy, the federal government gave evidence of an expanded role in urban affairs. Truman's Fair Deal, little of which survived the bitter partisanship of the post–World War II Congress, exerted comparatively little impact on cities; federal policies implemented in earlier decades that promulgated metropolitan decentralization continued to operate much as before. Still, the passage of a major housing bill after years of arduous effort and the promise of a rising level of federal support for urban reclamation gave progressives hope of considerable future change.[65]

2

DYNAMIC CONSERVATISM
AND THE CITIES

Historians have usually characterized the presidency of Dwight D. Eisenhower as a conservative Republican oasis in the midst of liberal Democratic administrations stretching from Franklin D. Roosevelt's New Deal to Lyndon B. Johnson's Great Society. A cautious conservative on economic affairs who managed to balance the federal budget three times, Eisenhower repeatedly avowed his commitment to private enterprise, lower taxes, and fiscal orthodoxy. No supporter of the nascent civil rights movement, he declined to endorse the U.S. Supreme Court's landmark decision in *Brown v. Board of Education* and thereafter paid little attention to the massive resistance movement sweeping the South. In matters regarding racial discrimination, offshore oil, and atomic energy development, he deferred to the authority of the states rather than the federal government. A conservative Republican who opposed many of the New Deal reforms that had been imbedded in the fabric of American life by the 1950s, he reluctantly acquiesced in popular programs such as Social Security but occasionally attempted to marshal partisan support on Capitol Hill and utilize the massive federal bureaucracy to minimize the impact of earlier legislation. His preference for limited government generally and his inclination to curtail federal involvement in local affairs specifically provided a sharp contrast to the New Deal–Fear Deal activism of the preceding years. The attempt to implement these philosophical proclivities—what Eisenhower termed "dynamic conservatism"—proved to be significant at a time of suburban expansion and central city retrenchment.[1]

Beginning in the late 1940s and continuing throughout the 1950s, as the United States enjoyed a period of prolonged and unprecedented prosperity, suburbs sprawled across the landscape while city officials, planners, and downtown businessmen lamented the decline of central cities. Automobile sales leaped from 5.4 million in 1954 to 7.4 million in 1955, as U.S. manufacturers introduced daring new designs and powerful V-8 engines in their new models, and streetcar suburbs abutting inner cities gave way to far-flung automobile suburbs. Metropolitan decentralization in the decade could be seen most clearly in a massive demographic shift; population rose a striking 56.3 percent in the suburbs and only 17.4 percent in central cities. Following the people who sought more living space beyond municipal boundaries, industry, retail, and jobs relocated to the metropolitan fringe as well. Acres of housing subdivisions, massive factories, and spacious shopping centers appeared in the suburbs, leeching tax dollars from aging central cities that increasingly possessed fewer resources with which to provide expensive municipal services. Millions of Americans enjoyed the many benefits of suburban living, but those left behind in declining central cities such as St. Louis, Cleveland, and Detroit had a less positive view of decentralization than did those living in Scarsdale, Levittown, and Park Forest. Recognition at midcentury that the United States was fast becoming a suburban nation led accordingly to concern for the fate of the urban core. What, if anything, should be done for the beleaguered central cities? And by whom?[2]

In the decade following World War II, many local businessmen and civic leaders mobilized their resources to save downtowns. Fearful of losing the middle class to the suburbs, mayors, city councils, and business groups created committees, commissions, and private-public partnerships to find solutions to the worsening problems caused by decentralization. In the aftermath of the Second World War, these groups took stock of the decay and blight that had crept across their cityscapes in the preceding decades and plotted how best to arrest plummeting property values and restore sagging central business districts to their former places of prominence. Long before Harry Truman's Fair Deal (especially the Housing Act of 1949) gave hope of substantial financial aid from Washington, local leaders were devising plans to build expressways, parking garages, and downtown office buildings. To civic leaders and government officials, it seemed only natural that the forces of private capital that had been responsible for building America's great industrial cities would take the lead in formulating a strategy for salvaging them.[3]

The gritty industrial city of Pittsburgh became the prototype of partnerships between city halls and big business. The iron and steel plants that dominated the local economy had long befouled the air with smoke and left a residue of soot and ash throughout the city, the environmental calamity having become so intolerable that corporate offices downtown threatened to flee the area. Under the leadership of Richard King Mellon, whose family controlled the Mellon Bank, Gulf Oil, Alcoa, and the area's largest coal company, the Allegheny Conference on Community Development launched a major redevelopment campaign that came to be known as the Pittsburgh Renaissance. The leading financial contributor to the Pennsylvania Republican Party, Mellon worked closely with Democratic mayor David Lawrence to forge a bipartisan coalition bent upon wholesale changes for the Steel City. Sweeping new antismoke ordinances forced through the city council literally brought sunlight back to the downtown and improved visibility an estimated 70 percent. A state-local partnership made possible the replacement of railroad yards and seedy warehouses at the Point (the confluence of the Ohio, Allegheny, and Monongahela rivers) with a state park and a complex of office towers, corporate headquarters, and a Hilton Hotel known as Gateway Center. The new Penn-Lincoln Parkway provided automobile access to the reconfigured central business district. *Newsweek* raved that Pittsburgh, no longer "the smoky city or the tired milltown," had "clear skies above it and a brand-new spirit below."[4]

Following the Pittsburgh model, plutocrats, chief executive officers, and corporate leaders across the nation endeavored to launch urban makeovers for their hometowns. Often enlisting the expertise of city planners, civil engineers, and other technocrats, the civic-minded businessmen formed community organizations like the Allegheny Conference to oversee the necessary reclamation work. In 1948 the business elite created the Greater Philadelphia Movement, and their counterparts in St. Louis followed with Civic Progress, Incorporated. In 1954 developer James Rouse and the chief executives of the one hundred largest corporations in the metropolitan region formed the Greater Baltimore Committee; that same year, the local business leadership created the Cleveland Development Foundation. In Chicago, real-estate mogul Arthur Rubloff enlisted city government in his daring plan to save the downtown by developing Upper Michigan Avenue to compensate for the decline of the traditional State Street retail hub. By the mid-1950s, New York City developers were adding 2 million square feet of new office space in Manhattan annually. In 1957 the chairman of that city's planning commission enthusiastically reported: "There are indications that not only is the flow from the city to the suburbs slowing, but that the reverse flow is picking up."[5]

In city after city, policy makers concluded that downtown revitalization depended upon improved highways to funnel workers and shoppers in and out of the city core. While bureaucrats in Washington continued to discuss the extent and nature of the federal government's role in improving automobile traffic in metropolitan areas, state and local authorities were passing bond issues, clearing land, and constructing freeways. In the early 1950s, Boston commenced work on the Central Artery to improve traffic flow in the city's sclerotic streets. By 1953 Detroit had spent or authorized $105 million for the John C. Lodge and Edsel Ford Expressways, and Pennsylvania had allocated funding for the construction of the Schuylkill Expressway in Philadelphia. In 1955 plans to improve automobile links among the five New York City boroughs proceeded with the completion of the Major Deegan Expressway between the Bronx and Manhattan and, despite heated protest from community groups, work continued on the Cross-Bronx Expressway. By 1957 Los Angeles had finished 223 miles in its developing labyrinth of freeways.[6]

Taking the lead on behalf of their cities, a vaunted cohort of mayors emerged after the Second World War to replace an earlier generation of urban leaders who had been known principally for their ineffectiveness and questionable character. As big-city newspapers and business executives noted, downtown revitalization seemed unlikely if municipal government continued to be viewed as a haven for corruption, cronyism, inefficiency, and petty politics. The new breed of mayors emerging in the 1950s, unlike their predecessors earlier in the century who sought primarily to manage ethnic loyalties and satisfy neighborhood constituencies, needed to cultivate good relations with the local business community, real-estate interests, and, increasingly, federal bureaucracies, in order to revitalize city centers. Mayors opposed to boss rule, such as Joseph Clark and Richardson Dilworth in Philadelphia, Hubert Humphrey in Minneapolis, Raymond Tucker in St. Louis, and Anthony Celebrezze in Cleveland, attached their urban reclamation efforts to a holistic reform platform; products of entrenched Democratic political machines such as Richard J. Daley of Chicago and Robert Wagner and Carmine DeSapio of New York City maintained their ties to disreputable party organizations even as they worked closely with Republican business elites. Whether reformers or "good bosses," the new breed mayors invariably turned their attention first to matters of municipal housekeeping. Having added more policemen and firemen to local forces, hastened garbage and snow removal, improved street lighting, and increased the number of parks and playgrounds, they forged alliances with the local business communities and used all the resources made available by state governments and private enterprise to reverse the sagging fortunes of their cities.[7]

During the late 1940s and early 1950s, the resuscitation of the inner cities resulted essentially from private funds and state aid. The most spectacular examples of that era's urban renaissance—Pittsburgh's Gateway Center, Philadelphia's Penn Center, Boston's Prudential Center, Chicago's Lake Meadows, and Detroit's riverfront development, to name just a few—occurred essentially without federal funding. Under the aggressive leadership of Robert Moses, New York City benefited immediately from the largesse made available by Title I of the 1949 Housing Act, but no other city did as well attracting federal dollars. The length of time necessary for cities to devise and submit redevelopment proposals and the bureaucratic logjams encountered in Washington minimized the amount of federal funds spent by the cities in the early 1950s, thereby reducing the impact of the legislation in the last years of the Truman administration. Despite heightened expressions of interest in urban affairs by Washington policy makers after World War II, it remained unclear as the 1952 presidential election approached whether a new occupant of the White House would capitalize upon the potential availability of federal resources.[8]

The Democratic Party had controlled the executive branch of the federal government for the previous two decades, and in 1952 the Republicans offered the nation's voters a clear alternative to New Deal–Fair Deal liberalism. The Republican presidential candidate, Dwight D. Eisenhower, promised a sharp turn away from the path taken by the Roosevelt and Truman presidencies. As the nation's greatest military hero, Eisenhower spurned the entreaties of both political parties after World War II and avoided politics while serving as president of Columbia University and supreme commander of NATO forces in Europe. When he finally agreed to seek the Republican presidential nomination in 1952, Eisenhower did so as a staunch conservative dedicated to reversing the corrosive effect of Democratic administrations that had been responsible for a dangerous expansion of government power. Railing against what he called the "whole-hog theory" of government, he promised to battle the "creeping socialism" that threatened individual freedom and business initiative. In an October 9, 1952, campaign speech in Los Angeles, he promised to preserve such social programs as Social Security, unemployment insurance, and public housing, but emphasized the preeminent importance of limiting government spending in order to balance the federal budget. Throughout the campaign, the Republican presidential aspirant reiterated several key themes—fiscal responsibility, reduced federal spending, limited government, and a clear repudiation of the agglomeration of power in Washington, D.C., by recent Democratic presidents. In describing his political philosophy as "dynamic conservatism," Eisenhower left no doubt that the federal government under his leadership would play no role in making conservatism dynamic.[9]

Not only did Dwight Eisenhower convincingly defeat Democrat Adlai E. Stevenson in 1952, but the outcome of the contest left the Republicans in charge of the Senate (49–47) and the House of Representatives (221–214). According to historian Gary W. Reichard's detailed study of the Republican-controlled Eighty-third Congress, conservatives fully in league with Eisenhower's agenda predominated on Capitol Hill after the election. Even more so than the new president, the fifty-nine freshmen Republicans (nine in the Senate and fifty in the House) thoroughly repudiated the free-spending, big-government culture that they believed Roosevelt and Truman had embedded in Washington. In his initial State of the Union address, Eisenhower identified a balanced budget as his "first order of business" and made clear his determination to curtail federal spending. "Getting control of the budget," he warned, "requires that State and local governments and interested groups of citizens restrain themselves in their demands upon the congress that the federal Treasury spend more and more money for all types of projects."[10]

To ensure that tax dollars were being put to the best use, the new president sought to improve the relations among federal, state, and local governments. A long career in the military had imbued Eisenhower with an appreciation for a well-defined organizational structure and clear lines of authority; as a laissez-faire conservative, he also possessed a reverence for the profit-minded efficiency of corporate capitalism and a firm belief in the inherent wastefulness and sloth of big government. Responding to his call for an investigation into the efficiency of American federalism, Congress appointed a commission on March 30, 1953. In its final report, issued on June 20, 1955, the Advisory Commission on Intergovernmental Relations underscored the need for decentralization and a carefully circumscribed role for the federal government. Accordingly, it urged that the primary responsibility for highway development be invested in the states with Washington agencies only providing technical assistance on problems of construction and maintenance. Similarly, the administration of public housing, urban renewal, and slum clearance should rest with municipalities appropriately supervised by the states. For philosophical as well as budgetary reasons, the commission also called for a cutback in the number of federal grants-in-aid to municipal governments.[11]

Following the recommendation of the Advisory Commission on Intergovernmental Relations, Eisenhower added to his cabinet a special assistant on state and local relationships. To occupy the vaguely defined post, the president chose Howard Pyle, an erstwhile radio personality and governor of Arizona who vigorously opposed the expansion of federal authority. Pyle faithfully echoed Eisenhower's views on the pitfalls of concentrated power in Washington and repeatedly advised states and municipalities to resist the temptation to become mere satellites orbiting around an omnipotent federal government. Perhaps because his experiences with relatively small Arizona cities left him unprepared to deal effectively with the needs and demands brought to his office by the mayors of larger Rust Belt cities, Pyle failed to cultivate good relations with urban leaders from the Northeast and Midwest. Mayors reported that he was likelier to lecture them than to listen and respond to their concerns. When Pyle left the position in 1959 to join the National Safety Council, Eisenhower abolished the post altogether.[12]

Before leaving the Advisory Commission on Intergovernmental Relations, Pyle recognized the importance of local issues by creating the Ad Hoc Committee on Metropolitan Area Problems. In October 1957 he welcomed to the committee's inaugural meeting representatives from several federal agencies, including the Department of Justice (DOJ); the Department of Health, Education, and Welfare (HEW); the Housing and Home Finance Agency (HHFA); the Department of Commerce; and the Bureau of the Budget—and then never convened the committee again during his last fifteen months in the cabinet. The lone voice for urban affairs in the White House after Pyle's departure belonged to Robert Merriam, who called three meetings of the Ad Hoc Committee on Metropolitan Area Problems in 1959–1960. A Chicago city alderman who had lost narrowly to Richard J. Daley in the 1955 mayoral election, Merriam accepted a job later that year at the Budget Bureau in Washington and in 1958 became deputy assistant to the president for interdepartmental relations. A recognized expert on metropolitan governance with a master's degree in political science from the University of Chicago, Merriam strongly argued that the federal government could ease the problems of city governments by improving relations among the Washington agencies that interacted directly with municipalities. In later years he concluded that "our only real accomplishment was that we finally got the Commerce highway people and the urban housing people to agree that they would consult with each other before either selected a site, either for a road or a project." Yet despite his genuine concern for the severity of the problems facing metropolitan America, Merriam stopped well short of advocating an enhanced federal presence at the local level as the solution. Touting administrative reform at various levels of government, he cautioned municipalities to avoid "the easy trail to Washington." Merriam spoke ardently in the White House about metropolitan problems but not in a manner that contradicted the Eisenhower administration's commitment to budget balancing and decentralized government.[13]

The efforts of Howard Pyle and Robert Merriam notwithstanding, the president's explications of dynamic conservatism contained few references to the problems confronting the nation's cities. His speeches and public comments articulated no specific urban programs. Before returning from NATO

headquarters in Europe and declaring his presidential candidacy in 1952, Eisenhower sought guidance from trusted advisers on policy issues with which
he had little familiarity. On the subject of the federal government's role in
housing, for instance, he turned to Aksel Nielsen, a wealthy Denver banker
and one of his frequent golfing partners. On the prospective candidate's behalf, Nielsen commissioned a study by three noted housing experts—Samuel
Neel, counsel for the Mortgage Bankers Association of America; economist
Miles Colean; and developer James Rouse. In a May 15, 1952, memorandum
prepared for Eisenhower's use "when you get to this country," the three experts provided a rudimentary summary of recent federal housing policy that
counseled circumspection in the future.[14] They wrote:

> The fight [over public housing] was acrimonious and the bitterness
> thereby engendered still persists. The outcome was the passage of the
> present program in which the federal government controls and sets the
> pattern for all local action and in many ways discourages local initiative
> in developing other—better—solutions. We believe it would be a great
> mistake for anyone seeking national office today to publicly discuss this
> subject merely as an "opponent" of public housing.[15]

Neel, Colean, and Rouse concluded by arguing for the primacy of state
and local control of housing programs and by endorsing the need for the
federal government to play only a supplementary role. During the 1952 campaign, Eisenhower commented infrequently about public housing and usually issued bland statements extolling the virtues of the private housing industry while also promising to give due consideration to the needs of slum
dwellers. In August the president of the National Association of Home
Builders (NAHB) reported that the Republican candidate had responded
negatively to a question about public housing, saying that "he wanted none
of it." Reformers immediately protested Eisenhower's purported repudiation of public housing, which prompted the candidate's aides to rejoin that
he had been misquoted. The furor subsided quickly, and most pundits
agreed with a *Journal of Housing* reporter's observation that Eisenhower
"has never clearly defined his attitude toward federal housing activities."
Following the advice of Republican senator Robert Taft, Eisenhower announced that, rather than make any decisions about housing in the heat of
the campaign, he intended to create a special commission later to offer recommendations on the government's role in providing low-income housing.
The commission would not issue its report until well after the inauguration,

probably not before the end of 1953, and no firm policy directions would emerge until then.[16]

Housing experts searching for clues to the new president's intentions eagerly awaited the appointment of a new chief administrator of the HHFA, the sprawling bureaucracy created during the Truman administration to oversee the federal government's myriad housing programs. Senator Taft recommended the selection of a successful businessman, neither a public-houser nor a real-estate man who unalterably opposed public housing, and urged Eisenhower to take his time in announcing the choice. Months passed without word from the White House concerning the HHFA, in part because Eisenhower initially devoted more attention to cabinet-level appointments of greater interest to him and in part because the new administration found it difficult to identify a candidate who was acceptable to all representatives of the housing industry. Nor could leading Republicans agree on what to do with the HHFA "colossus." Although Taft and most liberal party members contended that public housing should survive, many conservatives urged a thorough restructuring of the HHFA that would eliminate low-income housing altogether. The uncertainty of the agency's future no doubt made the administrative post less attractive and, as speculation mounted about why no selection had been forthcoming, a leading trade journal commented: "Few men of stature in the building industry were inclined to accept the $17,500 HHFA job only to be told to liquidate the agency."[17]

On February 25, 1953, Eisenhower announced his choice to administer the HHFA—Albert M. Cole, a Kansas Republican who had served four terms in the U.S. House of Representatives before being defeated for reelection the previous year. As a member of the House Banking and Currency Committee, Cole had become well known for his staunch opposition to public housing. He had voted against the Wagner-Steagall Housing Act of 1937, charging that it was socialistic, and opposed public housing generally because it "tends to destroy our form of government." The *St. Louis Post Dispatch* observed: "If the President had conducted a search for the appointee most likely to kill the 1949 Housing Act by administrative strangulation, he could hardly come up with a better choice." Cole's appointment, which Minnesota Senator Hubert Humphrey likened to "putting a fox in charge of the chicken coop," immediately generated opposition in liberal quarters. Representatives of organized labor, which had solidly supported public housing during the Roosevelt and Truman years, immediately notified Eisenhower of their displeasure. James G. Thimmes, chairman of the Housing Committee of the Congress of Industrial Organizations (CIO), sent the president a scathing telegram calling Cole's appointment "ridiculous and harmful." Walter Reuther, president of the United Auto Workers (UAW), noted in a letter to Eisenhower that the selection made no sense: "Mr. Cole throughout his Congressional career was a consistent opponent to public housing, the program he has been appointed to administer." The choice in fact made perfect sense, the president responded to Reuther, for Cole's understanding of public housing's shortcomings would allow him to devise "better and more economical" federal housing programs.[18]

On March 23, 1953, Cole urged the House Appropriations Committee to reduce the number of low-income housing starts for fiscal year 1954 from the 75,000 recommended by Harry Truman to 35,000. The decision for the reduction, said Cole, came from the White House pending a reassessment of the federal government's commitment to low-income housing. At an April 23 press conference, Eisenhower affirmed his intention to limit public housing construction to 35,000 units in fiscal year 1954 and to base decisions for subsequent years on recommendations made by a special government advisory committee he would soon appoint. Privately, Cole agreed with the president's go-slow strategy and seconded the decision to await the congressional committee's findings before taking substantive action.[19] He wrote Sherman Adams, the president's chief adviser: "It would seem most unwise for the Administration to put itself in the position of killing the public housing program as its first major action in the housing field. To do so would be to invite severe political criticism that the new Administration's primary concern in housing was apparently to deny adequate living accommodations to those citizens least able to obtain them."[20]

The president's decision not to propose any divisive housing legislation seemed prudent because of the composition of the Eighty-third Congress. Although Eisenhower had been elected by a huge majority in 1952, his coattails had been short. The Republicans nominally controlled both houses of Congress but by extremely narrow margins, enjoying majorities of only seven votes in the House and two in the Senate. In fact, because of the independence of some Republicans that resulted in Senate votes dividing evenly between the two parties, Vice President Richard Nixon often had to break ties in favor of the administration's initiatives.[21]

Partisan politics played a crucial role in determining the fate of public housing legislation during the 1950s, although support for and opposition to particular bills often cut across party lines. Most Democrats could be counted on to support increased expenditures for low-income housing, but a sizable bloc of southern conservatives in the party consistently opposed this and other social welfare measures. (A few Democrats from the South, progressives such as John Sparkman of Alabama and Burnett Maybank of South Carolina, not only broke ranks with their fellow Southerners but took leadership roles on behalf of public housing.) With but a few exceptions—Robert Taft of Ohio, Jacob Javits of New York, and Hugh Scott of Pennsylvania, most notably—the overwhelming majority of Republicans opposed low-income housing. This partisan divide became even sharper after the sudden death in July 1953 of Robert Taft, public housing's longtime champion in the Senate. The coalition of Republicans and southern Democrats, whose strength peaked early in the Eisenhower administration and declined gradually throughout the 1950s, doggedly strove to minimize the federal government's involvement in housing and to enlist the president as an ally in that effort.[22]

On September 12, 1953, Eisenhower finally appointed an ad hoc committee to establish a long-term housing plan. Chaired by Albert Cole, the twenty-three-member President's Advisory Committee on Government Housing Policies and Programs consisted primarily of banking, insurance, and real-estate luminaries, along with a token handful of reformers. On December 14, 1953, the committee issued a moderate report that made few controversial recommendations, proposed two new Federal Housing Administration (FHA) programs to stimulate investment in slum areas, and called for a continuation of public housing on a limited scale with some modifications. In an appendix to the general report, the Subcommittee on Housing for Low Income Families underscored the continued need for public housing and advanced a series of specific proposals for refining the Housing Act of 1949. For example, the subcommittee advocated lower density public housing based upon the construction of smaller projects on scattered sites throughout metropolitan areas. Urging an increase in government spending for slum clearance projects, the subcommittee cautioned that low-income families displaced as a result of such activity should be given preferential admission to public housing units. Under its new name, "urban renewal," urban redevelopment should be broadened so that slum clearance and new construction would be augmented by the rehabilitation of the existing housing stock. Finally, both the subcommittee and the committee affirmed the desirability of completing the 810,000 units of low-income housing authorized by Congress four years earlier—even if they stopped short of discussing the need for more construction. Given the makeup of the committee and the fears of public housing supporters, the recommendation to preserve the program even at a reduced level seemed remarkable; one disgruntled Republican legislator termed the committee report "demoralizing." At least for the moment, Eisenhower seemed to be seeking a "middle way" on the housing question that offered little change from existing programs.[23]

On January 25, 1954, Eisenhower sent to Congress a special message on housing that relied heavily on the recommendations of the Cole committee. The administration's housing proposal, which the president promptly submitted in the form of omnibus legislation, added to the urban redevelopment program of 1949 additional urban renewal opportunities based upon FHA financing for housing rehabilitation in slum areas. In order to create more investment opportunities in central cities that had nothing to do with housing, the law allowed local housing authorities to spend up to 10 percent of federal grants on projects not situated in predominantly residential areas. (Amendments to the Housing Act of 1961 later raised the amount of funds allocated for nonresidential uses to 30 percent.) The 1954 proposal also called for the construction of 140,000 public housing units over a four-year period, a continuation of the annual 35,000 unit standard established the year before. The president argued for the additional low-income housing units as a necessary concomitant to urban renewal, yet promised that "the continuance of this program will be reviewed before the end of the four-year period, when adequate evidence exists to determine the success of the other measures I have recommended."[24]

The Eisenhower administration's first major piece of housing legislation met with a tepid reception from both sides of the public housing question. The amendments to Title I signaling the shift from urban redevelopment to urban renewal elicited little comment in Congress as the fate of public housing attracted most of the attention. Reformers assailed the bill for seeking only 35,000 public housing units annually—a "token amount," according to Catherine Bauer, when more like 135,000 units a year were needed to make slum clearance and rehabilitation possible. Senator Burnet Maybank offered an amendment increasing the number of units constructed annually to 135,000 but received negligible support. Ira S. Robbins, president of the National Housing Conference, argued that the number of poorly housed lower- and working-class Americans necessitated the building of 200,000 units per year; the National Federation of Settlements and Neighborhood Centers concurred. Though relieved that Eisenhower had decided not to scuttle public housing altogether, reformers feared that the continued approval of such tiny amounts would eventually result in the program's elimination if only at a later date.[25]

On the other hand, real-estate and banking interests opposed the construction of any public housing at all and lobbied for passage of legislation (including the new urban renewal program) strictly on that basis. These conservatives enjoyed able representation in Congress, particularly in the House, where resistance to low-income housing continued to be stronger than in the Senate and where Republican Speaker Joseph W. Martin boasted that "public housing soon will become only a memory of the unlamented days of the managed economy." The House Banking and Currency Committee, following the leadership of its chairman, Republican Jesse Wolcott of Michigan, reported out the Housing Act of 1954 with no mention at all of low-income housing. The version of the bill approved by the Senate restored the 140,000 units provided in the president's original draft. In the reconciliation of the different versions of the bill, the House agreed to new construction equal to the number of units destroyed by slum clearance not to exceed 35,000 public housing units a year—in all likelihood, the congressmen assumed, less than 10,000 units annually. On August 2, 1954, Eisenhower signed a law whose provisions for public housing represented yet another dramatic reduction from the 1949 level. Jesse Wolcott exulted: "With these limitations, we conferees believe we have done a masterful job on public housing." The reformist National Housing Conference lamented that the outcome of the legislative struggle took "the President off the hook, and [killed] public housing at the same time."[26]

The Housing Act of 1954, which the Republican administration touted as the most significant piece of housing legislation ever enacted, coupled urban renewal with urban redevelopment initiatives to eradicate slums and blight in American cities during the 1950s and 1960s. Such reformist groups as the American Institute of Planners and the U.S. Conference of Mayors endorsed the law believing that the cause of low-income housing would benefit accordingly, but subsequent developments showed that slum clearance did not necessarily result in the construction of more dwellings for the poor. As Ira S. Robbins pointed out, the eradication of blight inherently did nothing to increase the supply of public housing and inevitably created the problem of relocating uprooted slum dwellers. Worse, the number of public housing units planned in 1949 had not been completed in any year and, as the shortage of decent low-income dwellings grew annually, the government made provisions for less and less. Wary liberals noted that the president offered no protest when the congressional leadership of his own party sliced public housing out of his legislation; only the actions of the Senate Democrats preserved the modest number of low-income units provided in the final bill. According to Eisenhower's biographer, Stephen E. Ambrose, the president intended (after the fulfillment of the commitment in the Housing Act of 1954) to replace government involvement in public housing with a package of long-term loans to private homeowners.[27]

In his January 1955 State of the Union address to Congress, Eisenhower asked for an amendment to the previous year's housing law that would limit the construction of public housing to 35,000 units during each of the next two fiscal years. "By that time," the president promised, "the private building industry, aided by the Housing Act of 1954, will have had the opportunity to assume its full role in providing adequate housing for low-income families." Builders took heart that Eisenhower's blueprint seemed to lay the groundwork for the elimination of public housing in favor of free enterprise. In his 1956 reelection campaign, the president made little effort to disguise his dissatisfaction with public housing. The Republican platform approved at the party's national nominating convention that summer made cursory mention of the topic and said nothing about future allocations. (The sole allusion in the platform neglected to note that the total number of low-income units built from 1953 to 1956 declined 7 percent from the amount constructed during the four years following the passage of the Housing Act of 1949.) A confidential memorandum assessing housing as an issue in the president's reelection campaign concluded: "The continuation of public housing has been accepted, but only upon the basis of the fulfillment of real need—and with a specific cut-off date; our leadership believed that private business would sufficiently develop their technology to build low cost private housing in such a volume that eventually the need for direct public housing aid would be dissipated."[28]

In his second term Eisenhower's innate suspicion of public housing became increasingly evident. The president asked for no new public housing construction but reluctantly signed the Housing Act of 1956, which authorized a total of 70,000 units for 1957-1958. In 1957 he signed a law authorizing another 35,000 units; in 1958 housing legislation passed the Senate but died in the House Rules Committee at the hands of its chairman, Virginia Democrat Howard Smith. Meanwhile, the administration refused to execute contracts for the total number of low-income housing units already authorized by Congress. "Merely increasing the backlog of authorized public housing units by some inflated figure," argued Albert Cole, "will not solve the problem." The HHFA authorized only 5,391 units in 1957, for example, and 24,293 in 1958. In her landmark article, "The Dreary Deadlock of Public Housing," Catherine Bauer assayed the sorry condition of public housing during Eisenhower's second term and sadly concluded that "after more than two decades, [it] still drags along in a kind of limbo, continuously controversial, not dead but never more than half alive."[29]

Eisenhower's long-simmering distaste for low-income housing became unmistakably clear in 1959. He requested no new public housing construction in the budget prepared for Congress, arguing that by 1960 the federal government would have provided shelter for approximately 2 million people in more than 475,000 public housing units with another 110,000 units under contract to be built. Lamenting the existence of a considerable backlog of projects, the president contended that the time had come for private industry to supplant Washington as the principal purveyor of low-income housing. He objected on ideological grounds to the federal government's involvement in activities that should be the purview of local authorities and pointed to the need for budgetary savings as he sought to enforce fiscal responsibility in the federal bureaucracy. As the historian of Eisenhower's fiscal policies noted, "the fact that the final tallies for fiscal 1959 were being written in glaring red ink just as the [housing] bill came for signature further strengthened his resolve to stop the next budget 'drifting over Niagara.'"[30]

On July 7, 1959, Eisenhower vetoed the $2.2 billion housing bill passed by Congress, calling it "extravagant" and "inflationary." (He had proposed a measure that authorized the spending of $810 million on various housing programs.) Charging—inaccurately—that the law allocated funds for the construction of 190,000 units of public housing at a time when over 100,000 authorized units remained unbuilt, he restated his belief that no more low-income units needed to be completed at all. The Senate fell nine votes short of the necessary two-thirds majority to override the veto, and Congress submitted a different version of the bill that summer that reduced the annual allotment of public housing starts from 45,000 to 37,000 units; Eisenhower responded with another veto. The president again chastised Congress for its spendthrift ways and rejected the need for public housing that, he claimed, "would be subsidized, on a basis that would cost the taxpayer many hundreds of millions of dollars over the next forty years." The Senate sustained his veto by five votes. On September 23, in the closing days of the legislative session, the president signed the Housing Act of 1959, which authorized the construction of 37,000 units of low-income housing. The following year, his last in the White House, Eisenhower declined to support omnibus legislation that included 25,000 public housing units and signed a "stop-gap" bill that made no mention of low-income housing construction. Public housing survived eight years of dynamic conservatism, but in a weakened state.[31]

Just as Eisenhower's early tolerance for public housing gave way to outright hostility by the middle of his second term, his administration also seemed to lose its initial enthusiasm for urban renewal. The ambitious expansion in

1954 of the urban redevelopment program created in 1949, what historian
Mark I. Gelfand called "the Republican professionals' gift to the GOP's business friends in the cities," proved to be extremely costly at a time when the
president became increasingly interested in fiscal belt-tightening. The
party's 1956 platform only devoted thirty-five words to urban renewal, causing frustrated HHFA officials to complain sarcastically that "the subject of
'Fisheries,' so dear to the hearts and minds of the rank and file of the American people, is given half a page, over three times as many words, and a separate title." In March 1957, responding to warnings from the Treasury Department of the urgent need for stringent budget cuts to forestall an
economic depression, the president requested drastic rescissions in the fiscal
year 1958 allocations he had submitted in January—including a draconian
reduction of $150 million in urban renewal funding. Having painstakingly
prepared extensive urban renewal applications in the years following passage
of the 1954 law, big-city mayors reacted bitterly to the news in 1957 that the
administration intended to cut spending on the program. In April a joint delegation of the United States Conference of Mayors (USCM) and the American Municipal Association (AMA) met with the president but found him unwilling to yield; the cities and states would have to take responsibility for
urban renewal, he explained. Led by Richard J. Daley of Chicago, Richardson Dilworth of Philadelphia, and Richard Lee of New Haven, a group of
Democratic mayors took their case to Capitol Hill, where by 1957 their party
held majorities in both the Senate and the House. Congress not only restored
the cuts in urban renewal proposed by the president but approved an additional $100 million; Eisenhower railed against the unwarranted and exces-
sive allocations for urban renewal but, having achieved his economies elsewhere in the budget, opted not to veto the bill.[32]

In his January 1958 budget message to Congress, the president asked for
an amendment that would require cities to pay half the cost of urban renewal
instead of the one-third they had been accustomed to providing. This latest
attempt at curtailing the federal government's participation in urban renewal failed, with big-city mayors again lobbying intensely in key congressional committees against program cuts, but Eisenhower at least succeeded
in negating congressional attempts to increase funding. Convinced that cities
could ill afford to contribute more to urban renewal and concerned that
Eisenhower's proposal needlessly antagonized big-city mayors, Albert M. Cole
vigorously argued against changing the program's funding formula. Discouraged by the prospects for urban renewal and uncomfortable with the increasingly conservative policies toward cities assumed by Eisenhower in the

latter years of his administration, Cole resigned from the HHFA in 1959 and accepted a lucrative job in industry.[33]

Albert Cole's tenure at HHFA had been surprisingly progressive in some respects—as a spokesman for urban interests, he advocated incremental increases in low-income housing and defended urban renewal—but he enthusiastically supported the Eisenhower administration's conservative policies on race. The president's definition of dynamic conservatism left minorities to fend for themselves in a rigidly segregated housing market that the federal government had helped to create. This tacit acceptance of residential segregation dovetailed with the Republican Party's forays into the South in search of white votes alienated by the Truman administration's tentative civil rights advances. As black migrants to the urban North became Democrats in overwhelming numbers, Republican paeans to local autonomy resonated in suburbs and the rural South. "The problems of racial discrimination are peculiarly local," Cole insisted. "I believe we should rely heavily on local responsibility and local wisdom to work out solutions." Affirming his devotion to the principles of economic and political freedom, he denied that the HHFA could—or should—battle racial discrimination in housing. Cole's successor, Norman P. Mason, likewise rejected plans to foster open occupancy and denied that government had any role to play in the burgeoning fair housing crusade. Under the leadership of both Cole and Mason, the federal government's position on housing and related urban affairs, buttressing the broad approach to the growing civil rights movement taken by the Eisenhower administration, accelerated the segregation of metropolitan America.[34]

Racial disturbances at public housing projects in Chicago and Louisville, as well as NAACP protests at the Levittown developments in Pennsylvania and New Jersey, raised concerns about the ability of state and local governments to deal with the problem of race and housing. In a 1955 cabinet meeting, Attorney General Herbert Brownell suggested the creation of an ad hoc committee to study the need for antidiscrimination measures by the federal government. Opinion within the cabinet divided, with some officials agreeing with Brownell and others opposed to the federal government's intrusion into state and local bailiwicks. Mutual Security Administrator Harold Stassen dismissed the legitimacy of the protests in Louisville, blaming the turmoil on communist rabble rousing. Eisenhower decided against forming a committee and, while condemning outright housing discrimination based upon race, argued that the federal government ought not "assume responsibility for ending discrimination in projects assisted through 'indirect activities' such as housing loan guarantee programs."[35]

To ensure that the HHFA honor the administration's position on race and housing, Cole set out to undermine the activities of the agency's Race Relations Service (RRS). In 1953 he chose Joseph R. Ray, an African American realtor, to replace the stubbornly outspoken Frank S. Horne as head of the RRS. Named a special assistant for minority studies, the unbowed Horne complained about his demotion and decried the passive acceptance of racial discrimination by the RRS under Ray's leadership. Horne used the occasion of the U.S. Supreme Court's ruling against "separate-but-equal" schools in May 1954 to increase criticism of the Eisenhower administration. The landmark *Brown v. Board of Education* decision, said Horne, firmly established the unacceptability of segregation in all walks of American life and presented the "opportunity" for "this Administration to remove all restrictions from the housing market." In 1955, citing the need to make budget cuts, Cole fired Horne and his assistant, Corienne Morrow. According to housing reformer Charles Abrams, Cole reported that the orders to terminate Horne's employment came directly from the Republican National Committee; the incident signaled the end of the HHFA as an advocate for racial desegregation by the mid-1950s. Even Joseph R. Ray, Horne's pliant successor, grumbled that correspondence that would normally be routed to the RRS was being sent to other offices—a clear sign, Ray noted, of "the gradual erosion of the duties and responsibilities" of the agency.[36]

The dismantling of the RRS raised important questions about whether the HHFA would attempt to enforce desegregation in housing along the lines that the Supreme Court had mandated for education in the *Brown* decision. In July 1954, after meeting with Eisenhower and several federal officials, Cole created the Advisory Committee on Minority Housing to formulate the administration's response. In September, he informed a meeting of the National Urban League of his refusal to "use our government aid as financial clubs" and reiterated his aversion to using leverage in Washington to effect desired outcomes in cities scattered across the nation. At a Minority Housing Conference in December, Cole suggested that 10 percent of new housing be set aside for minority occupancy in what Walter White of the National Association for the Advancement of Colored People (NAACP) likened to the "South African government's program of building separate communities for colored people." In the wake of the Housing Act of 1954 and the *Brown* decision, Cole recommended continued segregation coupled with a modest increase in the housing stock for African Americans—what the historian Arnold R. Hirsch caustically called a policy of "separate and adequate." In that sense, Hirsch noted, the Eisenhower administration "had yet to embrace *Plessy*, let alone *Brown*."[37]

Cole recognized that the nettlesome question of race and housing in metropolitan areas would focus on the Urban Renewal Administration (URA), which had been created by the Housing Act of 1954. The increased pace of slum clearance under the auspices of urban renewal in the 1950s necessitated the relocation of many poor African Americans, and Cole and others in the HHFA clearly saw the need for low-income housing to absorb the displaced minority populations. As Cole informed Connecticut Senator Prescott Bush, the small allocations for public housing included in the Housing Act of 1954 would serve solely to house the families uprooted by slum clearance. Public housing became an inner-city program tailored specifically to minority populations, leading many disenchanted African Americans to call urban renewal "negro removal." Indeed, minorities occupied 97 percent of the low-income housing constructed within urban renewal areas during the following years. As the Urban Renewal Administration shuffled poor black populations around metropolitan cores but carefully avoided suburban locations, the federal government became an easy target for racial integrationists who charged that housing policies in Washington promulgated segregation. By the end of the 1950s, noted the discouraged and newly outspoken Joseph R. Ray, the fact that the Urban Renewal Administration employed only one race relations officer in a program that almost exclusively involved African Americans seemed indefensible. Thanks to the urban renewal program launched in the 1950s, concluded Douglas S. Massey and Nancy A. Denton in their influential book, *American Apartheid*, "public housing projects in most large cities had become black reservations, highly segregated from the rest of society and characterized by extreme social isolation."[38]

As it did with urban renewal and the location of public housing, the Eisenhower administration continued to shore up the racial dividing lines that demarcated metropolitan areas through the policies of government financial agencies. In particular, the government's refusal to supervise the mortgage lending practices of private financial institutions curtailed credit to minorities and preserved racial segregation. Despite its long history of intervening in the housing market to safeguard property values, the Federal Reserve Board cited a lack of jurisdiction to justify its tolerance of discriminatory practices by member banks. The Federal Home Loan Bank Board declined to fashion a policy abrogating racial discrimination until 1961. The Federal Deposit Insurance Corporation (FDIC) announced remarkably that it "has no reason to believe that race is being used improperly by banks as a criterion in the making of real estate loans," all the evidence of redlining and the continued use of restrictive covenants throughout the nation notwithstanding.[39]

Most significant in underwriting metropolitan segregation, the FHA continued to serve the interests of white home buyers and to limit opportunities for African Americans who sought to purchase new housing. The FHA based its policies upon the assumption that an increased minority presence lowered property values. In order to preserve the desirability of a neighborhood, therefore, the FHA determined to maintain racial homogeneity. The agency roundly disputed the notion that racial bias drove underwriting decisions in any way, but at the same time the understanding of how inexorable market forces operated restrained the government from encouraging black occupancy in white neighborhoods. The Eisenhower administration avowed its commitment to "assure minorities equal opportunities to acquire good and well-located homes" and held a White House conference on housing for African Americans, but refused to intrude on local prerogatives or increase the amount of mortgage money available to minority borrowers. Section 220 of the Housing Act of 1954 sought to increase housing for minorities in urban renewal areas by allowing the FHA to insure mortgages on the basis of "acceptable risk" rather than the traditional "economic soundness" standard. Chary of guaranteeing loans in high-risk central cities and eager to maintain a low default record, however, the FHA approved few mortgages for minority homeowners under the auspices of Section 220. African Americans were able to acquire less than 2 percent of the federal mortgage insurance for new housing between 1946 and 1959. Moreover, although the FHA never guaranteed mortgages for the lion's share of homes in the private market, its policies and standards became the norm for financial institutions participating in the housing industry.[40]

Under the guidance of President Eisenhower and HHFA administrator Albert Cole, the federal government presided over the construction of more minority housing than ever before and virtually all of it under segregated conditions. Local housing authorities during the 1950s overwhelmingly built low-income units in the urban core and usually installed as residents nonwhite families recently displaced by slum clearance projects. Invoking a reverence for decentralized government, Washington bureaucracies deferred to the plans submitted by local agencies and supplied capital both through the public and private housing markets. In effect, the HHFA agreed to supply more housing for minorities in partial payment for downtown revitalization and the maintenance of segregation. A dual housing market based upon race developed rapidly as greater numbers of nonwhites resided in inner cities and largely white suburbs expanded across the landscape. The "American Apartheid" described by Massey and Denton took shape most clearly in the nation's largest cities.[41]

Metropolitan decentralization in the 1950s proceeded in part because of the dual housing market created by the federal government but also due to other policies emanating from Washington, D.C. Tax breaks for homeowners created an incentive for Americans to build new homes in the growing suburbs and created a huge subsidy that cost the U.S. Treasury billions of dollars annually. Deductions for mortgage interest payments and local property taxes had been relatively inconsequential before World War II, when only about 5 percent of Americans paid income taxes. Beginning in the Cold War era, when the Internal Revenue Service (IRS) collected taxes from virtually all wage earners, the incentive to build rather than rent became exceedingly attractive. The construction of new houses predominated in the suburbs, while multifamily dwellings remained more prevalent in inner cities, but a revision of the tax code in 1954 spurred the construction of more apartment buildings throughout metropolitan regions. The change that year allowed businesses to deduct the depreciation on their buildings in the first several years after construction rather than over the ensuing forty years, the length of time for "straight-line depreciation" specified by the U.S. Treasury Department in 1934. This new "accelerated depreciation" allowance quickly became a lucrative incentive for builders of all types of businesses, including multifamily dwellings. Because the incentive applied only to newly constructed buildings and not to the renovation of existing structures, investors instinctively looked at suburbs to take advantage of the opportunity. As historian Thomas W. Hanchett has noted, accelerated depreciation effectively made real-estate development a tax shelter. By the end of the decade, the number of new apartment complexes surpassed the number of new single-family structures in some suburbs.[42]

With any income-producing building qualifying for the accelerated depreciation deduction, real-estate development in the suburbs boomed in the 1950s and afterward. The relatively cheap cost of land on the metropolitan periphery provided inviting locations for offices, motels, retail outlets, factories, and other industrial sites, as well as rental housing. Because IRS regulations prohibited deductions for land depreciation, the comparatively high cost of real estate in inner cities discouraged developers. Suburban shopping centers appeared with increasing frequency after the 1954 tax code revision, drawing consumers away from the downtown department stores that had traditionally dominated retailing in metropolitan areas. Between 1953 and 1956 the number of shopping centers constructed annually in the United States tripled; the nation had approximately 13,000 shopping centers by 1970, almost all of them built in the preceding fifteen years. Again, federal taxation policies indirectly accelerated the movement of businesses and people to the suburbs.[43]

The federal government further heightened the attractiveness of suburban living by helping to extend the infrastructure necessary for residential development beyond existing urban and suburban boundaries. The problem of waste removal slowed home builders after the war, for example, when the U.S. Geological Survey, the American Water Works Association, the American Society of Civil Engineers, and several trade associations warned that private septic systems were creating dangerous levels of groundwater pollution. Increased federal assistance to state and local governments would allow developers access to public sewer lines and, most important, sewage treatment facilities. The Water Pollution Control Act of 1948, which expired on June 30, 1956, offered some assistance to state and local governments in the form of loans for the construction of sewage treatment plants. Calling water pollution a local problem, Eisenhower shied away from offering any encouragement to the congressmen seeking to pass new legislation to replace the expiring 1948 law. The AMA estimated that a sewage treatment program funded at $5.3 billion over ten years ($530 million annually) would be required for pollution abatement. Working closely with the AMA, Representative John Blatnik (Democrat, Minnesota), who chaired the House Subcommittee on Rivers and Harbors, drafted a bill that created federal grants-in-aid to communities ($100 million a year for ten years) for sewage treatment plants. Repeating his misgivings about the creation of a costly new federal grant program, Eisenhower nevertheless signed the Water Pollution Control Act of 1956 on July 9. The provision of potable drinking water, partially subsidized by the federal government, removed another potential obstacle to suburban growth.[44]

The federal government's greatest contribution to metropolitan decentralization came with the creation of the interstate highway system. The desirability of a transcontinental highway network that linked the nation's cities and also improved metropolitan traffic flow had been discussed as early as Franklin D. Roosevelt's second term, and larger cities had been building expressways after the Second World War with federal aid (a 50/50 financial match) from the Bureau of Public Roads. Having made urban redevelopment and public housing the keystones of its urban policy, the Truman administration declined to combine housing and highways in a comprehensive plan for the cities, left civil engineers in charge of highway construction, and made little progress toward completion of the national highway system outlined earlier by the BPR. Soon after Eisenhower assumed the presidency, however, the rapid rate of suburbanization and the lack of adequate roads to accommodate the exploding number of automobiles and trucks in cities and their surroundings brought a sense of immediacy to the problem of inadequate metropolitan transportation. As the Advisory Commission on Intergovernmental Relations made clear, the responsibility for action fell to the federal government because of the impossible clash of jurisdictions among the city, suburban, and state governments crying out for improved highways. Not only did the typical metropolitan area contain ninety-six local governmental entities, pointed out the commission, but metropolitan areas frequently straddled state lines; the New York City metropolitan region contained over 1,000 discrete government units, for instance, and Chicago another 960. At a time when few cities claimed effective local land use planning bureaus and virtually no regional transportation agencies existed, the need for involvement by the federal government seemed irrefutable even to the Eisenhower Republicans who normally warned against such centralization of power in Washington.[45]

As during the Truman years, a powerful coalition of interests advanced the idea of a national highway system with extensive metropolitan roadways. The highway lobby, comprised of the automobile manufacturers, the trucking industry, the oil companies, the construction industry, and a host of trade associations related to automobile production, foresaw greater profits, the creation of jobs, and a boon to the national economy engendered by the massive program. Mayors, local politicians, and downtown business interests jumped onboard as a way to deal with worsening traffic problems, revivify declining central business districts, and support the local building trades. Mayor Thomas D'Alesandro of Baltimore testified before Congress in 1956 that "traffic strangulation within cities is the major problem facing the country," and Nashville Mayor Ben West called the situation "desperate." Mindful that state highway engineers and officials would be making the critical design and location decisions, the American Association of State Highway Officials also supported the initiative on behalf of state highway engineers and administrators. Congressmen from heavily urbanized states in particular became keenly aware of the groundswell building in Washington in support of the popular proposal.[46]

In the early years of his presidency, the cautious Eisenhower predictably talked of abrogating the federal gasoline tax and expressed his hope that the states would assume full responsibility for road building. Overcoming his innate suspicion of large-scale domestic spending programs that potentially threatened his ability to balance the federal budget, however, he backed

away from his initial position and championed the legislation that created
the interstate highways. Several factors probably contributed to the president's decision to take a position that seemed contrary to his aversion to
government activism. Travel with a military caravan on a 1919 cross-country
trek designed to illustrate the inadequacy of the nation's highway system had
left Lieutenant Colonel Eisenhower with a strong and lasting belief in the
need for good highways; his exposure to the German autobahns during
World War II reinforced this idea that the United States needed good roads
for military reasons. In the threatening Cold War era, when the nation's military and civilian leadership worried about a possible nuclear attack
launched by the USSR, Eisenhower saw an extensive network of highways as
evacuation routes from the major cities that seemed likely targets of Soviet
missiles. As president, he also recognized the economic benefits of highway
construction that would employ tens of thousands of workers and stimulate
a sluggish economy over a projected decade and a half. Arthur F. Burns, a respected economist and head of the president's Council of Economic Advisors
(CEA), argued repeatedly in cabinet meetings that the administration should
use highway building as a countercyclical measure to stabilize the economy—and to good effect. According to Raymond J. Saulnier, Burns's successor at the CEA, "It is doubtful that any president has made a more systematic and sustained effort than Eisenhower to plan and utilize public
construction for countercyclical purposes." Finally, no one could deny the
need for serious action to address the nation's growing transportation problems. Eisenhower formally announced his support for interstate highways in
a speech delivered for him by Vice President Richard Nixon at the National
Governors' Conference on July 12, 1954.[47]

To prepare a detailed plan, Eisenhower appointed the President's Advisory Committee on a National Highway Program chaired by a long-time
confidant, retired U.S. Army General, and member of the General Motors
Board of Directors, Lucius E. Clay. In later years, Clay remembered that the
principal reason for the creation of such a massive public works program
had been to prepare for a possible economic recession. In the public hearings held by the committee on October 7–8, however, most of the testimony
offered by such groups as the Automobile Manufacturers Association, the
American Road Builders Association, the American Association of State
Highway Officials, the American Municipal Association, and the United
States Conference of Mayors dealt with the salubrious effect the interstate
highway system would have on city traffic. The committee report, issued in
January 1955, strongly recommended that the interstate highway system be

given "top priority" to improve the nation's defenses and bolster its economy. Emphasizing the need to expedite construction, the committee urged that the federal government abandon its 50/50 funding arrangement with the states and "assume principal responsibility" for the program's cost. Eisenhower praised the Clay Committee's efforts and used its recommendations as the heart of the legislation he sent immediately to Congress. Francis V. du Pont, whose family owned controlling interest in General Motors stock, replaced Thomas H. MacDonald as commissioner of the BPR in 1953, resigned the post he held for barely one year, and became a special assistant to the secretary of commerce so that he could devote all of his time to passing an interstate highway bill.[48]

The Clay Committee report received a mixed reception on Capitol Hill, despite the ardent efforts of the highway lobby, du Pont, and other supporters, and the Federal-Aid Highway Act of 1956 passed only after two years of haggling spanning both sessions of the Eighty-fourth Congress. The most controversial aspect of the bill involved the funding mechanism. Representatives of the powerful American Trucking Association objected to paying tolls as well as mandatory state and federal gasoline taxes. The Clay Committee proposed the sale of bonds to finance the project, but others argued for the extensive construction of toll roads, the implementation of user taxes on motor fuel and tires, or the use of general revenue. Many Democrats condemned Clay's reliance on bond sales as fiscally irresponsible because of the massive debt it would create; Senator Harry F. Byrd (Democrat, Virginia), a powerful member of the Finance Committee, called it "pork-barrel" politics. While some legislators wanted retention of the 50/50 formula for state and federal funding, others followed the Clay Committee's direction and proposed that the federal government assume 90 percent of the expense. John S. Bragdon, a West Point classmate of the president and army engineer who became the Coordinator of Public Works Planning in 1955, spoke avidly for the use of toll roads to pay for highway expansion. Having supported tolls at first, Eisenhower changed his mind and endorsed highway-user taxes in a special message to Congress in February 1955. The Republican-dominated House fell in line behind the president but, after hearing sixty-six witnesses during the summer, saw the majority coalition dissolve over the funding issue. In the Senate, an alternative to the Clay proposal submitted by Albert Gore Sr. (Democrat, Tennessee) that mandated prevailing wages for construction workers passed but ran afoul of conservatives in the House who fought to keep costs down. Congress adjourned in August 1955 without passing a highway bill.[49]

The legislative road proved to be much smoother in 1956, in large measure because the president and members of Congress had much to gain by passing a massive public works bill in an election year. Congressmen Hale Boggs of Louisiana and George Fallon of Maryland proposed a slightly revised version of the law introduced the previous year by the Eisenhower administration, and the House responded affirmatively by a vote of 388 to 19. Prodded by Majority Leader Lyndon B. Johnson, Democrats in the Senate accepted the broad outlines of the Boggs-Fallon proposal and approved it in a voice vote. Representatives of both the House and the Senate demonstrated a willingness to reconcile their differences in conference deliberations to accommodate the two versions. On June 26 the Senate approved the final draft by a vote of 89 to 1, and the House did so by acclamation. The president signed the Federal-Aid Highway Act of 1956 on June 29, 1956, authorizing the construction of a national highway system of 41,000 miles over the next thirteen years. With state governments paying for 10 percent of the cost of construction, the federal government would underwrite the remaining 90 percent of the National System of Interstate and Defense Highways from a highway trust fund drawn from excise taxes on motor fuel and tires.[50]

The key to breaking the legislative logjam, provided by Boggs and Fallon to solve the funding controversy, proved to be the ingenious highway trust fund. The IRS raised the levy on the motor fuel tax from two cents to three cents per gallon and the levy on new tires from five cents to eight cents per pound, compromise amounts designed largely to placate the powerful trucking industry. (A provision of the bill mandated higher user fees for heavy trucks.) Revenue raised under these auspices could be used only for new construction costs. Each year as road mileage increased, the amount of revenue in the trust fund would as well, so that the interstate highway program would develop a self-generating momentum apart from national economic fluctuations.[51] As one observer later noted with grudging admiration:

The money poured into the Trust Fund in a golden stream. Engineers across the land drew lines on maps, and the bulldozers followed, in increasing numbers. While each year Washington budget-makers strained to find the money for a thousand crying needs, and Congressional committee rooms echoed to the voices pleading for funds to pour on this or that hurt, the inviolable Highway Trust Fund plowed ahead under its own power.[52]

A staunch advocate of restraint by the federal government, President Eisenhower nevertheless championed what he himself termed the largest public works program "ever undertaken by the United States or any other country." The president and other conservatives justified building the interstate
highways as a defense measure at a time of heightened national security
interests. Eisenhower could rightly claim that the federal government only
provided funding, while state highway departments conducted the actual
building of the roadways. The pay-as-you-go structure of the highway trust
fund defused potential financial criticisms when the goal of budget balancing
remained a top priority in the administration. Such budgetary constraints reduced the influence of planners and eliminated significant additions such as
mass transit to the transportation strategy. Despite the unprecedented size
and cost of the interstate highway program, the 1956 legislation dealt primarily with civil engineering matters and to a great extent ignored the social
implications of roadway construction.[53]

The passage of the interstate highway law received praise from many
quarters—after all, policy analyst Daniel P. Moynihan archly observed, the
new program contained "something for everybody"—but the legislation had
surprisingly little to say about highways and cities. Unlike the 1939 and 1944
reports prepared by the BPR, which dealt extensively with both expressway
construction and slum clearance, the Clay Committee report made scant
mention of the potential impact of interstate highways on the urban environment. Clay himself later found it regrettable that his committee had devoted
so little attention to the "provision of throughways through the cities." This
omission seemed particularly egregious because $15 billion of the $27 billion
earmarked for interstate highway construction over the next decade would
be spent in urban areas. (The high cost of construction in the cities could be
explained by the fact that each mile of expressway completed in an urban
setting consumed twenty-four acres of land, each interchange eighty acres.)
The committee saw the interstates principally as facilitators of long-haul
traffic, provided few connections between the interstates and city roads, and
essentially ignored the social and economic problems that would be caused
by building the freeways in populated areas. "I'm not sure what the answer
is," Clay commented later, "the relationship of our big cities to the freeways." A 1959 report on the legislative intent of the Federal-Aid Highway
Act of 1956 prepared jointly by the Bureau of the Budget and the U.S. Department of Commerce affirmed that "the Interstate system is to serve national needs above local needs and that the interstate character of the system
should not be prejudiced by local considerations." According to several

accounts, Eisenhower himself believed for a long time that the interstates would only link far-flung urban places and expressed genuine surprise when discovering finally in 1959 that a significant portion of the interstate highways would actually pass through inner cities.[54]

As Clay, Eisenhower, and other influential policy makers expressed little concern about the impact of the expressways on inner cities, a consensus developed within the administration that one of the salutary benefits of the interstate program would be an acceleration of the rate of suburbanization. John S. Bragdon predicted to the Council of Economic Advisers in 1954 that the impetus given suburbanization by the completion of the high speed expressways would be "economically healthy."[55] The report of the Clay Committee went further, saying:

> We have been able to disperse our factories, our stores, our people; in short, to create a revolution in living habits. Our cities have spread into suburbs, dependent on the automobile for their existence. The automobile has restored a way of life in which the individual may live in a friendly neighborhood, it has brought city and country closer together, it has made us one country and a united people.[56]

While the White House looked forward to more suburbanization and big-city mayors and downtown businessmen lauded the new law's potential for reviving central business districts, urban planners and assorted liberal critics quickly identified serious flaws in the interstate highway blueprint. Concerned about having played virtually no role in conceptualizing or drafting the legislation, planners complained that no systematic thought had been given to the impact of highway construction on entire metropolitan areas. With the size of metropolitan regions predicted to double in the next twenty years, suggested planners, the location of interstate highways would surely affect how the growth would proceed. The results of a widely read 1956 Brookings Institution study, published the same year that Congress passed the fateful interstate legislation, argued forcefully that highways be completed in metropolitan areas only as part of a comprehensive transportation plan. Noting that such an undertaking was "too important to leave to the highway engineers," Massachusetts Institute of Technology Professor John T. Howard called the planning of the interstate system "a completely unconscious act. The designers of the system were conscious only of doing an excellent job of highway engineering." Howard praised civil engineers for their technical expertise but added: "It does not belittle them to say that, just as war is too important to leave to the generals, so highways are too important to leave to the highway engineers." Brookings Institution economist Wilfred Owen similarly observed that expressway construction had been conceived "strictly as engineering problems in which the only objective considered is that of keeping vehicles in rapid motion." Daniel P. Moynihan suggested a moratorium on interstate construction in urban areas until planning principles could be applied.[57]

One of the most important issues largely ignored by the Federal-Aid Highway Act of 1956 concerned the relocation of the residents displaced by housing demolition in urban areas. Early attempts to address the human cost of expressway construction failed in Congress despite extensive expert testimony and the determination of some legislators to provide adequate compensation for uprooted populations. Testifying in 1955 before the House Committee on Public Works, New York City's Robert Moses strongly lobbied for the payment of relocation expenses to renters, and the version of the final legislation passed by the House in 1956 included a provision for such reimbursement by the federal government. This arrangement encountered a roadblock in the White House where concerns about the program's cost led Eisenhower, his financial advisers, and his key Republican allies in the Senate to seek economy measures at every turn. The creation of the Highway Trust Fund quieted fears of excessive spending in the face of a potential recession, whereas the additional cost of relocation funding would have crept into the federal budget. Instead, the price tag for the interstates appeared as a separate item akin to the accounting of Social Security expenditures. Despite the efforts of Herbert Lehman (Democrat, New York), the Senate excised the relocation payment authorized by the House. In the conference committee that produced the final version of the bill, representatives of the House and the Senate excluded relocation funding. As the historian Raymond A. Mohl has noted, officials in the Eisenhower administration apparently overlooked the irony of refusing to provide relocation assistance for the highway program while allowing just such compensation for residents uprooted by urban renewal.[58]

The displacement of huge populations to make way for expressways in densely crowded urban neighborhoods sparked controversy in a number of cities in the 1960s and 1970s, with the first of the "freeway revolts" erupting at the end of the Eisenhower administration. In a pattern repeated frequently in the following decades nationwide, San Francisco activists mobilized successfully in 1959 to oppose the city's intention to extend the Embarcadero Freeway through Golden Gate Park and nearby middle-class neighborhoods.

Public opposition had failed in 1956 to derail the construction of the Embarcadero Freeway, a massive eyesore that separated the heart of the city from the scenic bay-front harbor, but the announcement of yet another construction project designed to serve the interests of downtown merchants and outlying commuters intensified public outrage three years later. A grassroots movement spearheaded by neighborhood organizations and supported editorially by the city's daily newspapers prevailed over the designs of local city planners and state officials. The San Francisco Board of Supervisors exercised the veto power provided by state law over the plans conceived by the California highway commission, and the city commenced consideration of mass transit as an alternative for improving downtown traffic. The highly publicized triumph of the grassroots associations over city hall in San Francisco portended additional conflict in coming years when highway engineers largely ignored the consequences of the technical work involved in extending the interstates into city neighborhoods.[59]

Nascent unrest over the location of expressways in urban neighborhoods at the close of the 1950s constituted the first rumblings of dissent over what had been a widely heralded program. For John S. Bragdon, a persistent advocate for limiting highway construction, the manifold problems of constructing the interstates in urban areas constituted the principal flaw of the Federal-Aid Highway Act of 1956. Even though he acknowledged that passage of the law meant that "the horse . . . was out of the stable," Bragdon continued in the last years of the Eisenhower administration to argue that the federal government should cease funding of expressways within metropolitan regions and cede that responsibility to municipal governments. In 1959, with the nation steeped in a severe economic recession, the president gave Bragdon the assignment of reviewing the interstate highway program to see if federal expenditures could be reduced. As Bragdon and the twenty-five members of his public works staff conducted their investigation and rumors spread of draconian cuts in expressway construction, big-city mayors from across the nation sent letters to Eisenhower voicing their grave concern. Within the federal bureaucracy in Washington, powerful constituencies squared off over the fate of the popular but expensive program. Officials at the BPR resented Bragdon's incessant demands for information and cooperated reluctantly; Bertram Tallamy, the federal highway administrator in charge of administering the interstate building effort, strongly opposed any changes in the 1956 legislation. Eager to reduce federal spending wherever possible, Bureau of the Budget personnel lined up solidly behind

Bragdon and the Public Works Planning Unit. Rumors of Bragdon's crusade to curtail interstate construction worried mayors, AMA officials, and other urban interests, all of whom remained as faithfully committed as ever to the need for more expressways. Mayor Ben West of Nashville told a congressional committee that "the Nation's cities will fight any such proposal to the bitter end."[60]

The months of heated internecine fighting came to a head in April when Eisenhower met with Bragdon, Tallamy, and other highway officials in the White House. In their subsequent accounts of what happened at the meeting, the two principal advocates gave different accounts of what transpired and of how the president reacted to their arguments. Bragdon and Tallamy especially differed in their descriptions of how Eisenhower reacted to his perusal of the "Yellow Book," the dense BPR manual that had been used in 1955–1956 to illustrate for congressmen where all urban routes of the interstate highway network would be situated. Tallamy reported that the president paid little attention to the "Yellow Book," but Bragdon suggested that Eisenhower seemed genuinely surprised at the extensiveness of the interstates' penetration into metropolitan areas. In any event, Eisenhower concluded that progress on the project "had reached the point that his hands were virtually tied" and that too much work had been done in and around cities to change courses. Bragdon resigned his post and accepted a position at the Civil Aeronautics Board shortly thereafter, and his successor at the Public Works Planning Unit, Floyd Peterson, submitted a cursory report in the Eisenhower administration's last days. For better or worse, the construction of interstate highways in metropolitan America would continue along paths determined by the civil engineers.[61]

Bragdon and other critics also questioned the Eisenhower administration's sole reliance on the automobile to solve urban transportation problems, lamenting the fact that little real consideration was being given to adding or improving mass transit. Many planners argued that building bigger highways merely created bigger traffic jams and that a more extensive highway network to accommodate automobiles only made sense as part of a comprehensive metropolitan transportation plan that also included a fuller complement of subways, elevated trains, commuter railroads, and other forms of rapid transit. Planners questioned both the blind adoration of the automobile and the thoughtless dismissal of mass transit as a viable solution to transportation needs. In his scathing critique of the automobile's influence on urban life, *The Highway and the City*, Lewis Mumford acidly noted: "The current American way of life is founded not just on motor transportation but on the religion of the motorcar, and the sacrifices that people are prepared to make for this religion stand outside the realm of rational criticism." Journalist Francis Bello agreed and pointed to the "endless sprawl" and traffic snarls in Los Angeles as "an example of what can happen to a city that worships the automobile." He added: "There is nothing wrong with mass transit that modern high-speed equipment could not cure." Many planners ruefully pondered the kind of improvement that would have been possible had a significant portion of the $27 billion authorized in the Federal-Aid Highway Act of 1956 been allocated to the cities' aging and declining public transportation systems.[62]

The movement to encourage federal aid to mass transit grew in the late 1950s as a number of commuter railroads operating in large east coast cities teetered on the verge of bankruptcy. The suburban lines of major railroads had been losing ridership and accumulating huge operating deficits since the end of World War II, and the severe economic recession of 1957 intensified the problem. Two successive Democratic mayors of Philadelphia, Joseph Clark and Richardson Dilworth, led the fight to obtain federal aid for the 100,000 daily riders of the city's commuter railroad lines. Before his election to the U.S. Senate in 1956, Clark tried unsuccessfully to get the Eisenhower administration to set aside funds for mass transit as an adjunct to its massive interstate highway program. Richardson Dilworth, Clark's successor in Philadelphia's city hall, sought to forge a coalition between big-city mayors and chief executive officers of the railroads to coax funding out of Washington for improvements to mass transit. He argued that cities could refurbish existing fixed rail lines and railroad cars for far less than the cost of building massive expressway systems, but many railroad executives balked at accepting government subsidies and preferred simply to cancel their passenger service altogether. Congress studied the problem, concentrating on the financial health of the railroads rather than the transportation needs of the cities. "Basically," concluded Florida Senator George Smathers, "the commuter service problem is a local one." The Transportation Act of 1958 brought the railroads financial relief by expediting the process by which they could eliminate their commuter lines, but it concerned big-city mayors who feared the onset of a severe transportation crisis.[63]

In January 1959, still reeling from the implications of the Transportation Act of 1958, Dilworth convened a meeting in Chicago of railroad executives and representatives of a number of cities that relied heavily upon commuter railroads. (Mayors and other urban officials attended from Allentown, Pennsylvania; Baltimore; Boston; Chicago; Cleveland; Detroit; Kansas City; Milwaukee; New York City; Philadelphia; St. Louis; and Washington, D.C.) Although some attendees expressed concern that federal aid might eventually lead to government takeover of the railroads—a view expressed most often by representatives from the midwestern cities, which depended less than eastern metropolises on commuter railroads—a rough consensus soon emerged on the need for financial assistance from Washington. The meeting dissolved without agreement on the necessary action that needed to be taken, but the participants appointed a committee under Dilworth's direction to draft specific proposals that could be turned into legislation. The Dilworth committee met in March 1959 in Philadelphia and wrote a report, "The Collapse of Commuter Service," which the AMA issued later that year. Based upon that report, Dilworth, representatives of the AMA, and James Symes, president of the Pennsylvania Railroad, drafted a bill that called for the U.S. Department of Commerce to make low-interest loans totaling $500 million to states, local governments, and metropolitan authorities for the improvement and maintenance of mass transit equipment and facilities.[64]

Dilworth and his compatriots found an eager ally on Capitol Hill, Senator Harrison Williams Jr. (Democrat, New Jersey). Williams introduced the bill crafted by Dilworth and Symes, after he and members of his staff had revised it, in March 1960. Passage of the measure seemed unlikely from the start, however, as Eisenhower announced immediately his intention to veto any mass transit legislation emerging from Congress during his last year in office. Eager to curb government spending, intent upon balancing the national budget one last time, and having retreated from his earlier support of urban renewal, the president vowed to oppose any additional local "raids" on the federal purse. Besides, Eisenhower intoned, disentangling rush hour traffic should remain a local matter. On June 27, 1960, after a brief and spiritless debate, the bill passed the Senate by voice vote; absent a defender of Senator Williams's fervor in the House, the bill never reached the floor for consideration. Federal aid for mass transit would have to await a Democratic administration.[65]

After eight years of "dynamic conservatism," many planners, big-city mayors, and other spokesmen for urban interests yearned for a Democratic administration that they hoped would devote greater attention to the problems of the nation's big cities. Uninterested in the complex of problems that

confronted cities in mid-twentieth century America, Eisenhower blithely ignored urban concerns during his two-term presidency. Lobbyists for such
interest groups as the United States Conference of Mayors, the American Municipal Association, and the National League of Cities saw their cause as essentially hopeless in the 1950s. "Under Ike, there was no sense in fighting,"
lamented a representative of the United States Conference of Mayors. "Ike
was not inclined to pay attention to cities, and insisted that he knew nothing
about them." New York City Mayor Robert F. Wagner Jr. said that local officials were "tired of being treated as special pleaders seeking unwarranted assistance to meet purely local problems, instead of what we really are: the
field grade officers who must daily and at first hand direct the battle against
the nation's prime domestic problems." A handful of officials in the administration—most notably Robert Merriam and, to a lesser degree, Howard
Pyle—presciently argued the need for more attention to urban problems, but
Eisenhower's interest never rose above a desire to improve the efficiency of
intergovernmental relations. The remarkable growth of suburbs and the related decline of inner cities seemed to the president the natural result of market forces, a matter of academic interest perhaps but not the cause for policy
formulation by the federal government. Besides, activism in Washington in-
fringed upon the bailiwicks of state and local governments while placing excessive demands on the federal Treasury. In his January 1960 State of the
Union message to Congress, Eisenhower denounced the temptation to provide additional federal aid to cities, saying: "I do not doubt that our urban
and other perplexing problems can be solved in the traditional American
method. In doing so we must realize that nothing is really solved and ruinous
tendencies are set in motion by yielding to the deceptive bait of the 'easy'
Federal tax dollar."[66]

Eisenhower's "dynamic conservatism" strove to minimize the impact of
the federal government on urban life, but his hands-off policy arguably constituted a form of "malign neglect." Opposed by a majority of the Democrats
and a few moderate Republicans on Capitol Hill, the Eisenhower administration fought a holding action to limit the construction of low-income housing
while seeking what Albert M. Cole called a "fair and feasible way to terminate the program." While minimizing the impact of public housing and other
initiatives that would have benefited inner-city homeowners, the federal government continued to foster the growth of suburbia. The authorization of the
interstate highways, the great domestic undertaking of the Eisenhower administration, further accelerated metropolitan decentralization and unearthed a host of other problems for cities that needed to be addressed by a

later generation of policy makers. In a penetrating analysis of the Eisenhower presidency, historian Robert Griffith noted that the interstate highway program "though producing enormous growth in the auto, oil, construction, and other related industries, laid an enormous if immeasurable tax upon the American people in the form of disintegrating cities, declining public transportation, air pollution, and wasteful energy consumption." More willing to confront these challenges than Eisenhower had been, the Democratic presidents of the 1960s would usher in an unprecedented age of federal involvement in urban affairs.[67]

3

THE NEW URBAN FRONTIER

The future of America's cities looked perilous in 1960. The remarkable post-war growth of suburbia mirrored the decline of the inner cities as the centrifugal movement of population, business, and tax dollars accelerated in the 1950s. Local efforts to fashion an urban renaissance, launched after World War II by a new breed of mayors in alliance with corporate executives, produced a number of noteworthy accomplishments but not in sufficient quantity to offset the overall downward trajectory. Large-scale highway and urban renewal projects funded in Washington, D.C., similarly offered hope, but the scope of federal commitment appeared wholly inadequate to the task of saving the cities. Democrats blamed the do-nothing policies of the Eisenhower administration for the worsening condition of urban America; the Republicans countered that the demographic changes of the previous eight years simply reflected the natural flow of population and wealth in a free society with government properly restrained. Either way, census data showed a clear picture of urban decline and suburban ascendance in the 1950s. From 1950 to 1960, while suburbs increased in population by more than 60 percent, the older cities of the Northeast and Midwest suffered the greatest losses. Boston, St. Louis, and Pittsburgh lost more than 10 percent of their populations; Detroit, Minneapolis, and Buffalo lost 7–10 percent; and New York City, Chicago, Philadelphia, Cleveland, Baltimore, and Cincinnati lost less than 5 percent.[1]

Population decline topped the list of serious problems confronting the cities, but a comparison of 1950 and 1960 census data revealed a number of other worrisome issues as well. Compounding the population loss, the middle classes led the suburban exodus. The median income of people living in the nation's largest metropolitan regions already exceeded the median income of those regions' core cities by 1950, and the disparity increased significantly during the next ten years. Further, the departure of the middle class meant fewer tax dollars for city halls starved for revenue. At the same time that the more affluent residents of the cities departed, the number of poor newcomers to the inner cities increased substantially. The arrival of southern blacks beginning during the Second World War and continuing in the late 1940s and 1950s, the so-called Second Great Migration, elevated the nonwhite populations of core cities to new heights. By 1960, for example, African Americans constituted more than one-fourth of the populations in Baltimore, Cleveland, Detroit, Philadelphia, and St. Louis. Changing racial demographics elevated racial conflict in these communities, while the influx of poor nonwhite immigrants put additional financial burdens on municipal budgets. Often poorly educated and lacking job skills, these recent arrivals paid few taxes but consumed city services at a rapid rate. The same could be said of such immigrants as Latinos and Appalachian whites. The arrival in the 1950s of Puerto Ricans in New York City, along with Appalachian whites in Chicago's Uptown and Cincinnati's Over-the-Rhine, put additional strains on those cities. The mounting problems confronting big-city mayors seemed daunting indeed by 1960.[2]

Unfortunately for the friends of America's cities, urban renewal was proving not to be the panacea envisioned by so many disparate groups in the postwar years. To be sure, the program scored a number of successes in deteriorating inner-city neighborhoods with the construction of gleaming new structures that improved the faces of downtowns. The list of impressive urban renewal creations included the Lincoln Center for the Performing Arts in New York City, the Charles Center in Baltimore, and the Gateway Center in Minneapolis, to name just a few; such institutions of higher education as Fordham University in New York City and Saint Louis University used urban renewal largesse to expand their campuses. Despite the completion of these glittering showplaces, however, a growing legion of skeptics questioned the value of urban renewal to the cities. By the early 1960s both conservatives and liberals were assailing the program as a questionable enterprise that spent exorbitant amounts of tax dollars while exacting an especially terrible toll on the city's working and lower classes. Looking at the inner-city residents who consistently bore the brunt of the federal program, African American author James Baldwin charged that urban renewal basically amounted to "Negro removal." Right-wing critics opposed the federal government's extensive involvement in local affairs and rued the expense of urban redevelopment as a harmful deviation from sound financial practice. In his polemical *The Federal Bulldozer*, conservative policy analyst Martin Anderson of the Joint Center for Urban Studies formulated a comprehensive critique of the

program and argued strenuously for its termination. He charged that the
federal government's intrusive presence in cities disrupted the private housing market, wasted millions of taxpayers' dollars, and uprooted hundreds of
small businesses in neighborhoods designated for redevelopment. The average length of time necessary to complete a project from inception to ribbon
cutting, determined Anderson, totaled an astonishing twelve years. Moreover, he contended, urban renewal projects devoted only 62 percent of new
construction dollars to housing, and over 90 percent of the replacement
housing arranged by the government charged rents that proved unaffordable
to displaced residents.[3]

Many members of the liberal intelligentsia grew equally disillusioned
with urban renewal, if for different reasons than conservative commentators.
Jane Jacobs cataloged the liberals' most trenchant criticisms in her romantic
The Death and Life of Great American Cities. Outraged by the New York
City renewal agency's designs on the Greenwich Village neighborhood in
which she lived, Jacobs composed a passionate defense of the well-worn portions of cities erroneously labeled slums by ravenous developers and Washington bureaucrats. Decrying wholesale neighborhood destruction, she
praised dense populations, the preservation of old buildings, and mixed economic functions—in short, the retention of the heterogeneity and diversity
that made metropolises vibrant and exciting places in which to live.[4] The toll
of urban renewal on the housing stock she calculated as follows:

> Low-income projects that become worse centers of delinquency,
> vandalism, and general social hopelessness than the slums they were
> supposed to replace. Middle-income housing projects which are truly
> marvels of dullness and regimentation, sealed against any buoyancy or
> vitality of city life. Luxury housing projects that mitigate their inanity, or
> try to, with vapid vulgarity . . . This is not the rebuilding of cities. This is
> the sacking of cities.[5]

The published attacks on urban renewal by Anderson, Jacobs, and others across the political spectrum resonated with much of the public because
of the program's disappointing outcomes in city after city. In many instances, charged local activists, federal bulldozers destroyed vital communities while exacerbating housing shortages. Moreover, massive public housing projects proved no substitute for cohesive neighborhoods. In the
celebrated case of Boston's West End, approximately 7,500 residents of a primarily Italian community singled out for removal vehemently objected and

mounted a protracted grassroots protest. The demonstrators lost their battle with city hall, then helplessly stood by as wrecking balls pulverized their homes and developers erected luxury apartment buildings. In later years, sociologist Herbert Gans's *The Urban Villagers* chronicled the Italian Americans' emotional attachment to their doomed neighborhood, and clinical psychologist Marc Fried wrote movingly about the grief experienced by the uprooted West Enders. Housing expert Chester Hartman contended that nearly one-half of these "slum dwellers" lived in perfectly good housing and reported that the median monthly rent for the 73 percent of dislodged people for whom the city found new housing subsequently rose from $41 to $71. Similar battles between local governments and grassroots groups in Chicago, Philadelphia, Buffalo, Cleveland, and other big cities, all ending in the destruction of viable neighborhoods, further tainted urban renewal's already declining reputation.[6]

Yet if urban renewal's decidedly checkered record of accomplishment called into question the initial enthusiasm that greeted its establishment, much support remained for the program that in 1960 still stood as the federal government's principal policy answer to the question of how to save urban America. If conservatives such as Martin Anderson lamented the inefficiency and logistical shortcomings of the federally funded venture, supporters pointed to the aesthetic gains downtown where dazzling glass-and-steel structures replaced crumbling tenements and rookeries. If Jane Jacobs and other liberals regretted the replacement of cozy neighborhood enclaves with sterile cookie-cutter megaliths, defenders noted the rise in assessed valuations downtown and the attendant increase in property tax revenues. The notion that urban reclamation depended upon saving the central business district continued to hold sway among policy makers at all levels. The operation of urban renewal may have fallen short of expectations, but big-city mayors and other local boosters felt that they could hardly turn their backs on federal aid in this or any other form; they remained eager suppliants for slum clearance funds in Washington, D.C. So when President Eisenhower curtailed urban renewal appropriations in the last years of his administration, the deficiencies in the program notwithstanding, city hall spokesmen lamented the reduction of federal aid at a time when the challenges of urban governance were clearly intensifying.[7]

In the 1960 presidential election, Democrats cited Eisenhower's inattention to urban affairs as a good example of how his administration's studied detachment held the nation back from achieving its full potential. Eisenhower's do-nothing conservatism allowed a number of the nation's critical domestic problems to worsen, the opposition charged, the deterioration of urban America being a clear example. When they identified the septuagenarian Eisenhower's age and health problems as a partial explanation for the alarming inactivity in the White House in the 1950s, the Democrats cheerfully pointed to their presidential candidate, Senator John F. Kennedy of Massachusetts, as a strong antidote to the recent torpor in Washington. Young and vigorous, the forty-three-year-old Kennedy promised in his campaign that year to quicken the pace of change and get the country moving again after the eight-year hibernation of the Eisenhower administration. In Kennedy, critics of the Republicans' indifference to urban affairs could not have found a better candidate. The grandson of a Boston mayor, congressman from an urban district, and senator from the nation's most urbanized state, Kennedy had a thorough and intuitive knowledge of city problems. Indeed, if elected, he would become the nation's first president born and raised in an urban environment.[8]

Kennedy had taken no leadership role in advancing urban interests during his generally undistinguished tenure in the U.S. Senate but, perhaps reflecting his growing interest in running for president, he took a number of steps in the late 1950s to position himself as a friend of the cities. In 1958, for example, he published an article, "The Shame of the States," in the *New York Times Magazine* that came to the defense of beleaguered cities struggling to deal with rising levels of crime, juvenile delinquency, traffic congestion, and poor housing stock. In the lengthy article, Kennedy blamed the cities' troubles on inadequate representation in state governments and in Washington. In his rendering, rural-dominated state legislatures that had stubbornly postponed reapportionment denied city halls the resources they needed to combat urban problems; the U.S. Congress, in turn, refused to direct funds to local governments in proportion to their needs. Later that year, at the annual meeting of the United States Conference of Mayors (USCM), Kennedy offered a seven-point "Urban Magna Carta" that recommended greater political representation for the cities. In 1959 he gave a similar address to the annual meeting of the American Municipal Association, calling the future of the nation's cities "the great unspoken issue in the 1960 election." On another occasion, he said: "The cities of America, their problems, their future, their financing, must rank at the top of any realistic list of 1960 campaign issues. This is the great unspoken, overlooked, underplayed problem of our time."[9]

Kennedy and the Democrats enjoyed the full support of the major urban lobbyists in 1960. The USCM and the American Municipal Association collaboratively wrote a comprehensive urban plank for inclusion in the Democratic and Republican party platforms that year; the Democrats incorporated the submission virtually word-for-word in the portion of their platform titled "Cities and Their Suburbs." Lambasting the Eisenhower administration's hostility to cities, the Democrats promised renewed attention to municipal concerns in the form of slum clearance, federal aid for transportation, metropolitan area planning, and greater funding for the improvement of municipal infrastructures. In contrast, the platform adopted by the Republican Party included only a brief section on housing that referred generally to governmental efforts "designed to supplement and not supplant private initiative." The Republican presidential nominee, Richard M. Nixon, talked about housing on several occasions at the outset of the campaign but increasingly avoided the issues that the Democrats had so skillfully co-opted. The Democratic Party could not be beaten on domestic issues, Nixon told the journalist Theodore H. White, so his campaign would concentrate on foreign policy matters.[10]

Within the Kennedy campaign, a number of urban policy advisors strongly urged the candidate to seize the ground that his opponent had willingly yielded and present a major speech devoted entirely to city problems. Boston Redevelopment Director Edward Logue, William Slayton of the National Association of Housing and Redevelopment Officials, Planning Professor William L. C. Wheaton of the University of Pennsylvania, and others persuaded Kennedy to announce a program for "the new urban frontier." Speaking to more than 450 municipal officials in October at the Urban Affairs Conference in Pittsburgh, Kennedy criticized the previous administration's treatment of the cities, dismissed Nixon's inchoate urban program as an "empty shell," and vigorously affirmed his support for the urban policies enumerated in the Democratic party platform. He also announced for the first time his support for the creation of a cabinet department devoted entirely to urban affairs. A clear and unequivocal pledge to give high priority to urban interests, Kennedy's Pittsburgh speech satisfied Slayton, Logue, Wheaton, and others interested in urban policy while underscoring the distinct differences between the two political parties on the issue.[11]

The fate of the cities never became the centerpiece of the 1960 presidential campaign, and both candidates understandably devoted most of their attention to U.S. interests abroad, developments in the Cold War, and a sluggish economy. The subject of housing came up only once in the famous televised debates, engaging the two candidates briefly before giving way to other topics. Robert C. Wood, an MIT political science professor and Kennedy adviser who later became the first undersecretary of the U.S. Department of Housing and Urban Development, later recalled that urban affairs remained secondary during the 1960 campaign and that foreign affairs always assumed primacy for the Democratic candidate. Still, Wood felt, "Kennedy was ahead of his time" in recognizing the salience of the issue before any other national politicians. With the enthusiastic support of the big-city mayors and the major urban lobbies and confident of securing comfortable electoral margins in the inner cities, Kennedy campaigned frequently in the suburbs to offset expected Republican majorities. In one of the closest presidential contests in history, the urban vote proved to be crucial for the Democrat as Kennedy carried twenty-seven of the forty largest cities. Thanks no doubt to his tireless courting of voters in suburbia, he also made a respectable showing among what had been predicted to be a constituency solidly in the Nixon column; he managed to increase the Democratic suburban vote in the nation's major metropolitan areas from 38 percent in 1956 to 49 percent in 1960. Kennedy fared poorly in the Great Plains, the Far West, and the smaller cities of the South, where opposition to the burgeoning civil rights movement favored the Republican candidate, but his success in the nation's great metropolitan regions proved essential to the Democratic victory. Looking at the electoral returns, New Haven Mayor Richard Lee exulted: "Kennedy is more than anything else the President of the cities."[12]

Kennedy's transition team appointed an unprecedented twenty-nine task forces in the weeks before the inauguration, and two of them explored pressing urban problems in significant ways. Along with groups to recommend policy directions in such areas as education, defense, economics, and the space program, the president-elect created on December 5, 1960, a twenty-three-member task force chaired by Senator Paul H. Douglas (Democrat, Illinois) to study the problem of depressed areas. Having spent considerable time during the campaign in strategically important West Virginia, Kennedy had become interested in the grinding poverty endured by the residents of the Appalachian mountains and had originally intended the task force to concentrate exclusively on that region. A product of Chicago's vital reform community who had been a champion of the urban poor harkening back to his association with Jane Addams and others at Hull House early in the twentieth century, Douglas argued that area redevelopment legislation should aid the poor in pockets of poverty existing in both urban and rural locations—especially communities with high unemployment caused by new technology and stiff competition from low-wage regions such as the South. Believing that such communities should not be abandoned to the vagaries of modernization, Douglas had unsuccessfully introduced an area redevelopment bill in 1956 and saw in Kennedy's election the opportunity for a second chance. He persuaded the president-elect to broaden the compass of the investigation beyond the hills and hollows of Appalachia. The task force conducted hearings in Washington, D.C., as well as in Charleston, West Virginia, before formulating a program national in scope.[13]

On New Year's Day, Douglas met with Kennedy in Palm Beach, Florida, to present him with the task force's four principal recommendations: (1) an immediate increase in the quantity and variety of the surplus food distributed to the needy; (2) creation of an experimental food stamp program as a pilot project in a number of counties throughout the nation; (3) passage of depressed area legislation to combat unemployment; and (4) special attention to the needs of the Appalachian poor. Kennedy promptly announced his support for the task force's proposals and began speaking publicly of the need for emergency legislation. As his first official act as president, still dressed in white tie and tails on the evening of the inauguration, he signed an executive order authorizing the expansion of the surplus food initiative and instructed the Department of Agriculture to implement the food stamp program.[14]

Kennedy identified area redevelopment as his first legislative priority, and on January 5, 1961, Douglas introduced a new bill, S. 1, which had been drafted with the assistance of White House staffers and cosponsored by forty-three other senators. The bill sought to attract private industry into areas with high and protracted unemployment rates by providing government incentives, allocating $300 million for loans in three separate funds of $100 million each for industrial areas, rural areas, and public facilities. Unlike the earlier version advanced by Douglas during the Eisenhower administration, the bill encountered very little opposition in Congress and passed both houses by lopsided vote margins. Douglas felt that the elimination of one of the bill's original sections that allowed for redeveloping a particularly poor neighborhood within a generally healthy urban area limited the legislation's effectiveness in cities by targeting rural areas excessively. Still, he lauded the final version of the bill signed by Kennedy on May 1, 1961, which authorized the Area Redevelopment Agency to spend $394 million over the next four years. The Area Redevelopment Act did not cure the nation's unemployment problem or bring massive changes to great numbers of declining urban neighborhoods, but it eased deplorable situations in a few chronically depressed sites. The Area Redevelopment Agency, which was replaced by the Economic Development Administration in 1965, served as a precursor to many of the Great Society programs that followed later in the decade.[15]

The Task Force on Housing and Urban Affairs, created on December 6, 1960, spoke more directly to the problems of the nation's major metropolises. Chaired by Joseph McMurray, a former New York State commissioner of housing, the task force also included two prominent bankers (Harry Held and Charles Wellman); the staff director of the House Subcommittee on Housing (John Barriere); and MIT political scientist Robert C. Wood. In two snowbound weekend hotel meetings, the five men completed what Wood called "a Noah's Ark" of a report ("everybody putting in their own piece") and then submitted the eighty-five-page document on December 30, 1960. The task force recommended additional money for low-income housing; more generous funding for urban renewal; increased attention to housing programs for college students, farm families, and the elderly; improved mass transit; liberalized Federal Housing Administration (FHA) requirements; and a new cabinet department for urban affairs. A report on the economy, prepared by the economist Paul A. Samuelson, also urged the president-elect to increase federal expenditures on housing. Housing construction had proved itself an effective tool for pulling the nation out of recessions, Samuelson reasoned, and increases in funding for low-income groups and the elderly provided economic stimuli that would have been disregarded by the private real-estate industry.[16]

The urban task force's recommendations, which Kennedy tentatively endorsed, echoed the support for the creation of a new cabinet department for cities he had announced in Pittsburgh. Believing that the person the new president chose as administrator of the Housing and Home Finance Agency (HHFA) would likely become the secretary of the new cabinet department, observers paid close attention to the appointment. Early speculation centered on Richard Lee, the respected mayor of New Haven and principal organizer of the October housing conference in Pittsburgh, and Joseph P. McMurray, the chair of the urban task force, but Kennedy surprised the experts when he announced the selection of Robert C. Weaver on December 31, 1960. As a Harvard-educated economist and author of two well-reviewed scholarly books, *Negro Labor* (1946) and *The Negro Ghetto* (1948), Weaver possessed impressive academic credentials. Having served in the Public Works Administration, the United States Housing Authority, the War Manpower Commission, and the War Production Board, he also boasted extensive experience in the federal government. Unlike the three men who had administered the HHFA since its inception in 1947, Weaver lacked extensive experience in the private housing industry. (Raymond Foley and Norman Mason had served as commissioners of the FHA, and U.S. Congressman Albert M. Cole had been the principal spokesman for real-estate and home building interests in the House of Representatives.) The nominee's credentials dealt entirely with government's role in housing, and he brought an unabashedly liberal perspective to discussions of urban affairs. An avid champion of public housing, regional planning, and an activist state, Weaver saw the HHFA not just as a federal bureaucracy charged with managing housing starts but also as a potential agent of reform for metropolitan America and the nation more broadly.[17]

At the time that Kennedy selected him to be HHFA administrator, Weaver was serving as vice chairman of the New York City Housing and Redevelopment Board and as chairman of the board of the National Association for the Advancement of Colored People. In those two administrative positions, the nominee had become nationally renowned as a champion of minority rights in housing. The choice of the African American Weaver allowed Kennedy to appoint a black person to a high position in his administration, in recognition of the important role played by minority voters in crucial northern states carried by the Democrats in the recent election—a goal made more urgent when Kennedy's attempt to appoint Chicago Congressman William L. Dawson postmaster general failed in mid-December. A civil rights moderate with considerable knowledge of housing and a keen understanding of how Washington bureaucracies operated, Weaver appeared to be a highly qualified choice as HHFA administrator. Controversy ensued, however, because some legislators expressed concern about Weaver's leftist politics and wondered how the traditionally good relations between the HHFA and the private housing industry would be affected. Of even greater concern to southern Democrats and other conservatives, the confirmation of Weaver would elevate an African American to the highest level ever in the executive branch of the federal government and then in all likelihood to a cabinet seat.[18]

Opposition to Weaver arose most visibly in the Senate where Southerners, many of whom had supported liberal housing legislation in the past with the understanding that open occupancy would not be enforced, looked askance at the appointment of someone they could not trust on this issue. A. Willis Robertson (Democrat, Virginia) and John Sparkman (Democrat, Alabama), chairmen of the Banking and Currency Committee and the Housing Subcommittee respectively, recoiled at the possibility of an integrationist heading the federal government's housing agency. At the February 1961 senate confirmation hearings, Robertson raised questions about the nominee's association with Communist organizations in the 1930s, and William Blakeley (Democrat, Texas) saw additional evidence of Communist involvement in the flattering reviews Weaver's books had received in left-wing publications. Robertson allowed witnesses to give their testimony only after the president submitted a letter affirming Weaver's loyalty. Next the nominee deflected a series of questions from the senators about a federal edict mandating open occupancy by correctly noting that such action could be taken only by the president and not by the HHFA. After the committee voted II to 4 in support of the nominee, the Senate confirmed Weaver by voice vote.[19]

A veteran of the housing reform movement and a passionate advocate for racial equality, Weaver believed in the complementariness of the two causes and sought to achieve the same goals at HHFA that he been pursuing throughout his public career. Hostile to real estate and financial institutions that fostered racial segregation, he suspected a number of federal agencies such as the FHA of acting solely as the representatives of the private housing industry. He also identified as a serious problem the longstanding autonomy of the FHA, which he likened to a free-standing feudal system, within the federal housing bureaucracy. He determined to bring the goals and operation of the FHA into conformity with the rest of the HHFA. The answer to the nation's housing problems, he firmly believed, came with an increased federal presence in the market, which would provide additional resources for low-income housing and inner-city redevelopment—not with greater autonomy for private residential and commercial builders.[20]

In order to transform the hidebound HHFA, Weaver sought to surround himself with like-minded housing experts who shared his dedication to reform. He lacked the authority to select all of his own subordinates but participated energetically when Kennedy appointed the commissioners of the HHFA's constituent agencies. Weaver chose labor's Jack Conway, who had served with distinction as Walter Reuther's assistant at the United Auto Workers since 1946, as deputy administrator. He enthusiastically agreed to the president's selection of Marie McGuire, the executive director of the San Antonio Housing Authority, to head the Public Housing Authority. Having won acclaim in San Antonio for building an innovative public housing project for the elderly, Victoria Plaza, and sharing Weaver's commitment to increasing the amount of low-income housing, McGuire became the first experienced public housing administrator to head the Public Housing Authority. Weaver assented to the appointment of Neil Hardy, a long-time HHFA official who enjoyed good relations with a number of leading real-estate developers, to administer the potentially troublesome FHA post. Believing it crucial to revitalize the stagnant urban renewal program, he reacted negatively when Kennedy staffers chose a politician (former Baltimore mayor Thomas

D'Alesandro) rather than an experienced housing official to supervise the ap-plication of Title I. Vigorously opposing what he called a patronage appoint-ment, Weaver held out for a month before the White House assigned D'Alesandro to another job and then successfully lobbied for William L. Slayton, who had worked at the National Association of Housing and Rede-velopment Officials and participated in several urban renewal projects.[21]

Weaver and his staff quickly began working on comprehensive housing legislation, based upon his belief in the indispensable role of government, which the new administration could submit to Congress. On March 9 Ken-nedy delivered a special message to Congress that summarized the housing bill he was sending to Capitol Hill. Believing the urban task force report to have been essentially useless as a legislative blueprint, Weaver and his aides crafted housing legislation offering no path-breaking innovations but rather prescribed the revitalization of traditional programs that had been allowed to atrophy during the Eisenhower era. The omnibus measure called for the completion of the 100,000 units of public housing authorized but never com-pleted by the Taft-Ellender-Wagner Housing Act of 1949, while seeking ad-ditional funding for increases in housing for the elderly, college students, and farm families. Attributing urban renewal's shortcomings to faulty conception and constrictive rules of operation, the bill increased the amount of funds to be used for nonresidential uses, allowed developers more freedom to craft broader and more ambitious projects, and proposed a startling $2.5 billion for urban renewal over four years. Emphasizing the importance of metropol-itan planning, a title of the law authorized $100 million in grants to preserve open land within rapidly expanding suburban areas as well as inner cities. The administration recognized the need for improved urban transportation but agreed to delay implementation of specific measures pending the out-come of a joint study by the HHFA and the Department of Commerce. Em-phasizing the desirability of comprehensive solutions to address complex metropolitan problems, the bill repeatedly urged systematic research and re-gional planning. With just a few exceptions, the Kennedy administration's proposal expanded current programs and increased funding for existing agencies.[22]

Weaver and his minions made sure to include provisions for the benefit of private housing and real-estate firms. FHA's Section 221 mortgage insur-ance program, which had originally been included in the Housing Act of 1954 on behalf of families displaced by urban redevelopment, would be expanded to include more low- and moderate-income families. Weaver's most ambi-tious creation in 1961, the Section 221 (d) (3) ("Below Market Interest Rate") program, encouraged private development of moderate-income housing by providing incentives to construct or repair rental structures of five or more units. Based upon the highly successful Mitchell-Lama program in New York City, Section 221 (d) (3) provided federal support for limited dividend corporations, cooperatives, and other nonprofit organizations as a means of increasing the supply of affordable rental housing for middle-income families. Weaver hoped that this unconventional program would assuage conservatives who might accept some involvement in the housing market by Washington short of outright government ownership.[23]

Despite Secretary Weaver's deliberate inclusion of programs to mollify the real-estate and construction lobbies, the private housing industry generally responded in predictably negative fashion. The U.S. Chamber of Commerce and the United States Savings and Loan League argued that public housing had proved a dismal failure in past decades and opposed funding for its continuation. The National Association of Real Estate Boards, the American Bankers Association, the Mortgage Bankers Association of America, and the Life Insurance Association of America inveighed against the expansion of FHA programs to serve middle-income families as a needless and unwarranted incursion into the private housing market. They especially resisted the proposal that empowered the FHA to issue no-down-payment, low-interest, forty-year mortgages for low- and moderate-income families to purchase houses. "This bill would extend a form of public housing to middle-income families," charged a real-estate industry spokesman. Little opposition developed in the housing industry to the modifications of Title I that relaxed the "predominantly residential" standard, no doubt because the creation of more opportunities for urban renewal meant more money-making opportunities for developers.[24]

The relatively minor "open land" provision, with its comparatively modest $100 million price tag, surprisingly became one of the most controversial pieces of the bill. The "open space" initiatives, which provided federal aid for municipalities to purchase land for parks and to acquire and preserve land until local government completed specific plans for public or private development, had been conceived primarily to encourage thoughtful suburban development. With Senate Minority Leader Everett M. Dirksen (Republican, Illinois) spearheading the opposition, congressional conservatives questioned the need for such generous funding for parks but saved special scorn for the "open space" proposal. Dirksen ridiculed what he saw as a useless and socialistic exercise in planning, suggesting sarcastically that a proposal dealing with open space should have originated in the Senate

Committee on Aeronautics and Space Sciences rather than the Senate Banking Committee. The Republican continued sardonically: "The committee should have hired some scientific talent from the Atomic Energy Commission and the National Aeronautics and Space Administration to come before it and spell out for us in clear and felicitous detail how this new venture into space will be made." Conservatives succeeded in limiting allocations for parks to a token amount and excised the amount for land reserves altogether, but the law authorized up to $50 million for federal grants to assist local agencies in acquiring land to be used as permanent open space.[25]

In at least one area of urban policy, Congress proved more daring than Kennedy and Weaver. Disregarding the administration's cautious refusal to propose additional funding for mass transit until additional study had been completed by the HHFA and the Commerce Department, Senator Harrison Williams Jr. (Democrat, New Jersey) insisted that an omnibus housing bill must address the cities' urgent need for transportation improvements. Williams had introduced the Urban Mass Transportation Act of 1961 in January but received no backing from the administration, which had determined to omit mass transit from its comprehensive legislation that year. Weaver expressed concern that "deficit-ridden transit networks" might siphon off funding available for housing programs and hesitated to engage in a turf battle with Commerce Secretary Luther Hodges, who argued strongly that control of mass transportation should be assigned to his bailiwick. (Weaver had just weathered a contentious confirmation battle against southern senators and might indeed not have relished a battle with Hodges, the segregationist former governor of North Carolina.) Williams attached his floundering bill to the administration's housing measure and scaled down the original $150 million appropriation to $50 million in loans for the acquisition and improvement of mass transit facilities and $25 million in grants for demonstration projects. In this much more limited form, the administration reluctantly approved its inclusion.[26]

The Democrats retained slender majorities in both houses of Congress after the 1960 election, having lost twenty seats in the House and one in the Senate, so passing legislation depended to a great extent on the administration's ability to maintain the loyalty of the party's sizable stable of southern conservatives. Fortunately for the fate of the Housing Act of 1961, a pair of Alabama Democrats friendly to housing reform occupied the chairmanships of the key committees (Banking and Currency) in the Senate and the House. Senator John Sparkman and Congressman Albert Rains had lost numerous battles for liberal housing legislation during the Eisenhower years, and both men welcomed the opportunity to support the new president's bill. In the Senate, Sparkman and other housing supporters defeated a series of crippling amendments offered by such conservative Republicans as Homer Capehart of Indiana and Everett Dirksen of Illinois. In the House, where opponents of housing legislation enjoyed a long record of success, Rains ruthlessly pushed the bill through committee hearings in what one bystander called "the worst railroad job I've ever seen." The bill's proponents acceded to the charges of fiscal irresponsibility by reducing the requested $2.5 billion for urban renewal by $500 million. When the representatives of suburbs and small towns objected during the floor debate to the monopoly on government largesse that the big cities would enjoy if the bill passed, Rains quickly proposed an amendment that added $500 million for the gas, water, and sewage improvements that appealed particularly to developing communities with incomplete infrastructures. Such extemporaneous horse trading paid off, and the bill passed in the House by a comfortable margin of 235 to 178. After the defeat of a motion to recommit introduced by Prescott Bush (Republican, Connecticut), the Senate passed the bill handily 64 to 25. Kennedy signed the bill into law on June 30, 1961.[27]

The Eighty-seventh Congress passed the Housing Act of 1961 with remarkable dispatch, elevating the hopes of its supporters in urban America, but the long-term results proved to be mixed. Kennedy partisans immediately called the housing law the most significant since 1949, but enthusiasm for its passage dissipated quickly. Because of the recession inherited from the Eisenhower administration, home construction lagged in 1961; in 1962 conditions began to improve in the suburbs, but inner cities continued to suffer. The amount of government-subsidized housing for the elderly increased substantially during the Kennedy years, but overall low-income housing construction never exceeded the rate achieved in the last year of the Eisenhower administration. The law's innovative attempts to increase federal support for moderate-income housing foundered, according to the National Commission on Urban Problems, because builders balked at the excessive red tape necessary to acquire loans, and local FHA field officers refused to embrace the program's social welfare goals. The Housing Act of 1961 specified appropriations only for the next few years, its supporters anticipating that HHFA staffers would submit a comprehensive housing bill during the presidential election year of 1964. In fact, the Housing Act of 1961 ended up being the most significant piece of urban legislation passed during the Kennedy administration.[28]

After the passage of the 1961 Housing Act, members of the Kennedy administration interested in urban affairs turned their attention to two policy goals—the establishment of a cabinet department for cities and the eradication of residential segregation—that proved exceedingly difficult to reach. Kennedy had endorsed both measures during the 1960 campaign. He had been especially critical of Eisenhower for condoning racial segregation in housing underwritten by the federal government, lamenting the fact that his predecessor had not taken any action to address what Kennedy portrayed as a straightforward problem. Matter-of-factly commenting that federally assisted housing could be "desegregated by the stroke of a presidential pen," Kennedy strongly suggested that he would issue such an executive order if elected president. When months went by after his inauguration without the new president fulfilling his promise, civil rights leaders who had avidly supported Kennedy grew restive. The White House feared that alienating the large and powerful contingent of southern Democrats in Congress by issuing the controversial executive order would jeopardize the chances of obtaining additional liberal legislation, a concern reinforced by the recognition that the Housing Act of 1961 would never have passed without the backing of John Sparkman, Albert Rains, and other Dixie legislators. Robert Weaver argued in the press for the greater importance of housing discrimination and for the postponement of legislative approval of the new cabinet post. Nevertheless, the president sent the cabinet department bill to Congress on April 18, 1961. During the 1961 Thanksgiving Day weekend at the Kennedy family compound in Hyannis Port, Massachusetts, the president and his aides discussed the sensitive situation and again decided to postpone signing the executive order until after the Department of Urban Affairs bill had been passed. According to presidential aide and speechwriter Theodore Sorensen, the Hyannis Port group gambled that they could get the Department of Urban Affairs bill through Congress that year and then the president could issue the executive order after the close of the congressional session when it would cause less of a stir; if the legislation failed to pass, the housing order could still be issued at a later time.[29]

The idea of a cabinet department for the cities, variously called the "Department of Municipalities," the "Department of Urbiculture," the "Department of Urban Affairs," and, in its most recent incarnation, the "Department of Urban Affairs and Housing," had been around for decades. President Kennedy contended that the elevation of the HHFA to cabinet rank would create "an awareness" of urban issues and provide "coordinated leadership" to federal programs for the cities. Perhaps most important, he argued, its

creation would be symbolic recognition of the importance of metropolitan issues in an America where 125 million people lived in urban and suburban
areas and only 13 million on farms or in small towns. The president could
have attempted to create the new cabinet post under the auspices of the Reorganization Act of 1949, which would have allowed either the Senate or the
House to kill the measure within sixty days, but chose the politically less controversial path of submitting a bill to Congress. Senator Joseph S. Clark
(Democrat, Pennsylvania), who introduced the administration's bill in the
Senate, praised the idea because it would give urban America "an equal
voice" in Washington for the first time and warned that the cities would be
"doomed" without increased aid from the federal government. The
administration's spokesman for the bill, Bureau of the Budget Director David
Bell, conceded that large cities already had indirect representation in Washington but argued that the new cabinet department would make their voice
direct and permanent. As expected, such organizations as the USCM, American Municipal Association, National Housing Conference, National Association of Housing and Redevelopment Officials, American Veterans Committee, and the American Federation of Labor–Congress of Industrial
Organizations enthusiastically endorsed the initiative. Representatives from
the American Institute of Planners and the American Institute of Architects
suggested that a cabinet department would give greater unity to the traditional hodgepodge of urban programs. Legislators from heavily urbanized
states and metropolitan districts, along with the mayors of the nation's largest cities, testified for the bill in Congress.[30]

Kennedy fully expected substantial opposition to the measure, and a variety of objections quickly surfaced from many different quarters. The National Association of Home Builders expressed concern about the FHA's loss
of autonomy in the new administrative structure, vowing to support the department only if the head of the FHA (not the department secretary) exercised exclusive control of mortgage insurance rates. The National Association
of Real Estate Boards took an even harder line, demanding that the federal
government terminate the public housing and urban renewal programs and
sell the FHA to private business. Echoing the charge that the new cabinet department would be nothing more than a handmaiden to Democratic big-
city mayors, NAREB President O. G. Powell predicted that passage of the
bill would "soon create a situation in which the mayors of our cities will
have nothing to do other than perform the ministerial task of distributing
federal money." Such organizations as the National Association of County
Officials and the Council of State Governments expressed their concern

about the potential damage to federalism by the aggrandizement of local governments. "Do we want to set up a department for direct dealings between Washington and the municipalities, which are adjuncts of the states?" asked Senator Everett M. Dirksen. He answered his own question negatively. A bipartisan coalition of conservatives in the Senate, which had already scotched the administration's Medicare and federal aid to education bills, eagerly joined in the effort to stymie what they perceived as another costly and ill-conceived liberal measure. Influential Senators John McClellan (Democrat, Arkansas), Sam Ervin (Democrat, North Carolina), Karl Mundt (Republican, South Dakota), and Carl Curtis (Republican, Nebraska) joined with Dirksen and other conservatives in railing against the creation of a new federal agency that would ally with corrupt big-city political machines.[31]

Despite the Kennedy administration's assurances that the new cabinet department would benefit cities, suburbs, and small towns alike, the charge that the bill overwhelmingly served big-city interests gained widespread currency and opened rifts between groups that did not normally join members of conservative coalitions. While the chief executives of core cities eagerly supported the legislation, mayors, city managers, and city commissioners in the suburbs frequently expressed reservations. Avid support for the legislation by the USCM, which was widely viewed as an organization controlled by the mayors of the nation's urban giants, seemed to substantiate the charges of a bias in favor of the largest cities. (The previous four presidents of the organization hailed from New York City, Los Angeles, Chicago, and Philadelphia.) Representative Glenn Cunningham (Republican, Nebraska), the former mayor of Omaha, Nebraska, claimed that the USCM was "dominated by a group of about six mayors from the huge metropolitan areas, and all the rest of us [were] just bystanders." He spoke at length during congressional hearings about the many challenges faced by medium-sized cities, which the national media largely ignored in their endless fascination with the great metropolises, and poignantly reported that small towns were "dying on the vine." Dismissing the need for such special interest legislation in favor of the relatively affluent and influential big cities, Cunningham called instead for the creation of a Department of Small Towns and Rural Affairs. His proposal gained no political traction but underscored the suspicion with which many suburban and small town residents viewed the proposed Department of Urban Affairs and Housing. As well, the president and his advisers understood the danger in having any measure they sent to Capitol Hill identified as a "big-city bill" because of the rural backgrounds and small town orientations of so many members of Congress.[32]

Additional opposition to the bill came from a powerful group of southern legislators who would not yield as long as the HHFA's Robert Weaver stood to become the first African American cabinet member. Kennedy had not explicitly indicated that he would appoint Weaver as the first secretary, but he had never denied that that had been his intention; policy makers at the White House and on Capitol Hill assumed that had been the president's plan. Although Kennedy had not made any promises, saying only that he would be a "logical contender," Weaver accepted the post at the HHFA thinking that the president had given him sufficient encouragement to believe that the cabinet post would be his. (Quizzed before the inauguration about possibly becoming the secretary of the Department of Health, Education, and Welfare, Weaver told two presidential emissaries that he preferred the new urban cabinet position because of his extensive experience in housing.) In 1961 increased civil rights agitation raised the level of anxiety among southern legislators about an African American at the head of an executive department who could use his position in the highest levels of government to encourage desegregation by tampering with federal housing programs and to expand the reach of federal power in other ways. As much as Kennedy felt obligated to make the appointment to repay northern black voters, he encountered a solid roadblock of congressional barons committed to placating their constituents by preserving segregation back home in the South.[33]

As Congress conducted hearings on the bill, Kennedy urged Weaver to maintain a low profile. When questioned about his prospects of becoming a cabinet secretary, Weaver declined to comment and studiously avoided making any remarks that would draw attention to his situation. Even though the outcome of the congressional deliberations would decide the fate of his agency, the HHFA administrator declined to appear on Capitol Hill and sent several subordinates to testify at the legislative hearings instead. No amount of care could airbrush Weaver out of the picture seen by the southern legislators, who had provided the necessary votes to pass the Housing Act of 1961, and even the region's moderates fell in line behind the unreconstructed racists. Failing to extract a private guarantee from the president that he would not appoint Weaver as secretary, the estimable John Sparkman reneged on an earlier statement in support of the bill and deserted the administration camp. Kennedy and his aides reluctantly accepted defeat, which became official on January 24, 1962, when the House Rules Committee, comprised mostly of Republicans and southern Democrats, killed the bill.[34]

Having failed at a conciliatory approach, Kennedy resolved to confront Congress forthrightly. In a press conference the same day that the House

Rules Committee had acted, he declared his intention of organizing the new cabinet department under the powers granted him by the 1949 reorganization law. He also announced his intention to appoint Robert Weaver secretary. "Obviously, if the legislation had been passed, Mr. Weaver would have been appointed," the president said. "It was well known on the Hill. The American people might as well know it." Kennedy's bold move made clear what Washington insiders had suspected for months and left Republicans complaining that the president had turned a legislative battle over government reorganization into a "racial issue." Privately, Kennedy chafed at the way his opponents had cloaked their motives in high-minded rhetoric. He said to Theodore Sorensen: "Imagine them [Republicans and southern Democrats] claiming that the bill was bad bureaucratic organization. They're against it because Weaver's a Negro and I'd like to see them say it." Having kept a low profile prior to the actions of the House Rules Committee, Weaver abruptly executed an about-face and became a prominent spokesman for the urban cabinet department. He told reporters that "a large segment of the population" would see resistance to an African American in the cabinet as the motivation for a vote against the legislation. If nothing else, Kennedy had put the party of Lincoln on the defensive with black voters in an election year.[35]

Now fully bathed in the limelight as it had not been before, the battle over the urban cabinet department moved into its second stage. According to the strictures of the 1949 reorganization law, either chamber of Congress could derail the executive action by voting it down within sixty days. Kennedy and his aides knew that conservative strength in the House made defeat of the measure there a "foregone conclusion"—Speaker of the House John McCormick, a loyal Kennedy ally, predicted as much early on—and resolved to increase the level of Republican discomfort by staging a full-scale debate in the Senate where the outcome remained legitimately in doubt. Before a full discussion could be concluded in the Senate, however, parliamentary maneuvering brought the matter to an abrupt close. When the House announced on February 19 its intention to bring the measure up for a vote immediately, Senate Majority Leader Mike Mansfield (Democrat, Montana) quickly requested a petition to discharge the measure from the Committee on Government Operations, where the crusty chairman, Arkansas Democrat John McClellan, was conducting hearings at a snail's pace. Bridling at the unseemly departure from orderly procedure and accusing the White House of interference with congressional prerogatives, the Senate defeated the discharge petition 58 to 42. As expected, the House rejected the Reorganization Plan the next day by a vote of 246 to 150.[36]

After the months-long struggle to create the Department of Urban Affairs and Housing collapsed so ignominiously, the press called the episode the worst legislative embarrassment of the Kennedy administration. *Newsweek* sniffed that White House operatives "maneuvered with all the finesse of third-rate precinct captains." The president admitted as much in his own analysis of the debacle, saying: "I played it too cute. It was so obvious it made them mad." Kennedy spoke of the inevitability of an urban cabinet department and predicted that the growing importance of the cities guaranteed success for urban forces sometime in the near future, but discontinued efforts for the balance of his time in the White House. The administration's 1963 budget mentioned a Department of Urban Affairs and Housing, but Congress never held hearings on the proposed legislation; Weaver termed its inclusion in the legislative agenda that year "a gesture." Public recognition of the worsening urban situation remained too slight, and southern resistance to any measure associated with the burgeoning civil rights movement too strong, for the creation of an urban cabinet department in the early 1960s.[37]

The issue of discrimination in housing, which Kennedy had deferred repeatedly since taking office, resurfaced in the spring and summer of 1962 as that year's congressional elections approached. Civil rights activists sent the president pens as a reminder of his 1960 pledge to end the practice with a stroke of the presidential pen, and picketers assembled outside the White House to shame the administration into action. Before reaching any conclusions about how best to handle the combustible issue, Kennedy waited for a report on housing from the Civil Rights Commission and conferred with a variety of advisers. Presidential confidant Theodore Sorensen explained that the crux of the matter became how best to respond to a series of questions regarding coverage: Would an executive order cover all or just some of the various housing activities subsidized by the federal government? Would it apply to housing in which government was only involved through mortgage guarantees? Would the order be retroactive? And potentially most troublesome of all, would the government become involved in housing built exclusively with bank loans? In other words, how deeply should Washington intrude into the affairs of the private housing industry to ensure compliance with an antidiscrimination directive? Sorensen recalled that the Federal Home Loan Bank Board, which supervised the activities of savings banks and savings-and-loans institutions, expressed a willingness to go along with the executive order; the Federal Deposit Insurance Corporation did not.[38]

Still unsure about the contents of the executive order he would issue, Kennedy decided to wait until after the congressional elections in November before wielding the presidential pen. Representatives of the construction industry warned that issuance of the order would reduce housing starts nationally by one-third, thereby slowing economic growth with disastrous political consequences. The president believed that the Democrats had potentially more to lose in the South than to gain in northern African American precincts. Any modest advances in civil rights could result in Democratic losses in southern congressional contests that might jeopardize the party's slender majorities in the House and Senate. On the other hand, Kennedy officials doubted that African American voters would be disgruntled enough by more delays to vote for the candidates of a Republican Party they perceived to be wholly unsympathetic to the civil rights movement. Northern Democrats representing suburban districts worried that an executive order banning discriminatory housing practices could drive white voters, many of whom had already fled the inner cities to escape racial change in their old neighborhoods, to support Republican candidates who had come out strongly against open housing. To Kennedy and his advisers, politics dictated another postponement until after election day.[39]

Waiting until after the election, Kennedy signed Executive Order 11063, which mandated the prevention of discrimination in housing provided wholly or partially with federal assistance, on November 10, 1962. His order applied only to new public housing and direct, guaranteed federal loans, however, and exempted all low-income units built or planned before November 20, 1962. Although in many respects a noteworthy breakthrough in the path to racial equality, the executive order fell short of its potential impact by severely limiting the scope of the federal government's influence in the private housing market. In its decision to restrict government involvement to federally financed housing and not to supervise transactions involving banks and savings and loan associations, the administration gave free reign to private builders and lenders in most of the housing constructed in the nation; the guidelines mandated by the presidential directive applied to less than 1 percent of the nation's housing units. Concerned that Weaver might resign when he discovered how narrowly conceived the executive order turned out to be, the president sent his brother, Attorney General Robert F. Kennedy, to report the bad news. Weaver complained at length privately but grudgingly accepted the political realities and voiced no public objections. To deflect attention away from the executive order, the White House made a brief announcement sandwiched between lengthy reports of Soviet bombers in Cuba and a potentially explosive border conflict between India and China. Closely monitoring developments thereafter, officials at the HHFA—and its successor, the Department of Housing and Urban Development—assessed the impact of Executive Order 11063 and found compliance erratic. Local housing authorities continued to perpetuate racial segregation through their site-selection practices, and private lending institutions awarded mortgages in customary fashion. In fact, as historians of the civil rights movement have noted, Kennedy's much-anticipated executive order altered racial patterns in housing imperceptibly if at all. Local ordinances, public attitudes, and the great disparity in income between blacks and whites combined to curtail the residential mobility of racial minorities. Until he left Washington in 1968 and brought his long career of public service to a close, Robert Weaver continually pushed the federal government to assume a larger role in combating metropolitan segregation.[40]

For the same reasons that he became involved in the struggle over racial discrimination in housing, Weaver believed that the HHFA should be responsible for all matters related to the nation's cities and suburbs. His interests included not just housing but also transportation, jobs, social welfare, education, and recreation, creating possible turf battles with the Departments of Commerce, Labor, Treasury, and Health, Education, and Welfare. He felt very strongly that the HHFA should have jurisdiction over mass transit programs, which had previously been situated in the Department of Commerce's Office of Transportation. Although willing to concede control over highways to the Bureau of Public Roads, which assumed responsibility for all road building in rural as well as in metropolitan areas, Weaver maintained that mass transit existed by definition only in urban areas. As a firm believer in regional planning, he saw the establishment of mass transit networks as an integral part of metropolitan development—as he put it, "Mass transit was not a matter simply of moving people and goods, but it was a part of the whole total planning for the urban complex." Finally, he argued for the placement of mass transit in the HHFA as a logical precursor to its likely location in the proposed Department of Urban Affairs and Housing. Department of Commerce officials pointed out the illogic of dividing various transportation functions among different government agencies, predicting inefficiency and duplication of effort as a consequence. Further, they rejoined, regional planning would be more difficult if different government agencies managed expressways and public transit systems. After a series of meetings that included Weaver and other HHFA officials, White House staff, representatives of the Budget Bureau, and the Under Secretary of Transportation, the HHFA prevailed in the bureaucratic tug-of-war and assumed control of the mass transit program in October 1961.[41]

Lines of authority between the housing and transportation bureaucracies remained blurred in the Kennedy administration, with mass transit assigned to the former and highways to the latter. On March 28, 1962, Robert Weaver of the HHFA and Orville Hodges of the Department of Commerce submitted a report to the president outlining potential avenues for cooperation between the two agencies. For example, they pledged joint action to provide suitable relocation housing for families displaced by federally assisted construction of highways and mass transit facilities. In metropolitan areas where local and state authorities agreed to undertake comprehensive planning, the HHFA and the Department of Commerce promised to contribute urban renewal and highway construction funding respectively. Commerce officials granted the HHFA administrator broad authority to conduct urban transportation research salient to housing issues. Weaver enjoyed considerable success at extending his agency's reach into areas previously reserved for the Department of Commerce, especially considering the failure to elevate the HHFA to cabinet-level status, but the perception persisted among mayors and other municipal officials that progress on urban transportation issues continued to lag behind the administration's attention to housing matters.[42]

On April 4, 1962, Kennedy submitted a message to Congress on transportation as a prelude to omnibus legislation that the White House submitted to the Senate and the House. The Federal-Aid Highway Act of 1962, which Congress passed later that autumn and the president signed into law on October 23, authorized the use of federal funds for relocation assistance payments to individuals and businesses displaced by highway construction programs in cities. The allocation of federal dollars for that purpose broke new ground but required approval by state governments while limiting outlays to $200 for individuals and $3,000 for businesses. Another portion of the legislation required that all federally aided highway projects in metropolitan areas approved after July 1, 1965, be based upon a "continuing comprehensive transportation planning process carried on cooperatively by States and local communities." In subsequent years, in order to maintain control of highway planning and avoid delays in interstate highway construction timetables, the Bureau of Public Roads and state highway departments frequently cooperated to avoid compliance with the law. Defining "continuing comprehensive transportation planning" broadly, bureau practices encouraged state authorities to bypass metropolitan planning agencies. Despite the best intentions of the administration, the drive to build expressways expeditiously again often superseded concerns about the impact on metropolitan land use. Still, the Federal-Aid Highway Act of 1962 established the precedent of requiring urban transportation planning as a condition of receiving federal funding and mandated that comprehensive transportation planning be conducted at the metropolitan—not just the city—level.[43]

Working closely with Senator Harrison Williams Jr. (Democrat, New Jersey), the White House introduced mass transit legislation in Congress in 1962 and 1963. In both cases, the administration sought $500 million for a federal matching grant program to help states and municipalities improve mass transportation. In 1962 the Senate Banking and Currency Committee passed the bill, which was debated on the floor briefly before being sent to the Commerce Committee for further study. The House Banking and Currency Committee approved the bill, but the Rules Committee refused to clear it for consideration on the floor. After the House foreclosed any chance of the bill's passage that year, Congress extended for six months the existing $50 million loan fund for mass transit created by the Housing Act of 1961. The mass transit bill championed by the administration in 1963, virtually an exact duplicate of the version that failed the year before, passed in the Senate after the White House accepted a reduction to $375 million for grant appropriations and a few other minor changes. Once again, however, the bill failed to obtain clearance from the House Rules Committee for floor consideration. In 1963, despite the dedicated work of Harrison Williams in the Senate and Albert Rains in the House, Republicans and conservative Democrats in Congress managed again to defeat mass transit legislation that they claimed would dangerously inflate the federal deficit. Besides, the conservatives argued, a problem in urban areas should appropriately be handled at the state or local levels. The $50 million mass transit loan fund created in 1961 expired on June 30, 1963. Congress passed the first significant mass transit bill in 1964 as part of Lyndon Johnson's Great Society.[44]

Defeats for mass transit legislation in 1962–63, the failure to create the Department of Urban Affairs and Housing, and the belated issuance of the executive order on housing discrimination, all of which the press portrayed as sharp setbacks for the Kennedy administration, led to the president's growing inattention to urban matters. Diverted by Cold War crises in Cuba, Germany, Laos, and Vietnam, the president seemed increasingly to concentrate on foreign policy—a development reflected in the budgets submitted to Congress that earmarked a preponderance of federal funds for the armed forces, military research and development, and a nascent space program. Disappointed mayors and other city boosters voiced their concerns, urging Kennedy to redeem the promises he made in 1960 about giving the cities their due. In January 1963, a USCM delegation urged the president to convene a White House conference to assess the state of the cities after two years of his leadership. In February, speakers at the annual meeting of the National Housing Conference expressed dismay at the administration's lackluster record on housing production and urban revitalization. When Kennedy addressed the organization's annual convention in June, USCM President Richard Lee announced that the White House Conference on Community Development would at last be held in December. Government officials and business executives would be chosen for a national commission that would plan the conference, the sessions of which would synthesize the latest thought on urban problems and present the president with the grist for a new urban program on the eve of his reelection year. Although the administration never made a public announcement canceling the conference, the decision to do so had been made before Kennedy's fateful trip to Texas in November. Earnestly preparing budgets that would be sent to Congress in an election year, neither Kennedy nor Weaver welcomed the distractions such a conference in December seemed likely to pose. They also wanted to avoid the unpleasantness of declining to support the ambitious funding proposals for cities that the conference attendees would surely propound. As they had done previously, policy makers at the White House and the HHFA decided in late 1963 that nettlesome urban problems could most profitably be addressed after an impending election.[45]

The assassination of President Kennedy on November 22, 1963, rendered moot any speculation about future directions the administration may have taken in urban affairs, leaving only a record compiled over a thousand days to consider. As in all efforts to evaluate the Kennedy presidency after its abrupt termination, any assessment of the administration's urban policy must evoke such terms as "brevity" and "incompleteness" more than "success" and "failure." Still, some broad brush strokes can be discerned in an unfinished picture. In the beginning, Kennedy spoke boldly about increased attention to festering urban problems and thereby excited the imaginations of local government officials, planners, and others who cared deeply about cities. His selection of Robert Weaver to administer the HHFA underscored the administration's support for traditional liberal policies staked out earlier by Truman but largely ignored by Eisenhower. Troubled relations with an essentially conservative Congress produced uneven results, the early and surprisingly easy passage of the Housing Act of 1961 offset by later reverses as an alliance of southern Democrats and Republicans gained the upper hand. By 1963 the unlikelihood of success on Capitol Hill and the president's preoccupation with foreign affairs relegated urban affairs to the background. The administration's inability to breathe life into the proposed Department of

Urban Affairs and Housing symbolized the disjuncture between the executive and legislative branches in Washington during the early 1960s. A Democratic president working with Democratic majorities in the Senate and the
House compiled a paltry record of urban legislation.

Frustrated in its dealing with Congress, the White House made a noteworthy breakthrough in the courts that benefited urban America in later
years. As Kennedy had pointed out as early as the 1950s, many city problems
owed to outmoded systems of political representation in which state legislatures continued to award disproportionate influence to rural areas with small
populations. Large cities, denied adequate home rule provisions and lacking
the financial resources commensurate with their size, increasingly struggled
to make ends meet. In the early days of the Kennedy administration, Attorney General Robert F. Kennedy submitted on behalf of the federal government an amicus curiae brief in a case before the U.S. Supreme Court involving Tennessee's failure to redistribute seats in the state legislature according
to population change. In *Baker v. Carr* (1962) the majority of the Court ruled
that cities possessed a constitutional right to challenge rural overrepresenta-
tion in state legislatures. In 1964, with Attorney General Kennedy personally
arguing the case against the gerrymandering Alabama state legislature, the
Supreme Court affirmed in *Reynolds v. Sims* the principle of "one person,
one vote" for apportionment. The decision that rural voters had no greater
right of representation than urban voters tipped the balance of electoral
power decidedly toward metropolitan America, a belated achievement of an
effort initiated in the Kennedy White House.[46]

The revival of urban renewal became another significant development of
the Kennedy years. Streamlined and reorganized by William Slayton, the
Urban Renewal Administration no longer brought projects to a halt with
interminable delays evaluating proposals. With an unprecedented level of
funding provided by the Housing Act of 1961, Slayton authorized expenditures for Title I grants in two years roughly equal to the amount spent during
the entire eight years of the Eisenhower administration. He insisted upon
closer supervision of local renewal authorities, appointed within the agency a
new commissioner for relocation to ensure that the Urban Renewal Administration no longer overlooked the plight of displaced residents, and instituted
a new level of cooperation with the Bureau of Public Roads so that its engineers did not begin building new expressways through the sites of planned
urban renewal projects. Of course, while many downtown businessmen and
developers welcomed the increased activity under Slayton, others viewed the
revival of urban renewal less enthusiastically. Although the Urban Renewal

Administration devoted more attention to building replacement housing, the number of new units never met the needs of the unfortunates left homeless by the wrecking ball. The use of eminent domain to dislodge homeowners and shopkeepers in the name of downtown revitalization, no matter how many income-producing businesses emerged to revive urban cores, still remained unpopular among some constituencies. The urban renewal bonanza of the early 1960s, though widely applauded by the business community, still received mixed notices from a wary public.[47]

The Kennedy administration likewise compiled an ambiguous record on low income housing, achieving some noteworthy reforms yet producing a strikingly low number of units at a time of growing need. Determined to infuse the struggling public housing program with new ideas and the kinds of social services never before offered to tenants, Weaver and McGuire experimented with new design and construction techniques. Plans to offer day care centers, career counseling, job placement services, and other social services in collaboration with the Department of Health, Education, and Welfare floundered because of bureaucratic foul-ups and lack of funding. Critics charged that a preoccupation with social improvement diverted precious resources into ancillary programs with fewer dollars left for constructing new units of low-income housing. In another significant departure from earlier practices, the Public Housing Authority devoted increasing amounts of public housing construction to elderly residents. From 1956, when they first became eligible for low-income housing, until 1960, the elderly received approximately 10–12 percent of total admissions. The real breakthrough came with the Housing Act of 1961, which allocated fully one-half of new public housing units to older people. By the end of 1964, tenants over sixty-five years of age occupied more than one-fourth of low-income units operated by the Public Housing Authority.[48]

Along with the production of a disappointing number of low-income units, Weaver's attempts to increase subsidized housing for working- and middle-class Americans sputtered as well. The showpiece of that effort, Section 221 (d) (3), sought unsuccessfully to launch a program for the rehabilitation and construction of middle-income rental housing. By the end of the Kennedy administration, by which time Weaver had hoped to start building approximately 50,000 middle-income units, construction under the Section 221 (d) (3) program had begun on fewer than 13,000 units. Many of the rank and file within the HHFA saw obtaining improved housing for working- and middle-class Americans as a less urgent goal than providing shelter for lower-income families, and the notion of additional government activity in

the private housing market met considerable resistance from the FHA bureaucracy. FHA Commissioner Neil Hardy shared Weaver's goal of making
all of the HHFA's constituent agencies conform to the broad policies adopted
at the highest administrative level, which meant for the FHA a loss of autonomy and in many respects a shift from a suburban to a metropolitan orientation. To reflect the HHFA's goal of improving central city housing, Hardy
appointed within the FHA an assistant commissioner for multifamily housing. Change came slowly and grudgingly to the FHA, however, as decades of
policy and practice could not be reversed overnight. As historian Mark I. Gelfand concluded, "Adding a social dimension to FHA's traditional business
activities would be a long and difficult task."[49]

Most of the urban initiatives launched during the Kennedy years involved long and difficult tasks, tackling intractable problems not likely to be
solved within a single, truncated presidential administration. Time after
time, the halting beginnings of urban programs designed in the New Frontier
became fully developed components of Lyndon Johnson's reform extrava-
ganza later in the 1960s. The War on Poverty, the heart of Johnson's Great
Society program, originated in a relatively obscure effort by Attorney General Robert F. Kennedy to reduce juvenile delinquency in the nation's cities.
Basing the New Frontier's activities on two experimental efforts, the Ford
Foundation's multisite Gray Areas demonstration project and Mobilization
for Youth in Harlem, the attorney general established the President's Committee on Juvenile Delinquency and Youth Crime in 1961. A special task
force, which the president commissioned in September 1963 to prepare an
antipoverty bill for the 1964 legislative session, relied almost entirely on the
staffers who had guided the administration's juvenile delinquency program.
President Kennedy never had the opportunity to act on the task force proposal, which had been completed in just three weeks, before his assassination.
In a series of meetings in December 1963 and January 1964, President Johnson demanded substantial changes in the antipoverty program conceived in
his predecessor's administration, but clearly the genesis of the resultant Economic Opportunity Act rested with Robert Kennedy's concern with juvenile
delinquency. During the course of his presidency, John F. Kennedy's interest
in poverty came to include urban America as well as rural Appalachia.[50]

The New Urban Frontier can perhaps best be seen as, first, the recognition of the importance of the cities and, second, the beginning of a considerable effort by the federal government to address urban problems. Kennedy
"remained unregenerately a city man," said his biographer, Arthur Schlesinger Jr., "deeply anxious about the mess and tangle of urban America." His

presidency consumed by Cold War crises and by the struggle to revive a
balky economy, he paid less attention to urban matters than he would have
liked or than his liberal supporters had hoped. He left a copious list of issues
plaguing America's large cities to his successor, involving low- and moderate-
income housing, urban renewal, residential segregation, mass transit, crime,
juvenile delinquency, and other problems that by the mid-1960s were said to
constitute an Urban Crisis. Much Great Society legislation dealing with
urban matters originated in embryonic Kennedy programs that failed to mobilize public opinion, fell short of obtaining legislative majorities, or languished at first before coming to fruition under Lyndon Johnson. A few
months after the martyred president's death, a political scientist observed:
"Kennedy will be remembered for many things, but in the long run, it may
well be that he will be best remembered as the first President to understand
the implications of the metropolitan revolution in the United States and as
the first to try to do something about it." The federal government became the
great benefactor of the cities under the leadership of Lyndon Johnson, a politician who seemed to be an unlikely friend of urban America.[51]

4

THE GREAT SOCIETY AND THE CITIES

The federal government's commitment to America's cities in the post–World War II era reached its apotheosis during the presidency of Lyndon B. Johnson. Many of the initiatives implemented during the Johnson years originated in the inchoate New Frontier reform program, and indeed many policy makers retained from the Kennedy administration created and administered the new federal agencies that came to life in the mid-1960s. Yet despite the sturdy ligatures connecting the urban programs of the two Democratic presidencies, it is clear that the scope of federal activity in Johnson's Great Society far exceeded the plans left on White House drawing boards on November 22, 1963, when President Kennedy died in Dallas. Some programs guided through Congress by Johnson during one of the most remarkable periods of legislative achievement in the nation's history dealt forthrightly with urban problems. Such laws as the Housing Acts of 1964 and 1965, the Urban Mass Transportation Act of 1964, the National Capital Transportation Act of 1965, the Demonstration Cities (Model Cities) Act of 1966, and the Housing and Urban Development Act of 1968 clearly took aim at America's troubled urban landscape; the creation of the U.S. Department of Housing and Urban Development in 1965 became perhaps the clearest example of the administration's commitment to solving urban problems. Other laws, such as the Elementary and Secondary Education Act of 1965 and the 1968 Civil Rights Act, although ostensibly concerned with other issues, touched on urban and suburban life in significant ways; likewise, the creation of the U.S. Department of Transportation in 1966 owed in part to the desire to address problems in the nation's metropolitan areas. The War on Poverty, with all of its constituent bureaucracies and programs, reverberated most clearly in the cities where the greatest number of poor Americans resided. Indeed, as the president asserted repeatedly, the attainment of the Great Society inevitably entailed the rehabilitation of the nation's foundering urban places.

The Johnson administration's ambitious legislative attempt to extend the fruits of a prosperous society to all Americans, the most significant reform program since the New Deal, unabashedly included a full-scale assault on urban problems.

Unlike John F. Kennedy, a cosmopolite from the bustling northeastern megalopolis who was thoroughly conversant with big-city issues, Lyndon B. Johnson hailed from an isolated small town on the cusp between the American South and Southwest. Raised in a community of fewer than 1,000 residents in the rugged hills of central Texas, Johnson spent his formative years in a poor rural environment that he later acknowledged seemed a world apart from the big cities he encountered after going to Washington, D.C., as a young New Dealer in the 1930s. Growing up, he recoiled at the destitution that surrounded him in the Southwest and vowed to aid the impoverished townsfolk who strove ceaselessly to make ends meet in a harsh land; that empathy resurfaced when he later observed the abject poverty of the urban slums and ghettos. If the teeming industrial cities seemed alien to Johnson, the needs and hopes of the struggling masses seemed all too familiar. An early and dedicated advocate of low-income housing, he worked feverishly as a freshman U.S. congressman in 1937 to secure a public housing project for Austin, the largest city in his legislative district. In the 1950s, as a Democratic Senate majority leader whose cautious conservatism often rankled his more progressive colleagues, he frequently joined the small but influential bloc of Southerners who voted for low-income housing and other measures to aid the urban poor. Johnson met frequently with delegations of big-city mayors during his tenure as Senate majority leader and won high praise from them for his openness, accessibility, and willingness to learn about urban problems. His painstaking leadership proved instrumental in passing the Civil Rights Acts of 1957 and 1960, two severely limited pieces of legislation noteworthy more for having laid the foundation for future successes than for any substantive reforms achieved in race relations at the time. Yet although some liberals rued his moderating influence on the civil rights measures in 1957 and 1960, the fact that a Southerner would work for such legislation in any form seemed remarkable at the time. The loss of John F. Kennedy appeared to be a terrible setback to those who championed urban causes, but these examples from Lyndon Johnson's days as Senate majority leader suggested that the new president might not be wholly indifferent to the plight of the millions of people living in American cities.[1]

The new president's great interest in urban America figured prominently in his administration's declaration of war on poverty. The Kennedy White

House had already embraced the idea of submitting an antipoverty bill to
Congress in 1964, and the secretaries of Health, Education, and Welfare
(HEW), Agriculture, Commerce, and Labor, along with the director of the
budget and the administrator of the Housing and Home Finance Agency
(HHFA), were hurriedly preparing legislation in November 1963. Asked immediately after Kennedy's assassination whether the cabinet members
should continue this work, Johnson replied affirmatively. This is "my kind of
undertaking," he enthused. "I'm interested. I'm sympathetic. Go ahead. Give
it the highest priority. Push ahead full tilt." Previous federal efforts at combating poverty, including a host of categorical and grant programs that provided aid for relief, housing, education, and job programs, operated independently and lacked a common purpose and effective coordination. Recalling
the impressive scale of the federal programs created by Franklin D. Roosevelt during the Great Depression, Johnson sought a program for the 1960s
that could rival if not surpass the New Deal. Averse to increasing federal
spending on welfare, though, the president wanted government to wage a
"war" on poverty solely by enhancing economic opportunity for the American people. Foreswearing tax increases, Johnson asked officials in his administration to create a program of education and job training that would allow
the people to better their skills and improve their own lot in life—government would offer, in the Johnson administration's formulation, a "hand up,
not a handout."[2]

At his January 8, 1964, State of the Union address, the president declared passionately: "This administration, today, here and now, declares un-
conditional war on poverty." He went on to note the difficulty of the task for,
he admitted, no civilization in history had ever vanquished poverty altogether. But no nation in history had ever amassed the riches that the United
States had, he added, and no nation had been able to marshal the resources
that the United States could to meet the challenge. All that this most affluent
of nations lacked was the will, the president noted as he implored his audience to join the antipoverty crusade. Even as Johnson exhorted the American
people in his State of the Union message, however, he had no legislation prepared to submit to Congress and no comprehensive battle plans for the War
on Poverty. The cabinet secretaries and other advisers engaged in the ongoing policy discussions in Washington were debating the nuts and bolts of a
program that remained largely conjectural in January 1964. How much
money would be dedicated annually to combat poverty? How would the
legislation be administered? Should the antipoverty effort be managed by
an existing federal bureaucracy such as a cabinet department, or should an

independent agency be created for that purpose? What role would the cities play? Would local governments enjoy considerable autonomy or would power be centralized to a great extent in the federal government?[3]

In addition to the need for better education, higher minimum wages, enhanced manpower training, and other programs to raise income levels, some administration officials insisted that "community action" be included in the War on Poverty. The amorphous concept of community action had grown out of the Ford Foundation's Gray Areas program of the late 1950s and early 1960s, an experiment designed by social scientists to address such urban problems as blight, juvenile delinquency, and inadequate schools. Advocating citizen participation as well as financial support from government and philanthropic foundations, the Ford Foundation program emphasized decentralization and community development. Paul Ylvisaker, who assumed control of the Gray Areas effort, parlayed his good contacts with social scientists holding important positions in the Kennedy administration into a successful effort to obtain numerous federal grants. Robert Kennedy in particular approved of Ylvisaker's ambitious plans for a national urban strategy, and by 1963 Gray Areas sites in New Haven, Philadelphia, and other eastern cities claimed to have achieved notable successes in establishing legal services for the poor and in opening job training offices. A limited experimental program tested only in a few cities, the Gray Areas project nonetheless had developed by late 1963 a large and loyal following among policy officials in the Kennedy administration; many of those policy officials remained in the Johnson administration and continued to laud community action as a vital part of any large-scale antipoverty effort.[4]

On February 1, 1964, Johnson appointed R. Sargent Shriver, head of the Peace Corps and brother-in-law to the late John F. Kennedy, to develop legislation for the War on Poverty. The president believed that getting the kind of immense antipoverty program he sought through the legislature would be extraordinarily challenging, and Shriver had been very successful at coaxing funding for the Peace Corps out of Congress. Shriver quickly assembled a task force to draw up the necessary legislation, meeting daily for a month and a half in the Peace Corps building. (The irrepressible Shriver eventually recruited 137 people to serve on the task force at one time or other.) The Task Force on Poverty—called the "Poor Corps" by Washington wags—included a variety of social scientists and policy makers who propounded a dizzying hodgepodge of programs. Representatives from the cabinet departments and a number of other federal agencies attended the meetings regularly, as did a number of mayors, governors, and policy makers with experience in antipoverty programs; occasionally Shriver brought in experts from university campuses and other locations. The task force members battled "chaos and exhaustion," commented one participant, but eventually drafted a series of recommendations out of the "beautiful hysteria of it all." With few exceptions, Johnson refrained from joining the deliberations and left the legislative specifics to the policy experts.[5]

On March 16, 1964, the president sent to Congress the Economic Opportunity Act (EOA) and requested an appropriation of $962.5 million to fund the War on Poverty. Title I of the law consisted of the Job Corps, an employment program targeting impoverished males between the ages of sixteen and twenty-one, and other work training and work-study initiatives. Title II created the Community Action Program, which would encourage the "maximum feasible participation" of poverty area residents and which would be administered by local agencies representative of their communities. Additional titles requested funding for such programs as Volunteers in Service to America, aid to migrant workers, loans for poor rural families, training for unemployed heads of households on welfare, and a federally financed loan program for businesses that would hire the hard-core unemployed. Title VI also provided for the creation of a new agency, the Office of Economic Opportunity (OEO), to administer the legislation's disparate components. Johnson indicated clearly to Congress his intention to appoint Sargent Shriver as the first head of OEO. In his message to Congress introducing the bill, the president spoke in general terms, avoided specifics about the operation of the various titles, and essentially limited his remarks to a broad discussion of government's role in increasing opportunity for the nation's poor.[6]

To offset the expected attacks in Congress, Johnson designated as the bill's chief sponsor conservative Democratic Representative Phil Landrum of Georgia. The defense of the bill by Landrum, an unreconstructed racist and longtime critic of any federal threats to local prerogatives, helped to deflect conservative charges of creeping socialism. Still, opposition came from all directions. Senate Minority Leader Everett Dirksen (Republican, Illinois) termed the bill "the greatest boondoggle since bread and circuses in the days of the ancient Roman empire—when the Republic fell." Republican Senator Barry Goldwater said: "The fact is that most people who have no skill, have had no education for the same reason—low intelligence or low ambition." In the United States, he continued, people get ahead "by merit and not by fiat." Richard Nixon called a press conference and termed the War on Poverty a "cruel hoax." In the legislative debates that followed, Republicans warned that passage of the EOA would create duplicative programs, add new layers to the bloated federal bureaucracy, and leach authority from state and local governments. Southern Democrats considered the War on Poverty a liberal smokescreen, a devious means of aiding African Americans and fomenting racial integration—an argument made at length by Republican Congressman William H. Ayres of Ohio. Seeking to exploit further the concerns of southern Democrats, Republicans offered an amendment ensuring that antipoverty funds would go to children attending Roman Catholic schools. Local officials welcomed the influx of federal dollars but saw community action as a potential threat to their autonomy in distributing the largesse. In congressional hearings, Chicago Mayor Richard J. Daley succinctly summarized his fellow mayors' dim view of "maximum feasible participation," saying, "We think the local officials should have control of this program."[7]

Calling the War on Poverty the most important item in the administration's reform package, Johnson drove his aides and congressional liaisons to pass the EOA at all costs. The president approved several compromises to ensure the bill's passage, discarding the provisions that underwrote family farms and provided loans for the inveterate unemployed. When Congresswoman Edith Green (Democrat, Oregon) objected that the bill authorizing the Job Corp only provided for the employment of men, the administration drafted an amendment to hire women as well. Southerners balked at the appointment of the defense department's Adam Yarmolinsky, a notorious leftist who had expedited the desegregation of military facilities, as deputy director of the OEO. At Johnson's insistence, Shriver reneged on his promise to appoint Yarmolinsky his second in command. The Senate passed the bill 61 to 34 on July 23, and the House followed suit by a vote of 226 to 185 on August 8. The president signed the measure into law on August 20. The bill authorized $947.5 million for the first year's antipoverty programs, just $15 million less than the amount requested by the president.[8]

Even after passage of the EOA in the summer of 1964, the substance of the War on Poverty remained murky to many people inside and outside of the Johnson administration. Never entirely conversant with the intricacies of the law, Johnson vaguely hoped that OEO's varied programs would reduce poverty levels but still remained indifferent about how the programs would actually work. Sargent Shriver, whom the president had coerced into accepting the OEO directorship, found himself in charge of a puzzling concatenation of programs including an urban Job Corps, Volunteers in Service to America, and the ill-defined community action initiative. Social scientists disagreed about the effectiveness of the legislative package approved by Congress, a reflection of the lack of consensus among poverty experts at the time about how best to raise income levels. Daniel Patrick Moynihan, who had served on the Shriver task force, concluded, "This is the essential fact: The government did not know what it was doing."[9] A leading historian seconded Moynihan's assessment twenty years later, saying, "When the Economic Opportunity Act was enacted, neither the President who sponsored it, the director-designate who would administer it, nor the congressmen who passed it really knew what they had done. Indeed, a history of the legislation might well be entitled . . . 'How Not to Fight Poverty.'"[10]

In the generally muddled picture of the antipoverty crusade after the passage of the EOA, the role of community action seemed most unclear. In *Maximum Feasible Misunderstanding*, a book whose title reflected the author's unsparing criticism of the War on Poverty, Daniel Patrick Moynihan remembered that "community action simply was not much on the minds of those who were most active in the Shriver task force." In his testimony before the House on Title II of the law, Attorney General Robert F. Kennedy attributed the success of the Justice Department's pilot programs to combat juvenile delinquency in Harlem and Washington, D.C., to the use of community action principles and urged the involvement of the urban poor as mandated by "maximum feasible participation." For the most part, however, community action elicited curiously little discussion in the House and the Senate. Chicago Mayor Richard J. Daley's congressional testimony warning that community action seemed to threaten a loss of control for city halls went unheeded. Although he prided himself on being a master of legislative detail who intuitively grasped the political implications of all congressional actions, Johnson failed to appreciate the potential divisiveness of Title II. In the rush to launch the War on Poverty, he apparently did not foresee how community action could pit mayors and city councils against neighborhood interests, whites against blacks, and the rich against the poor—in other words, the entrenched urban elites against the groups newly empowered by the EOA. In short, apart perhaps from a coterie of policy experts, few people in Washington understood the radical implications of the community action idea for the nation's cities. The War on Poverty would affect urban America in ways that were not altogether clear in 1964.[11]

In the preparation of legislation drafted specifically to address urban issues, Johnson at first closely followed the path of his predecessor. In a December 4, 1963, meeting with Princeton University historian Eric F. Goldman, the president speculated about the major domestic issues he would be confronting in the upcoming years. When Goldman suggested that "our cities, now heading for such disarray, appeared certain to be a prime problem,"

Johnson nodded affirmatively. "'The cities, yes,' he murmured. 'They are something I am going to have to learn a lot about.'" On January 27, 1964, just nineteen days after delivering his State of the Union address, Johnson gave his first speech to Congress on a single topic—housing. The president noted often during his talk the centrality of the housing program to the administration's War on Poverty, which he had dramatically proclaimed in his January 8 State of the Union address. His initial foray into housing followed closely the contours of previous Kennedy legislation, primarily adding flesh and sinew to the legislative skeleton already prepared by the HHFA for the 1964 congressional session. The "bare-bones" housing legislation Johnson was submitting to Congress, so called because the bill requested appropriations for just one year, included an extension of low-income housing construction (240,000 new units over four years) as well as an additional $1.4 billion for urban renewal. Like Kennedy's earlier proposals, the 1964 measure espoused subsidies for mass transit, an expansion of the open space program, and the establishment of a cabinet department for the cities. Responding to urban renewal's shoddy record of providing housing for uprooted residents, HHFA administrator Robert C. Weaver included in the bill two years of payments for displaced families. Another original proposal by the Johnson White House requested federal grants and loans for the planning and construction of entirely new communities (new towns) separate from existing metropolitan areas.[12]

Expecting the administration to submit a more ambitious omnibus bill in 1965, Congress passed the 1964 stopgap measure with relative ease. The Housing Act of 1964 authorized the expenditure of $1.13 billion for new and existing housing and urban renewal programs through September 30, 1965, and allocated federal grants totaling $350 million for mass transportation improvements in metropolitan areas. Johnson received most of what he had requested but prudently decided not to fight for two proposals that seemed to attract little support on Capitol Hill. Without backing from the big-city mayors and other powerful interest groups in Washington and vigorously opposed by private housing interests threatened by the considerable planning associated with the new towns idea, HHFA officials realized that the time had not yet come for this bold idea. The lack of enthusiasm for a cabinet level department for cities—dubbed "Urban Affairs and Housing" in its latest incarnation—likewise convinced the administration to trim its sails and try again in a year after the results of the 1964 election had perhaps improved its chances with a newly configured Congress. Some liberals considered the Housing Act of 1964 too timid and regretted that Johnson had not built upon the earlier Kennedy proposals more aggressively to make significant inroads on the housing front. "The President is going to have to lift the next housing bill out of the ruts of compromise and put it on a new intellectual level," editorialized the *New York Times.* "The public interest demands major changes in housing policy and urban planning." Overall, however, most observers considered the housing bill a good start for the new administration. Johnson signed the bill into law on September 2, 1964.[13]

Again following up on a Kennedy initiative, Johnson pushed for mass transit legislation in the spring of 1964. The Senate had passed a bill the previous year but, doubting that the necessary votes existed for passage in the House, the Democratic leadership there declined to ask the Rules Committee for consideration on the floor. Believing that sufficient pressure for mass transit existed on House Republicans from suburban districts in an election year, the new administration pressed forward eagerly. The president promised that "we are going to do our dead level best" to pass a mass transportation bill, and the Senate predictably approved the administration's measure on April 4 by a vote of 52 to 41. Even after the annual governor's conference meeting in Cleveland in June unanimously recommended federal aid for mass transit, however, the House Republican Policy Committee maintained its "unalterable opposition" to the measure. Congressman Albert Rains (Democrat, Alabama) offered the key amendment to break the logjam, proposing a reduction in federal funding from $500 million to $375 million. Thirty-nine Republicans deserted their party's leadership in the House, providing the necessary margin of victory in a 212 to 189 vote for passage. The Urban Mass Transportation Act of 1964, the first substantive allocation of federal funds for urban mass transit development, authorized the expenditure of $375 million over three years to help state and local governments improve existing systems and construct new facilities. The law mandated that federal grants and loans be awarded for comprehensive urban transportation systems in the planned development of metropolitan areas and that the awards be approved jointly by the HHFA administrator and the secretary of commerce; it also provided funding for research and development and for demonstration projects.[14]

While Johnson staffers labored for the housing and mass transit bills on Capitol Hill in the spring and summer of 1964, work proceeded to tie urban policy into the sweeping reform program the new administration was formulating. The president struggled for a pithy phrase to label the grandiose legislative package taking shape, briefly considering the "Better Deal" a possible choice because of his reverence for Franklin D. Roosevelt's New Deal.

He eventually settled on the Great Society, a slogan that historian Eric F. Goldman and speechwriter Richard Goodwin had adapted from Walter Lippmann's 1937 book, *The Good Society*. Johnson formally unveiled the Great Society program in his May 22 commencement address at the University of Michigan. A bold statement of national purpose that summoned Americans already blessed with plenty to strive for true greatness, the speech challenged an affluent populace to share its bounty with the less fortunate and reiterated the president's earlier call for a full-scale War on Poverty. Moreover, Johnson's impassioned speech made clear the centrality of the cities to any attempt at constructing the Great Society.[15] He said: "In the remainder of this century, urban population will double, city land will double, and we will have to build homes, highways, and facilities equal to all those built since this country was first settled. So in the next forty years we must rebuild the entire urban United States . . . Our society will never be great until our cities are great."[16]

To translate Johnson's soaring rhetoric into a coherent legislative program, White House officials decided to emulate the Kennedy example of commissioning task forces charged with drafting detailed blueprints for action. (An enthusiastic convert to the practice of utilizing presidential task forces to forge public policy, Johnson appointed 135 of them from 1964 to 1968.) Two weeks after the highly acclaimed University of Michigan address, Richard Goodwin and press secretary Bill Moyers met at economist John Kenneth Galbraith's house in Cambridge, Massachusetts, with two dozen academicians from Harvard University, MIT, Boston University, and a few other area institutions to discuss the topics for and composition of the task forces. In June, Moyers assembled fourteen task forces, asking them for their recommendations by November 15. Robert C. Wood, the MIT political scientist who had served on the Kennedy administration's Task Force on Housing and Urban Affairs four years earlier, agreed to chair the Task Force on Metropolitan and Urban Problems. Wood and the other ten members of the task force soon reached a consensus that their report should emphasize the importance of a holistic approach to solving metropolitan problems. The report produced by the group recommended continued reliance on existing programs such as public housing and urban renewal, a reaffirmation of the value of the new towns program, and, perhaps most important, an emphasis upon regional planning to address the needs of the burgeoning suburbs as well as the inner cities. The task force members urged the adoption of a federal program that would both revitalize aging urban cores and encourage the development of regional governance mechanisms to ensure measured metropolitan growth. The task force also broke new ground in proposing a program of rent supplements for the poor.[17]

As Wood later recalled, the task force members decided to embrace the increasingly popular notion of an "urban crisis" plaguing the United States. The sense of impending crisis, which Wood said he and his colleagues on the task force intended to underscore forcefully in their final report to the president, emanated in part from the eruption of racial violence in the summer of 1964. Even as the task force was meeting in Washington, the first in a series of riots occurred on July 16 in Harlem where a white New York City police lieutenant shot and killed a fifteen-year-old African American during a routine arrest. After a protest demonstration escalated into a battle between protesters and the police, African American mobs began attacking whites and looting and burning uptown Manhattan neighborhoods. The Harlem disturbance lasted for five days, by which time the rioting had spread to the Brooklyn ghetto of Bedford-Stuyvesant. Additional riots quickly followed in Rochester, New York, the Chicago suburb of Dixmoor, Illinois, and the New Jersey communities of Jersey City, Elizabeth, and Paterson. Nearly a month later, violence ensued in Philadelphia when two white policemen arrested a black woman for a minor traffic violation. Two weeks after Congress passed the Civil Rights Act of 1964, as the political rhetoric in that year's presidential election between Johnson and Republican Barry Goldwater intensified, the racial violence of that summer gave rise to increased discussion of a potential white backlash against the struggle for racial equality. A dramatic backdrop to the preparations being made in the White House for the 1965 legislative season, the turmoil in America's cities lent an air of immediacy to the formulation of the Great Society program.[18]

Following his landslide election over Barry Goldwater, Johnson sought to confirm his genuine interest in urban affairs by designating Vice President Hubert Humphrey the administration's principal liaison with the nation's mayors. A former mayor of Minneapolis, Minnesota, Humphrey had during his sixteen-year career in the U.S. Senate achieved an excellent rapport with the United States Conference of Mayors and the National League of Cities. The vice president enjoyed especially congenial relations with Mayors Richard J. Daley of Chicago, Robert Wagner Jr. of New York City, Richard Lee of New Haven, Henry Meier of Milwaukee, and Jerome Cavanagh of Detroit. In early 1965 Humphrey conferred with the mayors of more than one hundred cities to discuss the upcoming legislation of particular interest to the cities. He continued to meet with mayors during the rest of the Johnson administration, regularly scheduling gatherings with the chief executives of medium-sized communities and small towns as well as big cities. The vice president succeeded in granting the mayors unprecedented access to the White House, an important element in building support from the beginning for the inclusion of urban programs in the Great Society.[19]

Johnson read the final task force reports in December 1964, the month after the electorate had sent 68 Democrats and 32 Republicans to the Senate, and 295 Democrats and 140 Republicans to the House. He decided which policies to adopt as his own and sprinkled references to the new initiatives throughout his January 4, 1965, State of the Union address. He delivered in the following days a series of special messages to Congress that elaborated on the policy recommendations outlined in the January 4 speech, thereby designating a legislative agenda for 1965 and outlining with greater specificity the contours of the Great Society. On March 2, 1965, Johnson became the first president to deliver a special message to Congress on the status of the nation's cities. Unlike earlier presentations to joint meetings of the two legislative chambers that considered housing or some other specific issue related to cities, the president's March 1965 address dealt comprehensively with the broad array of challenges confronting metropolitan America. Johnson acknowledged the existence of an urban crisis, which he characterized as "one of the most critical domestic problems of the United States," and vowed to fight urban decay with all of the resources available to the world's wealthiest country. His prescription for the cities included the continuation and expansion of such programs as low-income housing, urban renewal, open land, and new towns; he seconded the call for more planning and metropolitan cooperation and a cabinet department for cities, while proposing the creation of two new groups: (1) a temporary national commission on building codes, zoning, taxation, and metropolitan development and (2) an Institute of Urban Development. He especially endorsed the use of rent supplements, which he praised as "the most crucial new instrument in our effort to improve the American city" as a potentially invaluable aid in providing shelter for moderate-income families.[20]

The Housing Act of 1965, which the White House promptly submitted to Congress, contained all of the programs Johnson had described in his special message on the cities and far surpassed the makeshift housing bill that the legislature had breezily accepted the year before. The colossal bill sent to Capitol Hill that spring proposed the construction of 240,000 new units of low-income housing over four years, designated $2.9 billion for urban renewal, increased housing allocations for the elderly, veterans, college students, and the physically handicapped, and included a modest rent

supplement program for moderate-income families. Section 23 authorized
persons of low income to lease existing units from private landlords with
government subsidies provided by local housing authorities. The bill also
provided for "turnkey" housing, by which a developer acquired land and
contracted with the local housing authority to construct public housing according to its specifications; after completion of the project, the developer
"turned the key" over to the city agency for rent to low-income families.
Stunning in its scope and complexity, the measure thrilled most liberal supporters of the Great Society and alarmed the traditional opponents of housing reform. The National Housing Conference and the American Federation
of Labor–Congress of Industrial Organizations (AFL-CIO) quickly jumped
on board, but many interest groups that usually endorsed federal aid to
housing, most notably the National Association of Housing and Redevelopment Officials, balked because HHFA, White House, and Bureau of the
Budget officials had drafted the legislation after virtually no consultation
with housing interest groups. Speaking for the U.S. Conference of Mayors,
Richard J. Daley of Chicago judged funding for new towns and rent supplements "unnecessary" and "premature," instead requesting increased allocations for public housing, urban renewal, and other traditional programs.[21]

The most controversial aspect of the housing bill proved to be rent supplements. Beginning in the 1950s, as disenchantment with public housing
mounted, some reformers had turned to rent certificates as an alternative
means of providing low-income housing. At a 1958 conference for the National Association of Housing and Redevelopment Officials, for example,
Catherine Bauer and Warren Jay Vinton made headlines with their endorsement of rent certificates to provide shelter for low-income families scattered
throughout urban areas. HHFA administrator Robert C. Weaver, who had
become intrigued with rent supplements before joining the Kennedy administration, introduced the below-market-interest-rate loan (Section 221 [d] [3])
program in 1961 for families who barely earned too much money to qualify for
public housing. The Section 221 (d) (3) program languished, with a total of
only 50,000 units completed during the Kennedy years, but Weaver remained
convinced that such subsidies held great promise as a means of addressing the
inadequacies of the nation's private housing market. By the time that Lyndon
Johnson became president, Weaver remained an avid supporter of public
housing for low-income families but saw rent supplements as the best way for
the federal government to underwrite moderate-income housing, and the 1964
Task Force on Metropolitan and Urban Problems shared his enthusiasm for
the program. Still, recognizing that the innovative program might seem too

daring to the staunch opponents of federal subsidies for housing, the HHFA administrator felt it unwise to give rent supplements too much emphasis in the 1965 housing law. As proposed in the legislation sent to Congress in March 1965, the comparatively modest sum of $150 million would be allocated for rent supplements between 1965 and 1968. Only new or renovated buildings developed by nonprofit or limited dividend companies receiving federally insured financing would be eligible to receive rent supplements.[22]

However narrowly conceived, rent supplements generated a firestorm of criticism from a variety of sources. Traditional defenders of the private housing market such as the United States Chamber of Commerce and the National Association of Real Estate Boards quickly weighed in against the proposal, the latter warning that rent supplements would soon be used in 40 percent of American households. At the same time, the champions of public housing saw rent supplements as a potential competitor for scarce federal dollars and objected to the diversion of resources to middle-income families when the basic necessities of the neediest families remained unmet. According to historian Alexander von Hoffman, industry lobbyists made the debate over rent supplements in Congress the most bitter housing battle since the passage of the seminal Taft-Ellender-Wagner law in 1949. Republicans in the House railed against the "socialistic subsidy formula" that threatened to undermine the "incentive of the American family to improve its living accommodations by its own efforts." In the Senate, liberal stalwarts Paul H. Douglas (Democrat, Illinois) and William Proxmire (Democrat, Wisconsin) feared that the new government largesse for middle-income families would harm public housing and urged that eligible income limits be lowered to extend the benefits of rent subsidies to the poor. Many big-city mayors, struggling to respond adequately to the needs of low-income residents, echoed the concerns expressed by Douglas and Proxmire that rent supplements would benefit suburbanites primarily while the poorer residents of the inner cities would continue to lack the bare rudiments of adequate shelter.[23]

In the spring and summer of 1965, paralleling the growing tension between inner cities and suburbs nationally, race became an important subtext in the intensifying congressional debate over rent supplements. Newspaper accounts describing the assault of civil rights demonstrators in Selma, Alabama, the struggle for voting rights legislation in Congress, and battles in northern communities over public school desegregation provided an uneasy backdrop to the discussion of federally-aided housing. After six days of rioting in the Watts area of Los Angeles, local officials counted thirty-four dead and 1,032 injured; with more than six hundred buildings damaged by arson and looting, property losses exceeded $40 million. When Douglas, Proxmire, and other liberals suggested that lowering the eligibility standards of the new rent supplement program could allow poor families to escape the barriers confining them to inner-city ghettos and barrios, conservatives inveighed against the possible invasion of homogeneous suburbs by unwanted minorities. Republican and Democratic legislators representing white working-class neighborhoods within core cities likewise objected that local governments lacking any control of rent supplements would have no means of managing racial residential change in their bailiwicks. Although Senator John Tower of Texas and other southern legislators denied that race figured in their opposition to rent supplements, their fulminations against forced integration left little doubt about what they feared.[24]

Fully engaged in the effort to push the voting rights and Medicare acts through the Eighty-ninth Congress—and poised to submit the next batch of Great Society laws, including measures to reform immigration policy and abrogate right-to-work legislation—the Johnson administration found its housing measure stalled in June by a decidedly minor component of the massive bill, the innocuous rent supplement program. Robert Weaver and Postmaster General Lawrence O'Brien, the president's most skilled political operative, lobbied intensely with housing interest groups and wavering congressmen on behalf of the housing bill. As a concession to the liberals whose expected support had not materialized, Senator Edmund Muskie (Democrat, Maine) introduced an amendment to lower the eligibility standard for rent supplements below the ceiling allowable for public housing. A vote in the House to recommit the bill to committee for the purposes of eliminating rent control failed by a vote of 208 to 202, and in the Senate an amendment by John Tower to expunge the program lost 47 to 40. With rent supplements narrowly preserved, the housing bill passed by comfortable margins in the Senate and the House. The president signed the Housing Act of 1965 into law on August 10, calling it the most important housing legislation since the landmark 1949 law. The final version of the bill retained the rent supplements provision but only for people who qualified for low-income housing; thus, an odd alliance of conservatives and liberals had subverted the original intention of the new program as conceived by Johnson and Weaver.[25]

Having gone to extraordinary lengths to preserve rent supplements in the omnibus housing bill, the administration continued to fight for its survival in subsequent years. When Congress considered its annual appropriations in October 1965, a conservative coalition led by two Republican congressmen from Michigan, James Harvey and House minority leader Gerald

Ford, secured enough votes to eliminate funding for the embattled program. Ford called rent subsidies a "pay-your-neighbor's-rent scheme" and a "radical revolutionary rent-subsidy gimmick," confidently predicting that the administration's dogged defense of the contentious program would be a useful issue for the Republicans in the 1966 elections. Johnson remained committed to the program and staged another intensive lobbying effort on Capitol Hill in 1966, but could not persuade all members of his party to provide full funding after Richard Russell of Georgia, the most influential southern Democratic senator, declared his opposition to rent supplements; Congress only appropriated half of the total requested by the administration that year. Moreover, Congress added a codicil that local governments must authorize all expenditures for rent supplements. In 1967, after elections the previous November had replaced a number of liberals in the House with conservatives who had campaigned against the costly domestic programs of the Johnson administration, the struggle over appropriations intensified; the White House had to settle that year for one-fourth of the amount it had requested for rent supplements. Despite the persistent lobbying of the Johnson administration, by 1968 Congress ended up appropriating only $42 million of the $150 million authorized in the Housing Act of 1965 for rent supplements. And just as they refused to authorize the construction of public housing within their boundaries, local governments exercised their veto power to limit the use of rent supplements in suburban areas. The Housing Act of 1965 took its place among the many significant Great Society measures passed by the Eighty-ninth Congress, but, despite the sustained efforts of Johnson, Weaver, and their acolytes, rent supplements never became an important tool to address the housing issues of middle-income families.[26]

The other major urban initiative that the president had listed in his March 2, 1965, special message to Congress, the creation of a cabinet department for the cities, finally seemed attainable in ways that it had not in previous years. Johnson declined to tackle the issue during his first year in the White House, but the huge majorities the Democrats enjoyed in both houses of Congress after the November 1964 election left the political landscape considerably more inviting to such a proposal. The president believed that the bill submitted to the Eighty-ninth Congress, which was virtually identical to the versions presented to the Eighty-seventh and Eighty-eighth Congresses, required only a few cosmetic changes to gain the necessary votes for passage. Trying to anticipate any possible roadblocks, the administration changed the name of the proposed cabinet department from "Urban Affairs and Housing" to "Housing and Urban Development." Giving housing top billing in the title would reassure the construction and banking industries that their interests remained paramount in the presidential cabinet. The choice of "urban development," with its implied emphasis upon the physical environment of the urban landscape, allayed concerns that the more nebulous "urban affairs" might encompass any and all topics remotely related to metropolitan life. The parsing of language in such fine detail mattered in the attempt to assuage the concerns of legislators poised to add another big piece of bureaucracy to a federal government already considered too ponderous in some quarters. Determined to avoid the kind of controversy that helped to derail Kennedy's earlier efforts, Johnson denied that any decision had been made to appoint Robert Weaver the new department's first secretary. The Civil Rights Act of 1964 and the impending passage of the voting rights bill may have signaled that southern obstructionists no longer could use the race issue with the same effectiveness, but Johnson was taking no chances.[27]

Reflecting the sense of inevitability about the new cabinet department, consideration of the administration's bill proceeded perfunctorily in Congress. The Democrats summoned the usual cast of characters—mayors, urban planners, labor unionists, and public housing officials—to testify in favor of the legislation. Some Republicans noted that such legislation would relegate state and local governments to subordinate roles, but, resigned to the certainty of the federal government devoting greater attention to urban affairs, most conservatives in Congress concentrated their objections on the efficacy of adding a new cabinet post. Always ready to challenge proposals designed to expand the size of the federal government, Republicans dismissed the value for cities as having to engage with yet another inefficient, wasteful Washington agency. An office of urban affairs and community development situated in the Executive Office of the President offered more benefit to mayors seeking "one-stop" service in the nation's capital, suggested Republican Congressmen Donald Rumsfeld of Illinois, Robert Griffin of Michigan, Florence Dwyer of New Jersey, and Republican Senator Hugh Scott of Pennsylvania. Surely a presidential aide with a small staff operating out of a White House office rather than a cumbersome bureaucracy would provide greater flexibility and quicker response to pressing urban problems, they argued. Charging that the Republican proposal seriously underestimated the scope and gravity of urban problems, Democrats urged the creation of a cabinet department as a clear statement of the importance of cities and as a sign of Congress's determination to deal with the urban crisis. The lone difference between the versions of the bill passed by the House and Senate involved the power of the Federal Housing Administration (FHA), which the construction and real-estate industries insisted must continue to operate independently. Congress adopted a proposal by the National Association of Home Builders that retained the FHA as a separate entity within the new agency under a federal housing commissioner who was also designated an assistant secretary. The law passed by comfortable margins in the House (217 to 184) and the Senate (57 to 33), and Johnson signed the law creating the Department of Housing and Urban Development (HUD) on September 9, 1965.[28]

Although Johnson had declined to designate Robert C. Weaver as the first secretary of HUD prior to the legislation's passage, Washington pundits considered the HHFA administrator the best-qualified candidate for the position and fully expected him to be appointed. So did Weaver. The legislation creating HUD would go into effect sixty days after the president signed the measure, so Weaver anticipated being named secretary—or at least acting secretary, pending congressional approval—by November 9, 1965. But in late October Johnson told Joseph Califano Jr., his senior domestic policy aide, that he did not want to make the appointment with Congress in adjournment and that he had not decided to name Weaver secretary of HUD. Califano broke the bad news to a shocked and angry Weaver, who felt that it would be "embarrassing, downright humiliating" not to be selected. He threatened to resign but, assured that he could still be chosen the first African American cabinet member, finally agreed to remain at his post until the president announced the appointment. While Johnson declined to discuss the matter and the press suggested a number of possible appointees during November and December, Weaver waited impatiently and publicly admitted that he desperately wanted the job.[29]

Why had Johnson not taken the anticipated step of immediately elevating his housing deputy to the cabinet post? Weaver had failed to establish warm relations with many legislators on Capitol Hill, a crucial requirement for any cabinet secretary seeking appropriations from congressional committees. Senate Majority Mike Mansfield (Democrat, Montana) had been disappointed with the HHFA administrator, especially with his handling of the rent supplement provision of the 1965 housing bill, and refused to support him for the HUD position. Detroit Mayor Jerome P. Cavanagh later remembered that many of the big-city mayors criticized Weaver's performance at the HHFA and spoke against his selection. Johnson liked Weaver personally and felt that he had proved himself a competent manager but doubted that the HHFA administrator could become the kind of charismatic leader needed to guide HUD in its infancy. According to presidential aide Harry McPherson, Weaver's incessant caution and frequent rhetorical lapses into bland "governmentese" frustrated Johnson and others who wanted more creative approaches to urban problem solving. McPherson believed Weaver's habitual circumspection typical of the African Americans in high-level government positions who always played it safe and avoided mistakes that could reflect negatively on their race. "Weaver is a supreme Negro bureaucrat," said McPherson, "and because he's Negro, I think, he's more bureaucratic than almost any white bureaucrat you want to find." Whatever the cause of Weaver's prudence, Johnson repeatedly commented that he wanted a more dynamic leader acting on behalf of the cities.[30]

Johnson considered a number of other candidates and consulted with dozens of stake holders in the appointment. Robert F. Kennedy confided in a telephone conversation with the president that he had not been impressed with Weaver and stated that his brother had never made any commitment that had to be honored; he also agreed with the president that there might be "some advantage to having a white man in there." Johnson mentioned to several confidants that he was seriously considering the noted financier and philanthropist Laurence Rockefeller for the post. The president also expressed his high regard for Ben Heineman, the chairman of the board of the Chicago and Northwestern Railroad who had served on several White House task forces, indicating to Mayor Richard J. Daley that he was thinking of appointing Weaver as secretary and Heineman as undersecretary—and then replacing Weaver with Heineman after a year or two. Heineman later recalled that he discussed the appointment with presidential aides Joseph Califano and Harry McPherson but declined to be considered and suggested instead United Auto Workers President Walter Reuther. Robert C. Wood, whom Johnson admired greatly, denied any designs on the position himself and gave Weaver an unqualified recommendation. In the end, after every major civil rights leader recommended the HHFA administrator, Johnson chose Weaver. On January 13, 1966, with little fanfare, Johnson appointed Weaver the first HUD secretary at a small White House ceremony arranged at the last moment; he also announced the appointment of Wood as undersecretary. The Senate Banking Committee approved after a hearing that lasted barely an hour, and the full Senate unanimously consented to the appointments later that day.[31]

The selection of the first HUD secretary, an unseemly tableau played out in the press over nearly three months, reflected poorly upon the president, left Weaver in an untenable position, and saddled the new agency with a multitude of questions about its leadership. Johnson had told Califano that he had to possess the unquestioned loyalty of the person he appointed at

HUD—he had to have "his pecker in my drawer," in the president's colorful phrase—and Weaver's quiet forbearance in the face of public humiliation left little doubt that he would be a compliant subordinate. Weaver had enjoyed the clear backing of the civil rights community, but the challenges to his selection from many other quarters and the number of names that surfaced as potential alternatives generated real doubts about the strength of his support within other interest groups. Johnson's clear lack of enthusiasm for the appointment seemed to indicate that lacking other viable alternatives he had reluctantly settled on Weaver, and rumors persisted that Robert C. Wood waited in the wings to replace the secretary if he stumbled—or perhaps even if he did not. Questions immediately surfaced about the HUD secretary's ability to act independently, to shape the policy debates about the future of the cities, and to chart a clear course of action for the new agency. Would HUD be simply a glorified housing agency or would it, under Weaver's leadership, fashion a broader urban vision? Would federal policies designed to aid the cities originate with Weaver, with others concerned with urban policy working in HUD and other federal agencies, or with the myriad task forces that the president continued to commission? The future of HUD as the primary voice of the cities in the federal government remained very much in doubt in 1965.[32]

The legislative bounty of 1965, the year that constituted the high water mark of the Great Society, included several other bills of importance to the cities. The first, the Elementary and Secondary Education Act, deviated from traditional education legislation that had allocated funds across the board for school construction and teacher salary increases. Instead, intent especially upon improving education in poor inner cities, the act provided more specialized types of aid for school districts with large numbers of children from low-income families. Like the War on Poverty, the Johnson administration's education program traced its roots to the Ford Foundation's inner-city work in the 1950s, one component of which sought to improve social conditions by resuscitating unidentified urban schools. Johnson pointed out that cities spent only about two-thirds as much as suburbs on education and that nearly two-thirds of tenth graders from poor neighborhoods in the nation's fifteen largest cities dropped out before receiving a high school diploma. As Education Commissioner Francis Keppel explained, the Elementary and Secondary Education Act would roughly double federal expenditures on public education, with the bulk of the new funds targeting poor children in order to break the cycle of poverty prevailing in urban America. Title I, the heart of the law, provided federal grants to the states on the basis of the following formula: the number of children from low-income families (under $2,000 a year) multiplied times 50 percent of each state's average expenditure per pupil. The U.S. Conference of Mayors unanimously endorsed the measure, which sailed through Congress in a mere three months; the House passed the bill by a vote of 263 to 153 and the Senate by a vote of 73 to 18. The president signed the bill in the presence of seventy-two-year-old Kate Deadrich Loney, who had been his first teacher, outside the dilapidated one-room schoolhouse he had attended as a four-year-old decades before.[33]

The Great Society also included measures to protect the environment. Contrary to the view of Johnson as a loyal servant of Texas oil interests indifferent if not hostile to ecological issues, the president frequently invoked the example of Theodore Roosevelt in seeking to conserve natural resources in the wilderness—and superseded Roosevelt's example by championing environmental measures in urban settings as well. Johnson inveighed against industrial miscreants that dumped their toxic waste indiscriminately, polluted the water, and befouled the air. The Water Quality Act of 1965, which the president signed on October 2, 1965, required the states to enforce water quality standards; the Clean Water Reclamation Act, which he signed on November 3, 1966, provided matching grants for the construction of sewage treatment plants. Enforcement of these laws proved problematic, requiring additional amendments in later years to guarantee the quality of drinking water in the cities. The report of the President's Task Force on Environmental Pollution documented the damage to the air by emissions from coal-burning factories and automobile exhaust, especially the air pollutants that fell back to earth as "acid rain." Public concern about air pollution grew after an ecological disaster in New York City on Thanksgiving Day, 1965, when an air inversion trapped lethal levels of soot in the atmosphere, suffocated eighty people, and left hundreds hospitalized. Johnson signed the Air Quality Act of 1967 on November 21, 1967, establishing stricter standards for automobile emissions and industrial pollution. Incomplete and underfunded, the Great Society's environmental legislation nonetheless constituted the federal government's initial steps to protect the urban masses from water- and air-borne pollutants.[34]

Passage in 1965 of a related environmental bill, the Highway Beautification Act, owed largely to the indefatigable work of the First Lady. At Lady Bird Johnson's request, the president in 1964 convened the Task Force on the Preservation of Natural Beauty to extend the earlier work on wilderness beautification to more populated areas. Using Washington, D.C., as a test case, the First Lady, the National Park Service, and private donors refurbished Pennsylvania Avenue between the White House and the Capitol and landscaped a series of parks throughout the city. Arguing that crumbling buildings, open sewage, and rabid rats presented greater threats to urban life than unsightly billboards and a dearth of green space, critics dismissed Mrs. Johnson and others interested in city beautification as effete members of the "daffodil and dogwood" set. The president informed Congress that he fully supported his wife's crusade, calling city beautification good for business and an important step in reviving the nation's flagging tourism industry. The bill finally passed by Congress restricted the use of billboards except in designated industrial areas and mandated the erection of fences around the junkyards and other eyesores adjacent to highways.[35]

The final noteworthy law for cities passed that year, the National Capital Transportation Act, brought to a close a campaign initiated earlier in the decade to build a subway in Washington, D.C. John F. Kennedy had been an enthusiastic supporter of a plan to build a subway in the nation's capital, but a bill introduced in Congress in 1963 providing for federal construction and operation of a rapid transit system failed in the House. Having lived for decades in Washington and encouraged by the passage of the Urban Mass Transportation Act of 1964, Lyndon Johnson quickly agreed to send a new bill to the Eighty-ninth Congress in 1965. Intending to placate the AFL-CIO, which had opposed the 1963 bill because it questioned whether federal operation of mass transit would limit such worker prerogatives as binding arbitration, the legislation offered in 1965 provided for a publicly owned system operated by a private company. By voice votes, the Senate and the House passed the National Capital Transportation Act authorizing the National Capital Transportation Agency to construct a 24.9 mile rail transit system at a total cost of $431 million—$150 million in grants (two-thirds from the federal government and one-third from the District of Columbia) and the sale of bonds to cover the balance of the cost. Johnson signed the measure on September 8. The Washington Metro, approved in 1965, a trunk line built almost exclusively within the District of Columbia, eventually grew to 106 miles and served patrons in the suburbs of northern Virginia and southern Maryland as well.[36]

By the end of 1965, onlookers marveled at the speed with which Johnson had managed to assemble the framework of his Great Society program. Driven by the insatiable taskmaster in the White House, the Eighty-ninth Congress had achieved a breathtaking legislative record of accomplishment. Building on an impressive start in 1964 and abetted by the outcome of that year's elections, which returned hefty Democratic majorities to Capitol Hill, the administration in 1965 secured Medicare and Medicaid, aid for primary

and secondary education, government loans for college students, a landmark voting rights law, immigration reform, environmental legislation, protection for consumers, and the creation of the National Endowment for the
Humanities and the National Endowment for the Arts, as well as several
lesser laws. Legislation directly targeting the cities included a major housing bill, a subway for the nation's capital, and, most important, the creation
of a cabinet department for urban affairs. Determined to confront the rising
urban unrest that seemed to worsen with each summer of his administration, the president felt the need to do even more for the nation's beleaguered
cities. With HUD finally created and its secretary firmly ensconced, Johnson
sought in 1966 a daring new program that would combine the resources of
the federal government's many agencies in a massive campaign to save
America's inner cities.

The president had been intrigued by a May 15, 1965, memorandum from
United Auto Workers President Walter Reuther proposing a "Marshall Plan
for the Cities." Rather than devising a generic program that would award
grants wholesale to American cities, as had been done routinely in the past,
Reuther proposed "a bold restructuring in six selected American cities of full
and complete organic neighborhoods for 50,000 people." He suggested that
six cities—Detroit; Chicago; Philadelphia; Washington, D.C.; Los Angeles;
and Houston—serve as test cases for an innovative federal program that
could be replicated on a much larger scale in the future. In Reuther's design,
the federal government would mobilize such disparate elements as business,
labor, local government, and community organizations into a powerful alliance to improve all aspects of urban life—housing, jobs, education, health
care, recreation, transportation, and public safety. Johnson distrusted the
labor leader but liked the audacity of his plan, thought it could be incorporated effectively into the existing Great Society framework, and believed that
federal involvement must go beyond housing in order to make a difference in
the aging central cities. At a September 17, 1965, White House meeting,
Reuther fleshed out his proposal to the president in greater detail and argued
persuasively that only the federal government (under the leadership of a
forceful president) could undertake such an enterprise. Johnson promptly
appointed another urban task force, chaired by HUD undersecretary Robert C. Wood, charged with effectuating Reuther's design for "demonstration
cities." Johnson also appointed Reuther to the task force, along with Whitney
Young of the Urban League, Kermit Gordon from the Budget Bureau, William Rafsky of the Philadelphia Redevelopment Authority, Charles Haar of
the Harvard University Law School, and industrialist Edgar Kaiser. Senator

Abraham Ribicoff (Democrat, Connecticut) and Ben Heineman, president of the Chicago and Northwestern Railroad, joined the group in November.[37]

The members of the task force quickly agreed with Reuther's central premise—that federal aid to the cities in the past had been distributed too diffusely and that the demonstration cities project must concentrate resources in a few communities to maximize effect—but many specifics remained to be determined. Questions arose about the relationship of the demonstration cities effort with other urban programs, specifically with HUD and the Community Action Program. At the same time, the task force discussed whether the Community Action Program should be left in an independent OEO or transferred to HUD. Walter Reuther and Ben Heineman forcefully argued in favor of the move to HUD because of the need to give the Community Action Program a strong organizational base; Kermit Gordon dissented, arguing against saddling the new agency with too many responsibilities and too many interests competing for too few dollars. Siding with Gordon, Whitney Young warned against taking any action until a HUD secretary had been appointed. With members of the task force unable to reach a clear consensus, Johnson decided to leave responsibility for the Community Action Program within an autonomous OEO and to assign demonstration cities to HUD.[38]

In the course of its meetings in the fall of 1965, the task force significantly reworked Reuther's original plan for six demonstration cities. Yielding to Senator Ribicoff's observation that political support would grow if a greater number of congressmen could vote for a measure that directly benefited their constituents, the task force increased the number of demonstration cities to sixty-six. The final bill that the president sent to Congress outlined a program for six large cities (population exceeding 500,000), ten medium-sized cities (250,000 to 500,000 population), and fifty small cities (population less than 250,000). Communities would submit proposals for federal funding and, with the selection process conducted judiciously by a special presidential commission, demonstration cities could be identified in a large number of states and congressional districts. The sixty-six communities selected for participation would be expected to avail themselves of the full panoply of federal programs already in existence so that this effort would dovetail, not compete, with the Community Action Program, the Job Corps, and other Great Society creations. Cities receiving grants must involve low-income communities, with demonstrable citizen involvement, in planning comprehensive neighborhood rehabilitation. Harkening back to the Community Action Program, the program called for full "citizen participation." The task force affixed a $2.3 billion price tag over six years on demonstration cities, the federal government paying 80 percent ($1.9 billion) and local authorities assuming responsibility for the remaining 20 percent. HUD would serve as the lead agency to administer the program.[39]

On January 26, 1966, Johnson unveiled Demonstration Cities while delivering his third message on housing to Congress. He requested funding for six urban initiatives, ranging from new towns to metropolitan development, but public attention focused on the $2.3 billion Demonstration Cities program that simultaneously sent cost-conscious, limited-government conservatives into apoplexy and left many liberals uncomfortable with the modest sum designated for the law. Republican Senator Everett M. Dirksen of Illinois observed that the plan had "all the prospects of becoming one of the greatest boondoggles this country has ever witnessed." Major metropolises such as New York City would need more funds, noted the *New York Times*, an inevitable result of spreading an inadequate amount of money across too many communities. Robert F. Kennedy, who had resigned as attorney general and had been elected senator from New York, called $2.3 billion a "drop in the bucket." Big-city mayors gave Demonstration Cities a qualified endorsement, hoping to receive some of the federal largesse, but also expressed concerns about the low funding levels. They also worried that grant-in-aid money already committed to hundreds of communities nationwide would be diverted to a select group of Model Cities; the U.S. Conference of Mayors would not endorse Demonstration Cities, for example, without receiving assurances that urban renewal funds would not be commandeered for the new program. To charges that Demonstration Cities meant a shocking extension of federal power, Johnson rejoined that state and local governments were expected to play a crucial role in the program's implementation. Congressional conservatives took aim at the appellation "Demonstration Cities," suggesting that the president had succumbed to the antics of antiwar and African American demonstrators in the cities; administration supporters soon adopted the less suggestive "Model Cities."[40]

With the threat of more racial violence in the cities looming in the spring and summer of 1966, the battle over Model Cities became one of the most bitter experienced by the Johnson administration. Several months after Democrats Paul Douglas of Illinois and Wright Patman of Texas introduced the bill in the Senate and the House respectively, the opposition seemed so strong that the *New York Times* on May 15 pronounced Model Cities dead. The administration shied away from using Douglas or Senator John Sparkman (Democrat, Alabama), both of whom faced difficult reelection campaigns that year against imposing Republican foes, as floor leaders for the bill. Unable to rely upon the two ablest and most informed senators to manage the controversial measure in the Senate Banking Committee and on the Senate floor, Johnson turned to the comparatively inexperienced Edmund Muskie (Democrat, Maine). Although affirming his broad sympathy with the objectives the president had outlined in his January 26 address, Muskie expressed concern about the needless complexity and ambiguity of the Model Cities legislation. In particular, he worried that the exceedingly complicated mechanism for allocating funds to the designated cities and a stringent desegregated housing provision would make the chances of passing the bill in its current form "slim." Only after several weeks of negotiation and the inclusion of a number of changes did Muskie agree to lead the fight for what he at last believed to be a vastly improved bill. Presidential aide Joseph Califano pointed out to the president that Muskie hailed from a small rural state that probably lacked a single community large enough to qualify for a Model Cities grant. "Well, he has one now," Johnson replied. "What one?" Califano asked. "Whatever one he wants," the president chortled. Portland, Maine, received one of the awards in the first round; Lewiston, Maine, in the second round.[41]

The administration expected fewer problems in the more liberal Senate than in the House but, even with Muskie's able leadership, the bill made grudging progress. Muskie needed the vote of Thomas J. McIntyre (Democrat, New Hampshire) to get the bill out of the Banking and Currency Committee's housing subcommittee. McIntyre faced reelection that year and hesitated to support a $2.3 billion bill that offered no benefit to his rural and small-town constituents. The administration agreed to request only $900 million for two years and not specify additional funding thereafter, a compromise that allowed McIntyre to claim that he had whittled down program cost; he provided the deciding vote in the subcommittee on July 23. The full committee passed the bill on August 10 by a vote of eight to six, and the debate on the Senate floor commenced as once again race riots erupted in the major cities of the Northeast and Midwest. Liberals Robert F. Kennedy, Abraham Ribicoff, and Jacob Javits (Republican, New York) questioned the value of a weakened Model Cities bill, while John Tower (Republican, Texas) led the conservative opposition against what he termed yet another attempt to solve problems by throwing federal dollars at them. A number of senators on both sides of the aisle grumbled about passing legislation simply to appease ghetto rioters.[42]

Even as the bill was being considered on the Senate floor, Ribicoff used his authority as chair of the Government Operations Committee's Subcommittee

on Executive Reorganization to conduct an investigation of the federal
government's role in urban affairs, to evaluate the Johnson administration's
record on behalf of the cities, and to assess the value of the Model Cities proposal. In the course of hearing testimony from Washington officials, big-city
mayors, and a variety of urban experts, Ribicoff and other members of the subcommittee repeatedly voiced their dissatisfaction with the administration's efforts on behalf of the cities. Secretary Weaver attempted to read prepared remarks about HUD's activities, but Ribicoff, Robert Kennedy, Jacob Javits,
Ernest Gruening (Democrat, Alaska), and Carl Curtis (Republican, Nebraska)
interrupted him repeatedly to enumerate the Johnson administration's deficiencies. The subcommittee afforded other administration spokesmen—OEO's
Sargent Shriver, Labor's Willard Wirtz, HEW's John Gardner, and Attorney
General Nicholas Katzenbach—the same rude treatment. New York City
Mayor John V. Lindsay testified about the shocking inadequacy of the requested $2.3 billion budget for Model Cities, contending that his city alone des-
perately needed $50 billion in federal aid; Detroit Mayor Jerome Cavanagh
upped the ante to a whopping $250 billion to solve the urban crisis in America.
The press gave extensive coverage to the sensational hearings in which, for the
most part, liberal Democrats savaged the White House for offering timid solutions to a massive problem. Furious at the way administration officials had
been ambushed at the hearings and suspecting that Robert Kennedy's criticisms amounted to the opening salvo in his 1968 presidential campaign, Johnson defended his record in a series of hastily scheduled appearances in the
Northeast. Weaver predicted a close vote in the Senate, and the administration
intensified its lobbying efforts in the late summer to ensure the crucial support
of liberal Democrats. The Senate passed the measure on August 19 by a comfortable margin of 53 to 22, but the unusually high number of abstentions (25)
underscored the ambivalence felt by many of the solons.[43]

The struggle continued in September and October in the House, where
even the reduction of initial funding to $900 million failed to appease the
hardy conservative opposition. Democrat William Barrett of Pennsylvania,
chairman of the key subcommittee of the Banking and Currency Committee,
had initially refused to fight what he knew would be an uphill battle until the
Senate had passed the bill. When a version of the legislation approved in the
upper chamber passed in Barrett's subcommittee and in the Banking and
Currency Committee itself, the House Republican Policy Committee rallied
all party members to defeat the measure. As in the Senate, debate reflected
the national preoccupation with race in the summer and fall of 1966—involving what the Model Cities bill would mean for the racial desegregation of

white neighborhoods, the location of public housing in suburbs, busing to achieve racial integration, and indeed how the nation was reacting to yet another summer of racial violence in the cities. Congressman Henry B. Gonzalez (Democrat, Texas), an avid supporter of the measure, proudly proclaimed: "The Demonstration Cities and Metropolitan Act of 1966 is the real antiriot bill of the 89th Congress."[44] A decidedly less enthusiastic congressman, Paul A. Fino (Republican, New York), openly appealed to the racial fears of his colleagues in urging defeat of what he called "the most far-reaching civil rights bill—however carefully disguised—that the White House has ever proposed." Fino fulminated:

> This program is a tool of black power . . . I can just imagine what kind of city demonstrations black power has in mind. They will demonstrate how to burn down shops and loot liquor stores. They will demonstrate how to throw Molotov cocktails at police cars. . . . Oh, yes, I can imagine the kind of demonstration program black power has in mind. Demonstration conflagration. Demonstration incineration.[45]

Concerned that the racist campaign being waged in the House might be gaining ground, Johnson mobilized a massive lobbying campaign in favor of Model Cities. He recruited the chief executive officers of twenty-two Fortune 500 Companies, led by Henry Ford II and David Rockefeller, to issue a statement of endorsement and to send telegrams to their congressmen urging passage of the bill. Convinced of the necessity for one last strong push from the White House, Johnson referred to Model Cities at an October 6 press conference as "one of the most important pieces of legislation for the good of all American mankind that we can act upon this session." After administration supporters defeated several amendments cutting allocations and acceded to an amendment stipulating that funding would not be used to achieve racial balance in the schools, the House passed the bill on October 14 by a vote of 178 to 141. A conference committee eliminated the few differences between the versions passed in the two chambers, and the president signed the Demonstration Cities and Metropolitan Development Act—which he thereafter insisted upon calling the Model Cities Act—on November 3, 1966. Having prevailed in arguably his most arduous struggle with the Eighty-ninth Congress, Johnson celebrated the passage of the measure and reiterated his high hopes for what he judged to be the administration's signal effort on behalf of the cities.[46]

Almost from the beginning, however, Model Cities suffered a series of setbacks that vitiated Johnson's optimism. Because of the paucity of funding and the glacial pace at which the federal government processed the necessary paperwork, the program sputtered in its infancy. In his January 1967 budget message, the president requested $662 million for the program in fiscal year 1968—but Congress appropriated just $212 million. By the May 1967 deadline for the first round of Model Cities planning grants, HUD had received 193 applications from forty-seven states, the District of Columbia, and Puerto Rico. On November 16, 1967, Weaver announced the award of planning grants to sixty-three cities; in March 1968, in what he called "round one and a half," the secretary chose twelve additional cities for funding. Reacting to the disappointment expressed by the many cities that HUD had not selected, Weaver and White House aides appealed to other federal agencies for additional grant funds for use in the second round of the competition. Jealously guarding their own resources at a time of budget cuts, OEO, Labor, and HEW contributed very little money. On September 6, 1968, Weaver identified the thirty-three communities that received second-round planning grants. HUD finally approved the first city for full funding on December 23, 1968, less than one month prior to the inauguration of a new president. Altogether, only nine cities received Model Cities funding during the Johnson administration.[47]

Allegations surfaced about politics permeating the Model Cities selection process. Along with the applications, Weaver provided the White House with a list of cities that included the name of each community's congressional representatives and whether or not they had voted for the bill—a perfect opportunity for political favoritism. Communities from the president's home state of Texas enjoyed great success in the competition. The selection of Austin, Houston, and San Antonio surprised no one, but awards to Eagle Pass, Texarkana, and Laredo seemed another matter. As well, Portland and Lewiston in Senator Edmund Muskie's home state of Maine; Butte and Helena in Senator Mike Mansfield's Montana; and Tulsa, Lawton, and McAlester in Representative Carl Albert's Oklahoma all received awards. The *Wall Street Journal* had great fun contemplating how Model Cities funds would eradicate urban blight in Pikesville, Kentucky, with its population of 4,754 souls. The newspaper observed that Pikesville enjoyed the good fortune of being located in the congressional district of Carl Perkins, chairman of the House Education and Labor Committee. Dismissing numerous press releases that affirmed the integrity of the merit-based selection process, critics labeled Model Cities just another pork barrel project directing funds into the coffers of the administration's political supporters at the expense of slum-ridden cities that continued to suffer without federal aid.[48]

Controversy also arose from the outset over the administration of Model Cities awards at the local level, a sticky problem that commenced with planning grants at the end of the Johnson years and continued with the program grants during the next presidential administration. Testifying before Congress in favor of the bill in 1966, Weaver affirmed that "this is a local program, to be planned, developed, and carried out by local people." Yet at other times the secretary confessed to having reservations about relinquishing all control to city halls, saying: "I don't think that we appropriate federal money with a blank check." The mayors whose cities received the infusion of federal funds wanted exactly that kind of autonomy, however, and rejected close supervision by distant Washington bureaucrats. HUD guidelines did not explicitly preclude existing city agencies from control over Model Cities planning but expressed a clear preference for new organizations created specifically for that purpose. In Chicago, municipal agencies entirely wrote the application submitted to HUD and ignored the protests of citizen groups representing the neighborhoods designated for Model Cities funding. Reluctant to alienate Mayor Richard J. Daley, a powerful Democrat and strong supporter of the president's domestic and foreign policies, HUD overlooked Chicago's transgressions and approved the city's planning application. This tension between HUD and Model Cities grant recipients, duplicated in other communities around the nation, contributed to the declining fortunes of what the president had hoped would be the linchpin in his design to aid the cities.[49]

The Johnson administration's other major legislative achievement of 1966, the creation of the U.S. Department of Transportation, seemed certain to affect urban America in some important ways. By the 1960s the regulation of the nation's highways, railroads, ports, canals, and airports fell to thirty-five agencies scattered throughout the federal government, most under congressional control. In 1960, in the name of greater efficiency and economy, President Eisenhower had advocated in his annual budget address the consolidation of the numerous agencies into a cabinet department. President Johnson quickly warmed to the idea of enhancing federal authority to improve the mobility and safety of Americans in transit and saw a federal department of transportation as an integral component of the Great Society. A 1964 Task Force on Transportation, under the leadership of UCLA economist George W. Hilton, recommended the creation of a cabinet department. The president instructed another task force on transportation created the following year to devise a workable plan, in Johnson's typically sweeping fashion, "looking not only to next year, but to 1980, the year 2000 and beyond." The president presented the idea to Congress in his January 12, 1966, State of

the Union Address, then ordered Budget Bureau Director Charles Schultze to
assemble yet another task force to formulate a concrete proposal. Chaired by
Assistant Budget Bureau Director Charles Zwick, the new task force acted
quickly and presented the White House with draft legislation within two
months. The proposal Johnson presented to Congress on March 2, 1966,
merged the Commerce Department's office of transportation, the Bureau of
Public Roads, the Federal Aviation Agency (FAA), the Coast Guard, the
Maritime Administration, and several smaller agencies into a new cabinet
department with jurisdiction over all manner of transportation modes—but
sharing responsibility with HUD for urban transportation.[50]

    The question of whether the responsibility for urban mass transit should
remain in HUD or be transferred to the new department perplexed members
of the Johnson administration from the start of deliberations. On the one
hand, Weaver argued that the kind of comprehensive urban planning that
HUD sought to undertake would be impossible without the control of rapid
transit. How does government make policy for urban improvement, queried
the secretary, without full attention to all matters of city life? On the other
hand, asked civil engineers and other policy makers, how could a new department effectively manage all the facets of the nation's transportation network without all modes of transportation included? What would be the point
of charging a government agency with responsibility for expressways but not
subways? With its members unable to reach a consensus, the Zwick task
force submitted its report to the White House without making a recommendation on the issue. Johnson and his aides found the matter equally perplexing and decided not to address urban mass transit in the bill submitted to
Congress. In his remarks accompanying the legislation, however, Johnson
explained that he would order the secretaries of HUD and Transportation to
confer and resolve the matter within one year of the law's passage. The issue
resurfaced in Congress, where many Democrats, led by Senator Abraham Ribicoff, largely favored Weaver, Wood, and the other liberals at HUD. The
Republican Policy Committee preferred the Department of Transportation,
which they expected to be controlled by engineers and technocrats who
would not allow the kind of social engineering for which HUD was already
becoming well known. With the debate over the creation of a department of
transportation centered for the most part on other issues, senators and representatives accepted the president's compromise to defer the decision about
urban mass transit for a year. Johnson signed the bill on October 15, 1966,
authorizing the Department of Transportation (DOT) to commence operations on April 1, 1967.[51]

Motivated no doubt by a combination of genuine philosophical differences and the goal of bureaucratic empire building, Weaver and Alan Boyd, the first transportation secretary, maneuvered to acquire control of urban mass transit. Boyd and his aides felt that, as a new agency still striving to establish an identity in Washington, DOT had to act aggressively before losing the momentum it had achieved in late 1966. Believing that all matters relating to urban transportation rightfully belonged in their bailiwick, they aggressively advanced their case for ownership of rapid transit.[52] DOT officials felt optimistic because of HUD's political liabilities. According to DOT Assistant Secretary for Administration Alan Dean:

In spite of the efforts of HUD, that department is known to be over its head in new programs, and there is much Congressional skepticism concerning HUD's ability to develop adequate technical expertise in urban transportation. Furthermore, the [DOT] is fundamentally less controversial and suspect among conservatives than HUD, which is necessarily involved in programs which do not yet have the degree of consensus enjoyed by the DOT and most of its functions.[53]

No less than Boyd, Weaver argued the case for his department as the best home for urban mass transit. Operating only in a handful of cities, its cause championed by few interest groups, and commanding a relatively small portion of the federal budget, contended the HUD secretary, rapid transit would get lost in DOT, overshadowed by the much larger federal highway program. A crucial factor shaping the orderly growth and development of cities and suburbs, mass transit coexisted symbiotically with other HUD grant programs such as Model Cities, urban renewal, public housing, open space, water and sewer facilities, and urban planning assistance. Attempting to utilize his agency's reputation as a liberal bastion, which DOT officials had identified as a significant debility, Weaver stressed the natural links between HUD and other War on Poverty programs designed to benefit lower income groups in urban ghettos.[54]

During the summer of 1967, negotiations continued between the two departments. Charles M. Haar, assistant secretary for metropolitan development in HUD, and Gordon Murray, special assistant for special projects in DOT, met several times without success. In August 1967, concerned about the lack of progress in the negotiations between HUD and DOT, presidential aide Joseph Califano instructed Weaver and Boyd to finalize their recommendation to the president; the secretaries met on September 19 but failed to reach agreement. Unable to resolve the issue by the October 1, 1967, deadline, Boyd sent to the Bureau of the Budget a recommendation that all mass transit functions be located in DOT. HUD officials disagreed, and the secretaries reported that mediation by Johnson or members of his staff would be necessary to resolve the issue. The president finally announced that mass transit functions should be transferred to DOT and ordered the two departments to work out the details. HUD Undersecretary Wood met with Secretary Boyd on January 2, 1968 to create a new organizational scheme according to the White House directive. In a February 26, 1968, message to Congress, based upon a February 8 report submitted by Weaver and Wood, the president announced a reorganization that created within the DOT a new Urban Mass Transportation Administration responsible for all grant awards as well as related research and development activities, effective on July 1, 1968. Under this new arrangement, the DOT secretary received the authority formerly vested in HUD under the Urban Mass Transit Act of 1964—with one exception. The HUD secretary still maintained the authority to undertake projects involving urban transportation systems related to the comprehensively planned development of urban areas. A September 9, 1968, memorandum of agreement signed by Weaver and Boyd formalized the unorthodox arrangement: DOT's Urban Mass Transportation Administration would be the new home of mass transit programs, but both departments would cooperate so that HUD continued to have a voice in the development and operation of rapid transit systems.[55]

While seeking congressional authorization for DOT and Model Cities, Johnson commissioned yet another task force on the cities in 1966. Chaired by Paul Ylvisaker, the latest urban task force deviated from its 1964 and 1965 predecessors by concentrating almost exclusively on the problem of racial discord. "The overriding problem of our cities is segregation by race and income," stated the final report. "No solutions to the nation's urban problems are valid unless they deal directly with the questions posed by segregation." Neither community action nor Model Cities seemed likely to enjoy any success, the report continued, unless the administration confronted the racial dimension of the urban conundrum directly. President Kennedy's carefully circumscribed 1962 executive order banning discrimination in housing had proved disappointing, a result underscored by the passivity of the Veterans Administration and the FHA during the Johnson years. The task force called for a new executive order that extended the mandate for open housing to all housing financed or insured by federal agencies. In short, suggested the task force, make open occupancy the centerpiece of federal urban policy and demand that the receipt of government aid be conditional upon suburbs genuinely seeking to achieve racial integration—daring recommendations in 1966.[56]

The status of Johnson's efforts on behalf of the cities remained unclear by early 1967, as evidenced by the title of the speech on urban and rural poverty that he gave to Congress on March 14—"America's Unfinished Business." Much of the uncertainty owed to the difficulties experienced by HUD, which within its first two years lost control over urban mass transit to DOT while assuming responsibility for the administration of Model Cities. Many legislators in Washington had explained their vote for Model Cities as a response to the frightful racial violence consuming urban America summer after summer in the 1960s, but, while a frustratingly elaborate application procedure stalled the flow of federal funds to municipal governments, the incidence of arson and looting reached new levels in 1967. As the number of casualties in the battles between rioters and law enforcement authorities rose again that year, the efficacy of the administration's efforts to aid the cities came into question. Enemies of the Great Society found the unprecedented expenditure of federal funds in urban locations hard to reconcile with the wanton destructiveness that had become commonplace in the decade's red-hot summers.[57]

Despite all that he had done to address urban problems, Johnson felt, the public perception continued to be that the riot-torn cities were undermining the Great Society at every turn. No president had done as much to improve the lives of ghetto dwellers, he believed, but the recurring racial violence embarrassed him and played into the hands of his enemies. Fearing a congressional investigation that would highlight the ineffectuality of his urban programs, the frustrated president instructed Vice President Humphrey to lead a cabinet discussion of new approaches that might be initiated. On July 23, 1967, even as Humphrey's group commenced its deliberations, the worst race riot of the decade erupted in Detroit. For the next several days, the president monitored events closely and forcefully responded to Republican charges that "rioting and violent civil disorders have grown to a national crisis since the present administration took office." Johnson feared that Michigan Governor George Romney, his likely opponent in the 1968 presidential election, was simultaneously delaying his appeal for federal troops for political reasons and blaming the president for failing to act decisively. Johnson finally dispatched federal troops to Detroit, he explained to a national television audience, "only because of . . . the undisputed evidence that Governor Romney of Michigan and the local officials in Detroit have been unable to bring the situation under control." Sensitive to Republican charges that the administration's generous reform program had created a climate that bred disrespect for authority, the president affirmed in the television address his unwavering commitment to law and order.[58]

On July 27, as federal troops were regaining control of the Detroit streets, Johnson addressed the nation on television again to discuss the measures his administration would be taking to address the racial violence pervading the nation's cities. First and foremost, he announced the formation of a bipartisan, blue ribbon commission on civil disorders with Otto Kerner, Democratic governor of Illinois, and John V. Lindsay, Republican mayor of New York City, serving as chairman and vice chairman respectively. Johnson saw the creation of the National Advisory Commission on Civil Disorders (known popularly as the Kerner Commission) as a preemptive strike against the rumored congressional investigation that he assumed would provide a forum for conservatives to level charges of pampering law breakers and for liberals to decry the inadequacy of the administration's urban programs. Although he publicly asked for a disinterested examination of the problem and insisted that the commission would enjoy complete autonomy in conducting its investigation, the president anticipated a ringing endorsement of his Great Society programs as the only viable solution to urban unrest. He fully expected the commission to recommend heightened congressional funding for Model Cities, rent supplements, and other programs that he still felt held the greatest likelihood of relieving the despair in inner-city ghettos.[59]

Johnson took the opportunity to endorse the administration's latest urban legislation, a rat extermination measure, which was mired in congressional committees with little chance of passage. (Senator Ribicoff had suggested the eradication of rats from the slums in the hearings he conducted the year before, and Weaver had agreed that the idea had merit.) The White House had originally submitted to Congress an omnibus housing bill that contained a $40 million allocation to cities for rat extermination. Unsure that a major housing bill could be passed in the increasingly combative Capitol Hill environment, HUD recommended going forward only with the rat extermination provision. Conservatives ridiculed what they contemptuously called the "civil rats bill," suggesting that the president release federal battalions of cats into the ghettos and slums and contemplating the appointment of a "high commissioner of rats." Johnson chided his opponents for belittling a measure designed to address a serious problem in urban life, defending his administration's attempt to protect innocent slum children who were being bitten by diseased vermin at an alarming rate. Congress defeated the legislation, another setback in 1967 for a White House that had few legislative achievements to show for the year. The press excoriated the heartless Republicans and southern Democrats for their callous indifference to a serious issue, and the Department of HEW subsequently established a rat extermination program of its own.[60]

By 1967 unrest was also growing with the Community Action Program, which had been an especially inviting target of the president's critics since its inception three years earlier. Whereas community action ostensibly entailed the transformation of local institutions dispensing services and the empowerment of the poor people receiving government aid, big-city mayors welcomed federal largesse but fully intended to maintain traditional lines of authority between city halls and the tumultuous neighborhoods. Almost immediately, tensions surfaced between the mayors who expected to exercise carte blanche in the distribution of federal dollars and Washington bureaucrats who wanted to do more than just provide cities with additional resources. In October 1964 the OEO's rejection of Philadelphia Mayor James Tate's antipoverty plan because of the failure to involve the poor in its creation sent a chilling message to city officials nationwide. The U.S. Conference of Mayors registered a vigorous protest because, as Baltimore Mayor Theodore McKeldrin wrote to the president, of the "almost unanimous feeling" that decisions about the poverty program were being made by bureaucrats "who do not understand the problems and operations of local governments." In Chicago, Mayor Richard J. Daley quickly co-opted the Community Action Program, appointed administrative boards that reported to him and not to neighborhood organizations, and, according to U.S. Congressman Adam Clayton Powell (Democrat, New York), achieved "minimum feasible participation of the poor." Under fire from local reformers and a congressional investigating committee, Daley took his case to the White House and won. The Chicago mayor's clout notwithstanding, public criticism continued unabated, and mayors in other cities continued to joust with OEO officials.[61]

At the annual meeting of the U.S. Conference of Mayors in St. Louis on June 1, 1965, two Democratic mayors outraged with the OEO's attempts to encourage maximum feasible participation (Sam Yorty of Los Angles and John Shelley of San Francisco) had submitted a resolution accusing the administration of fomenting "class struggle" and urged noncompliance with community action regulations. Believing that adoption of the resolution would embarrass the president, conference leaders requested a meeting with Vice President Hubert Humphrey and OEO officials. Daley, chair of the United States Conference of Mayors' War on Poverty Committee, and nine other mayors met with Theodore M. Berry (the administrator of OEO's antipoverty program) several days later in Washington. The delegation reported receiving reassurances that the administration would continue to be attentive to the mayors' concerns. Humphrey agreed "that the success of the program depends on very extensive leadership by local government and that's what [the mayors] are going to get." In the showdown between the community action advocates and the mayors who wielded such influence in the Democratic Party, the White House sided with the powerful men whose support the administration needed to govern effectively.[62]

Already troubled by the performance of the OEO, which seemed to be generating more complaints than accolades for the administration, Johnson listened to the mayors' lamentations with a sympathetic ear. The president questioned the loyalty of the "kooks and sociologists" at the OEO who seemed to him more intent upon raising the consciousness of poor people than upon administering good programs that brought credit to his presidency. With the cost of the Vietnam War rising exponentially in 1966, Johnson worked quietly with Congress to curtail federal spending on the antipoverty front. Whitney Young of the Urban League urged the president to repudiate any cutbacks in funding for the urban poor, but Johnson refused. When New Haven Mayor Richard Lee warned that "the war against poverty should not become a casualty of the war in Viet Nam," HUD Secretary Weaver rejoined that domestic programs had to yield to matters of higher priority dealing with national security. In 1967 Johnson told a liberal senator that the antipoverty program "was hardly his favorite program" but that "he was prepared to stick with it."[63]

Congress was not. Despite clear indication that OEO's modest level of spending had indeed reduced poverty levels in urban areas, the political landscape looked different on Capitol Hill in 1967 than it had in 1964. An alliance of Republicans and conservative Democrats seemed poised to terminate the War on Poverty, and Sargent Shriver spent virtually all of his time in 1967 on Capitol Hill lobbying to save the OEO. Conservatives questioned OEO's role in the race riots erupting in the nation's cities that summer, charging that government antipoverty workers were inciting the uprisings instead of acting as peacemakers. At the eleventh hour, Representative Edith Green (Democrat, Oregon) introduced an amendment to the EOA—what Republicans derisively termed the "bossism and boll weevil" amendment because of its appeal to big-city mayors and southern Democrats—that granted local governments the power to assume complete control of the antipoverty program. According to the *New Republic*, "the President has officially bid farewell to the original poverty program by asking Congress . . . to tie local community action programs to city hall." Maximum feasible participation had become a political liability and would have to be sacrificed to save the faltering War on Poverty. The Green Amendment defused the conservative attack on OEO, and Congress extended the agency's life for two more years—but in abridged form. The administration requested $2.06 billion in funding for fiscal year 1968, but Congress appropriated $1.77 billion. "OEO's dreary last years," observed the historian Allen J. Matusow, "were devoted to the twin goals of service and survival."[64]

By 1968 the disappointment with Johnson's urban initiatives mirrored the growing disenchantment with the Great Society altogether. Racial violence in the cities continued, and ambitious programs launched with great fanfare such as Model Cities produced few immediate results to justify the considerable expenditures authorized by Congress. As American involvement in Vietnam deepened, many policy makers explained the failure of domestic policies as a direct consequence of swelling military budgets that siphoned dollars away from needy urban neighborhoods. The president himself said as much in his January 17, 1968, State of the Union Address to Congress when he spoke eloquently about the poverty, unemployment, and crime endemic in the nation's slums but reluctantly admitted that not even the vast resources of the world's wealthiest country could simultaneously underwrite costly wars at home and abroad. The conflict in Southeast Asia would not last forever, but the struggle in the cities would have to be deferred at least for the moment. In the meantime, while continuing to request modest appropriations for existing programs, Johnson reintroduced a crime bill that Congress had rejected the previous year. Invoking the rising lawlessness in the cities, he asked Congress to pass the Omnibus Safe Streets and Crime Control Act with an appropriation of $100 million for fiscal year 1969 (double the amount he had requested in 1967). Johnson hoped the crime bill would be attractive to law-and-order conservatives who decried the recurrent violence in the slums as well as to liberals who would embrace the idea of making decaying neighborhoods safer for the poor people who often found themselves the victims of violence. Johnson seriously considered vetoing the final version of the Omnibus Safe Streets and Crime Control Act, which he felt Congress had ruined by deleting key gun control provisions and sanctioning wiretapping by federal, state, and local law enforcement officials in virtually unlimited fashion, but concluded that the bill "contains more good than bad" and signed it on June 19, 1968.[65]

At the end of February 1968, the president received an advance copy of
the report prepared by the National Advisory Commission on Civil Disorders. After conducting a seven-month investigation and compiling interviews
with mayors, rioters, ghetto residents, businessmen, law enforcement authorities, and innumerable witnesses in dozens of cities, the Kerner Commission concluded that the racial turmoil in America's cities stemmed from
chronic racism that had split the nation into separate and unequal black and
white societies. The commission railed against the doleful influence of the
federal government, which it said had been complicit in the maintenance of
ghettos, and prescribed the expenditure of vast sums of money to improve
education, housing, welfare, and job training. The estimated cost for these
program enhancements in fiscal year 1969 approached an astronomical $12
billion, more than doubling to $24.5 billion in fiscal year 1971; the president
estimated the price tag at an unrealistic $100 billion over the next several
years. The preliminary report infuriated Johnson, who suspected that Mayor
Lindsay and a few other liberals had gotten control of the commission and
rammed through a series of outrageous proposals. He thought their demands
for increased funding totally unrealistic but more fundamentally objected to
the imputation that his administration bore considerable responsibility for
the tragic events unfolding in the cities. Had he not done more than any
other president to arrest urban decline and oppose racism? He sent word of
his displeasure through emissaries to commission members, prodding them
to make more realistic recommendations and to provide details about potential funding sources, and became even angrier when they failed to respond.
The president threatened to reject the report or simply ignore it, but formally
accepted the 513-page document on February 29, 1968. In subdued fashion
the following month, he thanked the commission members for their efforts
and expressed his fundamental agreement with their goals. The dubious
criticisms of the Kerner Commission notwithstanding, he assured the nation
his administration would continue seeking solutions to the urban crisis.[66]

In April 1968, as a sign of his administration's abiding commitment to the
cities, the president announced the formation of the Urban Institute as a nonpartisan, nonprofit public policy organization designed to conduct research
related to government programs that addressed urban problems. The 1964
Task Force on Metropolitan and Urban Problems originally proposed the
creation of a federal think tank dealing with the cities, and Johnson mentioned the idea favorably in his 1965 special message to Congress on the cities,
but the concept remained vague for several years. In 1967 the president put
Robert Weaver in charge of creating the Urban Institute, but the selection of

the HUD secretary aroused concerns within the federal bureaucracy. Officials in other cabinet departments looked warily at the creation of a new agency as an example of HUD's empire building and argued the need for a broad perspective at the federal level on urban problems. As a result, OEO, the Departments of Transportation, Labor, HEW, Justice, and Commerce, as well as HUD, provided funding for the Urban Institute, and a protégé of Defense Secretary Robert McNamara, William Gorham, became its first president. In its infancy, the Urban Institute produced detailed evaluations of the Elementary and Secondary Education Act of 1965 and Model Cities program, calling for additional evaluation and more extensive technical assistance to the administration of Great Society programs.[67]

In seeking to make social progress without investing billions of dollars, the administration opted for the issue of fair housing hoping to secure legislation that would build on Kennedy's Executive Order 11063 to combat racial discrimination in urban neighborhoods and suburbs. Attorneys in the Justice Department had been comparing notes on the constitutionality of fair housing legislation since 1964, and the administration first introduced a bill in Congress in 1966. The idea of federal support of open occupancy proved to be anathema to many white homeowners, and the bill encountered the full force of a bipartisan anti–civil rights coalition in Congress that had lost to the liberals in 1964 and 1965 but remained a formidable opponent. Presidential aide Joseph Califano remembered that the issue "prompted some of the most vicious mail LBJ received on any subject and the only death threats I ever received as a White House assistant." The bill's supporters failed to muster the votes to break a filibuster mounted in the Senate by Southerners, and support for open housing became a lethal issue for several Democrats seeking reelection in 1966 against Republicans who opposed the measure; Paul H. Douglas, who had served as Senate floor leader for the bill, lost to Charles Percy in Illinois, and Governor Edmund "Pat" Brown lost to Ronald Reagan in California. Willing to accept the antidiscrimination provisions of the 1964 Civil Rights Act and the broadening of the franchise effected by the Voting Rights Act of 1965, many whites in the North as well as in the South balked at the prospect of residential desegregation.[68]

The administration persisted, submitting legislation in 1967 and again in 1968. Discussing the inadequacy of the Kennedy executive order and Title VI of the 1964 Civil Rights Act, Secretary Weaver noted in testimony before Congress in 1967 that existing federal nondiscrimination provisions applied only to about 4 percent of the nation's housing stock. Citing evidence that residential segregation was actually increasing, Johnson urged the passage of federal legislation that would bar discrimination in the sale and rental of all housing in the nation. The Civil Rights Act of 1967 stalled in committee, but in February 1968 Senators Walter Mondale (Democrat, Minnesota) and Edward Brooke (Republican, Massachusetts) introduced the administration's fair housing measure as an amendment to a bill already passed in the House and being considered by the Senate. The publicity surrounding the publication of the Kerner Commission report underscored the need for federal action and, presidential aide Joseph A. Califano Jr. noted, the president "was relentless. I mean there was no give. We were pushing, pushing, pushing. This was going to be done." The assassination of the Reverend Martin Luther King Jr. on April 4, which sparked another series of racial conflagrations in the nation's cities, added a sense of urgency to the passage of legislation prohibiting racial segregation. Johnson made an unabashed appeal to the House to approve the fair housing bill, which the Senate had passed by a vote of 71 to 20 on March 11, as a testament to the principles for which the martyred civil rights leader had stood. "What more can [you] do to achieve brotherhood and equality among all Americans?" the president asked congressmen in an April 5 letter to Speaker of the House John McCormack (Democrat, Massachusetts), House Majority Leader Carl Albert (Democrat, Oklahoma), and House Minority Leader Gerald Ford (Republican, Michigan). The most meaningful response legislators could make, Johnson answered, was to "enact [fair housing] legislation so long delayed and so close to fulfillment." The House passed the measure by a vote of 250 to 172 on April 10, and the president signed it into law the following day.[69]

The Civil Rights Act of 1968 declared equal housing opportunity the official policy of the U.S. government. When fully implemented in 1970, the law covered 80 percent of all private housing. Title VIII made discrimination illegal in all houses and rental units, prohibiting real-estate agents and brokers from refusing to sell or rent any dwelling on the basis of race, color, religion, or national origin. The law, which would be administered by the HUD secretary, outlawed blockbusting and other unsavory real-estate practices designed to maintain racial segregation. Any person who suspected foul play could file a grievance with the HUD secretary and, failing to receive satisfaction with the federal agency, could sue in federal court for injunctive relief. The U.S. Attorney General could bring a civil suit where a pattern of discrimination existed. The law also contained a series of antiriot provisions, part of the price the administration paid for passage.[70]

Along with the open housing law, Johnson also sought an omnibus housing bill in 1968 that would increase significantly the amount of low- and moderate-income housing available to the public. In a special message to Congress on February 22, 1968, devoted exclusively to urban problems, the president spoke movingly of how solving the urban crisis depended upon the provision of better housing. The Housing and Urban Development Act of 1968 established an ambitious ten-year goal of constructing or rehabilitating 26 million housing units, 6 million for low- and moderate-income families; in the first three years, $5.3 billion would be spent for 1.7 million units of low-income housing. The bill called for 300,000 housing starts in fiscal year 1969, an allocation of $230 million for fiscal year 1970 so that cities could plan for mass transit improvements, a HUD guarantee of $250 million of bonds for the planning and construction of new communities by private developers, and expansion of such existing programs as rent supplements and Model Cities. Following the examples of the Section 23 and turnkey programs initiated by the Housing Act of 1965, the measure sought to privatize low-income housing. Section 235 of the law, which provided federal subsidies for home purchases, and Section 236, which was designed for rental housing, employed FHA and Federal National Mortgage Administration (FNMA) instruments such as the below market interest rate and accelerated depreciation to induce builders to supply decent and affordable housing for low- and moderate-income families. Finally, the law partitioned the FNMA into two separate entities, a private corporation newly called the FNMA, which conducted the secondary mortgage market operations assigned to the old FNMA, and the Government National Mortgage Association (GNMA, or "Ginnie Mae"), a government-owned corporation that would guarantee mortgage-backed securities issued by private institutions other than FNMA. With typical bravado, Johnson called the bill submitted to Congress the most ambitious housing legislation ever sent to Capitol Hill.[71]

Title IV of the Housing and Urban Development Act of 1968 constituted the federal government's most significant attempt yet to encourage the creation of new communities, continuing a halting effort begun earlier in the decade. Title VII of the Housing Act of 1961 and Section 702 of the Housing and Urban Development Act of 1965 had provided federal aid for the construction of public facilities within new towns; Title IV of the Demonstration Cities and Metropolitan Development Act of 1966 had established a mortgage insurance program for that purpose. The 1968 law authorized a revolving fund for loan guarantees to private developers of new communities, who otherwise shied away from the considerable risks necessary in creating entire urban infrastructures for towns built from scratch. Weaver sought the cooperation of the secretaries of Transportation, HEW, Labor, Commerce, Interior,

and Agriculture in what administration officials assumed would be a collab-
orative effort. Because planners and developers would select sites for the new
towns nearby existing metropolitan areas, Secretary Boyd and others at DOT
expected that they would play a large role in securing external access as well
as establishing internal transportation systems. Although a relatively minor
part of the legislative package, the new towns proposal sparked considerable
interest among planners and developers as well as the bureaucrats at HUD
and DOT.[72]

Like the Civil Rights Act of 1968, the omnibus housing bill no doubt benefited from the increased interest in ameliorative urban legislation in the wake
of the King assassination. The housing measure moved through both chambers of Congress with remarkable ease that summer, sailing through the Senate by a vote of 67 to 4 on May 28, and the only major floor debate occurred in
the House over the income limits for the homeownership and rental assistance
programs. The original version invested the HUD secretary with the discretion to determine eligibility requirements, which prompted sharp resistance
from conservatives. Representative John B. Anderson (Republican, Illinois)
successfully offered amendments that limited eligibility under the homeownership and rental assistance programs to persons with incomes less than 30
percent higher than the ceiling for occupancy in public housing in their area.
With this limitation on HUD's authority and the guarantee by the Anderson
amendments that housing aid would be targeted to the neediest families, the
House passed the bill by a vote of 295 to 114 on July 10. Johnson signed the
Housing and Urban Development Act of 1968 on August 1, saying that "this
legislation can be the Magna Carta to liberate our cities."[73]

The increased role for the private sector in the omnibus housing law reflected the influence of the President's Committee on Urban Housing, popularly known as the Kaiser Committee, the members of which had worked collaboratively with the White House in 1968. Named after its chairman,
industrialist Henry F. Kaiser, the eighteen-member committee, which included eight members of the construction industry, three representatives of
financial institutions, and three trade unionists, heavily represented the
management and labor interests of the home building industry. The
committee's final report, issued on December 11, 1968, reiterated the goal of
26 million new and rehabilitated housing units completed by 1978—6 to 8
million of which would be federally subsidized units. To increase the availability of credit for home purchases, the committee offered a series of recommendations granting the Government National Mortgage Association greater
latitude in issuing securities. The Kaiser Committee ignored the social and

political aspects of public policy, declined to evaluate the Johnson record, and proffered a series of nuts-and-bolts recommendations aimed solely at increasing the housing stock. Unlike the Kerner Commission, the Kaiser Committee operated quietly and attracted little media attention. Johnson warmly welcomed its report.[74]

Not so the National Commission on Urban Problems, which had been created under the auspices of Section 301 of the Housing and Urban Development Act of 1965. Johnson selected to chair the commission Paul H. Douglas, a liberal Democrat who had played a major role in fashioning federal urban policy during his three terms in the U.S. Senate from 1949 to 1967. Although he had been a consistent supporter of Great Society legislation, the fiercely independent Douglas insisted upon crafting a disinterested report that moved beyond political advocacy to make substantive policy recommendations. Johnson formalized the appointment on January 12, 1967, and requested that he be given the commission's final report by December 31, 1968. For nearly two years, Douglas and the other fifteen members of the commission conducted a far-ranging investigation of urban life, assembling data at its temporary quarters in Washington, D.C., and receiving testimony from approximately 350 witnesses in twenty-two cities around the country, most notably in New Haven, Boston, Pittsburgh, Detroit, East Saint Louis, and Los Angeles. Much of the testimony dwelled upon the shortcomings—not just the good intentions—of federal programs created by the Johnson administration.[75]

Indeed, the commissioners heard from a steady stream of disgruntled public housing residents, community organizers, civil rights activists, and others who chided HUD as a remote, ineffective government bureaucracy that had constructed low-income housing at a snail's pace, maintained the public housing projects fitfully, and then responded indifferently to tenants' complaints. Witnesses further excoriated urban renewal for its wholesale destruction of housing in salvageable neighborhoods and for its wholly inadequate construction of replacement units. Municipal officials predictably defended the federal government's efforts, but the majority of witnesses—especially unscheduled speakers who took the opportunity afforded by the visiting commission to speak extemporaneously—painted a dispiriting picture of government indifference and lassitude.[76]

The commission provided a plethora of recommendations, many of which could be described as excessively ambitious. First, in response to the charge that the federal government had failed to deliver on the promise of the Taft-Ellender-Wagner Act nearly two decades before, the commission called for the construction of 2.0–2.5 million housing units annually, including

500,000 units devoted to low- and moderate-income families unable to secure satisfactory lodging in the private housing market. Furthermore, these
units should be built on scattered sites throughout metropolitan areas to foster racial integration. In addition, the commission report recommended the
construction of low-rise public housing only and outlined a series of steps to
be taken to improve the quality of life for residents of extant high-rise projects. Most provocatively, the commission urged that, if state and local housing authorities failed to make satisfactory progress in meeting the housing
needs of low- and moderate-income families, the federal government should
assume control and become the builder of last resort—in effect, prescribing a
return to the practice of the 1930s when the Public Works Administration directly built public housing. In all, the recommendations constituted a ringing
endorsement of the liberal vision for improving urban America by calling for
a larger role by the federal government and the investment of increasing
amounts of the nation's resources in the fight to save the declining cities.[77]

By the fall of 1968, the commission had published accounts of its hearings and individual studies of particular topics, so the tenor of its conclusions
had become widely known. Douglas forwarded copies of the final report to
Johnson and Weaver in early November and asked for a meeting with the
president so that the full commission could make a formal presentation of
the document. Angry at the report's criticisms of his administration, Johnson
refused to meet with the commission and instructed Douglas to submit the
report formally to President-elect Richard Nixon instead. HUD staffers attempted to suppress the report, but Douglas and members of the commission
staff sent photocopied materials to the *New York Times*, the *Washington Post*,
and the major wire services; they also handed out mimeographed copies to
reporters and other interested parties. On December 15 excerpts from the report appeared on the front page of the *New York Times* and hundreds of other
daily newspapers across the country. On December 31, as mandated by federal statute, the secretary of HUD submitted the commission report to Congress—but, to Douglas's chagrin, the version sent to Capitol Hill contained
less than half of the full report. Robert Wood, who replaced Weaver as HUD
secretary for the final twenty-seven days of the Johnson administration, refused to provide Congress with the portions of the study that criticized public housing, urban renewal, and other HUD operations. Wood explained that
he had excised the sections that had exceeded the commission's charter.
Douglas expressed regret that such censorship not only eliminated much of
the commission's analysis but also expunged more than fifty detailed recommendations that could have proved useful to congressional policymakers.[78]

The contretemps surrounding the report of the National Commission on Urban Problems seems in retrospect altogether predictable. The White House had, after all, given an equally frosty reception several months earlier to the Report of the National Commission on Civil Disorders. A lame-duck president in his last days in office with disastrously low ratings in public opinion polls—a proud man frustrated over his inability to extract the nation from a highly unpopular war in Southeast Asia at the same time that many of his prized legislative achievements were floundering due to inadequate funding—could not have welcomed criticism of yet another aspect of his administration. Johnson especially could not abide the accusation that so little progress had been made under his leadership in the quest to aid the cities. He had followed the recommendations of numerous task forces that called for increased federal involvement in the cities, mirroring his own inclination toward an activist presidency, and intensified his efforts as a response to the rising violence in urban America. With considerable justification, he contended that he had pushed more legislation through Congress to benefit urban American than had any of his predecessors in the White House. As with so many other negative assessments of the Great Society, Johnson saw his considerable efforts at achieving reform for the cities unappreciated by large segments of the public—by conservatives who condemned the urban programs as wasteful and wrongheaded and by liberals who always seemed to be clamoring for more programs and more funding.

Critics of the Great Society wasted little time in identifying the shortcomings of Johnson's efforts, alternately blaming a lack of clarity in program development, the ineffectiveness of government bureaucracies, and, perhaps most important, the crippling dearth of funding. Federal programs targeted at the cities frequently seemed to be perfect examples of these deficiencies. The urban education initiative foundered as the Elementary and Secondary Education Act's Title I benefits went all too often to children who did not need them. A HEW survey of elementary schools in 1967–68 found that the program benefited pupils from middle-class families rather than disadvantaged children with greater needs. The Community Action Program succeeded in raising the consciousness of local activists and straining the relationship between mayors and the Johnson administration while resulting in, as Daniel Patrick Moynihan put it, "maximum feasible misunderstanding." Model Cities, the putative centerpiece of the urban program, proved equally frustrating—and downright confusing. A full year after Congress created the program, Vice President Humphrey wrote a plaintive letter to a HUD official saying that he had been unable during recent speeches in Boston and Detroit to explain how Model Cities worked and asked for an explanation. "I want to get this for the President and, indeed, for myself," he admitted. In response, another HUD official told Humphrey that a community receiving a grant would not see any benefit for at least five years—not soon enough for the administration to receive any credit. Dividing inadequate sums of money among too many communities, battling constantly to retain the support of reluctant federal administrators who harbored serious reservations about the program, and awarding grants at a glacial pace according to an arcane process that no one seemed to comprehend, Model Cities achieved little by the time that Johnson left office.[79]

Although many of the administration's urban initiatives fell far short of the expectations set by the president's soaring rhetoric and the recurring turmoil in the inner cities may have seemed a product of neglect, Johnson devoted more attention to urban affairs than any other president in the twentieth century. He created three task forces to fashion recommendations, delivered five special messages to Congress to marshal support for his programs, and appointed two investigatory commissions to assess the nature of the urban crisis—a record that no other president could match. Furthermore, he could justly claim a number of significant achievements by the end of his tenure in the White House. The War on Poverty failed to lift all of the urban poor into the middle class, but the combination of sustained national economic growth (driven largely by the Vietnam War) and antipoverty programs roughly halved the poverty rate between 1960 and 1973; the elderly and African Americans enjoyed the greatest economic gains during those years. The various housing acts of the Johnson years substantially increased the number of new units and commenced a shift from public housing construction to the creation and management of subsidized housing by the private sector. If the enforcement provisions of the 1968 Civil Rights Act proved wanting in later years, the law nonetheless opened up the suburban housing market to blacks in ways that would have been impossible under Kennedy's limited 1962 executive order. The African American population in the suburbs increased nearly 50 percent in the 1970s, and by 1990 nearly one-fourth of black families resided in suburban locations. As Wendell Pritchett, Robert Weaver's biographer, has observed, "In terms of legislation Weaver's tenure oversaw the passage of more laws regarding the issues under his purview—housing production and antidiscrimination—than any period before or since."[80]

Regardless of the success or failure of the manifold urban programs, there could be little doubt that Johnson had expanded the federal government's presence in urban America. Federal grants-in-aid to the cities

rose from $7 billion in 1960 to $24 billion in 1970, most of the increase occur-
ring between 1964 and 1969. Within its first three years of operation, HUD
assumed responsibility for most of the federal programs. Robert Weaver,
Robert Wood, and their staff administered a disparate set of programs that
included traditional bellwethers such as public housing, urban renewal, and
FHA, along with new programs such as Model Cities and New Towns. The
agency presided over a diverse complex of housing programs, including Section 23, Section 235, Section 236, and turnkey housing, with an enhanced
emphasis upon providing moderate-income as well as low-income units.
Under the auspices of the Civil Rights Act of 1968, HUD also applied a new
set of fair housing rules that would potentially alter the racial makeup of
metropolitan areas. Other federal agencies in Washington, D.C., controlled
federal programs with ties to urban America—mass transit, community action, education, and job training, for example—but HUD clearly bore the
lion's share of the responsibility for the federal government's investment in
the cities. By the close of 1968, with the war in Vietnam claiming the nation's
resources at a stunning and accelerating rate, it seemed unclear whether this
new cabinet department could manage so complex a task or whether future
presidential administrations would be inclined to commit the federal
government's resources to the cities in the same manner that Lyndon Johnson had done. Would a Richard Nixon presidency be so interested in the fate
of the cities?[81]

5

NIXON AND THE NEW FEDERALISM

Richard Nixon's New Federalism marked the beginning of a steady decline in federal involvement in the cities. As part of a full-scale assault on many of the liberal achievements of the Kennedy and Johnson administrations, Nixon sought to weaken the ties between Washington, D.C., and urban America that had been nurtured during the previous eight years. Espousing the devolution of authority, he sought to weaken federal bureaucracies and strengthen local governments. Through the implementation of new policies such as revenue sharing and the substitution of block grants for categorical grants to cities, he endeavored to revolutionize the manner in which the federal government allocated resources. Just as the funding formulas of the Nixon administration favored suburbs over inner cities and the Sunbelt over the Rust Belt, so did decentralization inhibit the enforcement of federal civil rights statutes passed earlier in the 1960s; the New Federalism allowed suburban authorities to deflect plans for enhancing racial integration across municipal boundaries. The Nixon administration failed to transform the federal government's relationship with the cities immediately, yet ultimately initiated a series of policy shifts that laid the foundation for sweeping change in subsequent decades.

Nixon could hardly claim much of an electoral mandate at the outset of his presidency, for Democrats retained comfortable majorities in Congress after the 1968 election—57 to 43 in the Senate and 245 to 187 in the House. Instead of hastily dismantling Great Society agencies, therefore, Nixon retained some programs, eliminated others that had clearly lost political support, and even expanded a few. Rather than cut programs, he more often cut funding—invariably to the detriment of the Department of Housing and Urban Development (HUD). The Department of Transportation (DOT) fared somewhat better, spending unprecedented sums of money on urban mass transit but still generously underwriting the expressway construction that fueled suburban growth. Direct federal grants to local governments increased substantially during the Nixon years but not in ways that pleased the cities with the most urgent needs. At the president's direction, HUD increased low-income housing programs tied to the private market while terminating public housing construction. Nixon introduced innovative measures such as cash payments to the poor that pleased liberal Democrats more than many members of his own party, but he kept faith with conservatives in his pointed refusal to enlist federal agencies to reduce racial segregation in housing. As a consequence, his presidency allowed the suburbs to remain homogeneous havens for whites fleeing inner cities. Nixon's New Federalism could not be judged an abject disaster for the cities, but the policies of his administration left urban America in a much more precarious state than it had been when he took up residence in the White House.[1]

The political calculus of the late 1960s suggested that the new president might not be disposed to investing substantial resources in the cities—especially in the inner cities of the Northeast and Midwest, the struggling communities that were losing population, businesses, and tax dollars to the thriving suburbs and the Sunbelt. In the 1968 election, Nixon amassed impressive vote majorities in the middle-class tracts surrounding aging northern industrial cities and in a string of southern communities stretching from Virginia to southern California. He recorded some of his most lopsided victory margins over Democrat Hubert Humphrey in such places as Albuquerque, Phoenix, San Diego, and the prosperous communities of Orange County, California. Believing that the Great Society's categorical grant programs essentially favored Rust Belt metropolises and minority neighborhoods in central cities, Republican strategists saw no reason to continue rewarding solid Democratic constituencies. The shift in the political balance of power toward the suburbs nationally, benefiting the Republicans at the expense of the Democratic Party, threatened continued decline for the embattled inner cities.[2]

During the 1968 presidential campaign, Richard Nixon projected the image of a reasonable, experienced candidate who would calm the roiling waters that threatened to capsize the American ship of state. Following a series of shocking developments that year—the Tet Offensive, Lyndon Johnson's unexpected announcement that he would not seek reelection, the assassinations of Martin Luther King Jr. and Robert F. Kennedy, the tumult of the Democratic National Convention in Chicago that left the presidential candidacy of Hubert Humphrey in disarray, and the repeated outbreak of race riots in U.S. cities—the fifty-five-year-old former vice president promised calm, measured leadership. On the election's overriding issue, the future of

American military involvement in Southeast Asia, he spoke guardedly of a secret plan to end the war that would bring the troops home honorably. The portions of the Republican's speeches dealing with domestic issues condemned the previous eight years of Democratic leadership, inveighing against Lyndon Johnson's Great Society, denouncing violence in the streets, celebrating "law and order," and rejecting the busing of schoolchildren as the court-sanctioned means of enforcing desegregation. Praising the hardworking forgotten Americans who he said had suffered silently while liberals in Washington had permitted protesters, minorities, and members of the counterculture to dominate public discourse, the Republican candidate promised to heal the nation's wounds and reunite Americans in common cause. Blessed with a huge early lead in the campaign over his struggling Democratic opponent, he presented himself as a "new Nixon" wholly unlike the combative office-seeker of past years who had made so many enemies in politics and alienated much of the electorate. By his own admission, the "new Nixon" would be a centrist of moderate views, an effective manager of men and institutions who would restore amity to a troubled nation.[3]

In his acceptance speech at the Republican National Convention in Miami Beach that year, Nixon blamed the nation's domestic problems on the failed policies of the liberal Democratic presidencies of the 1960s. The deluge of government programs created by the Kennedy and Johnson administrations had not only failed to solve serious problems, he averred, but had in fact made them worse. Programs conceived in Washington, D.C., to aid the poor had raised "an ugly harvest of frustration, violence and failure across the land," and the shocking level of violence in American society stemmed in large part from the government's misguided responses to societal crises. "I say it's time to quit pouring billions of dollars into programs that have failed in the United States of America," the Republican candidate intoned and recommended instead the enlistment of "the greatest engine of progress ever developed in the history of man—American private enterprise." While forging a fruitful partnership with business, he continued, government should also be reduced in size and decentralized so that the prescribed growth of state and local governments would remediate the imbalances in American federalism wrought by liberal Democratic administrations. Nixon prescribed a New Federalism that would undermine the rule of elites in the nation's capital and return government to the people in their communities around the country.[4]

Although Nixon failed to address the urban crisis specifically in his Miami Beach address, he made passing reference to the plight of the cities.

"As we look at America, we see cities enveloped in smoke and flame," he noted. "We hear sirens in the night. . . . Did we come all this way for this?" As he made clear in the next several months during the campaign, the Republican candidate believed that his New Federalism provided the best answer to the difficult issues plaguing the cities. The regimentation engineered by Washington bureaucracies inevitably resulted in waste and inefficiency, ran Nixon's argument, just as the collusion between federal officials and Democratic mayors amounted to pork barrel politics that invariably left the cities with far fewer resources than lawmakers on Capitol Hill had promised. The New Federalism sketched by Nixon at the Miami Beach convention hinged upon revenue sharing, a system whereby federal grants would be dispatched directly to the states with few strings attached so that governors could allocate funds according to the specific needs of the communities under their jurisdiction. Revenue sharing appealed both to conservatives who sought to minimize the power of liberal Washington elites and to moderate Republicans and some Democrats who hailed the potential for municipal reform guided by good government forces at the local level.[5]

Nixon's promise of a New Federalism dedicated to reducing federal bureaucracies raised questions about the future of HUD and DOT, both of which had been created less than four years earlier as part of Lyndon Johnson's Great Society. Having vowed during the 1968 campaign to cut federal spending, terminate the unnecessary programs created by his spendthrift predecessors in the White House, instill fiscal responsibility, curtail the reach of Washington agencies, and restore freedom to state and local governments, the Republican candidate hinted that it would be necessary to disassemble much of the bureaucratic scaffolding erected by Johnson. Donald Rumsfeld, the new president's choice to administer the Office of Economic Opportunity, had characterized HUD as "another bureaucratic maze" that "confuse[d] the public, employ[ed] the faithful, and further waste[d] taxpayer dollars." Although Nixon stopped short of promising to eliminate HUD and DOT altogether, speculation abounded that these new agencies would be among the first casualties of the New Federalism. Such conjecture intensified when the president elect chose Michigan Governor George Romney as secretary of HUD and Massachusetts Governor John Volpe as secretary of transportation. Nixon appointed the two Republican governors to appease the party's moderate wing, according to conventional wisdom, and intended to emasculate or even abolish the two cabinet departments within the next four years. Neither Romney, an outspoken reformer and advocate of morality in politics, nor Volpe, an aggressive politician who reluctantly accepted the post at DOT after being passed over for the vice presidency, seemed likely to work effectively in the new Republican administration.[6]

In keeping with his intention to minimize the importance of cabinet secretaries and to garner advice and counsel primarily from new executive agencies operating in the White House, Nixon followed the recommendation of the Task Force on Housing and Urban Renewal to create an urban affairs advisory council. On January 23, 1969, he established by Executive Order 11452 the Council for Urban Affairs, a collection of cabinet secretaries and other high-ranking federal officials whose activities affected the nation's cities, for the purpose of "assisting the President in the development of a national urban policy, promoting the coordination of federal programs in urban areas, encouraging cooperation between all levels of government, and encouraging local decision making." The membership of the Council of Urban Affairs included Vice President Spiro Agnew, HUD Secretary George Romney, Transportation Secretary John Volpe, Health Education and Welfare Secretary Robert Finch, Labor Secretary George Shultz, Commerce Secretary Maurice Stans, Agriculture Secretary Clifford Hardin, and U.S. Attorney General John Mitchell. At the council's first meeting, Nixon noted that his administration had been saddled with such severe problems in the cities because of the inability of his predecessors in the White House to deal effectively with the escalating post–World War II urban crisis. In his estimation, Presidents Kennedy and Johnson had "tried to do things too fast, without much thought, and perhaps too politically."[7]

Rather than appoint Secretary Romney as the council's executive secretary, the president named his assistant for urban affairs, Daniel Patrick Moynihan. A Harvard University political scientist and recognized authority on race and social welfare in the cities who had served in the Kennedy and Johnson Labor Departments, Moynihan had achieved the reputation of a free-thinking Democrat who frequently parted company from prevailing liberal orthodoxies on social issues. In 1965 he completed a Labor Department study, "The Negro Family: The Case for National Action," widely known as the "Moynihan Report," which discussed black matriarchy at length but said comparatively little about racism. His analysis of ghetto life, which attributed the economic travails of African Americans to dysfunctional family life, struck many antipoverty activists and other liberals as blaming the victims. The chagrined Moynihan argued that critics ignored his identification of slavery as the primary cause of the problem and his celebration of the many African Americans who managed to escape the tangle of pathology in the inner cities, but the furor over his report persisted for years. In a brash 1967 speech to the leftist Americans for Democratic Action, Moynihan accused liberals of condescension in their approach to dealing with the problem of race in the cities, charging them with being enablers by excusing African American lawlessness. Many Republicans, including Nixon and his aides, praised Moynihan for warning members of Americans for Democratic Action that "liberals must divest themselves of the notion that the nation—and especially the cities of this nation—can be run from agencies in Washington." Impressively credentialed and yet independent of Democratic liberal elites, Moynihan seemed to the new president to be the perfect assistant for urban affairs.[8]

Moynihan confidently predicted that the Council for Urban Affairs would function like a domestic National Security Council—making him the Henry Kissinger of domestic policy. He counseled against moving too quickly to introduce new solutions for urban problems, cautioning that entrenched interest groups would fiercely protect their own turf. Moynihan warned Nixon: "All the Great Society activist constituencies are lying out there in wait, poised to get you if you try to come after them: the professional welfarists, the urban planners, the day-carers, the social workers, the public housers. Frankly, I'm terrified at the thought of cutting back too fast." Noting that no previous presidential administration had set out specifically to compose a national urban policy, he repeatedly regaled the president and others in the White House about the importance of such an undertaking. At Moynihan's urging, Nixon paid careful attention to the operation of the urban council during his first months in office. The president presided at ten of the first twelve meetings, typically spending two to three hours at each of them, and required that members of the group or their designated representatives attend faithfully. Council subcommittees presented reports on such topics as Model Cities, urban renewal, new towns, the Job Corps, the Office of Economic Opportunity, welfare reform, mass transit, land use and development, and black capitalism in the cities. The administration strove to foster good relations with the cities by inviting their representatives to attend meetings of the Council for Urban Affairs, big-city mayors attending on one occasion and the chief executives of medium-sized communities on another. At least at the outset of the Nixon administration, Moynihan achieved some success at highlighting the importance of urban affairs.[9]

Arguing that a comprehensive effort to deal with urban problems must deal with inner-city poverty, Moynihan urged a sweeping revision of the mechanism for providing relief to the nation's poor. Having long been critical of the existing welfare system, Aid to Families with Dependent Children (AFDC),

Nixon assigned the task of welfare reform to the Council for Urban Affairs. Moynihan initially favored Health Education and Welfare Secretary Robert Finch's Family Security System as an alternative to Aid to Families with Dependent Children, but judged its reliance upon a negative income tax potentially too controversial. He advocated instead the Family Assistance Program (FAP), which the administration introduced into Congress in August 1969. The FAP addressed what many conservatives identified as welfare's major shortcoming—Aid to Families with Dependent Children discouraged work through its termination of welfare benefits for the poor who found jobs—by supplying a federal stipend for anyone earning less than $720 per year. Providing a federal benefit as long as a family earned an amount of money below a designated poverty level and guaranteeing continued support if family income increased, the FAP both mandated a minimum level of government support and eliminated the disincentive for work. Moynihan called the Nixon proposal for a guaranteed annual income of $1,600 a year for a family of four the "most important piece of domestic legislation to come before the Congress in two generations." Genuinely original in its conception and daring in its challenge to social work conventions dating back generations, the FAP faced strong opposition from interest groups on both ends of the political spectrum. Conservatives balked at the very idea of a guaranteed income funded by tax dollars and calculated that, despite providing a work incentive, such a plan would necessitate increased spending on the poor. Suspicious of Nixon from the outset, the National Welfare Rights Organization and other liberal groups objected to the inadequacy of the federal stipends and expressed concerns about rigid eligibility requirements for aid recipients.[10]

Moynihan worked hard on behalf of the FAP for more than a year, lobbying on Capitol Hill, appearing on television and radio public affairs programs, and meeting with a variety of civil rights groups. He wrote a series of optimistic letters and memoranda to Nixon about the legislation's progress in Congress, all the while attempting to counter the increasingly popular perception that "the president isn't really behind [the FAP]." With a number of Republicans adamantly opposed to placing an income floor under every American family with children, the lack of support from congressional Democrats doomed the bill's prospects. When such consistent advocates of welfare reform as Albert Gore Sr. (Democrat, Tennessee), Eugene McCarthy (Democrat, Minnesota), and Fred Harris (Democrat, Oklahoma) promised the administration their votes but later reneged, the Senate Finance Committee rejected the measure. At odds with many members of his own party, meeting unexpectedly stiff resistance in Congress, and purportedly more concerned with other initiatives, Nixon lost interest in the FAP.[11]

On December 5, 1969, Nixon announced that Moynihan would be leaving his post to become the president's domestic adviser and that he would be replaced as executive secretary of the Council for Urban Affairs by his chief aide, John R. Price Jr. (At that time, Price also became the executive secretary of the newly created Rural Affairs Council.) While the administration characterized the personnel reshuffling as a promotion for both men—that is, as part of the president's effort to centralize the formulation of domestic policy in the White House—others referred to Moynihan as having been "kicked upstairs." The failure to marshal support for the FAP and the unfulfilled expectations of the Council for Urban Affairs, which held numerous meetings but claimed few actual achievements, left Moynihan, Nixon, and others disappointed. The Council for Urban Affairs met less frequently in 1970, as Price devoted increasing amounts of his time to the business of the Rural Affairs Council. In March 1970 the president proposed the creation of the Domestic Council as part of a broad executive reorganization, and the Council for Urban Affairs formally expired on July 1, 1970.[12]

With the demise of the Council for Urban Affairs, HUD became the federal government's principal organization for formulating policies related to urban matters, and George Romney replaced Moynihan as the administration's most visible advocate for the cities. Romney's rise in national politics owed to a spectacularly successful career in business and a faith-based dedication to public service. A self-avowed "do-gooder" who many journalists called "Saint George," Romney unabashedly advanced liberal causes in a Republican Party dominated by conservatives. Raised in humble circumstances, he became a millionaire in the automobile industry as president of American Motors. A devout Mormon who said that he had often encountered bias because of his religious beliefs, Romney became a champion of oppressed minorities and a civil rights activist during the Second World War. By the 1960s, he devoted increasing amounts of time to civic betterment activities. After serving as the vice president of the Michigan Constitutional Convention in 1961, he ran successfully for governor of the state in 1962, 1964, and 1966. In 1964 he opposed the presidential nomination of Barry Goldwater, decrying the Republican conservative's attempt to "buy the White House with the rights of others." President Johnson's landslide reelection that year immediately established Romney as the frontrunner for the Republican presidential nomination in 1968. As late as August 1967, he led Johnson 49 percent to 41 percent in the Gallup Poll and appeared to be safely ahead of his closest Republican rival, Richard Nixon. The political calculus shifted dramatically the following month when Romney suddenly renounced his earlier support for the nation's military activities in Vietnam, claiming to have been "brainwashed" by U.S. generals and diplomats during a recent visit to Southeast Asia. After his disastrous revelations about having been "brainwashed," Romney saw his candidacy unravel as Nixon secured the Republican nomination and narrowly defeated Democrat Hubert Humphrey in the election.[13]

Romney eagerly accepted Nixon's invitation to serve as secretary of HUD—after Whitney Young of the National Urban League declined the post—ignoring rumors that the president elect had never expected him to accept the offer. Nixon adviser John Ehrlichman believed that Nixon intended to bury his former rival in "a meaningless department, never to be noticed again." But having long affirmed the importance of citizen involvement in a democracy, Romney enthusiastically welcomed the opportunity for service. He saw HUD less as a bureaucratic and political dead end than as a diamond in the rough, a cabinet post of untapped potential where he could improve America's cities and aid the cause of race relations. An ambitious man of boundless energy, he came to HUD with an abundance of ideas and a penchant for innovation. Questioning, prodding, doubting, and arguing, he fully intended to expand HUD's profile while addressing the major domestic issues confronting the nation. By contrast, Nixon sought to centralize power in the White House and to reduce the influence of cabinet members. "Keep them away from me," he instructed his chief of staff, H. R. Haldeman, when cabinet secretaries clamored for presidential access. Romney quickly discovered that no one in the White House cared about his lengthy list of new programs, his blueprint for achieving racial amity, or his vision for an aggrandized HUD Department.[14]

Romney came to Washington, D.C., with enthusiasm and no shortage of original ideas, but he became exasperated almost immediately when the White House ignored his plans for a thorough reorganization of HUD. Convinced that the department had failed to reach its potential largely because of a faulty organizational structure and determined to apply the business acumen he had honed at American Motors, the new secretary announced in November 1969 a sweeping reorganization plan that left HUD staffers stunned. Asserting that the agency had been hamstrung since its creation by a slipshod organizational structure that amounted to a congeries of separate bureaucracies, he said that "our task is not to *reorganize*, but to *organize* for the first time." The reorganization included the complete transformation of the Federal Housing Administration (FHA), the component sections of which would be divided and redistributed to other portions of the agency. To an unprecedented degree, Romney relieved the FHA hierarchy of its traditional autonomy and arrogated its policy-making responsibility. At the same time, in keeping with the spirit of Nixon's New Federalism, Romney decentralized functions in HUD, increased the number of administrative regions from six to ten, and created twenty-three new area offices in cities throughout the country; by 1971 he added another twenty area offices. The creation of additional regional and local offices, the secretary argued, would improve efficiency by granting broader decision-making authority and eliminating frustrating delays while area officers waited for decisions from higher authorities. "You called for decentralization in Federal Government and HUD is delivering it," the secretary proudly reported to the president in October 1970.[15]

Yet even as the agency's employees struggled to master the new lines of authority and learn their new responsibilities, an ad hoc presidential committee was completing a revision of the cabinet structure as part of a comprehensive reorganization of the executive branch. In April 1969 Nixon appointed Roy L. Ash, the founder and chief executive officer of Litton Industries, to chair the President's Advisory Council on Executive Organization. Seeking to improve the president's control of the sprawling federal bureaucracy, the six-member Ash Council looked to the military and large business corporations for ways to create "straight lines of authority and accountability." (In addition to Ash, the council members included four business executives and John Connally, the Democratic governor of Texas.) The Ash Council report recommended the creation of a Department of Community Development, which would include HUD's housing programs, the Urban Mass Transportation Administration, and the Federal Highway Administration. In the president's new master plan for the organization of the executive branch, which he outlined in detail in his January 22, 1971, State of the Union Address to Congress, the number of cabinet departments would be reduced from twelve to eight. The Departments of State, Defense, Justice, and Treasury would remain largely unchanged; the others, including HUD, would be consolidated into four new departments (Community Development, Human Resources, Natural Resources, and Economic Development). According to this new design, HUD's organizational structure would be completely revamped and its exact status within the Department of Community Development indeterminate. Privately chagrined by the potential negative effects on HUD, Romney nevertheless joined Transportation Secretary John

Volpe in testifying before the House and the Senate in favor of the president's proposal. The Nixon plan for executive reform failed to attract the necessary backing from Congress but ended any consideration of the HUD reorganization in which Romney had invested so much time and care.[16]

Another of the HUD secretary's ambitious undertakings, "Operation Breakthrough," similarly met with indifference in the Nixon White House. Announced by Romney on May 8, 1969, Operation Breakthrough aimed to increase the production of low-income housing by fostering collaboration among the federal government, trade union officials, governors, mayors, and homebuilding industry leaders to develop new construction methods. Authorized by the Housing and Development Act of 1968, Operation Breakthrough allowed the HUD secretary to construct at least 5,000 dwellings a year for five years using a variety of new building technologies. With creative financing from HUD and private capital sources, suggested Romney, Operation Breakthrough would enable new single-family and multifamily housing units to be mass produced at lower cost than previously achieved by the private housing industry. In June 1969 HUD officially launched the program by requesting funding proposals from private builders. With the zeal of an auto salesman unveiling a new model to distributorships around the country, the secretary conducted a whirlwind series of meetings in Washington, D.C., New York, Illinois, Michigan, Pennsylvania, Texas, Ohio, Indiana, Florida, West Virginia, and Arkansas in the summer of 1969 to build up support for the new program. In February 1970 HUD selected twenty-two finalists out of the 236 proposals that had been submitted and, in order to expedite construction, offered Section 235 and 236 subsidies to the firms receiving funding. The initiative ultimately proved disappointing, however, neither reducing the cost of housing nor substantially increasing the production of low-income units. The companies receiving HUD assistance completed only fourteen of the original twenty-two authorized projects, building approximately 26,000 units in all. Because of the administration's unwillingness to underwrite the program adequately, Romney argued, Operation Breakthrough never amounted during its brief existence to more than an underfunded experimental program.[17]

Another rift between HUD and the White House developed over the fate of the Model Cities program of 1966, a holdover from the Great Society that Nixon and his aides looked forward to eliminating as soon as feasible politically. The principal response of the Johnson administration to the burgeoning urban crisis of the mid-1960s, Model Cities entailed local initiative in the development and implementation of plans to use federal grants for upgrading physical and social conditions in inner-city neighborhoods. Originally designed as a narrowly focused pilot program to be implemented in just a few big cities, Model Cities secured the necessary votes in Congress only by including sixty-six communities nationwide in the federal largesse authorized by the final version of the enabling legislation. Painfully slow to commence operation, the program remained largely in the planning stage by January 1969. Even so, stories of waste, favoritism, and inefficiency in the program's early days led conservative critics to label Model Cities a fatally flawed liberal answer to a problem best addressed by market forces—in short, another classic example of the danger in uncritically expanding federal power. The cities seemed to have benefited little at all since the Model Cities legislation had been passed three years before Nixon took office, and Democratic pleas for patience were wearing thin. Nixon had indicated repeatedly during the 1968 campaign that his approach to urban problems would likely deviate sharply from the nostrums offered by his Democratic predecessor, and Model Cities seemed to be a perfect target for the New Federalism.[18]

Nixon's plan to terminate Model Cities proved problematic, however, because several prominent members of the administration quickly emerged as defenders of the embattled program. A presidential task force chaired by conservative Harvard University political scientist Edward C. Banfield, an erstwhile New Dealer who by the late 1960s had become a bitter critic of the urban reform tradition, recommended that the new administration retain the Model Cities infrastructure to decentralize urban assistance programs and to fulfill Lyndon Johnson's faulty attempts to engage local communities and neighborhoods in urban reform efforts. The task force found that the Model Cities administration had awarded grants hastily, often denying to state and local governments a suitable role in the process, and opined that the program under Johnson had been "over-regulated and under-supported." Banfield and his colleagues recommended that federal aid be disbursed to project cities through revenue sharing rather than categorical grants-in-aid and concluded: "In our view, the Model Cities program has a limited but valuable part to play in the poorest neighborhoods of the central cities and their larger, older suburbs."[19]

Echoing the recommendation of the Banfield task force, both Romney and Moynihan acknowledged the unenviable record achieved by Model Cities in its first three years but argued for its preservation as the best means of confronting the nation's imposing urban problems. Better to address the deficiencies of a struggling program, they contended, than to waste the funds already spent and to devise a new program from scratch. When told by

Nixon that he wanted Model Cities "killed," Moynihan purportedly replied, "Now you worry about our treaties in Southeast Asia and I'll worry about our treaties with the cities." At the April 7, 1969, meeting of the Council for Urban Affairs, the program's defenders responded to Nixon's expressions of skepticism and at least for the moment forestalled any action leading to termination. "I can see in Model Cities one of the most horrible boondoggles in history," the president charged. Portraying the program as another muddled liberal attempt at utopianism, he sighed: "God knows, you turn the social planners loose and it is sorry." Backed by Moynihan and Transportation Secretary Volpe, Romney termed the elimination of Model Cities a potential political disaster because of the overwhelming support of the program by the nation's big-city mayors; Volpe added that many governors, having created state departments of community affairs to provide technical assistance to cities applying for Model Cities grants, would also be upset. Romney recommended that a committee of cabinet undersecretaries conduct a thorough study of the reasons for the poor performance by Model Cities and, based upon the group's findings, the reforms necessary to rescue the star-crossed venture could be implemented. The amended program would inevitably be vastly different, noted the HUD secretary, and the administration would garner the credit for having salvaged an ineffective, wasteful program.[20]

In the wake of the April 1969 Council for Urban Affairs meeting, Romney repeatedly affirmed the Nixon administration's commitment to the continuation of Model Cities. In June 1969, after White House budget projections for fiscal year 1970 included only $675 million for Model Cities grants instead of the $900 million authorized originally under the Johnson administration, Romney assured the program's supporters that additional funds would be forthcoming to make up the difference. Edmund Muskie, who had guided the Model Cities legislation through the Senate in 1966, praised Romney's consistent support of the program but raised questions about the firmness of the Nixon administration's desire to aid the cities. Such concerns resounded at HUD as well where Secretary Romney and Undersecretary Richard Van Dusen repeatedly protested the administration's continuing reductions in Model Cities funding. In an April 21, 1970, letter to Assistant Budget Bureau Director Richard P. Nathan, Van Dusen conceded the agency's ability to absorb a reduction of $128.5 million "without significant disruption" for fiscal year 1971 but contended that yet another funding cut would be calamitous politically. On behalf of Romney and the entire HUD leadership, Van Dusen wrote: "We believe that a clear Presidential commitment to the program is essential if we are to communicate to the urban constituency anything other than their abandonment." Although Nixon denied on April 30 that additional funding reductions reflected his administration's intention to undermine Model Cities, he confirmed the transfer of $120 million to a new program for compensatory education and desegregation activities. In December 1970, after perusing a preliminary budget prepared by the Office of Management and Budget (OMB), Romney protested vehemently to the president about additional cuts to Model Cities funding—and about OMB's proposal to terminate the program altogether as part of the administration's new revenue sharing initiative. Romney's protestations notwithstanding, budget reductions continued until President Nixon's successor, Gerald Ford, merged what remained of Model Cities into the revenue sharing program in 1974. Romney's unflagging defense of Model Cities earned him the plaudits of liberal Democrats on Capitol Hill and big-city mayors, while perhaps delaying its elimination for a few years, but finally could not stay the executioner's hand.[21]

Romney fought an uphill battle with the White House to fund another urban initiative conceived in the Johnson administration, the new towns (new communities) program. In response to the blight that had swept over so much of the nation's cities in the preceding decades, urban planners and urban reformers had offered a proposal patterned after Ebenezer Howard's garden cities model and the Great Depression–era Greenbelt Towns to construct wholly new communities outside of existing metropolitan regions. Not designed to be bedroom communities or satellite cities that depended entirely upon central cities for their existence, the new towns would spring from holistic planning and enjoy a solid economic foundation based on the creation of industrial and commercial zones as well as residential neighborhoods. Title IV of the Housing and Urban Development Act of 1968 had authorized the federal government to provide long-term loans and supplemental grants for up to 80 percent of the cost of providing public facilities (streets, water, sewerage, parks, and the like) for new towns. The boldness and sweep of the plan appealed to Romney, who immediately began lobbying to increase funding for new towns development. White House aides who had labeled Operation Breakthrough impractical pilloried the new towns venture as another example of the HUD secretary's unfortunate penchant for high-risk visionary schemes. Not until February 13, 1970, did the administration approve the first loan under Title IV for the creation of a new town. Disregarding the endorsement of his administration's Council for Urban Affairs, Nixon declined to support additional new towns funding in 1970 because of the "severe budgetary impact" it would engender.[22]

By 1970, however, a powerful coalition of interests had united in support of the new towns idea. Developer James Rouse, along with Nathaniel S. Keith, president of the National Housing Conference, and Walter Reuther, president of the AFL-CIO's Industrial Union Department, advocated expansion of the 1968 law to provide for an even greater government role in land acquisition and community development. Putting aside their concern about possible loss of revenue to the suburbs, the U.S. Conference of Mayors and the National League of Cities lent their endorsements as well. (In part, big-city mayors became less antagonistic because legislation proposed in 1970 provided for the federal government's funding of "new towns in town"—new communities formed on large tracts of land within municipal boundaries that some mayors assumed would simply constitute urban renewal on a massive scale.) An ad hoc subcommittee of the House Banking and Currency Committee held hearings in 1969–1970 and recommended expansion of the existing government program. Congressman Thomas Ashley (Democrat, Ohio) introduced the Housing and Urban Development Act of 1970, Title VII of which significantly increased the amount of federal loans and grants for new town development. White House aides repeatedly assailed the expansion of the new town provisions, going so far as to send telegrams to all state governors requesting their aid in opposing the measure, but the final version of the Housing and Urban Development Act of 1970 passed by Congress included Title VII. Unwilling to veto the omnibus housing law solely because of one troublesome section, Nixon signed the bill on December 31, 1970.[23]

Few new towns materialized, however, because the administration responded haltingly to the legislative mandate. Title VII stipulated that the program would be administered by the New Community Development Corporation, whose five members would be appointed by the president subject to Senate confirmation. Ostensibly independent yet situated within HUD, the corporation lacked an operating budget and an independent staff. Its charter members included three HUD officers, an undersecretary in the Department of Transportation, and one person from outside the executive branch (a New York businessman). Although the New Community Development Corporation supposedly oversaw the work of the Office of New Community Development (ONCD), which had been established by Title IV, the new corporation lacked the authority to approve preliminary applications. Title VII provided for fifty staff members in the ONCD, but HUD only allocated the funding for thirty, and the resultant understaffing led to a huge backlog of unprocessed new towns applications. ONCD staffers refused to schedule preapplication reviews with developers and, as a consequence, the logjam of applications for funding intensified.[24]

In addition to the structural and bureaucratic impediments, the OMB followed a presidential directive to cinch the federal purse strings. First, the OMB impounded the $3.5 million in application fees collected from prospective new town developers and refused to release the funds for the purpose of hiring new staff for the ONCD. Second, bowing to Nixon's preference for general revenue allocations rather than categorical grants to cities, the OMB would not disburse $5 million earmarked in Title VII for innovative planning. Most important, the OMB approved loan guarantees but repeatedly denied funding for the many grant programs authorized in the 1970 law. According to Congressman Ashley, Romney and ONCD Director William J. Nicoson never sought to undermine the new towns effort, but "they got shot down by the Office of Management and Budget . . . because OMB never went for the grants." Romney, who recommended to Nixon the creation of thirty new towns over a three-year period, agreed with Ashley that the White House had used OMB to throw up bureaucratic road blocks. As federal agencies complicated the application process to hinder program development and moved with excruciating deliberateness in processing the pending requests for funding, the number of applications dwindled. The New Communities administration itself reported, "Given the level of risk associated with large-scale development and the clear lack of support for Title VII at the Federal and local levels, few experienced large-scale developers were willing to undertake a Title VII project."[25]

In January 1972 Romney again protested when the White House authorized only a small portion of the new communities funding sought by HUD. He had not complained about the niggardly appropriations approved the year before during a period of fiscal belt-tightening, the secretary claimed, but another disappointing rejection of funding in 1972 at a time of hopeful economic projections left the clear impression that the administration simply lacked interest in new towns development. William J. Nicoson resigned the top post at ONCD later that year, and ten of his key subordinates quickly followed. By 1974 virtually all attempts at new community development had ceased, and in January 1975 HUD announced that ONCD would accept no additional applications for new town funding, all applications under review would be returned to developers, and available resources would be devoted only to refinancing existing projects. Limited to a much smaller scale than its proponents had envisaged, the new town program would be judged successful or not based upon the relatively few projects completed during the Nixon presidency.[26]

During the life of the program, under the auspices of Titles IV and VII, HUD provided loan guarantees and direct grants for thirteen new towns, including one new town within a town (Cedar-Riverside, near the Minneapolis central business district); one isolated community in an economically backward rural area (Soul City, North Carolina); and eleven towns near metropolitan areas—Flower Mound, Texas, twenty-two miles northwest of Dallas; Gananda, New York, twelve miles east of Rochester; Harbison, South Carolina, eight miles northwest of Columbia; Jonathan, Minnesota, twenty-five miles southwest of Minneapolis; Maumelle, Arkansas, twelve miles northeast of Little Rock; Newfields, Ohio, seven miles northwest of Dayton; Park Forest South, Illinois, thirty miles south of Chicago; Riverton, New York, ten miles south of Rochester; Shenandoah, Georgia, thirty-five miles southwest of Atlanta; St. Charles, Maryland, twenty-five miles southeast of Washington, D.C.; and The Woodlands, Texas, thirty miles north of Houston. In addition, three communities—Roosevelt Island, New York; Radisson, New York; and Park Central, Texas—received only grant assistance.[27]

HUD officials and real-estate experts readily identified the economic factors that undercut these new towns, citing as the primary reason for failure the inadequate financial aid from the federal government. Developers had to borrow heavily at unexpectedly high interest rates to acquire land, employ planners, construct houses, and market the product just to earn a modest return on their investments. When residential and industrial land sales lagged far below projections, developers charged prohibitively high rents that drove away potential buyers. As HUD staffers concluded, developers could pay their bills only if given a considerable write down on the cost of the land, an impossibility because of the scarce financial resources made available under the existing legislation. As early as 1965 a Johnson task force that recommended new towns had cautioned that no complement of loans from the federal government would suffice; instead, some sort of land bank would have to provide capital on a massive scale and developers would have to be granted the power of eminent domain to mitigate the high cost of land acquisition. Without these financial inducements, HUD's investments became irretrievably mired in debt.[28]

Compounding the problem of capital shortages, the new towns program commenced during the rapid decline of the real-estate market in the 1970s. Large-scale residential subdivisions typically ran deficits in their first five or six years, and the already fragile new communities program immediately ran headlong into a series of economic downturns. Because HUD's tortuous application process required at least fifteen months to complete, most of the

Title VII communities were unable to begin construction until 1972. A severe housing recession in 1974–1975, followed by another real-estate collapse and skyrocketing interest rates in 1979–1982, produced a wretched economic climate for investors. Crippled in their infancy, these new towns never fully recovered economically. At the same time, the surge in condominium construction and the sudden popularity of real-estate investment trusts provided more attractive outlets for precious capital in tight money markets. Many reformers counseled forbearance, urging HUD to absorb the losses and ride out the economic storm, but the financial situation for the new towns remained dismal for years after the end of the Nixon presidency.[29]

Almost from the beginning, HUD had begun taking remedial measures to salvage a portion of its investment. Following Riverton's near bankruptcy in 1974, the agency assumed a $1 million interest payment in 1975 for the financially distressed developers of Park Forest South. By 1976, all of the new communities that received federal loan guarantees, except The Woodlands, had declared bankruptcy or reported its likelihood. By 1981 HUD foreclosed on nine of the new towns that defaulted on their debt repayments and sold the land in those communities wholly or in sections to new developers; the agency refinanced three (St. Charles, Maumelle, and Harbison) that still offered some hope of survival. Only The Woodlands established economic viability. On September 30, 1983, after fifteen years and the expenditure of $590 million in unrecoverable loan guarantees and grants, HUD officially terminated the new towns effort.[30]

The failure to fund Model Cities and new towns reflected the administration's indifference to housing, the embattled officials at HUD concluded, especially to the provision of lodging for poor and working-class families. The minimalist approach to housing legislation that defined the Nixon years began with the omnibus housing bill sent to Congress in 1969, which proposed no new initiatives at all but rather authorized the extension of several programs due to expire on October 1, 1969, and the consolidation of others for cost-cutting purposes. New York City Mayor John V. Lindsay testified in the Senate that the administration bill fell far short of addressing "crisis conditions" in housing and warned that public housing faced "imminent collapse" unless the federal government produced additional funding. Ignoring Lindsay's jeremiads, Congress approved one- and two-year extensions of programs created under the Housing and Urban Development Act of 1968, which had authorized $5.3 billion for low-income housing. The Housing and Urban Development Act of 1969, which Nixon signed into law on December 24, provided $4.8 billion for fiscal years 1970 and 1971, less than the $4.9 billion originally approved by the House and $1.4 billion less than the $6.2 billion for fiscal years 1970, 1971, and 1972 approved by the Senate. Although disgruntled with the low level of funding in the law, reformers applauded the inclusion of a provision requiring the construction of a new low-income dwelling unit for each slum home razed as part of an urban renewal project. They also lauded the Brooke Amendment, which mandated that a family could be charged no more than 25 percent of its income for rent in a public housing unit and obligated the federal government to compensate local housing authorities for the expected loss of rental income.[31]

The administration followed a similarly cautious path in 1970, submitting housing legislation to Congress that spurned new initiatives in favor of a series of efficiency measures. Testifying before the Senate that year, Romney explained that "the intent of [the bill] was to consolidate and streamline the multitude of narrow and separate legislative authorities in the [HUD] Department's housing programs. The Administration bill sought to standardize the common elements in the existing authorities—income limits of families eligible to participate, definition of income and percentage of income families had to contribute in assisted housing." Faced with a second straight disappointing housing bill, several of the mayors appearing before congressional committees protested more forcefully in 1970 than they had the previous year. Hugh Curran, the mayor of Bridgeport, Connecticut, spoke at length about the urgent needs of communities confronting fiscal crises and said that the cities "find it rather difficult to concentrate on a proposal by HUD whose primary emphasis is restructuring of present housing programs." When John V. Lindsay characterized the bill as "a step backward" for the cities, Romney called the New York City mayor's remarks "irresponsible and inaccurate." The Housing and Urban Development Act of 1970, which Nixon signed into law on December 31, authorized just $2.8 billion for housing programs, provided a modest increase in funds for new towns development, included a new program for federal crime insurance, and, reflecting that congressional session's protracted debate over the seriousness of the nation's housing shortage, required that a report on urban growth be submitted biennially by the president to Congress. (The first biennial report, issued in 1972, dismissed the mandate of the 1970 law as too narrow and considered the rural as well as the urban situation as a means of formulating a national growth policy.) The final version of the law signed by the president eliminated a proposed $750 million for aid to public mass transit systems for the purpose of defraying annual operating deficits, interest charges, and other cost overrides.[32]

Romney testified in Congress in favor of the administration's 1969 and 1970 housing bills but complained privately about their limited scope. His restiveness increased as the administration reduced HUD's budget repeatedly throughout Nixon's first four years in office. The administration's Task Force on Urban Renewal submitted a negative report and recommended substantial cuts in the program's budget; the task force chairman, Martin Anderson, author of a highly critical book on urban renewal, commented sardonically that the program had compiled "a distinguished record of failure." The White House cut urban renewal funding 20 percent in its first budget and another 50 percent in its second. The first budget also included a significant number of personnel transfers and firings in HUD, all in the name of greater accountability, and the following year's budget reduced allocations for low-income housing construction and the virtual elimination of housing and community research projects. By 1971 the Nixon White House had nearly halved the HUD operating budget that existed during the last year of the Johnson administration. Romney argued that the structural reforms he implemented during his first year as secretary had vastly improved the agency's efficiency and dutifully implemented the mandated economies without public protest, but privately he challenged the wisdom of the budget cuts. In 1972 the secretary informed the president that the accumulated resource reductions, particularly the critical staff shortages created by a series of layoffs and forced retirements, had left HUD unable to discharge its responsibilities. Romney's assessment that year of the budget proposals for fiscal year 1974, which included a moratorium on subsidized housing and the outright elimination of several programs such as urban renewal and Model Cities, confirmed his earlier decision to resign in the near future. The net result of this "cold-hearted indifference to the poor and racial minorities," he warned the president, "could inflame the central cities and could contribute to eventually bringing Belfast to the streets of our cities."[33]

While Romney protested recurrent reductions in HUD's resource base, the agency confronted the most significant scandal in its brief history. A public outcry resulted from an investigation by the House Committee on Banking and Currency involving Section 235 of the Housing and Urban Development Act of 1968. Designed to enhance home ownership, Section 235 empowered the FHA to insure mortgages and subsidize monthly payments for low-income families. Tragically, the well-intentioned program turned into a scam for unethical real-estate speculators who bought decaying inner-city dwellings, slapped on coats of paint, and haphazardly made other superficial improvements before selling the houses at grossly inflated prices to unsuspecting buyers. HUD relaxed inspection requirements for Section 235 homes, a fatal error when local housing authorities failed to educate prospective homeowners about the importance of maintenance. In some instances, FHA officials looked the other way and received kickbacks. Unable to make their monthly payments or to find the money for repairs when water pipes burst, electrical wiring shorted out, or heating systems malfunctioned, tens of thousands of residents defaulted on their mortgages. In some instances, having invested as little as $200 in the decaying houses, low-income buyers simply slammed the door and walked away when problems arose. In 1973 a HUD investigation of the Section 235 program found 26 percent of renovated homes unfit for sale and 20 percent of mortgages in default. Owning thousands of repossessed houses of little or no value, the agency demolished the rickety structures and left acres of rubble and open spaces in inner-city Detroit, Philadelphia, Newark, Brooklyn, and other communities. The $2 billion Section 235 debacle, labeled the biggest scandal in housing history, added the taint of corruption to HUD's growing reputation for inefficiency and ineffectiveness. As a result of the Section 235 scandal, the agency's standing sank further in the Nixon White House.[34]

The ongoing wrangling between Romney and Nixon over HUD's declining fortunes in the administration reflected the fundamental tension between an activist department secretary with ambitious plans and a remote president who was devoting increasing amounts of his time to foreign affairs, but the most widely publicized aspect of the growing rift between the two men revolved around the issue of race and housing. By the late 1960s, the crusade for racial equality had shifted from the attainment of civil rights to the desegregation of housing—especially regarding the question of the federal government's role in fostering racial integration in the suburbs. Employing a "southern strategy" carefully crafted to lure Southerners into the Republican camp in 1968, Nixon had offered voters a respectable alternative that year to the heavy-handed race baiting of Alabama Governor George C. Wallace. Though more polished than Wallace's stark utterances, Nixon's unmistakable message resonated with voters in the South who opposed desegregation. Decrying the national press's tendency to "use the South as a whipping boy," he commented: "I wouldn't want to see a federal agency punish a local community" for opposing school integration. Political observers in the southern states reported that sizable numbers of lifelong Democrats were becoming "Nixiecrats" in 1968. As president, Nixon issued bland assurances that his administration opposed racial segregation but simultaneously affirmed the limits of federal power to enforce desegregation statutes; with a wink and a nod to suburban officials, the president also made it clear that his justice department had no interest in forcing integration on a resistant white populace in the South.[35]

Romney brought to his cabinet post a determination to address the problems of race relations, which he had been doing as a private citizen and elected official for more than twenty-five years. Having led the fight for open housing in Southeast Michigan during the Second World War, he served on the Detroit Victory Council after V-J Day to allay racial discord. He received the Action for Democratic Living Award from the Anti-Defamation League of Detroit in 1959 and in 1963 led an NAACP march for open housing into the affluent Detroit suburb of Grosse Pointe. Following the race riots that devastated America's cities in the summer of 1967, Governor Romney undertook a twenty-day, 10,000-mile trip across the nation to inspect conditions in the communities hardest hit by the civil disturbances. "The summer of 1967 was only an early taste of what may lie ahead," he concluded at the end of his sojourn. "America will be torn apart with civil guerilla warfare, beyond anything we have yet seen, if the majority response is punitive, instead of curative." A clash between a HUD secretary who clearly intended to situate racial desegregation at the center of his agency's agenda and a president who had exploited white backlash to further his own political prospects seemed inevitable.[36]

His initial misgivings aside, Romney took heart at the president's announcement shortly after his inauguration of a program to provide federal funds to cities devastated by the previous summer's race riots. As Daniel P. Moynihan explained at a press conference announcing the initiative, Nixon had conceived the idea for the reconstruction of riot-torn cities after a January 31, 1969, visit to the so-called burnt-out area of Washington, D.C., around the intersection of 7th and T Streets. Seeing that not a single building had been rebuilt since the April 1968 riots, the president requested that Romney investigate the situation in other large cities across the nation. When HUD regional directors reported the existence of similarly dismal conditions in twenty large cities, the president authorized the provision of $200 million for the rehabilitation effort. Referencing the inadequacy of the federal government's service delivery systems as one of the major reasons for the failure to improve urban America and specifically criticizing the Model Cities and urban renewal programs, Nixon justified the infusion of federal largesse as a last-ditch effort to salvage a disastrous situation worsened by the ineffectual Kennedy and Johnson administrations. Even as some city officials dismissed the program as a publicity stunt by the administration, HUD representatives immediately visited the twenty cities selected for aid to encourage immediate action. By February 1970, however, Romney reported to John Ehrlichman that momentum had been lost and that "lasting solutions must be developed on a more comprehensive, areawide basis." The secretary recommended that aid to the twenty cities be resumed under the auspices of conventional programs such as urban renewal, low-income housing, and the like.[37]

While urging federal aid to distressed inner-city slums, Romney also commented at length about the government's obligation to foster integration throughout entire metropolitan regions. Shortly after arriving in Washington, D.C., he announced HUD's Open Communities plan designed to enhance metropolitan dispersal of minorities by withholding federal funds for highways and infrastructure improvement from suburbs that maintained residential segregation through the use of exclusionary zoning practices. Condemning the "ominous trend toward stratification of our society by race and by income," the secretary vowed to utilize fully the powers invested in the federal government by the Civil Rights Act of 1968 and to hold accountable suburban communities that failed to meet their obligations under the law. Ignoring the strident protests of many local officials, he threatened severe financial consequences "if the suburbanites refuse to see their obligations, their opportunity."[38]

The first test of Romney's resolve came in 1970 in metropolitan Dayton, Ohio, where African Americans constituted 30 percent of the population in the core city but only 3 percent in the surrounding suburbs. To address the racial imbalance in the metropolitan region, the Miami Valley Regional Planning Commission (MVRPC) devised a fair-share housing plan to build 14,000 low-income housing units (mostly for minority occupation) in the five predominantly white suburban counties surrounding Dayton. The MVRPC design proposed the construction of only 1,700 low-income units in Dayton, with the remaining 12,300 units scattered throughout the neighboring communities. Suburban office holders and school officials vigorously opposed the proposal, but, citing the threat of sanctions for failing to comply with federal strictures, the forty-two-member MVRPC unanimously voted approval of the proposal in July 1970. Romney enthusiastically endorsed the vote, citing the Dayton Plan as a model for the nation, but saw the MVRPC plan dissolve when the federal government failed to provide the necessary subsidies for the 14,000 housing units and when other federal agencies dispatched grants to suburban governments with White House approval. The administration also prohibited Romney from denying HUD grants to Dayton suburbs that refused to construct low-income housing within their borders. Admitting defeat in June 1971, the secretary told the U.S. Commission on

Civil Rights: "The Dayton Plan is a great example [of metropolitan fair-share housing dispersal]. I'm all for it . . . But to undertake to bring this about through coercive means in my opinion would be self-defeating."[39]

The secretary ran afoul of the White House again when he threatened to withhold $20 million in urban renewal funds from the working-class Detroit suburb of Warren, Michigan, where the population of 180,000 included just twenty-eight African American families. Warren, Dearborn, and other communities ringing Detroit contained automobile factories that employed tens of thousands of minority workers but remained residentially segregated, in clear violation of the 1968 fair housing law. When the Warren city government chose to surrender federal funds rather than adopt a fair housing ordinance, Romney affirmed his support for HUD's Open Communities program. The national press gave increasing attention to the rising tensions in southeastern Michigan, and the White House dispatched Romney to reassure thirty-nine mayors of suburban Detroit communities that the Nixon administration had no policy of "forced integration of the suburbs." Angry white protesters confronted Romney after he met with the mayors, asking him why HUD was planning the construction of no low-income housing in the tony suburb of Bloomfield Hills where he lived just a few miles away. Nixon and his aides cringed at the newsreels of the Warren demonstrators jostling the secretary before a police detail arrived to extricate him from the shouting mob, the members of which were pounding on his car and brandishing invective-laced placards at television cameras. Asked at a press conference what he thought of Romney's Open Communities plan, the president responded that the federal government should promote racial integration "only to the extent that the law requires" and reiterated his position that "forced integration of the suburbs is not in the national interest."[40]

White House officials decried HUD's increasing involvement in the sensitive policy issue of suburban desegregation, pointing to the renegade secretary as the principal trouble maker. John Ehrlichman singled out Romney to the president for blame in a series of scathing memoranda, in one missive calling recent regrettable incidents "the result of what the Secretary perceives to be both his legal and moral obligation." In October 1970 he wrote Nixon: "This is a serious Romney problem which we will have to have as long as he is there. There is no approved *program* as such, nor has the White House approved such a *policy*. But he keeps loudly talking about it in spite of our efforts to shut him up. And he is beginning some administrative measures in that direction." Nixon tersely wrote in the margins of the confidential memorandum, "Stop this one." In November 1970, after months of dissembling and delaying, Ehrlichman at last agreed to schedule an appointment with the president so that Romney could make the case for his suburban housing policy of "forced integration." The meeting would allow Nixon to deny the charge that decisions on this volatile issue had been made without consultation with the HUD secretary, Ehrlichman explained to H. R. Haldeman, and "will make [Romney's] ultimate resignation more likely."[41]

The struggle between HUD and the White House came to a head shortly thereafter as Nixon made explicit his administration's position on race and the suburbs. In December 1970, in a tense White House meeting also attended by U.S. Attorney General John Mitchell, the president issued Romney a clear set of marching orders demanding unwavering compliance with the administration's position on metropolitan desegregation. Although Romney continued to lobby in cabinet meetings for a stronger push by the federal government in favor of residential desegregation, he publicly endorsed the president's opinion that change on the racial front must originate in local and state governments and institutions. On June 11, 1971, Nixon issued an 8,000-word coda, "Statement of Equal Housing Opportunity," which resoundingly underscored the difference "between discrimination because of race and discrimination because of economic status." His administration, the president made perfectly clear, would concern itself with the former but not with the latter; his justice department would "stick by the letter of the law in dealing with racial patterns in housing but . . . does not intend to go beyond the letter of the law." Testifying before the U.S. Commission on Civil Rights four days after the president had delivered his remarks, Romney pledged his complete support of the administration's position on race and housing. HUD remained committed to the ideal of open communities, the secretary said, and so did the president—if only by somewhat different measures. Romney never reconciled his own principles to Nixon's political expediency on the desegregation issue, but he lowered his profile in 1971–1972, refrained from openly assailing the administration's official stance, and periodically issued statements denying that his views on racial desegregation deviated significantly from the president's pronouncements on the subject. Publicly, at least, he remained a good soldier.[42]

Although he refrained from directly challenging administration policy on race and the suburbs, Romney continued to labor quietly behind the scenes to enforce the antidiscrimination provisions of the 1968 Civil Rights Act. In 1972, for example, he added eight new standards to be satisfied for the receipt of HUD housing subsidies. Under the new criteria, agency officials gave priority to applications that provided a variety of locations within metropolitan regions for housing minority families, refused to concentrate subsidized housing for minorities in one section of a metropolitan area, or provided aid to businesses located within certain areas of cities owned substantially by minority entrepreneurs. Another Romney innovation, Affirmative Marketing Regulations, prohibited discriminatory advertising or selling practices related to homes receiving HUD assistance and required these housing providers to submit marketing strategies for informing minority families of the availability of houses and apartments for sale or rent.[43]

Convinced that racial desegregation could only be achieved at the metropolitan level, Romney announced in January 1972 that he was launching Operation TACLE (Total American Community Living Environment) to encourage suburban integration through the implementation of regional plans for development. To initiate the program, HUD proposed to award a series of demonstration grants much as the Johnson administration had originally proposed to implement the Model Cities program. Romney lobbied the president and others in the White House but predictably found no enthusiasm for the plan. Nixon's January 20 State of the Union Address to Congress, presented less than two weeks after the secretary announced his new program, tellingly contained no mention of Operation TACLE—and, for that matter, little else about the explosive issue of race and the suburbs.[44]

Just as he supported residential desegregation, Romney also favored the racial integration of the nation's public schools. At a time when the courts sanctioned busing to achieve desegregation in education but many parents clung to the hallowed ideal of the neighborhood school, he pointed out that children of all races could live within a reasonable distance of their schools if the federal government removed the barriers to open housing. Opposed to court-ordered busing, Nixon instructed officials at Health Education and Welfare and at the Justice Department to dissemble and delay calls for desegregation. He wrote John Ehrlichman: "I want you personally to jump" on those cabinet departments "and tell them to *Knock off this Crap.* I hold them . . . accountable to keep their left wingers in step with my express policy—Do what the law requires and not *one bit more.*" In 1972 Nixon made resistance to court-ordered busing one of the centerpieces of his reelection campaign, and the U.S. Supreme Court, loaded with four of his appointees, subsequently handed down two landmark decisions that severely curtailed the movement to desegregate public schools. In a 1973 ruling, *San Antonio Independent School District v. Rodriguez*, the Court upheld the traditional practice of local funding for education and thereby ensured continued disparities in spending between inner cities and suburbs. In *Milliken v. Bradley* (1974), the Court overruled a lower court decision that ordered the merger of Detroit's predominantly black schools with the school districts of fifty-three suburbs to stimulate metropolitan desegregation. Based upon Chief Justice Warren Burger's reasoning, which absolved suburban school districts of intent and thereby vindicated the concept of de facto segregation, the *Milliken* decision protected white flight.[45]

The administration's defense of segregation in housing and education constituted yet another clear indication of the gulf between HUD and the White House. Romney clashed repeatedly with White House officials during his tenure as secretary, usually refraining from uttering any public criticism of decisions that he felt had been made more to boost the president's political fortunes than to benefit urban America. In addition to the many policy differences, the secretary's unceasing warfare with Nixon and his aides had to do with style as well as with substance. The straight-laced, moralistic Mormon secretary felt ill at ease in a White House where Nixon aides swore incessantly and scoffed at the importance of principle in politics. Proud of his image as an honest and forthright public servant, Romney bridled at the Machiavellian politics practiced in the Nixon White House and saw himself as a frequent victim of court intrigue. He chafed at his inability to secure an appointment with the president for months at a time and frequently had to settle for meetings with the standoffish domestic adviser, John Ehrlichman. Outraged by the president's increasing failure to convene the cabinet and by the attendant rise in influence of the White House staff, he called a rump meeting of other disgruntled secretaries in March 1971. At Nixon's instruction, Ehrlichman attended the meeting and strongly discouraged the attendees from scheduling any other such gatherings—abruptly quashing what became known in the White House as the "cabinet cabal."[46]

An uncomfortable fit from the start, the Nixon-Romney collaboration seemed doomed to fail sooner or later. Newspapers reported Nixon's dissatisfaction with Romney within the administration's first year, and speculation that the HUD secretary would be fired or resign arose soon thereafter. White House aides favored Office of Economic Opportunity director Donald Rumsfeld as Romney's replacement. In November 1970, Romney called a news conference specifically to deny that he was planning to submit his resignation, and he felt obliged to address the issue sporadically for the next two years. The final break came in August 1972, ostensibly because of the humiliating manner in which Nixon publicly dispatched Romney to Wilkes Barre, Pennsylvania, to monitor relief efforts in the wake of Hurricane

Agnes. Although newspapers reported this indignity as the "final insult," Romney said in his August 10, 1972, letter of resignation that lack of access to the president and poor relations with White House staff, notably with John Ehrlichman, had left him without an effective voice in the administration. The secretary intended to resign immediately, but, fearful of the impact of Romney's sudden departure on moderate Republican voters on the eve of the 1972 presidential contest, Nixon persuaded him to wait until after the election. Romney campaigned for the president that fall and complied with all White House initiatives until he left HUD after the inauguration. James T. Lynn, a Cleveland corporate lawyer then serving as undersecretary of Commerce, became the new HUD secretary.[47]

On January 8, 1973, just days before vacating his HUD office, Romney stated that the time had come to review the "entire Rube Goldberg structure" of federal urban development programs and declared a moratorium on the construction of government-funded housing. He had tried unsuccessfully to dissuade Nixon from taking such precipitous action, objecting to the "abrupt, across-the-board character of the moratorium which will cause widespread disruption in the housing industry and will prevent the Federal Government from keeping existing specific commitments for subsidized housing," but made the announcement as one of his last acts in office. The declaration of such a sudden policy shift sparked a bitter reaction among Democrats on Capitol Hill, who resented not having been consulted at all by the president and questioned whether such a moratorium could legally be applied without their consent. On July 20 the Senate voted to cancel the moratorium and provide a one-year extension of basic housing programs. Three days later, ruling that the executive branch could not negate laws duly passed by Congress, a federal district court found the moratorium illegal. The Senate passed a measure ordering HUD to resume the housing programs, but, acting under the threat of a presidential veto, the House recommitted the measure to a conference. In August the U.S. Supreme Court overrode the federal district court order that restored the suspended programs and upheld the executive action. In a September 19 report to Congress, Nixon reinstated the Section 23 program but confirmed his determination to halt the construction of new public housing units. In response to the charges of Senator William Proxmire (Democrat, Wisconsin) that the administration had killed the housing programs "in an attempt to cover up their own mismanagement," the president characterized public housing's failure as "comprehensive and long-standing."[48] He said, "I have seen a number of our public housing projects. Some of them are impressive, but too many are monstrous, depressing places—run down, overcrowded, crime-ridden, falling apart. . . . All across America, the Federal Government has become the biggest slumlord in history."[49]

The moratorium on the construction of government-funded housing dovetailed with another important component of the New Federalism, revenue sharing. "I reject the patronizing idea," Nixon told Congress, "that government in Washington, D.C., is inevitably more wise, more honest, and more efficient than government at the local or State level." During the administration's first year, Nixon proposed the remittance of a set portion of federal income taxes to the states with a minimum of federal restrictions on how the dollars should be spent—requiring only that a certain percentage of the funds be appropriated for the use of local governments. The funds provided in the first year would be a modest $1 billion in 1971 with the amounts gradually increasing to $5 billion by the mid-1970s. Such organizations as the United States Conference of Mayors, the National League of Cities, the National Housing Conference, and the AFL-CIO, all of which shared a stake in the preservation of existing grant programs, opposed the proposal. In 1969 and again in 1970, revenue sharing encountered stiff resistance in Congress, particularly from Democratic Congressman Wilbur Mills of Arkansas, who argued that additional federal taxes would be required to implement revenue sharing and that populous states containing large metropolitan areas such as New York, Illinois, Ohio, and Pennsylvania would suffer especially while less densely populated states with comparatively fewer and smaller urban places would benefit disproportionately. In 1971 the president altered his approach by requesting a $16 billion package for both general and special revenue sharing: $5 billion in general revenue sharing for states and cities to be spent without restriction and $11 billion in special revenue sharing funds for education, urban development, rural development, transportation, job training, and law enforcement (with local governments still enjoying considerable latitude in how money was spent on these projects). The decision to divide revenue sharing into two categories proved to be unfortunate, with critics faulting special revenue sharing as antithetical to the fundamental premise of the New Federalism, and the administration decided thereafter to return to a legislative initiative based solely upon general revenue sharing.[50]

In 1972 the administration's battle for general revenue sharing finally ended successfully. In response to Congressman Mills and others who warned that the potential cost of the initiative would necessitate an increase in taxes or the elimination of extant urban programs, the president promised that general revenue sharing would be an addition to and not a substitution for existing programs. Intense lobbying by a bipartisan coalition of mayors led by John V. Lindsay of New York City, Moon Landrieu of New Orleans, and Henry Maier of Milwaukee, which coveted the freedom to allocate federal resources without answering to Washington, D.C., bureaucrats, finally proved persuasive to liberals in Congress who had previously voted against revenue sharing and other measures presented as components of the New Federalism. Despite their concerns that the revenue sharing formula would divert funds to Republican strongholds in the suburbs and the flourishing cities of the Sunbelt, enough Democrats voted affirmatively to pass the bill. (Having developed a fanciful ambition to run for president that year, Mills tempered his opposition to revenue sharing in the hope of attracting the support of powerful local Democratic politicians.) The State and Local Fiscal Assistance Act of 1972 authorized the expenditure of $30.2 billion over five years, two-thirds of the total for local governments and one-third for the states, and Nixon signed the measure into law on October 20, 1972, in a well-publicized ceremony on the steps of Independence Hall in Philadelphia. In 1976 Nixon's successor, Gerald R. Ford, signed an extension of general revenue sharing that allocated an additional $25.6 billion for 3.75 years. Spreading federal dollars out widely to communities of various sizes and largely ignoring the pleas of the Rust Belt cities for special consideration, the federal government distributed more than $36 billion to thousands of local governments by 1980. Big-city mayors soon became disenchanted as they received no increase in funding—and sometimes fewer dollars—from the new federal program. "Revenue sharing," concluded the urban historian Carl Abbott, "was preeminently a *suburban aid* program."[51]

In keeping with the spirit of the decentralization embodied in revenue sharing, the administration prepared comprehensive legislation in 1972 designed to chart a new course in housing and community development. The Better Communities Act, a revision of a bill rejected by Congress in 1971, showcased Nixon's determination to rework housing policy through the lens of the New Federalism. According to the Better Communities Act, the federal government would distribute funds based upon need, and local governments would enjoy the freedom to use the money as they saw fit. Curtailing the unhealthy concentration of power in Washington, D.C., and eliminating the unavoidable waste and inefficiency that had doomed HUD since its inception, argued Nixon, the block grant approach would allow mayors and city councils the autonomy to spend federal dollars in the most effective manner possible. The housing act died in the House Rules Committee in 1972, and Congress narrowly failed to pass a similar measure in 1973, but, known as the

Housing and Community Development Act of 1974, it passed by overwhelming margins (76 to 11 in the Senate and 351 to 25 in the House) the following year; President Gerald R. Ford signed the bill on August 22, 1974.[52]

The most important housing bill since 1968, the Housing and Community Development Act of 1974 included two titles of major significance for cities—the Community Development Block Grant (CDBG) program and Section 8. Title I consolidated eight categorical assistance programs—Model Cities, urban renewal, open space, urban beautification, historic preservation, public facility loans, neighborhood facilities grants, and water and sewer grants—into CDBGs and allowed communities great latitude in spending the federal dollars they received in one installment. Cities could use the money on housing, public facilities, child care, and economic development, among other purposes, as they saw fit. The initial allocation of $8.4 billion for three years, which distributed funds according to population, poverty rates, and housing conditions, included a "hold-harmless" provision that protected communities that fared well under the old grant system by prohibiting changes in the funding formulas through 1977. Congress renewed the law in 1980 and again in 1983 but lowered allocations both times.[53]

Along with the reductions in funding after the expiration of the hold-harmless provision, several other factors exacerbated the harmful effect of CDBGs on aging central cities. As with general revenue sharing, the federal government disbursed grants over many more communities and thereby diluted the impact of funding on especially needy cities. CDBGs went not just to big cities but also to communities of 50,000 residents within metropolitan areas and to "urban counties" with populations exceeding 200,000. Many suburbs that had never previously received categorical grants of any kind received federal funds for the first time in the form of block grants. Although overall funding levels remained unchanged at first, 204 communities (181 central cities) received fewer federal dollars from block grants than they had from categorical grants. Meanwhile, between 1971 and 1974, federal funds increased to Dallas tenfold, Birmingham fivefold, Phoenix fourfold, and Houston fourfold. Title I of the 1974 Housing Act required cities to utilize block grants "principally [to] benefit people of low and moderate income," but provided HUD with no means to ensure compliance. Free to use federal funds without restriction, local officials spent money on a variety of pet projects (some of a highly questionable nature) and often ignored blighted neighborhoods saddled with a host of pressing needs. The CDBGs struck a blow for localism in a way that undermined the Great Society legislation designed to resuscitate the most vulnerable cities.[54]

The Housing and Community Development Act of 1974 also replaced the Section 23 leasing program with Section 8, which authorized HUD to invite local housing authorities to negotiate with the private sector for the supply of low- and moderate-income housing. Section 8 likewise authorized HUD to contract directly with private owners to construct federally subsidized units or to rehabilitate existing units. The law limited the federal government's activities to inspecting Section 8 units, certifying their acceptability, and reimbursing landlords for the difference between 25 percent of the renter's income and fair market value of the unit. In keeping with the spirit of the New Federalism, Section 8 shifted responsibility for low-income housing to private market forces and further circumscribed the federal government's role in the housing industry. Within a few months, with the federal government having retreated from its role in the construction of public housing, Section 8 became the principal provider of low- and moderate-income housing.[55]

The New Federalism's turn away from Great Society housing programs—as embodied in revenue sharing, CDBGs, Section 8 certificates, and shrunken budgets for HUD—confirmed the dire predictions of failure for George Romney's audacious plans. Having also come to Washington, D.C., with a brash agenda for DOT, John Volpe encountered many of the same frustrations working with the Nixon White House. A building contractor, public works administrator, and director of the Bureau of Public Roads (BPR) during the Eisenhower presidency before becoming the governor of Massachusetts, Volpe had established a reputation as an avid road builder. During his days in the Massachusetts statehouse, he had urged Congress to double the size of the interstate highway system nationally to meet the traffic increases expected in upcoming years. Critics expected that the new DOT secretary would "pave the country," and Harvard economist John Kenneth Galbraith warned at Volpe's Senate confirmation hearings that "if we don't keep an eye on him in Washington he'll cover the country in concrete." Both Volpe and Francis C. Turner, a highway engineer and former director of the BPR who assumed control of the DOT's Federal Highway Administration, "carried reputations as hard-line road builders" whose "bulldozer bias" portended an era of enhanced expressway construction for America's metropolitan areas. Neither man had expressed much interest in the construction of urban mass transit, instead reflexively advocating more highways as the solution to the transportation needs of growing metropolitan regions. The number of protests against expressway construction by the end of the Johnson administration caused some concern among road builders, but highway lobbyists expected Volpe and Turner to "stamp out" the incipient freeway revolt and "get the show on the road again."[56]

The expected paroxysm of expressway construction failed to materialize at the outset of the Nixon administration, however, as the president, the DOT secretary, and other top officials expressed the desire to create a more diverse intermodal transportation system for the cities. A task force on transportation, which presented its recommendations to the president elect in January 1969, called for additional mass transit and more careful attention to the location of urban expressways. So did a coalition of big-city mayors and corporate executives who talked about refusing federal highway aid without attendant funding increases for mass transit. Skillfully using the Council for Urban Affairs as a forum for exploring urban transportation options, Daniel Patrick Moynihan proved especially influential in making the case against the unchecked proliferation of expressways. Moynihan had long been touting the imposition of limits on urban highway construction, more mass transit, and holistic transportation planning in metropolitan areas, and, along with the renowned economist John Kenneth Galbraith, had taken a leadership position in the citizens' crusade to keep Boston's Inner Belt Expressway from being built through neighboring Cambridge. Tellingly, Moynihan created a permanent subcommittee on mass transportation in the Urban Affairs Council with Volpe (chair), Romney, and Commerce's Maurice Stans as members. In an influential 1969 journal article advocating a national urban policy, he proposed an increased role for the federal government in encouraging the reorganization of local governments as a response to the metropolitan problems (including transportation) that defied traditional solutions. Before leaving the administration and returning to Harvard in 1970, Moynihan persuasively argued that allowing local and regional administrative units rather than Washington bureaucracies to make decisions about expressways and mass transit fit comfortably with the ideals of the New Federalism.[57]

Nor did the anticipated drive for expressway construction materialize immediately at DOT after Moynihan's exit from the White House. From the outset, Volpe defied expectations by proposing a balanced system of highways and rapid transit in America's cities.[58] The automobile and the high-speed expressway, the new secretary stated, must be "tallied against other community and individual values—the need for elbow room, clean air, stable neighborhoods, more park land, and many others. So far, we have sought sheer mobility above every other consideration; other needs have been neglected, and the social equation is clearly out of balance."[59]

Demonstrating a new appreciation for urban imperatives and hopeful of shaping a transportation policy that would find favor in the Urban Affairs Council, the new secretary created the post of Assistant Secretary for Urban Systems and Environment. Volpe selected to fill the new position Seattle Mayor James D. Braman, who had won national acclaim by successfully defeating plans to construct a huge expressway and interchange that would have destroyed a city park and acres of minority housing and building mass transit instead. As a member of Nixon's task force on transportation, Braman had been influential in drafting recommendations for increases in federal funding for urban mass transit. He accepted the job at DOT only after receiving Volpe's assurance that he could continue to campaign with the National League of Cities and the U.S. Conference of Mayors for a federal mass transit trust fund similar to the trust fund that underwrote the interstate highway system. On the other hand, Francis C. Turner at the BPR remained a staunch advocate of expressway construction and criticized what he called the "anti-highway lobby." Having spent nearly forty years at the BPR, Turner feared that more attention to mass transit funding would come at the expense of the previously sacrosanct Highway Trust Fund. He found his views unpopular in Volpe's DOT and for the most part maintained a low profile at the Federal Highway Administration. According to DOT staffer James Burby, Volpe regretted Turner's appointment immediately and gave his subordinate clear instructions not to question the administration's policies in public speeches. Disgruntled by the new directions taken under Volpe, Turner retired in 1972 and accepted a position as a consultant to the U.S. House Public Works Committee, where he opposed increased mass transit funding.[60]

Volpe's declaration of DOT priorities genuinely surprised just about everyone, especially BPR engineers, highway lobbyists, and state and local officials who expected to receive carte blanche authority from Washington, D.C., to cover cityscapes with expressways. "Remember John A. Volpe, king of the open road, builder of mighty highways, the Joe Frazier of asphalt?" asked the *Boston Globe*. "Volpe now stands accused of being a traitor to his class, having been drummed out of the highwaymen's corps." According to James Burby, the chief attorney for the U.S. House Public Works Committee said about the DOT under Volpe's leadership: "We used to think the attitude downtown was bad in Alan Boyd's day, but this Administration is *totally* antihighway." To the consternation of his long-time aides and allies, Volpe had decided that he would be more than just a road builder as secretary of transportation.[61]

Volpe demonstrated his new appreciation for the impact of expressway building on the cities through his handling of "freeway revolts" in several U.S. cities. By the 1960s, at the same time that the displacement of population by urban renewal sparked heated protests across the country, resistance was increasing to the construction of massive expressways that swallowed up so much real estate in city after city. Protesters raised a number of objections to the inexorable spread of concrete across the cityscape, the wholesale destruction of neighborhoods, the displacement of residents and businesses, and the regrettable environmental consequences of increased vehicular traffic. Freeway revolts were percolating in a number of communities when Volpe took the helm at DOT, the most important test case revolving around the controversial Riverfront Expressway in New Orleans. The plan to build an expressway along the Mississippi River adjacent to the French Quarter, first proposed in 1946 by New York City's master builder Robert Moses, had drawn increasing citizen resistance throughout the 1950s and 1960s. Federal officials jettisoned the original plans for an elevated freeway in favor of a ground-level highway, but citizen groups continued to balk at the creation of any roadway that would despoil the environment of the city's most famous neighborhood; antifreeway activists held out for a tunnel or, better yet, no highway at all. After a visit to New Orleans that included an examination of the projected site as well as discussions with both advocates and opponents of the riverfront highway, Braman recommended the location of the expressway elsewhere. Noting that Interior Secretary Stewart Udall had designated the French Quarter a historic district in 1965 and citing a number of pending lawsuits challenging construction, Volpe announced the cancellation of the Riverfront Expressway in July 1969. The secretary also announced that the federal funding promised to the riverfront roadway would be allocated to the construction of an outer beltway, the Dixie Freeway, on the other side of the Mississippi River—which city elites likewise were never able to have built.[62]

Following the blockbuster New Orleans decision, DOT terminated several other expressway projects for which federal funding had already been committed. As Massachusetts governor, Volpe had staunchly backed the construction of Boston's Inner Belt Expressway despite vocal and persistent objection from Cambridge residents who would be displaced. Reversing his earlier stand, he approved Governor Francis Sargent's funding request for a new highway study for metropolitan Boston and thereby ended formal consideration of the Inner Belt Expressway. After the U.S. Supreme Court declined to approve the construction of a segment of Interstate 40 through Overton Park in Memphis and remanded the case to a lower court, Volpe terminated the project. Altogether, DOT decided not to underwrite or acquiesced in the decision not to build expressways in New York City, Chicago, Philadelphia, Baltimore, Cleveland, Milwaukee, Detroit, Pittsburgh, Providence, Seattle, San Antonio, and Washington, D.C. Volpe based his agency's decisions in many instances upon environmental consid- erations, citing the outcomes of the environmental impact studies for all fed- eral construction projects mandated by the National Environmental Policy Act of 1969. "Freeways that adversely affect our environment cannot be built," he proclaimed in 1970. According to the historian Raymond A. Mohl, a distinguished analyst of post–World War II federal transportation policy, "John Volpe exceeded even Alan Boyd as a freeway terminator."[63]

As construction of the increasingly unpopular urban expressways slowed and automobile traffic congestion increased, public demand for the refur- bishment and expansion of aging and inadequate public transit systems in- tensified. Surprisingly, given his history as a road builder, Volpe warmed quickly to DOT's support for mass transit and informed the *Wall Street Jour- nal* that he considered such aid his "number one priority." Told by Moyni- han that the president welcomed from DOT a proposal for a mass transit trust fund, Volpe and his aides began work immediately on a legislative package for submission to Congress. Transportation officials believed that strong support for urban mass transit existed in the White House and on Capitol Hill, but, perceiving a potential threat to the unique interstate fund- ing mechanism, the powerful highway lobby staunchly opposed the creation of another trust fund. Prodded by James Braman, DOT officials drafted a mass transit trust fund bill in the fall of 1969. Nixon refused to send the leg- islation to Congress, however, because of the opposition from Bureau of the Budget officials and White House economists (especially Arthur F. Burns) who questioned the wisdom of creating another autonomous trust fund over which the president would exercise no direct control. The DOT composed another mass transit trust fund bill in 1970 but again ran afoul of the high- way lobby and White House advisers. Instead, Congress passed legislation that made no mention of a trust fund and only approved expenditures from general appropriations. The Urban Mass Transportation Assistance Act of 1970 authorized $3.1 billion in grants and loans for state and local govern- ments over six years, earmarking small sums of money for subways in a hand- ful of cities and the remainder of the funds for buses in a multitude of loca- tions. The bill required that the DOT secretary choose projects for funding that best protected the environment. Senator Alan Cranston (Democrat, Cali- fornia) called the law "paltry . . . totally inadequate," but Senator Harrison A.

Williams Jr. (Democrat, New Jersey) considered the allocations all that could be "prudently" spent in the succeeding years. Its financial limitations aside, the spending authorized by the Urban Mass Transportation Assistance Act of 1970 far exceeded the limited amounts—never more than $175 million annually—authorized for urban mass transit in previous legislation.[64]

Volpe and Braman continued the fight for more urban mass transit funding overall, for additional access to the Highway Trust Fund, and for the creation of a trust fund specifically devoted to mass transit. The Federal-Aid Highway Act of 1973 authorized $3 billion from general revenues for the Urban Mass Transportation Administration (UMTA) and, in response to the freeway revolt, allowed communities to rescind allocations from the Highway Trust Fund for expressway construction and to use equivalent amounts for mass transit from the federal government's general fund. The Senate, environmental groups, and the White House backed a proposal to allow use of money in the Highway Trust Fund for mass transit projects, while the House and highway lobbyists fought to preserve the trust fund for highway use only. A compromise in the final bill mandated that all of the $780 million earmarked for urban construction in fiscal year 1974 be used for highways, allowed $200 million of the $800 million urban roads appropriation in the Highway Trust Fund for the purchase of buses in fiscal year 1975, and permitted any part of the $800 million slated for roads in the Highway Trust Fund to be spent for the construction of rail mass transit and the purchase of subway cars in fiscal year 1976. These comparatively modest inroads into the coffers of the Highway Trust Fund stopped short of a major policy shift, however, and the DOT crusade for a mass transit trust fund never succeeded during the Nixon era. In the three years following passage of the Federal-Aid Highway Act of 1973, the federal government spent $1 billion on mass transit and $19 billion for highways from the Highway Trust Fund. With federal spending on mass transit so meager by the early 1970s, the changes in the funding formula implemented by the Nixon administration made little difference for urban transportation. As the historian Raymond A. Mohl concluded, "Despite Volpe's conversion to mass transit, congressional infighting and highway lobbying kept the road builders in business and the American driver on the road."[65]

Incremental gains for urban mass transit frustrated many DOT officials who encountered a series of roadblocks to meaningful transportation reforms that would benefit the nation's cities. Like Romney at HUD, Volpe came to Washington, D.C., with great enthusiasm and a determination to implement change quickly. He bemoaned the frosty reception frequently afforded his ideas by the president and his aides and complained that politics trumped policy in the White House. Volpe reported that the president routinely avoided him at public functions and telephoned him only once during the years he served as secretary. Angry and frustrated that he could not obtain an appointment to see the president, Volpe once cornered Nixon at a White House prayer service and began reading to him from a three-by-five-inch index card explaining his policy agenda. Nixon asked for the resignations of all cabinet secretaries after his 1972 reelection; when Volpe grudgingly complied, the president quickly accepted. Volpe unhappily left Washington to become the U.S. ambassador to Italy, still grumbling about his shabby treatment at the hands of White House personnel. Nixon appointed Claude Brinegar, an oil company executive who promised to be more malleable than his assertive predecessor, the new DOT secretary.[66]

John Volpe at DOT and George Romney at HUD abruptly left office in January 1973, casualties of the administration's effort to purge troublesome secretaries from the cabinet. They had remained publicly loyal to the president during their four years of service but privately bridled at their personal treatment and at their lack of influence in the administration. They learned that the occupants of the White House made the important policy decisions and expected department secretaries to implement them unquestioningly. Both men found that the issues that animated their professional lives mattered little to Nixon and his aides, who clearly viewed HUD and DOT as remote outposts of the administration where former adversaries could be shunted to fulfill certain political purposes. After winning reelection, the president no longer needed to retain Romney and Volpe in the cabinet and replaced them with compliant functionaries James Lynn and Claude Brinegar. In the last months of the Nixon presidency, as the administration sought to balance the federal budget as part of its war on inflation, Lynn's principal responsibility became the identification of HUD programs that could be reduced or eliminated to cut costs.[67]

With power centralized in the White House, Nixon and his aides determined the policies that affected the nation's cities. During the administration's first year, Daniel P. Moynihan managed to keep the urban crisis at the center of domestic policy discussions. He spoke frequently in 1969 about the need for creating a comprehensive urban policy, but the demise of the Council for Urban Affairs and Moynihan's return to academia in 1970 meant reduced attention to the plight of the cities—a void left largely unfilled by HUD. Discussions about the need for an urban policy gave way to broader discourses about national growth, the former seen increasingly as a state and local matter and the latter still identified as an appropriate topic for federal involvement. As a consequence, urban policy in the Nixon White House simply became part of the drive for bureaucratic decentralization known as the New Federalism. Granting "wide administrative leeway" to state and local governments, revenue sharing reduced the capacity of government bureaucracies in Washington to decide how their allocations would be spent—and thereby weakened the sturdy ligatures between the federal government and the cities fashioned by the New Deal and the Great Society. In tandem with the moratorium on the building of more low-income housing, the Housing and Community Development Act of 1974 accelerated the shift away from construction toward rent subsidies. In the name of decentralization, Nixon dismantled Model Cities, curtailed new towns development, and limited enforcement of fair housing laws, but spared some Great Society programs that fostered local community development. Tailored to benefit suburbs and Sunbelt communities populated by Republican voters, the New Federalism created CDBGs and Section 8 vouchers, and granted more local autonomy to decide if and where expressways would be built; it also meant reduced funding for low- and middle-class housing programs and a retreat from racial desegregation in the cities and suburbs. As suburbanization continued apace and the financial condition of central cities worsened, Nixon offered urban America no bargain. Administration spokesman William Safire explained that the New Federalism "says to communities, 'Do it your own way.'" And, he might have said to the anxious mayors of the nation's big cities, make do with less assistance from Washington, D.C.[68]

By the time that the Watergate investigation climaxed with the president's resignation in August 1974, the relationship between Nixon and the mayors of the nation's largest cities had deteriorated drastically. Fiscal belt-tightening at HUD and other federal agencies left the denizens of city halls questioning the benefits of CDBGs, revenue sharing, and other components of the New Federalism. The spokesmen for big-city interests lamented their lack of a voice in an administration that seemed to assign urban affairs a consistently low priority while diverting more and more resources to suburban locations. "I'm not certain that Nixon is committed to an anti-cities strategy," said Seattle Mayor Wesley Uhlman, "but he's looking at the 1970 census and the fact that the new voting majority lies in the suburbs." Nixon's standing plummeted further in urban America as media coverage of the Watergate scandal revealed the administration's harassment of the U.S. Conference of Mayors (USCM). According to testimony and documents provided the Senate Watergate Committee, the White House plumbers secretly investigated the USCM's activities, the Internal Revenue Service audited the organization's Legislative Action Committee, and FBI agents interrogated and threatened to prosecute USCM staff members participating in lobbying efforts. The USCM took the administration to court, which ordered the suspension of all attempts to obstruct city lobbying efforts. Four days after Nixon resigned, a bipartisan delegation of mayors met with President Gerald R. Ford to effect a reconciliation between the White House and city hall. Ford received the mayors graciously, promised to listen respectfully to their ideas, and pledged a more welcoming environment in the White House than they had encountered during the Nixon years. It remained unclear, however, whether another conservative Republican administration would renounce—or at least temper—the policies of the New Federalism that were causing so much consternation in the cities.[69]

6

FORD AND THE NEW FEDERALISM

Before becoming president in 1974 Gerald R. Ford spent twenty-six years burnishing his conservative credentials in the U.S. House of Representatives. Faithfully representing the interests of his rock-ribbed Republican district, Ford voted against legislation authorizing federal spending for education, civil rights, transportation, low-income housing, and community development. A persistent critic of the Great Society's urban programs, he looked forward to the elimination of Model Cities, Community Action, and other liberal programs. He hardily endorsed the precepts of Richard Nixon's New Federalism, enthusiastically supporting block grants and other measures designed to empower state and local governments while reducing the influence of federal bureaucracies; as a key member of the Republican leadership in the House, he played an important role in the passage of the legislation that created general revenue sharing in 1972. Ford promised Americans a new style of leadership after the tendentious Nixon years, pledging a presidency based upon "communication, conciliation, compromise, and cooperation," but he made no mention of new policies or programs. Indeed, the actions affecting cities taken during his 875 days in office deviated little from those initiated by his predecessor. The New Federalism of Gerald Ford seemed much the same as the New Federalism of Richard Nixon. Unfortunately for urban America, however, Ford's New Federalism coincided with an acute economic downturn that led the occupants of city halls to call for more attention from Washington, D.C., and not less. To the chagrin of local officials, the president's commitment to conservative economic orthodoxy and his determination to restrain spending severely circumscribed the role the federal government played in the fate of the cities.[1]

When corruption charges forced Spiro T. Agnew to resign in late 1973, Richard Nixon selected House Minority Leader Gerald R. Ford of Michigan to replace the discredited vice president. The president purportedly favored

Secretary of the Treasury John Connally, a conservative Democrat from Texas, but figured that the popular Ford would encounter less difficulty being confirmed by the Congress. Unassuming, diligent, and hardworking, the Michigan congressman had achieved a solid if unspectacular record since coming to the House in 1948. A halting orator who lacked original ideas, Ford nonetheless won the respect of his colleagues because of his competency and reliability. Although he had clashed repeatedly with liberal Democrats over his conservative views, Ford remained well liked on both sides of the aisle because of his reputation for conviviality and fairness. Confirmed by lopsided margins in both houses of Congress, Ford took the vice presidential oath of office on December 6, 1973. Nixon had little regard for his new vice president's intelligence—a view he thought to be shared widely on Capitol Hill—and apparently believed that the prospect of a Ford presidency would deter impeachment proceedings as the Watergate scandal worsened. He was wrong. Faced with certain conviction in the Senate and removal from office, Nixon resigned and Ford became president on August 9, 1974. Claiming that the nation needed to move on and commence the healing of wounds left by Vietnam and Watergate, Ford quickly pardoned Nixon. He denied having agreed secretly to absolve Nixon of any wrongdoing in exchange for his appointment to the vice presidency and argued that his actions had spared the country the enervating investigations and legal proceedings that would inevitably have followed. Having brought the long national nightmare of Watergate to a close, the new president argued, he could confront the serious problems facing the United States in the mid-1970s.[2]

A severe economic recession that plagued the Ford administration from the start affected all decisions made about domestic policies, including aid to the cities. American prosperity, virtually uninterrupted since the close of the Second World War, faltered in the early 1970s. A $10 billion balance of payments deficit, slackened industrial productivity, and a $40 billion budget deficit by 1972 propelled the economy into a tailspin. Kept comfortably below 5 percent between 1955 and 1972, inflation skyrocketed to 8 percent in early 1973 and almost to 10 percent by the beginning of 1974. An Arab oil embargo launched by the Organization of Petroleum Exporting Countries (OPEC), made all the more effective by America's growing dependence upon Middle Eastern petroleum reserves, increased the prices of heating oil and gasoline by as much as 33 percent in the winter months of 1973–1974. The nation suffered for the first time from stagflation, the harrowing combination of rampant inflation and high unemployment rates—11 percent for the former and nearly 9 percent for the latter by 1975. The simultaneous rise in prices and unemployment obviated the federal government's past practice of inducing recessions to curb inflation, leaving Ford and his advisers baffled about the most effective way of dealing with the worst economic downturn since the Great Depression.[3]

Driven by his faith in traditional economic policies and an aversion to the government's use of Keynesian fiscal policy, Ford sought to reduce the ballooning federal deficit by cutting discretionary spending on social programs. Determined to lower inflation and balance the budget by slashing federal spending, the president vetoed thirty-nine bills in his first year in office that provided aid for education, health care, and other services. When the imposition of a temporary tax surcharge in 1974 resulted in an expanding budget deficit, he reversed himself and recommended tax cuts for individuals and businesses—but continued to hold the line on federal spending. Although the economic situation began to improve somewhat by mid-1975, Ford adhered to a fiscally cautious approach by proposing a permanent tax cut and additional reductions in federal spending. The administration's selection of inflation as "domestic enemy number one," willingness to tolerate rising unemployment, and reduction of government programs not surprisingly proved highly unpopular in city halls, where anxious mayors pleaded for additional financial aid from Washington, D.C.[4]

The steady decline of older Frostbelt cities, fueled by the flight of population, industry, and retail to the suburbs, had reached crisis proportions by the 1970s. During the decade, Cincinnati lost 15 percent of its population, Detroit lost 21 percent, and St. Louis lost 27 percent. The exit of the middle class deprived the cities of precious resources and exacerbated the problem of providing costly services when the poorer populations remaining in the cities paid far fewer dollars in taxes. Between 1965 and 1975, for example, New York City's operating expenses increased by 260 percent while tax revenue declined. With the American economy undergoing a painful deindustrialization, factory closings sent unemployment rates skyrocketing. Youngstown, Ohio, lost 20,000 jobs when its three steel mills shut down; the closing of the city's automobile tire factories cost nearby Akron twice that number. A dramatic reduction in steel making in 1972 left Gary, Indiana, with an unemployment rate of 40 percent. Between 1969 and 1976, New York City lost an estimated 542,000 jobs when factories, offices, and retail outlets relocated elsewhere. Not since the Great Depression, with its astronomical unemployment rates and rampant business failings, had the situation in urban America been so dire.[5]

Righting the nation's faltering economy, Ford maintained during the first days of his presidency, constituted the best national urban policy the federal government could offer the desperate cities. Liberated by the New Federalism from the flawed programs conceived in Washington, D.C., and possessing the resources generated by a vibrant economy, he believed city officials would be free to reverse decades of decline. Vice President Ford had outlined the benefits of decentralization to the leadership of the U.S. Conference of Mayors (USCM) on February 1, 1974, praising the progress made by the Nixon administration in housing and community development and especially highlighting the manner in which mass transit legislation in 1970 and 1973 had increased funding for the cities while allowing local authorities to identify their own transportation priorities. On August 14, just five days after replacing Nixon, Ford met with sixteen members of the USCM to promise them greater access to the White House than they had enjoyed during the previous administration and to affirm his goodwill toward the cities. The mayors spoke at length in the meeting about the deteriorating economic conditions in their communities and, while acknowledging the importance of reducing inflation, emphasized that rising unemployment was becoming their most serious problem; Mayor Kenneth Gibson of Newark, New Jersey, for example, noted that the 14 percent unemployment rate in his city more than doubled the reported national rate. The president and the mayors also discussed the prospects for imminent passage of housing and mass transit legislation proposed earlier that year by the Nixon administration. The president revealed that he would likely sign the housing law, which would provide additional funding and place the onus on local officials to act wisely on behalf of their cities without federal constraints. Admitting that he had during his career in the House consistently opposed federal subsidies for mass transit, Ford said that he might be willing to sign such a measure as president if the cost could be reduced; he urged the mayors to use whatever influence they possessed in Congress to produce a transportation bill that the president would not feel compelled to veto. Throughout the meeting, Ford combined expressions of goodwill toward the cities with reminders of his determination to subdue inflation, reign in federal spending, and balance the budget.[6]

On August 22, thirteen days after becoming president, Ford signed the Housing and Community Development Act of 1974, one of the foundations of the New Federalism, after both houses of Congress had passed the bill by hefty margins (76 to 11 in the Senate and 351 to 25 in the House). Title I of the law combined existing categorical grants into Community Development Block Grants (CDBGs)—the initial three-year allocation of $8.6 billion for CDBGs represented no reduction in federal funding for cities—and provided cities unprecedented autonomy in their expenditure. Title II rewrote the U.S.

Housing Act of 1937 to revise a number of assisted housing programs. The
law extended the Section 235 homeownership program and the Section 236
rental assistance program by two years but authorized only $75 million in
new funds, a fraction of the amount requested by liberal Democrats in Congress. Ford expressed satisfaction that the majority of the money earmarked
for assisted housing went to the new Section 8 program, which provided financial support to eligible low-income families occupying existing or substantially rehabilitated rental units. The president lauded the Housing and
Community Development Act of 1974 for reducing direct federal involvement
in urban affairs, ensuring greater autonomy for local authorities, and accelerating the movement from conventional public housing toward leased housing subsidies.[7]

Ford then turned his attention to the mass transit legislation being considered by Congress at that time. With the ardent support of big-city mayors
across the country, Representative John A. Blatnik (Democrat, Minnesota)
led the campaign on Capitol Hill. Following the conclusion of hearings in
Washington, D.C., Blatnik's House Public Works Committee heard additional testimony in New York City, Chicago, Boston, Los Angeles, San Diego,
San Francisco, Sacramento, and Atlanta. In July, New York City Mayor
Abraham Beame hosted a gathering of big-city mayors, labor officials, and
business leaders at Gracie Mansion to kick off a lobbying effort in support of
the legislation under review in Congress. The USCM's Legislative Action
Committee garnered additional publicity for the cause at the ceremony that
summer commemorating the opening of the Bay Area Rapid Transit system's
link between San Francisco and Oakland. The USCM even managed to re-
cruit Henry Ford II, the chairman of the Ford Motor Company and a long-
time friend of the president, as a supporter of the pending mass transit bill.[8]

On September 9, in his remarks to the International Conference on Urban
Transportation, Ford again recounted his past opposition to federal subsidies
for mass transit. Raiding the Highway Trust Fund to underwrite public transportation, he had long believed, "would lead to the Federal Government in
the local day-to-day transit operating matters." Noting that he had long
served in Congress as the representative of Michigan, the principal home of
automobile manufacturing, Ford affirmed his support of that industry.[9] He
said, "As we move to improve our transit systems, we must not lose sight of
one very important fact: The automobile is and will continue to be our chief
transportation vehicle. The automobile fits America's traditional lifestyle. No
matter how plush the bus, no matter how comfortable the train, Americans, to
one degree or another, will continue to drive their automobiles."[10]

Repeating the sentiments he had expressed in his earlier meeting with the USCM, however, the president also confirmed the need to improve the nation's urban transportation networks for the benefit of the expanding metropolitan populations. Although still reluctant to tamper with the Highway Trust Fund, Ford retreated from his earlier opposition to providing federal funds for operating expenses when the paucity of city resources jeopardized the continuation of mass transit service. He indicated his willingness to accept prudent legislation of limited scope that would enhance urban mass transit at a reasonable cost but not undermine his administration's commitment to fiscal responsibility.[11]

On November 26 Ford signed the National Mass Transportation Act of 1974, which authorized the expenditure of $11.9 billion over six years ($7.8 billion for capital grants and $4.1 billion for operating expenses) to aid the nation's financially troubled mass transit systems in communities with populations exceeding 50,000 people. (The law permitted the federal government to pay as much as 80 percent of the cost of capital projects and up to 50 percent of the cost of operating expenses.) Democrats in Congress had fought for a more generous measure carrying a $20 billion price tag, but, citing the need for fiscal restraint to fight inflation, the president sent word to Capitol Hill that he would accept no legislation costing more than $12 billion. The law broke new ground in allowing the federal government to provide subsidies for operating expenses as well as for construction costs. As the president noted in his remarks at the time of the bill's signing, the funding commitment for an unprecedented six years allowed communities for the first time to plan for long-term spending on mass transit.[12]

Big-city mayors and other defenders of the cities commended Ford's signing of major housing and mass transit bills within the first four months of his presidency but expressed concern about the person he chose to replace James Lynn as secretary of the Department of Housing and Urban Development (HUD). (Lynn became the director of the Office of Management and Budget, a position he held for the remainder of the Ford administration.) The president selected Carla Hills, a California attorney then serving as an assistant U.S. attorney general in the Civil Division for the post at HUD despite her total unfamiliarity with urban affairs. Hills "didn't pretend to know much about the housing industry," recalled Ford in his autobiography, but "I saw her lack of expertise as a plus. It was far better to pick someone from outside who would assimilate the necessary information and then decide the issues on their merits." Not everyone agreed. Urban interest groups, which had urged the president to choose a realtor, home builder, city planner, HUD official, or other experienced professional familiar with the field, questioned Ford's reasoning. A joint statement by the USCM and the National League of Cities predicted that "it will take her a year to eighteen months to learn the job, and by that time we will be in the midst of the next presidential election." The continued appointment of HUD secretaries who possessed little or no expertise in urban affairs—a description fitting James Lynn, Carla Hills, and to a lesser degree, George Romney—created the impression that Nixon and Ford invested little importance in the agency. The persistent rumor that the president selected Hills in deference to First Lady Betty Ford's persistent prodding further tainted the nomination and reinforced the idea that the president would follow Nixon's lead in consigning HUD to the second tier of cabinet departments.[13]

Hills's inexperience became an issue in Congress immediately. She underwent an unusually rigorous questioning at her Senate confirmation hearings on February 24, 1975, as Democrats took turns highlighting her lack of expertise with their detailed, sharply worded questions. Senator William Proxmire of Wisconsin took the lead for the Democrats, laying bare the nominee's shortcomings with relish and concluding that "this is no time for on-the-job training of a new Secretary of HUD." In the end, despite the expression of reservations by many legislators, the Senate confirmed the appointment by a vote of 85 to 5. The grumbling on Capitol Hill persisted when Hills testified before a congressional committee shortly after her confirmation and fared no better. Surrounded by her new subordinates at the agency, who for the most part appeared to share her lack of knowledge about the particulars of housing policy, the secretary made a disjointed presentation and failed to answer the most elementary questions about HUD programs. Hills's hard work and administrative skill eventually won over many of her congressional critics, but skepticism predominated at first.[14]

Ford met with Hills privately for the first time on April 30, 1975, seven weeks after her swearing-in ceremony, to discuss the administration's general approach to the cities as well as strategies for handling specific policy questions that would be confronting the new secretary in the coming months. The president expressed concern that the rapid growth of federal housing programs in the previous decade had led to the proliferation of government bureaucracies and underscored the need for more effective management in HUD. He pointed to the CDBG program as the cornerstone of his urban policy, urging its implementation as rapidly as possible, and emphasized housing rehabilitation and rental programs instead of new construction. Ford and Hills conferred about the need to accelerate the implementation of the Section

8 program, which had gotten off to such a slow start that no unit contracts had been awarded since passage of the enabling legislation in August 1974, and to clarify the status of the beleaguered Section 235 program. Suspended along with other federal housing programs in January 1973, Section 235 also faced a HUD investigation launched by Secretary Romney in response to charges of corruption and malfeasance. On April 15 the General Accounting Office had filed suit against the president, the Office of Management and Budget director, and the HUD secretary to release Section 235 funds impounded in 1973, and Hills reported that her agency's general counsel recommended release of the funds for use in a reformed program. To offset Section 235's high foreclosure and default rates, Hills subsequently revised eligibility rules to steer more aid to families at the higher end of the socioeconomic scale and released $264 million in funds for homeownership subsidies. The president and the secretary also spent considerable time at the meeting discussing the deplorable conditions in the housing industry, especially the drastic decline in housing starts and in the issuance of building permits, as well as the emergency housing legislation being considered in Congress to address these problems.[15]

Battered by rising prices, high interest rates, and dwindling demand during the recession, the housing industry in 1975 suffered through its worst year since World War II. The unemployment rate in the construction industry stood at an astronomical 22 percent in May. To ameliorate the problem, several legislators prepared emergency housing bills that spring. Senator William Proxmire's bill proposed that the federal government subsidize mortgage interest rates for middle-income homebuyers, Senator Edward Brooke (Republican, Massachusetts) introduced legislation that provided a $1,000 incentive payment for the purchase of a single family dwelling, and the measure submitted by Representative Henry Reuss (Democrat, Wisconsin) authorized a direct government subsidy to reduce interest payments. The Ford administration rejected them all. Secretary Hills commented: "We do not believe that we can spend our way out of the housing slump without inviting a new and more crippling inflationary spiral—in which housing would be the first to suffer." In June Congress passed a $1 billion emergency housing bill that the president had already warned he would not sign. The previous fall's elections had given the Democrats control of both houses of Congress, 61 to 38 in the Senate and 291 to 144 in the House, but not by the two-third margins necessary to override presidential vetoes unless several Republicans broke ranks. On June 24 Ford vetoed the measure, criticizing its excessive cost and vowing to instill the consumer confidence in the federal government essential to the housing market's recovery; the House sustained the veto the following day by a vote of 268 to 157.[16]

Recognizing the futility of continuing to battle for a broader program and hoping to finalize matters prior to the July 4 recess, Congress sent Ford an amended bill revised to satisfy the objections detailed in his veto message. On July 2 the president signed the Emerging Housing Act of 1975, which empowered the Government National Mortgage Association ("Ginnie Mae") to purchase $10 billion in mortgages and encouraged lenders to make mortgage funds available at below-market interest rates. The law also allowed HUD to make loans up to $250 a month for two years to unemployed homeowners who could not make their mortgage payments and to insure lenders against losses if they extended the same consideration to homeowners in financial distress. Because Congress had excised programs from the original bill that provided cash grants to middle-income families for housing down-payment costs and that reduced mortgage interest rates more substantially, Ford maintained that he had signed a law that provided relief to homeowners and yet maintained fiscal responsibility.[17]

A similar tableau unfolded in the summer of 1975 when congressional Democrats sought to provide additional aid to the cities by passing an emergency jobs bill. Congress passed a $5.3 billion emergency employment appropriations bill that would sustain and enhance the payment of benefits to unemployed workers after the beginning of the new fiscal year on July 1. Citing the potential havoc such legislation would wreak on the federal budget, Ford vetoed the bill on May 29. On June 4 the House voted 277 to 145 for the measure, falling five votes short of the necessary two-thirds majority to override the veto. As with the emergency housing bill, Congress quickly passed a more modest bill that assured the uninterrupted flow of unemployment compensation benefits to the unemployed after July 1; the president signed the Emergency Compensation and Special Unemployment Assistance Extension Act of 1975 on June 30. In his dealings with Congress over the emergency housing and unemployment bills, Ford accepted the need for limited federal action, gave ground grudgingly, and because Democrats lacked veto-proof majorities, succeeded in curtailing the scope of federal spending in the cities.[18]

The president's zealous protection of the federal purse strings exasperated urban officials struggling to make ends meet during the severe 1975 recession. Faced with declining revenues and the prospects of crippling budget deficits, city governments cut services, laid off personnel, proposed new taxes, and turned to the state and federal governments for increased financial aid. Legally obligated to balance budgets annually, city officials envied the federal government's ability to accumulate deficits and questioned Ford's reluctance to do so. At the July 1975 annual meeting of the USCM, the growing disenchantment with the president's budgetary priorities surfaced repeatedly. Seattle Mayor Wes Uhlman railed at the "cynicism" of the administration for requesting an 18 percent increase in military spending for fiscal year 1976 while skimping on federal aid to the cities. In his presidential address to the organization, San Francisco Mayor Joseph Alioto excoriated the administration for its readiness to aid private business and remove regulations that obstructed the operation of the free market while at the same time citing innumerable philosophical objections to the use of public resources on behalf of the commonweal. "Politically we are deep into a climate of negativism," charged Alioto. "The Ford administration is long on what it is against and very short on what it is for."[19]

The president declined to attend the annual USCM meeting in Boston, but Secretary Hills attended in his stead and delivered a forceful defense of the administration's urban record. She acknowledged the seriousness of the economic problems confronting urban America but asserted that "the crisis of the cities will not be solved by making their deficits part of a rapidly growing federal budget deficit." Likening an infusion of federal largesse to a physician treating symptoms while ignoring the underlying causes of an illness, she emphasized the need for local initiative to solve local problems. Reflexive reliance on HUD and other Washington bureaucracies only provided palliatives and allowed municipal governments to avoid making the kinds of difficult choices that could lead to effective and lasting change. "We need long-term solutions which are the product of the cities' initiative," the secretary stated. "Only then can the Federal Government's help be meaningful."[20]

Unconvinced by the administration's arguments for federal restraint, the USCM rallied around a proposal championed in Congress by Senator Edmund Muskie (Democrat, Maine) for countercyclical aid to the cities. As outlined in its July 1975 meeting, the USCM proposed that the federal government provide a $2 billion annual appropriation to the cities whenever the national unemployment rate exceeded 6 percent. On July 29 the Senate approved an amendment to a public works bill introduced by Muskie, William Brock (Republican, Tennessee), and Hubert Humphrey (Democrat, Minnesota) that contained the USCM's countercyclical initiative. Both houses of Congress approved a revised version of the bill containing the Muskie-Brock-Humphrey amendment in January 1976, but the president responded yet again with a veto. By a narrow margin, the Senate fell shy of the obligatory two-thirds vote to override. With economic conditions worsening in the early months of 1976, however, a reconfigured countercyclical bill met a different fate. Congress overrode the president's veto in July, and the Public Works Employment Act of 1976 provided $1.25 billion in federal aid for cities saddled with persistently high levels of unemployment. Because of the prolonged hardship in urban America, Congress finally mustered the votes necessary to pass legislation previously blocked by the president.[21]

Nothing underscored the tension between the penurious Ford presidency and cities teetering on the edge of economic catastrophe more than New York City's bankruptcy crisis in 1975. A number of U.S. communities battled financial calamity in the mid-1970s, but the travails of the nation's largest and wealthiest city became symbolic of the administration's growing reputation for indifference to the plight of urban America. In the 1950s and 1960s, during the mayoralties of Robert Wagner Jr. (1954–1965) and John V. Lindsay (1966–1973), New York City had begun deviating from the traditional custom of cities balancing their budgets annually, borrowing money only for capital improvements, and refraining from incurring debt to pay for operating expenses. By the time that Abraham Beame became mayor in 1974, New York City had accumulated a crushing $3 billion budget deficit and found it necessary to sell bonds and notes to pay the salaries and pensions of municipal employees, service its debts, and provide essential services. In early 1975, as Manhattan banks refused to underwrite additional loans and the New York State Assembly lent the city a portion of the funds needed to meet city payrolls, Beame and Governor Hugh Carey met with U.S. Treasury Secretary William Simon to seek federal assistance. Following the president's lead, Simon turned down the request for $1 billion in emergency funds. In a May 13 meeting with Beame and Carey, Ford offered several suggestions of how New York City could generate additional revenue—raising subway fares and charging tuition at community colleges, for example—but declined to provide federal aid and asserted that city officials must take the painful steps necessary to restore fiscal equilibrium. The president subsequently rejected additional pleas from the governor, forcing the state to create the Municipal Assistance Corporation (MAC) as a temporary agency to issue bonds and restructure New York City's debt. Disappointing bond sales and mounting debt led Governor Carey to sign the New York State Financial Emergency Act on September 9, which gave the state control of the city's finances. While the continued reluctance of Manhattan banks to purchase MAC bonds obviated the state's ability to provide financial aid, Ford still insisted that New York City must put its own fiscal house in order.[22]

Beame collaborated with other big-city mayors in preparing a bailout proposal for submission to Congress. Facing looming financial crises in their own communities and hoping that emergency federal aid for New York City would establish a helpful precedent, the members of the USCM's executive committee approved by a vote of thirteen-to-one Beame's plan for direct federal loans. USCM President Moon Landrieu of New Orleans and the other thirteen members of the executive committee met with Ford to discuss the worsening situation, arguing that the damage done by New York City to the municipal bond market across the country made it increasingly difficult for all cities to borrow money, but the president refused to budge from his opposition to federal involvement. On October 18 Landrieu testified on behalf of the USCM in Senate hearings and argued forcefully for federal intervention to forestall an economic upheaval that would damage urban America far beyond the banks of the Hudson River. Senators heard conflicting testimony, however. Although big-city mayors blamed New York City's plight on a crippling national recession, OPEC, and a number of intractable forces beyond the control of city hall, others excoriated the irresponsible financial policies of spendthrift mayoral administrations in the nation's largest city. Many conservatives echoed the sentiment of Senator Jake Garn (Republican, Utah), who suggested that "steps should be taken to allow the inevitable: the bankruptcy of New York City."[23]

Ford refused to yield as a number of prominent Democrats pilloried his unbending stance. Senator Henry "Scoop" Jackson of Washington charged that the president had declared "civil war" on New York City, and New York Representative Bella Abzug claimed that he had "branded New York as diseased, and now he wants to pull the plug." Calling Ford's position "immoral," Representative Edward I. Koch of New York said: "We are a city surrounded by the Mongol hordes, and I look at the window and the forces aren't those of barbarians; they are those of the White House."[24] In an impassioned speech to the National Press Club on October 29, the president forcefully rebutted his critics and once again reiterated his opposition to federal intervention. He said, "I can tell you now that I am prepared to veto any bill that has as its purpose a federal bailout of New York City to prevent a default. And I will tell you why. Basically it is a mirage. By giving a federal guarantee, we would be reducing rather than increasing the prospect that the city's budget will ever be balanced."[25]

The next day, the *New York Daily News* memorably headlined its account of Ford's speech: "Ford to City: 'Drop Dead.'" Although the president complained that the incendiary headline unfairly characterized the tenor of his remarks at the National Press Club, panicky New Yorkers found the five-word summary apt. Residents of the city and many others around the country considered his "Dutch Uncle approach" to the deepening crisis in New York City callous and insensitive.[26]

On November 26, following continued negotiations with the state of New York, Ford announced that he would seek the passage of legislation to provide credit for the delivery of essential services to the 8 million residents of New York City. The New York Seasonal Financial Act of 1975, passed by Congress five days later, authorized loans of $2.3 billion in each of the next three fiscal years; the city would be obligated at the end of each fiscal year to repay the loans at an interest rate 1 percent in excess of prevailing rates. The president explained his abrupt policy reversal by emphasizing that the fiscal soundness of the plan would ensure no additional cost to taxpayers, city officials would be held strictly accountable for repaying the loans, and Treasury Secretary William Simon would monitor developments in New York City carefully to ensure compliance with the conditions outlined in the legislation. A settlement in which state and local governments lived up to their financial responsibilities and expended all of their resources became possible, Ford insisted, only because he had refused to succumb for so long to a bailout based upon terms less favorable to the taxpayer. He concluded: "Only in the last month, after I made it clear that New York would have to solve its fundamental financial problems without the help of the Federal taxpayer, has there been a concerted effort to put the finances of the city and the State on a sound basis." The eleventh hour New York City bailout worked, but Ford's brinkmanship with local and state officials won few plaudits in city halls across the nation. Instead, the episode reinforced the image of the president as a tight-fisted defender of the bottom line who cared more about budget balancing than averting bankruptcy in the nation's preeminent city.[27]

In less publicized fashion, events in Detroit at the same time made clear the Ford administration's aversion to federal activism on behalf of the crisis-ridden cities. In April 1975 Mayor Coleman Young submitted to the White House "Moving Detroit Forward: A Plan for Urban Economic Revitalization," a blueprint for the economic revival of his struggling city. Elected mayor two years earlier on the platform of having promised wholesale redevelopment of Detroit's decimated downtown, Young called for the state and federal governments to underwrite nearly $3 billion in municipal improvements over the next five years. The mayor asked the Ford administration for $2.5 billion of the total in a combination of direct grants-in-aid, interest-free loans, low-interest public facility loans, and debt guarantees. In combination with state funds and private dollars, the federal largesse would provide $735 million for housing construction and rehabilitation, $730 million for public transit, $555 million for public service employment and job training programs, $526 million for riverfront development and the construction of industrial parks, $300 million for downtown commercial revitalization and neighborhood shopping center development, and $120 million for the improvement of the local police force. At a time when the federal government's entire CDBG program cost $2.2 billion, the audacity of the Detroit proposal staggered HUD administrators and White House officials.[28]

In his brief for "Moving Detroit Forward," Young based the ambitious proposal on the federal government's culpability in Detroit's collapse. Going beyond the standard argument that perilous times in urban America necessitated an infusion of resources from external sources, the mayor indicted Washington, D.C., agencies as the principal villains in his city's decline. With HUD holding more than 13,000 foreclosed homes in Detroit, fully one-third of the units repossessed by the federal agency nationwide, the federal government needed to admit its mistakes, absorb the losses, and commit the necessary resources for the city to salvage a modicum of its housing stock. "If Hurricane Edna wiped out a city somewhere, the federal government would pay to rebuild that city," Young explained. "Well, we've been hit by Hurricane HUD and it's up to them to do something about it." In addition to failed HUD programs, he argued, federal oil and energy policies, along with the imposition of safety requirements on the struggling automobile industry, had put thousands of Detroiters out of work. In short, Young concluded, his city had suffered especially because of misbegotten federal policies and should therefore be treated as a special hardship case among America's cities.[29]

HUD officials and White House staff viewed "Moving Detroit Forward" as hopelessly unrealistic and never considered responding affirmatively to its extensive wish list of federal grants and loans. Young sought an infusion of new dollars at a time when the Ford administration was poring over the federal budget carefully in search of places to save money. Funding the proposal would also set a precedent that could not be met for other communities and, the mayor's creative arguments notwithstanding, federal officials objected to the depiction of Detroit as uniquely deserving among the nation's big cities. The situation in Detroit proved problematic for several reasons, however, and the president and his advisers treated what they perceived to be a politically sensitive issue with considerable care. Ford had met with Young in Detroit on September 23, 1974—the only substantive one-on-one meeting with a big-city mayor the president had conducted during his time in office—and the leading politicians and businessmen in Michigan pushed hard for another conference to discuss the particulars of the new proposal. The president possessed a detailed knowledge of Detroit's disastrous condition and admitted that he felt a special responsibility for the well-being of the largest city in his home state. On April 30, 1975, Ford met in the White House with the mayor and a delegation of thirty business, civic, and labor leaders; he expressed his sympathy for the city's overwhelming set of problems but remained noncommittal about the possible provision of federal aid. Ford subsequently commissioned a special task force chaired by HUD Assistant Secretary David O. Meeker to evaluate "Moving Detroit Forward," and Secretary Hills met with Young on July 11 to discuss the city's sordid housing situation. In October, the task force met with local officials in Detroit for another round of talks but again made no promises to increase funding. As HUD's deputy assistant secretary for housing management summarized the administration's handling of the problem, "We say no, but we try to say it politely." The persistent Young kept badgering the Ford administration for additional aid but achieved little success until Detroit received several discretionary grants during the presidency of Jimmy Carter.[30]

Ford's hard line against increased federal assistance for New York City and Detroit came at a time when the threat of widespread municipal bankruptcies seemed real and the lingering housing recession continued to bedevil working- and middle-class families. By the end of 1975, an increasing number of congressmen joined big-city mayors and other urban interests in urging the president to deviate from the rigid path of fiscal responsibility he had chosen over a year earlier. In preparing the 1976 State of the Union message, the president and his advisers considered the possibility of creating new federal programs, especially to aid the moribund housing industry, but opted to maintain its commitment to fiscal restraint. In his lengthy January 19, 1976, address to the Congress, Ford made scant mention of urban conditions—two sentences on the "disappointing year in the housing industry in 1975" and three sentences urging a five-year extension of revenue sharing legislation so that local officials could continue to decide how federal allocations would be spent. The president's assessment of the state of the union made no explicit reference to the status of the cities and discussed only indirectly the ways in which the ailing economy affected the millions of people who resided in metropolitan areas.[31]

Ford's proposed budget for fiscal year 1977, which he released a few days after the State of the Union speech, similarly gave short shrift to the cities and elicited a predictably negative reaction from liberal Democrats in Congress and big-city mayors. At the USCM's Midwinter Conference on January 30, 1976, Senator Edmund S. Muskie excoriated the budget for its timid economic response to the recession and for its indifference to worsening urban conditions. "As an instrument of economic recovery," said Muskie, "the President promises only a slow, painful recovery that will hit hardest our large cities." The senator commented that the seriousness of urban problems had recently led *Business Week* to wonder if the United States would become "the world's first industrialized, urbanized country without important cities." On February 25, representatives of the USCM testified in Congress against the president's budget, charging that Ford's strategies to combat the recession provided generous federal aid for the private sector while ignoring state and local governments. Moon Landrieu of New Orleans, Kenneth Gibson of Newark, and Coleman Young of Detroit predicted that the budget's considerable increases in military funding, cuts in domestic spending, and acceptance of an intolerably high level of unemployment would inevitably ratchet up the fiscal pressure on the cities. Proposing that the federal budget grow by 5.5 percent in fiscal year 1977, the administration would increase federal assistance to state and local governments by just 1 percent. With inflation in excess of 8 percent, the three mayors calculated, the cities would absorb a $4.1 billion reduction in real dollars. Moreover, they noted that the federal government's addition of financial obligations to municipal authorities without the provision of more resources was contributing significantly to the cities' budgetary crises. Such unfunded mandates as increased contributions to the social security fund, mandatory compliance with new federal environmental standards, and additional financial responsibility for unemployment compensation would all require local governments to cut spending on essential services, raise taxes, borrow more money, or execute all three options in some undesirable combination. According to USCM spokesmen, endorsing the disastrous policies of the Ford administration would lead cities across the nation into the kind of financial crisis that had befallen New York City.[32]

Liberals also roundly condemned the Ford administration in the early months of 1976 for defending residential segregation in suburbia, which they saw as the continuation of policies established in the Nixon years. The issue resurfaced because of the U.S. Supreme Court's consideration of *Hills v. Gautreaux*, a case that had been ascending through the federal courts for a decade. In 1966 American Civil Liberties Union lawyers filed a class-action suit against the Chicago Housing Authority (CHA) on behalf of Dorothy

Gautreaux, three other public housing tenants, and two African Americans seeking to rent units in CHA projects. *Hills v. Gautreaux* charged the authority with violation of Title VI of the 1964 Civil Rights Act in systematically excluding blacks from public housing in white neighborhoods. In 1969 federal judge Richard Austin found for the plaintiffs and ordered the CHA to desegregate existing public housing projects and to construct new projects in integrated neighborhoods. At the direction of Chicago Mayor Richard J. Daley, the CHA filed an appeal, ceased all construction, and delayed compliance in existing projects. In 1974, having found HUD as well as the CHA culpable for segregated residential housing patterns, the U.S. Court of Appeals for the Seventh Circuit ordered both government agencies to prepare a metropolitan plan that would implement desegregation in the suburbs as well as the city. In 1975 the U.S. Supreme Court decided to hear an appeal filed by HUD secretary Carla Hills.[33]

The Ford administration vigorously opposed the circuit court's desegregation mandate. The president said he did not believe that "federal action should be used to destroy [the] ethnic treasure of existing neighborhoods," and Hills denied the need for federal activism in the suburbs. "Most communities do want to address [housing] needs," she asserted and predicted that HUD would not "find a lot of communities shirking their responsibility for subsidized housing." Areawide housing plans designed to disperse the urban poor would have a "chilling effect" on suburbs, argued the HUD brief submitted to the U.S. Supreme Court, because it potentially provided subsidized housing for tenants of inner-city public housing as well as for the suburbs' needy residents. On April 20, 1976, the Supreme Court affirmed the decision of the Court of Appeals by a vote of 8 to 0, upholding the principle of metropolitan relief and remanding the matter of how assisted housing would be built or leased to Judge Austin. Although the consequences of the *Gautreaux* decision turned out to be mixed, it seemed to many at the time that the inner city had won a notable victory over the suburbs—despite the Ford administration having clearly supported suburban defenders of segregation.[34]

By the spring of 1976, with the Democratic and Republican parties preparing their campaign machinery for that year's presidential election, Ford and his subordinates worried that negative perceptions of his presidency's urban policies could be very damaging to his candidacy. Although the president continued to believe in the New Federalism and other policies implemented by his and the Nixon administrations, he knew that a number of untoward events in 1975 had severely damaged his reputation with the USCM and other city leaders. At the same time, articles and editorials in the

press consistently depicted Ford as an uncaring and insensitive chief executive unmoved by the harsh urban conditions of the mid-1970s. In the early
months of 1976, White House personnel began readying a defense of the
administration's treatment of cities. The case for the president began with
recognition of the daunting challenges facing the nation's urban places, particularly the older cities of the Northeast and the Midwest, and continued
with the assertion that federal programs had historically exacerbated conditions in the cities. Policies originating in Washington, D.C., in the 1960s,
though often well-intentioned, had hastened white flight to the suburbs,
vastly expanded a wasteful and inefficient bureaucracy, and weakened local
autonomy. The Nixon and Ford administrations had taken useful first steps
to reverse the damage through the creation of revenue sharing and CDBGs,
the restoration of power in city halls, and the reduction of red tape by eliminating categorical grants. Most important, the Ford administration had
taken the necessary steps to curb the inflation that aggravated the cities' fiscal woes. "Our primary goal is to keep the rate of inflation down," noted
Carla Hills, "and the President is achieving this."[35]

On June 29 Ford formed the President's Committee on Urban Development and Neighborhood Revitalization to review the administration's efforts
on behalf of cities, to propose ways of improving relations between the federal government and local officials, and to recommend revisions to existing
urban policies. The committee, chaired by HUD Secretary Hills, included
Transportation Secretary William T. Coleman Jr.; Treasury Secretary William Simon; Commerce Secretary Elliott Richardson; Attorney General Edward Levi; Health, Education, and Welfare Secretary Forest David Mathews;
Labor Secretary William J. Usery Jr.; Agriculture Secretary John Knebel; and
several other federal officials. The president instructed Hills to announce the
formation of the committee in her speech before the USCM the following
day, making clear the administration's sustaining interest in urban affairs.
(A Ford administration official reported that the conferees gave Hills's
speech a cordial response, but most of the mayors remained skeptical about
the committee achieving anything substantive.) Committee members visited
Boston, Baltimore, Cleveland, Hartford, Newark, Pittsburgh, New Orleans,
San Diego, Oklahoma City, and Springfield, Illinois, before compiling an
interim report that they submitted to the president on October 21. Ford
praised the content of the report, which he described as "straight talk, not
vague or empty political promises," and endorsed its assessment that local
leaders "are looking for help in developing local solutions—not for political
promises of magic remedies from Washington."[36] The president provided a

succinct summary of the approach he had taken toward the cities: "Since I took office two years ago, my Administration has followed a clear urban policy: to provide the cities and their neighborhoods a fair share of Federal resources and the opportunity and flexibility to solve their own problems and manage their own growth and progress."[37]

At a press briefing that day, reporters peppered Hills with a series of pointed questions about the timing and substance of the report that they claimed raised anew the perception of the Ford administration's inattention to urban problems. "For eight years the Nixon-Ford Administration has been in charge of this problem and doesn't seem to have done much about it," observed a reporter. "Now, two weeks before the election, you are coming up with a plan for more efficiency." Hills denied any political calculations in releasing an interim report two weeks before election day and earnestly defended the administration's record. In response to a reporter's observation that the report made no mention of forthcoming initiatives, Hills explained that the major goal for the future would be to make policies already established by the administration more efficient and responsive to local exigencies. Unlike urban renewal, Model Cities, and other discredited policies of the past that merely threw money at problems and in the process made them worse, she continued, Ford urban efforts such as CDBGs, Section 8 housing, and revenue sharing had already demonstrated their cost effectiveness. As a conscientious steward of taxpayer dollars, HUD under her direction was demanding accountability from federal, state, and local officials. Finally, she emphasized that the administration remained committed to a number of principles for the improvement of cities—more efficient use of current resources rather than the provision of new federal funds, decentralization to promulgate local decision making, and, most important, the application of judicious economic policies to vanquish a recession that was draining city governments of their scarce resources.[38]

Denouncing the self-congratulatory pronouncements of the President's Committee on Urban Development and Urban Revitalization, Democrats in Congress sharply censured the administration's record on housing. In their telling, the thorny problems of the Nixon era had continued during the Ford years. In 1975 charges of graft and profiteering concerning the FHA's single-family mortgage insurance programs in Chicago had led to hearings by the Senate Banking, Housing, and Urban Affairs Committee. Secretary Hills investigated promptly and promised to implement a series of reforms, but the incident revived unpleasant memories of the recent HUD scandals under George Romney's leadership. Critics on Capitol Hill requested additional funding for the Section 8 and Section 235 programs as well as new construction to augment subsidies for existing housing; HUD officials countered that it made more economic sense to subsidize old units than to construct new ones. In 1976 congressional liberals urged the resumption of the discontinued public housing program that had, despite its imperfections, contributed a total of 1.2 million units since its inception to the nation's housing stock for low-income families. HUD officials strongly dissented, arguing that the "warehousing" approach of public housing had been thoroughly discredited in previous decades. The Congress and the White House eventually reached a compromise on the $850 million allocated for federally assisted housing programs in fiscal year 1977, specifying that the preponderance of new funds would go for rental subsidies and setting aside just $100 million for new construction. In signing the Housing Authorization Act of 1976, Ford noted that "the Congress has ignored both our unfortunate previous experience and the present success resulting from the Section 8 program. Reversing this record of progress, it voted to reinitiate a public housing program." The president reluctantly signed the bill, he explained, because of the legislature's agreement to limit the size of the construction program stringently.[39]

Ford's fiscal restraint in dealing with urban problems became a significant issue in that year's presidential election as the Democratic candidate, Jimmy Carter, accused the administration of neglecting the cities. "Today," said Carter during the campaign, "America's number one economic problem is our cities." He further pointed to Ford's vetoes of countercyclical public works and emergency housing legislation in 1975 as examples of the Republican's indifference to urban suffering. At the USCM annual meeting on June 29, 1976, Carter commented that the cities had been "political whipping boys" for the previous eight years of the Nixon and Ford presidencies. His election, Carter promised the mayors, would ensure that cities would have "a friend in the White House." Although he had renounced a federal bailout of New York City a year earlier, the Democratic candidate excoriated Ford for his handling of the crisis and promised if elected to meet with Mayor Beame and Governor Carey to extend federal aid beyond the three years stipulated by the New York City Seasonal Financial Act. Ford attempted to portray Carter as another tax-and-spend liberal Democrat whose vague campaign promises to aid the cities would inevitably entail the kinds of spendthrift policies his administration had struggled to curtail. The incumbent hewed to his economic policies as the best medicine for urban ills and decried expensive liberal nostrums that had failed to work in the past. Just as the economy and foreign affairs dominated the campaign generally, the September 23 presidential debate devoted to domestic affairs notably avoided the problems of the cities; the two candidates referred to urban issues during the debate only in response to questions dealing with broader economic concerns. Carter's narrow defeat of Ford on November 2 seemingly had little to do with the incumbent's urban policies.[40]

The fate of the cities played a decidedly minor role in the outcome of the 1976 presidential election, but vigorous criticism of the Ford administration's treatment of urban America continued unabated in liberal strongholds. During the confirmation hearings for a new HUD secretary in January 1977, Senator William Proxmire leveled a scathing indictment against the urban policies of both the Nixon and Ford administrations. The chairman of the Senate's Committee on Banking, Housing, and Urban Affairs and one of Congress's leading authorities on housing matters, Proxmire brought eight years of frustration to bear in his attack on the two Republican presidencies. He berated the Nixon-Ford administrations for failing to launch the Section 8 program in a timely fashion, for allowing thirteen new towns to flounder, for settling on voluntary compliance with desegregation statutes rather than strenuously enforcing civil rights laws in the suburbs, and for absorbing multimillion dollar losses from foreclosed properties due to corruption and incompetence in HUD. Proxmire further alleged that "many, many HUD workers are tired of working for administrations that, regardless of the commitment of the Secretary, [do] not really care very much about housing." Having been very critical of Carla Hills at her confirmation hearings in 1974, he offered grudging recognition in early 1977 of her subsequent work as secretary, absolved the HUD staff of primary responsibility for the disappointing performance of the previous two years, and laid blame for the housing disaster at the doorstep of the White House. Proxmire conceded that by the end of her tenure, Hills could talk about housing "in a reasonably intelligent way."[41] He wrote the secretary: "Given the fact that you had to work within an Administration which I believe cares little about meeting domestic needs; given the fact that you had little experience and had to spend some time learning; and given the fact that you were in the job for less than two years; I believe under the circumstances you have done a good job."[42]

For Proxmire and other critics of the New Federalism, the primary shortcomings of the Nixon and Ford administrations could be seen not just in dollars-and-cents issues but also in a change in the culture of the executive branch that represented the abandonment of Great Society efforts to nurture the cities. National funding for urban America remained a modest portion of the federal budget but continued to rise incrementally in the mid-1970s.

Thanks to the impact of revenue sharing and the disbursement of CDBGs, however, big cities lost ground economically as smaller cities and suburbs received more largesse from Washington, D.C. The middle class prospered at the expense of the lower and working classes, the South and West at the expense of the Northeast and Midwest. At the same time, Nixon and Ford gave less attention to the plight of the cities than to such domestic affairs as inflation control, bureaucratic reform, energy policy, and the environment. After Daniel Patrick Moynihan left the White House staff in 1970, no other presidential adviser emerged as a strong and consistent advocate for the formulation of a national urban policy in the Nixon and Ford administrations. The sudden creation of a special cabinet-level committee to examine city problems late in the Ford administration only drew attention to the lack of concern with those issues during the preceding years.[43]

Ford's New Federalism, in many ways simply a continuation of the course charted earlier by the Nixon presidency, nudged the cities toward greater autonomy during a harrowing economic recession that sent mayors scurrying, hat in hand, to Washington, D.C., for increased financial aid. The urban supplicants repeatedly came away empty handed, Carla Hills having told them that "the federal government is a pump-primer, not the well." The president's sober pronouncements to central cities about reducing fanciful expectations and living within their means stung all the more as the federal government distributed precious dollars to a much larger number of communities across the nation. Although the federal Treasury intervened only to rescue New York City, the urban fiscal crisis of the mid-1970s brought Cleveland, Detroit, Buffalo, and several other cities to the brink of bankruptcy before states or local financial institutions stepped in at the eleventh hour. The president's tightfistedness with New York City for so long before finally relenting evidenced an apparent disregard for urban problems that reverberated in city halls across America. Firmly committed to the notion that putting the economy on a sound footing constituted the best urban policy, Ford sought to steer the cities away from the direction chosen by Great Society liberalism. His "drop dead" proclamation to New York City sent a chilling message to urban America about the kind of support the cities could expect from Washington, D.C., in the future. Carter's defeat of Ford in the 1976 election signaled the apparent demise of the New Federalism and brought hope that the fate of the cities would once again assume a prominent policy position in the federal government.[44]

7

A NEW PARTNERSHIP WITH THE CITIES

The election of a Democratic president in 1976 ignited celebrations in city halls throughout the nation. Jimmy Carter's strident criticisms of the Ford administration's urban policies during the campaign and his promise to establish a new partnership involving the federal government, private industry, and the cities raised expectations that more resources would be forthcoming to the local officials who were still combating intractable economic problems. More so than any of his predecessors in the White House, Carter sought to formulate a comprehensive urban policy for his administration. Unable to marshal the necessary political support in the nation's big cities or in Congress, however, he found both the creation and the implementation of such a policy to be extraordinarily difficult. The U.S. economy continued to sputter in the late 1970s under the weight of soaring energy prices, low productivity, high unemployment, and elevated interest rates, forcing the president to subordinate his urban programs and policies to the need for fiscal restraint. The Carter administration succeeded somewhat in steering federal funds from suburbs and small communities to central cities, but such limited transfers dashed the hopes of liberals who anticipated something of an urban renaissance on the heels of what they viewed as two disastrous Republican presidencies. Without gainsaying the need to help urban America, Carter limited federal spending and reminded the cities of the need for sound business practices. While affirming his determination to bring social justice to the dispossessed and downtrodden in the cities, he also bridled at the excesses of liberalism in the 1960s. With its austerity budgets and penchant for cultivating private funding sources, the New Partnership followed the New Federalism's path of devolution and a reduced role for the federal government. Rather than reestablishing the kind of relationship between the cities and the federal government forged by the Great Society, Carter's presidency paved the way for the accelerated decentralization of the Reagan era.[1]

A newcomer to national politics in 1976, Carter was an unknown to much of the American electorate in that year's presidential campaign. After an abbreviated career as a nuclear engineer in the U.S. Navy, he managed his family's peanut farm in rural Georgia, served two terms in the state legislature, and, after an unsuccessful gubernatorial race in 1966, won election as governor in 1970. Listed by the national media as one of the progressive "New South" governors elected in the wake of the civil rights revolution, Carter called for an end to racial discrimination, sought to increase funding for education, and encouraged economic diversification in the historically agricultural region. Along with governors Reuben Askew of Florida, Dale Bumpers of Arkansas, James Hunt of North Carolina, and William Winter of Mississippi, Carter invested resources in education, roads, and other services that they hoped would lure new businesses to their underdeveloped states. He claimed as his greatest achievement the reorganization of the Georgia state government to increase efficiency by eliminating unnecessary agencies and streamlining the bureaucracy. As a presidential candidate, he forthrightly identified himself as a born-again Christian, spoke movingly about the need for morality in politics, and vowed to restore integrity and honesty in government. His campaign made much of his status as a Washington outsider and, drawing upon his success at reforming state government, promised to dismantle the wasteful federal bureaucracy. Inveighing against inefficiency and corruption as unfortunate byproducts of 1960s liberalism, Carter cultivated the image of a moderate, responsible reformer who would safeguard the interests of the hardworking middle class. He hoped to retain the electoral support of traditional Democratic constituencies in the Northeast and Midwest while recapturing southern voters who had embraced Republicanism in their flight from the Great Society's racial reforms. He pledged as president to bring a populist's sensibility to such issues as energy, conservation, health care, welfare, and the plight of the cities.[2]

Carter targeted the urban vote early as a key to winning the 1976 presidential election, and he assiduously courted big-city mayors and interest groups associated with the nation's big cities. Speaking at the annual meeting of the U.S. Conference of Mayors (USCM) on June 29, 1976, he presented a detailed analysis of the plight of urban America that sharply criticized the policies of the Nixon and Ford administrations. As governor of Georgia from 1971 to 1975, Carter maintained, he had experienced the same kind of frustration dealing with hidebound federal bureaucracies in Washington, D.C., that the mayors had felt during those years. He promised his audience a more empathetic and accessible administration, a new creativity in dealing with the difficult problems confronting the cities, and an end to the divisiveness that had characterized the recent Republican presidencies. In short, he promised better leadership. Specifically, he called for an extension of general revenue sharing, full enforcement of civil rights statutes barring residential segregation, additional housing for low-income families and the elderly, and, most important of all, a long-range, comprehensive, and consistent urban policy that would provide an effective and flexible strategy for dealing with the cities' problems. Decrying the defeatism that he said had recently predominated concerning the fate of the cities, Carter told the mayors: "I believe that, working together, we can turn the tide, stop the decay, and set in motion a process of growth that by the end of this century can give us cities worthy of the greatest nation on earth."[3]

In his address to the USCM and repeatedly throughout the campaign, Carter cautioned that the public sector alone could not revivify the cities and that any national campaign conducted on behalf of urban America by the federal, state, and local governments would fail without the participation of private enterprise. The New Partnership he envisioned for the cities required the use of federal funds "for use as a catalyst for private investment." Carter's speeches to Democratic audiences consistently promised a more salubrious climate in Washington, D.C., for city officials but also invoked the need for responsible spending at all levels of government. While pledging the cities "predictable and adequate financial support from the federal government," he shied away from specific references to the cost of programs. Republicans decried Carter's vagueness and complained that the increased funding for cities he was promising could not be provided simply by rooting out waste and inefficiency in government bureaucracies. Even members of Carter's staff acknowledged a tension during the campaign between Democratic mayors, who desperately sought funding increases for new and existing programs to ease the financial burdens on their cities, and the candidate's desire to address pressing urban issues without amassing greater deficits in the federal budget. According to Stuart Eizenstat, who later became President Carter's chief domestic adviser, political pressure from the mayors forced the candidate in 1976 to abandon responsible positions grounded in fiscal soundness. The Democratic candidate grudgingly agreed to endorse a proposal by New York City Mayor Abraham Beame to shift the burden for funding Aid to Families with Dependent Children from the cities to Washington, D.C., for example, despite his reservations about its considerable cost. Regrettably, Carter and his staff agreed, a winning electoral coalition could not be assembled that year without appeasing traditional Democratic constituencies in the cities.[4]

The outcome of the November 2 presidential election substantiated that assessment. Having narrowly defeated Gerald Ford and barely amassed 50 percent of the popular vote, Carter could indeed identify his healthy electoral majorities in the cities as the margin of victory. He received two-to-one or better victory margins in New York City, Boston, Philadelphia, Newark, Baltimore, Cleveland, Chicago, Detroit, Minneapolis, St. Louis, and Oakland. Without the huge electoral majorities he garnered in New York City, Philadelphia, Pittsburgh, Cleveland, Toledo, Milwaukee, St. Louis, and Kansas City, he would not have carried New York, Pennsylvania, Ohio, Wisconsin, and Missouri, which would have deprived him of the necessary electoral votes to win the election. Tom Tatum, the campaign's national director of urban affairs, reported that Carter received 70 percent of the urban vote nationwide, 85 percent of the African American vote, and 72 percent of the Jewish vote (which he characterized as "highly urban"). Moreover, the Democrat had won "solid margins" from southern urban areas. In all, Tatum informed the president in a "detailed debriefing memo" ten days after the election, "the urban elected officials, political leaders, and campaign workers and volunteers clearly did their work well."[5]

Disgruntled with the frugality of the Nixon and Ford presidencies, urban and minority voters cast their ballots overwhelmingly in 1976 for a return to the halcyon days of the Great Society and fully expected the new president to repay them accordingly. Ignoring Carter's history as a moderate, his recurrent criticisms of 1960s liberalism, and the qualifiers he carefully inserted into his campaign rhetoric, they articulated a series of expectations about the more generous aid to the cities expected of the new administration. One week after the election, one hundred mayors assembled in Chicago and sent the president elect an urgent plea for federal action. Warning that many cities faced the kind of fiscal crisis that had nearly bankrupted New York City, they requested a meeting with Carter as soon as possible to make their case for more financial assistance from Washington, D.C. At a December 14 meeting in Atlanta, a delegation from the USCM urged Carter to develop immediately a $20 billion urban investment program that would create thousands of jobs to meet the cities' unemployment problem; he listened sympathetically but postponed specific discussions until after taking office in January. Black Democratic mayors intended to hold Carter to a higher standard than they had held Nixon or Ford, explained Detroit Mayor Coleman Young, "for the simple reason that Jimmy Carter's platform certainly was more responsive to our perception of the needs of the city." Speaking on the television public affairs program *Face the Nation* on December 19, 1976, Mayor Young reported happily that the president elect was giving no signs of reneging on his commitments. "And it's refreshing for me to hear an elected candidate saying the same thing after an election, in terms of the programmatic approach, as he said before," said the mayor.[6]

Desiring a clear and unmistakable signal of the new administration's commitment to the cities, the mayors pressed hard to have one of their own selected as secretary of the Department of Housing and Urban Development (HUD). Mayors Coleman Young of Detroit and Kenneth Gibson of Newark reported having discussed with emissaries from the Carter camp the possibility of being appointed to the post, but they also confirmed that no offer had been tended. Instead, Carter chose Patricia Roberts Harris, a wealthy African American lawyer and veteran civil rights activist. The daughter of a Pullman porter, Harris had worked her way through Howard University, served as the associate director of the American Council on Human Rights, and earned a law degree from George Washington University, where she later taught. President Kennedy had appointed her co-chairperson of the National Women's Committee for Civil Rights, and President Johnson had appointed her ambassador to Luxembourg. After serving briefly as dean of the law school at Howard University, she joined a prestigious Washington, D.C., law firm. Successful, politically savvy, and well connected in the Democratic Party, Harris maintained close ties with the civil rights community (as a member of the National Association for the Advancement of Colored People Legal Defense Fund) and with corporate America (serving on the board of directors at IBM and Chase Manhattan Bank). She had compiled an impressive résumé but could claim no expertise in housing and urban affairs.[7]

Carter's choice of Harris disappointed the mayors, who wondered aloud whether HUD would once again be the forgotten department in the presidential cabinet. "The appointment of Mrs. Harris was made in order to meet the legitimate demands of blacks and women," commented John J. Gunther, chief of staff of the USCM. "However, in meeting these demands, Governor Carter had displayed striking insensitivity to the problems of the cities." Senator William Proxmire (Democrat, Wisconsin), chairman of the Senate Banking, Housing, and Urban Affairs Committee, seconded Gunther's reservations at Harris's confirmation hearings. Recalling that he had registered essentially the same objections at the confirmation hearings of the previous two HUD secretaries, James Lynn and Carla Hills, Proxmire bluntly told Harris: "What troubles me about your nomination is the absence of any really significant experience in housing and urban development." The senator acknowledged that the nominee was likely to be confirmed but insisted that the Senate would be repeating the mistake of approving the appointment of a HUD secretary whose limited knowledge and inexperience would significantly reduce the agency's effectiveness. He compared Harris's nomination to an enthusiastic football fan being chosen to coach the Washington Redskins or the Green Bay Packers.[8] Proxmire told the nominee:

> And yet when the President nominates, as three Presidents now have, three successive persons who are bright and scholarly lawyers with no visible record or experience in housing and urban development to head HUD—an agency with 15,000 employees and a multi-billion dollar budget—and to run a far more complex and important operation than a professional football team, there is nothing but warm and happy applause. And Mrs. Harris, from the rest of this committee and the Senate, that's about what you can expect to get this morning.[9]

Noting that the nominee worked for a distinguished Washington, D.C., law firm and speculating about the cost of the expensive clothing she was wearing that day, Proxmire asked Harris if she knew anything about the poor. "Sir," the indignant nominee retorted, "I am one of them." Other senators, most notably Edward Brooke (Republican, Massachusetts) and John Tower (Republican, Texas), strongly defended the nominee, who subsequently received an overwhelming confirmation vote.[10]

On January 18, 1977, two days before his inauguration, Carter sent Secretary Harris and seven other newly confirmed cabinet members to the USCM's annual mid-winter meeting to offer the mayors additional assurances of his good intentions. Treasury Secretary W. Michael Blumenthal told the mayors, "There is probably no issue that will concern this administration more and concern the President more than the question of jobs and the question of the cities," calling these matters the "top priority" of his department. Representatives of the incoming administration defended the president elect's decision to seek from Congress a $15 billion urban investment program rather than the $20 billion package proposed by the USCM at their Atlanta meeting the previous month. Newark Mayor Kenneth Gibson found less funding for an urban investment effort, along with Carter's recent comments expressing a general preference for tax cuts rather than increased spending on job creation, "extremely disappointing." The mayors likewise squirmed when Joseph A. Califano Jr., the new secretary of Health, Education, and Welfare (HEW), warned that "money does not come out of the sky" and that there "are no panaceas out there." At the close of the conference, several mayors complained about what they had heard from the cabinet secretaries but reiterated their support of the incoming administration. New York City Mayor Abraham Beame lamented the reduced size of the urban stimulus package but remained optimistic that relations would improve between the White House and the nation's city halls. Mayor Paul Soglin of Madison, Wisconsin, expressed considerable skepticism about the new president's intentions but added: "At least Carter is holding out some hope, which Nixon and Ford never did."[11]

After his inauguration, Carter set his sights on restoring order and rationality to a federal government that he saw as having grown unwieldy and unresponsive in recent decades. The failures of distended Washington bureaucracies, he believed, showed clearly in the ineffectual attempts to aid the nation's cities. Federal agencies had repeatedly wasted resources and the programs they had administered achieved few successes because of "jurisdictional uncertainty, duplication of effort, and lack of coordination." As Carter outlined during his campaign, the righting of past wrongs began with the creation of a comprehensive urban policy to chart a clear path for future reform—for developing the "new partnership" that would resuscitate the cities. On March 21, 1977, Carter created the Urban Regional Policy Group (URPG), chaired by HUD Secretary Harris, to develop a national urban policy and asked for a preliminary report from the group by early summer. (In the opening weeks of the new administration, the Treasury Department also formed an Office of Urban Finance, and the Office of Management and Budget [OMB] created an Urban Development Task Force.) The URPG membership included the secretaries of HEW, Treasury, Commerce, Labor, and Transportation, a representative from the Environmental Protective Agency, and several members of the president's domestic policy staff. Carter named Stuart Eizenstat and Jack Watson of his staff to serve as the group's liaison with the White House. From the beginning, jurisdictional disputes between the major domestic agencies, turf wars, and policy wrangles slowed progress to a crawl. According to a HUD official, some members of the cabinet departments had no interest at all in participating; others felt answerable only to their own constituents and not at all to Harris. HEW representatives complained about not understanding their agency's role in the URPG, while staff members from Labor and Transportation claimed to have been assigned too small a voice in the deliberations. Many of the participants feared that Harris would abuse her authority as chair of the group to advance HUD's agenda to the detriment of the other agencies. By the end of the summer, well past the deadline Carter had set for presentation of preliminary findings, Harris confessed that the URPG had nothing to report.[12]

In the absence of substantive action on urban issues by the White House, African American politicians and civil rights leaders protested loudly in the summer of 1977. Not only had the URPG seemingly disappeared into a bureaucratic black hole, they charged, but Carter had done virtually nothing for the cities during his first several months in the presidency. In June, Newark Mayor Kenneth Gibson upbraided the president for attempting to right the national economy "at the expense of the cities, the unemployed, and the poor." Vernon Jordan, the executive director of the National Urban League and one of the most prominent civil rights spokesmen in the nation, publicly lambasted Carter in July for failure to take action in the cities on behalf of minority populations. Speaking at the organization's national meeting with the president in the audience, Jordan said: "The sad fact is that what this Administration has not done . . . far exceeds its list of accomplishments." The Southern Christian Leadership Conference discussed sponsoring another March on Washington if Carter failed to respond soon. Publicly chastised, the president set a September deadline for a URPG report that contained a set of legislative initiatives to be included in his January 1978 State of the Union address. After discussions with domestic policy aides, Harris shifted primary responsibility for mobilizing the URPG from one of her HUD subordinates (Donna Shalala, assistant secretary for policy development and research) to another (Robert C. Embry Jr., assistant secretary for planning and development) and sought more help from Stuart Eizenstat. Infused with a sense of urgency, the group met more frequently in the late summer—but with little more success. When the URPG failed to deliver its recommendations in September, the White House first extended the deadline to mid-October and then to November 1.[13]

Stung by the criticism that his administration had been unsympathetic to the plight of the cities, Carter conducted a surprise visit to New York City's South Bronx on October 6. Leading a phalanx of reporters and television cameramen down Charlotte Street past crumbling tenements, abandoned auto chasses, and weed-covered empty lots, the president toured one of the nation's most infamous slums. Visibly disturbed as he gingerly picked his way through the rubble left by the fires that had denuded much of the area, Carter pledged federal aid to begin the process of rejuvenating the ravaged neighborhood. After returning to Washington, D.C., he instructed the URPG to sketch a proposal for the rehabilitation of the South Bronx that would "serve as a prototype for other blighted urban areas." In the following weeks, representatives from the Departments of HUD, Transportation, Commerce, Labor, HEW, and Interior, as well as the Small Business Administration, flocked to the South Bronx to confer with local officials, ministers, civil rights leaders, and neighborhood activists about strategies for community uplift. The film footage of the ashen-faced president walking through the hellish cityscape remained one of the iconic images of the late 1970s, and his promise of federal aid defused (at least for a few news cycles) the charges of administrative indifference to America's rapidly deteriorating urban cores.[14]

Despite broaching the possibility of additional federal funds for the South Bronx, Carter continued to favor relatively inexpensive proposals that would improve existing urban programs rather than new initiatives that required increased spending in the cities. As they deliberated in the summer and fall of 1977, the members of the URPG received a series of messages from the White House reminding them of the need for fiscal responsibility in the national urban policy they were formulating. In July Bert Lance, director of the OMB, wrote Harris a lengthy letter outlining the severe constraints that would be imposed on HUD's fiscal year 1979 budget. To achieve the president's avowed goal of balancing the federal budget by 1981, Lance explained, the White House was assigning cabinet secretaries strict spending "ceilings" that could under no circumstances be exceeded. The projections for HUD in fiscal year 1979 entailed personnel reductions, minimal increases in housing programs, and an end after September 30, 1977, to the mortgage purchase commitments made under the Emergency Home Purchase Assistance Act of 1974. Through the use of zero-base budgeting techniques, the OMB director added, HUD should eliminate ineffective initiatives and "hold programs to the lowest feasible levels." In the name of greater efficiency, members of the president's domestic policy staff called for streamlining, cost cutting, and administrative reorganization. Carter aide Jack Watson extolled the virtues of improved coordination between federal and local agencies as a means of "[producing] enormously increased benefits for the cities with dollars we already have."[15]

Several prominent members of the Carter administration touted neighborhood activism as the principal means of improving the cities without resorting to huge increases in federal funding. Underscoring the power of local voluntarism to combat the corrosive effects of poverty on the family, which had been an essential component of urban reform thought since the Progressive Era, these liberals rued the broad expansion of federal power engendered by the Great Society but appreciated the decentralization triggered by the War on Poverty's Community Action Program. Secretary Harris expressed a firm commitment to reviving urban neighborhoods, and the Social Gospel roots of the 1970s movement for neighborhood improvement appealed strongly to the religious convictions of the president and his wife, Rosalynn. Already suspicious of the massive, Washington D.C.-centered, liberal reform campaigns launched in the 1960s, Carter approved of small-scale community efforts conducted at the local level, with the federal government only providing guidance and a modicum of financial aid. Within the executive branch, two ardent communitarians in particular reinforced the president's predilections; Marcia Kaptur, a member of the domestic policy staff, and Monsignor Geno Baroni, a HUD assistant secretary, both argued persuasively for neighborhood revitalization as the centerpiece of a Carter urban policy. An urban planner and community organizer in Toledo and Chicago, the Polish-American Kaptur brought to the White House a strong preference for churches, community organizations, and other voluntary associations as the optimal agents of urban reform. A second-generation Italian immigrant and veteran of the civil rights movement, Monsignor Baroni had founded the National Center for Urban Ethnic Affairs to safeguard the interests of the white urban ethnic masses. Both Kaptur and Baroni spoke for working-class whites in inner-city neighborhoods who felt abandoned by the Great Society reform model. To avoid the alienation and divisiveness inevitably generated by the federal bureaucracies administering large-scale programs, Kaptur and Baroni warned, a comprehensive urban plan must avoid the temptation to assign HUD and other federal agencies additional responsibilities and instead assign control to grassroots activists.[16]

Kaptur, Baroni, and their acolytes in the administration defended a place-based as opposed to a people-based orientation in the debate about how best to aid the cities. The supporters of a place-based approach thought that distressed areas in older industrial cities, which had been undermined by deindustrialization, population loss, and the spread of blight, could be salvaged with the infusion of enough federal aid. In their view, the scale of intervention through earlier federal programs such as urban renewal, public housing, and Model Cities had always fallen far short of need. By contrast, those who favored a people-based strategy thought the reclamation of post-industrial cities impossible and instead lobbied for government policies that subsidized the movement of the poor toward the metropolitan periphery in pursuit of the jobs that were relocating to the suburbs. The most effective policy, according to Secretary of Labor Ray Marshall and Secretary of HEW Joseph A. Califano Jr., would include job-retraining programs, improved transportation for inner-city residents who could find no work in their immediate surroundings, and incentives for relocation to the suburbs as an antidote to inner-city deindustrialization. While many Democrats in the White House and on Capitol Hill recognized the government's historical role in promoting decentralization and resisted the call for surrendering core cities to ongoing decline, the people-based arguments of Marshall and Califano remained compelling politically if the Democrats hoped to attract suburban and Sunbelt voters. Moreover, as Califano argued, the fact that few members of Congress hailed from struggling core cities made a place-based urban plan an unlikely winner on Capitol Hill. Carter's preference for enhanced neighborhood involvement, public-private partnerships, generous tax incentives for industry, and government decentralization seemed possibly to be a way out of the people-place conundrum by luring investment capital back into the cities. The president's vision of an urban renaissance, as he made clear to the URPG, depended upon private investment, with the federal government playing a subsidiary role.[17]

Carter struck a blow for private-public partnerships and the targeting of federal funds to the distressed areas of older Rust Belt cities when he signed the Housing and Community Development Act of 1977 on October 12. The legislation identified as its primary goal stemming the population loss and disinvestment plaguing many of the nation's urban cores. The law allocated $12.5 billion for a variety of housing and community development projects, the largest sum of money appropriated for the cities during the Carter presidency, though decidedly less than the $20 billion earlier proposed by the USCM, and extended the Community Development Block Grant (CDBG) program for three more years. A component of the legislation, the Community Reinvestment Act of 1977, sought to end redlining and ensure that blacks received equal consideration for home loans by requiring that federal agencies monitor the lending practices of banks and savings-and-loan associations in low- and moderate-income neighborhoods. To complement the small-scale projects undertaken by the CDBGs, the law created Urban Development Action Grants (UDAGs) that underwrote the kinds of large-scale downtown revitalization originally attempted by the urban redevelopment and urban renewal efforts of the 1950s and 1960s. To overcome one of the major shortcomings of urban renewal, whereby land remained vacant for extended periods of time until developers could be identified, the government would make UDAG awards only after receiving the commitment of private funds. Congress appropriated $400 million annually in UDAG funding for fiscal years 1978, 1979, and 1980, seeking to encourage joint public-private partnerships in cities with the most acute problems. The law stipulated that

75 percent of the $400 million be allocated to cities with populations over 50,000 and the remaining 25 percent to smaller communities. Reflecting Carter's conception of the New Partnership and anticipating the urban plan still being compiled by the URPG, the UDAGs emphasized the use of public funds to "leverage" private investment in the cities.[18]

The formula by which UDAG funds would be allocated, which favored older industrial cities of the Northeast and Midwest, accounted for much of the opposition that surfaced in Congress to the Housing and Community Development Act of 1977. In addition to population and the prevalence of overcrowded housing, the key factors in the formula already in use for the dispensation of CDBGs, Harris argued for a new approach that considered the age of housing, the incidence of poverty, and "growth lag." (The secretary defined "growth lag" as the extent to which a city's population growth rate between 1960 and 1973 fell short of the average population increase of all cities during the period.) In the House of Representatives, Mark Hannaford (Democrat, California) opposed the new formula, arguing that "the taxpayers of the South and West [would], in effect, [be] taxed to support the revitalization of cities such as Newark and Detroit." Senator Jesse Helms (Democrat, North Carolina) contended that the Harris formula would consign 40 percent of UDAG funds to northeastern cities, 9 percent to the West, and 7 percent to the South. He protested: "I see no reason why the rest of the country should maintain a chronic bailout of the Northeast because the political leaders of that area refuse to put their houses in order." Title I of the final bill adopted a dual system—allowing grants to be awarded according to the calculation already in use for CDBGs or according to a second formula that counted population growth, poverty, and the age of housing—enabling HUD to give preference to older industrial cities.[19]

In December 1997 the URPG finally submitted a draft of its urban policy, "Cities and People in Distress," to the White House. Rather than the $5–7 billion price tag the domestic policy staff expected or the $6–10 billion cost predicted by the press, the 111-page document outlined programs requiring an additional $20 billion in annual funding. The product of prolonged bartering among several federal agencies, the plan enumerated programs without designating priorities and stopped well short of articulating an overall approach to urban reform. According to the *New York Times*, Carter dismissed the long, rambling document as nothing more than a "laundry list" of programs and responded to the group: "Don't tell me we'll spend more money all around, then we'll call it an urban policy. Give me something worth funding if you want more money." The next day, he informed aide

James McIntyre to omit any urban initiatives from the 1979 budget then under preparation. Convinced that the URPG could not complete a coherent urban policy in time for inclusion in his January State of the Union address, the president announced that he would postpone sending Congress a special message outlining his urban policy until March 15, 1978. The decision not to recommend additional funding for urban America, along with yet another delay in the announcement of an urban policy, led to more unrest in city halls. "What policy? What action?" groused Boston Mayor Kevin White. "They haven't done anything to date."[20]

The efforts of the URPG having been judged inadequate in the White House, the task of preparing an urban plan fell almost exclusively after December 1977 to HUD and members of the domestic policy staff. On January 20, after the president had delivered his State of the Union address with virtually no mention of urban issues, Eizenstat sent Carter a memorandum commenting at length on the urban policy that he and Harris were submitting under separate cover for the March 15 address. Alluding to the interminable delays over the previous ten months and the complaints about ineffective leadership in the URPG, Eizenstat said that the forthcoming urban policy "is designed to restore Secretary Harris' leadership in this area and provide her with a policy which she can announce publicly." He also noted that he and Harris had differed on several issues and that the vagueness of the resultant policy proposal reflected their inability to resolve those disagreements. Harris favored a policy that addressed primarily the needs of the "most distressed cities," for example, while Eizenstat sought the distribution of federal funding to a much larger number of communities. The HUD secretary also maintained less confidence in the ability of market forces to stimulate urban recovery, while Eizenstat preferred more limits on federal intervention in the cities. Pointing out the preponderance of the "most distressed cities" in the Northeast and Midwest, where only 20 percent of the nation's population lived, Eizenstat argued for a broad-based dispersal of aid to cities as the best strategy politically. "We simply cannot propose an urban policy that writes off the needs of 80 percent of the Nation's population," he argued.[21]

Carter responded to the Harris-Eizenstat draft with a clear statement of what he expected in an urban policy. He indicated that such a policy should have four emphases: no new money, greater attention to neighborhoods, a strong state role, and a strong private sector role. In February and March, HUD, the domestic policy staff, and James T. McIntyre, the new OMB director, continued to revise the draft. On March 23, four days before the rescheduled message to Congress unveiling the urban plan, the president received a detailed memorandum from Harris, Eizenstat, and McIntyre detailing their proposal. The plan generally remained faithful to the four policy emphases dictated by the president, extolling the inclusion of local and state governments along with the private sector in the path-breaking new partnership Carter had proposed more than a year earlier and deviating primarily in the call for a modest infusion of $600 million in new funds for the cities. The president initially balked at four recommendations in the plan—an Urban Development Bank, an extensive public works program, a targeted employment tax credit, and a differential investment tax credit—but relented the next day after meeting with Harris and Eizenstat, who argued convincingly for the political necessity of the measures. With only three days remaining before the formal presentation of the urban plan, however, Carter continued to question the excessive cost necessary for implementation.[22]

On March 24 Hamilton Jordan, the White House chief of staff and one of the president's oldest and closest confidants, wrote Carter a confidential memorandum notable for its frankness and political astuteness. Anticipating the president's reluctance to endorse an urban plan that included additional appropriations, Jordan argued the need for enhanced funding. "While I share your doubt that more federal dollars can increase substantially the quality of life in the American cities," he said, "the political, press and public reactions to your policy will be determined to a large extent by the amount of new money budgeted for it." Jordan predicted that the proposal of an urban plan that allocated only $600 million in new funds, which amounted to approximately one-tenth of 1 percent of the federal budget, would "be the single biggest political mistake we have made since being elected."[23] He sternly warned Carter of the political pitfalls of appearing to shortchange the cities, saying, "Mr. President, I do not see how we can continue to alienate key groups of people who were responsible for your election and still maintain our political base. The groups that make up the urban collation— blacks, Hispanics, labor, Democratic mayors, etc.—have been waiting all year for the 'comprehensive, major program' we promised them. A $600 million program will simply not receive serious political consideration."[24]

Carter finally presented his comprehensive urban plan, "The New Partnership to Conserve America's Communities" to Congress on March 27 and to 250 governors, mayors, and the heads of urban advocacy groups in the East Room of the White House the following day. The plan included a 13-page introduction, a 178-page memorandum that listed forty-three policy recommendations, and 18 pages of letters from federal agency officials explaining their views on the various initiatives. In the message he sent to Congress, the president said, "The urban policy I am announcing today will build a *New Partnership* involving all levels of government, the private sector, and neighborhood and voluntary organizations in a major effort to make America's cities better places in which to live and work." Forsaking the traditional reliance on increased appropriations for housing, transportation, and jobs programs, the president talked about the need for economic development, neighborhood revitalization, and intergovernmental cooperation. Federal aid alone would never suffice, Carter repeated again and again. "From the experience of the urban renewal program of the 1950s," he recounted, "we learned to be skeptical of what Reinhold Niebuhr once called 'the doctrine of salvation through bricks'—the idea that we can bulldoze away our urban problems." The plan included tax incentives and loan guarantees to lure private businesses (including defense contractors) into blighted urban areas, underwrote new Neighborhood Reinvestment Centers, and created a National Development Bank (governed jointly by the HUD, Transportation, and Commerce secretaries) authorized to guarantee investments in inner cities totaling $11 billion through 1981. The New Partnership clearly sought to shift the focus of urban policy away from Washington, D.C., toward a variety of communities scattered across the country.[25]

The announcement of Carter's much-anticipated urban plan elicited for the most part a negative reaction. Some legislators on Capitol Hill commended the New Partnership—for example, Representative Henry Reuss (Democrat, Wisconsin) praised the plan for "sett[ing] in motion a policy process that if sustained holds the promise of halting the deterioration of our urban centers"—but most of the people expressing an interest in urban affairs dismissed the plan as a cautious and severely limited approach that would commit too few federal resources to make a difference in the cities. Their expectations heightened by a full year of waiting, the critics found the proposal profoundly disillusioning in its limited scope. New York City Mayor Edward I. Koch judged the plan's paltry allotments to meet the nation's housing needs inadequate for the Empire State alone. The National Urban League's Vernon Jordan vented his frustration at length, calling the program "disheartening" and a "missed opportunity." The *New York Times* saw the plan as an unfortunate product of confusion, interagency rivalries, and bureaucratic compromises that survived largely because the president had ignored the matter for months while attending to more pressing economic problems and nettlesome foreign policy issues. Reporting that a deeply dissatisfied president had almost scrapped the plan on the very morning that it was scheduled to be announced,

Washington Post columnist David Broder lampooned the dense document as "'10 recommendations supported by 38 strategies' or maybe 10 strategies supported by 38 recommendations, plus 160 suggestions for improving old programs left scattered in five agencies—in short, a smorgasbord." Important policy questions, such as precisely how the National Development Bank would make funds available for urban investment, remained largely unanswered. A consensus quickly developed that the vague plan, which had supposedly been gestating for an entire year, appeared to have been fitted together hurriedly at the eleventh hour to meet an impending deadline.[26]

In the months following the formal introduction of the New Partnership in March, the legislative package attached to Carter's urban plan languished on Capitol Hill. The difficulty encountered by the administration owed to skepticism among liberal Democrats about the limitations placed upon government involvement, the political opposition of legislators on both sides of the aisle who objected to the preference afforded Rust Belt cities, concerns about undertaking additional financial commitments at a time of lingering inflation, and fear of a nascent taxpayers' revolt as presaged by the California electorate's adoption of the Proposition 13 tax limitation initiative. As a result of these political factors, Congress rejected or delayed consideration of virtually all of the bills submitted by HUD during the summer and fall of 1978. The Senate passed an amended version of the countercyclical revenue sharing measure adopted by Congress in 1976 that would have increased aid to cities with severe financial problems, but the House leadership decided not to call for a vote when its opponents threatened a parliamentary slowdown on the last day of the congressional session. Both the House and the Senate held hearings on legislation creating a two-year, $400 million program of grants for the development of urban revitalization programs by the states but took no further action. A three-year, $3 billion public works bill met stiff resistance, especially in the Senate, and the administration concluded that insufficient support for the measure existed to proceed to a vote; the White House similarly declined to press for action on the creation of the National Development Bank, ostensibly the centerpiece of the New Partnership, and opted to forestall consideration until 1979. Of the fifteen bills sponsored in 1978 by the administration in conjunction with the president's urban plan, the Ninety-fifth Congress passed only an urban mass transit provision attached to an omnibus highway bill.[27]

In 1977 the president directed a task force headed by Transportation Secretary Brock Adams to prepare a detailed report on existing federal surface transportation programs (highway networks and urban mass transit) as the first step in forming a comprehensive national program. According to Adams, the task force found a "crazy quilt" of aid programs with no consistent federal-local matching ratios for funding and no coherent philosophy governing the distribution of federal dollars to state and local governments. The secretary suggested the consolidation of a number of highway and mass transit programs as well as the establishment of a uniform federal-state matching grant formula that would be applicable to the vast majority of transportation projects. Based upon the task force's recommendations, the administration sent Congress on January 26, 1978, a transportation bill allocating $47 billion in federal aid for four years that represented an increase of just $472 million over existing levels of funding. The bill also proposed in the name of enhanced efficiency the merger of the Urban Mass Transportation Administration and the Federal Highway Administration within the U.S. Department of Transportation. To the disappointment of environmentalists and mass transit partisans, the measure preserved the Highway Trust Fund through 1983 and diverted none of its funds for public transportation aid. Mayors and others seeking more federal dollars for urban mass transit termed the funding grossly inadequate, but Carter defended the modest sum as a necessary part of his effort to balance the federal budget by fiscal year 1981. The critics also bridled at the fact that, as an additional cost-cutting measure, the legislation sought no new money for urban mass transit before fiscal year 1980. When Adams objected to the funding delay in his testimony before the House Ways and Means Committee and suggested that revenue from a proposed standby gasoline tax be earmarked for mass transit, the White House announced that the secretary had not been speaking on behalf of the administration.[28]

Determined to obtain funding for fiscal years 1978 and 1979, Senator Harrison A. Williams Jr. (Democrat, New Jersey) sponsored a bill to increase urban mass transit authorizations over a five-year period that passed on June 23. Dissatisfied with the Senate's handiwork, the House Public Works and Transportation Subcommittee on Surface Transportation, chaired by James J. Howard (Democrat, New Jersey), conducted hearings on a separate bill that combined highway and mass transit funding on a more generous scale than either the Senate or White House versions. In a September 30 press briefing, OMB Director James T. McIntyre called the House bill "currently the biggest threat to the budget pending in Congress," and he and Adams warned that Carter would veto the measure unless substantial cuts were made. The bill passed by the House authorized $61 billion over four years, more than $10 billion more than the version passed in the Senate. The president objected to the cost of the compromise measure negotiated by House and Senate conferees, which both houses of Congress accepted on October 15, but reluctantly agreed to trade his signature for several votes he needed in the House to pass the administration's energy package.[29]

The Surface Transportation Assistance Act of 1978, which Carter signed into law on November 6, provided $51.4 billion in federal aid for highways and urban mass transit over the next four years. Combining highway, public transportation, and highway safety authorizations in one omnibus measure for the first time, the law allocated $30.6 billion for highways, $13.6 billion for public transit, and $7.2 billion for highway safety. Although the White House succeeded in paring down the amount for the bill favored in the House, the final version of the law cost nearly $5 billion more than the administration had proposed ten months earlier. The law extended the Highway Trust Fund for five years, forestalled the use of Highway Trust Fund dollars for urban mass transit, and initiated a number of reforms in the way that state and local governments obtained federal dollars for transportation improvements. The administration had sought to decrease federal contributions to many projects, but state and local governments actually ended up paying smaller shares in the law's final version. Title III of the bill, the Federal Public Transportation Act of 1978, limited 85 percent of expenditures to municipalities with more than 750,000 population and reserved 15 percent for smaller communities; funds could be used for either capital or operating expenses. The Surface Transportation Assistance Act of 1978 allocated less financial assistance for mass transit than the cities had hoped to receive, a result once again of the president's eye on the federal government's bottom line.[30]

Urban interests also felt shortchanged by another piece of legislation signed by the president on November 6, 1978, after months of contentious bartering with Congress. The Revenue Act of 1978, which provided an $18.7 billion reduction for 4.3 million taxpayers in 1979, bore scant resemblance to the measure introduced by the administration the previous January. Having signed the bill without comment, Carter later complained that Congress had revised the rate schedules so dramatically that most Americans would pay more taxes in 1979 than they had in 1978. The law reduced the number of taxpayers who qualified for home ownership tax subsidies, thereby limiting the attractiveness of the suburbs for inner-city residents, but at the same time significantly increased benefits for businesses seeking to relocate by cutting corporate income tax rates and liberalizing the Investment Tax Credit. By permitting larger capital gains deductions, both in the allowable exclusion rates and in the new exemption for taxpayers fifty-five years and

older, the law privileged suburban areas over core cities. Economists predicted that the Investment Tax Credits' comparatively generous provisions
for business expansion in suburbia would prove more advantageous than the
less substantial extension of credit to rehabilitate buildings in use for more
than twenty years (most commonly in inner cities) permitted by the new law.
Because of the flight of industry in recent decades, claimed defenders of
inner cities, the provisions in the Revenue Act of 1978 lowering corporate
taxation would inevitably enhance metropolitan decentralization.[31]

Carter signed two measures at the end of the 1978 congressional session
that redounded to the benefit of the cities by providing federal aid for public
works and job training, in both instances accepting compromises to ensure
passage that left the bills' supporters only partially satisfied. In the first case,
the president angered many African American members of Congress with his
tepid support for the Humphrey-Hawkins full employment bill, which guaranteed "last resort" jobs to the hard-core unemployed, and with his insistence that the law contain an anti-inflation provision. A disastrous meeting
that included Carter, Vice President Walter Mondale, and the congressional
black caucus dissolved acrimoniously after a few angry legislators stormed
out in protest and some of those who remained began shouting at each other.
At a later peacekeeping session with those African American leaders, the
president vowed to increase administrative support for the Humphrey-
Hawkins bill in Congress. The final version of the law signed by Carter on
October 27 contained the original unemployment reduction provisions but
also set as a national goal reducing the inflation rate to 3 percent by 1983 and
eliminating it altogether by 1988. Many black leaders charged that the
administration's tardy and halfhearted advocacy, along with its demand of a
timeline for eradicating inflation, watered down what could have been more
effective unemployment legislation. In the second case, the president signed
a four-year extension of the Comprehensive Employment Training Act (CETA),
a job training and youth employment program originally passed in 1973,
after a series of compromises in Congress that eliminated approximately
100,000 public service jobs and held down wages. Again, liberal critics
charged, the administration should have provided more potent leadership for
critically important legislation to the unemployed youth of the inner cities.[32]

By the winter of 1978–1979, with inflation having risen to 9 percent and
Carter more determined than ever to balance the federal budget by the time
of his reelection campaign in 1980, the prospects for increased funding in
urban America seemed to be worsening. Alfred Kahn, the chairman of the
Council on Wage and Price Stability and the administration's designated

chief inflation fighter, warned local officials that "the prescribed medicine is restraint" for the struggling cities. Liberal Democrats in Congress continued to resist the president's attempts to cut domestic spending, an eventuality that seemed even likelier after Carter promised NATO allies that the United States would increase its contribution by an estimated $15 billion in fiscal year 1980. After the November 1978 election the Democrats retained control of both houses of Congress (58 to 42 in the Senate and 277 to 158 in the House), but the losses suffered by several influential liberals and moderates in both parties meant that the Ninety-sixth Congress would likely be more conservative and more partisan than its predecessor. Losses by longtime liberal stalwarts such as Dick Clark (Democrat, Iowa), Floyd Haskell (Democrat, Colorado), Thomas McIntyre (Democrat, New Hampshire), and Edward Brooke (Republican, Massachusetts), coupled with the reelection of Jesse Helms (Republican, North Carolina) and Strom Thurmond (Republican, South Carolina) and the election of such conservative Republicans as Thad Cochran of Mississippi and Roger Jepson of Iowa, promised a rightward shift in the Senate. The president's call for additional fiscal retrenchment, which he deemed necessary for both political and economic reasons, antagonized indispensable Democratic constituencies and drove cabinet secretaries to speak out against impending budget cuts in 1979. Labor Secretary Ray Marshall argued that cutbacks in job programs would only transfer people to the welfare rolls, and HUD Secretary Harris sent a blistering memorandum to the OMB saying that "she could not live with proposed reductions in her department."[33]

Carter's anti-inflation measures especially displeased African American legislators, mayors, and civil rights leaders whose expectations had been repeatedly dashed by what they had expected to be a beneficent Democratic administration. Instead, they believed, conditions in the inner-city ghettos had worsened during the first two years of a presidency that seemed more committed to budget balancing than to rewarding the needy voters who had been crucial in the 1976 victory over the Republicans. Unemployment among black teenagers, most of whom lived in urban cores, stood at an alarming 35.5 percent by the end of February 1979. Frustrated African Americans vandalized and looted stores in Washington, D.C., and Baltimore during the winter of 1978–1979 when they arrived for temporary work shoveling snow only to find that the few jobs advertised had already been distributed; many local officials attributed such examples of civil unrest to the failed policies of the uncaring Carter administration. As Louis Martin, the president's assistant for minority affairs, lamented: "They do not buy the linkage between the battle on inflation and the need to cut job programs."[34]

By the summer of 1979, a sense of crisis gripped the nation as the economy continued to worsen. Despite having identified the battle against inflation as his top priority, Carter had been unable to arrest the rise in prices throughout his term in office; inflation averaged 11 percent that year. At the same time, a burgeoning energy crisis resulted from sharp increases in the price of oil engineered by the Organization of Petroleum Exporting Countries, which raised prices four times in five months that year. Facing the prospects of much higher gas prices and possible fuel shortages, truckers rioted in Levittown, Pennsylvania; the police reported 100 injuries and more than 170 arrests. The governor of North Carolina mobilized the National Guard to protect truckers from mobs trying to halt the delivery of gasoline. According to public opinion polls, the American people's growing disquietude in the summer of 1979 stemmed as much from their dissatisfaction with the president as from bad economic news. The results of a June *New York Times*–CBS News poll confirmed Carter's plummeting popularity, giving him only a 33 percent approval rating. For eleven days in July, the president retreated to Camp David for a series of talks with government, business, labor, and religious leaders. On July 15 Carter delivered an address on the "crisis of the American spirit" to a national television audience. In what came to be known as his "malaise" speech, the president spoke extensively about the worrisome energy situation, exhorted Americans to remain confident, and called for shared sacrifice during troubled times. He said nothing about worsening conditions in the cities. Three days later, the president announced that he had asked all of his cabinet secretaries to submit "pro forma resignations" and had decided to accept five of them—from Treasury's J. Michael Blumenthal, HEW's Joseph A. Califano Jr., Energy's James Schlesinger, Transportation's Brock Adams, and HUD's Patricia Roberts Harris. (Harris immediately replaced Califano at HEW.) The sudden purge of the five cabinet members created the impression of a panicky administration fraying under the weight of economic exigency.[35]

Local officials hoped that the cabinet shakeup would afford them a stronger voice in the administration, for Carter replaced Harris and Adams with two respected big-city mayors: Maurice "Moon" Landrieu of New Orleans, a former president of the USCM, at HUD, and Neil Goldschmidt of Portland at Transportation. The leadership change promised to be especially striking at HUD, where the suave, congenial Landrieu followed the irascible Harris. From the outset of her tumultuous tenure as secretary, Harris had sought to shake up the department with new policies and personnel shifts. Her confrontational style and controversial appointments aroused enough

criticism in the department that she quickly received a warning memorandum from the White House that questioned her decision making. HUD Assistant Secretary Donna Shalala admiringly called Harris "tough as nails,"
but others in the agency less enamored of the secretary's abrasive style derisively referred to her as "the queen." Rumors persisted throughout Harris's
tenure that her volubility worked against HUD's interests in the White
House.[36] HUD Assistant Secretary Robert C. Embry Jr. remembered that
"Secretary Harris was a very strong and outspoken person, and she didn't
mind taking on the President or taking on the Office of Management and
Budget and making her case vigorously and forcefully. And she didn't back
down to anybody."[37]

Harris acted as a staunch advocate for the black urban poor, and civil
rights leaders valued her advocacy in the cabinet for their constituents. HUD
received modest increases in funding for low-income housing during the first
two years of the Carter administration but absorbed substantial budget reductions after 1978. Although never publicly questioning the fiscal limitations the White House imposed upon HUD's operation and always stopping
short of disagreeing openly with the president's penchant for fiscal restraint,
the secretary chafed privately at the restrictive policies the administration
adopted for the cities. Harris agreed with the president that public-private
partnerships held great promise for the rebuilding of American cities, but,
unlike Carter, she found much to laud in the urban renewal efforts of the
1950s and 1960s. She shared Carter's reverence for neighborhoods but regretted the paucity of funds made available for traditional low-income housing programs, which she continued to believe benefited the urban poor. With
one eye on the federal ledger, Carter shied away from the expense of providing adequate shelter to the urban masses and, in the view of HUD staffers,
discussed the need for more housing only as an antidote to unemployment in
the construction trades. Harris identified housing as "the single most important physical component of national urban policy."[38]

When Moon Landrieu became HUD secretary on September 24, 1979,
Congress was considering a series of amendments to existing housing legislation that would determine the level of federal support for UDAGs and several
other housing programs. The White House lobbied for the concentration of
funds in the new UDAG program as the most effective use of scarce resources, but many liberal Democrats resisted further cuts in subsidies for
older initiatives. Carter justified an increase in UDAG appropriations by noting that the amendments allowed the expenditure of more money in pockets
of poverty, especially distressed areas within otherwise economically healthy

cities—a change vigorously opposed by the representatives of Rust Belt cities who feared the loss of funds to thriving Sunbelt cities that possessed a relatively small number of isolated distressed neighborhoods. On December 21 the president signed the Housing and Community Development Amendments of 1979, a measure that Senator Harrison A. Williams Jr. called one "of the smallest efforts in assisted housing in recent years." The bill increased UDAG authorizations from $400 million to $675 million and allowed up to 20 percent of these funds to be spent in pockets of poverty within communities not designated as distressed, the Rust Belt legislators having acquiesced because of the huge increase in appropriations for the program. As well, the administration and the Congress cooperated to reduce housing programs for the needy. The amendments authorized $1.14 billion in federal aid for low-income housing assistance in fiscal year 1980—$1.06 billion for Section 8 vouchers, $195 million for public housing construction, and $50 million for the modernization of existing units—a sum expected to underwrite an estimated 250,000 housing units, down from the 360,000 units completed in 1979. In addition, Congress failed in 1979 to pass Carter's one-year, $1 billion infusion of federal funds to areas combating high unemployment. The emergency antirecession bill passed in the Senate by early August but stalled in the House, where two committee chairmen questioned the reliability of the unemployment statistics provided by local governments.[39]

Landrieu inherited administrative support for another housing measure making its way through Congress in the late summer of 1979, a substantial revision of the 1968 Fair Housing Act submitted by Democratic Representatives Don Edwards of California and Robert Drinan of Massachusetts. As chairman of the House Judiciary Committee's Subcommittee on Civil Rights Oversight, Edwards had become convinced that the compromises required to pass the 1968 law had critically impaired the federal government's ability to eradicate housing discrimination. Secretary Harris, who strongly advocated a more aggressive role for the federal government in rooting out residential segregation, had called the 1968 law "less than half a loaf" and charged that it "identified the problems but supplied only the most pallid of solutions." As early as 1971, the California congressman began holding hearings that laid bare the lack of enforcement provisions in the legislation and made the quest for fair housing an expensive and time-consuming enterprise with little chance of success. Contrary to the expectations shared by many legislators and civil rights advocates, the Edwards subcommittee found that the incidence of racial segregation in metropolitan America had increased since 1968. The Edwards bill authorized HUD to consider charges of housing discrimination brought by individuals or to initiate investigations on its own. Going far beyond the limits established in the 1968 law, which only allowed HUD to attempt to settle disputes between aggrieved persons and alleged violators, the measure empowered HUD to appoint administrative law judges who could issue cease-and-desist orders, levy fines up to $10,000, and assign compensation to the victims of discrimination; the Justice Department could also bring lawsuits in federal court when administrative remedies failed. The sweeping provisions of the bill prohibited discriminatory practices in a host of real estate practices, including rentals, sales, mortgages, repair and rehabilitation loans, and insurance. Despite the backing of the White House, HUD, and the Justice Department, the Edwards bill never reached the floor of the Senate or the House in 1979.[40]

In 1980 the administration continued to support fair housing legislation but failed to engineer passage of the first major civil rights legislation in more than a decade. In his January 21, 1980, State of the Union address to Congress, Carter called the fair housing bill "the most critical civil rights legislation before the Congress in years." Despite the president's hortatory rhetoric, the White House's tardy lobbying efforts and assignment of higher priority to other bills under consideration at that time led African Americans to characterize the administration's support as lukewarm. In the face of fierce lobbying by the National Association of Realtors and the Society of Real Estate Appraisers, Edwards and his House colleagues agreed to a series of accommodations with opponents that reduced the role played by liberal HUD personnel, allowed the Justice Department to appoint administrative law judges instead, and provided for the appeal of desegregation decisions to federal district courts. Passed by the House on June 12, the Edwards bill expired in the Senate, where Republicans and conservative Democrats conspired to derail all civil rights legislation. Countering the efforts at compromise by Democrats Robert C. Byrd of West Virginia and Edward M. Kennedy of Massachusetts, Republicans Strom Thurmond of South Carolina and Orrin Hatch of Utah insisted on two crucial changes that the bill's supporters found unacceptable: First, the conservative Republicans demanded that HUD not only be required to demonstrate that discrimination had occurred but also to prove intent on the part of alleged violators—a virtual impossibility in any legal proceeding. Second, they insisted on jury trials rather than administrative hearings for defendants, which made convictions highly unlikely in many southern communities. Hatch and Thurmond conducted a filibuster on the Senate floor that forestalled consideration of the bill when a cloture vote of 54–43 on December 9 fell six votes short of the necessary

three-fifths majority. The failure of the Ninety-sixth Congress to pass a fair
housing bill, which Carter as a lame-duck president presumably would have
signed, made future prospects for such legislation exceedingly bleak after the
November 1980 electoral triumph of Ronald Reagan and the Republicans.[41]

In 1980 the Carter administration issued two reports that assessed the
status and future prospects of the comprehensive urban policy presented two
years earlier. The first document, a response to the congressional mandate
that the executive branch report to the public every two years on the development of a national urban growth policy, drew heavily from the official
1978 report that had been tied directly to the New Partnership proposal. One
wag in 1980 called *The President's National Urban Policy Report* a "limp
and defensive reprise" of its predecessor, a fair assessment of a study with
limited goals and objectives. Indeed, the report reiterated the limitations
caused by "scarce funds," "tight budget constraints," and "current anti-
inflation efforts," all the while praising improved cooperation between government agencies, the development of better methods for measuring the effects of government action, guideline revision, and, most of all, prudent
spending in lean times. The report's final section, "An Urban Policy for the
1980s," prescribed continued cost-cutting, minimal federal activism, and enhanced public-private cooperation. Concerned that the update of the
nation's urban policy would generate negative headlines in the months before the presidential election, Carter offered little comment when the administration released the lackluster report with little fanfare after the close of the
summer's political conventions.[42]

The second document resulted from the work of a blue-ribbon commission appointed by the president on October 24, 1979, and chaired by William J.
McGill, the former president of Columbia University, to script a national
agenda for the 1980s. One of the ten reports prepared by the commission,
"Urban America in the Eighties: Perspectives and Prospects," recounted
Washington, D.C.'s history in urban development and ventured a series of
recommendations about the federal government's role during the coming
decade. Taking account of government's crucial role in the inexorable decentralization that had been ongoing in metropolitan America for decades, the
report judged the human and financial losses suffered by core cities unrecoverable. "Industrial cities such as Boston, Cleveland, and Detroit stand as
brick-and-mortar snapshots of a bygone era," concluded McGill and his colleagues. Instead of wasting resources on quixotic reform efforts, they suggested, HUD and other federal agencies should recognize the inevitability of
population loss in the cities and strive to ameliorate the undesirable effects of

demographic change on the affected cities and suburbs. In the recurring debate over whether government policy should primarily serve people or places, the commission came down forcefully for aiding the former. Misguided attempts to save hollowed-out urban cores could in fact be counterproductive by diminishing opportunities for geographically mobile workers.[43] The report concluded: "The federal government can best assure the well-being of the nation's people and the vitality of the communities in which they live by striving to create and maintain a vibrant national economy characterized by an attractive investment climate that is conducive to high rates of economic productivity and growth and defined by low rates of inflation, unemployment, and dependency."[44]

At first blush, such sentiments seemingly endorsed the New Partnership's emphasis on the public stimulation of private investment and the Carter administration's economic policies, especially the fight against inflation, as the centerpieces of urban policy. At the same time, however, the McGill Commission rejected the need for a comprehensive national urban policy at all. "There are no 'national urban problems,'" the report stated, "only an endless variety of local ones." The federal government could be most useful to urban residents by attending to changes in the tax code, income redistribution programs, and other financial nostrums designed to revitalize the national economy—and then to help people vacate the dying cities for more inviting locations on the urban periphery. The report offered a bleak forecast for urban America in the 1980s and provided a fitting coda to the administration's four years of caution, circumspection, and frugality.[45]

By the end of the Carter presidency, the optimism pervading urban America after the 1976 election seemed a dim memory. The URPG's halting attempts to formulate a comprehensive urban plan dissolved in bureaucratic inertia and agency infighting, leaving HUD and the White House domestic policy staff to salvage what they could from the effort. The policy announced tardily in March 1978—which amounted generally to a defeat for the aggressive ideas trumpeted by Harris and a victory for Carter, Eizenstat, and the OMB budget-balancers—cast the federal government in a supporting role and thrust private enterprise center stage. Congress eviscerated the program over the next several months, burying most of the bills in committees and voting down those measures that came to the floor. The centerpiece of Carter's New Partnership ended up being the UDAG program, which had been adopted as part of the Housing and Community Development Act of 1977 while the administration was still struggling to articulate an overall scheme for aiding the cities. UDAGs perfectly embodied the spirit of the New Partnership by combining two important goals of the administration—targeting federal support to the worst areas of the most distressed cities, thereby addressing the president's genuine compassion for poor families in the slums, and providing discretionary grants to builders so that private enterprise rather than government took the lead in urban revitalization. In what the president considered a vast improvement over the old urban renewal approach, which he felt relied much too heavily on a recurring infusion of federal dollars, HUD would "sweeten" development deals struck by city halls and profit-minded developers.[46]

A study conducted in 1979 of the first 241 UDAG grants awarded to 214 cities found that 42 percent went to cities in the Northeast, 30 percent to the Midwest, and 28 percent to the South and West. The federal government's contribution of $487 million generated $2.86 billion in private matching funds. As intended, federal spending primarily stimulated the construction of industrial and commercial structures instead of housing—$1.36 billion for industrial projects, $935 million for commercial projects, $291 million for new hotels, and $276 million for residential projects. The use of federal dollars in that fashion proved controversial, as some liberals rued the administration's preference for downtown real-estate development rather than neighborhood refurbishment and low-income housing. Remembering the vehement criticisms voiced years earlier of urban renewal, they objected to the displacement of low-income families and questioned the assertion that inner-city residents benefited from the development bonanza. Skeptics suggested that private investment would have taken place with or without federal funds, nodding knowingly when a Chicago developer who received a million-dollar UDAG subsidy to build high-rise apartments remarked: "The project would have gone ahead anyway . . . The actions grant was a lovely surprise—manna from heaven."[47]

Critics railed against HUD for forsaking low-income housing in favor of UDAG grants that provided $12 million for downtown redevelopment in Toledo, Ohio, and $10.5 million for a shopping center, housing project, and hotel complex in St. Louis; the volume of disapprobation rose during the 1980 campaign when the administration awarded $12.8 million in grants for department store and office construction in downtown Detroit and $6.4 million for luxury housing and a shopping complex in the Baltimore Inner Harbor. Such expenditures led urban policy expert Norman J. Glickman to say, "The overwhelming portion of the UDAG subsidy is not helping the poor but the [Donald] Trumps of the world." UDAG's undeniable success at stimulating downtown investment pleased others, however, who seconded Carter's belief that the federal government should only act as a catalyst for private development. James Rouse, the leading builder of urban festival market-places in the 1970s and 1980s, termed UDAGs "the most remarkable pro-gram dealing with the American city I have seen in my time." During the twelve years of the program's existence from 1978 to 1989, HUD awarded $4.6 billion in UDAG grants to approximately 3,000 development projects in more than 1,200 communities.[48]

The UDAG program sparked downtown redevelopment, particularly in the declining central business districts of older Rust Belt cities, but an in-crease in available office space and high-priced hotel rooms left many serious urban problems unanswered. Central cities of the Northeast and Midwest fared marginally better under Carter than they had under the Nixon and Ford administrations, both of which spread federal funds more widely to suburbs and small cities. The New Partnership's recipe of targeting, leverag-ing, public-private cooperation, and reduced government funding produced few immediate benefits for the cities, however. During the Carter years, urban unemployment and poverty rates inched upward, local budgetary cut-backs meant fewer dollars for the delivery of essential services, population loss to the suburbs continued apace, and the production of low-income hous-ing provided by the federal government slowed. The president's refusal to embrace a Keynesian approach to reviving the economy by uncinching the federal purse strings reverberated strongly among the most vulnerable in-habitants of the inner cities. African Americans who had initially backed the president grew restive as the administration seemed impervious to the dete-riorating conditions in the inner cities, and the worst racial violence since the combustible 1960s erupted in the summer of 1980. Overshadowing distur-bances in Boston, Wichita, and Chattanooga, a three-day conflagration in Miami's Liberty City neighborhood left 18 dead and more than 400 injured. By the time that police restored order and arrested 850 looters, arsonists, and snipers in Liberty City, property damage reached an estimated $100 million. However much he deplored the racial violence of 1980, Carter continued to believe that the cities would benefit most from a reduction of government. Carter never wavered from his conviction that private investment and neigh-borhood activism represented the future of urban America. Remaining faith-ful to the ideals of the New Partnership, he pointed the nation in a direction that policy makers in Washington, D.C., followed for the next generation.[49]

8

RONALD REAGAN'S NEW FEDERALISM

The 1980s indelibly bore the imprint of President Ronald Reagan, who won election in 1980 and reelection four years later on the strength of a few basic ideas that he presented skillfully to the American electorate. The "Great Communicator," as the laudatory media dubbed the Republican president, drove home in his campaign speeches and other public orations a series of seminal principles that amounted to religious articles of faith—the effect of big government had been deleterious and must be reversed; the United States needed a strong military to protect the nation's interests against the godless forces of international communism; and steep tax cuts would restore economic risk taking, invigorate the economy, and simultaneously eliminate budget deficits. Juxtaposed against a series of economic setbacks and foreign-policy disasters in the 1970s that left many Americans unsure of the nation's future prospects, Reagan's unshakable adherence to those core beliefs and his unwavering optimism proved to be reassuring tonics in troubled times. But while the Reagan years saw the creation of considerable new wealth and the accelerated enrichment of the wealthiest Americans, uneven economic growth during the decade resulted in increasing inequality between the haves and the have-nots. The number of Americans living below the poverty line increased dramatically, the incidence of infant mortality rose sharply, the evaporation of manufacturing jobs left blue-collar workers with a diminished standard of living, and the shrinking middle class suffered from net losses in income. The striking new inequality of the 1980s showed most clearly in the nation's big cities, where harried municipal officials battled not only worsening fiscal problems but also a new combination of urban calamities, including alarming rates of homelessness, the increase in murders and other violent crimes associated with a crack cocaine epidemic, and a frightening public health threat caused by acquired immune deficiency syndrome (AIDS). While Reagan chirped that "it's morning again in America," others observed that life in the nation's big cities had become more perilous than ever and wondered what yet another Republican president's promise of a New Federalism portended for urban America.[1]

In fact, the eight years of the Reagan presidency meant substantial reductions in federal aid and fiscal retrenchment for municipal governments. Administration spokesmen hailed market solutions for urban problems, invoking longstanding Republican criticisms of earlier federal programs aimed at the cities and praising the curative potential of supply-side economics. In Reagan's formulation, substantial tax cuts and prudent federal spending would create the healthy economic climate that would allow rising financial tides to lift all boats. The drive for privatization meant fewer dollars for public housing and the authorization of housing vouchers. As its principal response to the deterioration of the old industrial cities, the administration proposed the creation of enterprise zones that would harness the power of the private sector (with minimal government assistance) to stimulate investment in desiccated neighborhoods. To the chagrin of big-city mayors and other defenders of city interests, the administration repeatedly singled out such urban programs as low-income housing and mass transit for reduction or elimination as part of its quest for fiscal responsibility. Indeed, no federal agency absorbed more funding losses during the Reagan years than the Department of Housing and Urban Development (HUD), which saw its budget reduced by more than 50 percent from 1980 to 1988. The disclosure of a series of scandals at HUD, whereby businessmen and government officials enriched themselves at the expense of the urban poor, further undermined morale in the beleaguered agency. The administration's indifference to HUD programs and the degree to which greed overrode the public interest seemed to confirm not only a moral laxity born of the unchecked pursuit of profit but also the administration's pervasive uninterest in urban problems—what some Reagan critics charged constituted a wholesale abandonment of the cities.[2]

Beginning during the 1980 presidential campaign and continuing throughout his tenure in the White House, Reagan consistently made economic policy the centerpiece of his domestic agenda. Relentless criticism of the Carter administration's economic record became a winning strategy as the recession of the late 1970s lingered along with double-digit inflation and a 7.8 percent unemployment rate in May 1980. "I cannot and will not stand by while inflation and joblessness destroy the dignity of our people," a tearful Reagan told a television audience at the outset of the campaign. He relentlessly exploited Carter's inability to revive the economy, rhetorically asking the voters, "Are you better off than you were four years ago?" The key to addressing urban problems revolved around putting the nation's economic house in order, Reagan maintained, for "there is no better federal program than an expanding economy." Rather than repeating the flawed Democratic practice of pouring money indiscriminately into cities that failed to adjust to changing economic realities, his administration would strive to stabilize the unsettled economy, stimulate investment, and encourage cities to make the changes necessary to compete vigorously in a dynamic marketplace.[3]

As part of his pledge to cut frivolous federal spending, Reagan vowed to ease the tax burden on the hardworking middle class and the aspiring entrepreneurial class while demanding greater accountability of the unworthy poor. America's excessively progressive tax structure punished the successful and deprived them of incentives to work harder, said the candidate, while generously rewarding the indigent for their shiftlessness. In his stump speeches, he repeatedly charged that the nation's big cities teemed with hucksters feigning poverty to collect undeserved government handouts. Reagan often recounted the story of a Chicago "welfare queen" who drove a Cadillac and bilked the government for $150,000 by using eighty aliases, thirty different addresses, and a dozen Social Security cards. Journalists confirmed that no such person existed, but Reagan used the apocryphal story artfully to stigmatize the poor and build popular support for economic policies that would address the moral shortcomings in big-city slums and ghettos while reducing unnecessary social welfare spending. America had fought a war on poverty for nearly twenty years, he quipped, "and poverty won."[4]

In addition to a daring economic policy, Reagan promised a New Federalism that would vanquish the damaging dependency of state and local governments on federal largesse. As far back as 1975, articulating his philosophy as the rising star of the Republican Party, Reagan had said: "We can and must *reverse* the flow of power to Washington; not simply slow it or paper over the problem." In large measure, his call for decentralization owed to an aversion to big government at any level and a belief that Great Society excesses in particular had grossly inflated the federal bureaucracy. In Reagan's view, the federal usurpation of power began in the 1960s when state governments shirked their responsibilities to aid the cities. Governors and state leaders had acknowledged their obligations in the ensuing two decades, he adduced, and no excuse remained for the urban imperialism of ravenous Washington, D.C., agencies. The devolution of federal authority would empower city halls and private businesses while investing decision making in the hands of the authorities best suited to assess local conditions and allocate resources accordingly. Decentralization would enhance productivity as well as innovation, opportunity as well as accountability.[5] The administration argued:

> The virtues of Federalism historically have been diversity, creativity, and heterogeneity. With States and localities as innovators, the opportunities for experimentation are multiplied, while the consequences of failure are contained. States and localities are likely to imitate one another's successes and learn from one another's mistakes. They are likely to tailor programs to local circumstances and to profit from the ingenuity of citizens stirred to action by the prospect of having some influence on the outcome.[6]

After defeating incumbent Jimmy Carter in 1980, Reagan claimed a popular mandate to reduce the size of the federal government and return power to the states and cities. He won with 51 percent of the popular vote, to Carter's 41 percent and Independent John Anderson's 7 percent, and by a landslide in the electoral college, 489 to 49. Republicans also increased their numbers in the Senate from forty-one to fifty-three and gained thirty-three seats in the House, although the Democrats retained control of the lower chamber. With the exception of a speech in the South Bronx, where he accused Carter of reneging on promises to help declining urban neighborhoods, Reagan paid scant attention to inner cities during the 1980 campaign. The new president came into office with no debts to big-city mayors, black or Latino leaders, trade unions, or other interest groups that had loyally backed previous Democratic administrations. On the other hand, according to analyses of voting results, he enjoyed great support among the so-called Reagan Democrats (one-time blue-collar Democrats living in older suburbs who had voted Republican in recent decades). The outcome of the election indeed seemed to offer fertile ground for implementation of the New Federalism.[7]

In a March 2, 1981, speech to the Congressional City Conference of the National League of Cities, Reagan outlined the priorities of the new administration and explained how those goals could benefit the nation's cities. He acknowledged that reductions in federal funding for the cities would be forthcoming, arguing that the economic crisis demanded an end to business-as-usual budgetary practices. The expansion of power in Washington, D.C., had accounted for the shocking decline of the nation's cities in recent decades, he contended, by creating a maze of government regulations that inhibited entrepreneurialism and creativity. At one time exemplary paragons of enterprise and industry, America's cities had become subservient to an insatiable federal bureaucracy hungry for power. "Instead of assistance," Reagan charged, "the

Federal Government is giving orders." Worse, he went on, federal agencies gave orders without providing the necessary resources and thereby saddled municipalities with a series of unfunded mandates that exacerbated local funding shortfalls. Government had indeed been the problem, not the solution, and a curtailment of federal involvement constituted a necessary first step on the road to fiscal recovery.[8]

To oversee the reduction of federal influence in the cities, Reagan chose Samuel R. Pierce Jr. as secretary of HUD. A successful Wall Street lawyer who had long been active in the Republican Party, Pierce, an African American, had served as a New York state judge, undersecretary of Labor, and general counsel of the U.S. Department of the Treasury. Testifying before the Senate Banking Committee on January 13, 1981, Pierce agreed with the president that reducing inflation should be the new administration's first priority. The nominee pledged to reduce expenditures in his bailiwick to help with the critical task of budget balancing. "Therefore," he said, "I intend to quickly but carefully review the programs at HUD with a view toward cutting unnecessary costs." During Senate confirmation hearings nine days later, William Proxmire (Democrat, Wisconsin) discussed Pierce's dearth of experience with public housing and lack of knowledge about HUD and its programs but readily agreed with his cohorts that the nominee merited approval. Senators across the political spectrum, ranging from conservative Republican Strom Thurmond of South Carolina to liberal Democrat Alan Cranston of California, applauded the nominee's promise to cut federal spending and reduce wasteful government regulation.[9] Senator Daniel Patrick Moynihan (Democrat, New York) lavished extraordinary praise on Pierce, saying, "May I just begin with the observation that if there were more men such as he in the country, Presidents would have an easier time filling their Cabinets. There are few men in our time who have served with such distinction as Judge Pierce has in such a broad range of response [sic] positions in public and private life . . . He is in every respect a singular man."[10]

The membership of the Senate confirmed Pierce unanimously (98 to 0, with two members not voting) and promptly did the same for Reagan's nominee for secretary of the Department of Transportation (DOT), Drew Lewis. A wealthy businessman who had unsuccessfully run for governor of Pennsylvania in 1971, Lewis affirmed the Reagan plan for cost cutting in government and promised greater economy in DOT. In his senate confirmation hearings, he identified as a principal goal the gradual elimination of operating subsidies for urban mass transit. Like Pierce, Lewis received hardy endorsements from a varied group of senators and a unanimous confirmation vote.[11]

Having had the membership of his cabinet confirmed in short order, Reagan devoted the early months of his presidency to getting his economic plan through Congress. Based upon the Kemp-Roth version of supply-side economics favored by many conservative Republicans, the president's initiative called for steep tax cuts for employers and investors whose use of additional capital would lead to greater entrepreneurial activity; the resultant economic growth would raise personal income for businesses and businessmen, who would in turn pay more taxes. Thus, in theory at least, supply-side economics would result in economic growth and government's collection of more revenue despite lower tax rates. Reagan sought a 30 percent reduction of federal income taxes over three years, lower capital gains taxes, estate and gift tax reductions, and increased depreciation allowances on business investments. Along with this generous incentive package for business, his budget proposal sought to trim government expenditures by eliminating social welfare programs, transfer responsibility for other social programs to the states, reduce entitlement payments, and shrink the federal bureaucracy. The Economic Recovery and Tax Act of 1981 passed by Congress in July gave Reagan much, if not all, of what he sought—most notably tax cuts totaling 25 percent over three years (5 percent the first year and 10 percent each of the next two years) that benefited wealthy individuals and businesses disproportionately. The administration provided the Defense Department and military contractors with increased outlays while cutting funding for many domestic programs—including the abolition of the Comprehensive Employment and Training Act (CETA) jobs program and significant reductions in Social Security, Medicare, public housing, veterans' hospitals, college student loans, and other social programs. Budget Director David Stockman commented approvingly that the landmark 1981 tax law had laid the foundation for a "minimalist government . . . a spare and stingy creature which offered even-handed public justice but no more."[12]

The first budget submitted by the Reagan White House exacted an especially heavy toll on social welfare programs and the cities. The Omnibus Budget Reconciliation Act of 1981, which finalized federal expenditures for fiscal year 1982, harmed the lower-income and working-class residents of large cities in particular because of cuts in Aid to Families with Dependent Children (AFDC), food stamps, and Medicaid, as well as the elimination of CETA. The HUD budget allocated $18.2 billion for assisted housing (public housing and Section 8 vouchers for approximately 153,000 units), down from $30.9 billion (an estimated 260,000 units) in the last budget prepared by the Carter administration; it also increased from 25 percent to 30 percent the portion of their gross incomes that tenants of subsidized housing had to pay over the next five years. The fiscal year 1982 budget reduced federal funding for mass transit programs, which had been increasing steadily for several years, by 31 percent. The administration attempted to terminate the Urban Development Action Grant (UDAG) program—a curious action given that UDAGs had been designed specifically to stimulate private investment in blighted inner-city neighborhoods, a crucial element of the Reagan urban plan—but Congress authorized $500 million to retain the popular initiative for at least another year. According to a study conducted by Princeton University's Urban and Regional Research Center, the budget cuts implemented during the first year of the Reagan administration negatively affected urban governments more than suburban and rural governments. Some of the smaller communities escaped federal funding cuts entirely, and a few rural and suburban communities actually received federal aid increases. Moreover, older suburbs situated in the inner rings of metropolitan regions, which by the late twentieth century were experiencing many of the same severe problems plaguing distressed core cities, suffered deeper budget cuts than the less-densely populated, wealthier suburbs on the periphery.[13]

The stringent cuts in low-income housing and other federal programs affecting inner-city residents unsurprisingly provoked a sharp reaction from urban America. Newark Mayor Kenneth Gibson wrote Reagan to protest the drastic cuts in public housing funds and implored the president not to sacrifice the disadvantaged in the name of fiscal accountability. Richard Hatcher, the mayor of Gary, Indiana, and president of the U.S. Conference of Mayors (USCM), told the press that the administration's reduction of federal aid to the cities threatened to leave gaping holes in the nation's "social safety net" through which many of the "truly needy" would fall. U.S. Representative Cardiss Collins of Chicago, chairwoman of the House Government Operations Subcommittee on Manpower and Housing, objected strenuously to a change in the rent contribution formula that would consider the value of food stamps as income. She contended that the projected increase in rent for public housing tenants, as specified in the Omnibus Budget Reconciliation Act of 1981, would surely lead to more homelessness in urban America. U.S. Representative Jack Kemp (Republican, New York), a vocal proponent of supply-side economics who argued for the necessity of steep cuts in federal spending, nonetheless warned the president against the proposed reduction of funding for the nation's public transportation systems. Kemp argued that decades of neglect and disinvestment had left the mass transit networks of older cities with defective and unsafe infrastructures (rolling stock, track, signals, and the like) that had to be salvaged at all costs. He illustrated the seriousness of the crisis by pointing to the struggles of New York City's Metropolitan Transportation Authority to accommodate six million riders daily, including 85 percent of the commuters who worked in the Manhattan business district. Mass transit's worsening effectiveness in New York City, which served one-third of the nation's mass transit customers, was already causing declines in the city's productivity and commerce and inducing employers to relocate factories and corporate headquarters in other locations. "Perhaps unlike anywhere else," Kemp argued, "these mass transit systems are the link to survival."[14]

Undeterred by the criticism, Reagan continued to introduce in Congress the various measures comprising the New Federalism. He proposed assigning full funding responsibility to the states for AFDC and food stamps in exchange for the federal government assuming the cost for Medicaid, but mayors and governors balked at the exchange believing that state and local governments would be saddled with much steeper bills in the future. In his January 26, 1982, State of the Union address, the president announced his intention to submit legislation that would create enterprise zones in the depressed areas of the nation's cities. The administration adapted its enterprise zone proposal broadly from the "free trade zones" created in Great Britain under Prime Minister Margaret Thatcher. Offered as the antithesis of the Great Society's Model Cities program of the 1960s, which relied heavily on government subsidies and centralized planning, enterprise zones aimed to remove government influence and allow unfettered business to pursue profit freely. An enterprise zone bill introduced in the House in 1981 by Jack Kemp and Robert Garcia (Democrat, New York) and in the Senate by John Chafee (Republican, Rhode Island) had attracted some interest but fallen far short of passage. Under the auspices of the 1982 proposal, states and municipalities could apply to designate blighted urban areas as enterprise zones, and the federal government would provide a broad array of economic and tax incentives to attract new business investment to revitalize inner cities and small towns. "Some will say our mission is to save free enterprise," Reagan told Congress. "Well, I say we must *free* enterprise so that together we can save America."[15]

Desperate to attract funding of any sort to declining neighborhoods in their cities, many mayors and city officials endorsed enterprise zones. Republican Mayor George Voinovich of Cleveland and Democratic Mayor William Schaefer of Baltimore co-chaired a committee of mayors that lobbied on Capitol Hill for passage of the Reagan administration's legislation in 1982.

The major urban interest groups, the USCM and the National League of Cities, embraced the idea as well. "We've supported the concept of enterprise zones, long before President Reagan came into office," noted John Gunther of the USCM. The legislation stalled in Congress, however, as skeptics raised a series of questions about the potential viability of enterprise zones. Economists expressed doubt that tax incentives alone could lure businesses back into blighted neighborhoods, especially as the lingering recession of the early 1980s restricted credit and inhibited the growth of small businesses; they also noted that enterprise zone schemes ignored the high crime rates, poor transportation, limited labor supply, and other problems endemic to impoverished urban areas. Liberal critics of enterprise zones called the administration's bill a poor alternative to necessary legislation that would improve housing, education, and infrastructure. "They think it's a way of buying out from some really rough problems on the cheap," commented M. Carl Holman of the National Urban Coalition. The Urban Institute's George Peterson conceded that an enterprise zone could be useful for financially strapped cities, "but it in no way constitutes a national urban policy."[16]

On March 23, 1982, in a message to Congress transmitting the enterprise zone legislation, Reagan provided the details about the program he had broadly sketched out in the State of the Union address in January. The law authorized the HUD secretary to designate up to twenty-five zones in each of three years to apply for the package of federal incentives, with the number of awards dependent upon the quality of the applications. Tax concessions offered to businesses that chose to locate in the enterprise zones included a capital investment credit, an income tax credit to employers for payroll paid to employees working in the zones, a 50 percent credit to employers on wages paid to disadvantaged workers, and the suspension of capital gains taxes. As well, the White House recommended that state and local governments reduce taxes in the enterprise zones, modify zoning, permit, and building code requirements, and sponsor job training programs. The administration identified enterprise zones as its principal urban initiative and urged the passage of the necessary legislation as an innovative example of how private enterprise could spearhead inner-city redevelopment. Congress declined to pass the bill in 1982.[17]

In April 1982 the administration released the final report of the President's Commission on Housing, which had been constituted on June 16, 1981. The composition of the thirty-member commission, which included twenty-nine Republicans, three women, and two minorities, no doubt heavily influenced its analysis. The group included nineteen members from the banking, real estate, and construction industries, seven attorneys, and no representatives from the construction trades or consumer rights organizations. William McKenna, vice chairman of the Federal Home Loan Bank of California, chaired the commission, and former HUD secretary Carla Hills served as vice chairman. In its interim report released in October 1981, the commission had included a statement of principles that endorsed fiscal responsibility, encouraged the deregulation of housing markets, urged reliance on the private sector, and promoted an "enlightened federalism" with minimal government intervention in housing markets. The 277-page final report issued in April 1982 identified its primary recommendation as the reshaping of federal housing policies and programs to conform to the administration's economic philosophy. The report affirmed that "the genius of the market economy, freed of the distortions forced by government housing policies and regulations that swung erratically from loving to hostile, can provide for housing far better than Federal programs." In particular, the commission's findings unambiguously endorsed the administration's efforts to reduce the federal government's involvement in the provision of low-income housing. "The attack on federal housing" would proceed on several fronts, including the termination of existing construction programs; the demolition, conversion, and sale of public housing projects; the extraction of larger portions of tenants' income as the price for obtaining subsidized housing; and the creation of a new housing allowance program to replace government-operated units. Positing that excessive cost and not the substandard quality of lodging constituted the biggest housing hurdle confronting poor families in the cities, the commission advocated the use of vouchers as the federal government's primary program. Delicately sidestepping the sensitive issue of open housing, the final report briefly endorsed the maximum freedom of housing choice but also obliquely encouraged neighborhood stability.[18]

Three months after the release of the report of the President's Commission on Housing, the administration followed with the publication of the biennial national urban policy assessment mandated by the Housing and Urban Development Act of 1970. Long before HUD issued the *President's National Urban Policy Report* on July 8, 1982, a description of its contents had already generated considerable controversy. HUD Secretary Pierce had assigned the preparation of the report to Emanuel S. Savas, the agency's assistant secretary of Policy Development and Research. Before joining the Reagan administration, Savas had been a professor of public management at Columbia University's Graduate School of Business and director of its Center for Government Studies, as well as a first deputy city administrator in New York City under Mayor John V. Lindsay. In those positions in academia and municipal government, he had propounded a larger role for free enterprise and a diminished government presence in urban affairs. In the provision of low-income housing, that meant the use of vouchers to augment house-holders' purchasing power and to discourage reliance upon government aid. In the case of urban mass transit, it meant divesting government of owner-ship and turning existing public transportation networks over to private pur-veyors; government's role would be restricted to distributing vouchers to rid-ers rather than providing grants to service providers. Savas and other policy analysts in the Reagan administration believed that government had grown exponentially to serve the self-interests of politicians, bureaucrats, social workers and their clients, and the liberal intelligentsia. Because of the insidi-ous web of self-interest and entitlements spun since the 1960s, they con-cluded, government monopolies such as the post office, public housing au-thorities, the police, and social service agencies inevitably wasted money and delivered services inefficiently.[19]

With Pierce expressing no interest in determining a set of urban policy principles, Savas enjoyed great latitude chairing the Urban Policy Working Group that labored from June to December 1981 to prepare the biennial re-port. Under his guidance, the group composed a draft that forcefully extolled the virtues of laissez-faire economics and condemned federal activism as counterproductive. Still, not entirely pleased with the finished product, Savas embargoed the draft report in December and submitted his own version in May 1982. After HUD administrators made a few cosmetic changes suggested by the working group, Pierce submitted the second draft on June 18, 1982, to the president at a meeting of the Cabinet Council on Human Resources. Ob-jecting to the report's strident tone, harsh criticism of local governments, and refusal to recognize any contributions to urban life made historically by the federal government, the Cabinet Council rejected Savas's handiwork.[20]

Two days later, quoting extensively from the repudiated document, the *New York Times* reported that the White House had found the preliminary HUD study exceedingly ideological in its denunciation of past federal urban policies. The newspaper quoted the draft as saying that "excessive dependence of city governments and city dwellers on the federal govern-ment" had resulted in the loss "of local control and . . . influence over their destinies." Another excerpt charged that city officials had been reduced from "bold leaders of self-reliant cities to wily stalkers of federal funds." The leak of the document's intemperate language became a public rela-tions disaster for the administration, and Reagan and Pierce quickly dis-owned what they dismissed as the preliminary work of midlevel policy makers. The president reassured the public that "the federal government will not abandon its partnership with the nation's cities."[21]

White House efforts at damage control notwithstanding, big-city mayors recoiled at what they saw as yet another attack on urban America. San Francisco Mayor Diane Feinstein called the report "unbelievable," and Richmond, Virginia, Mayor Henry L. Marsh III termed the document a "declaration of war." Given that the news leak came while the USCM was holding its annual meeting in Minneapolis, Mayor Lee Alexander of Syracuse, New York, commented that "the timing almost seems to draw a battle line between mayors of the cities and the White House." Detroit Mayor Coleman Young bitterly lashed out at the Reagan administration, blaming many of the cities' problems on the federal government's mismanagement of the economy and other shortsighted policies.[22] Charles Royer, the mayor of Seattle and president elect of the National League of Cities, said of the urban policy draft: "It is a blueprint for surrendering America's cities. With this document, the federal government admits it is incapable of winning the battle for the cities and announces its intention to go AWOL. It is ironic that so much effort by so many creative minds has been expended to rationalize this desertion."[23]

Under pressure to submit the final report to Congress in July, Pierce ordered the Savas draft rewritten again. On July 8 HUD submitted yet another version to the president, who forwarded the report to Congress without his signature. Despite some changes in the language, the final report essentially reflected the analysis and recommendations made by Savas—including assertions that past federal policies had played an important role in triggering urban decline. In many instances, the final report simply replaced incendiary language with more moderate phraseology that conveyed essentially the same meaning.[24] For example, the phrase "from bold leaders of self-reliant cities to wily stalkers of federal funds" became "Increasingly, state and local officials and their constituents looked to Washington for leadership and the resources to deal with nearly every problem, however narrow its scope or intractable its cause. More often than not, the federal program did little more than demonstrate concern about an age-old condition and offer the illusion of progress."[25]

In a cover letter attached to the report, Pierce refrained from making derogatory comments about the federal government but reiterated the major arguments that had become the heart of the Reagan administration's urban policy. He emphasized the need for economic growth, alluded to the importance of greater decentralization of government, called for an expanded role for private initiative, and specifically touted enterprise zones as the principal means of creating jobs and resuscitating blighted neighborhoods. *The President's Urban Policy Report of 1982*, with its unambiguous call for enterprise zones, housing vouchers, and a reduced federal presence in the cities, still bore the clear imprint of Savas and other ideologues at HUD who sought a sharp break from earlier agency policies and practices. The report forcefully argued that the future of American cities depended upon the success of Reagan economic policies and the creation of a New Federalism.[26]

The final urban policy report, supposedly a more carefully written and less volatile document than the draft leaked to the press earlier, elicited an equally unfavorable reaction from mayors and urban spokesmen. New York City Mayor Edward Koch called the New Federalism "a sham and a shame." John Gunther, executive director of the USCM, ridiculed the idea that private industry could be counted upon to contribute financially to the provision of municipal services. He said: "Private people do not come in to build streets, sidewalks, sewers, water lines—that's something government does. And if government doesn't do it, the private sector will go some place that the government will."[27] Ferd Harrison, the mayor of Scotland Neck, North Carolina, and the president of the National League of Cities, said angrily that the organization

> *rejects* the notion that the federal government grants-in-aid to cities have contributed to the decline of cities . . . *rejects* the notion that the federal government does not have a future role to play in assisting cities . . . *rejects* the premise that the federal government should now disengage from all assistance to cities, leaving local communities to the vicissitudes of general economic forces.[28]

Neither the housing commission report, which came after forty months of contraction in the housing industry, the highest unemployment rate among construction workers since the 1930s, and continued decline in real-estate prices, nor the biennial urban policy report offered policy makers much guidance about how to deal with the worsening housing crisis. To aid the housing industry specifically and to stimulate the sluggish national economy generally, legislators in both houses of Congress introduced housing bills that spring. After Republicans rejected the measures submitted by Senator Donald Riegle (Democrat, Michigan) and Congressman Henry Gonzalez (Democrat, Texas) as too costly, discussion increasingly concentrated on an amendment to an urgent supplemental appropriations bill submitted by Senator Richard Lugar (Republican, Indiana) that allocated $5 billion in subsidies over five years for low- and middle-income families building new homes. Presenting the measure as an emergency jobs bill that would address the worsening unemployment rate and provide an immediate benefit to the moribund housing industry, Lugar responded to charges of fiscal irresponsibility by pointing to the expected increase in tax revenues generated by enhanced home ownership. A loyal supporter of the administration and passionate defender of supply-side economics, the Indiana senator went to great lengths to deny that his bill deviated from the fiscal circumspection espoused by the Reagan presidency. He lauded the "extraordinary potential of this legislation to put people back to work without creating a precedent for other legislation which many of us would oppose as truly expensive on a net basis."[29]

The White House rejected all the emergency housing bills proposed in 1982, even the least objectionable version authored by the conservative Lugar. Testifying in the House, HUD Secretary Pierce endorsed a bill offered by Representative J. William Stanton (Republican, Ohio) that proposed instead a reduction in funding for new and existing housing programs. Budget Director David Stockman sent a letter to the Senate explaining in detail the administration's opposition to the Lugar bill and warned of a presidential veto if the measure passed Congress. Lugar and Senator Jake Garn (Republican, Utah) met privately with Reagan on June 22, shortly after the bill had passed in the Senate by an impressive 69 to 23 margin, to argue the critical need for emergency housing legislation. The next day, unmoved by the arguments of the two influential Republican senators, Reagan vetoed the bill. "We cannot justify singling out one industry for special relief," said the president in his veto message. "The recession and high interest rates have created hardship and unemployment for farmers, small businesses, the thrift industry, automobile manufacturers and dealers and many others." Congress failed to override the veto but passed a modified bill the following month. Once again, Reagan vetoed the measure, and, once again, Congress fell short of the necessary votes to override. On July 18, 1982, the president signed the third version of the supplemental appropriations bill, absent the Lugar housing amendment, agreeing to an additional $5.4 billion in expenditures and $5.8 billion in rescissions for the 1983 fiscal year. (Reagan had originally requested $4.5 billion in additional appropriations and $7.7 billion in rescissions.) Despite the extreme economic hardship and the pleas of loyal administration allies on Capitol Hill such as Richard Lugar and Jake Garn, Reagan could not be convinced to meet the housing crisis with increased federal funding.[30]

The president did, however, support new legislation that congressional session designed to increase profits for savings and loan associations (S&Ls) and other "thrift institutions" that were earning low rates of return on home mortgages. On October 15, 1982, Reagan signed the Garn–St. Germain Act, which deregulated the thrift industry and encouraged high-stakes investments in what had been a low-risk, carefully supervised industry. The new law lowered the standards for opening S&Ls and virtually eliminated government oversight by the Federal Home Loan Bank Board, thereby encouraging rampant speculation ostensibly to stimulate housing construction and create jobs. Unrestrained speculators bought up locally owned S&Ls and made a series of reckless investments that the Federal Savings and Loan Insurance Corporation insured on behalf of the federal government. In the short run, the appearance of sprawling housing developments, suburban malls, downtown hotels, convention centers, and festival marketplaces seemed to vindicate deregulation, but the construction boom proved to be short-lived. The extent of faulty investment and fraud became clear only after Reagan left office, but taxpayers ultimately faced the prospect of covering losses with a bailout estimated to cost $500 billion over the coming decades. By the early 1990s, despite the riches accrued by private developers and S&L owners, inadequate housing continued to be a problem for moderate- and lower-income families.[31]

In 1983, despite the concerted opposition of the administration, Congress passed legislation that provided new authorizations for housing programs for the first time since 1980. The Housing and Urban-Rural Recovery Act of 1983 provided new funding for development programs, reduced rent levels for public housing tenants, and empowered the federal government to build new low-income rental housing for the first time since Reagan's election. As the Senate and the House considered slightly different versions of the bill during the spring and summer months of 1983, the president called the legislation a "major budget buster" and countered with a budget for fiscal year 1984 that cut funds sharply for subsidized housing and proposed instead an extensive program of cash vouchers for low-income families. Reagan called for families in subsidized housing to pay 30 percent of their income for rent, the elimination of the Section 8 program, a 50 percent reduction in funding for UDAGs, and vouchers for all subsidized housing constructed in fiscal year 1984, except for 10,000 units for the elderly and handicapped. Especially alarming to advocates of low-income housing, Reagan continued to seek deeper and deeper cuts in HUD budgets. Cushing Dolbeare, president of the National Low Income Housing Coalition, pointed out that the administration had

slashed allocations for public housing from $30.2 billion in 1981 to $8.65 billion in 1983 to a projected $515 million in 1984. "You don't have to have a lot
of money," rejoined HUD Secretary Pierce. "You need to spend it better."[32]

Although a broad bipartisan coalition in Congress supported the $17.6
billion housing authorization measure in 1983, Reagan's threat of a veto and
promise to cut federal aid to housing significantly created a legislative logjam
through the summer and autumn months. Congressman Fernand St. Germain (Democrat, Rhode Island), chairman of the House Banking, Finance,
and Urban Affairs Committee, finally ended the standoff by presenting the
White House with a "take it or leave it" legislative package that combined
the housing bill with a measure increasing the U.S. contribution to the International Monetary Fund (IMF) by $8.4 billion that the president desperately
wanted. The threat to defeat the IMF authorization bill proved persuasive
enough that Reagan dispatched Budget Director David Stockman and Treasury Secretary Donald T. Regan to negotiate with St. Germain and Senator
Jake Garn. Both houses of Congress approved the resultant compromise, and
the president signed the $15.6 billion bill on November 30. The Housing and
Urban-Rural Recovery Act of 1983 authorized $9.9 billion for subsidized
housing in fiscal year 1984 as opposed to the $515 million originally suggested
by the White House. Whereas the administration had sought no funds for
new public housing construction, the law allocated $1.3 billion for 7,500 new
units in cities and 2,500 units for Native American reservations. The law authorized a demonstration project for 15,000 housing vouchers—Reagan had
requested 80,000—and increased the allocations for housing assistance to
the elderly and handicapped from 10,000 to 14,000. The measure also saved
the UDAG program for three more years, providing $440 million for fiscal
years 1984, 1985, and 1986. In all, the law slowed the administration's drive
to abolish federal housing subsidies but failed to halt it altogether.[33]

For the next three years, as Congress failed to provide additional authorization legislation but managed to pass a series of temporary funding extensions, shrunken federal housing programs struggled along on shoestring
budgets and endured the administration's persistent attempts to cut spending and decentralize operations. In 1985 Reagan sought a moratorium on all
federal housing program expenditures but finally signed an appropriations
bill that permitted the construction of a token amount of new low-income
units. Similarly, Congress rejected the president's proposals to eliminate several community development programs but reduced funding significantly.
UDAGs and Community Development Block Grants (CDBGs) absorbed sizable funding cuts, for example, and Congress agreed to postpone until fiscal

year 1987 the administration's plan to cease the distribution of general revenue sharing funds to approximately 39,000 municipal governments. Reagan's call in 1985 for the creation of enterprise zones failed on Capitol Hill for
the fourth consecutive year, as did the attempt to expand the year-old demonstration program for housing vouchers.[34]

In January 1986, for the first time during the Reagan administration, the
White House announced that HUD would defer spending for the balance of
the fiscal year on housing and community development programs authorized
during the previous congressional session. The agency intended to cancel appropriations for the CDBG and UDAG programs, both of which the president
was rumored to have singled out for termination. Administration officials are
"trying to respond and reduce the federal deficit," noted HUD Deputy Assistant Secretary DuBois Gilliam. "It is as simple as that. These are the areas
that have been selected." Defenders of urban interests on Capitol Hill
quickly registered strong opposition to the administration's unprecedented
action. Canceling the UDAG program in the middle of an award cycle would
be catastrophic for those communities that had invested large amounts of
time and money in the preparation of applications, noted Republican Senator John Heinz of Pennsylvania. Congressman Carroll Hubbard Jr. (Democrat, Kentucky), chairman of the House Committee on Banking, Finance,
and Urban Affairs, warned that the proposed deferrals and rescissions would
especially harm the indigent, homeless, and elderly beneficiaries of federal
housing assistance. Senator Daniel Patrick Moynihan (Democrat, New York)
protested vigorously, arguing that "by slashing federal assistance under the
CDBG program, together with the termination of UDAG funding and the
proposed rescission of General Revenue Sharing funds, implies the Federal
Government is pulling the rug out from under our mayors, county executives, and town supervisors." Congressional opposition succeeded, at least
temporarily, in preventing the administration from refusing to authorize
housing funds allocated by Congress.[35]

While battling with Congress over deferrals and rescissions, the administration argued its case for reduced federal funding for housing in the 1986
national urban policy report. Like its 1982 and 1984 precursors, the 1986 report emphasized the importance of sustained economic growth, fiscal restraint, low inflation, public-private partnerships, and steady decentralization leading to increased empowerment for the cities. Having implemented
the policies and practices of the New Federalism for the previous five years,
claimed the report, the administration had achieved remarkable results in
attaining stability and renewing prosperity in urban America. The report

applauded the remarkable urban rejuvenation that had recently been oc-
curring in such cities as Philadelphia, Syracuse, and St. Louis and boasted:
"The impact of the Administration's urban policy is that in all regions of the
Nation, many cities are growing faster, urban decline is being reversed, and
slow-growth local economies are being revitalized." No longer relying passively on federal aid for redevelopment resources, claimed HUD officials,
municipal governments had learned how to deliver services more efficiently,
enforce regulations more effectively, and attract private sector investment
to compensate for lost federal funding. The report underscored the importance of self-sufficiency not only for cities but also for poor individuals living in depressed neighborhoods (especially single parents and the chronically indigent) who had become dependent upon government assistance.
HUD Secretary Pierce praised the report, criticizing only its failure to emphasize enough the success of the president's drug abuse initiative. Otherwise, he strongly supported the message that "on the whole cities are in
much better shape than before."[36]

By 1986 the Reagan administration had indeed dealt a serious blow to
the federal government's aid program for cities generally and reduced the
flow of housing funds specifically. Housing programs suffered deeper cuts
after 1981 than any other part of the federal budget, funding levels having
been slashed by roughly two-thirds from fiscal years 1981 through 1987.
Housing starts for all low-income housing programs (public housing, Section 8 construction and rehabilitation, Section 202 housing for the elderly
and handicapped, and Section 235 homeownership) fell from 183,000 units
in 1980, to 119,000 units in 1983, to 42,000 units in 1984, and to 28,000 units
in 1985. Outlays for CDBGs declined from $3.7 billion in 1981, to $3.5 billion in
1985, and to a proposed $3.1 billion for 1986; funds for UDAGs plummeted
from $675 million in fiscal year 1981 to $316 million in fiscal year 1986. The
sums awarded local housing authorities by the federal government for operating expenses, entirely inadequate from the beginning, increased from $1.1
billion in 1981 to $1.6 billion in 1984 but then dropped sharply to $1.2 billion
in 1985 and $1.0 billion in 1986. Reflecting the cuts in programmatic spend-
ing, HUD also suffered a 21 percent cut in the number of permanent full-
time staff between 1981 and 1986—including a 38 percent reduction in the
Washington, D.C., headquarters. Persistent cuts in programs and personnel
left many HUD employees convinced that decision making in the agency's
leadership, which spoke incessantly about the need for greater economy, revolved simply around the need to meet goals in budget reduction.[37]

Housing partisans who hoped for an end to the systematic emasculation of HUD and a renewed federal commitment to the cities became more optimistic after the results of the 1986 elections rearranged the political calculus on Capitol Hill. The Democrats won control of the Senate for the first time since 1980—they gained eight seats and held a comfortable 55 to 45 majority—and the party added five seats in the House to increase their majority to 253 to 182. With the knowledgeable and aggressive William Proxmire (Democrat, Wisconsin) ensconced as the new chairman of the Senate Banking Committee and Alan Cranston (Democrat, California) as the chairman of the Senate Banking Committee's Housing Subcommittee, the prospects for obtaining substantive housing legislation appeared even better—especially after the passage in 1987 of a bill to provide emergency aid to the staggering number of homeless in America's cities. The transient nature of the homeless population made the extent of the problem difficult to determine precisely, but estimates of the number targeted by the legislation ranged from 300,000 to 3 million. Reporting that nonprofit organizations operated 96 percent of homeless shelters, HUD argued that the private sector rather than government should take the lead in providing temporary housing. Reagan initially objected to the legislation, citing its excessive cost and "duplicative programs," but bowed to the overwhelming margins by which it passed in the Senate (65 to 8) and the House (301 to 115) and signed the Stewart B. McKinney Homeless Assistance Act on July 22, 1987. (The law was named after Republican Congressman McKinney of Connecticut, an ardent champion of aiding the homeless who had died earlier that year of complications due to AIDS.) The law, which authorized $443 million for fiscal year 1987 and $616 million for fiscal year 1988, created twenty-one programs supervised by seven different federal agencies that provided housing, food, and health care to the homeless. Critics called the measure an expensive welfare program that failed to reduce homelessness, and service providers noted the inadequacy of the resources provided to meet the growing need. Still, given the administration's record on social welfare provision, housing reformers saw passage of the McKinney Act as a hopeful sign.[38]

The administration continued to resist omnibus housing legislation, however, and the president threatened to veto any bill that included new programs and cost more than $15 billion (Reagan had indicated that $14 billion would be the most he could accept). The Office of Management and Budget balked at the creation of the Nehemiah Homeownership program, which provided grants to nonprofit organizations to assist moderate-income families in becoming homeowners of newly built or rehabilitated housing in depressed urban areas. It also balked at more extensive lead-based paint abatement requirements, among other instances of "wasteful spending." The fate of an omnibus housing bill remained uncertain as the first session of the 100th Congress adjourned in December 1987.[39]

On February 5, 1988, after months of wrangling with Congress, Reagan signed the Housing and Community Development Act of 1987. He thanked Republican Senators Jake Garn of Utah, Pete Domenici of New Mexico, Bill Armstrong of Colorado, and Phil Gramm of Texas, whom he termed the "four horsemen" of financial responsibility, for holding the spending line and transforming a "budget buster that would have reversed hard-won housing policy reforms into a rational, cost-effective bill that is fiscally responsible." He especially applauded the law's permanent authorization of the housing voucher program, which would serve as the cornerstone of the administration's public/private partnerships, as well as the elimination of "ineffective programs" such as the Solar Energy Bank, Rental Housing Development Grants, and Section 235 subsidies. The president also lambasted several regrettable elements of the compromise bill, most notably the price tag of $15 billion during fiscal year 1988 and $15.3 billion during fiscal year 1989 for housing and community development (less than the $16 billion measure passed by the House but more than the $14 billion ceiling the president had established earlier). He criticized as well the retention of the Nehemiah Homeownership program and the restrictions placed upon landlords and owners of government-assisted housing.[40]

The Housing and Community Development Act of 1987 likewise pioneered in establishing the means by which tenants could purchase the public housing projects in which they lived, an idea that the administration had been promulgating for several years. Reagan had become enamored of the idea after watching the attempts of the Margaret Thatcher government in Great Britain to privatize much of that nation's public housing stock in the early 1980s. "It's time that all public housing residents have the opportunity of homeownership," the president commented in 1985, and Congressman Jack Kemp quickly became an ardent advocate for the idea on Capitol Hill. In 1986 Congress failed to pass the Urban Homestead Act, introduced by Kemp, Congressman Walter Fauntroy (Democrat, District of Columbia), and Congressman Richard Armey (Republican, Texas), but the President's Commission on Privatization adopted its broad outlines the following year in the discussion over the housing authorization bill. "Whatever the flaws in the Kemp approach," wrote a White House aide to the president's chief of staff, Donald Regan, "the basic idea is sound, low cost, and helps address the 'compassion' issue." The Housing and Community Development Act of 1987 provided training and technical support for public housing residents to form new resident management corporations that would assume the responsibility of operating the projects. After successfully managing the projects for at least three years, the corporations could receive financial assistance from HUD to purchase the housing. The corporations could then continue to serve as landlords or sell units to low-income families. Taking ownership of their own housing would empower public housing residents, enthused Kemp and his allies, and also allow them to become entrepreneurs as well.[41]

Finally, the Housing and Community Development Act of 1987 established a Fair Housing Initiative program, whereby HUD could provide financial aid to government agencies or private entities working to end housing discrimination. The law authorized the federal government to spend $5 million in each of fiscal years 1988 and 1989 to promote the enforcement of fair housing legislation and to educate the public concerning the rights and responsibilities under those statutes. Reagan endorsed the fair housing provision when he signed the law, noting that families and individuals still confronted bigotry when attempting to buy or rent homes, and resolutely announced that racism would no longer be tolerated. The president praised HUD Secretary Pierce, whom he called "one of the unsung heroes of our Administration," for his "good sense and commitment" in leading the ongoing fight against discriminatory real-estate practices.[42]

The inclusion of the fair housing initiative in the 1987 housing bill failed to mollify civil rights leaders and other fair housing advocates, who remained critical of the president for his indifference to their cause. "Nowhere has HUD's performance in the 1980s been as disappointing as in the field of fair housing," former HUD secretary Robert C. Weaver commented in 1985. Nor did the critics perceive Pierce, the lone African American in the Reagan cabinet, as having been much of an advocate for antidiscriminatory action in housing. In fact, critics characterized racism at HUD under Pierce's leadership as "ongoing, pervasive and rampant." According to charges leveled by an organization called Blacks in Government, the HUD secretary tolerated such abuses against minority staff in his bailiwick as unfair transfers, threats of firings, and exclusion from decision making. An April 1, 1983, article in the *Wall Street Journal* by Timothy Schellhardt, "HUD Chief Pierce Gets Reputation for Reclusiveness, Lack of Interest," reported widespread dissatisfaction with the secretary's performance among African American members of the agency and among civil rights leaders. While offering examples of the secretary's inaccessibility, lack of knowledge about housing and community development, and powerlessness in the higher councils of the Reagan administration,

Schellhardt described Pierce's indifference to the plight of the urban poor
and isolation from the African American community. The article also recounted how Representative Henry Gonzalez, chairman of the House Banking Subcommittee on Housing, had characterized Pierce as a "Stepin Fetchit"
for his unbending loyalty to the administration's policy of reducing aid to
public housing. Impatient constituent groups, who had long referred to
Pierce as "Silent Sam" for his laconic administrative style, began calling him
"the dud at HUD." Black leaders especially criticized the secretary for failing
to propose a new fair housing bill despite repeatedly promising to produce a
new measure to improve the ineffective 1968 civil rights law.[43]

In a variety of ways, HUD under Pierce's leadership refrained from
using the existing tools to maximize compliance with fair housing statutes. In
1975, in an effort to encourage nondiscriminatory real estate practices, HUD
and the National Association of Realtors jointly developed Voluntary Affirmative Marketing Agreements, but later undermined this effort during the
Reagan years by creating Community Housing Resources Boards (CHRBs)
as the principal mechanism for enforcement. The boards proved ineffectual
for a number of reasons—they could not publicize the names of participating
real-estate firms, the exclusion from membership of any fair housing organization, and proscriptions against testing real-estate practices to determine
the legality of these transactions. Reductions in funding for the boards inhibited enforcement, as did cutbacks in HUD's collection of data on race and sex
that agency officials deemed essential for proving the existence of discrimination. A number of community groups sued HUD for its failure to make adherence to fair housing law a prerequisite for receipt of CDBG awards. HUD
in the 1980s abandoned the incentives, utilized during the Carter administration, to encourage compliance with fair housing requirements in suburbs
seeking federal funding for community development. "Although HUD maintained a small but dedicated staff to administer the fair housing program,"
concluded James A. Kushner, in his detailed study of fair housing during the
Reagan years, "the Department traditionally had treated fair housing as an
unwanted program."[44]

Culpability for the lack of progress on fair housing, many critics felt,
rested with the Reagan Justice Department even more than with HUD.
Under Attorneys General William French Smith and Edwin Meese, the Department of Justice (DOJ) passively accepted the clear shortcomings of Title
VIII of the 1968 Civil Rights Act and offered scant leadership in drafting a
new measure. DOJ lawyers, who brought approximately twenty to thirty fair
housing cases per year in the 1970s, prosecuted no more than five annually in

the early 1980s. The department announced that it would no longer challenge discriminatory land-use practices, such as exclusionary zoning, or seek housing remedies as settlements in desegregation cases. In the relatively few housing discrimination cases it elected to prosecute, the DOJ sought less compensation in the Reagan years than had been customary during the Carter administration. The department failed to prosecute banks that violated the Community Reinvestment Act, which outlawed racial discrimination in lending. Most infuriating to civil rights activists, the department also began demanding proof that discriminatory intent (not just effect) be present before litigating in land-use cases. In many instances, DOJ attorneys even used Title VIII to challenge affirmative action in housing. William Bradford Reynolds, the associate attorney general for civil rights, became the spokesman for the administration's contention that fair housing laws did not require integration and that the federal government should not be in the business of fostering desegregation. Espousing a narrow interpretation of civil rights legislation, Reynolds argued that "the natural consequences of people's choice of housing is not something the federal government ought to" regulate, even if it results in neighborhoods or entire communities being occupied wholly by people of one race.[45]

The administration's lackluster record on fair housing enforcement led to increased demand for new legislation, especially among congressional Republicans who feared that their party's consistent opposition to civil rights measures was becoming a political liability. In 1982 Congress renewed the landmark Voting Rights Act of 1965, contrary to Reagan's recommendation, allowing the Democrats to score another public relations triumph. To avoid another such "fiasco," leading Republicans in the House met with White House and DOJ officials in January 1983 and urged the White House to endorse new fair housing legislation before Democratic Congressman Don Edwards of California could introduce a bill. In his State of the Union address to Congress on January 23, the president promised to submit stronger fair housing legislation to Congress immediately. Secretary Pierce subsequently explained that the administration's bill would empower the DOJ both to bring suits more readily in federal district courts and to seek substantial civil penalties against those who violated fair housing statutes. The Leadership Conference on Civil Rights and other interested groups sought legislation that would enable HUD unilaterally to bring charges against defendants and administrative law judges to impose substantial fines on those who were found guilty. The Reagan proposal only allowed HUD to recommend that legal action be taken by the DOJ, which appeared to civil rights activists to have neither the resources nor the inclination to pursue fair housing cases aggressively. Disgruntled with the Reagan initiative and fearing that Senate Republicans would emasculate any bill passed in the House, Democrats decided in 1983 to table fair housing until they obtained majorities in both houses of Congress.[46]

In 1988, after having reclaimed control of the Senate two years earlier, having rejected Reagan's nomination of Robert Bork as a Supreme Court justice, and having passed a civil rights bill over Reagan's veto, emboldened Democrats returned to the issue of fair housing. Vice President George H. W. Bush, the presumptive Republican candidate for president that year, who was seeking to shore up his standing with the civil rights community, worked openly for passage of fair housing legislation. Congressman Edwards and Senator Edward M. Kennedy (Democrat, Massachusetts) introduced fair housing bills that empowered administrative law judges to levy monetary penalties, an action the Reagan DOJ rejected as unconstitutional. The legislation favored by the administration, viewed as equally unacceptable by congressional Democrats, required jury trials in courts of law to award damages. Congressman Hamilton Fish of New York, the ranking Republican member of the House Judiciary Committee, successfully suggested a middle ground suitable to both the Leadership Conference on Civil Rights and the powerful real-estate lobby. The Fish compromise gave parties charged by HUD with housing discrimination the choice of having their cases heard by administrative law judges, who could levy fines up to $50,000, or opting for a jury trial in federal court, where legal costs would be greater and punitive damages potentially larger. Congress passed the Fair Housing Amendments Act of 1988 by lopsided margins, the House by a vote of 376 to 23 on June 26 and the Senate by a vote of 94 to 3 on August 1. An enthusiastic Vice President Bush led cheers for the measure throughout the summer and urged the president to sign the bill. Reagan did so on September 13, lauding Bush's "enormous courage" in voting for the 1968 fair housing law as a freshman congressman from the South and hailing the hard work and perseverance of Secretary Pierce during the previous eight years.[47]

Even while delivering celebratory remarks at the signing ceremony, however, Reagan continued the administration's effort to circumscribe the impact of fair housing legislation. In particular, the president insisted that the racial discrimination explicitly prohibited by the new law must be intentional. After enumerating the unprecedented protections afforded victims of discrimination by the legislation, he added: "At the same time, I want to emphasize that this bill does not represent any congressional or executive branch endorsement of the notion, expressed in some judicial opinions, that Title VIII violations may be established by a showing of 'disparate impact' or 'discriminatory effects' of a practice that was taken without discriminatory intent. Title VIII speaks only to intentional discrimination."[48]

Senator Kennedy rebutted the president's comments the following day, saying: "Congress contemplated no such intent requirement" and "courts and others interpreting the act should not give weight to the president's attempt to obtain in a signing statement what he could not achieve in the legislation itself." Just as Reagan and Kennedy quarreled over the need to demonstrate intent to prosecute discrimination cases successfully, debate over the meaning and scope of the Fair Housing Amendments Act of 1988 continued in subsequent years. The law's enhanced enforcement measures clearly addressed some of the shortcomings inherent in Title VIII of the 1968 Civil Rights Act, and victims of discriminatory housing practices enjoyed greater opportunity for redress of grievances after 1988. Still, even with the provision of additional tools for combating discrimination, successful litigation would depend upon the kind of heightened vigilance, commitment to reform, and willingness to litigate not evidenced by HUD or the DOJ under Reagan. The federal government could become a more aggressive agent in rooting out racial discrimination in housing—and thereby alter the racial composition of metropolitan regions—but only at the direction of the political leadership. The full potential of the Fair Housing Amendments Act of 1988 could be achieved only in a presidency willing to utilize the power of the federal government in ways that Reagan's New Federalism had vigorously opposed.[49]

The Reagan administration's efforts to advance the cause of the New Federalism continued in its attempts to shift responsibility for urban mass transit to states and municipalities. Despite the federal government having increased the level of funding for capital assistance in 1962 and for operating assistance in 1974, cities ran huge budget deficits and struggled to provide adequate service in the early 1980s. In the long run, said Reagan administration officials, the best answer to the public transportation conundrum rested with severe funding reductions by agencies in Washington, D.C., leading eventually to the elimination of federal subsidies altogether. In the short run, the federal government should maintain a modicum of aid for maintenance and new equipment purchases while urging municipal authorities to attain greater self-sufficiency by raising fares, increasing local taxes, and denying wage and benefit increases to transit workers. The White House principally singled out public transit workers for blame, noting that labor accounted for 80 percent of the cost of operating mass transit systems and that wage increases for unionized transit workers both surpassed pay raises for other public employees and exceeded the rate of inflation between 1967 and 1980. Municipal officials countered that wage increases in recent years for chronically underpaid transit workers had merely closed the gap with other public employees and reminded the White House that New York City, Chicago, Cleveland, and St. Louis had recently raised fares or had announced future fare increases. Fare hikes inevitably led to declining ridership, local officials added, which in turn resulted in declining revenue and the demand for another round of fare increases. Without federal subsidies, local governments could not interrupt this cycle of rising consumer charges. Unmoved by such arguments, the administration cut mass transit operating assistance in the largest cities by 20 percent for fiscal year 1982, and Reagan announced as his goal the elimination of all operating subsidies after fiscal year 1984.[50]

In 1982 liberals on Capitol Hill hoped to pass an omnibus transportation bill that would increase funding for highway improvements and urban mass transit by raising gasoline taxes for the first time since 1959. They found an ally in Transportation Secretary Drew Lewis, who became an avid lobbyist for the bill even when Reagan made clear his opposition to legislation that required a tax increase of any sort. Lewis and congressional supporters described the highway and mass transit measure as a jobs bill, arguing that the expected revenue generated by raising the gasoline tax from four cents per gallon to nine cents per gallon would create an estimated 300,000 construction jobs—not an inconsiderable number as an economic recession persisted through 1982. Cognizant of the president's opposition to taxes but his tolerance of users paying for specific services, Lewis persuaded Reagan that the increased revenue bound for the Highway Trust Fund and used specifically for roadway improvements could legitimately be termed "user fees." The Transportation secretary's argument faltered over mass transit funding, however, where no clear link existed between the motorist and the subway rider. As late as December 1982, Reagan still threatened to veto any transportation bill that did not provide for the eventual elimination of federal subsidies for mass transit operation. The president finally surrendered to a powerful bipartisan coalition in Congress determined to obtain significant aid for transportation but only after securing a compromise on mass transit funding: he agreed not to veto legislation that included funding for mass transit operation beyond fiscal year 1984 in return for deep cuts in operating subsidies. The Surface Transportation Assistance Act of 1982, which Reagan signed on January 6, 1983, authorized a record $71 billion for highway construction, road repairs, and urban mass transit. The measure allocated one cent of the five-cent gasoline tax increase to mass transit funding, which amounted to $17.7 billion for public transportation in fiscal years 1983–1986, and created a new block grant program for capital and operating expenses.[51]

Within weeks of signing the Surface Transportation Assistance Act of 1982, however, the president introduced a budget for the coming fiscal year that severely reduced the amount of block grant funding designated for urban mass transit. Senator Alfonse D'Amato (Republican, New York) complained that Reagan appeared to be reneging on the "delicate compromise" between Congress and the White House concluded in December 1982. The proposed budget for fiscal year 1984 placed a cap on operating assistance that, D'Amato calculated, would reduce expenditures for mass transit operations more than 75 percent. Budget Director David Stockman responded to the senator's complaints by noting that the White House had consistently opposed federal assistance for mass transit operations, a position unaltered by the recent passage of the transportation act. The administration's goal continued to be the elimination of federal operating subsidies by 1985, affirmed Stockman. Elizabeth Dole, who replaced Drew Lewis as transportation secretary in February 1983, wrote D'Amato that the Surface Transportation Assistance Act of 1982 reflected the president's commitment to a continuing federal role in mass transit capital assistance—but also represented a "significant first step in reducing the level of Federal operating subsidies." The fiscal year 1984 budget would allow the Urban Mass Transportation Administration to earmark more resources for capital expenditures and fewer dollars for operating assistance, the latter having been determined by officials at DOT and the White House not to be a proper role of the federal government.[52]

Reagan's crusade against urban mass transit continued throughout his administration. The president's budget for fiscal year 1986 proposed cutting mass transit funding by two-thirds, including the elimination of federal aid for the construction of all new systems, as part of a $3.8 billion reduction overall for the DOT. Such cuts, said Los Angeles Mayor Tom Bradley, would "sound the deathknell for many of America's transit systems." According to a survey conducted by the American Public Transit Association, Bradley reported, the results of such action would be the loss of 203,000 jobs, the widespread cancelation of service in American communities regardless of size, and extreme hardship for the elderly, the handicapped, the poor, the young, and other dependent groups. A White House official responded to the mayor that the administration would still fulfill its legal obligation to spend the "penny gas tax" for urban mass transit authorized by the Surface Transportation Assistance Act of 1982 but intended to do so according to a new formula-based capital assistance program. Congress finally approved a 10 percent reduction for urban mass transit in the fiscal year 1986 budget and the following year cut by 2.5 percent ($21 million) funding for mass transit operating assistance in cities with populations of more than 1 million people.[53]

In 1987 the battle over mass transit funding continued as part of the debate over omnibus transportation legislation that attracted considerable attention as the last projected authorization bill of the interstate highway era. With 97.5 percent of the interstate system completed and the remaining portions having generated contentious disputes in affected communities, it seemed unlikely by the mid-1980s that any more urban expressways would be completed with interstate funding. Reagan balked at legislation passed by Congress that authorized nearly one hundred highway demonstration projects funded entirely by the federal government, the controversial Central Artery project in Boston that involved depressing an existing roadway and widening a planned tunnel, and substantial federal funds for mass transit capital and operating costs. Oblivious to the entreaties of the National Governors' Association, which argued the critical economic need for highway construction that year, the president threatened to veto what he termed a fiscally irresponsible bill that jeopardized the federal government's ability to meet the deficit reduction goals imposed by the Gramm-Rudman-Hollings Balanced Budget and Deficit Control Act of 1985. On March 27 Reagan vetoed the measure, which he claimed exceeded by $10 billion the amount he was willing to approve for transportation funding. The president went to the Capitol and begged Republican senators to sustain his veto, but Congress voted on April 2 to override. The Surface Transportation and Uniform Relocation Assistance Act of 1987 authorized $88 billion through fiscal year 1992, $70 billion for highways and $18 billion for urban mass transit programs.[54]

By the end of the Reagan administration's second term, White House officials claimed to have made good progress in establishing the New Federalism by holding the line on spending for urban mass transit and housing, by linking urban policy firmly to economic policy, and by devolving authority to state and local governments. The 1988 national urban policy report boasted that America's cities had rebounded during the previous eight years due to sustained economic growth, low inflation, sinking unemployment rates, and the rising productivity engendered by Reaganomics. Once the recession of 1981–1982 had dissipated, the report explained, the leadership of metropolitan regions in all geographical areas moved quickly to take advantage of the opportunities created by the revived economy. The housing situation had improved, benefiting perhaps more than any other industry from the decline in interest rates, and the middle class especially enjoyed access to more credit subsidies and tax incentives. Rather than constructing more housing for low-income families, the administration had wisely pioneered in the more efficient use of vouchers. The report recognized the "recalcitrance of some enduring social problems," including drug trafficking and abuse, underachieving public schools, and the failure of poor families to enter the economic mainstream. Local governments, private businesses, and religious institutions working together—not federal government intrusion into urban markets—offered the best hope of discovering solutions to such lingering social problems. The fashioning of an effective national urban policy agenda for the 1990s, the 1988 report concluded, depended upon the liberation of urban governments from the constrictive federal programs forged earlier and against which the Reagan administration had been warring for eight years.[55]

The New Federalism exacted an especially heavy toll on HUD, which lost resources, personnel, programs, and prestige during the Reagan years. When the president failed to recognize Secretary Pierce at a White House reception and addressed him as "Mr. Mayor," the widely reported incident symbolized the agency's plummeting influence. Having ranked fourth in 1981 among the eleven federal departments in funding level (behind only Treasury, Defense, and Health and Human Services), the agency fell to a ranking of eighth by 1988 (trailing Agriculture, Labor, Transportation, and Education, as well as Treasury, Defense, and Health and Human Services). The HUD budget, which amounted to 7 percent of the total federal budget in the Carter administration, declined to 1 percent by the end of the Reagan years. The number of full-time employees at HUD fell from approximately 16,000 in 1981 to 12,500 in 1988, a decline of 23 percent. Ten different people held the position of assistant secretary for housing during the eight years of the Reagan administration, the average length of stay totaling 8.4 months; the position remained vacant between January 1986 and May 1987. Because HUD underwrote and insured decreasing amounts of subsidized housing, assistant secretaries and their subordinates left or lost their jobs in what came to be perceived as a dead end within the agency. The loss of talented professionals in that area and indeed throughout HUD, many former employees argued, constituted a "brain drain" during the 1980s.[56]

HUD programs suffered along with the unsparing reductions in the agency's total budget. HUD administrators implemented an 85 percent cut in assisted housing expenditures, for example, and a 29 percent reduction in spending for CDBGs. The New Federalists reduced support for neighborhood development by eliminating the agency's Office of Neighborhoods,

Voluntary Associations, and Consumer Protection, as well as the assistant secretary position that had been responsible for neighborhoods under the Carter administration. After Reagan tried for years to eradicate the UDAG program, Congress did it for him in 1988; faced with a choice between funding a space station for the National Aeronautics and Space Administration or UDAGs, Congress chose the former and eliminated the latter. Rather than fight to preserve the shrinking budget of his agency, Pierce boasted that HUD's expenditures "were under budget" in six of the eight years of his tenure. Altogether, the secretary noted proudly, "HUD was under budget by more than $26.6 billion for the eight years of the Reagan administration."[57]

In addition to lauding his agency's sterling record of efficiency, Pierce later wrote about the "relentless campaign" waged at HUD when he was secretary against "fraud, waste, and mismanagement" that led to "more than 2,300 convictions of persons or firms doing business with HUD and more than $300 million in unnecessary expenditures avoided." Pierce's boastful comments seemed incomprehensible considering the massive scandals in HUD during the Reagan years, first uncovered by a congressional investigation in 1989. According to the findings of the House Government Operations Committee's Subcommittee on Employment and Housing, HUD officials, former highly ranked government appointees, and other Republican officeholders brazenly enriched themselves at the public expense during the 1980s. At a time of dramatic cutbacks in federal spending, defalcations at HUD cost the government between $4 billion and $8 billion. Rather than building low-income housing, the agency subsidized the construction of luxury apartments, swimming pools, golf courses, and the like for the cronies of HUD officials. An investigation by an independent counsel lasting nine years eventually led to seventeen convictions and the payment of more than $2 million in fines. In the panoply of scandals saturating the Reagan era, as *Newsweek* noted, the HUD imbroglio ranked as historically less significant than Iran-Contra and cost the taxpayers far less than the savings and loan swindle. "Yet in terms of breathtaking cynicism and hypocrisy, it's hard to match," the newsmagazine concluded. "Over eight years ostensibly respectable people effectively became poverty pimps, getting rich and powerful by subverting programs intended to help the poor."[58]

The congressional subcommittee at first investigated the operation of the Section 8 Moderate Rehabilitation Program (Mod Rehab), which had been created as part of the Housing and Community Development Act of 1978 to provide housing for low- and moderate-income families through the provision of tax breaks and rental subsidies to developers interested in renovating and

managing existing units. The 1978 law required Mod Rehab funds to be distributed evenly across the nation regardless of need, but a 1984 amendment
empowered the secretary to allocate funds anywhere without geographical
restriction. To obtain the lucrative tax credits and subsidies, developers
quickly discovered, they needed to hire Republican consultants who would
use their connections in the Reagan administration to secure the necessary
backing at HUD. Having obtained the promise of funding in Washington,
D.C., the developers could characterize their proposals to officials at local
housing authorities as a "done deal." Congressman Tom Lantos (Democrat,
California), chairman of the investigating subcommittee, scoffed that the
Mod Rehab awards selection process had "all the competitiveness and sus-
pense of professional wrestling."[59]

The influence peddling and cronyism uncovered in the investigation
proved shocking both because of the vast sums of money that changed
hands and because leading Republicans who had extolled the virtues of the
private sector and condemned the innate wastefulness of big government
cynically lined their own pockets with money from government programs.
The rogue's gallery of politically connected fixers, virtually none of whom
possessed any expertise in housing, included some of the most influential
figures in recent Republican administrations. Reagan's former secretary of
the Interior, James G. Watt, a fierce champion in the cabinet of a smaller
federal government who had scorned lobbyists "lured by the crumbs of subsidies, entitlements, and giveaways," accepted $420,000 for making a few
telephone calls on behalf of clients seeking HUD funding for housing projects. Testifying before the subcommittee, he admitted to having no profi-
ciency in housing matters and cheerfully acknowledged that the "system
was flawed." Frederick Bush, President-elect George H. W. Bush's 1988
campaign manager and ambassador-designate to Luxembourg, received
$215,000 in consulting fees for Mod Rehab and other HUD awards. John
Mitchell, Richard Nixon's attorney general during the Watergate era, received $75,000 for his lobbying efforts at HUD. Carla Hills, U.S. Trade Rep-
resentative under the Reagan administration, could at least point to her earlier tenure as HUD secretary in the Ford administration as evidence that she
knew something about housing; she earned $138,445 for her consultancy on
Mod Rehab projects, one of which subsequently defaulted on loans exceeding $300 million. In all, reported HUD Inspector General Paul Adams, Re-
publican consultants netted $5.7 million in fees from the Mod Rehab pro-
grams from 1984 to 1988.[60]

Lantos's subcommittee found that the Mod Rehab scam generated additional moneymaking opportunities for at least fourteen HUD officials who resigned and quickly reaped the benefit of their knowledge and agency connections as consultants. Having ignored the inspector general's warning in 1983 that overcharging by consultants was costing the Mod Rehab program millions of dollars annually, Undersecretary Philip Abrams resigned in 1984 and joined a consulting firm that obtained $133 million in renovation funds and $29 million in tax credits—largesse that included overcharges of $9.7 million, according to auditors employed by Congress. The company employing Abrams and two other former HUD officials (Philip Winn and Lance Wilson) obtained nearly one-eighth of the Mod Rehab awards distributed in an eleven-month period. Maurice Barksdale told the subcommittee that he earned $300,000 as a consultant on HUD projects after leaving the agency and made a $2,000 personal loan to HUD Deputy Assistant Secretary Dubois Gilliam. "On hindsight," Barksdale said of the personal loan, "perhaps it was not the right thing."[61]

Consultants thrived by ingratiating themselves with Pierce's executive assistant, Deborah Gore Dean, who oversaw the Mod Rehab awards and other HUD programs. A member of a wealthy and politically influential Republican family, the twenty-nine-year-old Dean went to work in the HUD mailroom, soon became Pierce's chief aide, and began authorizing the disbursement of funds with the use of an autopen bearing the secretary's signature. She interceded for influential Republicans, solicited donations, hosted receptions for consulting firms, and otherwise politicized HUD's grant programs—a process she justified in a *Wall Street Journal* interview saying that the Mod Rehab program was "set up and designed to be a political program." She also installed a number of her friends, who became known as the "brat pack," into high-level administrative positions in the agency. Dean refused to testify before the investigating subcommittee, invoking her Fifth Amendment right against self-incrimination. She did, however, maintain publicly that Pierce had authorized all of her actions. Dean became one of six HUD staffers indicted for criminal activities, and in 1994 a jury convicted her of perjury, concealing material facts, conspiracy to defraud the government, and accepting illegal gratuities. Her sentence reduced on appeal, Dean served one year of home confinement and paid a monetary fine.[62]

Investigators found that the corruption extended far beyond the borders of Washington, D.C. The lax supervision practiced at HUD allowed regional officials and private contractors employed by the agency to bilk the government for millions of dollars. A HUD audit in 1989 found $100 million missing from property sale accounts in fifty-three field offices nationwide. In Atlanta, for example, two escrow agents sold properties whose owners had defaulted on FHA-insured mortgages and illegally diverted $1.6 million from the sales into their own bank accounts. In the most widely publicized case, Marilyn Harrell, a closing agent who sold repossessed houses in Prince George's County, Maryland, admitted stealing $5.5 million in FHA funds. Ms. Harrell, who became known as "Robin HUD," donated most of her ill-gotten gain to charitable organizations and causes. "I was amazed that it went on for as long as it did," she confessed in a television interview. "But people kept coming for help and we had access to the monies and no one seemed particularly concerned."[63]

The lack of oversight extended to Capitol Hill, where members of Congress spent more time lobbying HUD officials for grants on behalf of their constituents than monitoring the agency's financial dealings. "HUD has been a honey pot not only for people trying to get influence but also for members of Congress," charged William Proxmire, chairman of the Senate Banking, Housing, and Urban Affairs Committee from 1986 to 1988. "There was very little criticism by members of our committee because they were looking to HUD to help them in their districts and in their states." No one prospered more than New York Senator Alfonse D'Amato, who served on the appropriations and housing committees and enjoyed extraordinary success in steering HUD grants to his family and friends. "D'Amato owned HUD," commented an agency staffer. Having discovered that a New York contracting firm that funneled D'Amato substantial campaign contributions subsequently received preferential treatment from HUD, a Senate Ethics Committee reprimanded the senator but stopped short of recommending that legal action be taken against him.[64]

The investigations and indictments called into question the role in the scandal played by "Silent Sam" Pierce, the only Reagan cabinet member to serve a full two terms. As an indifferent and distracted manager whose corporate administrative style entailed the delegation of responsibility entirely to his subordinates, Pierce claimed to have been so woefully removed from HUD's activities that he truly had no knowledge of the shady dealings going on around him. HUD staffers confirmed that Pierce spent little time in his office and exhibited virtually no curiosity about the programs and policies he was supposedly administering. At a meeting during his last year where officials discussed the Moderate Rehabilitation program, the secretary interrupted: "What is this Moderate Rehab program anyway?" A staff member present at the meeting told *Newsweek*, "There was stunned silence. I watched jaws drop around the room." Unwilling to hear bad news of any sort, the secretary ordered the public affairs office to elide critical newspaper articles from his daily press clippings. When subordinates supplied him with reports alleging malfeasance in the agency, Pierce told them, "Show me an indictment and I'll take action."[65]

Investigators questioned whether Pierce was guilty of more than willful ignorance, however. A HUD official charged that Pierce overrode agency policy to award funding for a housing project to his former law partner, and newspapers reported that the secretary intervened on numerous occasions to provide housing grants to friends and business associates. Refusing to testify voluntarily in the continuing investigation, Pierce finally responded to a subpoena and appeared before the congressional subcommittee on September 26, 1989. He invoked the protection of the Fifth and Sixth Amendments and refused to answer questions, becoming the first cabinet secretary to do so since the Teapot Dome scandal of 1922. In the end, Pierce struck a deal whereby he admitted to having fostered an environment in which his subordinates engaged in "improper and even criminal conduct" in return for which federal prosecutors declined to charge him with a crime.[66]

Unearthed shortly after the close of the Reagan administration, the HUD scandal served as an apt postscript for the agency's decline during the preceding eight years. Resistance on Capitol Hill to the New Federalism mitigated the impact somewhat of the Reagan administration's proposals for draconian funding cuts, and advocates of affordable housing enjoyed notable success in preserving allocations for operating subsidies and modernization of existing units. Nevertheless, the compromise budgets crafted annually by Congress and the White House left the agency with significantly fewer dollars each year. HUD's budget fell from $33.4 billion in 1980 to $10.2 billion in 1988, its allocations for assisted housing from $26.7 billion to $3.9 billion during those years. Routinely forced to economize, the agency pruned programs and eliminated personnel. Morale plummeted among the HUD employees who survived the periodic layoffs and furloughs, and many transferred to other agencies or served out their time in fear of more staff reductions. Demoralization increased with the recognition by career housing experts that HUD had become a dumping ground for political appointees, a perfect example of the kind of cronyism decried by the opponents of big government. The moral laxity at HUD surfaced as early as 1983 when Assistant Secretary Emanuel S. Savas, the principal architect of the drive to limit federal aid to cities, resigned facing charges of "abuse of office" for having his subordinates type and proofread during work hours the manuscript of a book he was preparing for publication. Most alarming, members of Deborah

Gore Dean's brat pack and other unqualified bureaucrats were undermining or destroying housing programs that had provided moderate- and low-income families affordable housing for decades. The New Federalism left HUD in a shambles.[67]

In addition to emasculating HUD, the administration succeeded in reducing overall federal assistance to the cities by 60 percent. During the Reagan years, the New Federalists managed to eliminate UDAGs, Section 235 housing, CETA, and general revenue sharing while significantly reducing funding for CDBGs, mass transit, legal services for the poor, job training, and public service employment—all of which put greater economic pressure on municipal budgets. The New Federalism took its greatest toll on the nation's largest cities, which relied most on the federal government for poverty-related services and funding for service delivery. Federal aid to cities with over 300,000 population decreased from $5.2 billion in 1980 to $3.4 billion in 1989, a 35 percent reduction. In 1980 these large cities received 22 percent of their funding from Washington, D.C., as compared to 6 percent by 1989. State governments also lost federal funds at a time when they needed to increase their matching dollars for AFDC and Medicaid benefits; state assistance as a percentage of city outlays fell far short of compensating for federal cuts, barely remaining static during the 1980s.[68]

Reduced federal funding for social welfare programs proved devastating in large cities, where the poor especially felt the effects of retrenchment. In low-income communities suffering from deindustrialization, capital flight, and housing deterioration, the shrinkage of the social safety net proved catastrophic for the underemployed, aged, disabled, and single mothers with children. Social scientists referred to this growing big-city population as the underclass, an increasingly visible group of indigents comprised largely of unemployed, welfare-dependent African Americans and Latinos who were increasingly losing their connections to the American mainstream. Reagan often proclaimed his compassion for society's unfortunates, but his administration's policies reduced levels of support for the "worthy" poor and insisted on making invidious distinctions that culled out an increasing number of "unworthy poor" from eligibility for federal aid. Because of cuts in grants to cities and in social welfare programs, the number of urban poor increased during the 1980s. The central city poverty rate swelled from 15.7 percent in 1979 to 21.5 percent in 1992; the percentage of poor people living in cities likewise rose from 37 percent in 1983 to 42 percent in 1992.[69]

Federal reductions in funding affected the cities significantly in the declining number of poor families receiving housing assistance. The number of available low-income housing units in the cities fell from 6.5 million in 1970 to 5.6 million in 1985, while the number of low-income households rose from 6.2 million to 8.9 million during the same years. The resulting disparity of 3.3 million units in the mid-1980s led to a dramatic increase in the number of homeless families and individuals. Having peaked in the Great Depression, the incidence of homelessness declined in the 1940s, 1950s, 1960s, and 1970s, only to rebound alarmingly in the 1980s. Along with Vietnam veterans, unemployed workers, the chronically mentally ill, and children, the growing number of homeless included an unprecedented number of one-parent, female-headed families. Many members of this rootless urban population slept in doorways, subway stations, and parks, surviving by scavenging, begging, and, in some cases, stealing. By the late 1980s, according to the best estimates, the homeless population swelled to more than 1 million people nationwide—as many as 600,000 on some nights. The president downplayed the problem, describing the homeless as mentally deranged or people who simply had chosen a footloose lifestyle. On a television news program, Reagan defended himself against charges of indifference toward the worsening problem by saying that "people who are sleeping on the grates . . . the homeless . . . are homeless, you might say, by choice."[70]

If homelessness and other urban problems intensified during the 1980s, Reagan continued to believe that the situation would only worsen with greater federal government activism. "Government is not the solution, it's the problem," he repeatedly intoned. His New Federalism insisted that the best solutions to America's problems rested with less government, lower taxes, and decentralization. Reagan rejected the idea that increases in federal aid to urban America prior to his administration owed to the incapacity of state and local governments to meet their financial obligations. The fate of the cities should be decided by the free market and local government, not by spendthrift bureaucrats in Washington, D.C., who usurped the authority of states and municipalities. Considering the reductions in grants and social welfare programs, the cities paid the lion's share of the cost for the domestic budget cuts enacted in the decade. The fiscal health of cities in the future would depend upon the fortunes of the economy and the ability of municipal governments to raise more revenue, attract more private investment, secure more foundation grants, and establish public-private partnerships—in short, to become more entrepreneurial. Residents of cities that failed to provide jobs and services should "vote with their feet," the president declared, and move to more prosperous communities. The failure of deregulation, signaled

by rampant overdevelopment and the massive bailout necessitated by the
S&L fiasco, remained unclear at the close of the 1980s. Reagan had not been
entirely successful in promoting privatism in urban America, to be sure, and
much remained to be done. Congress stopped short of officially adopting enterprise zones as national policy, even though thirty-seven states had created
them by the end of the decade, and the use of housing vouchers remained
limited. True believers in the New Federalism looked hopefully to the future,
confident that the election in 1988 of two-term Vice President George H. W.
Bush or conservative supply-sider Jack Kemp would complete the transformation begun by Reagan.[71]

9

GEORGE H. W. BUSH'S
NEW FEDERALISM

As a loyal two-term vice president, George H. W. Bush dutifully endorsed the policies and actions of the Reagan administration. Despite being a centrist Republican who had rejected supply-side economics and other staples of the party's right wing, the vice president raised no public objections to the conservative directions charted by Reagan's New Federalism. As president, Bush essentially followed the same urban policies developed during the preceding eight years; he continued to tout the importance of private business investment as the key to urban revitalization, the reduction of federal funding to the cities, and the virtues of decentralization. His selection of conservative Republican Congressman Jack Kemp as secretary of the Department of Housing and Urban Development (HUD) signaled the administration's commitment to enterprise zones as the best means of reinvigorating struggling neighborhoods in core cities and to promulgating homeownership for public housing tenants. At the same time, while remaining faithful to the fundamental principles of Reagan's New Federalism, Bush sought to distance himself from some of the less salutary developments of the preceding eight years in urban America. Faced almost immediately with the disclosure of the massive depredations at HUD in the 1980s, he charged Kemp with the wholesale reform of the scandal-ridden agency. As America's cities continued to struggle with disturbingly high rates of poverty and homelessness, Bush vowed to leaven sound economic policies with a measure of compassion that would ease the suffering of the underclass. Elevated levels of defense spending and an economic recession commencing in 1989 intruded, however, shifting the administration's funding priorities away from domestic programs. Bush's stirring promises of a "kinder, gentler Nation" notwithstanding, the amount of federal largesse made available to address acute resource shortfalls in urban America continued to decline. The residents of the nation's cities saw very little difference between the New Federalisms espoused by the Reagan and Bush presidencies.[1]

In 1988 Bush ran a presidential campaign that closely adhered to the ideals in favor with the Republican mainstream of that era. He opposed gun control, abortion, and an intrusive federal government; he favored low taxes, the death penalty, and prayer in the public schools. He demonized liberals for their profligate spending, softness on crime, and hostility toward the conventional values prevalent in an idealized Mid-America. Contrary to his image of affable gentility, Bush conducted a venomous campaign against the Democratic candidate for president, Massachusetts Governor Michael Dukakis. In a series of overheated television advertisements, Republicans portrayed Dukakis as an unpatriotic tax-and-spend liberal who cared more for the rights of criminals than for their victims. Capitalizing on the rising fear of crime in suburban America, the Republicans made the "revolving door prison policy" of Dukakis's governorship the centerpiece of their campaign—especially after Willie Horton, an African American murderer on a weekend furlough from a Massachusetts prison, severely beat and stabbed a hostage and raped his fiancée. Dukakis at first publicly defended the furlough program as a rehabilitative measure before finally discontinuing it in response to rising public outrage. Never before had "attacks on an opponent, rather than promotion of one's own agenda, [become] the primary target of a presidential campaign," commented *Time* of the Bush campaign. The negative tone of the campaign may well have contributed to the low voter turnout in 1988, as only 54.2 percent of the electorate cast ballots on November 8. Bush won with 53.4 percent of the popular vote to Dukakis's 45.6 percent and carried the electoral college by 426 to 111. The Democrats had hoped that Dukakis, a resident of suburban Brookline, would appeal to suburban voters, but election returns indicated that the Republicans successfully portrayed him as beholden to minorities, the poor, and other big-city interest groups. The Democrats maintained comfortable majorities in Congress, 259 to 174 in the House and 55 to 45 in the Senate.[2]

In his January 20, 1989, inaugural address, Bush delivered a speech noteworthy for its conciliatory tone, generous bipartisanship, and criticism of the outgoing administration. With a visibly startled Ronald and Nancy Reagan seated nearby, the president perfunctorily listed the achievements of his predecessor but then decried the rampant materialism of recent years, discussed the urgent need to reduce the ballooning federal deficit, and promised that "a new breeze is blowing." Repudiating the Reagan shibboleth that government intervention inevitably created problems, Bush predicted that his administration would launch a "new engagement in the lives of others—a new activism." At the same time, he acknowledged the crucial need for private philanthropy to combat poverty, homelessness, and other social ills in the cities. Leadership in the struggle against domestic problems must come from a "thousand points of light"—"all the community organizations that are spread like stars throughout the nation, doing good." As he had throughout the campaign, the president pledged to "make kinder the face of the nation and gentler the face of the world." In short, his New Federalism would pursue essentially the same goals identified by the Reaganites but in a more moderate fashion that would mitigate the impact on society's unfortunates.[3]

To administer his New Federalism in the cities, Bush selected Jack Kemp as secretary of HUD. A conservative ideologue and devout supply-sider with strong ties to the Reagan administration, Kemp seemed at first an odd choice to preside over the agency given the task of implementing kinder, gentler policies in urban America. As a nine-term congressman from Buffalo, New York, Kemp nonetheless had combined his devotion to low taxes and limited government with an undeniable passion for revitalizing the ailing inner cities and aiding the urban poor. Long an ardent supporter of civil rights and spokesman for urban causes, the former professional football player embraced social welfare concerns in a manner uncommon among Republican conservatives. As secretary of HUD, he promised to wage a second war on poverty. At a time when the incidence of homelessness in big cities had reached extraordinary proportions, Kemp argued for the feasibility of providing homeownership opportunities to low-income persons. He believed that the reclamation of cities depended upon the empowerment of distressed neighborhoods and poor people and that government could best facilitate an inner-city renaissance through the creation of enterprise zones and the encouragement of homeownership rather than rental housing subsidies. Kemp hoped that his ambitious agenda for the cities, based upon what the *Wall Street Journal* called his unique brand of "progressive conservatism," would flourish in a pragmatic Bush presidency that saw HUD as more than a convenient target for budget cuts.[4]

From the outset of his tenure at HUD, Kemp lobbied aggressively in the White House and on Capitol Hill for a measure he had been championing since 1980 in the House of Representatives—enterprise zones. In a 1989 HUD report he had commissioned, "Enterprise Zones in America: A Selected Resource Guide, II," Kemp outlined in detail how inner cities could flourish with fewer federal dollars by attracting private investment and luring small businesses into traditionally foreboding cityscapes. Government's role in the Kemp plan revolved around tax and regulatory incentives as inducements for investment. In July of that year, the president submitted a proposal to Congress for the inclusion of fifty enterprise zones in distressed urban and rural areas (fifteen each in 1990, 1991, and 1992, and five in 1993) as a first step in revitalizing the pockets of depression that remained impervious to the economic growth enjoyed by much of the nation in the 1980s. Congress passed a version of the administration bill but, according to Kemp, rendered the achievement "merely symbolic" by omitting any tax incentives for enterprise zones from its budget.[5]

Kemp found his grandiose plans for enterprise zones and other initiatives stalled in the first months of the Bush presidency, however, because of the unfolding revelations about fraud and mismanagement at HUD during the Reagan years. Stories outlining influence peddling and graft surfaced in local news outlets and trade publications during the summer of 1988, and network television and newspapers with national circulations began covering the story extensively in the spring of 1989. During the next four years, the *New York Times*, the *Washington Post*, the *Los Angeles Times*, and the *Wall Street Journal* collectively devoted more than 1,300 articles to the HUD scandal and Kemp's responses to the latest exposés of wrongdoing at the agency; the ABC, CBS, and NBC nightly news programs aired nearly 200 stories on the HUD imbroglio during the same time. Kemp announced in April 1989 that he was terminating HUD's Section 8 Moderate Rehabilitation (Mod Rehab) program, which the agency's inspector general had identified as the heart of the scandal, and congressional investigations commenced the following month that produced a steady stream of embarrassing headlines for the rest of the year. Having largely ignored the mundane operation of HUD during its steady eclipse in the 1980s, the press covered the developing scandal with relish in 1989 and faithfully reported Kemp's reactions to each salacious new disclosure.[6]

The various investigations into HUD operations in the Reagan administration proceeded on several fronts throughout 1989. The House Government Operations Subcommittee on Employment and Housing heard testimony from thirty-nine witnesses at eighteen hearings during the year, initially concentrating on the Mod Rehab program but eventually delving into numerous other programs administered by HUD. The Senate Banking Committee's HUD Investigation Subcommittee hired the president elect of the American Bar Association, Talbot "Sandy" D'Alemberte, to conduct its inquiry. The Justice Department initiated several criminal investigations and returned indictments against HUD employees, and the Senate Ethics Committee appointed a special counsel to evaluate the conduct of Senator Alfonse D'Amato (Republican, New York), who was accused of directing HUD business to political contributors and relatives. U.S. Attorney General Richard Thornburgh agreed to appoint a special prosecutor to examine the conduct of Kemp's predecessor, Samuel R. Pierce Jr. Kemp cooperated enthusiastically with the various probes, taking the opportunity to enhance his credentials as a reformer. "He was smart enough to get out in front on the scandal," commented a *Washington Post* reporter, "to denounce what happened and talk about reforms."[7]

As committees in both houses of Congress continued their investigations in 1989, Kemp and his aides composed a reform plan to salvage what remained of HUD's sullied reputation and to safeguard the agency from future damage. On October 31 the administration submitted to Congress a legislative package of reforms crafted at HUD and endorsed by the White House. Most notably, the bill established limitations on the use of discretionary funds such as Mod Rehab and sought to improve financial oversight by creating new supervisory positions within HUD. The administration proposals also required lobbyists and consultants to register and disclose fees, mandated that all funding decisions be made public, stipulated that waivers of any HUD regulations be approved by assistant secretaries and made public, enhanced the subpoena power of the agency's inspector general, and increased funding for auditing and monitoring activities. Kemp also sought to limit profits for developers by prohibiting them from receiving HUD subsidies and low-income tax credits. For the most part, House and Senate members applauded Kemp's efforts to drain the "swamp" of fraud at HUD. Senate Majority Whip Alan Cranston (Democrat, California), chairman of the Banking Committee's Housing Subcommittee, called the reform package "right on target."[8]

Some objections arose in the Democratic Congress to Kemp's efforts, however, as partisan and personal interests surfaced in the legislative process. Whereas Kemp emphasized the urgent need to pass reform bills so that systemic problems at HUD could be solved quickly and substantive housing issues could be considered, a number of Democrats rejected the wisdom of passing laws as the sole response to HUD's failures. Senator Cranston argued that Kemp's reform measures should be included in an omnibus housing bill, thereby increasing the likelihood of obtaining additional funding for HUD from a new Congress that was projected to be fiscally conservative. On the other hand, Representative Charles Schumer (Democrat, New York) contended that much of the needed reform could be handled administratively within HUD. Prolonged attention to a reform bill would be unnecessary, Schumer said, diverting attention from more important housing matters that would likely be prolonged until the following year. Other Democrats balked at Kemp's repeated references to "systemic flaws" as the explanation for the HUD scandals, discerning implicit criticisms of an agency that Republicans had long excoriated and fearing that the opportunistic secretary intended to conceal conservative policy changes in his "reform" package. House Banking Committee Chairman Henry Gonzalez (Democrat, Texas) blamed "people problems" in the Reagan administration for HUD's poor performance. "These programs work when people of good will are there to administer them," Gonzalez wrote Kemp.[9]

Although members of Congress applauded the Kemp plan's elimination of Mod Rehab, they resisted the eradication of all such discretionary programs. The secretary targeted for extinction two "slush funds," as he called them, of great popularity to Democrats and Republicans alike. Senators and congressmen had long inserted earmarks into the Community Development Block Grant discretionary fund, as witnessed by the twenty-five projects worth $20 million already tucked into the HUD budget for fiscal year 1990. A similar discretionary fund for subsidized housing construction empowered HUD officials to ignore requirements that funding be allocated to regions of the country equitably and allowed some legislators to obtain an extraordinary number of pork-barrel projects for their constituents. Although many legislators agreed in principle with Kemp's vow to keep HUD funds from being doled out as political favors, they continued to carp about specifics of the legislation that would potentially limit the ability of Congress to earmark projects for designated cities and states.[10]

The biggest obstacle to passage of Kemp's legislation proved to be Democratic insistence that HUD reform be linked directly with an omnibus housing bill. Hoping that major housing legislation would be able to pass on its own merits, the Democrats finally agreed to consider the Kemp measure independently. "The alternative," said Congressman Barney Frank (Democrat, Massachusetts), "is for Congress to be accused of having uncovered a scandal and not passing legislation to address it." The reform bill passed by Congress conformed very closely to the Kemp proposal, severely limiting the use of discretionary funds, demanding greater accountability by HUD, mandating that all funding decisions be made public, establishing a chief financial officer for HUD and a comptroller for the Federal Housing Administration (FHA), curtailing the ability of consultants and lobbyists to earn huge profits from HUD programs, and authorizing $25 million to monitor and evaluate HUD housing and community development programs. To defuse opposition related to the curtailment of earmarks, none of the changes in the measure affected projects already approved in appropriations bills. The president signed the Department of Housing and Urban Development Reform Act of 1989 on December 15.[11]

Devoting most of their time to the hearings and legislation addressing the HUD scandal and to bailout legislation for the crippled savings and loan industry, the members of Congress failed in 1989 to create new housing programs or renew existing ones. The banking committees in the Senate and the House held hearings on omnibus housing legislation, but neither panel took action in 1989. The administration exhibited no interest in the subject until late in the legislative session, when congressional Democrats threatened to delay passage of Kemp's HUD reform bill prior to the consideration of major housing legislation. The White House hastily prepared a $4.2 billion proposal, which Bush announced in Dallas, Texas, on November 10 at the annual meeting of the National Association of Realtors. The president's proposal adhered to the central tenet of the Reagan administration's housing policy—that the shortage of affordable middle- and lower-income housing owed to problems of affordability and not availability. "There is no better housing policy than a growing economy," Bush told the Realtors. Again following the lead of the Reagan administration, he called for an expansion of the housing voucher program and the creation of fifty enterprise zones in inner-city neighborhoods suffering from high unemployment and disinvestment. He also announced a series of housing and economic development initiatives called Homeownership and Opportunity for People Everywhere (HOPE) designed to allow public housing tenants to purchase their own homes. Chary of the privatism inherent in the president's proposal and eager for government to resume subsidizing the construction of low-income housing, Democrats in Congress rejected the administration's approach in the waning weeks of the legislative session. Senator Daniel Patrick Moynihan (Democrat, New York) charged that the president's proposal barely compensated for the deep cuts in federal housing subsidies inflicted during the 1980s. "With the proposed level of funding," said Barry Zigas, president of the National Low-Income Housing Coalition, "it's impossible to see any real dent in the crisis confronting low-income people." Although they disagreed about the level of federal support necessary to aid the cities, Bush, Kemp, and congressional leaders all concurred that the stage had been set for the passage of meaningful housing legislation in 1990.[12]

The White House clarified its goals for effective housing legislation in the 1990 national urban policy report prepared by Kemp and his HUD staff. Reflecting the secretary's abiding interest in eradicating inner-city poverty, the Bush administration's first biennial report on the cities emphasized that no successful urban policy could fail to address the fate of the underclass and the homeless. To attain the necessary combination of empowerment and opportunity necessary to improve the lot of millions of big-city residents, the administration listed six priorities: expand homeownership, create jobs and economic development through enterprise zones, empower the poor occupants of public housing through resident management and homesteading opportunities, enforce fair housing statutes, help make public housing drug free, and provide temporary shelter for the homeless until they could recover a measure of economic stability. The report conceded that fulfillment of the six priorities alone by federal legislation would not rehabilitate the cities, and success would also depend upon the activism of state and local governments, the private sector, and nonprofit institutions. Still, according to Kemp, the key to winning the second war on poverty rested with allowing all people to share in the cherished American dream of homeownership. Therefore, because of its unique role in government, HUD had a moral imperative to act.[13]

Housing advocates responded to the report with references to a critical shortage in low-income housing, a condition that had been worsening during the previous decade and that had reached crisis proportions by 1990. According to the National Association of Housing and Redevelopment Officials, the backlog of applicants for public housing numbered an estimated 800,000 to 1 million families nationwide, and many local housing authorities had stopped adding names to their waiting lists; another 1 million families were waiting on federal vouchers to subsidize their rents in private housing. Having campaigned on the pledge to complement hard-headed fiscal responsibility with compassion for the cities' poor and homeless, Bush expressed a willingness to work with lawmakers on Capitol Hill. Convinced that the future success of the Republican Party depended upon improving its electoral appeal to urban and minority voters, Kemp believed that the administration must increase economic opportunity for the inner-city poor. In addition to shepherding the HUD reform bill through Congress, he conducted a series of highly publicized tours through the nation's worst urban slums and paid a number of visits to public housing projects with records of successful tenant self-government, such as Kenilworth-Parkside in Washington, D.C., and Cochran Gardens in St. Louis. Frequently photographed trudging through the most benighted big-city neighborhoods, the secretary added to his image as a cost-cutting conservative a new reputation for empathy. If Congress and the executive branches differed on the types of programs best suited to help the urban poor, they agreed upon the pressing need for action.[14]

The principal difference between the administration on the one hand and congressional leaders and liberal housing reformers on the other hand remained whether the government should just help the poor pay rent in the private market or continue to subsidize the construction of low-income housing. Administration officials cited a 7.3 percent vagrancy rate for all rental units nationwide in 1989 as proof that an adequate supply of housing existed and cautioned against new construction as expensive and unnecessary. Construction advocates countered that national vacancy rates ignored regional variations, masking the severity of low-income housing shortages in the Rust Belt cities of the Northeast and Midwest. Moreover, they noted, the inclusion of apartments in uninhabitable buildings and luxury units affordable only to the affluent distorted the data and revealed little about the actual availability of housing suitable for poor families. The destructiveness of downtown redevelopment projects and the decline in government funding for low-income housing had combined to reduce the number of apartments renting for $150 to $300 per month from 10.1 million in 1974 to 8.5 million in 1985. During the same time span, the number of families living in poverty increased from 9.5 million to 13.9 million. Although the number of impoverished renters receiving subsidies from the government increased during the 1970s and 1980s, reported William C. Apgar, associate director of the Joint Center for Housing Studies at Harvard University, the growing incidence of poverty meant that the low-income housing shortage actually worsened. Could this problem be addressed adequately by a generous expansion of the voucher program, which would in theory spur private construction, or would it be necessary to add to the stock of public housing to meet the demand for low-income units?[15]

In 1990 Congress considered three omnibus housing bills, two of which originated on Capitol Hill and the third submitted by HUD embodying the sensibilities of Bush's New Federalism. The bill favored in the House, introduced by Representative Henry Gonzalez, primarily increased funding levels of existing programs and proposed the creation of a public-private partnership to encourage nonprofit groups to develop and manage low-income housing projects. The bill's Community Housing Partnership program would award grants to local governments and nonprofit organizations for the production of housing and also provide financial assistance to low- and moderate-income families interested in purchasing homes. The discussion in the Senate revolved around a bill cosponsored by Alan Cranston and Alfonse D'Amato that sought to make federal housing programs more responsive to local needs. The Cranston-D'Amato bill proposed a generous new $3 billion annual subsidy program—Housing Opportunity Partnerships—that would encourage the development of rental apartments for low-income families. It would also replace housing vouchers with a "rent credit" program, whereby the government responded to local need by either supplying assistance to tenants for the renewal of expiring Section 8 contracts or to tenants evicted by owners who refused to renew project-based agreements. The Gonzalez measure dealt almost exclusively with existing programs, while the Cranston-D'Amato bill shored up extant programs and also created a few new ones.[16]

The administration bill presented to Congress by Kemp, the most innovative of the three measures, introduced several new programs designed to allow low-income families and public housing tenants to become homeowners. HUD would distribute grants to public housing tenants so that they could buy their apartments and to nonprofit groups for the transfer of vacant single-family homes to low-income individuals. The measure also created a Shelter Plus Care program to provide rent subsidies and support services to homeless people struggling with alcoholism, drug addiction, or mental health concerns. Operation Bootstrap required local housing authorities to help low-income families achieve economic independence. Finally, HUD would designate fifty Housing Opportunity Zones in large cities where municipal governments would encourage the construction of affordable housing by repealing restrictive zoning laws and outmoded building codes.[17]

Officials at HUD and in the White House marshaled the full political weight of the administration in favor of the Kemp proposal and against the competing congressional bills. Kemp himself spearheaded the opposition to the Cranston-D'Amato bill in the Senate, charging that its empowerment of state and local agencies without effective safeguards constituted an open invitation to the kind of influence peddling that had recently plagued HUD. He warned that the $2 billion-a-year Housing Opportunity Partnership program also proved unsatisfactory by targeting only 12 percent of new housing units for families below the poverty line while allowing 20 percent for high-income families. Kemp quickly found a staunch ally in Senator Daniel Patrick Moynihan, who praised the innovativeness of the administration's proposal, saying that if the legislation were "90 percent Jack Kemp and 10 percent traditional, it would be a better bill." The HUD secretary threatened to resign if Congress passed the Gonzalez bill. In July the White House sent a letter to the House Rules Committee detailing Bush's determination to veto the Gonzalez bill in the event of its passage. The president would not sign any omnibus housing bill, the letter warned, that failed to authorize HUD's HOPE initiative, direct housing resources to the neediest low-income families, empower poor people in the housing marketplace, and meet the administration's standard of fiscal responsibility. In short, although the letter affirmed the president's desire to cooperate amicably with Congress in formulating housing legislation, the administration's political activities during the summer of 1990 made clear that the HUD proposal must be the centerpiece of any new bill. As an additional inducement, OMB Director Richard Darman promised senators that Bush would not veto any bill because of cost if it met the administration's policy objectives.[18]

The Cranston-Gonzalez National Affordable Housing Act of 1990, which the president signed on November 28, met the majority of the administration's policy objectives. Pundits called passage of the law, hailed widely as the most significant housing measure since the Housing and Community Development Act of 1974, another triumph for Kemp and the cornerstone of Bush's New Federalism. The president lamented that the law, which authorized $27.5 billion for fiscal year 1991 and $29.9 billion for fiscal year 1992, allocated 10 percent of that amount the first year and 15 percent the second year for the construction of rental housing for low-income families. Reiterating the administration's aim of enabling the poor to purchase their own homes rather than building more public housing projects, Bush said: "I do not believe that the earmarking of funds for new construction is consistent with the goal of providing States and localities with maximum flexibility to meet their specific affordable housing needs." Congressional Democrats managed to preserve an acceptable level of funding for conventional housing construction programs but also acquiesced to new HUD programs that Bush and Kemp envisioned as a significant step toward economic self-sufficiency and homeownership for the urban poor. In the president's words, the law made real progress toward making public housing "a springboard for independence, not a bottomless pit for dependency."[19]

The contours of Bush's New Federalism could be seen in several new programs created by the Cranston-Gonzalez National Affordable Housing Act of 1990. Title II of the law created Homeownership Made Easy (HOME) investment partnerships, which provided block grants to state and local governments for housing improvements. HOME grants, which required state and local governments to provide matching funds of 25 percent to 50 percent of project costs, could be used for the rehabilitation of substandard housing but not to subsidize public housing or provide rental assistance. Title IV of the law created the HOPE program to encourage the sale of public housing units to their tenants. HOPE grants could be used for the purchase of vacant, foreclosed, or decrepit single-family and multifamily properties as well as public housing. Title VIII created the Shelter Plus Care program, which provided lodging and social services for the homeless, and the AIDS Housing Opportunity Act, which provided grants to state and local governments for the care of persons with the disease. (The Title VIII programs sought to address the underlying causes of homelessness—mental illness, drug and alcohol addiction, dysfunctional families, and disease—and not just provide more shelter.) The law also founded the National Housing Trust to help first-time home buyers meet down-payment costs and afford mortgage interest rates and allocated $250 million for fiscal year 1991 and $521 million for fiscal year 1992. Finally, in response to growing concerns about losses in the FHA mortgage insurance fund, the law increased down-payment costs and annual insurance fees for home buyers. Briefly noting the law's many innovations, the press devoted the most attention to the HOPE program as a significant breakthrough in the administration's quest to foster homeownership for low-income families in the inner cities.[20]

The HOPE program, described by the press as the crown jewel of Kemp's grand design for saving the inner cities, floundered in its infancy because of inadequate funding. In 1991, the year after passage of the Cranston-Gonzalez Act, the White House and Congress eliminated all funding for HOPE grants. In the deliberations over the fiscal year 1992 appropriations bill, Kemp requested $865 million for HOPE, but the House initially offered only $361 million and the Senate an even more penurious $215 million. Bob Traxler (Democrat, Michigan) in the House and Barbara Mikulski (Democrat, Maryland) in the Senate led the opposition to HUD's request for HOPE funding, questioning the wisdom of selling precious public housing units and dismissing the notion that poor people could ever buy their own homes. In response to intense campaigns by housing lobbies and some city officials, members of Congress were seeking much higher levels of funding for the HOME Investment Partnerships program aimed at increasing the supply of low-income housing. Charging Congress with a "betrayal of low-income families" that amounted to a return "to the failed scandal-prone housing programs of the past," Kemp asked the president to veto the appropriations bill. Bush traded his support of HOPE grants for congressional support of two other measures of higher priority to the administration, the space station *Freedom* and increased funding for the National Aeronautics and Space Administration. To the chagrin of Kemp and other officials at HUD, the president signed the final budget bill on October 28 authorizing just $136 million for HOPE. "From the administration there was a yawn, from Congress there was sniper fire," grumbled Frank Keating, HUD's general counsel.[21]

The White House similarly showed little interest in aiding the cities when it formulated a major transportation bill in 1991. With a number of highway and mass transit authorization measures expiring on September 30 that year, Bush identified an opportunity not only to alter funding levels for existing programs but also to make important changes in federal transportation policy. U.S. Department of Transportation (DOT) Secretary Sam Skinner indicated that he considered the overhaul of the current system his most important undertaking as a cabinet officer and promised a comprehensive effort to pass a path-breaking bill that year. On February 13, with Skinner standing at his side in the White House, Bush presented an ambitious five-year, $105 billion plan that administration spokesmen called the most significant transportation legislation since the creation of the interstate highway system in 1956. The bill outlined the creation of a 155,000-mile National Highway System designed to connect the nearly completed interstate highways with existing and proposed feeder roadways to form an intricate network of roads spanning the country. In most instances, the expansion of the 47,000-mile interstate complex into a National Highway System would entail widening, repairing, and limiting access to existing two-lane highways. The law also provided states with more flexibility in spending funds authorized for transportation, in exchange for having to pay a greater share of the cost for road projects. The big loser in the proposed legislation appeared to be urban mass transit, which would receive only $16.3 billion in federal funds over the next five years. State and local governments would be obligated to contribute a larger percentage of the cost for mass transit capital projects, and the federal government would terminate operating assistance for 147 transit systems in large metropolitan areas.[22]

The administration's transportation bill produced a mixed response on Capitol Hill and elsewhere. The generous provisions for highway construction by the federal government, estimated at $14.3 billion in 1992 and $27.6 billion by 1996, amounted to a one-third increase in spending for the balance of the year and meant immediate infusions of money into a sluggish national economy. The legislation also provided state and local officials and civil engineers with more autonomy in making regional transportation plans and allowed for the construction and operation of more toll roads. On the other hand, the bill's advocacy of the massive National Highway System led New York Senator Daniel Patrick Moynihan to exclaim, "We built the interstate

system, you're not going to build another one!" Moynihan and others
blanched at the short shrift given public transportation by the administration, essentially replicating the harsh practices of the Reagan presidency.
Having absorbed a 50 percent reduction in federal funding since 1981, mass
transit systems in the nation's cities had repeatedly increased fares, cut service, and deferred maintenance on aging infrastructures. Jack Gilstrap, the
executive vice president of the American Public Transit Association, called
the administration measure's lavish spending on road building "a recipe for
more traffic jams, air pollution, and wasted energy." Mass transit advocates
capitalized upon the growing awareness of conservation issues, an especially
important consideration after Congress's passage of the Clean Air Act of
1990 established exacting standards for reducing pollution from motor vehicles in metropolitan areas. Legislators perceived the necessity of passing a
transportation bill that complemented the Clean Air Act, and the outbreak of
the Persian Gulf War in February 1991 underscored the need to lessen the
nation's dependence on foreign oil. For a host of reasons, continued neglect
of mass transit systems was becoming politically less tenable in many quarters by the early 1990s.[23]

Opposition to the DOT bill quickly took shape in Congress, where a bipartisan coalition of senators took exception to the administration's preoccupation with road building at the expense of urban mass transit. On April 25
Senators Moynihan, John Chafee (Republican, Rhode Island), Frank Lau-
tenberg (Democrat, New Jersey), and Steve Symms (Republican, Idaho) introduced an alternative to the DOT measure that quickly became known as
the Moynihan bill. The administration bill revolved around the commitment
of $44 billion to improve 150,000 miles of federal highways, including 47,000
miles of interstates. The Moynihan bill, by contrast, allocated just $14 billion
to roadways and approximately $45 billion to the states for use as they saw
fit—a freedom that the senators felt would inevitably lead to more funding
for urban mass transit. "We've poured enough concrete," said Moynihan. A
second area of dispute involved the states' share of financial contribution for
transportation projects, especially for urban mass transit. The administration measure proposed that the federal government pay 75 percent of the cost
for major highways and bridges, 60 percent for state road and transit programs, and 50 percent for new mass transit spending. The New York
senator's bill proposed a 75/25 federal-state split for all highway construction and maintenance, as well as for mass transit capital projects.[24]

Competing interest groups recognized the vast sums of money at stake in
the congressional deliberations and avidly campaigned for and against the

two proposals. The American Trucking Association, the American Automobile Association, and other highway lobbyists strongly backed the DOT bill, with its traditional emphasis on road building. Because the proposed funding increases would come from higher gasoline taxes, which the highway lobbies characterized as user fees paid by motorists and truck drivers, they contended that the longstanding federal proclivity for road building should continue. On the other side of the argument, a broad coalition that included the American Public Transit Association, environmentalist groups, municipal governments, and urban planners rued the ill effects of an automobile-centered national transportation policy that they argued had outlived its usefulness. Owing to the growing concern with air pollution and expressway traffic congestion, public transportation partisans won many converts on Capitol Hill. "We have demonstrated our ability to build highways to move *vehicles*," commented Representative Norman Y. Mineta (Democrat, California). "Now we must tackle the more difficult challenge of moving *people* within the heavily congested urban and suburban communities connected by these highways."[25]

The battle between the White House and Capitol Hill proved to be prolonged and rancorous, arguably one of the most contentious struggles that developed between the executive and legislative branches during the Bush presidency. In an address to a joint session of Congress on March 6, 1991, the president had identified the transportation bill as one of his top two legislative priorities that year and urged Congress to pass the measure within one hundred days. In his remarks to the American Association of State Highway and Transportation Officials in the White House Rose Garden on June 21, Bush charged that the expensive Moynihan measure relied too heavily on federal spending and thereby jeopardized adequate funding for other programs such as aviation safety, education, health care, and drug enforcement. More important than the issue of cost, said the president, the Senate bill shortchanged the national highway system and funded urban mass transit too generously—thereby undermining the two elements that comprised the heart of DOT's initiative. Equally determined to produce landmark legislation in 1991, Moynihan observed that he had been issuing warnings about the nation's misguided infatuation with the automobile since 1960 and had as a cabinet member and as a U.S. senator seen the federal government make a series of regrettable policy choices inimical to metropolitan America. He agreed with Bush that a holistic new transportation policy must allow states and cities greater freedom in determining how tax dollars would be spent, but he also insisted that municipal governments and regional authorities submit detailed plans for all forms of transportation—not just highways—before receiving federal funding. In Moynihan's design, federal highway money must be fungible, and cities must have the option of building and maintaining mass transit instead of more expressways.[26]

After months of excruciating negotiations between DOT and congressional committees, punctuated by Skinner's threats of a presidential veto, both houses of Congress approved a compromise bill on November 27. Skinner criticized the legislation for its excessive cost and its inclusion of federal funding for mass transit operating assistance, but urged the president to sign the bill anyway. After all, he noted, the final bill contained twelve of the sixteen key initiatives Bush listed in his February 13 White House address introducing the legislation. Bush signed the $151 billion bill on December 18 at a muddy road-building site outside Euless, Texas, saying little to the small crowd of construction workers and dignitaries in attendance about sweeping changes in national transportation policy. Instead, he informed them that the measure would pump $11 billion into the economy and pay for 600,000 jobs. He enthused that the bill "will enable us to build and repair roads, fix bridges, and improve mass transit; keeps Americans on the move, and help the economy in the process. But really, it is summed up by three words: jobs, jobs, jobs. And that's the priority."[27]

The Intermodal Surface Transportation Efficiency Act (ISTEA) of 1991 authorized $151 billion over six years, $119.5 billion for highways and $31.5 billion for urban mass transit. The law satisfied the administration by allocating $38 billion for creation of the 155,000-mile National Highway System and by granting state and local governments greater flexibility in the expenditure of federal transportation dollars. ISTEA designated a portion of the highway funds to transportation "enhancements," including such environmental and aesthetic improvements as the conversion of abandoned rail lines to bicycle trails, the rehabilitation of historic transportation buildings, and the creation of new wetlands. To meet the requirements of the 1990 Clean Air Act, the bill provided states $6 billion in grants to devise strategies for the reduction of congestion and pollution. The legislation pleased urban interests by allocating an unprecedented $31.5 billion for mass transit, by far the largest sum since the federal government began making contributions for that purpose in 1964, with nearly $5 billion earmarked for fifty-seven new rail and bus systems. Significantly, states could spend half—or with the approval of DOT, up to 100 percent—of their federal highway allocations on mass transit. Congress later strengthened the law in 1998 with passage of the Transportation Equity Act for the Twenty-first Century, which allocated

$222 billion for highway and mass transit improvements through 2003. Like ISTEA, this act afforded local officials greater discretion in the use of federal dollars and increased funding for mass transit.[28]

Much of the enthusiasm over the passage of ISTEA in 1991 dissipated the following year, however, as the administration cut back on funding for transportation programs. When Bush threatened to veto any appropriations bill that exceeded his budget request, Congress allocated $1.2 billion less for highway and mass transit programs than in fiscal year 1992. The appropriations bill signed by Bush on October 6, 1992, reduced highway funding slightly but inflicted much deeper cuts in the amount targeted for urban mass transit. Whereas ISTEA had called for $5.2 billion in mass transit spending for fiscal year 1993, the revised sum totaled only $3.8 billion. The administration explained the reductions in terms of the need for fiscal responsibility, and again budgetary belt-tightening fell most heavily on urban mass transit.[29]

Despite the prospect of more mass transit funding under the auspices of ISTEA, the wholesale assault on corrupt programs and practices at HUD, and passage of the important Cranston-Gonzalez Act, the administration continued to receive sharply critical notices for its treatment of urban America. Contrary to Bush's talk during the 1988 campaign of tempering hardheaded economic policy with compassion, the federal government's tepid support of the cities had remained consistent since the close of the Reagan administration. In 1992 more than 42 percent of poor people in the United States lived in inner cities, up from 30 percent in 1968. Because of a large and growing federal budget deficit, the product of a steep economic downturn in 1989, scant hope existed for an increase in grant awards to municipalities. Congress had passed antirecession, countercyclical legislation in 1976 over Gerald Ford's veto and in 1977 and 1978 with Jimmy Carter's approval, creating short-term public works and public service jobs, but it stopped short of doing so in 1990 and 1991 under the threat of a Bush veto. New York City Mayor David Dinkins singled out the deleterious effect of federal funding cutbacks in explaining the mounting problems he was confronting. Federal funds comprised 19.4 percent of New York City's budget in 1980, he observed, but only 9.7 percent in 1990.[30] Equating the actions of the Bush and Reagan administrations toward the cities, Dinkins said: "Since 1980 our creativity in meeting the challenges of urban America has been severely tested, not by any disappearance of will on the part of the people, but by the painful withdrawal of the federal government from American urban life, in housing and child care, in mass transit and public education, in drug enforcement and medical services. The federal government has been on the retreat."[31]

Kemp initially received high marks from big-city mayors for avowing the administration's commitment to aiding the urban poor, but a lack of results soon dampened their enthusiasm. The media reported that Kemp's rivals within the cabinet had effectively isolated him, minimizing his influence with the president, and that his exclusion from the administration's inner circle continued to marginalize HUD in Washington officialdom. Seeing little evidence that the president intended to live up to his 1988 campaign rhetoric, mayors and city officials grumbled that Kemp appeared to be the only high-level figure in the Bush administration who cared about cities. Kemp himself seemed to be taking Bush to task when he said, "The White House is the epicenter of national policy. There are problems of poverty and despair and economic decline in many people's neighborhoods which the president has both a moral and political obligation to address."[32]

Even though Kemp remained a frequent and forceful spokesman for urban America, his effectiveness as an administrator increasingly came into question. As a self-professed "bleeding heart conservative," the HUD secretary earned high praise for his advocacy on behalf of the urban poor and homeless, but critics maintained that the agency was making few strides in alleviating the wretched conditions in the inner cities—a situation that Kemp's defenders attributed to the powerful forces arrayed against him in the administration. Despite the secretary's early success at rooting out corruption in HUD, the press, state and local officials, and members of the housing industry reported that the administration of the agency's programs failed to improve under Kemp's direction. HUD had been quick to excise troubled programs but slow to furnish replacements. Fixated on his own agenda of fostering homeownership among public housing tenants, which was proceeding at a glacial pace, the secretary neglected existing programs to provide affordable rental housing for the poor and effective management of the department. The HOME Investment Partnership program had committed only 4 percent of its $1.5 billion allotment by 1992, a result largely attributable to the crippling restrictions enforced by HUD. Builders and government officials complained that HUD failed to process paperwork efficiently in the Kemp years, in large measure because the fear of scandal and an overabundance of caution led to a bureaucratic paralysis. "Jack was a little traumatized," said Congressman Barney Frank (Democrat, Massachusetts). "Often nothing at all happened because the department was so anxious to make sure that nothing bad would happen." Long delays in approving contracts and authorizing expenditures brought hundreds of proposed projects to a halt and left local housing authorities frustrated and angry. Some critics argued that the ambitious Kemp moved tentatively to authorize new projects and policies for fear of making mistakes that would taint his reputation for probity and jeopardize his political career; others attributed the secretary's inertia to his proclivity for "sexy, empower-the-poor" issues rather than the "nuts-and-bolts technical" concerns of administration. In either case, said Senator Barbara Mikulski, the Maryland Democrat who chaired the appropriations subcommittee that oversaw HUD's budget, "I think he's lost a great deal of steam. Quite frankly, I'm distressed."[33]

Kemp's declining reputation improved somewhat—and the Bush administration's standing in urban America declined further—as a result of the harrowing Los Angeles race riot on April 29–May 4, 1992. The outbreak of violence stemmed from an incident on March 3, 1991, when highway patrolmen pursued a speeding motorist, Rodney King, an African American, on the Foothill Freeway for nearly eight miles before he stopped driving and resisted arrest. A bystander used his video camera to film the white policemen subduing and beating King with clubs as he lay helpless on the ground. The defense managed to move the trial of the four policemen charged with using excessive force to nearby Simi Valley, California, a predominantly white suburban enclave with a reputation for conservative, law-and-order politics. The trial, which concluded more than a year after the incident, attracted a huge television audience and uncovered a number of unsettling facts about the way the understaffed and poorly trained Los Angeles Police Department customarily treated minorities. Ignoring the damning evidence provided by the witness's home video footage, the all-white jury ruled the brutal clubbing of King within the statutory limits prescribed for the treatment of uncooperative criminal suspects. On April 29, 1992, the jury found three of the defendants not guilty and deadlocked in the case against the fourth policeman. Reports of the controversial verdicts spread quickly, sparking a conflagration of rioting, looting, and arson in the Los Angeles metropolitan area. By the time that federal troops had combined with local police to restore order several days later, the toll of the riot included 55 killed and 2,300 injured, approximately 800 buildings destroyed by fire, and an estimated $1 billion in property damage. Race riots followed in Atlanta, Birmingham, Chicago, and Seattle.[34]

The rampage triggered by the frustrating verdict in the Rodney King trial laid bare the racial and ethnic tensions boiling beneath the surface in the nation's second largest metropolitan region and elsewhere. To many residents of America's inner cities, the Rodney King incident seemed emblematic of the shoddy treatment afforded people of color by predominantly white police forces. The violence in Los Angeles could be explained in part by the uneasy relations between poor African Americans trapped in a deteriorating inner city and unsympathetic white policemen, who many ghetto residents viewed as members of an occupying military force, but other factors contributed as well. Rampaging African Americans in Los Angeles assaulted white motorists, dragging them out of their cars and trucks and beating them viciously without provocation. Blacks fought against Latinos, and both groups attacked Asian American small business owners whose modest but steady economic progress served as daily reminders to ghetto and barrio residents of their own lack of upward mobility. The arrival of large nonwhite immigrant populations had increased the heterogeneity of America's metropolises, intensifying economic competition and straining relations between groups of varying cultural backgrounds. The hopes engendered by the civil rights breakthroughs of the 1960s had gone largely unfulfilled in later decades for African Americans, many of whom saw the crumbing of the inner cities as a symbol of the government's failure to deliver on the promises made at a more hopeful time.[35]

The Rodney King riots rekindled discussions about the failure of government to deal adequately with the problems of poverty, unemployment, and crime in the inner cities and specifically called into question the record of the Bush administration in that regard. Subject to intense media scrutiny as the events in Los Angeles unfolded, the White House stumbled to formulate a quick and effective response to the civil disorder. Despite having conferred with Los Angeles Mayor Tom Bradley six months earlier about the likelihood of racial violence in the city, Bush hesitated initially before telling Chief of Staff Sam Skinner that he wanted to address the nation on television. The president finally delivered his speech on May 1, two days after the onset of the rioting, condemning the wanton violence and destruction sweeping southern California and recounting the steps he had already taken to restore order. Emphasizing the robustness of his response, he described the military presence dispatched to the riot area—3,000 National Guardsmen, 3,000 members of the Seventh U.S. Infantry, 1,500 U.S. Marines, and 1,000 federal riot-trained law enforcement officers (FBI, U.S. Marshals, U.S. Border Patrol, and the like). On the one hand, Bush condemned the lawlessness in unmistakable terms. "It's been the brutality of a mob, pure and simple," he intoned. "And let me assure you: I will use whatever force is necessary to restore order. What is going on in L.A. must and will stop. As your President, I guarantee you this violence will end." On the other hand, he lamented the poor state of race relations that led to such behavior, expressed concern about the questionable verdict in the King case, and promised that the U.S. Justice Department would conduct an independent criminal investigation into the events of March 1991. Adding further to the impression of the administration's vacillating and unsure response to the crisis, Bush waited five days before traveling to Los Angeles for a tour of the riot site and meetings with community leaders.[36]

Secretary Kemp reacted immediately to the events in Los Angeles, identifying an opportunity to elevate HUD's profile in the administration and to link the outbreak of civil unrest with the failure to enact programs he had long been espousing. On May 2 he urged the president to consider the rioting in South Central Los Angeles, the epicenter of the disturbance, the product of forces undermining the viability of big cities throughout the nation. The tone of his remarks contrasted sharply with Bush's earlier characterization of the unrest as "the brutality of a mob, pure and simple." Instead, Kemp called the riot a "cry of help." Chronic poverty among African Americans trapped in inner-city ghettos "undermines respect for the law, it undermines respect for property, both your neighbor as well as the community," he said. While chiding Congress for failing to pass his proposals during the preceding three years, Kemp also challenged the White House to intensify its war against poverty, crime, drugs, and despair.[37]

On May 4 Kemp sent a detailed memorandum to the president listing the key initiatives that could then be advanced successfully in Congress. The secretary recommended the creation of vast numbers of enterprise zones throughout the country, the allocation of an additional $93 million in Community Development Block Grant funds, the promotion of youth job training programs in inner cities, the reduction of taxes on wages for low-income people by increasing the Earned Income Tax Credit, and the stimulation of investment by cutting the capital gains tax rate. The arson and vandalism in Los Angeles underscored the point that public housing tenants and renters of slum properties had no stake in their communities and no reason to preserve order, Kemp maintained, so the government should strive to expand property ownership, homeownership, and resident management through the HOPE initiative. In these and other ways, exhorted the secretary, the federal government could take the lead in "greenlining the inner city."[38]

Although nominally the voice of the administration on urban affairs, Kemp repeatedly found his counsel ignored in the White House. Excluded from high-level meetings during and immediately after the riots, the secretary chafed at not being able to exert greater influence in the area of his expertise. Bush consulted Health and Human Services Secretary Louis W. Sullivan, an

African American, to get "the sensitivities that a black man can provide" in
analyzing the Los Angeles race riot. Instead of Kemp, the president put
David Kearns, the deputy secretary of Education, in charge of a federal delegation to meet with California officials after the disturbance while the HUD
secretary remained in Washington, D.C. Kemp persisted in sending unsolic-
ited memoranda to the president offering advice and recounted his views in a
number of interviews with the press, while the members of the news media
continued to portray him as a forlorn figurehead with very little influence in
the White House.[39]

As Kemp recited his pleas for enterprise zones and enhanced homeownership, the discourse on the riots quickly descended into partisan bickering
over which political party or branch of government could plausibly be
blamed for past policy failures in the cities. On May 4 press secretary Marlin
Fitzwater ascribed the recent outbreak of civil discord to the failed social
welfare programs of the 1960s and 1970s launched during Democratic presidencies. Asked by reporters whether he was in fact blaming the Johnson and
Carter administrations for the riots, Fitzwater responded affirmatively. Despite the best efforts of Reagan and Bush, he explained, the "destructive
forces of the social welfare programs of the '60s and '70s" continued to poi-
son the federal government's presence in the cities. Pressed to name specific
federal programs responsible for worsening urban conditions, he replied, "I
don't have the list with me," and then added, "You are all quite aware of
those programs, and they have failed. You could take a look at study after
study." The press secretary also echoed remarks offered earlier that day by
the president blaming the Democrats in Congress for failing to pass measures
proposed by his administration that would have mitigated problems in
neighborhoods such as South Central Los Angeles. Congress perpetuated the
mistakes of the Johnson and Carter administrations and, by denying ghetto
residents a stake in their communities and pride in homeownership, exacerbated a precarious situation. In short, Fitzwater concluded, the Bush administration was "paying the price" for the shortcomings of the flawed social
welfare programs that originated a generation earlier.[40]

Democrats defended the Great Society's urban and antipoverty legislation, demanding that Fitzwater and others in the White House be specific in
their condemnation of past programs. House Speaker Thomas S. Foley
(Democrat, Washington) called the press secretary's claims "totally absurd"
and countered: "There hasn't been a single program identified in this general
sweeping criticism of the legislation of the '60s." In the face of the Democratic attack, administration officials backtracked somewhat and tempered

their earlier remarks. Not all Great Society programs had been disastrous, they conceded, and Bush acknowledged having recommended increased spending on Democratic measures that had proven to be effective. But at the same time, the president refused to disown Fitzwater's remarks totally. "In the past decade, spending is up, a number of programs are up," Bush told a gathering of newspaper publishers on May 6. "And yet, let's face it, that has not solved many of the fundamental problems that plague our cities."[41]

Democrats lost no time in blaming Bush for the tragic events in Los Angeles and for his "malign neglect" of the troubled inner cities. At a meeting of the Democratic Leadership Council on May 2, Arkansas Governor Bill Clinton accused the president of fostering racial discord and thereby causing the riots through his systematic neglect of the inner cities. Kemp accused Clinton of demagoguery and demanded that the Arkansas governor apologize to the president and the American people. On May 8, in his response to a speech given earlier that day by Bush to a group of Los Angeles politicians and community leaders, Clinton reproached White House officials for ignoring some of the commonsensical proposals for aiding the inner cities advanced by Kemp in previous years. Referring to the HUD secretary as the "black sheep" of the administration, Clinton noted that Bush and his closest aides had belatedly taken notice of urban problems only when the Los Angeles riots made the situation impossible to ignore any longer. "I just hope that there will be some conviction behind it," he said of the administration's eleventh-hour pledge to increase federal aid to inner-city ghettos and barrios.[42]

Both the administration and Congress pledged their cooperation in passing an emergency bill for riot-torn Los Angeles and long-term, far-reaching legislation for all cities. On May 13 Bush announced that the Federal Home Loan Bank Board would provide $600 million in low-interest loans to individuals and businesses victimized by the riots. In addition, Congress passed, and on June 22 the president signed, a quick-fix emergency bill to provide disaster relief for sections of Los Angeles damaged by the uprising and funds for repairs to downtown Chicago following massive flooding there in April. The bill earmarked $495 million to the Federal Emergency Management Agency for disaster assistance and $500 million to the Small Business Administration for loans. The negotiations over a comprehensive urban aid package proved more problematic, however, as Republicans and Democrats could not reconcile their considerably different proposals. In a meeting with Democratic congressional leaders on May 12, Bush presented a six-point plan that reiterated the initiatives repeatedly forwarded by HUD in recent years—enterprise zones, reductions in capital gains taxes, more generous funding for

HOPE, subsidies for parents who wished to send their children to private schools, welfare reform, and a "weed and seed" initiative to "weed out" criminals and "seed" targeted neighborhoods with funds for social programs such as Head Start and job training. (A National Public Radio reporter commented puckishly that Bush had finally discovered his urban policy—hiding in Kemp's desk drawer.) Democrats in Congress responded with a $9 billion proposal not unlike the administration plan in many of its particulars but underwritten on a much grander scale. The Democrats wanted more money for social programs across the board, but they also sought additional funding for urban mass transit and a crime control bill opposed by Republicans in the Senate.[43]

The various urban aid bills being considered in Washington, D.C., paled in comparison with the massive federal spending on the cities deemed necessary by big-city mayors. At its annual meeting, the membership of the United States Conference of Mayors (USCM) recommended in June a $35 billion package that included $6 billion for a community development jobs program, $5 billion for public works, $4 billion for improved transportation, $3 billion for job training, and $2 billion for small business loans. Bush declined an invitation to attend the USCM conference, but Kemp showed up to seek the mayors' support for enterprise zones and the HOPE program. He spoke of the need for an "audacious, dramatic effort" in "waging—and this time winning—a new war on poverty" and posited that "an alliance between a radical, bleeding-heart, progressive-conservative HUD secretary and equally activist mayors from across the political spectrum would be unbeatable." The enthusiasm among the mayors generated by Kemp's speech had no impact on the officials on either end of Pennsylvania Avenue who endeavored unsuccessfully to draft a politically tenable and fiscally responsible urban aid measure.[44]

A number of factors subverted the attempt to pass comprehensive urban legislation in the wake of the Los Angeles riot. The debate in Congress revolved around enterprise zones, with Democrats refusing to include the generous benefits that Bush deemed necessary to attract businesses to invest in declining inner-city neighborhoods, and the unacceptable price tag of adding this legislative package to a federal budget already bulging at the seams. The stringent Budget Enforcement Act of 1990, which stipulated that all new legislation passed by Congress be accompanied by tax increases or cuts in existing outlays, left little room for new initiatives. The 1990 law also mandated that any reductions in defense spending be applied to lowering the budget deficit. Big-city mayors and others argued that the King riots demonstrated the need for immediate action, the concerns about red ink notwithstanding, and wondered what happened to the expected peace dividend created by the end of the Cold War. House Armed Services Committee Chairman Les Aspin (Democrat, Wisconsin) suggested toppling the budget wall separating defense and domestic spending to commandeer $6 billion for an urban aid bill. "We've got to decide whether we're for people or budgets," Kemp said. "I'm for budget constraints, but there's an urgent unmet need to create wealth and opportunity in the inner city." No one else in the administration echoed those sentiments, however. "This isn't going to be a tax–increase bill," warned Budget Director Richard Darman, in a statement more reflective of the view from the White House. Many Democrats on Capitol Hill shied away from the cost of yet another large spending bill as well. "Let's face it, we're short of money, and just reaching in our pockets and asking how much is not going to do the job," said Representative Julian Dixon (Democrat, California). "It's not a Republican problem that we face," commented Kurt Schmoke, the Democratic mayor of Baltimore. "I met with the Democratic leadership of the House, and these people just don't get it."[45]

Partisan politics in a presidential election year formed the backdrop for the legislative gridlock that developed in the summer of 1992. Bush's concentration on foreign affairs during the preceding three years, especially the successful conduct of the war against Iraq, had for a time elevated his popularity but also left him vulnerable to charges of indifference to domestic affairs—allegations peaking in 1992 because of the Los Angeles riots and a stubbornly anemic economy. The president hoped to cooperate with Congress in producing legislation affirming his compassion for the urban underclass but, owing to financial limitations, only at a limited cost. At the same time, the incumbent president's most significant challenge for the nomination came from the principal spokesman for the Republican Party's right wing, Patrick J. Buchanan, who had praised the verdict in the Rodney King case and demanded a tough law-and-order stance by the White House after the riots. Bush's consideration of a large-scale urban aid bill, chided Buchanan, indicated the administration's willingness to be blackmailed by urban insurrectionists. "This orgy of violence and lynching cannot be used to shake down the American taxpayer for another Great Society," he warned darkly. Bush spoke optimistically about striking a deal with the Democrats, but his plan for urban recovery essentially recycled earlier proposals trumpeted by Kemp and either rejected by Congress or funded minimally. And economic and political priorities gave the president little room for compromise.[46]

Democrats in Congress felt constrained by political pressures as well. If the executive and legislative branches cooperated to pass a major urban aid bill in the months immediately preceding the election, they feared, Bush would reap the lion's share of the credit and shore up the major weakness on his presidential résumé. In effect, the Democrats would be handing Bush an antidote to their insistent claim that he could not successfully manage the country's economic and social problems. In addition, at a time when the party's strategy for reclaiming the presidency depended upon quashing its image as the single-minded champion of the dependent urban classes and upon attracting middle-class and suburban voters, many influential Democrats worried about seeming too zealous in pursuit of another expensive social welfare law. These concerns resonated strongly with the prospective presidential nominee, Bill Clinton, who pushed the Democratic Party to distance itself from New Deal–Great Society liberalism and cultivate a broader electoral appeal. A former president of the centrist Democratic Leadership Council, Clinton counseled fiscal responsibility, restrained government, and the forging of new links between the poor and middle-class interests. David Mason, an analyst with the conservative Heritage Foundation, observed: "If the Democrats sign up for nothing more than Great Society programs, they run the risk of exacerbating their old image."[47]

In 1992, despite the impetus provided by the Rodney King riots, Republicans and Democrats in Congress lacked the political will to address the worsening problems of urban America. Representative Vin Weber of Minnesota, a close friend and ally of Kemp, represented the Republicans in the negotiations. The HUD secretary maintained a high profile on Capitol Hill during the summer working both sides of the aisle in search of common political ground. A cadre of Democrats, most notably Representative Charles B. Rangel of New York, House Majority Leader Richard Gephardt of Missouri, and Senator Edward M. Kennedy of Massachusetts, labored feverishly to effect a compromise, but their attempts to forge consensus never transcended the political and economic impediments blocking passage. Many legislators, especially Democrats, shied away from Kemp's beloved enterprise zones. Representative Thomas Downey (Democrat, New York) scoffed at the utility of such empowerment schemes as a means of aiding the urban poor, saying: "I think it would be more cost-effective to dump the money out of an airplane over the ghettos." A $3 billion urban aid bill proposed by Representative John Conyers Jr. (Democrat, Michigan) failed to pass, and the second session of the 102nd Congress ended without the adoption of major urban aid legislation.[48]

Unable to agree on comprehensive urban aid legislation, Congress endeavored at the same time to pass a bill reauthorizing the Cranston-Gonzalez National Affordable Housing Act of 1990. In the two years since passage of the housing bill, pointed out its supporters in HUD and on Capitol Hill, implementation of the key HOPE and HOME programs had stalled. Congress had provided no funding for either program in its appropriation bill for fiscal year 1991 and only $136 million for HOPE in the fiscal year 1992 budget. Moreover, stricter requirements for FHA loans implemented by the 1990 housing law had severely reduced the number of families who could obtain low-interest mortgages and led members of the real-estate industry to seek relaxation of the two-year-old standards. Kemp hoped that a new housing law would further deemphasize the federal government's role in construction while providing more aid to public housing tenants and low-income renters for home purchases. Much of the discussion in Congress dealt with an increase in violence against elderly residents of public housing projects after the mentally disabled, drug addicts, and juvenile delinquents became eligible for admission to government-assisted housing under a broadened definition of disability. Consideration of bills in the House and Senate proceeded desultorily at first, but the tempo of activity quickened after the Rodney King riots, as several legislators suggested that the violence constituted in large measure a cry for better housing. What began as limited legislation to fine-tune programs conceived two years earlier became much more expansive—and accordingly generated much more legislative contentiousness. Additional impetus for legislation came in August when the National Commission on Severely Distressed Public Housing, which had been charged in 1989 with formulating a comprehensive plan for action nationwide, presented its final report to Congress. The commission recommended the rehabilitation or replacement of 86,000 public housing units and the pursuit of private and nonprofit management options.[49]

Members of the Senate worked closely with the White House in preparing a bill that followed HUD's lead to reduce the federal government's role in subsidized housing, but the version taking shape in the House veered sharply in another direction. Under the direction of its chairman, Representative Henry Gonzalez, the House Subcommittee on Banking, Finance, and Urban Affairs gave short shrift to the HOPE program and agreed to relax standards for FHA mortgage loans. Seeing the advances he had made in the 1990 law threatened, Kemp became intensely active in Capitol Hill negotiations. "As much as I want to work with you to produce a housing bill in this Congress," he wrote Gonzalez, "I must advise you that the Administration does not intend to start these discussions over issues that have already been debated at length and resolved in the National Affordable Housing Act [of 1990]." Kemp threatened a presidential veto if the housing reauthorization bill produced on Capitol Hill deviated from the vital principles outlined two years earlier—most important, the expansion of the HOPE program, increased power for poor people in the marketplace, and enhanced safeguards for the FHA's family insurance fund.[50]

The final bill approved by the House on October 5 and by the Senate on October 8, which allowed local housing authorities to designate separate housing for the aged and disabled, allocated $32.5 billion for fiscal year 1993 and $34 billion for fiscal year 1994. Kemp approved of the law in some respects but resolutely opposed the proposed resolution of some fundamental issues. He applauded the generous allocations for the next two fiscal years, which represented healthy funding increases over the amounts approved in 1990. Congress authorized $855 million for mortgage subsidies and down-payment assistance so that public housing tenants could become homeowners under the auspices of the Urban Revitalization Demonstration (HOPE VI) program, for instance, including $40 million for the new Youthbuild program, whereby disadvantaged youths would acquire construction skills by helping to build low-income housing. Kemp also praised the groundbreaking lead-based paint hazard reduction provision that created rules to reduce lead-based paint poisoning in private and federally subsidized housing. As a response to research indicating that lead poisoning affected 3 million children under the age of six, especially in public housing projects completed in the 1950s and 1960s, HUD would issue grants to state and local governments for lead-based-paint hazard reduction. The secretary would not support the bill, however, because of revisions made to the 1990 reforms on FHA mortgage loans. He wrote Budget Director Richard Darman requesting that the president veto the measure, which passed in the House by a margin of 377 to 37 and in the Senate by voice vote. Ignoring the very public position staked out by Kemp, Bush signed the Housing and Community Development Act of 1992 on October 28.[51]

Kemp suffered an even more disheartening defeat a few days later when the president vetoed a tax bill that contained a demonstration program for the creation of dozens of enterprise zones. Anticipating a veto after passing the legislation but thinking that Bush might change his mind after the November 3 election, Congress took the unusual step of holding the bill on Capitol Hill rather than forwarding it immediately to the White House for the president's consideration. The day after losing the election to Bill Clinton, however,

Bush vetoed the tax bill. "The original focus of the bill—to help revitalize America's inner cities—has been lost in a blizzard of special interest pleadings," explained the president. By terminating the enterprise zone provision, the president dealt one last blow to the heart of Kemp's design for renewing the inner city and confirmed that a wide gulf existed between HUD and the White House.[52]

As he himself admitted, Kemp compiled an ambiguous legacy at HUD. He earned high marks within the agency and throughout the federal bureaucracy for dealing effectively with the scandals of the Reagan administration. "The department was a leaking, listing hulk [in 1988]," said Frank Keating. "We radically reformed it." Kemp's success at regenerating a bureaucracy burdened by corruption and favoritism and his penchant for new ideas did much to improve HUD's tarnished image. He boasted of introducing innovative new programs that would revolutionize the federal government's role in inner cities, claiming to have put 55,000 public housing tenants "on the path" to homeownership. In fact, HOPE transferred no public housing units to tenant ownership during the Bush years, at a time when the 55,000 families cited by the secretary occupied only 4 percent of the nation's 1.4 million public housing units and more than 1 million families were on waiting lists for admission to public housing. Indeed, HUD made few inroads into providing homeownership opportunities for low-income families. Kemp listed as his greatest "failure" never being able to push through Congress legislation to create significant numbers of enterprise zones, which would channel capital and credit into America's hemorrhaging inner cities.[53]

The White House's reluctance to invest heavily in HUD programs bespoke a continuing concern about budget deficits and, despite the president's promises of more compassion for society's unfortunates, an indifference to the problems of inner-city residents. Stuart Butler, the director of domestic policy at the conservative Heritage Foundation, ascribed the administration's halfhearted attempts to foster social welfare legislation of importance in urban America—what he drolly referred to as Bush's "Skirmish on Poverty"—to several factors: the president's infatuation with foreign policy; White House aides' distrust of the ambitious Kemp, the only member of the cabinet who had run for president in 1988 and whom they suspected would again; the consistent opposition to urban initiatives by the three most influential economic policy makers in the administration, Treasury Secretary Nicholas Brady, Budget Director Richard Darman, and White House Chief of Staff John Sununu; the fear that a Democratic Congress would pander to urban interest groups and convert streamlined programs into wasteful bureaucratic

monstrosities; and the lack of enthusiasm from traditional Republican voting
blocs in the suburbs and the Sunbelt. The administration routinely pointed
to Capitol Hill to explain the lack of progress in addressing problems in the
cities, noted Butler, but in fact the White House evinced decidedly less interest than members of the legislative branch in urban affairs.[54]

In the Bush administration, as during the Reagan years, the New Federalism translated into declining levels of federal spending in urban America.
The nonpartisan Center on Budget and Policy Priorities in Washington,
D.C., reported that spending, adjusted for inflation, fell 82 percent on all
subsidized housing programs, 66 percent on low-income housing, 63 percent
on employment and job training programs, and 40 percent for community
development, community service, and social service block grant programs
between 1981 and 1992. Overall, federal aid to cities declined by more than 50
percent during that time, and funds for both General Revenue Sharing and
Urban Development Action Grants (UDAGs) disappeared altogether. According to a study undertaken by the National League of Cities, federal
spending for municipal programs increased slightly from 1988 to 1992, due
to small increases in CDBGs, job training programs, and mass transit funding, although the proportion of the federal budget devoted to municipal aid
continued to fall. A 1991 survey by the USCM found that, while budgets in
the fifty largest U.S. cities rose by an average of 95 percent between 1980 and
1990, federal contributions declined from 17 percent of municipal spending
to 6 percent. The New Federalism of the Bush presidency again called for
greater self-reliance on the part of urban America.[55]

Bush deviated somewhat from Reagan in enforcing fair housing statutes
more conscientiously, but only in a manner that still discouraged suburban
desegregation. Owing to the passage of the Fair Housing Amendments Act
of 1988, which Vice President Bush had enthusiastically supported, the
number of complaints alleging housing discrimination and the monetary
compensation awarded successful litigants increased nearly tenfold since
the Reagan administration. Assessing the Bush administration's performance in 1991, John Relman of the Washington Lawyers' Committee for
Civil Rights and Urban Affairs identified some shortcomings—a sizable
backlog of unresolved complaints and relatively small damage awards provided to victims, for instance—but overall gave the Bush Justice Department high marks for pursuing "a policy of aggressive enforcement." Yet the
administration's heightened attention to housing discrimination stopped
well short of an attempt to desegregate the suburbs. As the fulcrum of
Kemp's policy to reclaim inner cities, HOPE aimed to sell public housing

units to tenants and encourage low-income families to purchase and reha-bilitate homes where they resided; homeownership became an incentive for minorities and the poor to remain in blighted neighborhoods. Bush's affir-mation of fair housing pertained solely to inner cities and older suburbs, noted the reporter Thomas Byrne Edsall, and he "imposed minimal 'costs' for social responsibility."[56]

In his unsuccessful run for reelection in 1992, Bush continued to boast about his record on fair housing just as he extolled the wisdom of his administration's policies toward urban America. His effusive campaign rhet-oric seemed unpersuasive to many urban voters, however. Dramatic cuts in low-income housing subsidies, funding reductions for other HUD programs, and rising levels of urban poverty and homelessness called into question the efficacy of Bush's "muted conservatism" for the cities. Enterprise zones, HOPE, and other innovations designed to address the plight of the inner-city poor made little headway despite Kemp's insistent efforts to engage the pres-ident and his aides. Indeed, cynics insisted, only the lethal Los Angeles riots and the presidential election campaign in 1992 belatedly elevated the profile of the cities among White House policy makers. The fate of the cities re-mained, as it had been during the Reagan years, subordinate to economic conditions and other domestic issues.[57]

10

BILL CLINTON AND A "THIRD WAY"
FOR URBAN AMERICA

After the twelve years of the Reagan and Bush administrations, both of
which preached the virtues of a new federalism and reduced the flow of resources to urban America, big-city mayors hoped that the election of a
Democrat in 1992 would revive the Great Society liberalism of the 1960s.
Liberals expressed ambivalence at the outcome of the election, however,
unsure that a Clinton presidency would necessarily spark a renewal of the
federal government's commitment to the cities. As the five-term governor
of Arkansas, Bill Clinton had taken progressive stances on such social issues as abortion and health care but carefully positioned himself as a "New
Democrat" with a moderate message tailored for middle-class voters in the
suburbs. As cofounder and chairman of the centrist Democratic Leadership Conference (DLC), he had espoused "an ideas-based movement focused on shaping a specific mainstream alternative identity for the [Demo-
cratic] party." (Some liberals within the party archly suggested that DLC
stood for "Democrats for the Leisure Class.") His speeches frequently attacked the huge budget deficits created by the Reagan-Bush tax cuts and
extolled fiscal responsibility at a time when big-city mayors clamored for
funding increases. Indeed, the DLC tailored its positions on urban issues to
the examples set by white politicians who succeeded black mayors in New
York City, Chicago, Los Angeles, Philadelphia, and other cities. Having
governed during the lean years of the 1980s, those white mayors preached
budget-tightening, tax relief, curtailment of costly social programs, and
tougher law enforcement—and less reliance upon federal largesse. They
frequently repudiated affirmative action and quotas in municipal hiring
and rejected a rights-based liberalism in favor of public-private partnerships when appealing to minority voters. In their belief that strengthening
community institutions offered more promise than reflexively funneling
more federal dollars into distressed cities, the DLC's urban policy experts

questioned the need for the Clinton administration to develop an urban policy at all.[1]

On the other hand, Clinton had received high marks from liberals during his time as head of the Progressive Policy Institute in the early 1990s and had earned a large following among women and minorities through his repeated demonstrations of empathy for society's unfortunates. He had forged such a close and enduring relationship with African Americans that the novelist Toni Morrison later called him the nation's first black president. During the campaign and in the hopeful winter months of 1992–1993 after his election, Clinton promised that mayors and local officials would once again be welcome in the corridors of federal power—that they would be given "a seat at the table." The Democratic candidate's effusive campaign references to the New Deal and the Great Society and his promise to build on the legacy of those reform movements encouraged the people who hoped for a sharp break from the urban policies of the Reagan-Bush years.[2]

At least in symbolic ways, Clinton's actions in the White House validated that optimism. Unlike Reagan and Bush, Clinton maintained a highly visible presence in the nation's cities during his presidency. As a frequent worshipper at inner-city black churches and a visitor at public housing projects, Clinton orated movingly about society's responsibility to combat racism and poverty; surrounded by civil rights leaders and African American politicians, many of whom had been his friends for many years, he affirmed his administration's commitment to improving the quality of life in inner-city ghettos. Reagan and Bush had seldom met with big-city mayors to discuss their concerns and rarely accepted invitations to speak at the national meetings of the United States Conference of Mayors (USCM) and the National League of Cities, but Clinton made time to meet with the mayors in a variety of venues. He selected two big-city mayors, Henry Cisneros of San Antonio and Federico Peña of Denver, as the secretaries of Housing and Urban Development (HUD) and Transportation, respectively. He likewise appointed Donna Shalala, former assistant secretary of HUD and board member of the New York City Municipal Assistance Corporation, as secretary of Health and Human Services and Robert Rubin, a Wall Street investment banker who had advised the mayor of New York City on urban policy, to head the National Economic Council (NEC). Unlike his Republican predecessors, he had stocked the upper tiers of the executive branch with experienced policy makers who were fully conversant with the condition of the cities.[3]

Yet despite a number of apparent differences from his Republican predecessors, Clinton failed to enact policies that increased federal support of

urban America. Determined to eliminate the mammoth budget deficits he
had inherited, reluctant to reduce defense appropriations, and hesitant to
propose an unpopular tax increase, Clinton opted repeatedly for curtailing
domestic spending. As well, partisan politics presented a constant challenge
for a two-term president who failed to amass popular vote majorities in either of his elections. Clinton triumphed in 1992 with only 43 percent of the
popular vote, owing his winning plurality to the fact that third-party candidate H. Ross Perot secured a surprising 19 percent, and won reelection four
years later with 49 percent of the vote. Unable to rely upon the backing of a
bifurcated Democratic Party and opposed by a rejuvenated Republican
Party that regained control of both houses of Congress in 1994, Clinton tra-
versed a treacherous political terrain that complicated the task of passing
any sort of reform legislation; the impeachment battle that consumed much
of his second term further undermined whatever political credibility he enjoyed on Capitol Hill. Thus constrained by economic and political forces, the
president advanced revised proposals for enterprise zones and other cautious
initiatives popular with earlier Republican administrations, cut back on traditional liberal programs such as low-income housing, and presided over a
major overhaul of the nation's welfare system. His attempt to find a "third
way" to address urban problems fell short of quelling the partisan rancor
suffusing Washington, D.C., kept the federal government on a path of reduced funding for local governments, and left the defenders of urban America bemoaning the continuing deterioration of the cities.[4]

To shape his inchoate plans for an innovative urban policy, Clinton selected Henry Cisneros as secretary of HUD. After studying urban planning
at the Harvard School of Government, Cisneros had returned to his native
San Antonio and entered politics. As mayor of the city from 1981 to 1989 and
president of the National League of Cities, he became nationally known for
engineering government-industry partnerships in failing neighborhoods. In
1989, owing to his son's medical problems and the disclosure of his extra-
marital affair with a constituent, Cisneros decided not to seek reelection as
mayor and opened a successful financial consulting company. He returned
to public life after the 1992 Watts riot, which convinced him of the urgent
need for renewed attention to big-city ghettos. His varied experiences as a
popular urban politician and a successful entrepreneur made him the perfect choice to preside over the president's proposed marriage of hardheaded
pragmatism and entrepreneurialism; his openness to experimentation and
history of cultivating good relations with the financial community reinforced Clinton's repudiation of the Democrats' longstanding reputation for

hostility toward big business. Cisneros seemed ideally suited to wean cities from their dependence upon federal largesse by creating public-private partnerships. "If there is one man who was born to be HUD secretary," said Jack Kemp, testifying in the Senate over the selection of his successor, "It is Henry Cisneros." Agreeing with Kemp, members of the Banking, Housing and Urban Affairs Committee recommended approval by a vote of 19 to 0. The discussion on the Senate floor the following day proceeded cursorily, moving the nomination briskly toward confirmation. Only Lauch Faircloth (Republican, North Carolina) offered negative comments, criticizing HUD for operating too many programs for the homeless and questioning the nominee sharply about whether he would cut the agency's budget to help reduce the federal deficit. The Senate confirmed Cisneros by voice vote on January 21.[5]

From the outset of the Clinton presidency, members of the Domestic Policy Council (DPC) and an ad hoc urban task force struggled to formulate a coherent approach to the problems of the cities—an approach that would confirm the administration's genuine interest in the issue but at the same time specify the parameters that distinguished the "third way" from earlier strategies that had been found wanting. "Urban economic and community development has been a graveyard for liberal Democrats for decades," observed Paul Dimond, a member of the Domestic Policy Council, who warned that the Clinton administration must avoid the "place-based" urban programs that "have consumed much public treasure and many political careers for little return." Dimond and other White House officials outlined a plan for spending tax dollars wisely, encouraging public-private partnerships, fostering individual responsibility, and, wherever possible, limiting the activities of government in the marketplace. Echoing the words of prior Republican administrations, Clinton aides maintained that government's most useful contribution to urban welfare would be to direct a national economic recovery. In preparing for a February 5 meeting with the USCM, HUD Secretary Henry Cisneros urged the president to emphasize the potential for federal housing and community development efforts to stimulate the national economy. At the meeting with the mayors, Clinton outlined how his attention to two matters—bringing health care costs in line with inflation and getting banks to lend freely again—would provide more aid to cities than anything else the federal government could do. Those two changes would increase economic activity among the people who would pay more taxes to local governments, the president explained, providing municipal governments with desperately needed revenue. A resurgent national economy would help the cities immeasurably, and government support of community development would also bolster the administration's economic stimulus package by creating jobs.[6]

Deliberations in the spring of 1993 over the creation of urban policy proceeded exactly one year after the race riots that devastated southern California. The civil unrest that followed the controversial verdict in the Rodney King case, which had been announced on April 29, 1992, gave Bill Clinton and other Democrats the opportunity to pillory President Bush's inattention to rising racial tension and to the decline of the inner cities. Keenly aware of the impending anniversary of that event, members of the urban task force believed that the mishandling of the King riots by the Republican administration had been an important factor in Clinton's 1992 victory. Furthermore, they agreed with community leaders that conditions in South Central Los Angeles had continued to deteriorate in the year since the riot. Despite promises from Washington, D.C., to aid with the physical and emotional rehabilitation of the riot-torn ghetto, the Bush administration had reduced funding earmarked for reconstruction of the riot area from the fiscal year 1993 budget. Few businesses in Watts had been rebuilt, the number of guns on the streets had increased, the promise of new development projects had gone unrealized, and demoralized neighborhood residents had lost faith in the government's promises to address problems rampant in inner-city ghettos. The task force members recommended the appointment of a cabinet member as a presidential emissary to Watts—someone other than HUD Secretary Cisneros, who had just been designated the administration's liaison with South Florida after Hurricane Andrew—as well as a new plan to coordinate federal assistance to the area damaged by the riot and to stimulate nonprofit initiatives by foundations and philanthropy-minded businesses. In addition to establishing credible policies that would appease public officials and community leaders in Los Angeles, a necessity to forestall another outbreak of violence where wounds from the previous year's violence had not yet healed, White House policy makers also urged immediate action on two long-term policy initiatives that would constitute the core of the president's third way— the enterprise zone/community development bank proposal and crime/community policing plans, both of which they intended to introduce publicly in April. The anniversary of the Rodney King riots would serve as an opportunity to contrast Bush's indifference with the Clinton administration's short- and long-term plans to save the cities.[7]

Optimism in America's cities dimmed in the first months of 1993, however, when the Republican Congress eviscerated the administration's $16.3

billion economic stimulus package. The supplemental appropriations bill, a grab bag of diffuse measures designed less to address long-term economic and social problems than to stimulate the economy immediately, included public works projects to create jobs and spur economic development in cities, provide summer employment for youths, and enhance social welfare programs for the poor. Republicans and conservative Democrats in Congress refused to support massive spending before the government made any attempt to reduce the federal budget deficit. Conservatives on Capitol Hill vehemently objected to measures targeted for the cities, especially a proposed $2.5 billion increase in the Community Development Block Grant program and a $1.2 billion allocation for transportation (public bus systems, subway and light rail projects, airport refurbishment, and capital improvements for Amtrak). The House approved the bill relatively quickly, but a Republican filibuster in the Senate withstood four unsuccessful cloture motions. Democratic sponsors finally deleted everything from the bill except a $4 billion emergency appropriation to continue payment of unemployment benefits for the remainder of the fiscal year. A chagrined Clinton signed the truncated bill on April 23, grumbled mayors and urban lobbyists, without having devoted much time or expended much political capital to salvaging something for the cities. Even more demoralizing to the cities than the loss of additional funding, the defeat of the stimulus package seemed to reflect the administration's tepid commitment to passing a major piece of legislation devoted primarily to furthering urban interests.[8]

The cities received some good news in 1993 with the expansion of the Earned Income Tax Credit, which benefited low-income working families with children, and the passage of legislation creating enterprise zones. The enterprise zone bill sent to Congress by Clinton that spring, the centerpiece of the administration's efforts to aid the cities, resembled legislation first introduced on Capitol Hill more than a decade earlier by Republicans. Attempts to provide federal funding for the program foundered during the Reagan and Bush administrations, but by the early 1990s approximately 2,000 enterprise zones had been created in forty states—including Arkansas under Governor Clinton. States had provided low-interest loans, reduced sales and local property taxes for businesses that located in declining neighborhoods, and offered tax credits to firms that hired employees locally, but economists argued that financial constraints on the states limited the scope and effectiveness of the endeavor; only the federal government could provide the necessary resources to stimulate investment in otherwise uninviting locales. Clinton acknowledged the importance of the federal government's participation but insisted that grassroots organizations and local governments must take the lead in designing projects for funding. Committed to insuring the financial soundness of his administration's enterprise zone proposal, he mandated cooperation among communities, the federal government, and the private sector. The president demanded that local governments, despite their precarious economic situations, provide some financial commitment through in-kind contributions, technical assistance, or some other nonmonetary contribution. Clinton said that the enterprise zones detailed in the administration's bill would empower people and community organizations, provide maximum flexibility, cut red tape, minimize the role of the federal government, and invest limited government funds judiciously.[9]

In contrast to the more ambitious legislation submitted earlier, some of which provided for the creation of as many as three hundred enterprise zones, Clinton sent Congress a much more modest bill. The streamlined Clinton plan posited the creation of ten "empowerment zones," which stood to receive the lion's share of the tax breaks, and one hundred "enterprise communities," which would obtain lesser benefit packages, as selected by the secretary of HUD. Of the $4.1 billion requested in new tax breaks over five years, the plan allocated $3 billion for employment and training wage credits for businesses in the ten empowerment zones and the remaining $1 billion for other tax credits in all 110 communities. The bill also provided for the chartering of a national network of community development banks, empowered to lend money from a federal Community Banking and Credit Fund, and Community Partnerships Against Crime, a HUD program to reduce crime in public housing. An enterprise board of domestic agency cabinet secretaries would supervise the programs. As the principal spokesman for the bill, Cisneros outlined four themes that underscored the centrality of enterprise zones to the administration's preeminent goal of community empowerment—economic responsibility, community responsibility, family responsibility, and individual responsibility. White House officials boasted that the emphasis on community empowerment, which moved well beyond the shopworn argument between liberals and conservatives over federal spending increases on the one hand and tax breaks for business on the other hand, constituted nothing less than the reinvention of government.[10]

Clinton's use of enterprise zones as the cutting edge of his "third way" predictably stirred opposition from both conservatives and liberals, the former for still investing too much power in government at the expense of market solutions and the latter for its limitations in the face of calamitous urban conditions that cried out for a massive infusion of federal dollars. Denouncing the administration's proposal for failing to offer adequate incentives for business investment in the inner city, Jack Kemp called for the elimination of all capital gains taxes for anyone who worked or invested in an enterprise zone. "We need to let the marketplace work," he intoned. Senator Joseph Lieberman (Democrat, Connecticut) charged that the proposal created too few "real" zones and too many "quasi-zones." Citing the need to curb spending so that a tax increase could be avoided, conservatives in the Senate eliminated the enterprise zone proposal from the deficit-reduction bill to which it had been attached in the House. The thirty-eight members of the Congressional Black Caucus, who constituted an influential bloc of votes in a closely divided Congress, refused to support any bill lacking the Clinton proposal and ultimately negotiated the reduction of an energy tax favored in the Senate in exchange for a scaled-back version of the enterprise zone plan. Title XIII of the Omnibus Budget Reconciliation Act of 1993, which the president signed on August 10, allocated $2.5 billion in tax incentives over five years for Empowerment Zones/Enterprise Communities (EZ/EC) and $1 billion over two years for a social services block grant for the enterprise zones. The law created nine empowerment zones (six urban and three rural) as well as ninety-five enterprise communities (sixty-five in urban areas and thirty in rural areas). The social services block grant provided $100 million to each of the urban enterprise zones, $40 million to each of the rural empowerment zones, and $2.95 million for each of the enterprise communities. The law contained no capital gains tax cut, allowing instead a capital gains tax deferment for stock in some small businesses, and eliminated the enterprise board. On September 9, ignoring the wishes of the congressional majority, Clinton created the President's Community Enterprise Board, comprised of representatives from seventeen federal agencies and chaired by Vice President Al Gore, to assist him in implementing community empowerment efforts in distressed urban and rural areas.[11]

Skepticism about the EZ/EC provision, the heart of the congressional battle over the Omnibus Budget Reconciliation Act of 1993, persisted after passage of the bill. EZ/EC differed from the Republican version propounded throughout the 1980s by Jack Kemp and others in three principal ways—its addition of social service grants to tax incentives for private enterprise, the requirement of community planning at the local level, and the inclusion of a supervisory board within the federal government to monitor the selection and administration of enterprise zones. The selection of a small number of cities on a competitive basis, a process of designating urban laboratories that resembled the approach utilized earlier by Model Cities, deviated from the free market approach favored by conservatives. Critics further faulted EZ/EC for awarding enterprise communities a "consolation prize" of $2.95 million in social service grants, a token amount by any yardstick. As the evaluation of applications submitted by dozens of communities proceeded in 1993–1994, mayors and legislators questioned the fairness of the selection process and the potential importance of political influence. Again, as in the case of Model Cities, concerns arose about a federally funded urban program becoming simply another opportunity for Democrats to disburse pork to their political allies in the nation's big cities. Finally, what would happen to the thousands of communities not selected for aid—and to the fortunate few cities chosen for inclusion when funding elapsed in the future?[12] Even the administration's spokesman for the program in the House, Charles B. Rangel (Democrat, New York), confessed to an initial lack of enthusiasm for the idea. He said: "I rejected the whole concept under Reagan. But people came to me and said, 'How can it hurt?' So I just said, 'What the hell.' But when it started looking like the urban policy for the nation, it was obviously inadequate."[13]

By the June 1994 application deadline, HUD received 74 applications from cities seeking urban empowerment zones and 219 applications from municipalities pursuing designation as urban enterprise communities. In evaluating the applications, HUD Assistant Secretary Andrew Cuomo and others on the interagency committee considered the merits of the proposals and sought evidence of community participation. On December 20, 1994, the White House announced the six cities awarded empowerment zone funding—Atlanta, Baltimore, Chicago, Detroit, New York City, and Philadelphia/Camden. (The administration also selected as its three rural empowerment zones the Kentucky Highlands, Mid-Delta, Mississippi, and the Rio Grande Valley, Texas). Yielding to the intense disappointment in several cities with powerful Democratic mayors, the administration also awarded $125 million in HUD grants to Los Angeles and $90 million to Cleveland, as well as $25 million in social services block grants to Boston, Houston, Kansas City, and Oakland. After the designation of empowerment zones and enterprise communities, very little happened in the designated cities as the wheels of the federal bureaucracy turned in slow motion. Vice President Gore's Community Enterprise Board scheduled no meetings until the summer of 1995, and HUD failed to complete memorandums of agreement with the empowerment zone cities until the early months of 1996. The administration finally allocated money for the empowerment zones in the waning months of 1996, more than two years after cities originally applied for funding.[14]

As the administration meticulously laid the groundwork for the creation of enterprise zones, which would affect only a small number of communities and not show results for several years, Cisneros hoped to commence substantive reform of the nation's assisted housing programs. His bold agenda for HUD included demolishing many of the sterile high-rise towers that loomed over blighted neighborhoods, improving the enforcement of fair housing legislation, and enhancing the geographic mobility of low-income families that had been trapped in the inner city. Through the use of Section 8 vouchers, he hoped to move tenants of subsidized housing projects out of the distressed areas to which they had long been confined and to break down the barriers separating cities and suburbs within metropolitan regions. Through his advocacy of the EZ/EC program and vigorous desegregation measures, the secretary indicated his intention of pursuing both "people" and "place" approaches to urban redevelopment.[15]

At Cisneros's urging, the administration implemented two small pilot programs designed to increase the mobility of the inner-city poor. The Moving to Opportunity demonstration project, based upon action taken in metropolitan Chicago in the 1970s as a result of a federal court ruling in the *Gautreaux* case, provided Section 8 vouchers, moving expenses, day care stipends, and counseling to approximately 7,500 renters receiving welfare payments in New York City, Chicago, Boston, Los Angeles, and Baltimore to allow them to move to better neighborhoods. The two-year, $235 million initiative generated immediate resistance in the metropolitan regions surrounding the five cities and a torrent of negative publicity in the media. A *Wall Street Journal* columnist lambasted Moving to Opportunity for "sowing chaos in suburban neighborhoods, rewarding those who are dependent on the state, and alienating middle class Americans who end up paying for apartments that they themselves could not afford." The program fared little better on Capitol Hill where Senator Barbara Mikulski of Maryland, the ranking Democrat on the Banking, Housing, and Urban Affairs Committee, expressed sympathy for the idea of helping families flee what she called "zip codes of pathology" but called Moving to Opportunity "too controversial." Congress quickly cancelled the funding for the second year. Cisneros said, "We learned not to offer a program like this during an election year, when people are looking for a wedge issue and are not above frightening people with questions of race." The second pilot project, the Bridges to Work program, allocated $17 million for four years to provide ghetto residents in Baltimore, Chicago, Denver, Milwaukee, and St. Louis with better transportation so that they could work in the suburbs.[16]

The Moving to Opportunity and Bridges to Work programs grew out of the secretary's longtime interest in reducing the "spatial separation" between the races and socioeconomic classes in the inner cities and the suburbs. Cisneros wrote in the introduction of *Interwoven Destinies: Cities and the Nation*, a collection of essays published shortly after he became HUD secretary, about how government subsidies had historically favored suburban sprawl and about how metropolitan-wide strategies would be necessary to renew inner cities. Under the secretary's guidance, HUD hosted conferences and sponsored research projects concerning the need to address metropolitan and regional problems rather than dealing solely with urban and suburban issues separately. Nevertheless, the increased scholarly attention to metropolitanism failed to generate meaningful policy initiatives. Like its predecessors, the Clinton administration found affluent suburbs extremely resistant to working in tandem with the core cities that anchored their metropolitan regions—especially when cooperation across municipal boundaries meant breaking down residential barriers that separated communities by race and social class.[17]

Cisneros spoke frequently about the importance of fair housing, pointing out that homebuyers and renters continued to be denied lodging because of their skin color or family status, and identified the issue as one of HUD's top priorities. The agency undertook more vigorous enforcement of existing fair housing statutes, and the Civil Rights Division of the Justice Department followed suit. The administration attempted to hold local housing authorities accountable for promulgating racial segregation through their location of public housing projects in certain neighborhoods—in the most notable case, seizing control of low-income units in Vidor, Texas, to grant African Americans occupancy—but in most instances singled out the real estate and mortgage industries for their role in blocking desegregation efforts. In a variety of ways, HUD and the Civil Rights Division of the Justice Department targeted banks and other lending institutions to encourage fair lending practices. HUD provided grants to local fair housing groups that monitored banks granting mortgages in their communities and then published online analyses of the banks' lending practices with regard to race and income. Perhaps most significantly, the administration instructed federal bank regulators to consult those findings when deciding whether to approve or deny bank mergers and acquisitions. Fair housing advocates gave the administration high marks for increasing the pressure on lending institutions, an effort that allowed more minority home buyers to obtain mortgages, but rued its failure to pass legislation that would expand the scope of the Community Reinvestment Act of 1977. Indeed, the percentage of home purchase loans institutions approved under the auspices of the act decreased from 36.1 in 1993 to 29.5 in 2000.[18]

Frustrated with the halting progress achieved in the administration's early days, Cisneros made the case for more extensive federal activity on behalf of the cities in a November 24, 1993, memorandum to the president. "Our nation's cities and communities are in deeper trouble than I imagined when you nominated me to be Secretary of HUD a little less than a year ago," began Cisneros, who went on to applaud Clinton's efforts but noted that more needed to be done. He lauded the president's call for "civic engagement and moral renewal" in a recent speech in Memphis, Tennessee, that emphasized the importance of individual initiative in combating urban problems but warned that Americans would respond: "Yes, Mr. President, we hear you, but we need your help. We need you to do something." Cisneros acknowledged that, indeed, the president had done a good deal to aid the cities, much more than many people realized. In addition to the EZ/EC program, noted the secretary, the administration's list of accomplishments included, among others, augmentation of the Earned Income Tax Credit, the permanent extension of low-income housing tax credits, avid enforcement of fair housing laws, and enactment of anticrime legislation. These varied achievements constituted the threads of a program that needed to be woven together into a "coherent fabric of urban policy," argued the secretary, a goal attainable only through vigorous presidential leadership. "I do believe it is important that you speak to your urban base," said Cisneros, "and describe what you are doing for poor and working people." Otherwise, the critique after the Memphis speech would persist that the administration was offering less an urban program than a potpourri of self-help ideas.[19]

In the summer of 1994, presumably in response to Cisneros's urging, the White House formed a committee within the executive branch to recommend how the administration could forge a comprehensive urban policy. Carol Rasco, head of the Domestic Policy Council, Robert Rubin, head of the National Economic Council, and Jack Quinn, deputy chief of staff to the vice president, convened a series of meetings and worked with staff at the Office of Management and Budget to prepare recommendations. In October the committee released a draft report listing a series of steps to be taken in response to the concern expressed by mayors, minority groups, and inner-city residents that the administration had paid inadequate attention to urban issues. Echoing Cisneros, the committee listed as one of its prime objectives the unification of "disparate, fragmented, and overlapping 'urban' problems across federal agencies." Beyond fulfilling existing commitments to the

EZ/EC initiative, the report urged a second phase of community empowerment whereby the administration would encourage inner cities to build linkages to the private sector with special attention to such issues as crime, youth, and jobs. The report also recommended the elimination of brownfields as a major impediment to economic development in distressed urban areas. In all of the administration's activities on behalf of the cities, the report emphasized, the federal government should avoid any top-down model and insist upon community empowerment. Ideally, improved coordination among government agencies and greater community activism would lessen the need for additional resources.[20]

Although sentiment within the White House for greater federal involvement in the cities was increasing in 1994, concern over the election that year acted as a powerful countervailing force. The press widely interpreted a series of setbacks in the first two years of the Clinton administration, most notably concerning the status of gays in the military, gun control, and the establishment of a national health care system, as the rejection of big government liberalism. Having unsuccessfully backed those reforms, the president seemed to have reneged on his 1992 campaign promises of government restraint and more private-public cooperation. A number of investigations into the financial dealings of the president and the first lady, as well as charges of sexual harassment against the president, raised serious questions about ethical standards in the White House. As a special prosecutor's inquiries moved from failed land deals in Arkansas and the firing of White House travel agents to the president's sexual peccadilloes, public opinion polls indicated that public trust in government had reached an all-time low. Repudiating liberalism and trying to distance the Democratic Party from its New Deal–Great Society roots, Clinton backed legislation designed to appeal to conservative and moderate constituencies. The administration's reauthorization bill for federal housing programs, which Congress failed to pass, included more money for care of the homeless and enforcement of fair housing statutes but displeased liberals by recommending substantial cuts for public housing operating subsidies and modernization accounts. The reauthorization bill likewise requested additional funds for such unobjectionable items as the Section 202 program, which provided federal assistance to builders of housing for the elderly, and the HOME program, which offered matching grants to cities and states for affordable housing. Clinton also proposed a welfare reform bill designed to increase personal responsibility and limit the length of time that indigents could receive federal assistance. The USCM expressed concern about the stringency of the welfare reform bill, which failed to attract enough

Democratic support for passage, especially objecting to steep entitlement cuts that would hurt the most vulnerable segments of the urban population.[21]

To burnish his law and order credentials, the president secured passage of a $30.2 billion crime bill in 1994. Public opinion polls showed that voters ranked high crime rates at or near the top of their list of concerns, and mayors and big-city police chiefs lobbied avidly for increased federal involvement in what had historically been perceived as a local issue. Democrats in Congress summoned Republican mayors such as Rudolph Giuliani of New York City and Richard Riordan of Los Angeles to testify in favor of the Clinton crime bill, hoping to demonstrate that support of the measure cut across party lines. The bill signed by the president on September 13 allocated unprecedented sums of federal dollars for a number of grants to state and local governments—$8.8 billion for police departments, $7.9 billion for the construction of prisons, and $6.9 billion for crime prevention programs. The law also created dozens of new federal capital crimes, mandated life sentences in prison for third-time violent offenders, and banned nineteen types of semi-automatic assault weapons. The Republican opposition in Congress had argued for more stringent measures—including more funding to hire policemen, less gun control, harsher sentencing guidelines, and far fewer dollars for crime prevention programs—but Clinton justifiably claimed that the crime bill set new benchmarks for providing financial aid to state and local law enforcement authorities.[22]

The crime bill drew a mixed reaction from city officials and members of the urban lobby, who tempered their praise for a measure that offered additional resources to needy cities with expressions of concern. On the one hand, local officials eagerly welcomed the $8.8 billion for police departments at a time when many communities had had to cut allocations for law enforcement because of budgetary shortfalls. The new law mandated that 85 percent of the $8.8 billion be used to put more patrolmen on the streets and the remaining 15 percent for training and equipment to enhance community policing programs that emphasized closer community-police relations at the grassroots level. Of the $6.9 billion for crime prevention, HUD would allocate $1.6 billion for direct aid to poor communities (according to a formula that considered relative poverty, unemployment, and local tax rates) for education, substance abuse treatment, and job training programs. Crime prevention would also underwrite programs that created or expanded urban parks, boys and girls clubs in public housing, and midnight basketball leagues. On the other hand, as much as they welcomed the influx of federal funds to enhance their crime-fighting efforts, big-city mayors regretted that the largesse could not be earmarked for more compelling problems. As one policy analyst put it, "The busy and new-to-Washington bees over in the White House seem determined to land in every public policy flower in the field—except the ones on which the mayors would like to see them alight." Many members of the Congressional Black Caucus called the bill too punitive, decrying its imbalance in favor of law enforcement rather than crime prevention; wary African American legislators provided almost half of the thirty-four Democratic votes against passage. Rather than providing significant funding increases for public housing, Community Development Block Grants, job training, and Project Head Start, the Clinton administration had seemingly chosen to shore up its standing with the political center by placing more uniformed policemen on the streets, building more prisons, and lengthening jail terms.[23]

Dismissing Clinton's eleventh-hour move to the electoral center as so much political expediency, his opponents on Capitol Hill continued to depict him as a traditional Democratic champion of free-spending, intrusive government. House Minority Whip Newt Gingrich (Republican, Georgia) skillfully exploited the president's flagging popularity by drafting a Republican "Contract with America," a list of ten goals that included a pledge to cut taxes, a constitutional amendment that mandated a balanced federal budget, legislative line-item vetoes, severe limitations on welfare, a prohibition of U.S. soldiers being placed under United Nations command, the expansion of death penalty provisions, and the abolition of one or more cabinet departments. Gingrich pronounced the 1994 election a referendum on Democratic liberalism and big government, effectively drowning out Clinton's protestations that his administration stood for fiscal responsibility, welfare reform, free trade, law and order, and local empowerment. The election results in November 1994 devastated the Democratic Party. In the most pronounced electoral swing in the modern era, the Republicans gained nine seats in the Senate, fifty-four seats in the House, and eleven governorships. With a majority in the Senate (52 to 48) for the first time since 1986 and a majority in the House (230 to 204) for the first time since 1954, the Republican Party arguably wielded more legislative power in the national government after the 1994 election than at any time since the Second World War. So did conservatives. The election of seventy-three freshman Republicans to the House, many of them Southerners ideologically to the right of Gingrich, underscored the conservative triumph that year. "The nails are in the coffin," observed a leader of the moderate DLC. "New Deal liberalism . . . is dead and buried."[24]

Republican majorities in the 104th Congress moved quickly to implement the Contract with America, which posed an immediate threat to the plans conceived in the White House for developing a more cohesive urban policy. The conservative drive to cut taxes, maintain high levels of defense appropriations, and shrink the federal deficit required considerable reductions in domestic spending across the board. Despite the fact that HUD had already absorbed substantial cuts—Cisneros had eliminated twenty-one of the agency's eighty-one field offices, terminated 1,500 staff members, and pared the agency's budget by $800 million—congressional foes of the administration targeted the cities for further reductions. First, Congress specified $16.5 billion in rescissions from the fiscal year 1995 budget approved the year before. HUD absorbed $6.3 billion of the retroactive cuts, mostly from its public housing and Section 8 allocations, which amounted to a 24.9 percent decrease in the agency's budget. After initially vetoing the bill and salvaging some funding for the Community Development Funding Institutions program and AmeriCorps, the national service program, Clinton signed the measure in July 1995. Second, Congress pursued additional spending reductions for HUD in the epic struggle over the fiscal year 1996 budget. Clinton's proposed budget cut HUD's base budget and staff, but his congressional antagonists demanded even more reductions. The battle concluded in April 1996, seven months into the fiscal year, after several presidential vetoes and two shutdowns of the federal government—from November 14 to November 19, 1995, and from December 16, 1995, to January 6, 1996. The president managed to save some programs, such as Community Development Funding Institutions and AmeriCorps, but the final fiscal year 1996 budget once more eviscerated HUD by eliminating all new Section 8 vouchers and exacting deep cuts in public housing, existing Section 8 allocations, and other urban programs. Robert Reischauer, the former director of the Congressional Budget Office, called the damage to municipal governments and the urban poor in 1996 "historically unprecedented."[25]

The survival of HUD seemed genuinely at risk. The Contract with America had called for the elimination of cabinet departments as a means of shrinking the federal government, and the deep budget cuts inflicted upon HUD following the landslide Republican win in November 1994 made the agency a logical choice for eradication. "You could abolish HUD tomorrow morning and improve life in most of America," charged Gingrich, who went on to explain why the agency was being singled out for expulsion. "Its 'weak constituency,'" he said, "makes it a prime candidate for cuts." Republicans Lauch Faircloth of North Carolina and Sam Brownback of Kansas introduced bills in the Senate and the House respectively to dismantle HUD, and a bill championed by Rick Lazio (Republican, New York), chair of the House Banking

Committee's Subcommittee on Housing and Community Opportunity, proposed the repeal of the Wagner-Steagall Housing Act of 1937 and the 1969 Brooke Amendment, which limited the amount of rent that public housing tenants paid based upon their income. White House staff discussed cooperation with the Republicans, openly considering the selection of HUD as a sacrificial lamb so that other agencies and programs might withstand the conservative onslaught. The president agreed that such action might be unavoidable, and only the remarkable efforts of Secretary Cisneros saved the agency from termination.[26] Michael Stegman, assistant secretary of HUD for policy development and research commented: "This was a brutal time. Henry [Cisneros] did an extraordinary job of protecting HUD, an agency targeted for elimination. He spent an enormous amount of time justifying the need for a cabinet-level department aimed at urban areas and the poor."[27]

Cisneros sought nothing less than the reinvention of HUD, fashioning a daring plan, "Reinvention Blueprint," that he shared with the White House and then released to the public. Besides changing the name of the agency to the "Department of Community Investment and Housing," a modification designed to emphasize a new commitment to economic development, he proposed consolidating HUD's sixty existing programs into three block grants: the Community Opportunity Fund, devoted to emphasizing job creation and cleaning up brownfield sites; the Affordable Housing Fund for the administration of all assisted housing programs; and a Housing Certificate Fund, which would combine all vouchers and rental housing subsidies. State and local governments would administer the three block grants, a situation that Cisneros believed would be extremely popular with the governors and mayors who would exercise exclusive control over expenditures. The FHA would become an autonomous, government-owned corporation that would address its financial problems with flawed HUD programs and return to the business of providing insurance for first-time homebuyers and others who had been unable to obtain suitable housing in the private market.[28]

In its most controversial section, Reinvention Blueprint called for the eventual elimination of public housing. Conceding that a half century of federal policy had consigned the poor to warehouses for society's most dysfunctional families, Cisneros flatly stated that the federal government must "get . . . out of the business of public housing." The federal government should begin by severing all ties with public housing authorities, he said, leaving local and state officials to deal with chronic financial and managerial problems. Utilizing the HOPE VI model, the federal government would aid in the demolition of high rise projects and provide vouchers to relocate the displaced residents. HUD would gradually withdraw operating subsidies from local housing authorities, which would then compete with private land-lords, nonprofit corporations, and other housing providers for the business of low-income tenants who received federal vouchers. Ideally, Cisneros noted, HUD would employ vouchers exclusively. No longer directly involved in the provision of low-income housing, HUD would serve as a catalyst for change and as senior partner in an intergovernmental consortium guiding local col-laborations. The federal government would also regulate the limited amount of financial aid to the states and localities based upon their success at meet-ing specific performance goals. The boldness and sweep of the secretary's proposal testified to the seriousness of the threat confronting HUD. "Nobody else could have gotten away with demolishing public housing," remembered Assistant Secretary of Housing, Federal Housing Commissioner Nicolas Ret-sinas. "Cisneros was immune from criticism."[29]

The concessions offered by Cisneros elicited starkly different reactions from the supporters and opponents of HUD. Fearful that the federal govern-ment would be abandoning public housing tenants to the vagaries of the pri-vate housing market, the Council of Large Public Housing Authorities, the Low Income Housing Information Service, the National Housing Law Proj-ect, and other advocacy groups accused the secretary of capitulation. The rhetoric in Reinvention Blueprint invoking decentralization, intergovern-mental cooperation, and freedom of choice, they feared, simply provided cover for the wholesale desertion of the inner cities. The tenor of the secretary's remarks received a much more favorable reception in the 104th Congress, where Republicans continued to prune housing appropriations from the federal budget while encouraging HUD officials to explore policy reforms. Cisneros diverted the discussion away from the mechanics of cabi-net reconfiguration to a narrower consideration of agency reform. His ploy rescued the agency from a congressional death sentence in 1995, but officials at HUD and the White House recognized that the postponement of action would likely be temporary. "Proponents of [HUD's] elimination will be back," cautioned Cisneros. "We will be hunted."[30]

Having secured a reprieve for his agency, Cisneros continued in the sum-mer of 1995 to argue within the administration for the creation of a compre-hensive urban program. Despite the imposing barriers presented by the des-iccated federal budget and a hostile Congress, the secretary implored Clinton to act decisively on behalf of urban America. Despairing that continued inac-tion by the government had resulted in the loss of inner-city youth to gangs, drugs, and guns, he argued in a long August 9 memorandum to the president that events of that summer compelled an immediate response from the White House to forestall further unsustainable setbacks for urban America. According to many local leaders, the sudden outbreak in the preceding months of civil unrest in several communities—especially Indianapolis, Los Angeles, and Coconut Grove (outside Miami)—bespoke the inevitability of wider disturbances throughout the nation. At the same time, noted Cisneros, the administration was running the risk of losing the battle for the cities to the political opposition. Despite having imposed what the HUD secretary called "unconscionable" budget cuts, the Republicans under the leadership of Speaker of the House Gingrich were criticizing recent Democratic presidencies as ineffectual and promising hard-headed new economic policies that purportedly would benefit the cities more than the discredited liberal nostrums of past decades. Gingrich had appeared before the USCM to present the Republican case, and his think tank, the Progress and Freedom Foundation, was meeting with mayors and other city officials to discuss the kinds of innovative policies that could be included in a projected Contract with America's Cities. Mayor Norm Rice of Seattle applauded Gingrich's efforts and remarked that he and other mayors hoped to see similar displays of interest by the administration. As the White House began preparing the last budget it would submit to Congress before the close of the president's first term, Cisneros argued, a strong statement in defense of cities needed to be made. He said that the creation of a handful of empowerment zones and a larger number of enterprise communities, all inadequately funded, fell far short of an authentic urban program.[31]

Yet at a time when city officials called out for more aid from the federal government, the administration responded with retrenchment in preparation for the president's reelection campaign in 1996. Members of the Domestic Policy Council (DPC) and the National Economic Council (NEC) discussed the feasibility of pursuing a second round of competition for empowerment zones in deference to the remarkable response in 1994. More than five hundred communities had submitted proposals for urban and rural EC/EZ awards, reflecting an unprecedented outburst of community organizing and strategic planning that could easily and quickly be translated into a second batch of worthwhile applications. Regardless of whether Congress approved a second round of EC/EZ grants, the policy makers argued, the president would receive credit for having demonstrated a continuing commitment to the cities. Even so, despite the enthusiastic support for a second round of awards by HUD, the DPC and the NEC recommended to Clinton that the program be deferred due to inadequate funding. In a teleconference with

the president on June 20, 1995, the members of the USCM expressed their
concern with the penuriousness of the projected budget toward urban America. Mayor Rice of Seattle commented that the Community Development
Block Grant program, which he described as the mayors' "priority program," did not appear at all on Clinton's list of protected programs that year.
The president responded that certain "necessary cuts" had to be made to
avoid the "unacceptable pain" of curtailing funding for education, Medicare,
and other domestic programs. To the growing dismay of the mayors, financial exigency continued to trump attention to urban concerns.[32]

In 1996 the administration edged even further to the political right at the
expense of the urban poor. Promising sweeping reform at his State of the
Union address that year, the president proclaimed: "The era of big government is over." Foreshadowing one of the most controversial acts of his presidency, Clinton affirmed his 1992 campaign pledge to "end welfare as we
know it" by reducing the length of time that welfare recipients could receive
federal aid. In 1995 government appropriations for approximately 13.4 million people receiving cash payments from Aid to Families with Dependent
Children (AFDC), the federal-state entitlement program created in 1935 that
provided assistance to low-income families, totaled $22.6 billion. According
to Clinton, new legislation was needed to reduce the staggering cost of public
assistance at a time of budget overruns, to address the abuses in a highly unpopular system that fostered welfare dependency, to provide work incentives, and to encourage individual responsibility. Clinton vetoed two measures favored by congressional conservatives in late 1995 and early 1996,
calling them excessively harsh, but continued to express his desire to approve
legislation that met the goals he set for sweeping welfare reform. A small but
dedicated core of Democrats in Congress led by Senator Daniel Patrick Moynihan of New York staunchly opposed Republican proposals for terminating
AFDC, which they argued would exact inordinately steep cuts in food stamps
and aid to legal immigrants. On July 29 representatives of more than a dozen
civil rights, religious, and low-income advocacy organizations met with Clinton urging him not to sign a Republican bill gaining momentum in Congress.
"It appears that Congress has wearied of the war on poverty and decided to
wage war against poor people instead," Hugh Price, the president of the National Urban League, said to the president.[33]

Disregarding the objections of the liberal spokesmen, as well as the opposition of the secretaries of HUD, Health and Human Services, and Labor,
the president signed the Personal Responsibility and Work Opportunity Reconciliation Act of 1996 on August 22. Clinton expressed concern about the

excessive reductions in food stamps and aid to legal immigrants but praised the legislation overall as a necessary corrective to a welfare system desperately in need of overhaul. The new law replaced AFDC with the Temporary Assistance to Needy Families program, which provided state authorities considerable discretion in allocating block grants provided by the federal government. The Personal Responsibility and Work Opportunity Reconciliation Act stipulated that heads of low-income households would relinquish federal aid after two years if they had not found employment and could not receive benefits for more than five years during their lifetimes. The Temporary Assistance to Needy Families program immediately pared the number of people receiving public aid to an estimated 12.2 million and reduced necessary funding to $20.3 billion; public aid rolls numbered fewer than six million recipients by 2000. Along with greater economy, unemployed families and individuals would break the bonds of welfare dependency and enter the labor market.[34]

Dismayed that a Democratic president had signed legislation that countermanded more than sixty years of social welfare policy, liberals inveighed against what many termed an act of craven political expediency. Congressman Charles Rangel bitterly admitted that passage of the law constituted a "big political victory" for Clinton but voiced his displeasure that "my president will boldly throw one million into poverty." Marian Wright Edelman, president of the Children's Defense Fund, charged that the president's signature "makes a mockery of his pledge not to hurt children. It will leave a moral blot on his presidency and on our nation." Moynihan agreed that the elimination of AFDC would hit hardest the youngest members of low-income families, decrying the law's premise that "the behavior of certain adults can be changed by making the lives of their children as wretched as possible. This is a fearsome assumption." He called the Personal Responsibility and Work Opportunity Reconciliation Act the "most brutal act of social policy since Reconstruction."[35] Asked by reporters what he would say to the furious Democrats who had been so critical of the law, Clinton responded:

> We saved medical care. We saved food stamps. We saved child care. We saved the aid to disabled children. We saved the school lunch program. We saved the framework of support. What we did was to tell the states, now you have to create a system to give everyone a chance to go to work who is able-bodied, give everyone a chance to be independent. And we did—that is the right thing to do.[36]

Having cooperated with the president to reform the nation's welfare system, Republicans in Congress also sought in 1996 to pass legislation that would fundamentally overhaul public housing. Representative Rick Lazio and Senator Connie Mack (Republican, Florida), who chaired the House and Senate banking committees responsible for overseeing housing issues, introduced bills purporting to consolidate funding for public housing and low-income rental assistance and to transfer federal authority for subsidized housing to local housing authorities. Concurring with the wisdom of devolving power from HUD to local housing authorities and combining scattered federal housing programs into block grants, Cisneros worked with Lazio, Mack, and Senator Christopher Bond (Republican, Missouri) to craft legislation that would make the provision of public housing more efficient. Congress adjourned in 1996 without reconciliation of the two bills because of the inability to win support in the Senate for the more extensive measure passed in the House. Senators balked at two provisions of the Lazio bill—the repeal of the Wagner-Steagall Act of 1937 and the elimination of the Brooke Amendment, which required local housing authorities to fix tenant rents at 30 percent of their income.[37]

Later that summer, Clinton signed a housing appropriations bill that confirmed the administration's rightward drift. In an influential article in the October 20, 1996, edition of the *New York Times Magazine*, Jason De-Parle reported that the president had the previous month signed a budget authorizing the construction of no new low-income housing. In the halcyon days of the early 1970s, the federal government had built as many as 400,000 units annually. The number declined to an average of approximately 100,000 units per year during the two Reagan terms and to around 75,000 a year during the Bush administration. Contrary to the expectations of public housing advocates, the number fell further to 40,000 a year during the first years of the Clinton administration. At a time when the federal government was spending $66 billion annually on mortgage insurance and property tax deductions for middle-income homeowners—about four times the amount allocated for low-income housing subsidies—HUD was devoting increasing proportions of its dwindling budget for repairing, preserving, and replacing public housing units rather than building new ones and for evicting gang members and drug dealers from the crime-ridden projects. In his remarks at the September 26 signing ceremony for the authorization legislation, Clinton said little about the absence of funding for new public housing units; instead, he reported that the bill would allow HUD to accelerate the demolition of the nation's worst public housing projects and provide more livable housing in the future. HUD secretaries traditionally measured their progress by the growth of the subsidized housing inventory, DeParle noted, but Cisneros faced the prospect of possibly being the first to preside over an actual decline in the number of low-income units.[38]

In January 1997, shortly after Clinton's reelection, Cisneros announced his resignation from HUD under a cloud of scandal. In March 1995 U.S. Attorney General Janet Reno had appointed an independent counsel to investigate allegations that Cisneros lied to FBI investigators about illegal payments to a former mistress during background checks prior to his appointment as HUD secretary. (In December 1997 the Justice Department indicted Cisneros on eighteen counts of conspiracy, giving false statements, and obstruction of justice; two years later, he negotiated a plea agreement and paid a $10,000 fine.) Whatever shortcomings the Clinton administration may have had, mayors, urban lobbyists, and other liberals praised Cisneros for his work at HUD during the previous four years. First and foremost, insiders credited him with indispensable leadership in saving the agency in 1995, when Republicans sought to terminate its existence and top officials in the White House seemed willing to go along. Cisneros received high marks for investing the new HOPE VI program, which had been conceived at the end of the Bush administration, with energy and resources. He immediately brought a degree of professionalism and sound business practices to an agency that had compiled a poor record of performance and struggled with a series of scandals since its inception. He had also improved HUD's accounting procedures and internal management systems. "In the 1980s, HUD was drifting and losing talented people," observed Eric Belsky, the research director of the Millennial Housing Commission. "Under Cisneros, HUD was the embodiment of 'good government.' There was an emphasis on re-energizing the agency and making it work more effectively."[39]

Clinton appointed Andrew Cuomo, who had served the previous four years as assistant secretary of HUD for Community Planning and Development, to succeed Cisneros as agency secretary. Whatever ambitious plans Cuomo may have had for halting the retrenchment ongoing at HUD during recent decades, he faced the same financial limitations and political pressures that had confounded Cisneros in the preceding four years. At Cuomo's senatorial confirmation hearings, conservative Republicans referred to HUD as a "bloated and poorly run bureaucracy" and warned the secretary designate to expect a continuation of lean financial times due to diminishing resources. Republican Senator Lauch Faircloth, who had introduced a bill in the 104th Congress to eliminate the department, accused HUD of having become a "massive Washington bureaucracy" that had "lost sight of its mission." Senator Richard C. Shelby (Republican, Alabama) concurred, threatening continued loss of funding. In response, Cuomo announced the continuation of the downsizing initiated by his predecessor. Under his plan, a massive reorganization of HUD would include job cuts leading to the reduction of the agency workforce by nearly 30 percent over the next four years. He also pledged to decentralize the agency's operation, ceding more authority for the management of public housing to local field offices. The Senate unanimously confirmed Cuomo on January 29, 1997, amid much bipartisan praise for his qualifications and experience—but not until Republicans made clear that their kind words for the nominee had no bearing on the plans they harbored for the agency he would lead.[40]

In 1997 Representative Lazio and Senator Mack reintroduced legislation to reconfigure public housing by elevating poor families from government dependency to self-sufficiency. As in the previous year, Republicans in Congress declared their intention of achieving sweeping changes in the operation of public housing to complement the reform of welfare effected in 1996; the bills passed in their respective chambers of Congress, but the legislative session ended before the House and Senate could agree on a measure to send to the president for his signature. Also, as in the previous year, the version passed in the House called for abrogation of the Wagner-Steagall Act and a revision of the Brooke Amendment that would allow local housing authorities to charge tenants a greater percentage of their income for rent. In contrast to the deliberations in 1996, however, Cuomo maintained a greater distance than Cisneros had from the Republicans in Congress. The secretary criticized the Lazio bill in particular for directing a disproportionate share of scarce resources to the working poor and forcing the poorest public housing residents—those unable to pay more than 30 percent of their income for lodging—out of subsidized housing and onto the streets. He also lobbied on Capitol Hill for an administration measure that retained the 1937 housing law and combined numerous HUD programs into two revenue streams, one for capital expenditures and the other for operating expenses.[41]

After three years of legislative wrangling, Congress passed a major alteration of public housing in 1998. The Quality Housing and Work Responsibility Act, which Clinton signed on October 21, amended the Wagner-Steagall Act, devolved authority from the federal government to state and local housing authorities, and changed income requirements to allow for a greater mix of incomes in public housing. The bill also required that 75 percent of Section 8 vouchers be reserved for people making less than 30 percent of the median income in the locality. While legislators from both political parties believed that the quality of life for low-income residents would improve if more working tenants lived in public housing, liberal Democrats insisted on protecting the interests of the very poor. The final bill required that local housing authorities reserve at least 40 percent of public housing for the very poor (those earning 30 percent or less of an area's median income). The bill also required that able-bodied adult residents of public housing devote at least eight hours a month of service to their communities or to an approved economic self-sufficiency program; local housing authorities would terminate the leases of tenants who failed to comply with the community work requirement. "This bill completely overhauls America's indefensible current public housing system," boasted Speaker of the House Newt Gingrich. "This bill could almost be considered the second stage of the Republican welfare plan."[42]

Although sustained economic growth persisted throughout the second Clinton administration, pockets of privation remained in large American cities. As HUD officials put it, "The bright light of America's current economic success has not illuminated all corners of our country." Encouraged by Cuomo to address the plight of the urban poor, Clinton initiated conversations with Republican leaders in Congress about passing an antipoverty bill. He visited big-city slums and depressed rural areas throughout the summer and fall of 1999 to publicize the fate of the 32 million Americans (11.8 percent of the population) who continued to live in penury. On his travels, Clinton urged the expansion of his EZ/EC program and touted the virtues of a "new markets" initiative that provided tax credits, low-interest loans, and other incentives to attract capital to high-risk urban neighborhoods. In November 1999, the president and Speaker of the House Dennis Hastert (Republican, Illinois) announced their mutual support of a bipartisan bill blending the Democratic and Republican community development proposals into landmark antipoverty legislation. The bill would extend the life of the thirty-one existing empowerment zones, create nine new ones, underwrite a new markets package, and include two new Republican programs to aid the cities— the creation of forty "renewal communities" (empowerment zones with additional regulatory relief and an exemption from capital gains taxes) and the expansion of "charitable choice" opportunities (allowing the use of federal funds to support faith-based substance abuse programs in inner cities). Clinton and Hastert agreed to cooperate fully in securing passage of the bipartisan bill by the following year. "We may be wrong," said the president of the goal he shared with the Speaker, "but we actually believe that we can bring the benefits of free enterprise to poor people."[43]

Although the White House hoped that the Clinton-Hastert entente would engender a spirit of bipartisan cooperation on Capitol Hill, the path to passing an omnibus antipoverty bill in 2000 proved to be a tortuous one. To a great extent, the difficulty stemmed from the parties' very different philosophies on how best to aid the indigent in America's cities. Committed as ever to market solutions, Republicans envisioned the federal government's role as limited to providing capital gains tax and regulatory relief. Secondarily, they hoped to underwrite the work of faith-based organizations dedicated to helping the poor help themselves. Even the New Democrats who rejected their party's traditional practice of providing federal grants to city halls favored a substantial role for the federal government in administering subsidies for private investment—an approach that many Republicans felt still involved too much centralized planning in Washington, D.C. These philosophical differences appeared most clearly in the distinction between Clinton's empowerment zones and the Republicans' renewal communities, the latter adding capital gains tax exclusion and regulatory relief to the former's menu of tax incentives. In its final form, the community renewal bill that Clinton signed on December 21, 2000, included a series of compromises that allowed both parties to claim victory for their pet nostrums. The legislation expanded the number of empowerment zones to forty, allotted funding for forty renewal communities, provided new markets tax credits, and underwrote charitable choice. In its most elemental form—in its inclusion of tax credits, capital gains tax relief, and federal funding for faith-based antidrug programs, instead of jobs programs, construction of low-income housing, and other federal grants to cities—the antipoverty package represented the culmination of Clinton's two-term exploration of a third way for government to aid urban America.[44]

Clinton's eight years in the White House saw a striking improvement in the national economy, but questions remained about how much the administration's third way aided the cities. To be sure, the country enjoyed a remarkable economic recovery from the lingering recession of the Bush years. Per capita income increased, wages for unskilled workers rose after a fifteen-year decline, unemployment decreased to the lowest level since the 1960s, and home ownership rates soared to an all-time high. The nation's poverty rate fell substantially, aiding African Americans, Latinos, and the urban poor along with other groups. Rising tides did indeed lift all boats, and policies initiated by the Clinton administration, such as the raising of the minimum wage rate and the expansion of the Earned Income Tax Credit, clearly contributed to the improved condition of the urban poor. Thanks in some measure no doubt to the 1994 crime bill, the government reported the

lowest felony rates in three decades. The residents of America's cities benefited, according to White House officials, from the "stealth" urban agenda
pursued by the president. Without fanfare, went the argument, Clinton
boosted cities by reviving the national economy, opening inner-city neighborhoods to unprecedented infusions of investment capital, rewarding work
and devaluing welfare, creating empowerment zones, providing local law enforcement officials with more resources for improving public safety, and in-
stituting other reforms to lure the private sector back into the forsaken
neighborhoods of the ailing cities. By resisting overt interventions into local
affairs and insisting on fiscal responsibility in spending on urban programs,
domestic policy aide Bruce Reed commended the president, "you succeeded
where LBJ failed."[45]

White House officials lauded Clinton's third way for engineering a dramatic economic turnaround, restoring the "vital center" of American politics
by nudging the Democratic Party back into the electoral mainstream and
laying the foundation for an inner-city revival based upon private investment, but many liberals expressed disappointment with the sum and substance of the two-term administration. With a Democratic president presid-
ing over a strong economy, they asked, how had the cities not fared better?
By the White House's own admission, unemployment and poverty rates remained unacceptably high—a nagging problem that continued to plague
inner cities much more than suburbs. Despite economic data showing reduced poverty levels and enhanced remuneration for the working class, the
gulf between the highest and lowest socioeconomic classes continued to expand during the 1990s; the gap between the rich and the poor in America remained the widest of any industrial nation. Marian Wright Edelman, president of the Children's Defense Fund, saw the economic upswing of the
Clinton years as a missed opportunity, saying: "We should be ashamed we
haven't made more progress in this economy. . . . What's going to happen
when a recession comes?" An official in the Department of Health and
Human Services agreed: "We've clearly made gains in this administration.
But I think we missed an opportunity to do even better."[46]

Furthermore, disgruntled liberals warned, the president's success at
creating a framework for increased private investment in the cities by no
means ensured that empowerment zones, renewal communities, new markets, and exceedingly generous packages of tax incentives would inject
enough capital into failing big-city neighborhoods to offset the continued
loss of federal funding. Big-city mayors applauded many aspects of devolution, at least in principle, and warmly welcomed corporate investment in

their communities but wondered about the price to be paid in diminishing grant dollars. Clinton's record on federal aid to the cities certainly gave them pause. Rather than reversing the downward trend in urban spending that prevailed in the 1970s and 1980s, the administration unquestioningly ranked deficit reduction and budget balancing as its top priorities. The seminal Clinton initiatives such as the EZ/EC program and new markets, operating initially on a limited scale and funded sparingly, produced few immediate results and paled in comparison with the federal government's past expenditures for urban uplift.[47]

The administration's treatment of housing, which many observers considered the key barometer in measuring the federal government's assistance to urban America, won few plaudits from the cities. From the outset of his administration, Clinton failed to identify housing as a majority priority. Under Cisneros, HUD survived a partisan assault aimed at dismantling the department but absorbed substantial budget reductions; Cuomo found it necessary to implement further economies. The agency's strategy for the provision of low-cost housing during the eight years of the Clinton administration included the construction of fewer subsidized units, the accelerated use of HOPE VI funding to demolish distressed public housing projects, and the utilization of Section 8 vouchers to redistribute public housing renters to better neighborhoods. The viability of HOPE VI depended upon the success in finding suitable lodging for uprooted tenants, which became problematic when the appropriation bills passed by Congress in 1995, 1996, and 1997 provided no new funding for Section 8 vouchers. The situation caused grave concern as the contracts for thousands of Section 8 units negotiated in the 1970s and 1980s expired in the mid-1990s and the government's commitment to meeting the projected multibillion dollar cost of renewal remained questionable. Legislation passed in 1997 and 1999 permitted a restructuring of Section 8 contracts, which maintained the viability of the popular program and allowed HUD to avoid a financial disaster, but the decision of 10 percent of landlords at that time to opt out of government subsidization in favor of market-rate rentals eliminated an estimated 87,000 units of low-income housing. Between 1991 and 1999, the number of units available to low-income families in American communities decreased by 940,000. Administration officials hoped that passage of the Community Renewal Tax Relief Act of 2000, which increased allocations to the states for Low Income Housing Tax Credits, would stimulate the construction of subsidized housing by offering more tax incentives to private developers.[48]

Repeatedly avowing his determination to balance the federal budget, Clinton initially cooperated with Congress to keep a tight rein on spending for urban mass transit as well as low-income housing. As the national economic climate improved during the 1990s, the president responded to the liberal call for substantial increases in funding for public transportation to offset the deep cuts of the Reagan-Bush years. In his first year in office, Clinton sought and received a tiny budget increase for transit programs that elevated funding to the level reached in the final Carter budget (fiscal year 1981). The following year, however, the administration's commitment to a "shrinking purse" produced cuts in operating assistance for mass transit and grants to purchase buses and build terminals. In 1995 Clinton proposed an overall reduction in spending for transportation programs, resulting in a 12 percent cut in allocations for bus and commuter rail systems. Vice President Al Gore repeatedly lobbied for increased aid to mass transit as a key component in reviving inner cities and reducing traffic congestion and urged transferring federal dollars from highway construction to mass transit systems, but the administration continued to seek modest increases for transportation funding in deference to fiscal responsibility.[49]

Owing to the widespread popularity of allocations for highways and commercial aviation, Congress in the 1990s regularly approved funding increases for road repairs, automobile and truck safety measures, and airport construction; year after year, mass transit and Amtrak received the smallest sums from transportation budgets. In the budget approved for fiscal year 1996, for example, Congress increased aid for highways but cut allocations for every other mode of transportation. Budgets that reduced amounts for mass transit usually eliminated money for new projects first and preserved some funds for state and local governments to be used for operating assistance. In deference to the importance of mass transit to the millions of New York City commuters, Senator Alfonse D'Amato (Democrat, New York) led the fight for increased federal support of urban mass transit during the Clinton years; the majority of legislators on Capitol Hill, recognizing the reliance of most Americans on the automobile, sought enhanced highway funding for their districts and states. When federal budgetary surpluses mounted and the national economic picture improved in the mid-1990s, House Transportation and Infrastructure Committee Chairman Bud Shuster (Republican, Pennsylvania) and Senate Environment and Public Works Committee Chairman John Chafee (Republican, Rhode Island) recommended that the portion of gasoline taxes used for deficit reduction instead be spent for additional highway construction and other infrastructure enhancements.[50]

In the wake of the Bush-era economic recession, with budgetary deficits having been converted into surpluses, federal policy makers approved the most significant transportation legislation of the Clinton years. On June 9, 1998, the president signed the Transportation Equity Act for the Twenty-first Century (TEA-21), a six-year, $217 billion bill that increased by 40 percent the federal allocations authorized by the Intermodal Surface Transportation Efficiency Act (ISTEA) of 1991. Consolidating many of the gains won in the 1991 law, TEA-21 increased flexibility in the use of federal funds by municipal governments. Clinton initially balked at the legislation's steep cost, expressing concern that TEA-21 "must be within the balanced budget and should not crowd out critical investments in education, child care, health care, or threaten our budget discipline," and considered a veto if Congress failed to eliminate a number of earmarks to reduce the price tag. In the end, however, he concluded that the measure "does a lot more good than harm, much more." Increasing funding for both highways and mass transit, providing $176 billion for the former and $41 billion for the latter, the 1998 measure assumed special significance in its endorsement of ISTEA's bequest of authority for transportation investments to local authorities. Most important, TEA-21 conformed to the decentralization that defined the Clinton administration's third way.[51]

Several factors bolstered Clinton's announced intention to develop a third way for the improvement of urban America—the need to address a worrisome federal deficit by curbing domestic spending, the dramatic electoral turnaround in 1994, Republican control of Congress for six of the president's eight years in office, and Clinton's own ideological predisposition to practice a politics of moderation. The alliance between New Democrats and Republicans in the 1990s led to devolution of authority, fiscal restraint, reduced spending on urban programs, and a heightened reliance on private capital to regenerate the cities. The 1996 Democratic Party platform boasted that "Republicans talked about shifting power back to the states and communities—Democrats are doing it." Although Henry Cisneros and Andrew Cuomo escaped the opprobrium directed by urban liberals at many of their predecessors and generally received acclaim for their leadership of an embattled agency, HUD during the 1990s continued its steady decline in size, resources, and influence. To many disgruntled liberals, talk of a stealth urban policy was meant to obscure the absence of any policy at all. The Clinton administration seemed more the logical extension of the Republican presidencies that preceded his than a throwback to the Democratic activism that characterized the 1960s.[52]

11

THE FATE OF CITIES

In the years immediately after the Second World War, the federal government devoted few resources directly to city governments. The United States spent approximately fifty times as much money on the military as on metropolitan problems in the 1950s and early 1960s, not surprisingly so as the nation became embroiled in the Cold War against Communist nations, but also allocated four times as many dollars to agriculture as on urban development. The situation changed dramatically in the 1960s as recurrent race rioting, the declaration of a war on poverty, and the widespread recognition of an urban crisis in America led to the provision of unprecedented amounts of federal aid to the cities. According to the Advisory Commission on Intergovernmental Relations, the ratio of federal grants awarded state and local governments to the amount of revenue generated locally increased from 11.5 percent in 1950, to 16.8 percent in 1960, to 22.9 percent in 1970, to 31.7 percent in 1980. Declining Rust Belt cities of the Northeast and Midwest in particular benefited from the increased largesse flowing from Washington, D.C. By the end of the 1960s, for example, Pittsburgh received ninety-one cents from the federal government for every dollar spent by the city; Newark and Cleveland followed closely behind, garnering sixty-four cents and sixty cents respectively. Faced with the loss of population, jobs, industry, and retail to suburban and Sunbelt locations, the mayors of ailing inner cities warned of their inability to deal with intensifying fiscal crises and gladly accepted as much financial aid as the federal government was willing to provide.[1]

Identifying himself as a progressive who sought to continue the New Deal policies of his predecessor, Franklin D. Roosevelt, Harry Truman came into the White House when cities desperately needed federal aid to address problems left festering during the Great Depression and the Second World War. Truman's Fair Deal reform program foundered, sidetracked by the urgent needs of demobilization and conversion to a peacetime economy, the cost of waging war in Korea, and the effective opposition of a Republican-dominated Congress. Confronted with a severe postwar housing shortage, he successfully championed path-breaking legislation that established goals for low-income housing and created a framework for urban redevelopment largely underwritten by federal aid. Bowing to the political necessity of addressing the volatile housing issue, Truman postponed action to create extensive urban highway networks. The Truman administration achieved few legislative breakthroughs, but passage of the Taft-Ellender-Wagner Housing Act of 1949 signaled the beginning of a large-scale effort to revive declining inner cities and raised hopes of an expanded federal presence in urban America in future years.

The presidency of Dwight Eisenhower constituted a step backward from increasing New Deal–Fair Deal engagement in urban affairs. At a time of rapid suburbanization and concomitant problems for inner cities, Eisenhower's "dynamic conservatism" emphasized limited government and fiscal restraint. Despite never halting public housing construction altogether, the president nevertheless managed to reduce the number of low-income units completed in the cities. The interstate highway system, which boasted enthusiastic support from urban and suburban quarters, increased metropolitan decentralization, diverted resources away from public transportation, and contributed significantly to the decline of core cities. The creation of the ingenious Highway Trust Fund established a solid financial foundation for the federal government's support of automobility and left mass transit partisans at a disadvantage they struggled unsuccessfully to overcome. Although Eisenhower likely failed to understand the details of highway construction in urban America, the federal government's policy of underwriting expressways determined the character of metropolitan growth in the 1950s and decades thereafter.

In contrast to Eisenhower, John F. Kennedy spoke often about the major issues confronting America's cities and brought to the White House an urban sensibility that led big-city mayors and others to anticipate a dramatic policy turnaround in Washington, D.C. The expected urban renaissance directed from the nation's capital mostly failed to materialize during the truncated Kennedy presidency, however. Cold War crises and sluggish economic growth limited the administration's achievements in urban areas, delaying the implementation of ambitious plans to fight poverty in the inner cities, improve housing, and combat racial segregation. Still, the policy failures of the Kennedy years laid the foundation for the impressive achievements of the Johnson era. If New Frontier policy makers celebrated few legislative successes on

Capitol Hill, the Kennedy presidency legitimated the idea of increased federal involvement in urban affairs and spawned a series of proposals that became law later in the 1960s.

The nation's distressed cities figured prominently in the Great Society's grand reform design, both because of the concentration of poor people in the slums and because of the racial discord concentrated in urban America during the decade's red-hot summers. Lyndon Johnson's War on Poverty, though flawed in conception and hamstrung by limited funding, nevertheless reduced the number of indigent individuals and families in American cities. Embracing the Taft-Ellender-Wagner Housing Act's goal of "a decent home and a suitable living environment" for every American family, the Johnson administration succeeded in passing new housing legislation and substantially increasing subsidies for the construction of homes for low-income families. Title IV of the Housing and Urban Development Act of 1968 sought to expand the housing stock by creating new towns subsidized by the federal government. Building on the promise of John F. Kennedy's cautious Executive Order 11063, the Civil Rights Act of 1968 extended the guarantee of fair housing to an estimated 80 percent of dwellings in American communities and substantially opened suburban housing markets to African Americans for the first time. The Urban Mass Transportation Act of 1964 broke new ground in authorizing federal funds for the improvement of existing transit systems and the construction of new facilities. Determined to wage a comprehensive federal war on urban decline that merged and enhanced extant housing, transportation, and antipoverty initiatives, the White House and Congress created the Model Cities program. At the height of 1960s liberalism, the Johnson administration crafted a new partnership between the federal government and the cities that friends and foes alike saw as breathtaking in its reach and importance.[2]

The Great Society's ambitious urban agenda began to unravel quickly, however. The escalating financial demands of war in Vietnam siphoned money away from domestic programs, and the president and Congress began negotiating funding cuts in urban programs as early as 1967. Aggressively repudiating Great Society liberalism, Richard Nixon announced a New Federalism designed to retract the reach of the federal government and sever the newly created federal-urban linkages. The Nixon administration declared a moratorium on public housing construction and used revenue sharing, which subsumed the Model Cities apparatus, to pave the way for greater decentralization. The Housing and Community Development Act of 1974, signed by Nixon's successor, Gerald Ford, created the Section 8 rental assistance program, which nudged low-income housing from government toward the private sector, and fashioned Community Development Block Grants consolidating eight federal programs to give cities greater latitude in spending aid from Washington, D.C. Title VII of the Housing and Urban Development Act of 1970 increased the amount of federal aid available for new towns, but the Nixon and Ford administration's stingy appropriations effectively terminated the effort by 1975. Nixon ignored the entreaties for increased aid to the cities advanced by Department of Housing and Urban Development (HUD) Secretary George Romney, whose dedication to residential desegregation the president found particularly irksome. Cultivating political support in Republican suburban enclaves and preserving the southern strategy he had employed so skillfully in the 1968 presidential campaign, Nixon declined to enforce civil rights statutes that threatened metropolitan settlement patterns. Espousing fealty to the same goal of metropolitan decentralization, Ford challenged the Gautreaux decision and defended segregation in the suburbs. Surveying the continued decline of inner cities, Ford likewise followed Nixon's lead in blaming the situation on the failed liberal policies of the past.

Defying expectations that the election of a Democrat would in some measure restore the ruptured federal-urban ties of the 1960s, Jimmy Carter instead propounded a New Partnership with the cities that seemed to share much in common with the approach favored by his Republican predecessors hailing back to Herbert Hoover's associationalist approach of the 1920s. In his 1978 State of the Union message, Carter said: "Government cannot solve our problems. . . . Government cannot eliminate poverty, or provide a bountiful economy, or reduce inflation, or save our cities." To the consternation of traditional liberal constituencies, the Carter administration proposed tiny increases in funding for public housing in 1977–1978 and acceded to cuts in 1979–1980. Urban Development Action Grants, created as the centerpiece of the Housing and Community Development Act of 1977, sought to leverage private investment in the struggle to resuscitate declining inner cities—unfortunately in a manner that, according to liberal critics, devoted far too few dollars to the task and excessively benefited private investors. African Americans expressed disaffection at the president's surprising preference for decentralization and private initiatives, criticizing him especially for failing to pass fair housing legislation in 1979–1980. Carter hoped to become the first president to devise a federal urban policy and formed an Urban Policy Research Group for that purpose. Constrained by the president's insistence on stringent economy measures and unwavering insistence on limited government action, however, the research group floundered interminably before finally producing a prolix report and a series of policy recommendations that quickly perished in Congress. In all, Carter's New Partnership seemed to be cut from the same cloth as the New Federalisms of the Republican administrations bracketing his own.[3]

Ronald Reagan's New Federalism continued the reduction of the federal government's presence in urban America with a vengeance. Beginning in 1981, the Reagan administration targeted social programs and public works for draconian cutbacks in federal spending—all to the detriment of the cities. The White House recommended market solutions for urban problems, touting vouchers for low-income families unable to find suitable housing and enterprise zones for inner-city redevelopment. No cabinet-level federal department suffered as severely as HUD, which saw its budget reduced by more than half during the Reagan years. Under the desultory leadership of Secretary Samuel R. Pierce Jr., the agency endured declining morale and the drastic loss of resources and influence; a series of shocking scandals surfaced as well, leaving HUD in a shambles at the end of the 1980s. Pierce evinced little interest in pursuing fair housing in metropolitan areas, an indifference shared by Republican conservatives in the Department of Justice. The White House imposed severe economies on urban transportation as well, cutting the funding for mass transit by nearly one-third in 1983 and bargaining aggressively with Congress thereafter to minimize appropriations. The Surface Transportation and Uniform Relocation Assistance Act of 1987, which continued the usual practice of allocating lavish amounts for highways and much more modest sums for public transportation, passed over the president's veto. In 1988, after the administration had failed repeatedly to eliminate Urban Development Action Grants, Congress terminated the program in the name of fiscal necessity. Impervious to the rising level of distress in the cities, most obvious during the 1980s in the alarming increases in poverty and homelessness, Reagan persisted in celebrating market solutions and the decline of government.[4]

George H. W. Bush objected to the hard edges of Reagan's domestic policies and promised a kinder, gentler New Federalism but continued along the same path of domestic spending cuts that boded ill for the cities. Following the arc of the preceding eight years, federal funds for low-income housing continued to decline during the Bush years. HUD Secretary Jack Kemp forthrightly confronted the sordid scandals left over from the previous administration and managed to burnish the agency's tarnished reputation but instituted an intricate system of checks and balances that deterred productivity. Kemp became a forceful spokesman for urban America in the administration, but his advocacy of enterprise zones and other innovative measures to revivify distressed inner-city neighborhoods won few converts in the White House. The Cranston-Gonzalez Housing Act of 1990, which created the Homeownership and Opportunity for People Everywhere (HOPE) program, deemphasized the role of the federal government by empowering the private real-estate market, and the Intermodal Surface Transportation Efficiency Act (ISTEA) of 1991 equipped state and local governments with greater authority to spend federal funds earmarked for transportation. Declining federal revenues for the cities during the Bush years brought continuing increases in poverty and homelessness rates in urban communities.[5]

Heavily influenced by the Democratic Leadership Council's politics of moderation, Bill Clinton's "third way" for America's cities signaled yet another triumph for devolution and decentralization. Borrowing the idea of enterprise zones from the Reagan and Bush administrations, Clinton made the Empowerment Zones/Enterprise Communities design the centerpiece of his urban program. Having proclaimed in his 1996 State of the Union address that "the era of big government is over," the president cooperated that year with congressional Republicans to "end welfare as we know it." Displeased with the federal government's role in providing low-income housing and willing to entertain discussion of dissolving HUD, Clinton approved a housing reform measure two years later that Republicans portrayed as a companion piece to the earlier welfare reform law. The Quality Housing and Work Responsibility Act, which he signed in 1998, amended the Wagner-Steagall Act of 1937, granted additional autonomy to local public housing authorities, and required public housing residents to perform community service to retain their lodging subsidies. The Community Renewal Act of 2000, the product of close cooperation between the White House and conservative Republicans in Congress, further emphasized the role of the private sector in inner-city redevelopment and served as a fitting coda to Clinton's third way. The president and other centrist Democrats boasted that the residents of America's cities benefited from the national economy's resurgence in the 1990s and from the "stealth" urban policies that encouraged private investment in decaying inner-city neighborhoods and shifted authority from Washington, D.C., to state capitals and city halls. Clinton's promise to "reinvent" government, constrain federal bureaucracies, and enlist the private sector in urban revitalization ended a three-decade-long flight from the policies of the Great Society that presumed government beneficence and placed federal agencies at the heart of the effort to aid the troubled cities.[6]

The retreat from the Great Society's urban policies unfolded along with—and in part resulted from—HUD's inability to serve as a strong advocate for the cities in the federal government. President Johnson and others in the White House believed in 1965 that granting big-city mayors, urban renewal directors, municipal organizations, planners, and other urban interest groups a seat in the presidential cabinet symbolically affirmed the importance of the cities to the national agenda. As the historian Mark I. Gelfand has shown in *A Nation of Cities*, the creation of HUD represented the culmination of a protracted effort that commenced during the New Deal to legitimize urban reform and tie the federal government firmly to that effort. "Between 1933 and 1965 a revolution occurred in federal-city relations," Gelfand concluded. "Making best use of that revolution will be in the hands of later generations." As a series of presidential administrations opted for devolution in the last decades of the twentieth century, however, HUD proved to be a weak voice for urban liberalism and an ineffective champion of declining big cities against a succession of New Federalisms.[7]

At the time of HUD's creation in 1965, the proponents of a cabinet department dedicated to the concerns of the nation's cities envisioned an agency with a broad reach and substantial authority to formulate urban policy comprehensively. They hoped that, unlike its predecessor, the Housing and Home Finance Agency, HUD would enjoy responsibility for all community development efforts as well as housing affairs—in short, that it would become responsible for more than just bricks and mortar. Almost immediately, however, problems surfaced between the bailiwicks that uneasily coexisted within the department. Lacking a clear and coherent mission, the agency implemented a number of policies that often worked at cross-purposes. The sharpest divisions prevailed between programs seeking urban redevelopment while serving the interests of the middle class (mortgage insurance, sewer and water grants, urban renewal, Community Development Block Grants, Urban Development Action Grants, and new towns) and programs for low-income families (Model Cities, public housing, Section 235 and 236 subsidies, and Section 8 vouchers). The chasm separating HUD's various units grew so vast, reported an agency official, that staff members of the various branches labored in virtual isolation and rarely communicated with each other.[8]

At the same time, constraints on HUD's authority relative to other cabinet departments and the limitations placed on its portfolio indicated that the new agency would likely become a glorified version of the Housing and Home Finance Agency elevated to cabinet rank. A number of federal bureaus that administered housing programs, most notably the Veterans Administration, the Federal Home Loan Bank Board, and the Farmers Home Administration, remained outside of HUD's authority. Given the Federal Housing Administration's traditional autonomy within the Housing and Home Finance Agency and earlier federal agencies, HUD could hardly claim to dictate all aspects of federal housing policy. The creation of the Department of Transportation in 1966 left HUD with no responsibility for mass transit or urban freeways. The War on Poverty assigned antipoverty programs, despite their salience for big-city slums, ghettos, and barrios, to the independent Office of Economic Opportunity, and in later decades the Department of Health, Education, and Welfare (and its successor, Health and Human Services) assumed control of most social welfare endeavors. The Departments of Agriculture, Commerce, Education, Interior, Labor, and Treasury all claimed jurisdiction at one time or another over federal programs that served significant urban populations. Statutory limits on HUD's authority made the formulation of comprehensive urban policies a virtual impossibility.[9]

Deprived of sole responsibility for addressing urban problems, HUD often became the lead agency charged with coordinating the efforts of several other cabinet departments. HUD officials subsequently struggled to convene representatives of the participating groups, create and sustain interest in urban programs of questionable importance to the others, coax financial contributions from wary bureaucrats eager to safeguard their own scarce budgets, and find consensus among constituencies with competing interests—armed in most instances only with their own persuasiveness. HUD encountered these formidable hurdles early on, beginning with the intercabinet machinations over funding the Model Cities program at a time when the Vietnam War was draining resources from all agencies in Washington, D.C. Ongoing competition with the Department of Transportation over highway building and mass transit funding in metropolitan areas aptly illustrated the perennial problem of "feuding fiefdoms."[10]

Unlike many of the other cabinet departments with which it competed for resources, HUD lacked an influential, cohesive, and generously funded clientele that consistently and ably supported the agency's policy-making efforts in the White House and on Capitol Hill. Instead, a loose and malleable coalition of interest groups arrayed across the political spectrum came together sporadically in defense of assorted urban issues. The homebuilding industry, consisting of developers, bankers, mortgage lenders, Realtors, materials manufacturers, and trade unions, shared the common goal of increased housing construction and always sought generous subsidies from the federal government. HUD sometimes found it difficult to reconcile the single-minded aims of the housing industry with the community development goals espoused by consumers, environmentalists, and neighborhood activists. Moreover, while consistently supportive of housing construction as economically and socially beneficial, the agency had to deal with the inherent tensions between the defenders of the private housing market and subsidized low-income housing advocates, between suburban expansion and inner-city redevelopment.

Mayors, city managers, and other urban officials formed one of HUD's principal clienteles but seldom wielded significant power in Washington, D.C., political power struggles. A few big-city mayors won reelection like clockwork and built formidable power bases at the state and national levels—as the estimable Richard J. Daley did in Chicago, for instance—but electoral turnover minimized the clout of most urban chief executives. Beset by a welter of intractable problems, mayors more often came to the nation's capital as worried supplicants than as aggressive power brokers. The mayors of big cities and smaller communities often disagreed about major policy issues, with the former likelier to be active in the U.S. Conference of Mayors and the latter joining the National League of Cities. Although the different organizations occasionally joined forces and lobbied together on Capitol Hill and some mayors belonged to both groups, more commonly the two memberships harbored different views. Among the members of these large, diverse organizations, consensus on major issues often proved difficult to obtain. According to political scientist Suzanne Farkas, "[U.S. Conference of Mayors] members tend to factionalize along the lines of North-South on civil rights issues, liberal-conservative on issues bearing on 'federal participation,' and small city-large city on issues such as mass transit, rent supplements, and civilian review boards."[11]

The urban poor—and those individuals and organizations who spoke for them—remained by definition one of HUD's least powerful constituencies. Bereft of resources, politically unorganized, disfranchised, and immobile, the working poor and the indigent in the inner cities suffered as the popularity of people-based antipoverty plans supplanted place-based approaches. The bureaucracies created by the unsuccessful Community Action Program and Model Cities experiment disappeared by the 1980s, leaving a smattering of antipoverty foundations, community organizations, religious groups, and inner-city missions in their wake. Sporadically uninvolved with federal policy regarding welfare, employment, public safety, and other key issues in slums and ghettos, HUD's activities affected the urban poor principally through the low-income housing units subsidized in various ways by federal funds. High-rise public housing gave way to Section 8, HOPE VI, and other attempts to relocate the poor into units built by private enterprise with government assistance—even as moneymaking enterprises replaced the low-income projects as part of urban redevelopment plans in distressed neighborhoods. The modest amount of replacement housing provided to the uprooted public housing tenants, who could no longer afford to reside in the units built on cleared land, testified to the powerlessness of the poor in the big-city real-estate deals concocted by profit-making private concerns and underwritten by government.

Created in part as a response to racial unrest in urban America and linked in the public imagination with the civil rights movement, HUD quickly became an important benefactor of racial minorities in the cities. Because the persistence of poverty, crime, drug use, and other social problems in ghettos and barrios emerged as a prominent part of the urban crisis, the crusade for racial uplift and the effort to save the declining inner cities seemed inextricably linked. In the last decades of the twentieth century, as national politics turned rightward, conservative politicians decried the inequities and "reverse racism" of affirmative action, and African Americans clung to the hard-fought gains of the civil rights era, vulnerable racial minorities viewed HUD as one of the few hospitable outposts in Washington, D.C. Beginning with Robert Weaver and continuing with Patricia Roberts Harris, Samuel Pierce, and Henry Cisneros, the selection of members of racial minorities as HUD secretaries underscored the agency's special attention to the plight of the heterogeneous cities.

Standing tenth in seniority among cabinet departments, saddled with impotent clienteles, and unable to establish its control of urban matters across jurisdictional boundaries, HUD suffered from lack of power and prestige in the executive branch. Significant scandals during the Nixon and Reagan administrations further damaged HUD's standing in Washington, D.C., leading political insiders to comment that the infamy surrounding the agency served as both a cause and a consequence of the inability to attract and retain an effective staff. Recruitment of first-rate administrators with considerable experience in government and business to such an unattractive cabinet post proved difficult, and presidents typically selected HUD secretaries to grant representation to particular electoral groups or to repay political or personal debts—a standard resulting in the frequent choice of minorities and women, lending a modicum of demographic diversity to a cabinet otherwise composed overwhelmingly of white males. Few HUD secretaries possessed prior experience in housing or urban affairs, and some Republican presidents appointed men to the post who appeared indifferent or openly hostile to the worsening situation in the inner cities; believing that James Lynn and Samuel Pierce had been appointed specifically to dismantle the department, liberal critics labeled them "executive saboteurs." Consigned to the outer ring of the cabinet, HUD secretaries fought incessantly for access to the president and influential White House aides. Most HUD secretaries served with little fanfare and made few headlines during their tenure in office; George Romney and Jack Kemp took a different path, gaining considerable media attention for loudly propounding alternatives to administration policy, but enjoyed little success and left Washington, D.C., having failed to elevate HUD's profile in the executive branch.[12]

Exacerbating all of HUD's liabilities, the federal government imposed a series of economy measures that left the agency unable to satisfy even the most modest expectations. Through a series of budget reductions, moratoriums, rescissions, and impoundments, Congress deprived HUD of adequate resources—in some cases failing to provide necessary allocations for programs the national legislature had recently approved. Shortfalls began to mount in the late 1960s because of the Vietnam War, and the 1970s brought inflation and an unprecedented energy crisis that drove mortgage rates up and sent the housing industry into a prolonged recession. HUD absorbed the lion's share of the domestic spending cuts mandated by the Reagan and Bush administrations—its portion of the federal budget falling from 7.5 percent in 1978 to 1.3 percent in 1990—and continued to suffer during the 1990s under a Clinton administration pursuing a fiscally responsible third way that steered resource-starved cities away from the federal government toward private investors. By the end of the twentieth century, HUD spent considerably less money and employed far fewer people than it had during the halcyon days of the Great Society. In the end, commented urban economist Anthony Downs, the agency became nothing more than "an ineffective symbolic gesture of concern."[13]

HUD's shortcomings resulted from the severity of the challenges facing urban America, to be sure, but they also underscored the fundamental policies effected by the federal government throughout the second half of the twentieth century. Presidential administrations varied significantly in the strength of their commitments to inner-city reclamation, but the federal government's generosity toward the cities ebbed overall beginning in the 1970s; ameliorative policies emanating from Washington, D.C., after the Second World War never obviated the damage done in earlier decades. Having

instituted a series of policies that underwrote centrifugal population movement, enhanced an already powerful suburban lure, and left inner cities to
fend for themselves in a hazardous economic climate, the federal government
interceded sporadically to mitigate the situation in urban America—an ineffective intervention that the historian Alice O'Connor has aptly likened to
"swimming against the tide." Large-scale, generously funded public policies
fueled metropolitan decentralization while modest sums spent for community development in inner cities proved hopelessly inadequate. By the end of
the twentieth century, as federal allocations for low-income housing totaled
no more than a few billion dollars annually, the federal government subsidized home ownership at the rate of $90 billion a year; the home mortgage
interest deduction alone more than doubled the amount of government largesse afforded public housing budgets, Section 8 vouchers, and other housing programs for the inner-city poor. Officials in Washington, D.C., jealously
guarded the purse strings of the Highway Trust Fund, which for many years
remained sacrosanct in the federal budget, and allocations for freeways
dwarfed the paltry sums designated for urban mass transit. In an era of rising defense appropriations, escalating costs for such entitlement programs as
Social Security and Medicare, and a growing disposition to rely on the financial acumen of the financial community, a succession of presidential administrations found budgetary relief by cutting aid to the cities and trumpeting
public-private partnerships. Both Republicans and Democrats invoked
"devolution" and "decentralization" to defend as sound policy decisions
their repeated funding reductions for urban America. Tacitly ratifying
decades of policymaking in the nation's capital that underwrote metropolitan decentralization and dismissing the Great Society as an expensive failure,
the federal government in the last three decades of the twentieth century
turned a blind eye to the fate of the cities.[14]

NOTES

PREFACE

1. Mark I. Gelfand, *A Nation of Cities: The Federal Government and Urban America, 1933–1965* (New York: Oxford University Press, 1975).
2. On the pitfalls of creating a national urban policy, see Joshua Sapotichne, "Reconstructing National Urban Policy: Agenda-Setting in a Complex Policy Area" (Ph.D. diss., University of Washington, 2009).
3. See Iwan Morgan, *The Age of Deficits: Presidents and Unbalanced Budgets from Jimmy Carter to George W. Bush* (Lawrence: University Press of Kansas, 2009).

INTRODUCTION

1. Raymond A. Mohl, "Shifting Patterns of American Urban Policy since 1900," in *Urban Policy in Twentieth-Century America*, ed. Arnold R. Hirsch and Raymond A. Mohl (New Brunswick, N.J.: Rutgers University Press, 1993), 1–4; Alice O'Connor, "Swimming against the Tide: A Brief History of Federal Policy in Poor Communities," in *Urban Problems and Community Development*, ed. Ronald F. Ferguson and William T. Dickens (Washington, D.C.: Brookings Institution Press, 1999), 77–88; Mark I. Gelfand, *A Nation of Cities: The Federal Government and Urban America, 1933–1965* (New York: Oxford University Press, 1975), 3–22; and Peter Dreier, John Mollenkopf, and Todd Swanstrom, *Place Matters: Metropolitics for the Twenty-first Century*, 2nd rev. ed. (Lawrence: University Press of Kansas, 2004), 126.
2. Eric J. Karolak, "'No Idea of Doing Anything Wonderful': The Labor-Crisis Origins of National Housing Policy and the Reconstruction of the Working-Class Community," in *From Tenements to the Taylor Homes: In Search of an Urban Housing Policy in Twentieth-Century America*, ed. John F. Bauman, Roger Biles, and Kristin M. Szylvian (University Park: Pennsylvania State University Press, 2000), 60–80; Kenneth T. Jackson, *Crabgrass Frontier: The Suburbanization of the United States* (New York: Oxford University Press, 1985), 192. Also see Christian Topalov, "Scientific Urban Planning and the Ordering of Daily Life: The First 'War Housing' Experiment in the United States, 1917–1919," *Journal of Urban History* 17 (November 1990): 14–45; Kristin M. Szylvian, "Industrial Housing Reform and the Emergency Fleet Corporation," *Journal of Urban History* 25 (July 1999): 647–690; and Roy Lubove, "Homes and 'A Few Well Placed Fruit Trees': An Object Lesson in Federal Housing," *Social Research* 27 (Winter 1960): 469–486.

3. Janet Hutchison, "Shaping Housing and Enhancing Consumption: Hoover's Interwar Housing Policy," in Bauman, Biles, and Szylvian, *From Tenements to the Taylor Homes*, 81–101; Mark S. Foster, *From Streetcar to Superhighway: American City Planners and Urban Transportation, 1900–1940* (Philadelphia: Temple University Press, 1981), 46–50; Jackson, *Crabgrass Frontier*, 174–186. Also see Ellis Hawley, "Herbert Hoover, the Commerce Secretariat, and the Vision of the 'Associative State,'" *Journal of American History* 61 (June 1974): 116–140.

4. Roger Biles, *A New Deal for the American People* (DeKalb: Northern Illinois University Press, 1991), 207–209; Mohl, "Shifting Patterns of American Urban Policy since 1900," 8–9.

5. Biles, *A New Deal for the American People*, 210 (first quotation); Roger Biles, *Big City Boss in Depression and War: Mayor Edward J. Kelly of Chicago* (DeKalb: Northern Illinois University Press, 1984), 23 (second quotation).

6. Sidney Fine, *Frank Murphy: The Detroit Years* (Ann Arbor: University of Michigan Press, 1975), 299–300 (first quotation); Howard Chudacoff and Judith E. Smith, *The Evolution of American Urban Society*, 3rd ed. (Englewood Cliffs, N.J.: Prentice Hall, 1988), 240 (second quotation); Biles, *A New Deal for the American People*, 210–211.

7. Gertrude S. Fish, "Housing Policy during the Great Depression," in *The Story of Housing*, ed. Gertrude Sipperly Fish (New York: Macmillan, 1979), 185–186; Jackson, *Crabgrass Frontier*, 193–195; Biles, *A New Deal for the American People*, 24 (quotation).

8. Gelfand, *A Nation of Cities*, 24 (Tugwell quotations), 55 (Roosevelt quotations). Also see Charles H. Trout, "The New Deal and the Cities," in *Fifty Years Later: The New Deal Evaluated*, ed. Harvard Sitkoff (New York: Alfred A. Knopf, 1985), 133–153.

9. Ibid., 381 (Ford quotation); Jackson, *Crabgrass Frontier*, 195 (Tugwell quotation).

10. Biles, *A New Deal for the American People*, 211–212; Paul K. Conkin, *Tomorrow a New World: The New Deal Community Program* (Ithaca: Cornell University Press, 1959), 329 (quotation). Also see Joseph L. Arnold, *The New Deal in the Suburbs: A History of the Greenbelt Town Program, 1935–1954* (Columbus: Ohio State University Press, 1971).

11. Jason Scott Smith, *Building New Deal Liberalism: The Political Economy of Public Works, 1933–1956* (Cambridge, UK: Cambridge University Press, 2006), chap. 1; Biles, *A New Deal for the American People*, 212.

12. Biles, *A New Deal for the American People*, 212–213; Smith, *Building New Deal Liberalism*, chap. 1.

13. Raymond A. Mohl, "Planned Destruction: The Interstates and Central City Housing," in Bauman, Biles, and Szylvian, *From Tenements to the Taylor Homes*, 229–230; Biles, *A New Deal for the American People*, 223.

14. Robert P. Ingalls, *Herbert H. Lehman and New York's Little New Deal* (New York: New York University Press, 1975), 182 (quotation); Gail Radford, "The Federal Government and Housing during the Great Depression," in Bauman, Biles, and Szylvian, *From Tenements to the Taylor Homes*, 102–106; Jackson, *Crabgrass Frontier*,

222–223. Also see Gail Radford, *Modern Housing for America: Policy Struggles in the New Deal Era* (Chicago: University of Chicago Press, 1996).

15. Mary Susan Cole, "Catherine Bauer and the Public Housing Movement" (Ph.D. diss., George Washington University, 1975), 352n; Biles, *A New Deal for the American People*, 215 (quotations). Also see Timothy McDonnell, *The Wagner Housing Act: A Case Study of the Legislative Process* (Chicago: Loyola University Press, 1957); J. Joseph Huthmacher, *Senator Robert F. Wagner and the Rise of Urban Liberalism* (New York: Athenaeum, 1971); and Roger Biles, "Nathan Straus and the Failure of U.S. Public Housing, 1937–1942," *Historian* 53 (Autumn 1990): 33–46.

16. Radford, "The Federal Government and Housing during the Great Depression," 107 (quotation); Biles, *A New Deal for the American People*, 213–214.

17. Christopher Howard, *The Hidden Welfare State: Tax Expenditures and Social Policy in the United States* (Princeton: Princeton University Press, 1997), 49–53; O'Connor, "Swimming against the Tide," 91; Radford, "The Federal Government and Housing during the Great Depression," 104–108.

18. Jackson, *Crabgrass Frontier*, 197–203. For a fuller discussion of these New Deal agencies and racial segregation, see Kenneth T. Jackson, "Race, Ethnicity, and Real Estate Appraisal: The Home Owners Loan Corporation and the Federal Housing Administration," *Journal of Urban History* 6 (August 1980): 419–452.

19. Jackson, *Crabgrass Frontier*, 213 (quotation). Also see Arnold R. Hirsch, "With or Without Jim Crow: Black Residential Segregation in the United States," in Hirsch and Mohl, *Urban Policy in Twentieth-Century America*, 84–94; and Douglas S. Massey and Nancy A. Denton, *American Apartheid: Segregation and the Making of the Underclass* (Cambridge, Mass.: Harvard University Press, 1993).

20. Roger W. Lotchin, "The Metropolitan-Military Complex in Comparative Perspective: San Francisco, Los Angeles, and San Diego, 1919–41," *Journal of the West* 18 (July 1979): 19–30; Mohl, "Shifting Patterns of American Urban Policy since 1900," 11–12. Also see Philip J. Funigiello, *The Challenge to Urban Liberalism: Federal-City Relations during World War II* (Knoxville: University of Tennessee Press, 1978); Roger W. Lotchin, *Fortress California, 1910–1961: From Warfare to Welfare* (New York: Oxford University Press, 1992); Gerald D. Nash, *The American West Transformed: The Impact of the Second World War* (Bloomington: Indiana University Press, 1985); Bruce J. Schulman, *From Cotton Belt to Sunbelt: Federal Policy, Economic Development, and the Transformation of the South, 1938–1980* (New York: Oxford University Press, 1991); and Harvard Sitkoff, "Racial Militance and Interracial Violence in the Second World War," *Journal of American History* 58 (December 1971), 661–681.

21. Kristin M. Szylvian, "The Federal Housing Program during World War II," in Bauman, Biles, and Szylvian, *From Tenements to the Taylor Homes*, 121–132.

22. Ibid., 132–133.

23. Philip J. Funigiello, "City Planning in World War II: The Experience of the National Resources Planning Board," *Social Science Quarterly* 53 (June 1972): 91–104; Funigiello, *The Challenge to Urban Liberalism*, 165–185; Gelfand, *A Nation of Cities*, 100–103; David R. Goldfield and Blaine A. Brownell, *Urban America: A History*, 2nd ed. (Boston: Houghton Mifflin, 1990), 339–340. Also see Otis Graham, *Toward a*

Planned Society: From Roosevelt to Nixon (New York: Oxford University Press, 1976); and Patrick D. Reagan, *Designing a New America: The Origins of New Deal Planning, 1890–1943* (Amherst: University of Massachusetts Press, 1999).

24. Kenneth T. Jackson, "A Nation of Cities: The Federal Government and the Shape of the American Metropolis," *Annals of the American Academy of Political and Social Science* 626 (November 2009): 11–20; O'Connor, "Swimming against the Tide," 77–83. The historian Brian Balogh argues that the federal government played an even larger role in national affairs in the nineteenth century than is generally understood—but largely behind the scenes. See Brian Balogh, *A Government out of Sight: The Mystery of National Authority in Nineteenth-Century America* (Cambridge, UK: Cambridge University Press, 2009).

CHAPTER 1. THE FAIR DEAL AND THE CITIES

1. Alonzo L. Hamby, *Man of the People: A Life of Harry S. Truman* (New York: Oxford University Press, 1995), 248–260; Richard O. Davies, *Housing Reform during the Truman Administration* (Columbia: University of Missouri Press, 1966), 31 (quotation).

2. Kristi Andersen, *The Creation of a Democratic Majority, 1928–1936* (Chicago: University of Chicago Press, 1979); Samuel J. Eldersveld, "The Influence of Metropolitan Party Pluralities in Presidential Elections since 1921: A Study of Twelve Key Cities," *American Political Science Review* 43 (1949): 1189–1206; Richard Sauerzopf and Todd Swanstrom, "The Urban Electorate in Presidential Elections, 1920–1996," *Urban Affairs Review* 35 (September 1999): 75–77.

3. *Public Papers of the Presidents of the United States: Harry S. Truman, 1945* (Washington, D.C.: Government Printing Office, 1961), 292 (quotation).

4. Robert M. Fogelson, *Downtown: Its Rise and Fall, 1880–1950* (New Haven, Conn.: Yale University Press, 2001), 392 (quotation).

5. Margaret Pugh O'Mara, "Uncovering the City in the Suburb: Cold War Politics, Scientific Elites, and High-Tech Spaces," in *The New Suburban History*, ed. Kevin M. Kruse and Thomas J. Sugrue (Chicago: University of Chicago Press, 2006), 63–66. For a fuller discussion, see Margaret Pugh O'Mara, *Cities of Knowledge: Cold War Science and the Search for the Next Silicon Valley* (Princeton, N.J.: Princeton University Press, 2005).

6. Ann Markusen, Peter Hall, Scott Campbell, and Sabina Deitrick, *The Rise of the Gunbelt: The Military Remapping of Industrial America* (New York: Oxford University Press, 1991), 6–7, 25, 231. Also see Bruce J. Schulman, *From Cotton Belt to Sun Belt: Federal Policy, Economic Development, and the Transformation of the South, 1938–1980* (Durham, N.C.: Duke University Press, 1994), esp. chap. 6; Andrew Kirby, ed., *The Pentagon and the Cities* (Newbury Park, Calif.: Sage, 1992); and Ann Markusen and Joel Yudken, *Dismantling the Cold War Economy* (New York: Basic Books, 1992), esp. chaps. 7 and 8.

7. Frank Fisher, "Rebuilding Our Cities," *Nation* 161 (August 8, 1945): 130; Mark I. Gelfand, "Cities, Suburbs, and Government Policy," in *Reshaping America:*

Society and Institutions, 1945–1960, ed. Robert H. Bremner and Gary W. Reichard (Columbus: Ohio State University Press, 1982), 265; David W. McCullough, *Truman* (New York: Simon & Schuster, 1992), 470.

8. *New York Times,* December 13, 1945; *Public Papers of the Presidents of the United States: Harry S. Truman, 1945,* 533–534; Laura McEnaney, "Nightmares on Elm Street: Demobilizing in Chicago, 1945–1953," *Journal of American History* 92 (March 2006): 1265–1275.

9. Wilson W. Wyatt Sr., *Whistle Stops: Adventures in Public Life* (Lexington: University Press of Kentucky, 1985), 59; *Public Papers of the Presidents of the United States: Harry S. Truman, 1945,* 534–535; Davies, *Housing Reform during the Truman Administration,* 44 (quotations).

10. Wyatt, *Whistle Stops,* 65–70; Davies, *Housing Reform during the Truman Administration,* 45 (quotation); "The Promise of the Shortage," *Fortune* 33 (April 1946): 101–102.

11. Wyatt, *Whistle Stops,* 67–70; Richard O. Davies, *Defender of the Old Guard: John Bricker and American Politics* (Columbus: Ohio State University Press, 1993), 109 (first quotation); *New York Times,* May 23, 1946 (second quotation). The congressional debates are covered in *Congressional Record,* 79th Cong., 2nd Sess., March 1, 4, 5, 6, 1946.

12. J. Joseph Huthmacher, *Senator Robert F. Wagner and the Rise of Urban Liberalism* (New York: Atheneum, 1971), 322–325; Davies, *Housing Reform during the Truman Administration,* 33–39. The best source on Robert A. Taft's role in the postwar housing debate is James T. Patterson, *Mr. Republican: A Biography of Robert A. Taft* (Boston: Houghton Mifflin, 1972).

13. Richard O. Davies, "'Mr. Republican' Turns 'Socialist': Robert Taft and Public Housing," *Ohio History* 73 (Summer 1964): 135–143; Huthmacher, *Senator Robert F. Wagner and the Rise of Urban Liberalism,* 323–325; "Housing: Poor Hope," *New Republic* 115 (December 9, 1946): 749; "The Promise of the Shortage," 101–103.

14. *New York Times,* May 23, 1946; "The Housing Mess," *Fortune* 35 (January 1947): 81; Bryant Putney, "Obituary for Veterans' Housing," *Nation* 163 (December 21, 1946): 722–723; Douglas Knerr, *Suburban Steel: The Magnificent Failure of the Lustron Corporation, 1945–1951* (Columbus: Ohio State University Press, 2004), 69.

15. Bryant Putney, "Obituary for Veterans' Housing," 723 (quotation); *New York Times,* November 13, 1946; Davies, *Housing Reform during the Truman Administration,* 155n41; Knerr, *Suburban Steel,* 84–85.

16. *New York Times,* October 3, 1946; Bryant Putney, "Obituary for Veterans' Housing," 722 (quotation).

17. Wyatt, *Whistle Stops,* 72–84; "The Shape of Things," *Nation* 163 (November 16, 1946): 541; Bryant Putney, "Obituary for Veterans' Housing," 722–723; *Public Papers of the Presidents of the United States: Harry S. Truman, 1946* (Washington, D.C.: Government Printing Office, 1962), 490.

18. Wyatt, *Whistle Stops,* 86; Putney, "Obituary for Veterans' Housing," 722 (quotation).

19. McEnaney, "Nightmares on Elm Street," 1275; Roger W. Caves, "An Historical Analysis of Federal Housing Policy from the Presidential Perspective: An Intergovernmental Focus," *Urban Studies* 26 (February 1989): 63; *Public Papers of the
Presidents of the United States: Harry S. Truman, 1947* (Washington, D.C.: Government Printing Office, 1963), 313 (quotations).

20. Mark I. Gelfand, *A Nation of Cities: The Federal Government and Urban
America, 1933–1965* (New York: Oxford University Press, 1975), 245–248; William
L. C. Wheaton, "The Evolution of Federal Housing Programs" (Ph.D. diss., University of Chicago, 1953), 140–160; Davies, *Housing Reform during the Truman Administration,* 62–63; Undated Truman Statement, Harry S. Truman Papers, Official File
63, box 364, folder January–March 1949, Harry S. Truman Presidential Library, Independence, Mo.

21. Caves, "An Historical Analysis of Federal Housing Policy from the Presidential Perspective," 63; Gelfand, *A Nation of Cities,* 247–248; Davies, *Housing Reform
during the Truman Administration,* 59–64.

22. Davies, *Housing Reform during the Truman Administration,* 64–68.

23. Ibid., 68–72; Richard H. Rovere, *Senator Joe McCarthy* (New York: Harper
& Row, 1959), 107–108; *New York Times,* August 20, 1947.

24. John H. Mollenkopf, *The Contested City* (Princeton: Princeton University
Press, 1983), 75 (first quotation); "Last Chance for Houses," *New Republic* 119 (May
24, 1948): 8; *New York Times,* June 11, 1948; Richard O. Davies, *Housing Reform during the Truman Administration,* 79 (second quotation).

25. *Public Papers of the Presidents of the United States: Harry S. Truman, 1948*
(Washington, D.C.: Government Printing Office, 1964), 392 (quotations); Davies,
Housing Reform during the Truman Administration, 83–84.

26. "Should the President Call Congress Back?" memorandum, June 29, 1948,
Clark Clifford Papers, box 33, folder 1948, July 27 Message, Harry S. Truman Presi-
dential Library, Independence, Mo.; Thomas C. Reeves, *The Life and Times of Joe
McCarthy: A Biography* (New York: Stein and Day, 1982), 148.

27. Reeves, *The Life and Times of Joe McCarthy,* 148–151; Caves, "An Historical
Analysis of Federal Housing Policy from the Presidential Perspective," 63; *New York
Times,* August 11, 1948 (quotations). On the significance of housing in the 1948 campaign, see R. Alton Lee, "The Turnip Session of the Do-Nothing Congress: Presidential Campaign Strategy," *Southwestern Social Science Quarterly* 44 (December 1963):
256–267; Mollenkopf, *The Contested City,* 75.

28. Davies, *Housing Reform during the Truman Administration,* 104–105; *U.S.
Statutes at Large,* 63, pt. 1:413 (quotation); Roger Biles, *Crusading Liberal: Paul H.
Douglas of Illinois* (DeKalb: Northern Illinois University Press, 2002), 58; Raymond M.
Foley to Elmer B. Staats, February 24, 1949, Papers of Harry S. Truman, Official File
63, box 364, folder January–March 1949, Harry S. Truman Presidential Library, In-
dependence, Mo.; Hilary Ballon, "Robert Moses and Urban Renewal," in *Robert
Moses and the Modern City: The Transformation of New York,* ed. Hilary Ballon and
Kenneth T. Jackson (New York: W. W. Norton, 2007), 97. Also see Jeanne R. Lowe,
Cities in a Race with Time: Progress and Poverty in America's Renewing Cities (New

York: Random House, 1967); and Scott A. Greer, *Urban Renewal and American Cities: The Dilemma of Democratic Intervention* (Indianapolis: Bobbs-Merrill, 1965).

29. Statement of Raymond M. Foley, February 3, 1949, Raymond M. Foley Papers, box 3, folder Housing Act of 1949, Harry S. Truman Presidential Library, Independence, Mo.; *Congressional Record*, 81st Cong., 1st sess., April 19, 1949, 95, pt. 4:4730 (quotation); *New York Times*, April 20, 1949; Thomas Sancton, "Housing and Segregation," *Nation* 168 (April 30, 1949): 490.

30. Davies, *Defender of the Old Guard*, 137–139; *Congressional Record*, 81st Cong., 1st sess., April 20, 1949, 95, pt. 4:4802 (quotation).

31. Paul H. Douglas, "A Senator's Vote: A Searching of the Soul," *New York Times Magazine*, April 30, 1950, 42; *Congressional Record*, 81st Cong., 1st sess., April 21, 1949, 95, pt. 4:4857 (quotation); Davies, *Defender of the Old Guard*, 138; Biles, *Crusading Liberal*, 59–60.

32. Davies, *Housing Reform during the Truman Administration*, 109–110 (NAREB quotations); Harry Truman to Sam Rayburn, June 17, 1949, Papers of Harry S. Truman, Official File 63, box 364, folder June–December 1949, Harry S. Truman Presidential Library, Independence, Mo. (Truman quotations); Roger W. Caves, "An Historical Analysis of Federal Housing Policy from the Presidential Perspective," 64.

33. Davies, *Housing Reform during the Truman Administration*, 112; James T. Patterson, *Grand Expectations: The United States, 1945–1974* (New York: Oxford University Press, 1996), 141–142, 166; *Public Papers of the Presidents of the United States: Harry S. Truman, 1949* (Washington, D.C.: Government Printing Office, 1964), 382 (quotation).

34. Fogelson, *Downtown*, 379 (quotation). On Robert Moses and New York City, see Joel Schwartz, *The New York Approach: Robert Moses, Urban Liberals, and Redevelopment of the Inner City* (Columbus: Ohio State University Press, 1993); and Robert A. Caro, *The Power Broker: Robert Moses and the Fall of New York* (New York: Alfred A. Knopf, 1974). On Chicago, see Arnold R. Hirsch, *Making the Second Ghetto: Race and Housing in Chicago, 1940–1960* (Cambridge, UK: Cambridge University Press, 1983). On St. Louis, see Joseph Heathcott, "The City Quietly Remade: National Programs and Local Agendas in the Movement to Clear the Slums, 1942–1952," *Journal of American History* 34 (January 2008): 221–242. On Detroit, see Thomas J. Sugrue, *The Origins of the Urban Crisis: Race and Inequality in Postwar Detroit* (Princeton: Princeton University Press, 1996).

35. Roger Biles, "Public Housing and the Postwar Urban Renaissance, 1949–1973," in *From Tenements to the Taylor Homes: In Search of an Urban Housing Policy in Twentieth-Century America*, ed. John F. Bauman, Roger Biles, and Kristin M. Szylvian (University Park: Pennsylvania State University Press, 2000), 144–145; Catherine Bauer, "Redevelopment: A Misfit in the Fifties," in *The Future of Cities and Urban Redevelopment*, ed. Coleman Woodbury (Chicago: University of Chicago Press, 1953), 9 (first quotation); Alice O'Connor, "Swimming against the Tide: A Brief History of Federal Policy in Poor Communities," in *Urban Problems and Community Development*, ed. Ronald F. Ferguson and William T. Dickens (Washington, D.C.: Brookings Institution Press, 1999), 96 (second quotation).

36. Alexander von Hoffman, "Vision Limited: The Political Movement for a U.S. Public Housing Program, 1919–1950," Taubman Center for State and Local Government, John F. Kennedy School of Government, Harvard University, May 1996, 74–75; Mollenkopf, *The Contested City*, 79; Biles, "Public Housing and the Postwar Urban Renaissance," 144–145.

37. "Co-op Houses," *Architectural Forum* 84 (January 1946): 90–95; Paul K. Conkin, *Tomorrow a New World: The New Deal Community Program* (Ithaca: Cornell University Press, 1959), 202–210; Hoffman, "Vision Limited," 71–72.

38. Kristin M. Szylvian, "Cooperative Home Ownership and the Housing Act of 1950," paper presented at the Annual Meeting of the Social Science History Association, October 10, 1996; Davies, *Housing Reform during the Truman Administration*, 118–120. Szylvian is finishing a book on the cooperative housing movement that deals extensively with the 1949 and 1950 legislation.

39. Raymond A. Mohl, "Shifting Patterns of American Urban Policy since 1900," in *Urban Policy in Twentieth-Century America*, ed. Arnold R. Hirsch and Raymond A. Mohl (New Brunswick, N.J.: Rutgers University Press, 1993), 14–15; Kenneth T. Jackson, *Crabgrass Frontier: The Suburbanization of the United States* (New York: Oxford University Press, 1985), 190–230. Also see Robert C. Weaver, *The Negro Ghetto* (New York: Harcourt Brace, 1948); and Charles Abrams, *Forbidden Neighbors: A Study of Prejudice in Housing* (New York: Harper, 1955).

40. Arnold R. Hirsch, "Searching for a 'Sound Negro Policy': A Racial Agenda for the Housing Acts of 1949 and 1954," *Housing Policy Debate* 11 (2000): 397 (quotation); Arnold R. Hirsch, "'Containment' on the Home Front: Race and Federal Housing Policy from the New Deal to the Cold War," *Journal of Urban History* 26 (January 2000): 180; Oral History Interview with Philleo Nash, November 9, 1966, 526–528, Harry S. Truman Presidential Library, Independence, Mo.

41. Arnold R. Hirsch, "Choosing Segregation: Federal Housing Policy between *Shelley* and *Brown*," in Bauman, Biles, and Szylvian, *From Tenements to the Taylor Homes*, 212 (quotations); Arnold R. Hirsch, "With or Without Jim Crow: Black Residential Segregation in the United States," in Hirsch and Mohl, *Urban Policy in Twentieth-Century America*, 90–91; David Rusk, *Cities without Suburbs*, 3rd ed. (Washington, D.C.: Woodrow Wilson Center Press, 2003), 25.

42. Martha Biondi, *To Stand and Fight: The Struggle for Civil Rights in Postwar New York City* (Cambridge, Mass.: Harvard University Press, 2003), 121–136; Benvenga is quoted on p. 125, Horne on p. 224.

43. Hirsch, "Choosing Segregation," 216 (quotation); Hirsch, "Searching for a 'Sound Negro Policy,'" 400–401.

44. "Address by Robert C. Weaver at National Conference on Discrimination in Housing," May 20, 1952, Philleo Nash Papers, box 41, folder Housing . . . 1947–51, Harry S. Truman Presidential Library, Independence, Mo.; Hirsch, "Choosing Segregation," 216; Hirsch, "Searching for a 'Sound Negro Policy,'" 413 (quotation).

45. Hirsch, "Searching for a 'Sound Negro Policy,'" 404–407; Unsigned Letter to Lee F. Johnson, September 28, 1950, Philleo Nash Papers, box 56, folder Minorities—

Negro—Detroit '50, Harry S. Truman Presidential Library, Independence, Mo. Also see Arnold R. Hirsch, *Making the Second Ghetto: Race and Housing in Chicago, 1940–1960* (Cambridge, UK: Cambridge University Press, 1983); and Martin Meyerson and Edward C. Banfield, *Politics, Planning, and the Public Interest: The Case of Public Housing in Chicago* (New York: Free Press, 1955).

46. Hirsch, "Choosing Segregation," 217–218; Roger Biles, *Illinois: A History of the Land and Its People* (DeKalb: Northern Illinois University Press, 2005), 257.

47. Hirsch, "Searching for a 'Sound Negro Policy,'" 408–409 (quotation). Also see Hirsch, *Making the Second Ghetto*, chap. 4.

48. "Report of the Resolutions Committee of the 43rd Annual Convention of the [NAACP], June 28, 1952, Oklahoma City, Oklahoma," Philleo Nash Papers, box 56, folder Minorities—Housing—1951, 52, Harry S. Truman Presidential Library, Independence, Mo. (first quotation); "Address by Robert C. Weaver at National Conference on Discrimination in Housing" (second quotation); Philleo Nash to Harry S. Truman, memorandum, June 23, 1952, Philleo Nash Papers, box 57, folder Minorities—Negro—Memorandum, Harry S. Truman Presidential Library, Independence, Mo. Also see Arnold R. Hirsch, "Less than Plessy: The Inner City, Suburbs, and State-Sanctioned Residential Segregation in the Age of Brown," in *The New Suburban History*, 33–56.

49. David M. P. Freund, "Marketing the Free Market: State Intervention and the Politics of Prosperity in Metropolitan America" in *The New Suburban History*, 19 (quotation). Also see David M. P. Freund, *Colored Property: State Policy and White Racial Politics in Suburban America* (Chicago: University of Chicago Press, 2007), especially chap. 5; and Thomas W. Hanchett, "The Other 'Subsidized Housing': Federal Aid to Suburbanization, 1940s–1960s," in Bauman, Biles, and Szylvian, *From Tenements to the Taylor Homes*.

50. David M. P. Freund, *Colored Property*, 190–195; Andrew Wiese, *Places of Their Own: African American Suburbanization in the Twentieth Century* (Chicago: University of Chicago Press, 2004), 129–142.

51. Barry Checkoway, "Large Builders, Federal Housing Programs, and Postwar Suburbanization," in *Critical Perspectives on Housing*, ed. Rachel G. Bratt, Chester Hartman, and Ann Myerson (Philadelphia: Temple University Press, 1986), 125–127; Delores Hayden, *Redesigning the American Dream: The Future of Housing, Work, and Family* (New York: W. W. Norton, 1984), 6–8; Hanchett, "The Other 'Subsidized Housing,'" 166 (quotation). Also see Barbara Kelly, *Expanding the American Dream: Building and Rebuilding Levittown* (Albany: State University of New York Press, 1993).

52. David R. Goldfield and Blaine A. Brownell, *Urban America: A History* (Boston: Houghton Mifflin, 1990), 292; Raymond A. Mohl, "Planned Destruction: The Interstates and Central City Housing," in Bauman, Biles, and Szylvian, *From Tenements to the Taylor Homes*, 229–230; Thomas H. MacDonald, "The City's Place in Post-War Highway Planning," *American City* 58 (February 1943): 42–44. Also see Mark I. Foster, *From Streetcar to Superhighway: American City Planners and*

Urban Transportation, 1900–1940 (Philadelphia: Temple University Press, 1981);
W. Stull Holt, *The Bureau of Public Roads: Its History, Activities, and Organization*
(Baltimore: Johns Hopkins University Press, 1923); and Norman Bel Geddes, *Magic
Motorways* (New York: Random House, 1940).

53. Thomas H. MacDonald, "The Case for Urban Expressways," *American City*
62 (June 1947): 92–93; Richard O. Davies, *The Age of Asphalt: The Automobile, the
Freeway, and the Condition of Metropolitan America* (Philadelphia: J. B. Lippincott,
1975), 12–13; Fogelson, *Downtown*, 317 (quotation); Edward Weiner, *Urban Transportation Planning in the United States: An Historical Overview* (Westport, Conn.:
Praeger, 1999), 17.

54. Owen D. Gutfreund, *Twentieth-Century Sprawl: Highways and the Reshaping of the American Landscape* (New York: Oxford University Press, 2004),
40–41.

55. Foster, *From Streetcar to Superhighway*, 153 (first quotation); Bruce Seely,
Building the American Highway System: Engineers as Policy Makers (Philadelphia:
Temple University Press, 1987), 203; Gelfand, *A Nation of Cities*, 224; Mark H. Rose,
Interstate: Express Highway Politics, 1941–1956 (Lawrence: University Press of Kan-
sas, 1979), chap. 3; Mohl, "Planned Destruction," 232 (second quotation).

56. George F. Emery, "Urban Expressways," in *American Planning and Civil
Annual*, ed. Harlean James (Washington, D.C.: American Planning and Civic Association, 1947), 127; Rose, *Interstate*, 57 (quotation); Harold M. Mayer, "Moving People and Goods in Tomorrow's Cities," *Annals of the American Academy of Political
and Social Science* 242 (November 1945): 116. Also see Cliff Ellis, "Professional Conflict over Urban Form: The Case of Urban Freeways, 1930 to 1970," in *Planning the
Twentieth-Century American City*, ed. Mary Corbin Sies and Christopher Silver (Baltimore: Johns Hopkins University Press, 1996).

57. *Congressional Quarterly Almanac*, 80th Cong., 2nd sess., 1948, vol. 4, 284;
81st Cong., 2nd sess., 1950, vol. 6, 602–606. Seely, *Building the American Highway
System*, 193, 200, 202.

58. Harry S. Truman to Senator Dennis Chavez, August 17, 1950, Official File
129, box 678, folder OF 129 (1949–50), Harry S. Truman Presidential Library, Independence, Mo.; Thomas H. MacDonald, "The Case for Urban Expressways," 92–93;
Bruce Seely, *Building the American Highway System*, 194 (quotation); Mohl,
"Planned Destruction," 230–231; Rose, *Interstate*, 61–62.

59. Raymond A. Mohl, "The Interstate and the Cities: Highways, Housing, and
the Freeway Revolt," research report prepared for the Poverty and Race Research Action Council, 2002, 7–8, copy in the author's possession.

60. Gelfand, *A Nation of* Cities, 226; Seely, *Building the American Highway
System*, 194; Rose, *Interstate*, 59 (quotation).

61. Seely, *Building the American Highway System*, 194; Walter Blucher, "Moving
People," *Virginia Law Review* 36 (November 1950): 849; Gelfand, *A Nation of Cities*,
231 (quotation).

62. Janet R. Daly Bednarek, *America's Airports: Airfield Development, 1918–1947*
(College Station: Texas A&M University Press, 2001), 10; Paul Barrett, "Cities and

Their Airports: Policy Formation, 1926–1952," *Journal of Urban History* 14 (November 1987): 117 (quotation); Roscoe C. Martin, *The Cities and the Federal System* (New York: Atherton Press, 1965), 91–92; Roger W. Lotchin, *Fortress California, 1910–1961: From Warfare to Welfare* (New York: Oxford University Press, 1992), 248; Robert B. Fairbanks, "A Clash of Priorities: The Federal Government and Dallas Airport Development, 1917–1964," in *American Cities and Towns: Historical Perspectives*, ed. Joseph F. Rishel (Pittsburgh: Duquesne University Press, 1992), 167.

63. Barrett, "Cities and Their Airports," 129 (quotations); Bednarek, *America's Airports*, 153; Lotchin, *Fortress California*, 252; *Congressional Quarterly*, 79th Cong., 2nd sess., 1946, vol. 2, 355–356.

64. Rose, *Interstate* (quotation), 61.

65. Ibid., 65.

CHAPTER 2. DYNAMIC CONSERVATISM
AND THE CITIES

1. Eisenhower biographies and studies of his presidency contain very little mention of urban policy. See Stephen E. Ambrose, *Eisenhower: The President* (New York: Simon & Schuster, 1984); Robert F. Burk, *Dwight D. Eisenhower: Hero and Politician* (Boston: Twayne, 1986); Elmo Richardson, *The Presidency of Dwight D. Eisenhower* (Lawrence: University Press of Kansas, 1979); Charles C. Alexander, *Holding the Line: The Eisenhower Era, 1952–1961* (Bloomington: Indiana University Press, 1975); R. Alton Lee, *Dwight D. Eisenhower: Soldier and Statesman* (Chicago: Nelson-Hall, 1981); Fred I. Greenstein, *The Hidden-Hand Presidency: Eisenhower as Leader* (New York: Basic Books, 1982); and Robert Griffith, "Dwight D. Eisenhower and the Corporate Commonwealth," *American Historical Review* 87 (February 1982): 87–122. On Eisenhower's fiscal conservatism, see Iwan W. Morgan, *Eisenhower versus "The Spenders": The Eisenhower Administration, the Democrats and the Budget, 1953–1960* (New York: St. Martin's Press, 1990).

2. Jon C. Teaford, *The Metropolitan Revolution: The Rise of Post-Urban America* (New York: Columbia University Press, 2006), 72.

3. Ibid., 58–59; Mark I. Gelfand, *A Nation of Cities: The Federal Government and Urban America, 1933–1965* (New York: Oxford University Press, 1975), 164–165.

4. Jon C. Teaford, *The Rough Road to Renaissance: Urban Revitalization in America, 1940–1985* (Baltimore: Johns Hopkins University Press, 1990), 108–109; Roy Lubove, ed., *Pittsburgh* (New York: New Viewpoints, 1976), 177–181; Teaford, *The Metropolitan Revolution*, 54 (*Newsweek* quotation). Also see John F. Bauman and Edward K. Muller, *Before Renaissance: Planning in Pittsburgh, 1889–1943* (Pittsburgh: University of Pittsburgh Press, 2006).

5. Teaford, *The Rough Road to Renaissance*, 105–120; Teaford, *The Metropolitan Revolution*, 58 (quotation).

6. Thomas H. O'Connor, *Building a New Boston: Politics and Urban Renewal, 1950–1970* (Boston: Northeastern University Press, 1993), 82–88; Mark H. Rose,

Interstate: Express Highway Politics, 1941–1956 (Lawrence: University Press of Kansas, 1979), 65; Teaford, *The Metropolitan Revolution*, 58–59.

7. Teaford, *The Rough Road to Renaissance*, 54–66. Also see Roger Biles, *Richard J. Daley: Politics, Race, and the Governing of Chicago* (DeKalb: Northern Illinois University Press, 1995); and Warren Moscow, *The Last of the Big-Time Bosses: The Life and Times of Carmine DeSapio and the Rise and Fall of Tammany Hall* (New York: Stein & Day, 1971).

8. Gelfand, *A Nation of Cities*, 164–165. On Moses and Title I in New York City, see Robert A. Caro, *The Power Broker: Robert Moses and the Fall of New York* (New York: Vintage Books, 1975); and Joel Schwartz, *The New York Approach: Robert Moses, Urban Liberals, and Redevelopment of the Inner City* (Columbus: Ohio State University Press, 1993).

9. Gary W. Reichard, *The Reaffirmation of Republicanism: Eisenhower and the Eighty-third Congress* (Knoxville: University of Tennessee Press, 1975), 10.

10. Ibid, 14n34; *Public Papers of the Presidents of the United States: Dwight D. Eisenhower, 1953* (Washington, D.C.: Government Printing Office, 1961).

11. The Commission on Intergovernmental Relations, "A Report to the President for Transmittal to the Congress," June 1955, 215–216, 226–227, 232, Meyer Kestnbaum Files, box 4, File Commission on Inter-Governmental Relations (14), Dwight D. Eisenhower Presidential Library, Abilene, Kans.; "Remarks of Robert E. Merriam," October 22, 1956, Robert Merriam Records, box 9, folder Metropolitan Areas, Dwight D. Eisenhower Presidential Library; John J. Gunther, *Federal-City Relations in the United States: The Role of the Mayors in Federal Aid to Cities* (Newark: University of Delaware Press, 1990), 196.

12. "Remarks of Robert E. Merriam"; Gelfand, *A Nation of Cities*, 176–179.

13. Oral History Interview with Robert Merriam, 98 (first quotation), Dwight D. Eisenhower Presidential Library; "Remarks of Robert E. Merriam"; Robert Merriam, "Partners or Rivals?" *National Municipal Review* 45 (December 1956): 532–536;Gelfand, *A Nation of Cities*, 182 (second quotation).

14. Aksel Nielsen to Dwight D. Eisenhower, May 20, 1952, White House Central Files, Official File 120, box 612, folder Housing 1953-1, Dwight D. Eisenhower Presidential Library. For an overview of Eisenhower and public housing, see Roger Biles, "Public Housing Policy in the Eisenhower Administration," *Mid-America* 81 (Winter 1999): 5–25.

15. Memorandum to Aksel Nielsen, May 15, 1952, White House Central Files, Official File 120, box 612, folder Housing 1953-1, Dwight D. Eisenhower Presidential Library.

16. Ibid; "Builders Say Ike 'Wants None' of Public Housing; General's Aides Say It Isn't So," *House and Home* 2 (October 1952): 36 (first quotation); "The Washington Scene—What Will Housing, Slum Clearance Picture Be in 1953?" *Journal of Housing* 9 (December 1952): 430 (second quotation).

17. Robert Taft to Herbert Brownell, December 17, 1952, White House Central Files, Official File 120, box 612, folder Housing 1953-1, Dwight D. Eisenhower Presidential Library; "GOP Hits Snag Finding New HHFA Chief So Lame Ducks Are Retained," *House and Home* 3 (February 1953): 104–105 (quotation).

18. "The Fox in Charge," *New Republic* 129 (March 9, 1953): 7 (Humphrey quotation); "Administrative Strangle," *New Republic* 128 (April 6, 1953): 9 (newspaper quotation); "Eisenhower Finally Picks New Boss for HHFA: Former Representative Albert Cole," *House and Home* 3 (March 1953): 140 (Thimmes quotation); Walter P. Reuther to Dwight D. Eisenhower, March 6, 1953, White House Central Files, Official File 24, box 201, folder Housing and Home Finance Agency, 1953, Dwight D. Eisenhower Presidential Library; Dwight D. Eisenhower to Walter P. Reuther, April 1, 1953, White House Central Files, Official File 24, box 201, folder Housing and Home Finance Agency, 1953, Dwight D. Eisenhower Presidential Library. The Senate confirmed Cole's appointment by a vote of 64–18.

19. "Administrative Strangle," 9; "Requests and Authorization of Additional Units of Low-Rent Public Housing," White House Central Files, Official File 120, box 616, folder 1959-2, Dwight D. Eisenhower Presidential Library.

20. Albert Cole to Sherman Adams, July 17, 1953, White House Central Files, Official File 120, box 613, folder Housing 1953-1, Dwight D. Eisenhower Presidential Library.

21. Alexander, *Holding the Line*, 24.

22. Albert Cole to Sherman Adams, October 21, 1953, White House Central Files, Official File 120, box 613, folder Housing 1953-2, Dwight D. Eisenhower Presidential Library; Reichard, *The Reaffirmation of Republicanism*, 119–125; James T. Patterson, *Mr. Republican: A Biography of Robert A. Taft* (Boston: Houghton Mifflin, 1972), 611–612.

23. The President's Advisory Committee on Government Housing Policies and Programs, "A Report to the President of the U.S.," December 14, 1953, White House Central Files, Official File 120-B, box 617, folder Advisory Committee on Government Housing Policies and Programs—3, Dwight D. Eisenhower Presidential Library; D. Bradford Hunt, "How Did Public Housing Survive the 1950s?" *Journal of Policy History* 17 (2005): 206 (quotation).

24. "Message to the Congress on Housing," January 25, 1954, Dwight D. Eisenhower Papers as President, box 6, folder Message to Congress on Housing, 25 January 1954," Dwight D. Eisenhower Presidential Library (quotation); *Public Papers of the Presidents of the United States: Dwight D. Eisenhower, 1954* (Washington, D.C.: Government Printing Office, 1960), 197.

25. Catherine Bauer, "Three-Way War in Housing: Lenders v. Builders v. Reformers," *Reporter* 10 (June 22, 1954): 20 (quotation); U.S. Senate Committee on Banking and Currency, *Hearings before the Committee on Banking and Currency*, 83rd Cong., 2nd sess., 1954, pt. 1: 677, 829, 996.

26. *New York Times*, January 24, 1954 (Martin quotation), August 21, 1954; Nathaniel S. Keith, *Politics and the Housing Crisis since 1930* (New York: Universe Books, 1973), 113–114; "Housing Act of 1954," *Journal of Housing* 11 (August–September 1954): 261; *Public Papers of the Presidents of the United States: Dwight D. Eisenhower, 1954*, 675; Reichard, *The Reaffirmation of Republicanism*, 128 (Wolcott and NHC quotations).

27. U.S. Senate Committee on Banking and Currency, *Hearings before the Committee on Banking and Currency*, 836; John Sparkman, "Demand Exceeds Supply," *New Republic* 132 (January 17, 1955): 13; Ambrose, *Eisenhower*, 158. For a discussion

of the very different reasons that reformers and builders supported urban redevelopment, see Catherine Bauer, "Redevelopment: A Misfit in the Fifties," in *The Future of Cities and Urban Redevelopment*, ed. Coleman Woodbury (Chicago: University of Chicago Press, 1953), 7–25.

28. "Ike Asks 'Firm' 35,000-Unit-a-Year Program but Hints End of Public Housing in 1958," *House and Home* 7 (February 1955): 41 (quotation); Keith, *Politics and the Housing Crisis since 1930*, 118; Biles, "Public Housing Policy in the Eisenhower Administration," 18–19; William A. Ulman, "Proposal for Analysis of Housing and Its Relationship to the Political Campaigns of 1956," Bryce N. Harlow Papers, box 11, folder Housing #4, Dwight D. Eisenhower Presidential Library.

29. Biles, "Public Housing Policy in the Eisenhower Administration," 19–20; "Statement with Regard to Senator Clark's Speech before the National Housing Conference," Department of Housing and Urban Development, Subject Correspondence Files: Albert M. Cole, HHFA, 1953–58, box 12, folder National Housing Conference, National Archives II, College Park, Maryland (first quotation); Biles, "Public Housing and the Postwar Urban Renaissance," 147 (second quotation).

30. Ambrose, *Eisenhower*, 488; *Public Papers of the Presidents of the United States: Eisenhower, 1959* (Washington, D.C.: Government Printing Office, 1960), 84; "Ike Asks: Kill Public Housing, Boost VA Interest Rate," *House and Home* 15 (February 1959): 41; Morgan, *Eisenhower versus "The Spenders,"* 146 (quotation).

31. Press Release, "To the Senate of the U.S.," July 7, 1959, White House Central Files, Official File 120, box 616, folder 1959, Dwight D. Eisenhower Presidential Library; press release, "To the Senate of the U.S.," September 4, 1959, White House Central Files, Official File 120, box 616, folder 1959, Dwight D. Eisenhower Presidential Library(quotation); *Public Papers of the Presidents of the United States: Dwight D. Eisenhower, 1959*, 641; Comptroller General of the U.S., "Report to the Congress of the U.S.: Audit of Public Housing Administration, Housing and Home Finance Agency, fiscal year 1959," March 1960, White House Central Files, Official File 25-E, box 207, folder Public Housing Administration: 7, Dwight D. Eisenhower Presidential Library; Morgan, *Eisenhower versus "The Spenders,"* 146–147; Congressional Quarterly Service, *Housing a Nation* (Washington, D.C.: Congressional Quarterly Service, 1966), 40–41.

32. Gelfand, *A Nation of Cities*, 176 (first quotation), 185–87, 286 (second quotation); Jeanne R. Lowe, "Rebuilding Cities—and Politics," *Nation* 186 (February 8, 1958): 118–120.

33. Gelfand, *A Nation of Cities*, 191, 194, 420n57; Ashley A. Foard and Hilbert Fefferman, "Federal Urban Renewal Legislation," *Law and Contemporary Problems* 25 (Autumn 1960): 672–684; Gunther, *Federal-City Relations in the United States*, 199–200.

34. Charles Abrams, "Segregation, Housing, and the Horne Case," *Reporter* 13 (October 6, 1955): 31; Robert F. Burk, *The Eisenhower Administration and Black Civil Rights* (Knoxville: University of Tennessee Press, 1984), 115 (quotation).

35. Burk, *The Eisenhower Administration and Black Civil Rights*, 112–113.

36. Arnold R. Hirsch, "Choosing Segregation: Federal Housing Policy between *Shelley* and *Brown*," in *From Tenements to the Taylor Homes: In Search of an Urban*

Housing Policy in Twentieth-Century America, ed. John F. Bauman, Roger Biles, and Kristin M. Szylvian (University Park: Pennsylvania State University Press, 2000), 219 (Horne quotations); Abrams, "Segregation, Housing, and the Horne Case," 30–33; Arnold R. Hirsch, "Searching for a 'Sound Negro Policy': A Racial Agenda for the Housing Acts of 1949 and 1954," *Housing Policy Debate* 11 (2000): 422 (Ray quotation).

37. Hirsch, "Searching for a 'Sound Negro Policy,'" 424 (first quotation); Hirsch, "Choosing Segregation," 219 (second quotation).

38. Hirsch, "Searching for a 'Sound Negro Policy,'" 425–427; Hirsch, "Choosing Segregation," 221; Douglas S. Massey and Nancy A. Denton, *American Apartheid: Segregation and the Making of the Underclass* (Cambridge, Mass.: Harvard University Press, 1993), 57 (first quotation); Arnold R. Hirsch, "Less than Plessy: The Inner City, Suburbs, and State-Sanctioned Residential Segregation in the Age of Brown," in *The New Suburban History*, ed. Kevin M. Kruse and Thomas J. Sugrue (Chicago: University of Chicago Press, 2006), 56 (second quotation).

39. Burk, *The Eisenhower Administration and Black Civil Rights*, 122. In *Colored Property*, historian David M. P. Freund argues that federal agencies not only expanded their influence in the private housing market after World War II but also persuaded homebuyers that market forces, not government policies, resulted in racial exclusion. David M. P. Freund, *Colored Property: State Policy and White Racial Politics in Suburban America* (Chicago: University of Chicago Press, 2007).

40. Freund, *Colored Property*, 187–190; Andrew Wiese, *Places of Their Own: African American Suburbanization in the Twentieth Century* (Chicago: University of Chicago Press, 2004), 138–140; Gelfand, *A Nation of Cities*, 221 (quotation).

41. Hirsch, "Searching for a 'Sound Negro Policy,'" 430–432; Massey and Denton, *American Apartheid*, 55–58.

42. Thomas W. Hanchett, "The Other 'Subsidized Housing': Federal Aid to Suburbanization, 1940s–1960s," in Bauman, Biles, and Szylvian, *From Tenements to the Taylor Homes*, 172–173; "There Are Big Profits in Small Apartments and Duplexes," *House and Home* 20 (July 1961): 166–167; Victor Gruen, *The Heart of Our Cities: The Urban Crisis—Diagnosis and Cure* (New York: Simon & Schuster, 1964), 267.

43. Thomas W. Hanchett, "U.S. Tax Policy and the Shopping-Center Boom of the 1950s and 1960s," *American Historical Review* 101 (October 1996): 1082–1110; Hanchett, "The Other 'Subsidized Housing,'" 172–173. Also see John Jakle, Keith Sculle, and Jefferson Rogers, *The Motel in America* (Baltimore: Johns Hopkins University Press, 1996).

44. Adam Rome, *The Bulldozer in the Countryside: Suburban Sprawl and the Rise of American Environmentalism* (Cambridge, UK: Cambridge University Press, 2001), 103–110; George Christopher to Dwight D. Eisenhower, March 19, 1958, John Bragdon Records, box 3, folder American Municipal Association, Dwight D. Eisenhower Presidential Library; John J. Gunther, *Federal-City Relations in the United States*, 196–199; Hanchett, "The Other 'Subsidized Housing,'" 170–171.

45. Raymond A. Mohl, "Ike and the Interstates: Creeping toward Comprehensive Planning," *Journal of Planning History* 2 (August 2003): 240–242.

46. Rose, *Interstate*, 41–54; Gary T. Schwartz, "Urban Freeways and the Interstate System," *Southern California Law Review* 49 (March 1976): 487 (quotations); Bernard J. Frieden and Lynne B. Sagalyn, *Downtown, Inc.: How America Rebuilds Cities* (Cambridge, Mass.: MIT Press, 1989), 20–22.

47. Mohl, "Ike and the Interstates," 243–244; Dwight D. Eisenhower, *The White House Years: Mandate for Change, 1953–1956* (New York: Doubleday, 1963), 548; Raymond A. Mohl, "The Interstates and the Cities: Highways, Housing, and the Freeway Revolt," Research Report, Poverty and Race Research Action Council, 2002, 13 (quotation); Raymond J. Saulnier, *Constructive Years: The U.S. Economy under Eisenhower* (Lanham, Md.: University Press of America, 1991), 233; Bruce Seely, *Building the American Highway System: Engineers as Policy Makers* (Philadelphia: Temple University Press, 1987), 214.

48. Oral History Interview with Lucius D. Clay, April 17, 1971, OH-285, 923–925, Dwight D. Eisenhower Presidential Library; "Report of the United States Conference of Mayors for Submission to the Subcommittee on Roads of the House Committee on Public Works, Hearings on the Federal Aid Highway Program," U.S. President's Advisory Committee on a National Highway System Records, 1954–55, box 4, folder Hearings (1), Dwight D. Eisenhower Presidential Library; "Summary of Public Hearings, President's Advisory Committee on a National Highway Program, October 7–8, 1954," U.S. President's Advisory Committee on a National Highway System Records, 1954–55, box 2, folder Subject File-Hearings-October 7–8, 1954 (5), Dwight D. Eisenhower Presidential Library; Owen D. Gutfreund, *Twentieth-Century Sprawl: Highways and the Reshaping of the American Landscape* (New York: Oxford University Press, 2004), 54; Gelfand, *A Nation of Cities*, 225 (quotations); Seely, *Building the American Highway System*, 214.

49. Mark H. Rose, "Reframing American Highway Politics, 1956–1995," *Journal of Planning History* 2 (August 2003): 216; Richard O. Davies, *The Age of Asphalt: The Automobile, the Freeway, and the Condition of Metropolitan America* (Philadelphia: J. B. Lippincott, 1975), 15–23; *Public Papers of the Presidents: Dwight D. Eisenhower, 1955* (Washington, D.C.: Government Printing Office, 1959), 275–280; Seely, *Building the American Highway* System, 215 (quotation); Tom Lewis, *Divided Highways: Building the Interstate Highways, Transforming American Life* (New York: Viking, 1997), 95–120; Mohl, "Ike and the Interstates," 244–245; Rose, *Interstate*, 79–80.

50. Rose, *Interstate*, 87–92.

51. Daniel P. Moynihan, "New Roads and Urban Chaos," *Reporter* 22 (April 14, 1960): 16.

52. Davies, *The Age of Asphalt*, 23.

53. Schwartz, "Urban Freeways and the Interstate System," 438 (quotation); Mohl, "Ike and the Interstates," 238–239.

54. Moynihan, "New Roads and Urban Chaos," 14 (Moynihan quotation); Lewis, *Divided Highways*, 153; Gelfand, *A Nation of Cities*, 228; Oral History Interview with Lucius D. Clay, 925–926 (Clay quotations); "Report on Legislative Intent with Respect to the Location of Interstate Routes in Urban Areas and the Concept of Local Needs in Section 116 of the Federal-Aid Highway Act of 1956," September 1959, John

Bragdon Records, box 38, folder Highways-Legislative Intent-Urban Areas, Dwight D. Eisenhower Presidential Library; Mohl, "Ike and the Interstates," 254; U.S. Department of Commerce, "Federal Transportation Policy and Program," February 1960, Robert Merriam Files, box 14, folder Transportation, Dwight D. Eisenhower Presidential Library; Schwartz, "Urban Freeways and the Interstate System," 445.

55. J. S. Bragdon to Council of Economic Advisers, memorandum, November 2, 1954, John Bragdon Records, box 83, folder Transportation-Highways, Urban, Dwight D. Eisenhower Presidential Library.

56. Moynihan, "New Roads and Urban Chaos," 19.

57. Gelfand, *A Nation of* Cities, 229; Mohl, "Ike and the Interstates," 245 (first and second Howard quotations); Moynihan, "New Roads and Urban Chaos," 19 (third Howard quotation); Wilfred Owen, *Cities in the Motor Age* (New York: Viking 1959), 32 (Owen quotation).

58. Martin Anderson, *The Federal Bulldozer: A Critical Analysis of Urban Renewal, 1949–1962* (Cambridge, Mass.: MIT Press, 1964), 56–57; Eisenhower, *Mandate for Change*, 127–128; Moynihan, "New Roads and Urban Chaos," 16; Mohl, "Ike and the Interstates," 250.

59. Mohl, "The Interstates and the Cities," 58–59; William Issel, "'Land Values, Human Values, and the Preservation of the City's Treasured Appearance': Environmentalism, Politics, and the San Francisco Freeway Revolt," *Pacific Historical Review* 68 (November 1999): 611–646; Joseph A. Rodriguez, *City against Suburb: The Culture Wars in an American Metropolis* (Westport, Conn.: Praeger, 1999), 24–26.

60. Rose, *Interstate*, 95 (first quotation); Lewis, *Divided Highways*, 145–150; Mohl, "Ike and the Interstates," 254–256; Schwartz, "Urban Freeways and the Interstate System," 487 (second quotation).

61. Rose, *Interstate*, 95 (quotation); Mohl, "Ike and the Interstates," 255; Lewis, *Divided Highways*, 151–152.

62. Lewis Mumford, *The Highway and the City* (New York: Harcourt, Brace, and World, 1963), 234 (Mumford quotation); Mohl, "Ike and the Interstates," 247 (Bello quotations).

63. Gelfand, *A Nation of* Cities, 231–234; "Crisis in City Transit," *Architectural Forum* 106 (June 1957): 109; George M. Smerk, *Urban Mass Transportation: A Dozen Years of Federal Policy* (Bloomington: Indiana University Press, 1974), 35; Michael N. Danielson, *Federal-Metropolitan Politics and the Commuter Crisis* (New York: Columbia University Press, 1965), 39 (quotation).

64. Smerk, *Urban Mass Transportation*, 35–37; Gelfand, *A Nation of Cities*, 233–234; Danielson, *Federal-Metropolitan Politics and the Commuter Crisis*, 100–106.

65. Smerk, *Urban Mass Transportation*, 38–39; Gelfand, *A Nation of Cities*, 234 (quotation); Danielson, *Federal-Metropolitan Politics and the Commuter Crisis*, 109–113.

66. Suzanne Farkas, *Urban Lobbying: Mayors in the Federal Arena* (New York: New York University Press, 1971), 62 (first quotation); Gelfand, *A Nation of Cities*, 194 (second quotation); *Public Papers of the Presidents of the United States: Dwight D. Eisenhower, 1960–61* (Washington, D.C.: Government Printing Office, 1961), 14–15 (third quotation).

67. Gilbert Y. Steiner, *The State of Welfare* (Washington, D.C.: Brookings Institution, 1971), 142 (Cole quotation); Griffith, "Dwight D. Eisenhower and the Corporate Commonwealth," 106 (Griffith quotation).

CHAPTER 3. THE NEW URBAN FRONTIER

1. Jon C. Teaford, *The Rough Road to Renaissance: Urban Revitalization in America, 1940–1985* (Baltimore: Johns Hopkins University Press, 1990), 122–124.

2. Ibid., 124–127. Also see Mitchell Gordon, *Sick Cities* (New York: Macmillan, 1963).

3. William L. Slayton to Wolf von Eckardt, December 1, 1963, William L. Slayton Papers, box 3, folder 12/63, John F. Kennedy Presidential Library, Boston; Martin Anderson, *The Federal Bulldozer: A Critical Analysis of Urban Renewal, 1949–1962* (Cambridge, Mass.: MIT Press, 1964).

4. Jane Jacobs, *The Death and Life of Great American Cities* (New York: Vintage, 1961).

5. Ibid., 4.

6. Herbert J. Gans, *The Urban Villagers* (New York: Free Press of Glencoe, 1962); Marc Fried, "Grieving for a Lost Home: Psychological Costs of Relocation," in *The Environment of the Metropolis*, ed. Leonard J. Duhl (New York: Basic Books, 1963); Chester Hartman, "The Housing of Relocated Families," in *Urban Renewal: The Record and the Controversy*, ed. James Q. Wilson (Cambridge, Mass.: MIT Press, 1966). Also see Thomas H. O'Connor, *Building a New Boston: Politics and Urban Renewal, 1950–1970* (Boston: Northeastern University Press, 1993). On the Chicago battle, see George Rosen, *Decision-Making Chicago Style: The Genesis of a University of Illinois Campus* (Urbana: University of Illinois Press, 1980); and Roger Biles, *Richard J. Daley: Politics, Race, and the Governing of Chicago* (DeKalb: Northern Illinois University Press, 1995), 74–77.

7. Teaford, *The Rough Road to Renaissance*, 160–161.

8. Mark I. Gelfand, *A Nation of Cities: The Federal Government and Urban America, 1933–1965* (New York: Oxford University Press, 1975), 292–293.

9. John F. Kennedy, "The Shame of the States," *New York Times Magazine*, May 18, 1958, 12, 37–38, 40; *New York Times*, December 1, 1959; Gelfand, *A Nation of Cities*, 295 (first quotation); Michael N. Danielson, *Federal-Metropolitan Problems and the Commuter Crisis* (New York: Columbia University Press, 1965), 112 (second quotation). Also see William O'Hallaren, "A Fair Share for the Cities," *Reporter* 21 (November 12, 1959): 22–24.

10. Francis E. Rourke, "Urbanism and the National Party Organizations," *Western Political Quarterly* 18 (March 1964): 155; Kirk H. Porter and Donald Bruce Johnson, *National Party Platforms, 1840–1964* (Urbana: University of Illinois Press, 1966), 617 (quotation); Theodore H. White, *The Making of the President, 1960* (New York: Atheneum, 1961), 206.

11. Oral History Interview with William L. Slayton, February 3, 1967, 2–3, John F. Kennedy Presidential Library; Gelfand, *A Nation of Cities*, 304 (quotation).

12. Oral History Interview with Robert C. Wood, January 29, 1968, 10, John F. Kennedy Presidential Library; Theodore H. White, *The Making of the President, 1960*, 353–354; Joseph K. Zikmund, II, "Suburban Voting in Presidential Elections, 1948–1964," *Midwest Journal of Political Science* 12 (May 1968): 248; Gelfand, *A Nation of Cities*, 306 (quotation).

13. Roger Biles, *Crusading Liberal: Paul H. Douglas of Illinois* (DeKalb: Northern Illinois University Press, 2002), 153; Paul H. Douglas, *In the Fullness of Time: The Memoirs of Paul H. Douglas* (New York: Harcourt Brace Jovanovich, 1971), 518–519; Alice O'Connor, "Swimming against the Tide: A Brief History of Federal Policy in Poor Communities," in *Urban Problems and Community Development*, ed. Ronald F. Ferguson and William T. Dickens (Washington, D.C.: Brookings Institution Press, 1999), 97–98.

14. Biles, *Crusading Liberal*, 153. The January 2, 1961, issue of the *New York Times* included the full text of the task force report.

15. *Congressional Quarterly Almanac, 1961*, 87th Cong., 1st sess., 1961, vol. 17, 76, 247–249; Herbert S. Parmet, *JFK: The Presidency of John F. Kennedy* (New York: Penguin, 1983), 77, 97; Roger Biles, *Crusading Liberal*, 153–154; Douglas, *In the Fullness of Time*, 519–522; Alice O'Connor, "Swimming against the Tide," 98–99.

16. "Report of the Task Force on Housing and Urban Affairs for President-Elect John F. Kennedy," December 30, 1960, John Barriere Papers, box 1, John F. Kennedy Presidential Library; "The New Frontier for Housing," *House and Home* 19 (February 1961): 132–139; Alexander von Hoffman, "The Quest for a New Frontier," working paper on the history of housing policy, August 6, 2007, 17–18, in possession of the author.

17. Hoffman, "The Quest for a New Frontier," 18; A. H. Raskin, "Washington Gets 'The Weaver Treatment,'" *New York Times Magazine*, May 4, 1961, 16, 30. Also see Wendell E. Pritchett, *Robert Clifton Weaver and the American City: The Life and Times of an Urban Reformer* (Chicago: University of Chicago Press, 2008).

18. Oral History Interview with Robert C. Weaver, November 19, 1968, 20–23, Lyndon B. Johnson Presidential Library, Austin; Harold Wolman, *The Politics of Federal Housing* (New York: Dodd, Mead & Co., 1971), 83–84; Raskin, "Washington Gets 'The Weaver Treatment,'" 16, 30.

19. Oral History Interview with Robert C. Weaver, May 6, 1964, 56, 68, John F. Kennedy Presidential Library; Oral History Interview with Robert C. Weaver, November 19, 1968, 24.

20. Oral History Interview with Robert C. Weaver, May 6, 1964, 55–56, John F. Kennedy Presidential Library; Oral History Interview with Robert C. Weaver, October 1, 1964, 232–234, John F. Kennedy Presidential Library.

21. Nathaniel S. Keith, *Politics and the Housing Crisis since 1930* (New York: Universe Books, 1973), 140–141; Oral History Interview with Marie McGuire, April 3, 1967, John F. Kennedy Presidential Library; Oral History Interview with William L. Slayton, February 3, 1967, 4–5; Gelfand, *A Nation of Cities*, 314–315.

22. *Public Papers of the Presidents: John F. Kennedy, 1961* (Washington, D.C.: Government Printing Office, 1962), 163–169; Robert C. Wood, *The Necessary Majority:*

Middle America and the Urban Crisis (New York: Columbia University Press, 1972), 40; Oral History Interview with William L. Slayton, February 3, 1967, 6; Hoffman, "The Quest for a New Frontier," 20–23; Danielson, *Federal-Metropolitan Politics and the Commuter Crisis*, 156–158.

23. Hoffman, "The Quest for a New Frontier," 22.

24. Ibid., 24 (quotation); Gelfand, *A Nation of Cities*, 318–321.

25. Congressional Research Service, *A Chronology of Housing Legislation and Selected Executive Actions, 1892–1992* (Washington, D.C.: Government Printing Office, 1994), 95; *Public Papers of the Presidents of the United States: John F. Kennedy, 1961*, 167; *Congressional Record*, 87th Cong., 1st sess., June 8, 1961, 107, pt. 8:9891 (quotation); Nathaniel S. Keith, *Politics and the Housing Crisis since 1930*, 143.

26. Raskin, "Washington Gets 'The Weaver Treatment,'" 36; Danielson, *Federal-Metropolitan Politics and the Commuter Crisis*, 158 (quotation); Alan Altshuler and David Luberoff, *Mega-Projects: The Changing Politics of Urban Public Investment* (Washington, D.C.: Brookings Institution Press, 2003), 182; Gelfand, *A Nation of Cities*, 319; Congressional Research Service, *A Chronology of Housing Legislation and Selected Executive Actions, 1892–1992*, 95; Royce Hanson, "Congress Copes with Mass Transit, 1960–64," in Frederic N. Cleaveland and associates, *Congress and Urban Problems* (Washington, D.C.: Brookings Institution, 1969), 321–326.

27. Keith, *Politics and the Housing Crisis since 1930*, 143; Oral History Interview with William L. Slayton, February 3, 1967, 6; Gelfand, *A Nation of Cities*, 319–320; Hoffman, "The Quest for a New Frontier," 26–28.

28. National Commission on Urban Problems, *Building the American City: Report of the National Commission on Urban Problems to the Congress and to the President of the United States* (Washington, D.C.: Government Printing Office, 1968), 147; Keith, *Politics and the Housing Crisis since 1930*, 145; Hoffman, "The Quest for a New Frontier," 26–27.

29. Carl M. Brauer, *John F. Kennedy and the Second Reconstruction* (New York: Columbia University Press, 1977), 43 (quotation); Oral History Interview with Robert C. Weaver, July 8, 1964, 158–159, John F. Kennedy Presidential Library; John J. Gunther, *Federal-City Relations in the United States: The Role of the Mayors in Federal Aid to Cities* (Newark: University of Delaware Press, 1990), 203; Parmet, *JFK*, 258–259; Oral History Interview with Theodore Sorensen, May 3, 1964, 122–123, John F. Kennedy Presidential Library. Also see Nick Bryant, *The Bystander: John F. Kennedy and the Struggle for Black Equality* (New York: Basic Books, 2006); and Mark Stern, *Calculating Visions: Kennedy, Johnson, and Civil Rights* (New Brunswick, N.J.: Rutgers University Press, 1992).

30. John B. Willman, *The Department of Housing and Urban Development* (New York: Praeger, 1967), 23; Wendell E. Pritchett, "Which Urban Crisis? Regionalism, Race, and Urban Policy, 1960–1974," 6, unpublished paper in possession of the author (quotations); Gelfand, *A Nation of Cities*, 324–328; Judith Heimlich Parris, "Congress Rejects the President's Urban Department, 1961–62," in Cleaveland, *Congress and Urban Problems*, 191.

31. "Federal Legislative Matters Affecting Housing and Home Finance Agency," July 19, 1961, HHFA Records, Reel 5, Lyndon B. Johnson Presidential Library; Pritchett, "Which Urban Crisis?" 7 (first quotation); Willman, *The Department of Housing and Urban Development*, 27 (second quotation); Gelfand, *A Nation of Cities*, 328–330.

32. Suzanne Farkas, *Urban Lobbying: Mayors in the Federal Arena* (New York: New York University Press, 1971), 126; Gelfand, *A Nation of Cities*, 329.

33. Oral History Interview with Robert C. Weaver, November 19, 1968, 21 (quotation); Brauer, *John F. Kennedy and the Second Reconstruction*, 127–128.

34. Gelfand, *A Nation of Cities*, 331–332; *New York Times*, January 17, 22, 25, 1962.

35. Oral History Interview with Theodore Sorensen, May 3, 1964, 122; Brauer, *John F. Kennedy and the Second Reconstruction*, 129 (first quotation); *New York Times*, January 26, 1962 (second quotation); Theodore C. Sorensen, *Kennedy* (New York: Harper & Row, 1965), 481 (third quotation); "Mousetrapped," *Newsweek* 59 (February 5, 1962): 22; Wendell E. Pritchett, "Which Urban Crisis?" (fourth quotation).

36. *New York Times*, January 30, 1962; Brauer, *John F. Kennedy and the Second Reconstruction*, 129–131; Gelfand, *A Nation of Cities*, 333–335.

37. "Debacle," *Newsweek* 59 (March 5, 1962): 24 (first quotation); Gelfand, *A Nation of Cities*, 335 (second quotation), 446n77 (third quotation); Willman, *The Department of Housing and Urban Development*, 30.

38. Oral History Interview with Theodore Sorensen, May 3, 1964, 122–123; Sorensen, *Kennedy*, 480.

39. Gelfand, *A Nation of Cities*, 447n99; Brauer, *John F. Kennedy and the Second Reconstruction*, 206–207.

40. Roger Biles, "Public Housing and the Postwar Urban Renaissance, 1949–1973," in *From Tenements to the Taylor Homes: In Search of an Urban Housing Policy in Twentieth-Century America*, ed. John F. Bauman, Roger Biles, and Kristin M. Szylvian (University Park: Pennsylvania State University Press, 2000), 151; Oral History Interview with Robert C. Weaver, November 19, 1968, 25–27; David M. P. Freund, "Democracy's Unfinished Business: Federal Policy and the Search for Fair Housing, 1961–68," *Poverty and Race in America: The Emerging Agendas*, ed. Chester Hartman (Lanham, Md.: Lexington Books, 2006), 174; Brauer, *John F. Kennedy and the Second Reconstruction*, 208–211.

41. Oral History Interview with Robert C. Weaver, June 16, 1964, 138 (quotation), John F. Kennedy Presidential Library; Lee C. White to Theodore C. Sorensen, memorandum, April 13, 1961, Lee C. White Papers, box 17, folder Mass Transit 1961, Mar. 10–May 25, 1961, John F. Kennedy Presidential Library.

42. "Urban Transportation: Joint Report to the President by the Housing and Home Finance Administrator and the Secretary of Commerce," March 28, 1962, HHFA Records, Reel 2, John F. Kennedy Presidential Library; "Highway–Mass Transit Coordination," August 31, 1965, Department of Transportation Records, RG 398, General Correspondence, 1958–1967, box 7, folder Transportation Task Force Originals of Sept. 2, 1965 Submission, National Archives II, College Park, Md.

43. "Highway–Mass Transit Coordination"; *Congressional Quarterly Almanac*, 87th Cong., 2nd sess., 1962, vol. 18, 449–451; Thomas A. Morehouse, "The 1962 Highway

Act: A Study in Artful Interpretation," *Journal of the American Institute of Planners* 35 (May 1969): 160–168; Edward Weiner, *Urban Transportation Planning in the United States: An Historical Overview* (Westport, CT: Praeger, 1999), 33–34; Royce Hanson, "Congress Copes with Mass Transit, 1960–64," 328–333.

44. *Congressional Quarterly Almanac*, 87th Cong., 2nd sess., 1962, vol. 18, 561–564; *Congressional Quarterly Almanac*, 88th Cong., 1st sess., 1963, vol. 19, 556–562; Hanson, "Congress Copes with Mass Transit, 1960–64," 328–347.

45. Keith, *Politics and the Housing Crisis since 1930*, 147–150; Gelfand, *A Nation of Cities*, 340–341.

46. Arthur M. Schlesinger Jr., *A Thousand Days: John F. Kennedy in the White House* (Boston: Houghton Mifflin, 1965), 660. The Kennedy administration's participation in the reapportionment cases is detailed in Victor S. Navasky, *Kennedy Justice* (New York: Atheneum, 1971).

47. Oral History Interview with William L. Slayton, February 3, 1967; Gelfand, *A Nation of* Cities, 337–339. For a sampling of opinions on urban renewal during those years, see "Rebuilders of Cities—or a New Pork Barrel?" *Business Week* (December 7, 1963): 64–70; Hubert Kay, "The Third Force in Urban Renewal," *Fortune* 70 (October 1964): 130–133; "Cities: The Renaissance," *Time* 79 (March 23, 1962): 19; and John C. Sparks, "The Fallacy of Urban Renewal," *Reader's Digest* 81 (October 1962): 114–116.

48. Gilbert Y. Steiner, *The State of Welfare* (Washington, D.C.: Brookings Institution Press, 1971), 148–150; Oral History Interview with Marie McGuire, April 3, 1967, John F. Kennedy Presidential Library; Biles, "Public Housing and the Postwar Urban Renaissance, 1949–1973," 155; Gelfand, *A Nation of Cities*, 337. The Kennedy administration pioneered in the provision of public housing on Indian land. See Roger Biles, "Public Housing on the Reservation," *American Indian Culture and Research Journal* 24, no. 2 (2000): 49–63.

49. Wood, *The Necessary Majority*, 41; Robert C. Weaver, *The Urban Complex* (Garden City, NY: Doubleday, 1964), 197–200; Gelfand, *A Nation of Cities*, 339 (quotation).

50. Allen J. Matusow, *The Unraveling of America: A History of Liberalism in the 1960s* (New York: Harper & Row, 1984), chap. 4; O'Connor, "Swimming against the Tide," 99–102; Schlesinger, *A Thousand Days*, 660–661.

51. Gelfand, *A Nation of Cities*, 347 (quotation).

CHAPTER 4. THE GREAT SOCIETY AND THE CITIES

1. On Lyndon Johnson's formative years, see Robert Dallek, *Lone Star Rising: Lyndon Johnson and His Times, 1908–1960* (New York: Oxford University Press, 1991); Robert A. Caro, *The Years of Lyndon Johnson: The Path to Power* (New York: Alfred A. Knopf, 1982); and Robert A. Caro, *The Years of Lyndon Johnson: Means of Ascent* (New York: Alfred A. Knopf, 1990). On Johnson as Senate majority leader, see Robert A. Caro, *The Years of Lyndon Johnson: Master of the Senate* (New York: Alfred A. Knopf, 2002); for a somewhat different assessment than Caro offers of

Johnson's role in the passage of the 1957 and 1960 Civil Rights Acts, see Roger Biles, *Crusading Liberal: Paul H. Douglas of Illinois* (DeKalb: Northern Illinois University Press, 2002). On Johnson and the big-city mayors, see Oral History Interview with Anthony J. Celebrezze, January 25, 1972, Lyndon B. Johnson Presidential Library, Austin, Tex. For a vivid description of the liberal expectations of a Johnson presidency after the Kennedy assassination, see Arthur M. Schlesinger Jr., *Journals: 1952–2000* (New York: Penguin, 2007).

2. Irving Bernstein, *Guns or Butter: The Presidency of Lyndon Johnson* (New York: Oxford University Press, 1996), 95 (first quotation); James T. Patterson, *Grand Expectations: The United States, 1945–1974* (New York: Oxford University Press, 1996), 535 (second quotation).

3. *Public Papers of the Presidents of the United States: Lyndon B. Johnson, 1963–1964* (Washington, D.C.: Government Printing Office, 1965), 1:114 (quotation); Bernstein, *Guns or Butter*, 97–98.

4. Alice O'Connor, "Community Action, Urban Reform, and the Fight against Poverty: The Ford Foundation's Gray Areas Program," *Journal of Urban History* 22 (July 1996): 586–625. Also see Alice O'Connor, *Poverty Knowledge: Social Science, Social Policy, and the Poor in Twentieth-Century U.S. History* (Princeton: Princeton University Press, 2001), chap. 5.

5. "The Office of Economic Opportunity during the Administration of President Lyndon B. Johnson, November 1963–January 1969," vol. 1, pt. 1, 28, box 1, Lyndon B. Johnson Presidential Library (first quotation); Robert Dallek, *Flawed Giant: Lyndon Johnson and His Times, 1961–1973* (New York: Oxford University Press, 1998), 77 (second and third quotations); Bernstein, *Guns or Butter*, 101–102.

6. *Public Papers of the Presidents of the United States: Lyndon B. Johnson, 1963–1964*, 1:375–380; *Congressional Quarterly Almanac*, 88th Cong. 2nd sess., 1964, vol. 20 (Washington, D.C.: Congressional Quarterly Service, 1965), 215.

7. *Congressional Quarterly Almanac*, 88th Cong., 2nd sess., 1964, vol. 20, 215–218; Patterson, *Grand Expectations*, 539 (Dirksen quotation); "The Office of Economic Opportunity during the Administration of President Lyndon B. Johnson," 43 (Nixon quote), 44 (Goldwater quote); House Committee on Education and Labor, *Hearings before the Subcommittee on the War on Poverty Program of the Committee on Education and Labor*, 88th Cong., 2nd sess., 1964, pt. 2, 767 (Daley quotation).

8. *Congressional Quarterly Almanac*, 88th Cong., 2nd sess., 1964, vol. 20, 208; Bernstein, *Guns or Butter*, 107–111; Dallek, *Flawed Giant*, 110–111.

9. Allen J. Matusow, *The Unraveling of America: A History of Liberalism in the 1960s* (New York: Harper & Row, 1984), 125–126; Daniel P. Moynihan, *Maximum Feasible Misunderstanding: Community Action in the War on Poverty* (New York: Free Press, 1969), 170 (quotation).

10. Dallek, *Flawed Giant*, 111.

11. Moynihan, *Maximum Feasible Misunderstanding*, 86 (quotation); *Congressional Quarterly Almanac*, 88th Cong., 2nd sess., 1964, vol. 20, 218; Oral History Interview with James C. Gaither, May 12, 1980, 7, Lyndon B. Johnson Presidential Library; Matusow, *The Unraveling of America*, 243–244. Also see Noel A. Cazenave,

Impossible Democracy: The Unlikely Success of the War on Poverty Community Action Programs (Albany: State University of New York Press, 2007).

12. Eric F. Goldman, *The Tragedy of Lyndon Johnson* (New York: Alfred A. Knopf, 1969), 91 (quotations); *Public Papers of the Presidents of the United States: Lyndon B. Johnson, 1963–1964*, 1:237–240; *Congressional Quarterly Almanac*, 88th Cong., 2nd sess., 1964, vol. 20, 274–283; Michael N. Danielson, *Federal-Metropolitan Politics and the Commuter Crisis* (New York: Columbia University Press, 1965), 194–195.

13. *Public Papers of the Presidents of the United States: Lyndon B. Johnson, 1963–1964*, 1:237–240; *Congressional Quarterly Almanac*, 1964, 88th Cong., 2nd sess., 1964, vol. 20, 274–283; Mark I. Gelfand, *A Nation of Cities: The Federal Government and Urban America, 1933–1965* (New York: Oxford University Press, 1975), 357–362; Alexander von Hoffman, "Let Us Continue: Housing Policy in the Great Society, Part One," 4–10, http://www.jchs.harvard.edu/publications/governmentprograms/w09-3_von_hoffman.pdf.

14. *Congressional Quarterly Almanac*, 1964, 88th Cong., 2nd sess., 1964, vol. 20, 558 (quotations); Edward Weiner, *Urban Transportation Planning in the United States: An Historical Overview* (Westport, Conn.: Praeger, 1999), 42–43; "Highway-Mass Transit Coordination," August 31, 1965, U.S. Department of Transportation Records, RG 398, General Correspondence, 1958-1967, box 7, folder Transportation Task Force Originals of Sept. 2, 1965 Submission, National Archives II, College Park, Md.; Suzanne Farkas, *Urban Lobbying: Mayors in the Federal Arena* (New York: New York University Press, 1971), 169–170; *Public Papers of the Presidents of the United States: Lyndon B. Johnson, 1963–1964*, 2:850.

15. William E. Leuchtenberg, "The Genesis of the Great Society," *Reporter* 34 (April 21, 1966): 36; Dallek, *Flawed Giant*, 80–84; Goldman, *The Tragedy of Lyndon Johnson*, 166–167.

16. *Public Papers of the Presidents: Lyndon B. Johnson, 1963–1964*, 1:705.

17. David W. Welborn and Jesse Burkhead, *Intergovernmental Relations in the American Administrative State: The Johnson Presidency* (Austin: University of Texas Press, 1989), 30; Leuchtenberg, "The Genesis of the Great Society," 37–38; Oral History Interview with Robert C. Wood, October 19, 1968, 7–10, Lyndon B. Johnson Presidential Library, Austin, Tex. The other ten members of the task force were Professors Martin Meyerson, Catherine Bauer Wurster, W. Norman Kennedy, and Nathan Glazer of the University of California; Professor Raymond Vernon of Harvard University; Paul Ylvisaker of the Ford Foundation; Detroit Mayor Jerome Cavanagh; *Atlanta Constitution* editor Ralph McGill; psychiatrist Karl Menninger; and banker Saul Klaman. Gelfand, *A Nation of Cities*, 452n60.

18. Oral History Interview with Robert C. Wood, October 19, 1968, 11–12; Theodore H. White, *The Making of the President, 1964* (New York: Atheneum, 1969), 221–242; Matusow, *The Unraveling of America*, 139–140; Robert M. Fogelson, *Violence as Protest: A Study of Riots and Ghettos* (Garden City, New York: Anchor Books, 1971), 1–2. Also see Wendell E. Pritchett, "Which Urban Crisis? Regionalism, Race, and Urban Policy, 1960-1974," *Journal of Urban History* 34 (January 2008): 266–286.

19. "Suggested Remarks for the Vice President," Hubert H. Humphrey Papers, box 150.E.5.3B, folder General. Subject Files. Mayors: 1st Conf. March 8, 1965. Cor. and Misc., Minnesota Historical Society Library, St. Paul. Additional folders in box 150.E.5.3B detail Humphrey's many meetings with the mayors in 1965–1966.

20. Demetrious Caraley, "Congressional Politics and Urban Aid," *Political Science Quarterly* 91 (Spring 1976): 30–32; Leuchtenberg, "The Genesis of the Great Society," 38–39; Gelfand, *A Nation of Cities*, 369–371; *Public Papers of the Presidents: Lyndon B. Johnson, 1965* (Washington, D.C.: Government Printing Office, 1966), 1:7, 232 (first quotation), 237 (second quotation).

21. Hoffman, "Let Us Continue," 13; Gelfand, *A Nation of Cities*, 371; Biles, "Public Housing and the Postwar Urban Renaissance, 1949–1973," in *From Tenements to the Taylor Homes: In Search of an Urban Housing Policy in Twentieth-Century America*, ed. John F. Bauman, Roger Biles, and Kristin M. Szylvian (University Park: Pennsylvania State University Press, 2000), 156; Nathaniel S. Keith, *Politics and the Housing Crisis since 1930* (New York: Universe Books, 1973), 161–162.

22. "Three Views on How Public Housing Should Be Revamped," *House and Home* 14 (November 1958): 53; Hoffman, "Let Us Continue," 13–16.

23. "Questions about the Rent Supplement Plan," *Journal of Housing* 22 (March 1965): 127–128; Keith, *Politics and the Housing Crisis since 1930*, 161–162; Hoffman, "Let Us Continue," 18 (quotations).

24. Hoffman, "Let Us Continue," 19–20; Bernstein, *Guns or Butter*, 383–387.

25. Keith, *Politics and the Housing Crisis since 1930*, 163–164; Hoffman, "Let Us Continue," 20–24; "Aborted Revolt," *Newsweek* 66 (July 12, 1965): 16.

26. Hoffman, "Let Us Continue," 23–25; "Weaver's Frustrating Year—Errors, Politics Mar HUD Start," *House and Home* 29 (October 1966): 12–14; National Commission on Urban Problems, *Building the American City: Report of the National Commission on Urban Problems to the Congress and to the President of the United States* (Washington, D.C.: Government Printing Office, 1968), 149–151.

27. *Congressional Quarterly Almanac*, 89th Cong., 1st sess., 1965, vol. 21 (Washington, D.C.: Congressional Quarterly Service, 1966), 383; Gelfand, *A Nation of Cities*, 375–379. On the choice of Weaver as HUD's first secretary, see Wendell Pritchett, *Robert Clifton Weaver and the American City: The Life and Times of an Urban Reformer* (Chicago: University of Chicago Press, 2008), chap. 14.

28. "The Department of Housing and Urban Development during the Administration of President Lyndon B. Johnson, November 1963–January 1969," vol. 1, pt. 1, 19, box 1, Lyndon B. Johnson Presidential Library; *New York Times*, March 12, 1965; *Congressional Quarterly Almanac*, 89th Cong., 1st sess., 1965, vol. 21, 382–387; Oral History Interview with Kermit Gordon, November 12, 1980, 12, Lyndon B. Johnson Presidential Library; Emmette S. Redford and Marlan Blissett, *Organizing the Executive Branch: The Johnson Presidency* (Chicago: University of Chicago Press, 1981), 26; Gelfand, *A Nation of Cities*, 375–379.

29. Oral History Interview with Robert C. Weaver, November 19, 1968, 35–36, Lyndon B. Johnson Presidential Library; Joseph Califano Jr., *The Triumph and*

Tragedy of Lyndon Johnson: The White House Years (New York: Simon & Schuster, 1991), 128 (quotation).

30. Telephone conversation with Roy Wilkins, November 4, 1965, LBJ Telephone Conversations, Miller Center, University of Virginia, http://www.millercenter.virginia .edu/academic/presidentialrecordings/johnson; Califano, *The Triumph and Tragedy of Lyndon Johnson*, 128; Oral History Interview with Jerome P. Cavanagh, March 6, 1979, 28–29, Lyndon B. Johnson Presidential Library; Oral History Interview with Harry McPherson, April 9, 1969, 17 (quotation), Lyndon B. Johnson Presidential Library; Oral History Interview with Kermit Gordon, November 12, 1980, 13, Lyndon B. Johnson Presidential Library.

31. Pritchett, *Robert Clifton Weaver and the American City*, 265 (quotation); telephone conversations with Martin Luther King Jr. (January 4, 1965), Abraham Ribicoff (September 1, 1965), Robert F. Kennedy (September 13, 1965), Richard J. Daley (December 1, 1965), William Proxmire (January 17, 1966), LBJ Telephone Conversations, Miller Center; Oral History Interview with Ben W. Heineman, January 26, 1976, 5–6, Lyndon B. Johnson Presidential Library; Harry C. McPherson Jr. to Lyndon B. Johnson, December 13, 1965, White House Central Files, EX FG 170, box 252, folder Dept. of HUD 11/21/65–01/25/66, Lyndon B. Johnson Presidential Library; Califano, *The Triumph and Tragedy of Lyndon Johnson*, 129–130.

32. Califano, *The Triumph and Tragedy of Lyndon Johnson*, 127 (quotation).

33. *Congressional Quarterly Almanac*, 89th Cong., 1st sess., 1965, vol. 21, 275–282; Julie Roy Jeffrey, *Education for Children of the Poor: A Study of the Origins and Implementation of the Elementary and Secondary Education Act of 1965* (Columbus: Ohio State University Press, 1978), 35; Bernstein, *Guns or Butter*, 193; Matusow, *The Unraveling of America*, 221.

34. Bernstein, *Guns or Butter*, 273–298.

35. Randall B. Woods, *LBJ: Architect of American Ambition* (New York: Free Press, 2006), 665 (quotation); Bernstein, *Guns or Butter*, 298–306.

36. *Congressional Quarterly Almanac*, 89th Cong., 1st Sess., 1965, vol. 21, 672; Zachary M. Schrag, *The Great Society Subway: A History of the Washington Metro* (Baltimore: Johns Hopkins University Press, 2006), 57–63.

37. Charles M. Haar, *Between the Idea and the Reality: A Study in the Origin, Fate, and Legacy of the Model Cities Program* (Boston: Little, Brown, 1975), 35–36 (quotations); Woods, *LBJ, Architect of American Ambition*, 690; Califano, *The Triumph and Tragedy of Lyndon Johnson*, 130; Oral History Interview with Robert C. Wood, October 19, 1968, 18–22, Lyndon B. Johnson Presidential Library; Oral History Interview with Ben W. Heinemann, January 26, 1976, 23, Lyndon B. Johnson Presidential Library; Oral History Interview with Harry McPherson, April 9, 1969, 15–17, Lyndon B. Johnson Presidential Library.

38. Oral History Interview with Robert C. Wood, October 19, 1968, 22; Redford and Blissett, *Organizing the Executive Branch*, 39, 99–101.

39. *Public Papers of the Presidents: Lyndon B. Johnson, 1966* (Washington, D.C.: Government Printing Office, 1967), 1:82–91; Haar, *Between the Idea and the Reality*, 46; Bernstein, *Guns or Butter*, 461–463; Califano, *The Triumph and Tragedy*

of Lyndon Johnson, 131; "Observations," Administrative History of HUD, box 2, folder Vol. II, pt. II [2 of 2], Lyndon B. Johnson Presidential Library (quotation).

40. *Public Papers of the Presidents: Lyndon B. Johnson, 1966,* 1:82–91; Helen B. Shaffer, "Housing for the Poor," *Editorial Research Reports* 1 (March 4, 1966): 163–165; Haar, *Between the Idea and the Reality,* 75 (Dirksen quotation), 79 (Kennedy quotation); *New York Times,* January 27, March 5, 1966; Joseph Califano, *The Triumph and Tragedy of Lyndon Johnson,* 131; "Administrative History of HUD," 44, box 2, folder Vol. II, Pt. II [2 of 2], Lyndon B. Johnson Library; Farkas, *Urban Lobbying,* 207; Oral History Interview with Harry McPherson, April 9, 1969, 16–17, Lyndon B. Johnson Presidential Library.

41. *New York Times,* May 15, 1966; Haar, *Between the Idea and the Reality,* 59–60; Biles, *Crusading Liberal: Paul H. Douglas of Illinois* (DeKalb: Northern Illinois University Press, 2002), 189; Oral History Interview with Ben W. Heineman, January 26, 1976, 23; Edmund S. Muskie to Lyndon Johnson, June 16, 1966, Edmund S. Muskie Papers, box 593, folder 2, Edmund S. Muskie Archives and Special Collections Library, Bates College, Lewiston, Me. (Muskie quotation); Califano, *The Triumph and Tragedy of Lyndon Johnson,* 132 (Johnson and Califano quotations).

42. *New York Times,* November 4, 1966, clipping, Edmund S. Muskie Papers, box 594, folder 1; Bernstein, *Guns or Butter,* 465–466; Dallek, *Flawed Giant,* 320–321.

43. *New York Times,* August 16, 21, 29, 1966; Wendell E. Pritchett, *Robert Clifton Weaver and the American City,* 293–297; Jeff Shesol, *Mutual Contempt: Lyndon Johnson, Robert Kennedy, and the Feud That Defined a Decade* (New York: W. W. Norton, 1997), 244–246; Gareth Davies, *From Opportunity to Entitlement: The Transformation and Decline of Great Society Liberalism* (Lawrence: University Press of Kansas, 1996), 135–142.

44. *Congressional Record,* 89th Cong., 2nd sess., October 13, 1966, 112, pt. 20:26628.

45. Ibid., 26612–26613.

46. Dallek, *Flawed Giant,* 321; *Public Papers of the Presidents of the United States: Lyndon B. Johnson, 1966,* 2:1120 (quotation), 1309; *New York Times,* October 7, 1966; Bernstein, *Guns or Butter,* 466–467.

47. U.S. Department of Housing and Urban Development, *The Model Cities Program: A Comparative Analysis of the Planning Process in Eleven Cities* (Washington, D.C.: Government Printing Office, 1970), 7; "The Department of Housing and Urban Development during the Administration of President Lyndon B. Johnson, November 1963–January 1969," vol. 1, pt. 1, chap. 5, pp. 16–40, box 1; Charles M. Haar, *Between the Idea and the Reality,* 143–147; Oral History Interview with Jerome P. Cavanagh, March 6, 1979, 31, Lyndon B. Johnson Presidential Library.

48. "Cities Selected for Model City Planning Grants," news release, November 16, 1967, Edmund S. Muskie Papers, box 763, folder 6; Bernstein, *Guns or Butter,* 468; *Wall Street Journal,* November 24, 1967, clipping, "Administrative History of HUD," box 2, folder Vol. II, Pt. II [1 of 2], Lyndon B. Johnson Presidential Library.

49. Haar, *Between the Idea and the Reality,* 235 (Weaver quotations); U.S. Department of Housing and Urban Development, *The Model Cities Program,* 9–10;

Roger Biles, *Richard J. Daley: Politics, Race, and the Governing of Chicago* (DeKalb: Northern Illinois University Press, 1995), 169–170.

50. *Public Papers of the Presidents: Lyndon B. Johnson, 1966*, 1:6–7, 255; "Highlights of the President's Transportation Message," April 1966, Department of Transportation Records, RG 398, General Correspondence, 1958–1967, box 4, folder 1966 Transportation Message, National Archives II, College Park, Md.; Mark H. Rose, Bruce E. Seely, and Paul F. Barrett, *The Best Transportation System in the World: Railroads, Trucks, Airlines, and American Public Policy in the Twentieth Century* (Columbus: Ohio State University Press, 2006), 137–143; "Planes, Trains, Ships, Roads: An Official Look Ahead," *U.S. News and World Report* 60 (January 24, 1966): 48–49; Dallek, *Flawed Giant*, 313 (quotation); "History of the Department of Transportation in the Lyndon B. Johnson Administration (November 22, 1963—January 21, 1969)," chap. 1, pp. 5–7, vol. 1, pt. 1, box 1, Lyndon B. Johnson Presidential Library; Oral History Interview with Alan S. Boyd, November 20, 1968, 18–20, Lyndon B. Johnson Presidential Library.

51. "History of the Department of Transportation in the Lyndon B. Johnson Administration (November 22, 1963—January 21, 1969)," chap. 1, pp. 7–8, 42; "Republican Policy Committee Statement on Department of Transportation," August 10, 1966, Administrative History of DOT, vol. 1, pt. 1, 1–2, box 1, Lyndon B. Johnson Presidential Library; "The Department of Housing and Urban Development during the Administration of President Lyndon B. Johnson, November 1963—January 1969," vol. 1, pt. 1, chap. 6, p. 34, box 1, Lyndon B. Johnson Presidential Library; "Policy Guides for the DOT/HUD Study of Urban Transportation Problems," June 6, 1967, Department of Transportation Records, RG 398, General Correspondence, 1967–72, box 1, folder Allocation of Funds & Staff Between HUD & DOT, National Archives II; Oral History Interview with Alan S. Boyd, November 20, 1968, 23–24, Lyndon B. Johnson Presidential Library; *Public Papers of the Presidents: Lyndon B. Johnson, 1966*, 2:1188–1189.

52. "DOT/HUD Urban Transportation Study, from Asst. Sec. for Administration," June 26, 1967, Department of Transportation Records, RG 398, General Correspondence, 1967–1972, box 11, folder Mass Urban Transportation, National Archives II.

53. Ibid.

54. "Administratively Confidential Memorandum for Joseph Califano, Jr. [from Alan Boyd]," n.d., Department of Transportation Records, RG 398, General Correspondence, 1967–1972, box 12, folder Mass Urban Transportation, National Archives II; Robert C. Weaver to Joseph A. Califano Jr., October 7, 1967, Department of Transportation Records, RG 398, General Correspondence, 1967–1972, box 14, folder Urban Mass Transportation Functions, National Archives II.

55. "Urban Mass Transportation," Administrative History of the DOT, vol. 1, pt. 3, pp. 14–18, box 2, Lyndon B. Johnson Presidential Library; "The Department of Housing and Urban Development during the Administration of President Lyndon B. Johnson, November 1963—January 1969," box 3, folder Vol. II, Pt. III [2 of 2], Lyndon B. Johnson Presidential Library; "Administratively Confidential Memorandum for Joseph Califano, Jr. [from Alan Boyd]," n.d., Department of Transportation

Records, RG 398, General Correspondence, 1967–1972, box 12, folder Mass Urban Transportation, National Archives II; *Public Papers of the Presidents: Lyndon B. Johnson, 1968–69* (Washington, D.C.: Government Printing Office, 1970), 1:269–271; "Agreement between the Secretary of the Department of Housing and Urban Development and the Secretary of the Department of Transportation," Administrative History of the Department of Transportation, box 2, folder Vol. I, Narrative History, Pt. III [2 of 2], Lyndon B. Johnson Presidential Library.

56. "1966 Task Force on Cities," 4 (quotation), 171, White House Central Files, box 4, Lyndon B. Johnson Presidential Library; Oral History Interview with James C. Gaither, November 19, 1968, 19, Lyndon B. Johnson Presidential Library.

57. *Public Papers of the Presidents: Lyndon B. Johnson, 1967*, 1:340–344.

58. Ibid., 2:715–717; Califano, *The Triumph and Tragedy of Lyndon Johnson*, 213–218; Dallek, *Flawed Giant*, 414 (quotations). The standard account of the 1967 Detroit race riot is Sidney Fine, *Violence in the Model City: The Cavanagh Administration, Race Relations, and the Detroit Race Riot of 1967* (Ann Arbor: University of Michigan Press, 1989).

59. *Public Papers of the Presidents: Lyndon B. Johnson, 1967*, 2:721–726; Califano, *The Triumph and Tragedy of Lyndon Johnson*, 219–220.

60. Barefoot Sanders to President Johnson, July 21, 1967, White House Central Files EX FG 170, box 253, folder 05/01/67–07/27/67, Lyndon B. Johnson Presidential Library; Oral History Interview with Robert C. Weaver, November 19, 1968, Tape Two, 15–17, Lyndon B. Johnson Presidential Library; Dallek, *Flawed Giant*, 415 (first quotation); Pritchett, *Robert Clifton Weaver and the American City*, 302–303 (second quotation).

61. Matusow, *The Unraveling of America*, 246 (first quotation); Biles, *Richard J. Daley*, 108 (second quotation).

62. "Proposed Resolution Referred to the Executive Committee of the U.S. Conference of Mayors, June 1, 1965, by the Committee on Resolutions," Hubert H. Humphrey Papers, box 150.E.5.4F, folder General. Subject Files. Mayors: U.S. Conf. Ann. Mtg., May 29–June 2, 1965 (first quotation); David M. Welborn and Jesse Burkhead, *Intergovernmental Relations in the American Administrative State*, 69–70; John J. Gunther, *Federal-City Relations in the United States: The Role of the Mayors in Federal Aid to Cities* (Newark: University of Delaware Press, 1990), 224–225; Biles, *Richard J. Daley*, 108; Matusow, *The Unraveling of America*, 250 (second quotation).

63. David W. Welborn and Jesse Burkhead, *Intergovernmental Relations in the American Administrative State*, 76 (first and third quotations); Dallek, *Flawed Giant*, 334 (second quotation).

64. "The Office of Economic Opportunity during the Administration of President Lyndon B. Johnson, November 1963–January 1969," vol. 1, pt. 1, chap. 4, p. 569 (second quotation), p. 601 (first quotation), box 1, Lyndon B. Johnson Presidential Library; Moynihan, *Maximum Feasible Misunderstanding*, 142; Matusow, *The Unraveling of America*, 270 (third quotation).

65. *Public Papers of the Presidents: Lyndon B. Johnson, 1968–69*, 1:25–33, 179–186, 725 (quotation); Dallek, *Flawed Giant*, 549.

66. Califano, *The Triumph and Tragedy of Lyndon Johnson*, 260–262; Dallek, *Flawed Giant*, 515–556. Also see National Commission on Civil Disorders, *Report of the National Commission on Civil Disorders* (New York: Bantam, 1968).

67. Fred Bohen to Joe Califano, March 8, 1968, Presidential Task Force Subject File: Gaither, box 49, folder Urban Institute, Lyndon B. Johnson Presidential Library; J. Irwin Miller, McGeorge Bundy, Kermit Gordon, Robert S. McNamara, Richard E. Neustadt, and Cyrus Vance to the Board of Trustees of the Urban Institute, memorandum, March 5, 1968, Presidential Task Force Subject File: Gaither, box 49, folder Urban Institute, Lyndon B. Johnson Presidential Library; James A. Smith, *The Idea Brokers: Think Tanks and the Rise of the New Policy Elite* (New York: Free Press, 1991), 151–153.

68. "To Fulfill These Rights," White House Conference, June 1–2, 1966, Legislative Background, Fair Housing Act of 1968, box 1, folder 1966 Preparation of the Message (4), Lyndon B. Johnson Presidential Library; Califano, *The Triumph and Tragedy of Lyndon Johnson*, 276 (quotation); Biles, *Crusading Liberal*, 188–199.

69. "Statement of Robert C. Weaver, Sec. of [HUD] before the Subcommittee on Housing and Urban Affairs of the Senate Banking and Commerce Committee on S. 1358, the Fair Housing Act of 1967," August 21, 1967, Legislative Background, Fair Housing Act of 1968, box 4, Lyndon B. Johnson Presidential Library; "Nondiscrimination in Housing—Title VIII of the Civil Rights Act of 1968," Legislative Background, Fair Housing Act of 1968, box 1, folder 1966—Preparation of the Bill (1), Lyndon B. Johnson Presidential Library; Dallek, *Flawed Giant*, 517 (first quotation); Woods, *LBJ, Architect of American Ambition*, 840; Lyndon Johnson to John McCormack, April 5, 1968, White House Central Files, Confidential File, box 66, folder LE/HU2, 4/1/68–8/31/68, Lyndon B. Johnson Presidential Library (second and third quotations); *Congressional Quarterly Almanac*, 90th Cong., 2nd sess., 1968, vol. 24, 153–154.

70. "The Department of Housing and Urban Development during the Administration of President Lyndon B. Johnson, November 1963–January 1969," chap. 8, p. 2, vol. 1, pt. 1, box 1, Lyndon B. Johnson Presidential Library; *Congressional Quarterly Almanac*, 90th Cong., 2nd sess., 1968, vol. 24, 153–154.

71. *Public Papers of the Presidents: Lyndon B. Johnson, 1968–69*, 1:253–262; *Congressional Quarterly Almanac*, 90th Cong., 2nd sess., 1968, vol. 24, 313–314; Roger W. Caves, "Housing and Urban Development Act of 1968," in *The Encyclopedia of Housing*, ed. Willem van Vliet (Thousand Oaks, Calif.: Sage Publications, 1998), 259–260; Kent W. Cotton, *Housing in the Twenty-first Century: Achieving Common Ground* (Cambridge, Mass.: Harvard University Press, 2003), 217; Biles, "Public Housing and the Postwar Urban Renaissance, 1949–1973," 156.

72. Robert C. Weaver to Alan S. Boyd, September 11, 1968, and Robert H. Bruton to Deputy Assistant Secretary for Policy Development, memorandum, September 17, 1968, Administrative History of the Department of Transportation, box 2, folder Vol. I, Narrative History, Pt. IV [2 of 2], Lyndon B. Johnson Presidential Library.

73. *Congressional Quarterly Almanac*, 90th Cong., 2nd sess., 1968, vol. 24, 323; *Public Papers of the Presidents: Lyndon B. Johnson, 1968–69*, 2:866 (quotation).

74. Charles E. Connerly, "President's Committee on Urban Housing (Kaiser Committee)," in Vliet, *The Encyclopedia of Housing*, 425–426. See the President's Committee on Urban Housing, *A Decent Home: The Report of the President's Committee on Urban Housing* (Washington, D.C.: Government Printing Office, 1969).

75. National Commission on Urban Problems, *Building the American City*, vii; Charles E. Connerly, "National Commission on Urban Problems (Douglas Commission)," in Vliet, *The Encyclopedia of Housing*, 381; Biles, *Crusading Liberal*, 204.

76. Biles, *Crusading Liberal*, 205–206.

77. National Commission on Urban Problems, *Building the American City*, 180–192; Biles, *Crusading Liberal*, 206.

78. *New York Times*, December 15, 1968; Biles, *Crusading Liberal*, 207–208; Joseph Foote, "As They Saw It: HUD's Secretaries Reminisce about Carrying Out the Mission," *Cityscape* 1 (September 1995): 73–74.

79. Jeffrey, *Education for Children of the Poor*, 127–128; Moynihan, *Maximum Feasible Misunderstanding*, xiii–xiv; Hubert H. Humphrey to Ken Gray, memorandum, August 25, 1967 (quotation), Neal Peterson to Hubert H. Humphrey, memorandum, September 7, 1967, Hubert H. Humphrey Papers, box 150.D.20.7(B), folder General. Project Files. Model Cities, 1967; Oral History Interview with James C. Gaither, May 12, 1980, Lyndon B. Johnson Presidential Library; Bernard J. Frieden and Marshall Kaplan, *The Politics of Neglect: Urban Aid from Model Cities to Revenue Sharing* (Cambridge, Mass.: MIT Press, 1975), 234–235.

80. Peter Dreier, John Mollenkopf, and Todd Swanstrom, *Place Matters: Metropolitics for the Twenty-first Century* (Lawrence: University Press of Kansas, 2004), 132–136; Dennis R. Judd and Todd Swanstrom, *City Politics: Private Power and Public Policy* (New York: Longman, 1998), 199; Pritchett, *Robert Clifton Weaver and the American City*, 323 (quotation). On the Great Society's impact on the poverty rate, see James T. Patterson, *America's Struggle against Poverty, 1900–1980* (Cambridge, Mass.: Harvard University Press, 1981).

81. Judd and Swanstrom, *City Politics*, 217; Dreier, Mollenkopf, and Swanstrom, *Place Matters*, 134.

CHAPTER 5. NIXON AND THE NEW FEDERALISM

1. James T. Patterson, *Grand Expectations: The United States, 1945–1974* (New York: Oxford University Press, 1996), 704–705; Paul E. Peterson, "The Changing Fiscal Place of Big Cities in the Federal System," in *Interwoven Destinies: Cities and the Nation*, ed. Henry G. Cisneros (New York: W. W. Norton, 1993), 193–194; Dennis R. Judd and Todd Swanstrom, *City Politics: Private Power and Public Policy* (New York: Longman, 1998), 213–214; Alice O'Connor, "Swimming against the Tide: A Brief History of Federal Policy in Poor Communities," in *Urban Problems and Community Development*, ed. Ronald F. Ferguson and William T. Dickens (Washington, D.C.: Brookings Institution Press, 1999), 108–113.

2. John H. Mollenkopf, *The Contested City* (Princeton: Princeton University Press, 1983), 122–127; David R. Goldfield and Blaine A. Brownell, *Urban America: A History*, 2nd ed. (Boston: Houghton Mifflin, 1990), 388–389; Michael J. Rich, *Federal Policymaking and the Poor: National Goals, Local Choices, and Distributional Outcomes* (Princeton: Princeton University Press, 1993), 72–80. Also see Kevin Phillips, *The Emerging Republican Majority* (New Rochelle: Arlington House, 1969).

3. On Nixon and the 1968 presidential campaign, see Theodore H. White, *The Making of the President 1968: A Narrative History of American Politics in Action* (New York: Simon & Schuster, 1970); Rick Perlstein, *Nixonland: The Rise of a President and the Fracturing of America* (New York: Scribner, 2008); and Patterson, *Grand Expectations.*

4. "The Office of Economic Opportunity during the Administration of President Lyndon B. Johnson, November 1963–January 1969," vol. 1, pt. 1, box 1, Supplement, p. 11, Lyndon B. Johnson Presidential Library, Austin, Tex. (first quotation); White, *The Making of the President 1968*, 318 (second and third quotations).

5. White, *The Making of the President 1968*, 316 (quotation); Perlstein, *Nixonland*, 396.

6. Melvin Small, *The Presidency of Richard Nixon* (Lawrence: University Press of Kansas, 1999), 40; Mollenkopf, *The Contested City*, 128 (quotation).

7. James W. Gaynor to Richard Nixon, December 16, 1968, Daniel P. Moynihan Papers, box 285, folder Housing: Public Housing Programs, 1968–69, Library of Congress, Washington, D.C.; *Public Papers of the Presidents: Richard Nixon, 1969* (Washington, D.C.: Government Printing Office, 1971), 12; press release, Office of the White House Press Secretary, January 23, 1969, Daniel P. Moynihan Papers, box 264, folder Council for Urban Affairs: General, 1969–1970 (first quotation); Memorandum for the Staff Secretary, April 14, 1969, White House Central Files, FG 6-12 (Council for Urban Affairs), box 1, Nixon Presidential Materials, National Archives II, College Park, Md. (second quotation); Godfrey Hodgson, *The Gentleman from New York: Daniel Patrick Moynihan, A Biography* (Boston: Houghton Mifflin, 2000), 160–161.

8. Daniel P. Moynihan, "The Negro Family: The Case for National Action," March 1965, Office of Policy Planning and Research, U.S. Department of Labor, Daniel P. Moynihan Papers, box 66, folder The Negro Family: Drafts, 1965 and Undated, # 2; Perlstein, *Nixonland*, 394–395 (quotation). Also see Daniel P. Moynihan, "Poverty in Cities," in *The Metropolitan Enigma: Inquiries into the Nature and Dimensions of America's "Urban Crisis,"* ed. James Q. Wilson (Cambridge, Mass.: Harvard University Press, 1968), 367–385; and Alice O'Connor, "The Privatized City: The Manhattan Institute, the Urban Crisis, and the Conservative Counterrevolution in New York," *Journal of Urban History* 34 (January 2008): 339.

9. A. James Reichley, *Conservatives in an Age of Change: The Nixon and Ford Administrations* (Washington, D.C.: Brookings Institution Press, 1981), 70 (quotation); John Osborne, "Moynihan at Work in the White House," *New Republic* 160 (March 22, 1969): 11–13; Daniel P. Moynihan, "Policy vs. Program in the '70's," *Public Interest* 20 (Summer 1970): 91; "Talking Points for the President for the First Meeting of the Council for Urban Affairs," January 23, 1969, Daniel P. Moynihan

Papers, box 264, folder Council for Urban Affairs: Meeting, 1/23/69; "Progress Report to the President: Activities of the Urban Affairs Council," June 10, 1969, White House Central Files, FG 6-12 (Council for Urban Affairs), box 2, folder 5/6/69—6/12/69, Nixon Presidential Materials; Memorandum for the President's File, February 11, 1970, White House Central Files, FG 6-12 (Council for Urban Affairs), box 3, folder 12/10/69—2/28/70, Nixon Presidential Materials. Also see Daniel P. Moynihan, "Toward a National Urban Policy," *Public Interest* 17 (Fall 1969): 3–20.

10. "Dr. Daniel Patrick Moynihan Interviewed," July 24, 1970, p. 2, Daniel P. Moynihan Papers, box 276, folder Family Assistance Plan: Correspondence, August 1970; John Robert Greene, *The Limits of Power: The Nixon and Ford Administrations* (Bloomington: Indiana University Press, 1992), 48–49; Joan Hoff, *Nixon Reconsidered* (New York: Basic Books, 1994), 123–135. Also see Daniel P. Moynihan, *The Politics of a Guaranteed Income: The Nixon Administration and the Family Assistance Plan* (New York: Random House, 1973); Vincent Burke, *Nixon's Good Deed: Welfare Reform* (New York: Columbia University Press, 1974); and Hodgson, *The Gentleman from New York*, 122–180.

11. Daniel P. Moynihan to Richard M. Nixon, memorandum, January 20, 1970, White House Special Files, John D. Ehrlichman Files, box 38, folder Family Assistance, 1970, Nixon Presidential Materials; Daniel P. Moynihan to Robert P. Mayo (Director of the Budget), January 15, 1970, White House Special Files, John D. Ehrlichman Files, box 38, folder Family Assistance, 1970, Nixon Presidential Materials (quotation); Moynihan, "Policy vs. Program in the '70's," 99–100; *New York Times*, November 21, 1970, clipping, Daniel P. Moynihan Papers, box 282, folder Family Assistance Plan: Senate Votes, 1970.

12. Press release, December 5, 1969, White House Central Files, FG 6-12 (Council for Urban Affairs), box 3, Nixon Presidential Materials; Greene, *The Limits of Power*, 50–51 (quotation); Royce Hanson, *The Evolution of National Urban Policy, 1970–1980: Lessons From the Past* (Washington, D.C.: National Academy Press, 1982), 9–11.

13. Clark R. Mollenhoff, *George Romney: Mormon in Politics* (New York: Meredith Press, 1968), 290–314; T. George Harris, *Romney's Way: A Man and an Idea* (Englewood Cliffs, N.J.: Prentice-Hall, 1967), 82, 217–229; George Romney, *The Concerns of a Citizen* (New York: G. P. Putnam's Sons, 1968), 60 (quotation).

14. Small, *The Presidency of Richard Nixon*, 36; *Boston Globe*, June 27, 1970 (first quotation); Perlstein, *Nixonland*, 360 (second quotation).

15. George Romney to Richard Nixon, memorandum, October 31, 1969, George Romney Papers, Post-gubernatorial Career Series, box 13, folder The President—Ehrlichman 1969, Bentley Historical Library, Ann Arbor, Mich.; "Organizational Overhaul Announced by Romney," November 7, 1969, George Romney Papers, Post-gubernatorial Career Series, box 13, folder The President—Ehrlichman 1969 (first quotation); Horace B. Bazan, "The Fragmentation of FHA: A Study of the 1969 Reorganization of the Department of Housing and Urban Development and the Resulting Red Tape, Slow Service, Inefficiency, and Incapacity to Control Losses, Including Suggestions for Improvement," prepared for the Mortgage Bankers Association of

America, June 1974; Brian D. Bayer, *Cities Destroyed for Cash: The FHA Scandal at HUD* (Chicago: Follett, 1973), 156; George Romney to Richard Nixon, October 20, 1970, White House Central Files, Subject Files, FG 24, box 2, folder 10/1/70–12/31/70, Nixon Presidential Materials (second quotation).

16. *Public Papers of the Presidents: Richard Nixon, 1971* (Washington, D.C.: Government Printing Office, 1972), 56–57; *Congressional Quarterly Almanac*, 92nd Cong., 1st sess., 1971, vol. 27 (Washington, D.C.: Congressional Quarterly Service, 1972), 767–768; Hoff, *Nixon Reconsidered*, 59 (quotation); Peri E. Arnold, *Making the Managerial Presidency: Comprehensive Reorganization Planning, 1905–1996*, 2nd ed. (Lawrence: University Press of Kansas, 1998), 277–293; M. Carter McFarland, *Federal Government and Urban Problems: HUD, Successes, Failures, and the Fate of Our Cities* (Boulder: Westview Press, 1978), 44–45.

17. Richard C. Van Dusen to John Ehrlichman, memorandum, March 18, 1969, Richard C. Van Dusen Files, 1969–72, box 74, folder WH 1–2, 1969, National Archives II, College Park, Md.; George Romney to James Keogh, memorandum, September 19, 1969, George Romney Papers, Post-gubernatorial Career Series, box 2, folder Cabinet Meetings 1969; Office of Technology Assessment, *Technology, Trade, and the U.S. Residential Construction Industry: A Special Report* (Washington, D.C.: Government Printing Office, 1986), 24–25; McFarland, *Federal Government and Urban Problems*, 172–175.

18. Joseph Foote, "As They Saw It: HUD's Secretaries Reminisce about Carrying Out the Mission," *Cityscape* 1 (September 1995): 74. On Model Cities, see McFarland, *Federal Government and Urban Problems*, and Bernard J. Frieden and Marshall Kaplan, *The Politics of Neglect: Urban Aid from Model Cities to Revenue Sharing* (Cambridge, Mass.: MIT Press, 1975).

19. "Summary of the Model Cities Task Force Report," Daniel P. Moynihan Papers, box 287, folder Local Governments: President's Task Force on Model Cities, 1969, #1 (first quotation); E. C. Banfield, "Draft of Task Force Report on Model Cities," November 13, 1969, p. 9, Arthur F. Burns Papers, box A26, folder Model Cities, Gerald R. Ford Presidential Library, Ann Arbor, Mich. (second quotation). Banfield's conservative reputation was solidified by the publication of *The Unheavenly City* (Boston: Little, Brown, 1970) and *The Unheavenly City Revisited* (Boston: Little, Brown, 1974).

20. Christopher C. DeMuth, "Deregulating the Cities," *Public Interest* 44 (Summer 1976): 127 (first and second quotations); *Portland (Me.) Evening Express*, April 7, 1969, clipping, Edmund S. Muskie Papers, box 1105, folder 6, Edmund S. Muskie Archives and Special Collections Library, Bates College, Lewiston, Me.; Small, *The Presidency of Richard Nixon*, 190; Richard C. Van Dusen to John Ehrlichman, memorandum, March 18, 1969, minutes, Meeting of the Council for Urban Affairs, April 7, 1969, Daniel P. Moynihan Papers, box 265, folder Council for Urban Affairs: Meetings, 4/7/69 (third and fourth quotations); George Romney to James Keogh, memorandum, September 19, 1969, George Romney Papers, Post-gubernatorial Career Series, box 2, folder Cabinet Meetings 1969.

21. "Secretary Romney's Statement on Model Cities," April 28, 1969, George Romney Papers, Post-gubernatorial Career Series, box 12, folder Urban Affairs Council and

Moynihan; Edmund S. Muskie to George Romney, October 29, 1969, Edmund S. Muskie Papers, box 1105, folder 6; Richard C. Van Dusen to Richard P. Nathan, memorandum, April 21, 1970, George Romney Papers, Post-gubernatorial Career Series, box 9, folder Model Cities and New Towns Sub-Com. (quotation); George Romney to Richard Nixon, December 30, 1970, George Romney Papers, Post-gubernatorial Career Series, box 13, folder President and Ehrlichman—1971. Also see Frieden and Kaplan, *The Politics of Neglect*, 199–204.

22. George Romney to John D. Ehrlichman, memorandum, May 12, 1971, Richard C. Van Dusen Files, 1969–72, box 74, folder WH 1–2, 1971–70; John D. Ehrlichman to George Romney, May 28, 1970, George Romney Papers, Post-gubernatorial Career Series, box 13, folder The President—Ehrlichman 1970 (quotation); George Romney to Richard Nixon, memorandum, January 6, 1972, George Romney Papers, Post-gubernatorial Career Series, box 14, folder Ehrlichman and President 1972. For background on the new towns program, see Roger Biles, "New Towns for the Great Society: A Case Study in Politics and Planning," *Planning Perspectives* 13 (April 1998): 113–132; and Donald Canty, ed., *The New City* (New York: Frederick A. Praeger, 1969).

23. Biles, "New Towns for the Great Society," 118–121; Jack A. Underhill, "New Communities Planning Process and National Growth Policy," in *The Contemporary New Communities Movement in the United States*, ed. Gideon Golany and Daniel Walden (Urbana: University of Illinois Press, 1974), 89–90; Raymond J. Burby and Shirley F. Weiss, *New Communities USA* (Lexington, Mass.: D. C. Heath, 1976), xviii, 60; Hugh Mields Jr., "The Politics of Federal Legislation for New Community Development," in *New Community Development: Planning Process, Implementation, and Emerging Social Concerns*, ed. Shirley F. Weiss, Edward J. Kaiser, and Raymond J. Burby (Chapel Hill: Center for Urban and Regional Studies, 1971), 249, 255–259.

24. Biles, "New Towns for the Great Society," 121–123; Underhill, "New Communities Planning Process and National Growth Policy," 92–93.

25. Biles, "New Towns for the Great Society," 123 (quotations); George Romney to Richard Nixon, May 22, 1970, General Records of the Department of Housing and Urban Development, Office of the Under Secretary, Richard Van Dusen Files, 1969–72, RG 207, box 50, folder New Communities, 1970–1972; New Communities Administration, Department of Housing and Urban Development, *New Communities: Problems and Potentials* (Washington, D.C.: Government Printing Office, 1976), 1–7.

26. New Communities Development Corporation, "PD&R Evaluation Report," General Records of the Department of Housing and Urban Development, NCD Corporation, Briefing Books, RG 207, box 8, "July 10, 1975"; Biles, "New Towns for the Great Society," 123–124.

27. New Communities Administration, Department of Housing and Urban Development, *New Communities*, 4–14; Mary-Margaret Wantuck, "Those New Towns, Fifteen Years Later," *Nation's Business* 71 (October 1983): 43; Biles, "New Towns for the Great Society," 124–125.

28. Cedar-Riverside Project Area Committee, "Position on Solution to the New Community Development Crisis," January 9, 1976, General Records of the Department of Housing and Urban Development, New Community Development Corporation, RG

207, box 11 (Briefing Books), December 10, 1976-1; Biles, "New Towns for the Great Society," 125-126.

29. Wantuck, "Those New Towns, Fifteen Years Later," 43; Biles, "New Towns for the Great Society," 126.

30. New Community Development Corporation, "New Communities Budget for FY 1984," General Records of the Department of Housing and Urban Development, NCDC, Briefing Books, RG 207, box 18, September 14, 1982-3; Helene V. Smookler, "Administration Hara-Kiri: Implementation of the Urban Growth and New Community Development Act," *Annals of the American Academy of Political and Social Science* 422 (November 1975): 137-138; "Can 'New Towns' Survive the Economic Crunch?" *Business Week* 2367 (February 10, 1975): 43-44; Richard Karp, "Building Chaos: The New Town Program Is a Multimillion-Dollar Mess," *Barron's National Business and Financial Weekly* 56 (September 6, 1976): 8-12; and Wantuck, "Those New Towns, Fifteen Years Later," 42-43. On the new towns, see Nicholas Dagen Bloom, *Suburban Alchemy: 1960s New Towns and the Transformation of the American Dream* (Columbus: Ohio State University Press, 2001); George T. Morgan Jr. and John O. King, *The Woodlands: New Community Development, 1964–1983* (College Station: Texas A&M University Press, 1987); and Frederick Steiner, *The Politics of New Town Planning: The Newfields, Ohio, Story* (Athens: University of Ohio Press, 1981).

31. *Congressional Quarterly Almanac*, 91st Cong., 1st sess., 1969, vol. 25 (Washington, D.C.: Congressional Quarterly Service, 1970), 393 (quotations); Caroline Nagel, "Brooke Amendments," in *The Encyclopedia of Housing*, ed. Willem van Vliet (Thousand Oaks, Calif.: Sage Publications, 1998), 34.

32. *Congressional Quarterly Almanac*, 91st Cong., 2nd sess., 1970, vol. 26 (Washington, D.C.: Congressional Quarterly Service, 1971), 729 (first quotation), 734 (second quotation), 735 (third and fourth quotations); Elizabeth J. Agius and Harold L. Wolman, "The President's National Urban Policy Report as a Policy Document: A History and Analysis of the First Twenty Years," in *National Urban Policy: Problems and Prospects*, ed. Harold L. Wolman and Elizabeth J. Agius (Detroit: Wayne State University Press, 1996), 31.

33. Martin Anderson to Richard Nixon, memorandum, December 4, 1969, Daniel P. Moynihan Papers, box 287, folder Local Governments: President's Task Force on Model Cities, 1969, #1 (first quotation); George Romney to Richard Nixon, memorandum, December 9, 1969, Richard C. Van Dusen Files, 1969-72, box 74, folder WH-1, 1970-1969 (2); George Romney to Richard Nixon, December 30, 1970, George Romney Papers, Post-gubernatorial Career Series, box 13, folder President and Ehrlichman—1971; George Romney to Richard Nixon, August 10, 1972, George Romney Papers, Post-gubernatorial Career Series, box 13, folder Meeting with President—8/12/72; George Romney to Richard Nixon, December 28, 1972, George Romney Papers, Post-gubernatorial Career Series, box 14, folder Ehrlichman and President 1972 (second quotation). Also see Martin Anderson, *The Federal Bulldozer: A Critical Analysis of Urban Renewal, 1949–1962* (Cambridge, Mass.: MIT Press, 1964).

34. Wright Patman to George Romney, January 7, 1971, George Romney Papers, Post-gubernatorial Career Series, box 11, folder Patman, Wright House Banking

Committee; Bayer, *Cities Destroyed for Cash*, 220–225; Roger Biles, "Public Housing and the Postwar Urban Renaissance, 1945–1973," in *From Tenements to the Taylor Homes: In Search of an Urban Housing Policy in Twentieth-Century America*, ed. John F. Bauman, Roger Biles, and Kristin M. Szylvian (University Park: Pennsylvania State University Press, 2000), 156; Carl Abbott, *Urban America in the Modern Age: 1920 to the Present* (Arlington Heights, Ill.: Harlan Davidson, 1987), 126–127.

35. Perlstein, *Nixonland*, 342 (quotations). Also see Dean J. Kotlowski, *Nixon's Civil Rights: Politics, Principle, and Policy* (Cambridge: Harvard University Press, 2001); Christopher Bonestia, *Knocking on the Door: The Federal Government's Attempt to Desegregate the Suburbs* (Princeton: Princeton University Press, 2006); Charles M. Lamb, *Housing Segregation in Suburban America since 1960: Presidential and Judicial Politics* (Cambridge: Cambridge University Press, 2005); and Kevin M. Kruse and Thomas J. Sugrue, eds., *The New Suburban History* (Chicago: University of Chicago Press, 2006). Several of the essays in this collection are pertinent to the topic of race and housing in the late 1960s and early 1970s, but the actions of the Nixon administration are most evident in Lassiter, "'Socioeconomic Integration' in the Suburbs: From Reactionary Populism to Class Fairness in Metropolitan Charlotte," 120–143.

36. Mollenhoff, *George Romney*, 63; Harris, *Romney's Way*, 203–205; Romney, *The Concerns of a Citizen*, 23, 54 (quotation); Thomas J. Sugrue, *Sweet Land of Liberty: The Forgotten Struggle for Civil Rights in the North* (New York: Random House, 2008), 442–445.

37. Press release, April 8, 1969, Richard C. Van Dusen Files, 1969–72, box 79, folder WH 2-1, 1971–1969, p. 1 (first quotation); *Public Papers of the Presidents: Richard Nixon, 1969*, 269; George Romney to James Keogh, memorandum, September 19, 1969, George Romney Papers, Post-gubernatorial Career Series, box 2, folder Cabinet Meetings 1969, p. 2; George Romney to John D. Ehrlichman, memorandum, February 27, 1970, Richard C. Van Dusen Files, 1969–72, box 74, folder WH-1, 1972–1970, p. 2 (second quotation). The twenty cities in the HUD study were Washington, D.C., Detroit, Newark, Baltimore, New Haven, Boston, New York City, Pittsburgh, Providence, Rochester, Wilmington, Los Angeles, Chicago, Cleveland, Akron, Kansas City, Memphis, Louisville, Nashville, and Tampa.

38. W. Dennis Keating, *The Suburban Racial Dilemma: Housing and Neighborhoods* (Philadelphia: Temple University Press, 1994), 41–43; Dean J. Kotlowski, *Nixon's Civil Rights*, 54–59; Charles M. Lamb, *Housing Segregation in Suburban America since the 1960s*, 62–84; Matthew D. Lassiter, *The Silent Majority: Suburban Politics in the Sunbelt South* (Princeton: Princeton University Press, 2006), 305 (quotations).

39. Keating, *The Suburban Racial Dilemma*, 42–43; Lassiter, *The Silent Majority*, 305; Michael N. Danielson, *The Politics of Exclusion* (New York: Columbia University Press, 1976), 262 (quotation).

40. Danielson, *The Politics of Exclusion*, 222–225; Lassiter, *The Silent Majority*, 306; *Public Papers of the Presidents: Richard Nixon, 1970* (Washington, D.C.: Government Printing Office, 1971), 1106 (quotations).

41. John D. Ehrlichman to Richard Nixon, undated memorandum, George Romney Papers, Post-gubernatorial Career Series, box 15, folder President 12/2 (first quotation); John Ehrlichman, *Witness to Power: The Nixon Years* (New York: Simon & Schuster, 1982), 218 (second quotation); John D. Ehrlichman to Bob Haldeman, memorandum, November 30, 1970, White House Central Files, Subject Files, FG 24, box 2, folder 10/1/70–12/31/70, Nixon Presidential Materials.

42. *Public Papers of the Presidents: Richard Nixon, 1970*, 1106 (first quotation); Danielson, *The Politics of Exclusion*, 227–228; George Romney to John N. Mitchell, January 7, 1971, George Romney Papers, Post-gubernatorial Career Series, box 1, folder Attorney General and Mitchell; *Houston Chronicle*, June 15, 1971, clipping, Richard C. Van Dusen Files, 1969–72, box 77, folder WH 1–8, 1971 (second and third quotations); Citizens Commission on Civil Rights, "The Federal Government and Equal Housing Opportunity: A Continuing Failure," in *Critical Perspectives on Housing*, ed. Rachel G. Bratt, Chester Hartman, and Ann Meyerson (Philadelphia: Temple University Press, 1986), 311–312; "Statement of Secretary George Romney to the United States Commission on Civil Rights," June 15, 1971, Richard C. Van Dusen Files, 1969–72, box 77, folder WH 1–8, 1971.

43. McFarland, *Federal Government and Urban Problems*, 190.

44. *New York Times*, January 5, 1972; *Public Papers of the Presidents: Richard Nixon, 1972* (Washington, D.C.: Government Printing Office, 1974), 34–41.

45. George Romney to the Vice President, February 19, 1970, White House Central Files, Subject Files, FG 24, box 1, folder 1/1/70—3/31/70, Nixon Presidential Materials; Patterson, *Grand Expectations*, 733 (quotation). Also see Gerald Frug, "The Legal Technology of Exclusion in Metropolitan America," in Kruse and Sugrue, *The New Suburban History*, 205–219.

46. *Boston Globe*, June 27, 2007; Kenneth R. Cole Jr. to John Ehrlichman, memorandum, February 22, 1970, White House Central Files, Subject Files, FG 24, box 1, folder 1/1/70–3/31/70; Ehrlichman, *Witness to Power*, 107–110; Small, *The Presidency of Richard Nixon*, 40.

47. Kotlowski, *Nixon's Civil Rights*, 53, 61; "News Conference," November 25, 1970, George Romney Papers, Post-gubernatorial Career Series, box 14, folder President 12/2; Richard Nixon to George Romney, memorandum, August 7, 1972, George Romney Papers, Post-gubernatorial Career Series, box 13, folder Meeting with President—8/12/72; *Washington Post*, , August 13, 1972, clipping, Nixon Presidential Materials, White House Special Files, John D. Ehrlichman Files, box 25, folder George Romney; George Romney to Richard Nixon, August 10, 1972, George Romney Papers, Post-gubernatorial Career Series, box 13, folder Meeting with President—8/12/72; Foote, "As They Saw It," 76.

48. Congressional Quarterly, *Urban America, Policies and Problems* (Washington, D.C.: Congressional Quarterly, 1978), 6A (first quotation); George Romney to the President, December 28, 1972, George Romney Papers, Post-gubernatorial Career Series, box 14, folder Ehrlichman & President 1972, p. 1 (second quotation); *Congressional Quarterly Almanac*, 93rd Cong., 1st sess., 1973, vol. 29 (Washington, D.C.: Congressional Quarterly Service, 1974), 429. Christopher Bonestia argues that, in part,

Nixon opted for the housing moratorium to provide cover for the administration's refusal to pursue integration in suburbs. Bonestia, *Knocking on the Door*, 136–139.

49. *Public Papers of the Presidents: Richard Nixon, 1973* (Washington, D.C.:
Government Printing Office, 1975), 807.

50. *Public Papers of the Presidents: Richard Nixon, 1971*, 55 (quotation); *Public
Papers of the Presidents: Richard Nixon, 1969*, 643, 665–668; memorandum for Sen-
ior Administration Officials, June 24, 1970, Daniel P. Moynihan Papers, box 302,
folder Revenue Sharing, 1968–70; Wilbur Mills, "Comments on Revenue Sharing,"
January 26, 1971, White House Special Files, John D. Ehrlichman File, box 25, folder
Revenue Sharing, Wilbur Mills, Nixon Presidential Materials; Charles J. Orlebeke to
Secretary Romney, April 1, 1971, George Romney Papers, Post-gubernatorial Career
Series, box 11, folder Revenue Sharing; Benjamin Kleinberg, *Urban America in Trans-
formation: Perspectives on Urban Policy and Development* (Thousand Oaks, Calif.:
Sage, 1995), 189–195; Reichley, *Conservatives in an Age of Change*, 158; Timothy
Conlan, *New Federalism: Intergovernmental Reform from Nixon to Reagan* (Washing-
ton, D.C.: Brookings Institution Press, 1988), 30–35.

51. *Public Papers of the Presidents: Richard Nixon, 1973*, 39–40; Paul R. Dom-
mel, "Distributional Impacts of General Revenue Sharing," in *The Urban Impacts of
Federal Policies*, ed. Norman J. Glickman (Baltimore: Johns Hopkins University
Press, 1980), 542–543; Greene, *The Limits of Power*, 63–64; "The Mayors' Revolt,"
Newsweek 77 (May 24, 1971): 94; Julian E. Zelizer, *Taxing America: Wilbur D. Mills,
Congress, and the State, 1945–1975* (Cambridge, UK: Cambridge University Press,
1998), 333; William A. Caldwell, *How to Save Urban America* (New York: Signet,
1973), 227–228; Reichley, *Conservatives in an Age of Change*, 160; Abbott, *Urban
America in the Modern Age*, 130 (quotation).

52. *Public Papers of the Presidents: Richard Nixon, 1973*, 173; *Congressional
Quarterly Almanac*, 92nd Cong., 2nd sess., 1972, vol. 28 (Washington, D.C.: Congressional Quarterly Service, 1973), 633–635; *Public Papers of the Presidents: Richard
Nixon, 1974* (Washington, D.C.: Government Printing Office, 1975), 83; *Public Papers
of the Presidents: Gerald R. Ford, 1974* (Washington, D.C.: Government Printing Office, 1975), 43–44; *New York Times*, August 23, 1974.

53. Peter Dreier, John Mollenkopf, and Todd Swanstrom, *Place Matters: Metropolitics for the Twenty-first Century* (Lawrence: University Press of Kansas, 2004),
136–137; Mollenkopf, *The Contested City*, 131–132; Goldfield and Brownell, *Urban
America*, 389.

54. Goldfield and Brownell, *Urban America*, 389 (quotation); Judd and Swanstrom, *City Politics*, 227–228; Mollenkopf, *The Contested City*, 135; Susan S. Fainstein
and Norman I. Fainstein, "Economic Change, National Policy, and the System of Cities," in *Restructuring the City: The Political Economy of Urban Redevelopment*,
ed. Susan S. Fainstein, Norman I. Fainstein, Richard Child Hill, Dennis Judd, and
Michael Peter Smith (New York: Longman, 1983), 19.

55. Charles E. Connerly and Y. Thomas Liou, "Community Development Block
Grant," in *The Encyclopedia of Housing*, 64–65; Congressional Quarterly, *Urban
America, Policies and Problems*, 9-A; John F. Bauman, "Jimmy Carter, Patricia

Roberts Harris, and Housing Policy in the Age of Limits," in Bauman, Biles, and Szylvian, *From Tenements to the Taylor Homes*, 253–254.

56. Raymond A. Mohl, "The Interstates and the Cities: The U.S. Department of Transportation and the Freeway Revolt, 1966–1973," *Journal of Policy History* 20, no. 2 (2008): 208 (quotations); Kathleen Kilgore, *John Volpe: The Life of an Immigrant Son* (Dublin, N.H.: Yankee Publishing, 1987), 175.

57. Alan Altshuler and David Luberhoff, *Mega-Projects: The Changing Politics of Urban Public Investment* (Washington, D.C.: Brookings Institution Press, 2003), 177; "Report of the President-Elect's Task Force on Transportation," January 5, 1969, Daniel P. Moynihan Papers, box 305, folder 8, Library of Congress; Daniel P. Moynihan, "New Roads and Urban Chaos," *Reporter* 22 (April 14, 1960): 13–20; Moynihan, "Toward a National Urban Policy," 10–12; Osborne, "Moynihan at Work in the White House," 11–13; Mohl, "The Interstates and the Cities," 208.

58. Edwin A. Bock, *Between Mayors and Nixon: Secretary Volpe's Mass Transit Bill* (Syracuse, N.Y.: Inter-University Case Program, 1980), 12–13.

59. Mohl, "The Interstates and the Cities," 210.

60. Minutes, 15th Meeting, Council for Urban Affairs, July 11, 1969, pp. 8–9, Daniel P. Moynihan Papers, box 265, folder Council for Urban Affairs: Meetings, 1969 11 July; Bock, *Between Mayors and Nixon*, 13–14; Kilgore, *John Volpe*, 177; D. C. Oliver, "In the Footsteps of a Giant: Francis C. Turner and Management of the Interstate," *Transportation Quarterly* 48 (Spring 1994): 199–220; James Burby, *The Great American Motor Sickness: Or Why You Can't Get There from Here* (Boston: Little, Brown, 1971), 306; Mohl, "The Interstates and the Cities," 217.

61. Mohl, "The Interstates and the Cities," 216–217 (quotations); Kilgore, *John Volpe*, 172–188; Burby, *The Great American Motor Sickness*, 307.

62. Mohl, "The Interstates and the Cities," 214–215. On the Riverfront Expressway episode, see Richard O. Baumbach Jr. and William E. Borah, *The Second Battle of New Orleans: A History of the Vieux Carre Riverfront-Expressway Controversy* (Tuscaloosa: University of Alabama Press, 1981); Priscilla Dunhill, "Reconciling the Conflict of Highways and Cities," *Reporter* 38 (February 8, 1968): 23; and Beverly H. Wright, "New Orleans Neighborhoods under Siege," in *Just Transportation: Dismantling Race and Class Barriers to Mobility*, ed. Robert D. Bullard and Glenn S. Johnson (Gabriola Island, B.C., Canada: New Society Publishers, 1997), 121–144.

63. "Volpe Reprieves Overton Park," *Audubon* 75 (March 1973): 122; Russell E. Train, "The Environmental Record of the Nixon Administration," *Presidential Studies Quarterly* 26 (Winter 1996): 185–196; Mohl, "The Interstates and the Cities," 216 (quotations). Also see Kenneth R. Geiser Jr., *Urban Transportation Decision Making: Political Processes of Urban Freeway Controversies* (Springfield, Va.: National Technical Information Service, 1970), 331–335.

64. Mohl, "The Interstates and the Cities," 212 (first quotation); minutes, 15th Meeting, Council for Urban Affairs, July 11, 1969, pp. 8–12, Daniel P. Moynihan Papers, box 265, folder Council for Urban Affairs: Meetings, 1969 11 July; Bock, *Between Mayors and Nixon*, 20–47; Alan L. Dean and James M. Beggs, "The Department of Transportation Comes of Age: The Nixon Years," *Presidential Studies Quarterly* 26

(Winter 1996): 212; *Congressional Quarterly Almanac*, 91st Cong., 2nd sess., 1970, vol. 26, 331 (second and third quotations); Kilgore, *John Volpe*, 187; *Public Papers of the Presidents: Richard Nixon, 1970*, 848–849.

65. *Congressional Quarterly Almanac*, 93rd Cong., 1st sess., 1973, vol. 29, 435–452; Denis Hayes, "Can We Bust the Highway Trust?" *Saturday Review* 54 (June 5, 1971), 48–53; George M. Smerk, *The Federal Role in Urban Mass Transportation* (Bloomington: Indiana University Press, 1991), 108–122; Alan Altshuler with James P. Womack and John R. Pucher, *The Urban Transportation System: Politics and Policy Innovation* (Cambridge, Mass.: MIT Press, 1979), 36; Mohl, "The Interstates and the Cities," 214 (quotation).

66. Kilgore, *John Volpe*, 189, 197–198; Small, *The Presidency of Richard Nixon*, 40; Dean and Beggs, "The Department of Transportation Comes of Age," 213–215.

67. Richard Nixon to James T. Lynn, July 18, 1974, White House Central Files, Subject Files, FG 24, box 4, folder 7/1/74—End, Nixon Presidential Materials.

68. O'Connor, "Swimming against the Tide," 110; Royce Hanson, *The Evolution of National Urban Policy, 1970–1980: Lessons from the Past* (Washington, D.C.: National Academy Press, 1982), 18; Sugrue, *Sweet Land of Liberty*, 522 (quotations).

69. "The Mayors' Revolt," 94 (quotation); Presidential Address by Joseph Alioto, July 6, 1975, Carla Hills Papers, box 47, folder U.S. Conference of Mayors—7/8/75.

CHAPTER 6. FORD AND THE NEW FEDERALISM

1. Fred Greenstein, *The Presidential Difference: Leadership Style from FDR to Clinton* (New York: Free Press, 2000), 113–116; James T. Patterson, *Restless Giant: The United States from Watergate to Bush v. Gore* (New York: Oxford University Press, 2005), 93 (quotation); Royce Hanson, *The Evolution of a National Urban Policy, 1970–1980: Lessons from the Past* (Washington, D.C.: National Academy Press, 1982), 29.

2. On the Ford presidency, see John Robert Greene, *The Presidency of Gerald R. Ford* (Lawrence: University Press of Kansas, 1995); John Robert Greene, *The Limits of Power: The Nixon and Ford Administrations* (Bloomington: Indiana University Press, 1992); Yanek Mieczkowski, *Gerald Ford and the Challenges of the 1970s* (Lexington: University Press of Kentucky, 2005); A. James Reichley, *Conservatives in an Age of Change: The Nixon and Ford Administrations* (Washington, D.C.: Brookings Institution Press, 1981); Douglas Brinkley, *Gerald R. Ford* (New York: Times Books, 2007); Robert T. Hartmann, *Palace Politics: An Inside Account of the Ford Years* (New York: McGraw-Hill, 1980); and Gerald R. Ford, *A Time to Heal: The Autobiography of Gerald R. Ford* (New York: Harper & Row, 1979).

3. Iwan W. Morgan, *Deficit Government: Taxing and Spending in Modern America* (Chicago: Ivan R. Dee, 1995), 123–124; William H. Chafe, *The Unfinished Journey: America since World War II*, 5th ed. (New York: Oxford University Press, 2003), 430–433.

4. Morgan, *Deficit Government*, 124–126; Patterson, *Restless Giant*, 96–98; Greene, *The Presidency of Gerald R. Ford*, 71 (quotation).

5. David R. Goldfield and Blaine A. Brownell, *Urban America: A History*, 2nd ed. (Boston: Houghton Mifflin, 1990), 385–387; Howard P. Chudacoff and Judith E. Smith, *The Evolution of American Urban Society*, 6th ed. (Upper Saddle River, N.J.: Pearson Prentice Hall, 2005), 284; S. Paul O'Hara, "Envisioning the Steel City: The Legend and Legacy of Gary, Indiana," in *Beyond the Ruins: The Meanings of Deindustrialization*, ed. Jefferson Cowie and Joseph Heathcott (Ithaca: Cornell University Press, 2003), 230. Also see Barry Bluestone and Bennett Harrison, *The Deindustrialization of America: Plant Closings, Community Abandonment, and the Dismantling of Basic Industry* (New York: Basic Books, 1982).

6. John J. Gunther, *Federal-City Relations in the United States: The Role of the Mayors in Federal Aid to Cities* (Newark: University of Delaware Press, 1990), 238; Suzanne de Lesseps, "Urban Mass Transit," *Editorial Research Reports* 2 (October 17, 1975): 758; Tod R. Hullin to James Lynn, memorandum, August 26, 1974, David O. Meeker Files, box 18, folder Meeting w/ Mayors, 8/16/74, Gerald R. Ford Presidential Library, Ann Arbor, Mich.

7. *Congressional Quarterly Almanac*, 93rd Cong., 2nd sess., 1974, vol. 30 (Washington, D.C.: Congressional Quarterly Service, 1975), 345–360; *Public Papers of the Presidents: Gerald R. Ford, 1974* (Washington, D.C.: Government Printing Office, 1975), 42–43; Ford, *A Time to Heal*, 240.

8. Gunther, *Federal-City Relations in the United States*, 239–240.

9. *Public Papers of the Presidents: Gerald R. Ford, 1974*, 107–110, 111 (quotation).

10. Ibid., 110.

11. Ibid., 107–112.

12. *Congressional Quarterly Almanac*, 93rd Cong., 2nd sess., 1974, vol. 30, 695; *Public Papers of the Presidents: Gerald R. Ford, 1974*, 664–666; Lesseps, "Urban Mass Transit," 756.

13. Jim Cannon to the Vice President, memorandum, April 28, 1975, F. Lynn May Files, box 20, folder Vice President's Briefings, Gerald R. Ford Presidential Library; Joseph Foote, "As They Saw It: HUD's Secretaries Reminisce about Carrying out the Mission," *Cityscape* 1 (September 1995): 77–78; Ford, *A Time to Heal*, 240–241 (quotations); *Congressional Quarterly* Almanac, 94th Cong., 1st sess., 1975, vol. 31 (Washington, D.C.: Congressional Quarterly Service, 1976), 419.

14. Irwin Ross, "Carla Hills Gives 'The Woman's Touch' a Brand-New Meaning," *Fortune* 92 (December 1975): 122 (quotations); M. Carter McFarland, *Federal Government and Urban Problems. HUD: Successes, Failures, and the Fate of Our Cities* (Boulder: Westview Press, 1978), 46.

15. James E. Connor to the President, undated memorandum, James M. Cannon Files, box 17, folder March 1975, Gerald R. Ford Presidential Library; Jim Cannon to the Vice President, memorandum, April 28, 1975, F. Lynn May Files, box 20, folder Vice President's Briefings; Carla A. Hills to James M. Cannon and James T. Lynn, memorandum, April 18, 1975, L. William Seidman Files, box 187, folder Carla A. Hills (1), Gerald R. Ford Presidential Library; *Congressional Quarterly Almanac*, 94th Cong., 1st sess., 1975, vol. 31, 420; Ross, "Carla Hills Gives 'The Woman's Touch' A Brand-New Meaning," 164.

16. *Congressional Quarterly Almanac*, 94th Cong., 1st sess., 1975, vol. 31, 419–421, 440; James E. Connor to the President, undated memorandum, James M. Cannon Files, box 17, folder March 1975; Ross, "Carla Hills Gives 'The Woman's Touch' a Brand-New Meaning," 164 (quotation); *Public Papers of the Presidents: Gerald R. Ford, 1975*, pt. 1 (Washington, D.C.: Government Printing Office, 1977), 858–863.

17. *Congressional Quarterly Almanac*, 94th Cong., 1st sess., 1975, vol. 31, 421; *Public Papers of the Presidents: Gerald R. Ford, 1975*, pt. 1, 909–910; Mieczkowski, *Gerald Ford and the Challenges of the 1970s*, 86–87; Demetrios Caraley, "Congressional Politics and Urban Aid," *Political Science Quarterly* 91 (Spring 1976): 21.

18. *Public Papers of the Presidents: Gerald R. Ford, 1975*, pt. 1, 736–737, 897; *Congressional Quarterly Almanac*, 94th Cong., 1st sess., 1975, vol. 31, 793; Caraley, "Congressional Politics and Urban Aid," 21.

19. Transcript, "Meet the Press," July 6, 1975, p. 25, Ronald H. Nessen Files, box 69, folder Meet the Press—July 6, 1975, Gerald R. Ford Presidential Library (first quotation); Caraley, "Congressional Politics and Urban Aid," 19–20; presidential address by Joseph Alioto, Boston, July 6, 1975, Carla Hills Papers, box 47, folder U.S. Conference of Mayors—7/8/75—Speeches by Others, Hoover Institution Archives, Stanford, Calif. (second quotation).

20. Carla Hills Speech, July 8, 1975, Carla Hills Papers, box 47, folder U.S. Conference of Mayors—7/8/75—CAH Speech.

21. Gunther, *Federal-City Relations in the United States*, 244–245; Caraley, "Congressional Politics and Urban Aid," 20–21.

22. Greene, *The Presidency of Gerald R. Ford*, 90–92; Gunther, *Federal-City Relations in the United States*, 241; Richard A. Loverd, "Presidential Decision Making during the 1975 New York Financial Crisis: A Conceptual Analysis," *Presidential Studies Quarterly* 21 (Spring 1991): 254–255. On the New York City bankruptcy crisis, see Robert W. Bailey, *The Crisis Regime: The MAC, the EFCB, and the Political Impact of the New York City Financial Crisis* (Albany: State University of New York Press, 1984).

23. Gunther, *Federal-City Relations in the United States*, 241–242; *Congressional Quarterly Almanac*, 94th Cong., 1st sess., 1975, vol. 31, 444; *Congressional Quarterly Almanac*, 94th Cong., 2nd sess., 1976, vol. 32 (Washington, D.C.: Government Printing Office, 1976), 355 (quotation).

24. Ford, *A Time to Heal*, 315.

25. Ibid., 318–319.

26. *Chicago Daily News*, October 30, 1975 (first quotation); Brinkley, *Gerald R. Ford*, 127 (second quotation).

27. *Congressional Quarterly Almanac*, 94th Cong., 1st sess., 1975, vol. 31, 448; Ford, *A Time to Heal*, 331; Mieczkowski, *Gerald Ford and the Challenges of the 1970s*, 153; Muchnick, "Death Warrant for the Cities?" *Dissent* 23 (Winter 1976): 29–30; *Public Papers of the Presidents: Gerald R. Ford, 1975*, pt. 2, 1903 (quotation).

28. "Meeting to Discuss Detroit," April 9, 1975, James M. Cannon Files, box 43, folder Sec. Hills, 4/9/75, Gerald R. Ford Presidential Library; June Manning Thomas, *Redevelopment and Race: Planning a Finer City in Postwar Detroit* (Baltimore: Johns Hopkins University Press, 1997), 153–154.

29. Transcript, "Meet the Press," July 6, 1975, p. 26, Ronald H. Nessen Files, box 69, folder Meet the Press—July 6, 1975, Gerald R. Ford Presidential Library; Paul H. O'Neill to Warren Rustand, undated memorandum, F. Lynn May Files, box 7, folder Detroit, 4/30/75; *Detroit Free Press*, May 5, 1975, clipping, F. Lynn May Files, box 6, folder Detroit (1) (quotation).

30. "General Comments," undated, Carla Hills Papers, box 8, folder Detroit—Meeting w/ Mayor Young & Max Fisher; Carla A. Hills to Coleman A. Young, August 21, 1975, F. Lynn May Files, box 7, folder Detroit (2); "Meeting to Discuss Detroit," *Detroit Free Press*, May 5, 1975, clipping, undated memorandum from Deputy Assistant Secretary for Housing Management, F. Lynn May Files, box 7, folder Detroit (2) (quotation); Thomas, *Redevelopment and Race*, 154 .

31. Tod Hullin to Jim Cannon, September 18, 1975, James M. Cannon Files, box 51, folder Sec. Hills, 9/19/75, Gerald R. Ford Presidential Library; *Public Papers of the Presidents: Gerald R. Ford, 1976–77* (Washington, D.C.: Government Printing Office, 1979), 35 (quotation), 39.

32. "Remarks by Senator Edmund S. Muskie, U.S. Conference of Mayors' Midwinter Conference, Friday, January 30, 1976," p. 2 (first and second quotations), Steven G. McConahey Files, box 30, folder USCM—General; "Statement of Moon Landrieu, Kenneth Gibson, and Coleman Young on Urban Priorities and the President's FY 77 Budget before the Joint Economic Committee," February 25, 1976, pp. 4–5, 8–9, 15, Steven G. McConahey Files, box 30, folder USCM—General.

33. Roger Biles, *Richard J. Daley: Politics, Race, and the Governing of Chicago* (DeKalb: Northern Illinois University Press, 1995), 171–173; Elizabeth Warren, *The Legacy of Judicial Policy-Making: Gautreaux vs. Chicago Housing Authority, the Decision and Its Impacts* (New York: University Press of America, 1988), 12–18; Devereux Bowly, *The Poorhouse: Subsidized Housing in Chicago, 1895–1976* (Carbondale: Southern Illinois University Press, 1978), 189–193; Alexander Polikoff, *Waiting for Gautreaux: A Story of Segregation, Housing, and the Black Ghetto* (Evanston: Northwestern University Press, 2006), chap. 3.

34. *New York Times*, April 29, 1976; Michael N. Danielson, *The Politics of Exclusion* (New York: Columbia University Press, 1976), 355, 357 (quotations); Bowly, *The Poorhouse*, 193; Polikoff, *Waiting for Gautreaux*, 149–155; Charles M. Lamb, *Housing Segregation in Suburban America since 1960* (Cambridge: Cambridge University Press, 2005), 230–231.

35. Lynn May to John Rhinelander, Dave Meeker, and Charles Orlebeke, May 24, 1976, David O. Meeker Files, box 22, folder Urban Policy, 1970–1980 (2); Carla Hills, "White House Briefing with Conference of Mayors," January 29, 1976, Carla A. Hills Speeches, box 2, File 1/29/76, Gerald R. Ford Presidential Library (quotation).

36. Jim Cannon to Jim Connor, memorandum, July 2, 1976, James M. Cannon Files, box 38, folder Meeting with Sec. Hills, 8/13/76, Gerald R. Ford Presidential Library; "Meeting with the President's Committee on Urban Development and Neighborhood Revitalization," July 21, 1976, James M. Cannon Files, box 38, folder Meeting with President, 7/21/76; Steve McConahey to James Cannon, memorandum, July 16, 1976, Stephen G. McConahey Papers, box 30, folder U.S. Conference of

Mayors, General, Gerald R. Ford Presidential Library; Hanson, *The Evolution of National Urban Policy, 1970–1980*, pp. 35–36; "Statement by the President," October 21, 1976, p. 1, Ronald H. Nessen Files, box 54, folder HUD, 10/19/76—10/21/76 (quotations). Also see *Public Papers of the Presidents: Gerald R. Ford, 1976–77*, 2598–2601.

37. "Statement by the President," October 21, 1976, p. 1, Ronald H. Nessen Files, box 54, folder HUD, 10/19/76—10/21/76.

38. "Statement by the President and Press Conference of Carla A. Hills," October 21, 1976, p. 4 (quotation), Ronald H. Nessen Files, box 54, folder HUD, 10/19/76—10/21/76; "Interim Report of the Committee on Urban Development and Neighborhood Revitalization," F. Lynn May Files, box 18, folder Questions and Answers, Gerald R. Ford Presidential Library.

39. Don Morrow to Carla A. Hills, June 26, 1975, Carla A. Hills to William Proxmire, July 11, 1975, and William Proxmire and Adlai E. Stevenson to Carla A. Hills, August 1, 1975, all in Carla Hills Papers, box 13, folder Chicago FHA Scandal Correspondence; *Congressional Quarterly Almanac*, 94th Cong., 2nd sess., 1976, vol. 32, 342–345; *Public Papers of the Presidents: Gerald R. Ford, 1976–77*, 2126 (quotation).

40. "Carter on the Cities," p. 1, David Gergen Files, box 15, folder Debate Background—Cities, Gerald R. Ford Presidential Library (quotations); "Urban Problems," Michael Raoul-Duval Papers, box 25, folder Debate Briefing Book—Domestic Issues, Gerald R. Ford Presidential Library; Carla A. Hills to James E. Connor, September 21, 1976, Michael Raoul-Duvall Papers, box 26, folder Debate Working Papers, 9/23/76; Gunther, *Federal-City Relations in the United States*, 245; *New York Times*, September 24, 1976; Ron Nessen, *It Sure Looks Different from the Inside* (New York: Simon & Schuster, 1978), 263–277.

41. William Proxmire to Carla A. Hills, January 31, 1977, pp. 1–2, Patricia Roberts Harris Papers, box 81, folder Hills, Carla A., Library of Congress, Washington, D.C. (first quotation); Ross, "The Woman's Touch," 164 (second quotation).

42. William Proxmire to Carla A. Hills, January 31, 1977, p. 3, Patricia Roberts Harris Papers, box 81, folder Hills, Carla A., Library of Congress, Washington, D.C.

43. Kent W. Colton, *Housing in the Twenty-first Century: Achieving Common Ground* (Cambridge: Harvard University Press, 2003), 218–220; Paul E. Peterson, "The Changing Fiscal Place of Big Cities in the Federal System," in *Interwoven Destinies: Cities and the Nation*, ed. Henry G. Cisneros (New York: W. W. Norton, 1993), 193–194; Susan S. Fainstein and Norman I. Fainstein, "Economic Change, National Policy, and the System of Cities," in *Restructuring the City: The Political Economy of Urban Redevelopment*, ed. Susan S. Fainstein, Norman I. Fainstein, Richard Child Hill, Dennis Judd, and Michael Peter Smith (New York: Longman, 1983), 19; Alice O'Connor, "Swimming against the Tide: A Brief History of Federal Policy in Poor Communities," in *Urban Problems and Community Development*, ed. Ronald F. Ferguson and William T. Dickens (Washington, D.C.: Brookings Institution Press, 1999), 110; Hanson, *The Evolution of a National Urban Policy, 1970–1980*, 84.

44. Carla Hills, "White House Briefing with Conference of Mayors," p. 5, January 29, 1976, Carla A. Hills Speeches, box 2, file 1/29/76, Gerald R. Ford Presidential Library (quotation); Muchnick, "Death Warrant for the Cities?" 30; Charles J. Orlebeke,

"Chasing Urban Policy: A Critical Retrospect," in *The Future of National Urban Policy*, ed. Marshall Kaplan and Franklin James (Durham: Duke University Press, 1990), 196; Jon C. Teaford, *The Metropolitan Revolution: The Rise of Post-Urban America* (New York: Columbia University Press, 2006), 138–139.

CHAPTER 7. A NEW PARTNERSHIP WITH THE CITIES

1. For general discussions of the Carter presidency's urban policies, see Thomas J. Sugrue, "Carter's Urban Policy Crisis," in *The Carter Presidency: Policy Choices in the Post-New Deal Era*, ed. Gary M. Fink and Hugh Davis Graham (Lawrence: University Press of Kansas, 1998), 137–157; Harold L. Wolman and Astrid E. Merget, "The Presidency and Policy Formulation: President Carter and the Urban Policy," *Political Studies Quarterly* 10 (Summer 1980): 402–415; Demetrios Caraley, "Carter, Congress, and the Cities," in *Urban Policy Making*, ed. Dale Rogers Marshall (Beverly Hills: Sage, 1979), 71–98; and Alice O'Connor, "Swimming against the Tide: A Brief History of Federal Policy in Poor Communities," in *Urban Problems and Community Development*, ed. Ronald F. Ferguson and William T. Dickens (Washington, D.C.: Brookings Institution Press, 1999), 111–113.

2. James T. Patterson, *Restless Giant: The United States from Watergate to Bush v. Gore* (New York: Oxford University Press, 2005), 108–109; William H. Chafe, *The Unfinished Journey: America since World War II*, 5th ed. (New York: Oxford University Press, 2003), 436–437; Sugrue, "Carter's Urban Policy Crisis," 137–140. On the Carter presidency, see Burton I. Kaufman and Scott Kaufman, *The Presidency of James Earl Carter, Jr.*, 2nd rev. ed. (Lawrence: University Press of Kansas, 2006); Erwin C. Hargrove, *Jimmy Carter as President: Leadership and the Politics of the Public Good* (Baton Rouge: Louisiana State University Press, 1988); and Jimmy Carter, *Keeping Faith: Memoirs of a President* (New York: Bantam Books, 1982). On the gubernatorial years, see Gary M. Fink, *Prelude to the Presidency: The Political Character and Legislative Leadership Style of Governor Jimmy Carter* (Westport, Conn.: Greenwood Press, 1980).

3. "Address by Jimmy Carter on Urban Policy to the United States Conference of Mayors in Milwaukee," June 29, 1976, p. 4, Office of Chief of Staff Files, box 140, folder Urban Policy, 6/29/76—3/22/78, Jimmy Carter Presidential Library, Atlanta (quotation); Royce Hanson, *The Evolution of National Urban Policy, 1970–1980: Lessons from the Past* (Washington, D.C.: National Academy Press, 1982), 39.

4. Undated entry, B-5, Patricia Roberts Harris Papers, box 16, folder Briefing Books: Administration: HUD (undated), Library of Congress, Washington, D.C. (first quotation); "Carter on the Cities," undated memorandum, p. 1, David Gergen Files, box 15, folder Debate Background—Cities, Gerald R. Ford Presidential Library, Ann Arbor, Mich. (second quotation); Oral History Interview with Stuart Eizenstat, January 29, 1982, p. 10, Jimmy Carter Presidential Library; *Washington Post*, October 20, 1976.

5. Caraley, "Carter, Congress, and the Cities," 94; Tom Tatum to Jimmy Carter, memorandum, November 12, 1976, Office of Chief of Staff Files, box 4,

folder [Election Review—Urban Affairs, 11/12/76] [O/A 10,622], Jimmy Carter Presidential Library (quotations).

6. *New York Times*, November 9, 1976; John H. Mollenkopf, *The Contested City* (Princeton: Princeton University Press, 1983), 273; John J. Gunther, *Federal-City Relations in the United States: The Role of the Mayors in Federal Aid to Cities* (Newark: University of Delaware Press, 1990), 246; transcript, *Face the Nation*, December 19, 1976, Ronald H. Nessen Files, box 65, folder Face the Nation—12/19/76, p. 6, Gerald R. Ford Presidential Library (quotations).

7. Transcript, *Face the Nation*, December 19, 1976, pp. 2, 9; John F. Bauman, "Jimmy Carter, Patricia Roberts Harris, and Housing Policy in the Age of Limits," in *From Tenements to the Taylor Homes: In Search of an Urban Housing Policy in Twentieth-Century America*, ed. John F. Bauman, Roger Biles, and Kristin M. Szylvian (University Park: Pennsylvania State University Press, 2000), 249–250.

8. Gunther, *Federal-City Relations in the United States*, 246 (first quotation); "Opening Statement of Senator William Proxmire," January 10, 1977, p. 1, Carla Hills Papers, box 17, folder Harris, Patricia Roberts, Hoover Institution, Palo Alto, Calif. (second quotation).

9. "Opening Statement of Senator William Proxmire," January 10, 1977, p. 4.

10. Bauman, "Jimmy Carter, Patricia Roberts Harris, and Housing Policy in the Age of Limits," 249.

11. *New York Times*, January 19, 1977 (quotations); Gunther, *Federal-City Relations in the United States*, 246.

12. *Public Papers of the Presidents: Jimmy Carter, 1977* (Washington, D.C.: Government Printing Office, 1977), 1:485; Helen Leavitt, "No Easy Solutions: In Search of an Urban Policy," *New Leader* 61 (January 30, 1978): 12; Sugrue, "Carter's Urban Policy Crisis," 141 (quotation); Jimmy Carter to Cabinet Secretaries, memorandum, March 21, 1977, Carter Presidential Papers, Staff Offices, DPS—Eizenstat, Subject File, box 302, folder Urban Policy [CF, O/A 49] [5], Jimmy Carter Presidential Library; Orin Kramer to Stu Eizenstat, memorandum, April 20, 1977, Carter Presidential Papers, Staff Offices, DPS—Eizenstat, Subject File, box 308, folder Urban Policy—Economic Initiatives [CF, O/A 49] [2], Jimmy Carter Presidential Library; Joseph Foote, "As They Saw It: HUD's Secretaries Reminisce about Carrying out the Mission," *Cityscape* 1 (September 1995): 81–82; William W. Goldsmith and Michael J. Derian, "Toward a National Urban Policy—Critical Reviews: Is There an Urban Policy?" *Journal of Regional Science* 19 (February 1979): 94–95; Wolman and Merget, "The Presidency and Policy Formation," 403–404.

13. *New York Times*, June 14, 1977 (first quotation); Harold L. Wolman and Astrid E. Merget, "The Presidency and Policy Formation," 404 (second quotation); Hanson, *The Evolution of National Urban Policy, 1970–1980*, 40–41; Oral History Interview with Stuart Eizenstat, January 29, 1982, p. 25; Yvonne Scruggs, "HUD's Stewardship of National Urban Policy: A Retrospective View," *Cityscape* 1 (September 1995): 49–50; Sugrue, "Carter's Urban Policy Crisis," 138.

14. Kaufman and Kaufman, *The Presidency of James Earl Carter, Jr.*, 93 (quotation); Evelyn Gonzalez, *The Bronx* (New York: Columbia University Press, 2004),

127–135. Also see Jill Jonnes, *South Bronx Rising: The Rise, Fall, and Resurrection of an American City* (New York: Fordham University Press, 2002).

15. Bert Lance to Patricia Roberts Harris, July 12, 1977, Patricia Roberts Harris Papers, box 21, folder Housing: Presidential Meeting, 1977 (first quotation); Sugrue, "Carter's Urban Policy Crisis," 142 (second quotation).

16. Sugrue, "Carter's Urban Policy Crisis," 142–145; Bauman, "Jimmy Carter, Patricia Roberts Harris, and Housing Policy in the Age of Limits," 250–251. For more on Kaptur's views, see Ed Marciniak, *Reviving an Inner-City Community* (Chicago: Department of Political Science, Loyola University, 1977); and Marcia C. Kaptur, "East Humboldt Park Copes with the Chicago 21 Plan," *Planning* 43 (August 1977): 14–16. On Baroni, see John T. McGreevey, *Parish Boundaries: The Catholic Encounter with Race in the Twentieth-Century Urban North* (Chicago: University of Chicago Press, 1996), 230; and Geno Baroni, "The Neighborhood Movement in the United States from the 1960s to the Present," in *Neighborhood Policy and Planning*, ed. Phillip L. Clay and Robert M. Hollister (Lexington, Mass.: Heath, 1983). More generally, see Robert Halpern, *Rebuilding the Inner City: A History of Neighborhood Initiatives to Address Poverty in the United States* (New York: Columbia University Press, 1995).

17. Sugrue, "Carter's Urban Policy Crisis," 146–148; *New York Times*, January 25, 1978; Caraley, "Carter, Congress, and the Cities," 71. Also see Margaret Weir, *Politics and Jobs: The Boundaries of Employment Policy in the United States* (Princeton: Princeton University Press, 1992).

18. *Public Papers of the Presidents: Jimmy Carter, 1977* (Washington, D.C.: Government Printing Office, 1977), 2:1777–1778; Congressional Quarterly, *Urban America, Policies and Problems* (Washington, D.C.: Congressional Quarterly, 1978), 69 (quotation); *Congressional Quarterly Almanac*, 95th Cong., 1st sess., 1977, vol. 33 (Washington, D.C.: Congressional Quarterly Service, 1977), 126; Dennis R. Judd and Todd Swanstrom, *City Politics: Private Power and Public Policy* (New York: Longman, 1998), 201; Michael J. Rich, "UDAG, Economic Development, and the Death and Life of American Cities," *Economic Development Quarterly* 6 (May 1992): 150–151; Susan S. Jacobs and Elizabeth A. Roistacher, "The Urban Impacts of HUD's Urban Development Action Grant Program, or, Where's the Action in Action Grants?" in *The Urban Impacts of Federal Policies*, ed. Norman J. Glickman (Baltimore: Johns Hopkins University Press, 1980), 335.

19. *Congressional Quarterly Almanac*, 95th Cong., 1st sess., 1977, vol. 33, 133 (first quotation), 137 (second quotation).

20. Bert Carp to Stu Eizenstat, November 17, 1977, Carter Presidential Papers, Staff Offices, DPS—Eizenstat, Subject Files, box 308, folder Urban Policy (2) 11/77 [O/A 6346], Jimmy Carter Presidential Library; Stu Eizenstat and Bert Carp to the President, December 12, 1977, Carter Presidential Papers, Staff Offices, DPS—Eizenstat, Subject File, box 38, folder Urban Policy (Most Active) [OIA 6516] [2], Jimmy Carter Presidential Library; *New York Times*, December 18, 1977 (first quotation); Wolman and Merget, "The Presidency and Policy Formation," 405–406; Kaufman and Kaufman, *The Presidency of James Earl Carter, Jr.*, 94; "The Mayors Call for Help," *Time* 110 (December 12, 1977): 12 (second quotation).

21. Stu Eizenstat to Jimmy Carter, memorandum, January 20, 1978, Carter Presidential Papers, Staff Offices, DPS—Eizenstat, Subject File, box 309, folder Urban Policy (Most Active) [O/A 6516] [2], Jimmy Carter Presidential Library.

22. Hanson, *The Evolution of a National Urban Policy, 1970–1980*, 42; Wolman and Merget, "The Presidency and Policy Formation," 406–408; Bauman, "Jimmy Carter, Patricia Roberts Harris, and Housing Policy in the Age of Limits," 256.

23. Hamilton Jordan to President Carter, memorandum, March 24, 1978, Office of Chief of Staff Files, box 37, folder Urban Policy, 3/24/78, Jimmy Carter Presidential Library.

24. Ibid.

25. *Congressional Quarterly Almanac*, 95th Cong., 2nd sess., 1978, vol. 34 (Washington, D.C.: Congressional Quarterly Service, 1979), 45-E (first quotation); "Text of President Carter's Announcement of Urban Policy," March 27, 1978, p. 1, Patricia Roberts Harris Papers, box 34, folder Briefing Books: Urban & Regional Policy Group: Urban Policy: Announcement, March 27, 1978, Library of Congress (second quotation); *Public Papers of the Presidents: Jimmy Carter, 1978* (Washington, D.C.: Government Printing Office, 1979), 1:581, 587–588; Bauman, "Jimmy Carter, Patricia Roberts Harris, and Housing Policy in the Age of Limits," 256–257; Scruggs, "HUD's Stewardship of National Urban Policy," 54; Sugrue, "Carter's Urban Policy Crisis," 148–149.

26. Bauman, "Jimmy Carter, Patricia Roberts Harris, and Housing Policy in the Age of Limits," 257 (first quotation); Congressional Quarterly, *Urban America, Policies and Problems*, 13, 14 (second and third quotations); *New York Times*, April 2, 1978; *Washington Post*, March 29, 1978, clipping, Records of the White House Office of Counsel to the President, box 48, folder Urban Policy, 3/8/78 [CF, O/A 122], Jimmy Carter Presidential Library; Ray Horton to Daniel P. Moynihan, April 10, 1978, Daniel P. Moynihan Papers, Pt. 2, box 2369, folder 2, Library of Congress.

27. *Congressional Quarterly Almanac*, 95th Cong., 2nd sess., 1978, vol. 34, 23, 313–315; Richard P. Nathan, *A New Agenda for Cities* (Albany: Nelson A. Rockefeller Institute of Government, 1992), 38.

28. Congressional Quarterly, *Urban America, Policies and Problems*, 75; *Congressional Quarterly Almanac*, 95th Cong., 2nd sess., 1978, vol. 34, 542 (quotation); Helen Leavitt, "Back to the Trolley: Shifting Gears in Urban Transportation," *New Leader* 61 (March 1978): 12–13.

29. *Congressional Quarterly Almanac*, 95th Cong., 2nd sess., 1978, vol. 34, 27, 536–440, 550 (quotation).

30. Ibid., 536–543.

31. Ibid., 219–220; Kathy Jean Hayes and David L. Puryear, "The Urban Impacts of the Revenue Act of 1978," in Glickman, *The Urban Impacts of Federal Policies*, 451–464.

32. *Congressional Quarterly Almanac*, 95th Cong., 2nd sess., 1978, vol. 34, 17, 272–279; Kaufman and Kaufman, *The Presidency of James Earl Carter, Jr.*, 134–135.

33. Thomas J. Sugrue, "Carter's Urban Policy Crisis," 151 (first quotation); Kaufman and Kaufman, *The Presidency of James Earl Carter, Jr.*, 139–140 (second quotation)

34. Kaufman and Kaufman, *The Presidency of James Earl Carter, Jr.*, 169.

35. Patterson, *Restless Giant*, 127–128; Bruce J. Schulman, *The Seventies: The Great Shift in American Culture, Society, and Politics* (New York: Free Press, 2001), 135; *Public Papers of the Presidents: Jimmy Carter, 1979* (Washington, D.C.: Government Printing Office, 1980), 2:1237 (first quotation); Kaufman and Kaufman, *The Presidency of James Earl Carter, Jr.*, 177–178 (second quotation).

36. Gunther, *Federal-City Relations in the United States*, 248; unsigned memorandum to Patricia Roberts Harris, undated, Patricia Roberts Harris Papers, box 154, folder White House Correspondence May–June 1977, Library of Congress; Foote, "As They Saw It," 79 (first quotation); Bauman, "Jimmy Carter, Patricia Roberts Harris, and Housing Policy in the Age of Limits," 250 (second quotation); Steve Travis to Bert Carp, memorandum, November 29, 1977, Carter Presidential Papers, Staff Offices, DPS—Eizenstat, Subject File, box 308, folder Urban Policy (2) 11/77 [O/A 6346].

37. Foote, "As They Saw It," 79.

38. Peter Dreier, John Mollenkopf, and Todd Swanstrom, *Place Matters: Metropolitics for the Twenty-first Century*, 2nd ed. rev. (Lawrence: University Press of Kansas, 2004), 138; Steve Coyle to Patricia R. Harris, memorandum, July 18, 1977, Patricia Roberts Harris Papers, box 53, folder Carter: Urban Policy Statements, Library of Congress; John F. Bauman, "Jimmy Carter, Patricia Roberts Harris, and Housing Policy in the Age of Limits," 255 (quotation).

39. *Congressional Quarterly Almanac*, 96th Cong., 1st sess., 1979, vol. 35 (Washington, D.C.: Congressional Quarterly Service, 1980), 314 (quotation), 315–321; Rich, "UDAG, Economic Development, and the Death and Life of American Cities," 152. After Harris resigned as HUD secretary on August 3, 1979, Undersecretary Jay Janis became acting secretary and served in that capacity until Landrieu was sworn in on September 24, 1979. Foote, "As They Saw It," 83.

40. *Congressional Quarterly Almanac*, 96th Cong., 1st sess., 1979, vol. 35, 390 (quotation); Graham, "Civil Rights Policy in the Carter Presidency," 210–211; Charles M. Lamb, *Housing Segregation in Suburban America since 1960* (Cambridge: Cambridge University Press, 2005), 180–181.

41. *Public Papers of the Presidents: Jimmy Carter, 1980–1981* (Washington, D.C.: Government Printing Office, 1981), 1:118–119 (quotation); *Congressional Quarterly Almanac*, 96th Cong., 2nd sess., 1980, vol. 36 (Washington, D.C.: Congressional Quarterly Service, 1981), 373–377; Graham, "Civil Rights Policy in the Carter Presidency," 211–212.

42. *The President's National Urban Policy Report, 1980* (Washington, D.C.: Government Printing Office, 1980); Charles Orlebeke, "Chasing Urban Policy: A Critical Retrospect," in *The Future of National Urban Policy*, ed. Marshall Kaplan and Franklin James (Durham: Duke University Press, 1990), 198; Charles Orlebeke, "The President's National Urban Policy Report," *Journal of the American Planning Association* 48 (Winter 1982): 116 (quotations); Eisinger, "The Search for a National Urban Policy, 1968–1980," *Journal of Urban History* 12 (November 1985): 14–15; Hanson, *The Evolution of National Urban Policy, 1970–1980*, 52.

43. *Public Papers of the Presidents: Jimmy Carter, 1979*, 2:2014; President's Commission for a National Agenda for the Eighties, *Urban America in the Eighties:*

Perspectives and Prospects (Washington, D.C.: Government Printing Office, 1980), 5–25, 102; Sugrue, "Carter's Urban Policy Crisis," 152 (quotation); Orlebeke, "Chasing Urban Policy," 198; Eisinger, "The Search for a National Urban Policy, 1968–1980," 14–15.

44. President's Commission for a National Agenda for the Eighties, *Urban America in the Eighties*, 101.

45. Ibid., 102–106; Robert C. Wood, *Whatever Possessed the President? Academic Experts and Presidential Policy, 1960–1988* (Amherst: University of Massachusetts Press, 1993), 156 (quotation); Nathan, *A New Agenda for Cities*, 39–40.

46. Rich, "UDAG, Economic Development, and the Death and Life of American Cities," 150–151; Mollenkopf, *The Contested City*, 278–279.

47. Susan S. Jacobs and Elizabeth A. Roistacher, "The Urban Impacts of HUD's Urban Development Action Grant Program, or Where's the Action in Action Grants?" 336–348, 359; Congressional Quarterly, *Urban America, Policies and Problems*, 69–70; William K. Tabb, "The Failures of National Urban Policy," in *Marxism and the Metropolis: New Perspectives in Urban Political Economy*, ed. William K. Tabb and Larry Sawers (New York: Oxford University Press, 1984), 258–259; *New York Times*, March 26, 1982 (quotation).

48. Rich, "UDAG, Economic Development, and the Death and Life of American Cities," 150 (quotations); Mollenkopf, *The Contested City*, 279. Also see Nicholas Dagen Bloom, *Merchant of Illusion: America's Salesman of the Businessman's Utopia* (Columbus: Ohio State University Press, 2004).

49. *New York Times*, June 1, 1980; Hanson, *The Evolution of National Urban Policy, 1970–1980*, 59–65; Kaufman and Kaufman, *The Presidency of James Earl Carter, Jr.*, 221–222; Sugrue, "Carter's Urban Policy Crisis," 152.

CHAPTER 8. RONALD REAGAN'S
NEW FEDERALISM

1. William H. Chafe, *The Unfinished Journey: America since World War II*, 5th ed. (New York: Oxford University Press, 2003), 455–457; Haynes Johnson, *Sleepwalking through History: America in the Reagan Years* (New York: W. W. Norton, 1991), 242–244; Demetrios Caraley, "Washington Abandons the Cities," *Political Science Quarterly* 107 (Spring 1992): 2; James T. Patterson, *Restless Giant: The United States from Watergate to Bush v. Gore* (New York: Oxford University Press, 2005), 153 (Reagan quotation). On the Reagan presidency, see Michael Schaller, *Reckoning with Reagan: America and Its President in the 1980s* (New York: Oxford University Press, 1992); Robert Dallek, *Ronald Reagan: The Politics of Symbolism* (Cambridge: Harvard University Press, 1999); Lou Cannon, *President Reagan: The Role of a Lifetime* (New York: Simon and Schuster, 2000); Garry Wills, *Reagan's America: Innocents at Home* (New York: Penguin, 2000); and W. Elliot Brownlee and Hugh Davis Graham, eds., *The Reagan Presidency: Pragmatic Conservatism and Its Legacies* (Lawrence: University Press of Kansas, 2003).

2. David C. Schwartz, Richard C. Ferlanto, and Daniel N. Hoffman, *A New Housing Policy for America: Recapturing the American Dream* (Philadelphia: Temple University Press, 1988), 47. On Reagan and the cities, see George E. Peterson and Carol W. Lewis, eds., *Reagan and the Cities* (Washington, D.C.: Urban Institute Press, 1986); Richard P. Nathan, Fred C. Doolittle, and Associates, *The Consequences of Cuts: The Effects of the Reagan Domestic Program on State and Local Governments* (Princeton: Princeton Urban and Regional Research Center, 1983); Harold Wolman, "The Reagan Urban Policy and Its Impacts," *Urban Affairs Quarterly* 21 (March 1986): 311–335; Robert Benenson, "Reagan and the Cities," *Editorial Research Reports* 2 (July 23, 1982): 531–548; Norman J. Glickman, "Economic Policy and the Cities: In Search of Reagan's Real Urban Policy," *Journal of the American Planning Association* 50 (Autumn 1984): 471–478; and Neal M. Cohen, "The Reagan Administration's Urban Policy," *Town Planning Review* 54 (July 1983): 304–315.

3. Schaller, *Reckoning with Reagan*, 27 (first quotation); Patterson, *Restless Giant*, 148 (second quotation); Cohen, "The Reagan Administration's Urban Policy," 304 (third quotation).

4. Peter Dreier, "Reagan's Legacy: Homelessness in America," 3, http://www.nhi.org/online/issues/135/reagan.html; Schaller, *Reckoning with Reagan*, 77 (quotation).

5. U.S. Department of Housing and Urban Development, *The President's National Urban Policy Report, 1982* (Washington, D.C.: Government Printing Office, 1982), 4–32; Timothy J. Conlan, *New Federalism: Intergovernmental Reform from Nixon to Reagan* (Washington, D.C.: Brookings Institution, 1988), 223 (quotation); Cohen, "The Reagan Administration's Urban Policy," 305–306.

6. Cohen, "The Reagan Administration's Urban Policy," 306.

7. Patterson, *Restless Giant*, 149–150; Peter Dreier, John Mollenkopf, and Todd Swanstrom, *Place Matters: Metropolitics for the Twenty-first Century*, 2nd rev. ed. (Lawrence: University Press of Kansas, 2004), 138–139.

8. "Remarks at the Mid-Winter Congressional City Conference of the National League of Cities," March 2, 1981, pp. 5–6, Public Papers of Ronald Reagan, Ronald Reagan Presidential Library, http://www.reagan.utexas.edu/archives/speeches/public papers.html.

9. *Congressional Record*, 97th Cong., 1st sess., January 22, 1981, vol. 127, pt. 1, 753 (Pierce quotation), 754–757, 779; Joseph Foote, "As They Saw It: HUD's Secretaries Reminisce about Carrying out the Mission," *Cityscape* 1 (September 1995): 85.

10. Irving Welfeld, *HUD Scandals: Howling Headlines and Silent Fiascoes* (New Brunswick, N.J.: Transaction Publishers, 1992), 71.

11. *Congressional Record*, 97th Cong., 1st sess., January 22, 1981, vol. 127, pt. 1, 757–760, 779.

12. Schaller, *Reckoning with Reagan*, 45 (quotation).

13. *Congressional Quarterly Almanac*, 97th Cong., 1st sess., 1981, vol. 37 (Washington, D.C.: Congressional Quarterly Service, 1982), 28; Nathan, Doolittle, and Associates, *The Consequences of Cuts*, 6–8, 92, 115, 118, 146; Michael J. Rich, "UDAG, Economic Development, and the Death and Life of American Cities," *Economic Development Quarterly* 6 (May 1992): 151. John J. Gunther, chief of staff of the USCM,

credited pressure from his organization for saving UDAGs. John J. Gunther, *Federal-City Relations in the United States: The Role of the Mayors in Federal Aid to Cities* (Newark: University of Delaware Press, 1990), 251–252.

14. Kenneth A. Gibson to Ronald Reagan, January 11, 1982, WHORM Subject File, Federal Aid to Housing (FA004), box 33, folder 052600–059999, Ronald Reagan Presidential Library, Simi Valley California; John J. Gunther, *Federal-City Relations in the United States*, 254 (Hatcher quotations); Cardiss Collins to Ronald Reagan, telegram, April 7, 1982, WHORM Subject File, Housing (HS), box 1, folder 070000–072203, Ronald Reagan Presidential Library; Jack Kemp to Ronald Reagan, April 9, 1981, WHORM Subject File, Federal Aid to Transportation (FA007), box 50, folder 020000–024999, Ronald Reagan Presidential Library (Kemp quotation).

15. *Congressional Quarterly Almanac*, 97th Cong., 2nd sess., 1982, vol. 38 (Washington, D.C.: Congressional Quarterly Service, 1983), 68; William K. Tabb, "The Failures of Urban Policy," in *Marxism and the Metropolis: New Perspectives in Urban Political Economy*, ed. William K. Tabb and Larry Sawers (New York: Oxford University Press, 1984), 267; *Public Papers of the Presidents: Ronald Reagan, 1982* (Washington, D.C.: Government Printing Office, 1983), 1:76 (quotation); Paul Pierson, *Dismantling the Welfare State? Reagan, Thatcher, and the Politics of Retrenchment* (Cambridge: Cambridge University Press, 1994), 75–87; Glickman, "Economic Policy and the Cities," 474; Marc Bendick Jr. and David W. Rasmussen, "Enterprise Zones and Inner-City Economic Revitalization," in *Reagan and the Cities*, ed. George E. Peterson and Carol W. Lewis (Washington, D.C.: Urban Institute Press, 1986), 103–104.

16. Benenson, "Reagan and the Cities," 546–548.

17. "Message to the Congress Transmitting Proposed Enterprise Zones Legislation," March 23, 1982, pp. 1–5, Public Papers of Ronald Reagan, Ronald Reagan Presidential Library, http://www.reagan.utexas.edu/archives/speeches/1982/32382b.htm; *Congressional Quarterly Almanac*, 97th Cong., 2nd sess., 1982, vol. 38, 68; *Public Papers of the Presidents: Ronald Reagan, 1982*, 1:352–353.

18. Shannon Fairbanks to Karna Small Stringer, memorandum, June 1, 1982, WHORM Subject File, Housing (HS), box 2, folder 101971, Ronald Reagan Presidential Library; Samuel R. Pierce Jr. to Working Group on Housing Policy, memorandum, September 28, 1982, WHORM Subject File, Cabinet Council Files, box 27, folder FG 010-02 (077512–077513); Chester Hartman, "Housing Policies under the Reagan Administration," in *Critical Perspectives on Housing*, ed. Rachel G. Bratt, Chester Hartman, and Ann Meyerson (Philadelphia: Temple University Press, 1986), 363 (quotations).

19. Roger S. Ahlbrandt Jr., "Ideology and the Reagan Administration's First National Urban Policy Report," *Journal of the American Planning Association* 50 (Autumn 1984): 479–481; E. S. Savas, *Privatization: The Key to Better Government* (Chatham, N.J.: Chatham House, 1987), xi, 142, 196.

20. Roger S. Ahlbrandt Jr., "Ideology and the Reagan Administration's First National Urban Policy Report," 479–481; Richard Child Hill, "Federalism and Urban Policy: The Intergovernmental Dialectic," in *The Changing Face of Fiscal Federalism*, ed. Thomas R. Swartz and John E. Peck (Armonk, NY: M. E. Sharpe, 1990), 40,

53n16. For a full explication of Savas's views, see his *Privatization: The Key to Better Government*; "A Positive Urban Policy," *Urban Affairs Quarterly* 18 (June 1983): 447–453; and *Privatization and Public-Private Partnerships* (New York: Seven Bridges Press, 2000).

21. *New York Times*, June 20, 1982 (first and second quotations); Benenson, "Reagan and the Cities," 535 (third quotation).

22. Benenson, "Reagan and the Cities," 535 (quotations); George E. Peterson, "Urban Policy and the Cyclical Behavior of Cities," in *Reagan and the Cities*, ed. George E. Peterson and Carol W. Lewis (Washington, D.C.: Urban Institute Press, 1986), 17.

23. Peterson, "Urban Policy and the Cyclical Behavior of Cities," 11.

24. Ahlbrandt, "Ideology and the Reagan Administration's First National Urban Policy Report," 482–483.

25. *New York Times*, July 10, 1982.

26. Ahlbrandt, "Ideology and the Reagan Administration's First National Urban Policy Report," 482–483; Savas, "A Positive Urban Policy for the Future," 447–453; Pierson, *Dismantling the Welfare State?* 87; Wolman, "The Reagan Urban Policy and Its Impacts," 311–312; Cohen, "The Reagan Administration's Urban Policy," 304.

27. Benenson, "Reagan and the Cities," 533 (first quotation), 534 (second quotation).

28. Ibid., 533–534.

29. Richard G. Lugar to other U.S. senators, June 17, 1982, Robert Kabel Files, box 4, folder Lugar Housing Bill, Ronald Reagan Presidential Library (quotation); *Congressional Quarterly Almanac*, 97th Cong., 2nd sess., 1982, vol. 38, 71; William G. Johnson, "Housing Policy under the Reagan Presidency: The Demise of an Iron-Triangle," *Policy Studies Review* 10 (Winter 1991–1992): 80–81.

30. Johnson, "Housing Policy under the Reagan Presidency," 81; "Talking Points: Reasons to Oppose the Lugar Bill," March 23, 1982, WHORM Subject File, Federal Aid to Housing (FA004), box 33, folder 086000–091999, Ronald Reagan Presidential Library; "Meeting with Senator Richard Lugar and Senator Jake Garn," June 21, 1982, Robert Kabel Files, box 4, folder Lugar Housing Bill; *Public Papers of the Presidents: Ronald Reagan, 1982*, 1:814–816; "Veto Message on Urgent Supplemental and Housing Stimulus Bill," June 23, 1982, Office of Speechwriting, Speech Drafts, box 43, folder Veto Message on Urgent Supplemental and Housing Stimulus Bill, Ronald Reagan Presidential Library (quotation); *Congressional Quarterly Almanac*, 97th Cong., 2nd sess., 1982, vol. 38, 205, 212.

31. Raymond A. Mohl, "Shifting Patterns of American Urban Policy since 1900," in *Urban Policy in Twentieth-Century America*, ed. Arnold R. Hirsch and Raymond A. Mohl (New Brunswick, N.J.: Rutgers University Press, 1993), 24–25; Schaller, *Reckoning with Reagan*, 108–115.

32. "Talking Points against Gonzalez Amendments to H.R. 1; Housing and Urban-Rural Recovery Act of 1983," July 11, 1983, WHORM Subject File, Federal Aid to Housing (FA004), box 34, folder 151000–156999, Ronald Reagan Presidential Library (first quotation); *Congressional Quarterly Almanac*, 98th Cong., 1st sess., 1983,

vol. 39 (Washington, D.C.: Congressional Quarterly Service, 1984), 280 (second quotation); Pierson, *Dismantling the Welfare State?* 89.

33. *Congressional Quarterly Almanac*, 98th Cong., 1st sess., 1983, vol. 39, 277–283 (quotation on p. 277); Johnson, "Housing Policy under the Reagan Presidency," 81–82.

34. George V. Voinovich to Ronald Reagan, January 31, 1985, WHORM Subject File, Federal Aid to Housing (FA004), box 34, folder 272000–279965, Ronald Reagan Presidential Library; *Congressional Quarterly Almanac*, 99th Cong., 1st sess., 1985, vol. 41 (Washington, D.C.: Congressional Quarterly Service, 1986), 22, 303–305.

35. *Washington Post*, January 29, 1986, clipping, Daniel P. Moynihan Papers, pt. 2, box 1842, folder HUD Programs UDAG Legislation and Policy, General, 1985–1989, Library of Congress, Washington, D.C. (first quotation); John Heinz to Ronald Reagan, January 7, 1987, WHORM Subject File, Federal Aid to Housing (FA004), box 35, folder 386000–494999, Ronald Reagan Presidential Library; Carroll Hubbard to Ronald Reagan, February 7, 1986, WHORM Subject File, Federal Aid to Housing (FA004), box 35, folder 348000–385999, Ronald Reagan Presidential Library; Daniel Patrick Moynihan to Ronald Reagan, March 5, 1986, Daniel P. Moynihan Papers, pt. 2, box 1836, folder HUD Programs, CDBG, Legislation and Policy Correspondence, 1984–1987, Library of Congress (second quotation). Also see Daniel Patrick Moynihan to Ronald Reagan, January 6, 1987, Daniel P. Moynihan Papers, pt. 2, box 1842, folder HUD Programs UDAG Legislation and Policy, General, 1985–1989, Library of Congress.

36. "1986 National Urban Policy Report," July 25, 1986, p. 8, WHORM Subject File, Domestic Policy Council Files, box 70, folder FG010-03 (317/66)-1, Ronald Reagan Presidential Library (first quotation); "Executive Summary of the 1986 National Urban Policy Report," July 25, 1986, pp. 1–2, Thomas F. Gibson III Files, box 1, folder HUD (1), Ronald Reagan Presidential Library; "Minutes, Domestic Policy Council," August 6, 1986, p. 2, WHORM Subject File, Domestic Policy Council Files, box 70, folder FG010-03 (317166)-1, Ronald Reagan Presidential Library (second quotation).

37. *Congressional Quarterly Almanac*, 100th Cong., 1st sess., 1987, vol. 43 (Washington, D.C.: Congressional Quarterly Service, 1988), 685; Hartman, "Housing Policies under the Reagan Administration," 363–365; Mary K. Nenno, "Reagan's '88 Budget: Dismantling HUD," *Journal of Housing* 44 (May–June 1987): 106; Pierson, *Dismantling the Welfare State?* 88.

38. *Congressional Quarterly Almanac*, 100th Cong., 1st sess., 1987, vol. 43, 509 (quotation), 682–691; Willem van Vliet, ed., *The Encyclopedia of Housing* (Thousand Oaks, Calif.: Sage Publications, 1998), 560–561.

39. *Congressional Quarterly Almanac*, 100th Cong., 1st sess., 1987, vol. 43, 682–691; Joseph R. Wright Jr. to Phil Gramm, October 30, 1987, David Bokorny Files, box 1, folder Housing [1], Ronald Reagan Presidential Library (quotation); Johnson, "Housing Policy under the Reagan Presidency," 82.

40. "Presidential Remarks: Signing Ceremony for Housing Bill, Friday, February 5, 1988," Office of Speechwriting, Speech Drafts, box 380, folder Signing Ceremony for Housing Bill, Feb. 5, 1988 [1], Ronald Reagan Presidential Library (quotations);

Public Papers of the Presidents: Ronald Reagan, 1988(Washington, D.C.: Government Printing Office, 1990), 1:176–178; Congressional *Quarterly Almanac*, 100th Cong., 1st sess., 1987, vol. 43, 682–691; Pierson, *Dismantling the Welfare State?* 91.

41. "Presidential Remarks: Signing Ceremony for Housing Bill, Friday, February 5, 1988," 2–3; Pierson, *Dismantling the Welfare State?* 87; Jack Kemp to Donald Regan, February 4, 1987, WHORM Subject File, Housing (HS), box 12, folder 612000–End, Ronald Reagan Presidential Library (first quotation); T. Kenneth Cribb Jr. to the President, memorandum, November 20, 1987, T. Kenneth Cribb Files, box 2, folder Housing [2], Ronald Reagan Presidential Library; Gary L. Bauer to Donald Regan, February 10, 1987, WHORM Subject File, Housing (HS), box 12, folder 612000–End, Ronald Reagan Presidential Library (second quotation).

42. "Presidential Remarks: Signing Ceremony for Housing Bill, Friday, February 5, 1988," 3.

43. Robert C. Weaver, "The First Twenty Years of HUD," *Journal of the American Planning Association* 51(Autumn 1985): 469 (first quotation); "Statement of Protest," n.d., Melvin Bradley Files, box 5, folder Department of HUD (2 of 4), Ronald Reagan Presidential Library (second quotation); *Los Angeles Times*, "HUD Chief Accused of 'Blatant Racism,'" July 13, 1982, clipping in Melvin Bradley Files, box 5, folder Department of HUD (3 of 4), Ronald Reagan Presidential Library; *Wall Street Journal*, "HUD Chief Pierce Gets Reputation for Reclusiveness, Lack of Interest," April 1, 1983, clipping in Edwin Meese Files, box 30, folder HUD—Sec. Samuel R. Pierce Jr., Ronald Reagan Presidential Library (third, fourth, and fifth quotations).

44. *Washington Post*, "Fair Housing," April 21, 1983, clipping in Melvin Bradley Files, box 5, folder Department of HUD (2 of 4), Ronald Reagan Presidential Library; Hartman, "Housing Policies during the Reagan Administration," 374–375; Gary Orfield, "Separate Societies: Have the Kerner Warnings Come True?" in *Quiet Riots: Race and Poverty in the United States*, ed. Fred R. Harris and Roger W. Wilkins (New York: Pantheon Books, 1988), 110; James A. Kushner, "Federal Enforcement and Judicial Review of the Fair Housing Amendments Act of 1988," *Housing Policy Debate* 3 (1992): 547 (quotation).

45. *Washington Post*, "Fair Housing," April 21, 1983, clipping in Melvin Bradley Files, box 5, folder Department of HUD (2 of 4), Ronald Reagan Presidential Library; Hartman, "Housing Policies under the Reagan Administration," 375; Orfield, "Separate Societies," 110; Dreier, "Reagan's Legacy," 2; Kushner, "Federal Enforcement and Judicial Review of the Fair Housing Amendments Act of 1988," 545–546; *Washington Post*, "Fair Housing Law Questioned," July 11, 1984, clipping in Christena Bach Files, box 1, folder Fair Housing [1], Ronald Reagan Presidential Library (quotation).

46. Michael M. Uhlmann to Edwin L. Harper, January 13, 1983, WHORM Subject Files, Housing (HS), box 3, folder 112000–117772, Ronald Reagan Presidential Library; *Presidential Papers of the Presidents, 1983* (Washington, D.C.: Government Printing Office, 1983), 1:107; untitled speech by Samuel R. Pierce Jr., undated, pp. 1–2, Christena Bach Files, box 1, folder Fair Housing [3], Ronald Reagan Presidential

Library; Hugh Davis Graham, "The Surprising Career of Federal Fair Housing Law," *Journal of Policy History* 12, no. 2 (2000): 222–224.

47. *Congressional Quarterly Almanac*, 100th Cong., 2nd sess., 1988, vol. 44 (Washington, D.C.: Congressional Quarterly Service, 1989), 68–73; Graham, "The Surprising Career of Federal Fair Housing Law," 224–225; "Presidential Remarks: Signing Ceremony for Fair Housing Act, Tuesday, September 13, 1988," p. 2, Phillip Brady Files, box 1, folder Fair Housing Amendment [3], Ronald Reagan Presidential Library; Charles M. Lamb, *Housing Segregation in Suburban America since 1960: Presidential and Judicial Politics* (Cambridge: Cambridge University Press, 2005), 186 (quotation); Greene, *The Presidency of George Bush*, 18; Foote, "As They Saw It," 86.

48. "Presidential Remarks: Signing Ceremony for Fair Housing Act, Tuesday, September 13, 1988," 3.

49. *Washington Post*, "Playing Games with Fair Housing," September 18, 1988, clipping, Phillip Brady Files, box 1, folder Fair Housing Amendment [3]; Kushner, "Federal Enforcement and Judicial Review of the Fair Housing Amendments Act of 1988," 585–587.

50. Benenson, "Reagan and the Cities," 537–539; *Congressional Quarterly Almanac*, 97th Cong., 2nd sess., 1982, vol. 38, 22; Nathan, Doolittle, and Associates, *The Consequences of Cuts*, 118.

51. *Congressional Quarterly Almanac*, 97th Cong., 2nd sess., 1982, vol. 38, 22, 315–322; Bill Green et al. to Ronald Reagan, December 6, 1982, WHORM Subject File, Federal Aid to Transportation (FA007), box 51, folder 110000–115999, Ronald Reagan Presidential Library.

52. Alfonse D'Amato to Ronald Reagan, February 3, 1983 (first quotation), David A. Stockman to Alfonse D'Amato, March 24, 1983, Elizabeth Hanford Dole to Alfonse D'Amato, May 2, 1983 (second quotation), WHORM Subject File, Federal Aid to Transportation (FA007), box 51, folder 116000–129999, Ronald Reagan Presidential Library; *Congressional Quarterly Almanac*, 97th Cong., 2nd sess., 1982, vol. 38, 316.

53. *Congressional Quarterly Almanac*, 99th Cong., 1st sess., 1985, vol. 41 (Washington, D.C.: Congressional Quarterly Service, 1986), 268, 437; Tom Bradley to Ronald Reagan, February 27, 1985 (first quotation), Lee L. Verstandig to Tom Bradley, March 19, 1985 (second quotation), WHORM Subject File, Federal Aid to Transportation (FA007), box 52, folder 289000–290999, Ronald Reagan Presidential Library; *Congressional Quarterly Almanac*, 99th Cong., 2nd sess., 1986, vol. 42 (Washington, D.C.: Congressional Quarterly Service, 1987), 28.

54. Elizabeth H. Dole to Howard H. Baker Jr., memorandum, March 3, 1987, WHORM Subject File, Federal Aid to Transportation (FA007), box 53, folder 473400–484699, Ronald Reagan Presidential Library; Bill Clinton et al. to Ronald Reagan, March 24, 1987, WHORM Subject File, Federal Aid to Transportation (FA007), box 53, folder 472651–472785, Ronald Reagan Presidential Library; "Statement by the President," March 20, 1987, Anthony Dolan Files, box 51, folder Veto Announcement of Highway and Transportation Bill, Ronald Reagan Presidential Library; *Public Papers of the Presidents: Ronald Reagan, 1987* (Washington, D.C.:

Government Printing Office, 1989), 1:266; "President Ronald Reagan and the Surface Transportation and Uniform Relocation Assistance Act of 1987," U.S. Department of Transportation, http://www.fhwa.dot.gov/infrastructure/rw01e.cfm; *Congressional Quarterly Almanac*, 100th Cong., 1st sess., 1987, vol. 43 (Washington, D.C.: Congressional Quarterly Service, 1988), 25, 331.

55. "The President's National Urban Policy Report, 1988," p. 2, WHORM Subject File, Domestic Policy Council Files, box 81, folder FG010-03 (490767)-5, Ronald Reagan Presidential Library (quotation); "White Paper: President's Housing Policy," August 6, 1987, T. Kenneth Cribb Files, box 2, folder Housing Bill—8/14/87, Ronald Reagan Presidential Library.

56. Gunther, *Federal-City Relations in the United States*, 254–255; Schaller, *Reckoning with Reagan*, 116; Nenno, "Reagan's '88 Budget," 104–105; Schwartz, Ferlanto, and Hoffman, *A New Housing Policy for America*, 47; Welfeld, *HUD Scandals*, 148 (quotation).

57. Schwartz, Ferlanto, and Hoffman, *A New Housing Policy for America*, 47; Hill, "Federalism and Urban Policy," 45; Rich, "UDAG, Economic Development, and the Death and Life of American Cities," 151; *Congressional Quarterly Almanac*, 100th Cong., 2nd sess., 1988, vol. 44, 23; Foote, "As They Saw It," 85 (quotation).

58. Foote, "As They Saw It," 86 (first, second, and third quotations); Johnson, *Sleepwalking through History*, 179–180; Welfeld, *HUD Scandals*, 72; "The HUD Ripoff," *Newsweek* 114 (August 7, 1989): 16 (fourth quotation).

59. Eric Addison, "HUD: The Real Scandal," *Journal of Housing* 46 (November/December 1989): 288.

60. "The HUD Ripoff," 19 (first quotation); Johnson, *Sleepwalking through History*, 180; Addison, "HUD," 288.

61. "The HUD Ripoff," 20–21; Addison, "HUD," 292 (quotation).

62. Johnson, *Sleepwalking through History*, 182–183; *Wall Street Journal*, May 25, 1989 (first quotation); Addison, "HUD," 288–289; "The HUD Ripoff," 18 (second quotation); *New York Times*, February 25, 1994.

63. Addison, "HUD," 289.

64. "The HUD Ripoff," 20 (first quotation), 21 (second quotation); Leonard Lurie, *Senator Pothole: The Unauthorized Biography of Al D'Amato* (New York: Carol Publishing Group, 1994), 457–462.

65. "The HUD Ripoff," 17 (first and second quotations), 18 (third quotation).

66. Ibid., 18; Eric Addison, "HUD," 290–293; Irving Welfeld, *HUD Scandals*, 72; Mark Grossman, *Political Corruption in America: An Encyclopedia of Scandals, Power, and Greed* (Santa Barbara: ABC-Clio, 2003), 173 (quotation).

67. Johnson, "Housing Policy under the Reagan Presidency," 70; D. Bradford Hunt, *Blueprint for Disaster: The Unraveling of Chicago Public Housing* (Chicago: University of Chicago Press, 2009), 265–266; Schaller, *Reckoning with Reagan*, 116; Johnson, *Sleepwalking through History*, 168, 182–183. Also see D. Bradford Hunt, "Rethinking the Retrenchment Narrative in U.S. Housing Policy History," *Journal of Urban History* 32 (September 2006): 937–950.

68. Dreier, "Reagan's Legacy," 2; Caraley, "Washington Abandons the Cities," 7–12.

69. Cohen, "The Reagan Administration's Urban Policy," 308–310; Alice O'Connor, "Swimming against the Tide: A Brief History of Federal Policy in Poor Communities," in *Urban Problems and Community Development*, ed. Ronald F. Ferguson and William T. Dickens (Washington, D.C.: Brookings Institution Press, 1999), 113–115; Dreier, Mollenkopf, and Swanstrom, *Place Matters*, 140; Glickman, "Economic Policy and the Cities," 471–478. Also see Frances Fox Piven and Richard A. Cloward, *The New Class War: Reagan's Attack on the Welfare State and Its Consequences* (New York: Pantheon, 1982). The first extensive discussion of the underclass came in Ken Auletta, *The Underclass* (New York: Random House, 1982). Also consult Michael B. Katz, ed., *The "Underclass" Debate: Views from History* (Princeton: Princeton University Press, 1993).

70. Schwartz, Ferlanto, and Hoffman, *A New Housing Policy for America*, 201–205; Schaller, *Reckoning with Reagan*, 78–79; Dreier, "Reagan's Legacy," 4 (quotation).

71. Patterson, *Restless Giant*, 162 (first quotation); Thomas J. Sugrue, *Sweet Land of Liberty: The Forgotten Struggle for Civil Rights in the North* (New York: Random House, 2008), 524; Caraley, "Washington Abandons the Cities," 6–7; Sandra S. Osbourn, "The Federal Government and the Entrepreneurial City," *Congressional Research Service Review*, clipping, Daniel P. Moynihan Papers, pt. 2, box 2369, folder Urban Issues, 1987–1988, Library of Congress; Dennis R. Judd and Todd Swanstrom, *City Politics: Private Power and Public Policy* (New York: Longman, 1998), 235 (second quotation); Robert C. Wood, *Whatever Possessed the President? Academic Experts and Presidential Policy, 1960–1988* (Amherst: University of Massachusetts Press, 1993), 158; Mohl, "Shifting Patterns of American Urban Policy," 25–26; O'Connor, "Swimming against the Tide," 114.

CHAPTER 9. GEORGE H. W. BUSH'S
NEW FEDERALISM

1. Yvonne Scruggs, "HUD's Stewardship of National Urban Policy: A Retrospective View," *Cityscape* 1 (September 1995): 55 (quotation).

2. James T. Patterson, *Restless Giant: The United States from Watergate to Bush v. Gore* (New York: Oxford University Press, 2005), 224 (first quotation); Herbert S. Parmet, *George Bush: The Life of a Lone Star Yankee* (New York: Scribner, 1997), 349 (second quotation); Thomas Byrne Edsall, *Chain Reaction: The Impact of Race, Rights, and Taxes on American Politics*, with Mary D. Edsall (New York: W. W. Norton, 1991), 215–227; John Robert Greene, *The Presidency of George Bush* (Lawrence: University Press of Kansas, 2000), 37–39; *Congressional Quarterly Almanac*, 100th Cong., 2nd sess., 1988, vol. 44 (Washington, D.C.: Congressional Quarterly Service, 1989), 6-A.

3. *Public Papers of the Presidents: George Bush, 1989* (Washington, D.C.: Government Printing Office, 1990), 1:1–4 (quotations); *New York Times*, January 21, 1989; Greene, *The Presidency of George Bush*, 54.

4. Joseph Foote, "As They Saw It: Secretaries Reminisce about Carrying out the Mission," *Cityscape* 1 (September 1995): 87–88; William R. Barnes, "Urban Policies and Urban Impacts after Reagan," *Urban Affairs Quarterly* 25 (June 1990): 564–565; *Wall Street Journal*, February 16, 1989 (quotation). Many of Kemp's fundamental ideas are presented in his *An American Renaissance: Strategy for the 1980s* (New York: Harper & Row, 1979).

5. Scruggs, "HUD's Stewardship of National Urban Policy," 56; George Bush to Dan Rostenkowski, July 25, 1989, Daniel P. Moynihan Papers, pt. 2, box 1836, folder HUD Programs, Economic Dev. Zones, General, 1987–1990, n.d., Library of Congress, Washington, D.C.; U.S. Department of Housing and Urban Development, Office of Policy Development and Research, "The President's National Urban Policy Report, 1990," 11/20/90, 12–13, Records Management, White House Office of Records Management (WHORM), FG 23, box 311, folder Case No. 199292, George H. W. Bush Presidential Library, College Station, Tex.; *Washington Post*, July 9, 1990 (quotation).

6. Andre Shashaty, "Jack Kemp's Free Ride," *American Journalism Review* 15 (May 1993): 18; "The HUD Ripoff," *Newsweek* 114 (August 7, 1989): 16–22; Eric Addison, "HUD: The Real Scandal," *Journal of Housing* 46 (November–December 1989): 287–295.

7. *Congressional Quarterly Almanac*, 101st Cong., 1st sess., 1989, vol. 45 (Washington, D.C.: Congressional Quarterly Service, 1990), 27, 631; Shashaty, "Jack Kemp's Free Ride," 18 (quotation).

8. *Public Papers of the Presidents: George Bush, 1989* (Washington, D.C.: Government Printing Office, 1990), 2:1704–1705; *Congressional Quarterly Almanac*, 101st Cong., 1st sess., 1989, vol. 45, 633 (quotations).

9. *Congressional Quarterly Almanac*, 101st Cong., 1st sess., 1989, vol. 45, 635 (quotations).

10. Ibid., 634–638.

11. Ibid., 635 (quotation); Richard G. Darman to George Bush, memorandum, December 13, 1989, WHORM, FG 23, box 310, folder 096365 [1 of 3], George H. W. Bush Presidential Library.

12. *Congressional Quarterly Almanac*, 101st Cong., 1st sess., 1989, vol. 45, 653; *Public Papers of the Presidents: George Bush, 1989*, vol. 2, 1492 (first quotation); *New York Times*, November 11, 1989, clipping, Daniel P. Moynihan Papers, pt. 2, box 1847, folder National Affordable Housing Act, Press, 1988–1991, n.d., Library of Congress (second quotation).

13. U.S. Department of Housing and Urban Development, Office of Policy Development and Research, "The President's National Urban Policy Report, 1990," 10–16.

14. *New York Times*, October 12, 1990, clipping, vertical file, subject file, box 37, folder HUD, 9/25/90–12/26/90, George H. W. Bush Presidential Library; *Congressional Quarterly Almanac*, 101st Cong., 2nd sess., 1990, vol. 46 (Washington, D.C.: Congressional Quarterly Service, 1991), 632; Shashaty, "Jack Kemp's Free Ride," 19.

15. American Jewish Committee et al. to George Bush, March 28, 1990, WHORM, box 4, folder HS [128130–163968]; *Congressional Quarterly Almanac*, 101st Cong., 2nd sess., 1990, vol. 46, 632–633.

16. *Congressional Quarterly Almanac,* 101st Cong., 2nd sess., 1990, vol. 46, 634–635.

17. Ibid., 635.

18. *Buffalo News,* June 23, 1990, clipping, Daniel P. Moynihan Papers, pt. 2, box 1847, folder National Affordable Housing Act, Press, 1988–1991, n.d. (quotation); Jill Zuckman, "Politically Resonant Decisions Loom over Housing Aid," *Congressional Quarterly Weekly Report* 48 (September 8, 1990): 2829–2834; *Nation's City Weekly,* July 16, 1990, clipping, Daniel P. Moynihan Papers, pt. 2, box 1847, folder National Affordable Housing Act, Press, 1988–1991, n.d.; *Congressional Quarterly Almanac,* 101st Cong., 2nd sess., 1990, vol. 46, 640.

19. Morton J. Schussheim, "The Cranston-Gonzalez National Affordable Housing Act: Key Provisions and Analysis," *CRS Report for Congress,* January 31, 1991, in Daniel P. Moynihan Papers, pt. 2, box 1847, folder National Affordable Housing Act Reports, 1988–1991, n.d., Library of Congress; *Public Papers of the Presidents: George Bush, 1990* (Washington, D.C.: Government Printing Office, 1991), 2:1701 (first quotation); "Remarks by the President in Signing Ceremony for National Affordable Housing Act," November 28, 1990, p. 2, Speech File Draft Files, box 76, folder Signing Ceremony for National Affordable Housing Act," 11/28/90, George H. W. Bush Presidential Library (second quotation).

20. Nathan J. Schwartz, "Cranston-Gonzalez National Affordable Housing Act (P.L. 101–625)," in *The Encyclopedia of Housing,* ed. Willem van Vliet (Thousand Oaks, Calif.: Sage, 1998), 94–95; Schussheim, "The Cranston-Gonzalez National Affordable Housing Act"; *Public Papers of the Presidents: George Bush, 1990,* 2:1700; Foote, "As They Saw It," 88–89.

21. *Congressional Quarterly Almanac,* 102nd Cong., 1st sess., 1991, vol. 47 (Washington, D.C.: Congressional Quarterly Service, 1992), 334, 516, 518; Shashaty, "Jack Kemp's Free Ride," 20 (quotation).

22. *New York Times,* February 14, 1991, clipping, vertical file, subject file, box 63, folder DOT, 1/3/91–3/23/91, George H. W. Bush Presidential Library; *Public Papers of the Presidents: George Bush, 1991* (Washington, D.C.: Government Printing Office, 1992), 1:141; *Congressional Quarterly Almanac,* 102nd Cong., 1st sess., 1991, vol. 47, 137–138.

23. Robert A. Peck, "Daniel Patrick Moynihan and the Fall and Rise of Public Works," in *Daniel Patrick Moynihan: The Intellectual in Public Life,* ed. Robert A. Katzmann (Washington, D.C.: Woodrow Wilson Center Press, 1998), 77–81; Godfrey Hodgson, *The Gentleman from New York: Daniel Patrick Moynihan, A Biography* (Boston: Houghton Mifflin, 2000), 225 (first quotation); *Washington Post,* June 22, 1991, clipping, vertical file, subject file, box 63, folder DOT, 6/19/91–9/14/91, George H. W. Bush Presidential Library; *New York Times,* February 14, 1991 (second quotation).

24. "Statement (As Amended) by Senator Daniel Patrick Moynihan on the Surface Transportation Efficiency Act of 1991," *Congressional Record,* clipping, Daniel P. Moynihan Papers, pt. 2, box 2844, folder Transportation 1991–1996; Robert A. Peck, "Daniel Patrick Moynihan and the Fall and Rise of Public Works," 80 (quotation);

New York Times, May 22, 1991, clipping, vertical file, subject file, box 63, folder DOT, 3/24/91—6/18/91, George H. W. Bush Presidential Library.

25. *New York Times*, May 22, 1991; *Washington Post*, June 22, 1991 (quotation).

26. *Public Papers of the Presidents: George Bush, 1991*, vol. I, p. 705; *Congressional Quarterly Almanac*, 102nd Cong., 1st sess., 1991, vol. 47, 10-E; *Washington Post*, June 22, 1991; *Congressional Record* clipping, 1–7; Robert A. Peck, "Daniel Patrick Moynihan and the Fall and Rise of Public Works," 80 .

27. *Congressional Quarterly Almanac*, 102nd Cong., 1st sess., 1991, vol. 47, 137–138; Samuel K. Skinner to George Bush, memorandum, November 26, 1991, Chief of Staff Files, John Sununu Files, box 105, folder Skinner (Transportation)—1991, George H. W. Bush Presidential Library; *New York Times*, December 19, 1991; *Public Papers of the Presidents: George Bush, 1991* (Washington, D.C.: Government Printing Office, 1992), 2:1632 (quotation).

28. Hodgson, *The Gentleman from New York*, 337–338; Samuel K. Skinner to George Bush, memorandum, November 26, 1991; Peck, "Daniel Patrick Moynihan and the Fall and Rise of Public Works," 81; *Congressional Quarterly Almanac*, 102nd Cong., 1st sess., 1991, vol. 47, 137–138; David Rusk, *Cities without Suburbs*, 3rd ed. (Washington, D.C.: Woodrow Wilson Center Press, 2003), 119. Also see Mark H. Rose, Bruce E. Seely, and Paul F. Barrett, *The Best Transportation System in the World: Railroads, Trucks, Airlines, and American Public Policy in the Twentieth Century* (Columbus: Ohio State University Press, 2006).

29. *Congressional Quarterly Almanac*, 102nd Cong., 2nd sess., 1992, vol. 48 (Washington, D.C.: Congressional Quarterly Service, 1993), 669–675.

30. "The Economic Crisis of Urban America," *Business Week* (May 18, 1992): 38–40; Ronald Berkman, Joyce F. Brown, Beverly Goldberg, and Tod Mijanovich, eds., *In the National Interest: The 1990 Urban Summit with Related Analyses, Transcript, and Papers* (New York: Twentieth Century Fund, 1992), 1; Demetrios Caraley, "Washington Abandons the Cities," *Political Science Quarterly* 107 (Summer 1992): 15–16.

31. Berkman et al., *In the National Interest*, 17.

32. Scruggs, "HUD's Stewardship of National Urban Policy," 56; David Mervin, *George Bush and the Guardianship Presidency* (New York: St. Martin's Press, 1996), 36–37 (quotation).

33. Shashaty, "Jack Kemp's Free Ride," 16 (first quotation); *Dallas Morning News*, December 19, 1991, clipping, White House Office of Chief of Staff, Sam Skinner Files, box 6, folder Memos and Correspondence, December 1991 [2 of 3], George H. W. Bush Presidential Library; *Washington Post*, December 29, 1992, clipping, vertical file, subject file, box 54, folder HUD, 8/14/92—12/31/92, George H. W. Bush Presidential Library (second quotation); *New York Times*, October 12, 1990, clipping, vertical file, subject file, box 37, folder HUD, 9/25/90—12/26/90, George H. W. Bush Presidential Library (third, fourth, and fifth quotations).

34. Patterson, *Restless Giant*, 244–245; Haynes Johnson, *Divided We Fall: Gambling with History in the Nineties* (New York: W. W. Norton, 1994), 170–200.

35. Patterson, *Restless Giant*, 245.

36. *Public Papers of the Presidents: George Bush, 1992–93* (Washington, D.C.: Government Printing Office, 1993), 1:685 (quotation); Greene, *The Presidency of George Bush*, 169; *Congressional Quarterly Almanac*, 102nd Cong., 2nd sess., 1992, vol. 48, 339–340.

37. *Washington Post*, May 3, 1992, clipping, vertical file, subject file, box 54, folder HUD, 1/1/92–6/3/92, George H. W. Bush Presidential Library (quotations); "Department of Housing and Urban Development Emergency Response to the Crisis in Los Angeles," n.d., Daniel Casse Files, box 1, folder L.A. Riots [2 of 2], George H. W. Bush Presidential Library.

38. Jack Kemp to George Bush, memorandum, May 4, 1992, Records Management, WHORM, FG 23, box 311, folder Case No. 321366–337925, George H. W. Bush Presidential Library.

39. *Washington Post*, May 3, 1992 (quotation); "Press Briefing by Marlin Fitzwater," May 4, 1992, White House Press Office Files, Marlin Fitzwater Files, box 18, folder Los Angeles [Riots & Recovery] [3], George H. W. Bush Presidential Library; Charles Kolb, *White House Daze: The Unmaking of Domestic Policy in the Bush Years* (New York: Free Press, 1994), 227.

40. "Press Briefing by Marlin Fitzwater," May 4, 1992 (quotations); *Presidential Papers of the Presidents: George Bush, 1992–93*, 1:687–688; Dennis R. Judd and Todd Swanstrom, *City Politics: Private Power and Public Policy* (New York: Longman, 1998), 214.

41. *Congressional Quarterly Almanac*, 102nd Cong., 2nd sess., 1992, vol. 48, 340 (quotations); *Presidential Papers of the Presidents: George Bush, 1992–93*, 1:704–708.

42. "The Economic Crisis of Urban America," 44 (first quotation); "Statement by Housing and Urban Development Secretary Jack Kemp," May 3, 1992, WHORM, FG 23, box 311, folder Case No. 321366–337925, George H. W. Bush Presidential Library; *Presidential Papers of the Presidents: George Bush, 1992–93*, 1:730–732; "Governor Clinton's Response to President Bush's Address to the Boys and Girls Club of America," May 8, 1992, Daniel Casse Files, box 1, folder L.A. Riots [1 of 2] (second and third quotations).

43. *Congressional Quarterly Almanac*, 102nd Cong., 2nd sess., 1992, vol. 48, 341–342; *Presidential Papers of the Presidents: George Bush, 1992–93*, 1:759–763; Michael J. Rich, "Riot and Reason: Crafting an Urban Policy Response," *Publius: The Journal of Federalism* 23 (Summer 1993): 117–121; Kolb, *The Unmaking of Domestic Policy in the Bush Years*, 228; Scruggs, "HUD's Stewardship of National Urban Policy," 56.

44. Rich, "Riot and Reason," 125; David Rusk, *Inside Game, Outside Game: Winning Strategies for Saving Urban America* (Washington, D.C.: Brookings Institution Press, 1999), 129.

45. *Congressional Quarterly Almanac*, 102nd Cong., 2nd sess., 1992, vol. 48, 341–343 (quotations); Rich, "Riot and Reason," 121.

46. *Congressional Quarterly Almanac*, 102nd Cong., 2nd sess., 1992, vol. 48, 340, 342; Kolb, *The Unmaking of Domestic Policy in the Bush Years*, 228.

47. *Congressional Quarterly Almanac*, 102nd Cong., 2nd sess., 1992, vol. 48, 340. Also see William Schneider, "The Suburban Century Begins," *Atlantic Monthly* 270 (July 1992): 33–44.

48. *Congressional Quarterly Almanac*, 102nd Cong., 2nd sess., 1992, vol. 48, 345; Rich, "Riot and Reason," 124 (quotation).

49. *Congressional Quarterly Almanac*, 102nd Cong., 2nd sess., 1992, vol. 48, 367–368; National Commission on Severely Distressed Public Housing, *Final Report of the National Commission on Severely Distressed Public Housing: A Report to the Congress and the Secretary of Housing and Urban Development* (Washington, D.C.: National Commission on Severely Distressed Public Housing, 1992), 1–10.

50. Jack Kemp to Henry B. Gonzalez, May 13, 1992, WHORM, box 3, folder HS [328810], George H. W. Bush Presidential Library.

51. *Congressional Quarterly Almanac*, 102nd Cong., 2nd sess., 1992, vol. 48, 367–375; *Public Papers of the Presidents: George Bush, 1992–93* (Washington, D.C.: Government Printing Office, 1993), 2:2060–2061.

52. Rich, "Riot and Reason," 127; "Memorandum of Disapproval for the Revenue Act of 1992," November 4, 1992, George H. W. Bush Presidential Library, http://bushlibrary.tamu.edu/research/papers/1992/92110401.html.

53. Shashaty, "Jack Kemp's Free Ride," 18 (second quotation), 22 (first quotation); Foote, "As They Saw It," 88 (third quotation).

54. *Washington Post*, May 24, 1992; Rachel Bratt and W. Dennis Keating, "Federal Housing Policy and HUD: Past Problems and Future Prospects of a Beleaguered Bureaucracy," *Urban Affairs Quarterly* 29 (September 1993): 25; Caraley, "Washington Abandons the Cities," 17–19.

55. Rich, "Riot and Reason," 115–117.

56. John P. Relman, "Federal Fair Housing Enforcement under President Bush: An Assessment at Mid-Term and Recommendations for the Future," in Citizens' Commission on Civil Rights, *New Opportunities: The Civil Rights Record of the Bush Administration Mid-Term* (Washington, D.C.: Citizens' Committee on Civil Rights, 1991), 117 (first quotation); Charles M. Lamb, *Housing Segregation in Suburban America since 1960: Presidential and Judicial Politics* (Cambridge, UK: Cambridge University Press, 2005), 186–190; Edsall, *Chain Reaction*, 230 (second quotation). Also see Christopher Bonastia, *Knocking on the Door: The Federal Government's Attempt to Desegregate the Suburbs* (Princeton: Princeton University Press, 2006), 145–166.

57. Peter Dreier, John Mollenkopf, and Todd Swanstrom, *Place Matters: Metropolitics for the Twenty-first Century* (Lawrence: University Press of Kansas, 2004), 139–140; Edsall, *Chain Reaction*, 230 (quotation).

CHAPTER 10. BILL CLINTON AND A "THIRD WAY" FOR URBAN AMERICA

1. John Mollenkopf, "Urban Policy at the Crossroads," in *The Social Divide: Political Parties and the Future of Activist Government*, ed. Margaret Weir (Washington,

D.C.: Brookings Institution Press, 1998), 473 (first quotation); Kenneth S. Baer, *Reinventing Democrats: The Politics of Liberalism from Reagan to Clinton* (Lawrence: University Press of Kansas, 2000), 7 (second quotation); Jon F. Hale, "The Making of the New Democrats," *Political Science Quarterly* 110 (Summer 1995): 28–29.

2. Jonathan Walters, "Not a Local Hero Anymore," *Governing* 6 (September 1993): 32.

3. Peter Dreier, John Mollenkopf, and Todd Swanstrom, *Place Matters: Metropolitics for the Twenty-first Century*, 2nd rev. ed. (Lawrence: University Press of Kansas, 2004), 141; Mollenkopf, "Urban Policy at the Crossroads," 475–476.

4. James T. Patterson, *Restless Giant: The United States from Watergate to Bush v. Gore* (New York: Oxford University Press, 2005), chap. 10; Dreier, Mollenkopf, and Swanstrom, *Place Matters*, 140–146.

5. *Congressional Quarterly Almanac*, 103rd Cong., 1st sess., 1993, vol. 49 (Washington, D.C.: Congressional Quarterly Service, 1994), 427 (quotation).

6. Paul Dimond to Gene Sperling and Bruce Reed, memorandum, February 21, 1993, Domestic Policy Council, Bruce Reed Subject Files, box 105, folder 12, William J. Clinton Presidential Library, Little Rock, Ark. (quotation); William Fulton, "HUDdling with Henry Cisneros," *Planning* 59 (September 1, 1993): 18; Henry Cisneros to Mack McLarty et al., memorandum, February 1, 1993, Domestic Policy Council, Bruce Reed Subject Files, box 118, folder 10; *Public Papers of the Presidents: William J. Clinton, 1993* (Washington, D.C.: Government Printing Office, 1994), 1:58.

7. Urban Task Force to George Stephanopoulos, memorandum, March 17, 1993, Domestic Policy Council, Bruce Reed Subject Files, box 118, folder 8; Lynn A. Curtis to Mack McLarty III and Robert E. Rubin, memorandum, July 26, 1993, Domestic Policy Council, Bruce Reed Subject Files, box 108, folder 1.

8. *Congressional Quarterly Almanac*, 103rd Cong., 1st sess., 1993, vol. 49, 706–709; Henry Cisneros to Mack McLarty et al., memorandum, February 1, 1993; Walters, "Not a Local Hero Anymore," 31–32.

9. Paul Dimond, Sheryll Cashin, and Paul Weinstein to Working Group on Enterprise Zones, memorandum, March 3, 1993, Domestic Policy Council, Bruce Reed Subject Files, box 108, folder 11; *Congressional Quarterly Almanac*, 103rd Cong., 1st sess., 1993, vol. 49, 422; David Rusk, *Inside Game, Outside Game: Winning Strategies for Saving Urban America* (Washington, D.C.: Brookings Institution Press, 1999), 264.

10. Bruce Reed and Gene Sperling to the President, memorandum, April 19, 1993, Clinton Administration History Project, NEC, box 43, folder 9, William J. Clinton Presidential Library; *Congressional Quarterly Almanac*, 103rd Cong., 1st sess., 1993, vol. 49, 422; Bruce Reed and Gene Sperling to the President, June 9, 1993, Domestic Policy Council, Bruce Reed Subject Files, box 105, folder 12.

11. *Congressional Quarterly Almanac*, 103rd Cong., 1st sess., 1993, vol. 49, 422 (first quotation); Bruce Reed to the President, memorandum, September 13, 1993, Domestic Policy Council, Bruce Reed Subject Files, box 108, folder 1 (second quotation); Bill Clinton to the Vice President et al., memorandum, September 9, 1993, Clinton Administration History Project, OVP, box 60, folder 11; *Public Papers of the*

Presidents: William J. Clinton, 1993 (Washington, D.C.: Government Printing Office, 1994), 2:1356–1357.

12. Mollenkopf, "Urban Policy at the Crossroads," 479–480; Alice O'Connor, "Swimming against the Tide: A Brief History of Federal Policy in Poor Communities," in *Urban Problems and Community Development*, ed. Ronald F. Ferguson and William T. Dickens (Washington, D.C.: Brookings Institution Press, 1999), 116–117.

13. Nicholas Lemann, "The Myth of Community Development," *New York Times Magazine*, January 9, 1994, 28.

14. Todd Stern to the President, May 27, 1994, Clinton Administration History Project, NEC, box 43, folder 10; NEC-DPC Principals to the President and the Vice President, memorandum, April 14, 1995, Domestic Policy Council, Carol Rasco Subject Files, box 12, folder 2; Mollenkopf, "Urban Policy at the Crossroads," 480–482. Also see Marilyn Gittell, Kathe Newman, Janice Brockmeyer, and Robert Lindsay, "Expanding Civic Opportunity: Urban Empowerment Zones," *Urban Affairs Review* 33 (March 1998): 530–558.

15. James Bovard, "Suburban Guerilla," *American Spectator* 27 (September 1994): 26–32; Llewellyn H. Rockwell Jr., "The Ghost of Gautreaux," *National Review* 46 (March 7, 1994): 57; Mollenkopf, "Urban Policy at the Crossroads," 478; Charles M. Lamb, *Housing Segregation in Suburban America since 1960* (Cambridge: Cambridge University Press, 2005), 190–193.

16. Rockwell, "The Ghost of Gautreaux," 57; Bovard, "Suburban Guerilla," 26; *Wall Street Journal*, August 4, 1994 (first quotation); *New York Times*, March 28, 1995 (second, third, and fourth quotations); Dreier, Mollenkopf, and Swanstrom, *Place Matters*, 145; Lamb, *Housing Segregation in Suburban America since 1960*, 193–195. Also see John Goering and Judith D. Feins, eds., *Choosing a Better Life: Evaluating the Moving to Opportunity Social Experiment* (Washington, D.C.: Urban Institute, 2003); and Margaret Pugh, *Barriers to Work: The Spatial Divide between Jobs and Welfare Recipients in Metropolitan Areas* (Washington, D.C.: Brookings Institution Center for Urban and Metropolitan Policy, 1998).

17. Fulton, "HUDdling with Henry Cisneros," 18 (quotation); Henry G. Cisneros, ed., *Interwoven Destinies: Cities and the Nation* (New York: W. W. Norton, 1993), 17–29; Henry G. Cisneros to President Bill Clinton, memorandum, August 9, 1995, Domestic Policy Council, Bruce Reed Subject File, box 128, folder 6; Dreier, Mollenkopf, and Swanstrom, *Place Matters*, 146.

18. Henry G. Cisneros, "Legacy for a Reinvented HUD: Charting a New Course in Changing and Demanding Times," *Cityscape* 1 (September 1995): 151; Mollenkopf, "Urban Policy at the Crossroads," 484–485; Malcolm Bush and Daniel Immergluck, "Research, Advocacy, and Community Reinvestment," in *Organizing Access to Capital: Advocacy and the Democratization of Financial Institutions*, ed. Gregory D. Squires (Philadelphia: Temple University Press, 2003), 159–162; Dreier, Mollenkopf, and Swanstrom, *Place Matters*, 144–145. Also see Mara S. Sidney, *Unfair Housing: How National Policy Shapes Community Action* (Lawrence: University Press of Kansas, 2003); Peter Dreier, "The Future of Community Reinvestment: Challenges and Opportunities," *Journal of the American Planning Association*

69 (August 2003): 341–353; and Gregory D. Squires, "Introduction: The Rough Road to Reinvestment," in Squires, *Organizing Access to Capital*, 1–26.

19. Henry G. Cisneros to President Bill Clinton, November 24, 1993, Clinton Administration History Project, NEC, box 43, folder 9.

20. Carol H. Rasco, Bob Rubin, and Jack Quinn to Leon Panetta, memorandum, July 18, 1994, Clinton Administration History Project, NEC, box 43, folder 11; Christopher Edley Jr. to Carol Rasco, Robert Rubin, and Jack Quinn, memorandum, August 11, 1994, Domestic Policy Council, Carol Rasco Meetings, Travels, Events, box 58, folder 5; "Urban Policy Options," October 22, 1994, Domestic Policy Council, Bruce Reed Subject Files, box 128, folder 5 (quotation).

21. *Congressional Quarterly Almanac*, 103rd Cong., 2nd sess., 1994, vol. 50 (Washington, D.C.: Congressional Quarterly Service, 1995), 408–409; William H. Chafe, *The Unfinished Journey: America since World War II*, 5th ed. (New York: Oxford University Press, 2003), 503–505; Patterson, *Restless Giant*, 341–342; "Statement by the United States Conference of Mayors on the President's Welfare Reform Proposals," June 14, 1994, Domestic Policy Council, Bruce Reed Subject Files, box 118, folder 10.

22. *Congressional Quarterly Almanac*, 103rd Cong., 2nd sess., 1994, vol. 50, 273–294.

23. Ibid.; Walters, "Not a Local Hero Anymore," 31 (quotation).

24. Chafe, *The Unfinished Journey*, 503–504; Patterson, *Restless Giant*, 344 (quotation).

25. *Public Papers of the Presidents: William J. Clinton, 1995* (Washington, D.C.: Government Printing Office, 1996), 2:1896–1899; Patterson, *Restless Giant*, 371–372; Mollenkopf, "Urban Policy at the Crossroads," 490 (quotation).

26. Dennis R. Judd and Todd Swanstrom, *City Politics: Private Power and Public Policy* (New York: Longman, 1998), 245 (quotations); *Congressional Quarterly Almanac*, 104th Cong., 1st sess., 1995, vol. 51 (Washington, D.C.: Congressional Quarterly Service, 1996), 8–13; Mollenkopf, "Urban Policy at the Crossroads," 492; Rachel G. Bratt, "Housing for Very Low-Income Households: The Record of President Clinton, 1993–2000," *Housing Studies* 18 (July 2003): 624; Dreier, Mollenkopf, and Swanstrom, *Place Matters*, 141–142.

27. Bratt, "Housing for Very Low-Income Households," 624.

28. Henry Cisneros to Robert Rubin, December 5, 1994, Domestic Policy Council, Bruce Reed Subject Files, box 114, folder 8; Cisneros, "Legacy for a Reinvented HUD," 145–152; Mollenkopf, "Urban Policy at the Crossroads," 490–491; Judd and Swanstrom, *City Politics*, 245–246.

29. Henry Cisneros to Robert Rubin, December 5, 1994; Mollenkopf, "Urban Policy at the Crossroads," 491; Cisneros, "Legacy for a Reinvented HUD," 145; Bratt, "Housing for Very Low-Income Households," 624 (quotation).

30. Judd and Swanstrom, *City Politics*, 246; Mollenkopf, "Urban Policy at the Crossroads," 491; Cisneros, "Legacy for a Reinvented HUD," 151 (quotation).

31. Henry G. Cisneros to President Bill Clinton, memorandum, August 9, 1995, Domestic Policy Council, Bruce Reed Subject Files, box 128, folder 6; "Teleconference with U.S. Conference of Mayors," June 20, 1995, Domestic Policy Council, Bruce Reed

Subject Files, box 118, folder 10; Yvonne Scruggs, "HUD's Stewardship of National Urban Policy: A Retrospective View," *Cityscape* 1 (September 1995): 58–59.

32. NEC-DPC Principals to the President and the Vice President, April 14, 1995; "Teleconference with U.S. Conference of Mayors," June 20, 1995 (quotations); Laura Tyson, Gene Sperling, and Paul Dimond to the President, memorandum, February 12, 1996, Clinton Administration History project, NEC—Empowerment Zones, box 43, folder 11.

33. *Public Papers of the Presidents: William J. Clinton*, 1996 (Washington, D.C.: Government Printing Office, 1998), 2:79 (first quotation); Baer, *Reinventing Democrats*, 1; Dreier, Mollenkopf, and Swanstrom, *Place Matters*, 143 (second quotation); *Congressional Quarterly Almanac*, 104th Cong., 2nd sess., 1996, vol. 52 (Washington, D.C.: Congressional Quarterly Service, 1997), 6–23 (third quotation).

34. *Public Papers of the Presidents: William J. Clinton*, 1996, 2:1325–1328; George Stephanopoulos, *All Too Human: A Political Education* (Boston: Little, Brown, 1999), 420; Patterson, *Restless Giant*, 374–376.

35. *Congressional Quarterly Almanac*, 104th Cong., 2nd sess., 1996, vol. 52, 6–24 (first, second, and third quotations); Patterson, *Restless Giant*, 375 (fourth quotation).

36. *Public Papers of the Presidents: William J. Clinton, 1996*, 2:1328.

37. *Congressional Quarterly Almanac*, 104th Cong., 2nd sess., 1996, vol. 52, 7–21; "House Bill Advances Key Clinton Public Housing Reforms but Cisneros Says 'Harmful Provisions Must Be Dropped,'" News Release, May 8, 1996, Clinton Administrative History Project, HUD, box 31, folder 3.

38. Jason DeParle, "Slamming the Door: The Year That Housing Died," *New York Times Magazine*, October 20, 1966; Dreier, Mollenkopf, and Swanstrom, *Place Matters*, 145; *Congressional Quarterly Almanac*, 104th Cong., 2nd sess., 1996, vol. 52, 10–91; *Public Papers of the Presidents: William J. Clinton, 1996*, 2:1676–1678; Judd and Swanstrom, *City Politics*, 247.

39. Bratt, "Housing for the Very Low-Income Households," 625.

40. *Congressional Quarterly Almanac*, 105th Cong., 1st sess., 1997, vol. 53 (Washington, D.C.: Congressional Quarterly Service, 1998), 7–11 (quotations); Jesse Goldstein, "These Dems Want to Run New York. We Want to Know More: What Andrew Cuomo's HUD History Tells the City," *City Limits* 27 (September 1, 2002): 16.

41. *Congressional Quarterly Almanac*, 105th Cong., 1st sess., 1997, vol. 53, 7–12.

42. *Congressional Quarterly Almanac*, 105th Cong., 2nd sess., 1998, vol. 54 (Washington, D.C.: Congressional Quarterly Service, 1999), 20–14.

43. "HUD's New Role in Building New Markets," p. 102, Clinton Administrative History Project, HUD, box 31, folder 1 (first quotation); *Congressional Quarterly Almanac*, 106th Cong., 2nd sess., 2000, vol. 56 (Washington, D.C.: Congressional Quarterly Service, 2001), 17–11 (second quotation); *New York Times*, November 5, 1999; Dreier, Mollenkopf, and Swanstrom, *Place Matters*, 144.

44. *Congressional Quarterly Almanac*, 106th Cong., 2nd sess., 2000, vol. 56, 17–15; "HUD's New Role in Building New Markets," 102–106.

45. Bruce Reed to the President, memorandum, November 29, 2000, Clinton Administration History Project, Domestic Policy Council—Documentary Annex II, box

17, folder 5 (quotation); *New York Times*, November 26, 2000; Dreier, Mollenkopf, and Swanstrom, *Place Matters*, 142.

46. U.S. Department of Housing and Urban Development, *The State of the Cities, 2000: Megaforces Shaping the Future of the Nation's Cities* (Washington, D.C.: U.S. Department of Housing and Urban Development, 2000), v; Bratt, "Housing for Very Low-Income Households," 623–627; Dreier, Mollenkopf, and Swanstrom, *Place Matters*, 142; *New York Times*, December 26, 2000 (quotations).

47. Mollenkopf, "Urban Policy at the Crossroads," 493–494.

48. U.S. Department of Housing and Urban Development, *The State of the Cities, 2000*, 93; *Public Papers of the Presidents: William J. Clinton, 2000* (Washington, D.C.: Government Printing Office, 2002), 3:2778–2779; Bratt, "Housing for Very Low-Income Households," 614, 624–625; Dreier, Mollenkopf, and Swanstrom, *Place Matters*, 145; Willem van Vliet, ed., *The Encyclopedia of Housing* (Thousand Oaks, Calif.: Sage Publications, 1998), 344–345. Also see Henry G. Cisneros and Lora Engdahl, eds., *From Despair to Hope: HOPE VI and the New Promise of Public Housing in America's Cities* (Washington, D.C.: Brookings Institution Press, 2009).

49. *Congressional Quarterly Almanac*, 103rd Cong., 1st sess., 1993, vol. 49 (Washington, D.C.: Congressional Quarterly Service, 1994), 663; *Congressional Quarterly Almanac*, 103rd Cong., 2nd sess., 1994, vol. 50 (Washington, D.C.: Congressional Quarterly Service, 1995), 530 (quotation); *Congressional Quarterly Almanac*, 104th Cong., 1st sess., 1995, vol. 51. (Washington, D.C.: Congressional Quarterly Service, 1996), 2–19, 11–69; *New York Times*, May 5, 1999.

50. *Congressional Quarterly Almanac*, 104th Cong., 1st sess., 1995, vol. 51, 11–69; Dreier, Mollenkopf, and Swanstrom, *Place Matters*, 139; Bratt, "Housing for Very Low-Income Households," 622–623; *New York Times*, March 5, 1998; *Congressional Quarterly Almanac*, 105th Cong., 2nd sess., 1998, vol. 54 (Washington, D.C.: Congressional Quarterly Service, 1999), 24–27. Consult the volumes of the *Congressional Quarterly Almanac* for mass transit allocations in the 103rd, 104th, 105th, and 106th Congresses.

51. Paul G. Lewis and Eric McGhee, "The Local Roots of Federal Policy Change: Transportation in the 1990s," *Polity* 34 (Winter 2001): 205–229; *Congressional Quarterly Almanac*, 105th Cong., 2nd sess., 1998, vol. 54, 24–14 (first quotation), 24–26 (second quotation).

52. John Kincaid, "De Facto Devolution and Urban Defunding: The Priority of Persons Over Places," *Journal of Urban Affairs* 21 (Summer 1999): 138 (quotation). Also see Peter Eisinger, "City Politics in an Era of Federal Devolution," *Urban Affairs Review* 33 (January 1998): 308–325.

CHAPTER 11. THE FATE OF CITIES

1. William K. Tabb, "The Failures of National Urban Policy," in *Marxism and the Metropolis: New Perspectives in Urban Political Economy*, ed. William K. Tabb and Larry Sawers (New York: Oxford University Press, 1984), 255–256.

2. *United States Statutes at Large*, 81st Cong., 1st sess., 1949, 63, pt. 1, 413 (quotation); Mara S. Sidney, *Unfair Housing: How National Policy Shapes Community Action* (Lawrence: University Press of Kansas, 2003), 32–33. The creation of this federal-city partnership is best explicated in Mark I. Gelfand, *A Nation of Cities: The Federal Government and Urban America, 1933–1965* (New York: Oxford University Press, 1975).

3. Michael Peter Smith, *City, State, and Market: The Political Economy of Urban Society* (New York: Basil Blackwell, 1988), 54; William K. Tabb, "The Failures of National Urban Policy," 257 (quotation); Rachel G. Bratt and W. Dennis Keating, "Federal Housing Policy and HUD: Past Problems and Future Prospects of a Beleaguered Bureaucracy," *Urban Affairs Quarterly* 29 (September 1993), 21; Royce Hanson, *The Evolution of National Urban Policy, 1970–1980: Lessons from the Past* (Washington, D.C.: National Academy Press, 1982), 51.

4. Raymond A. Mohl, "The Transformation of Urban America since the Second World War," in *Essays on Sunbelt Cities and Recent Urban America*, ed. Robert B. Fairbanks and Kathleen Underwood (College Station: Texas A&M University Press, 1990), 22–23; Bratt and Keating, "Federal Housing Policy and HUD," 9–11; Kent W. Colton, *Housing in the Twenty-first Century: Achieving Common Ground* (Cambridge: Harvard University Press, 2003), 220, 242 .

5. Bratt and Keating, "Federal Housing Policy and HUD," 14.

6. *Public Papers of the Presidents: William J. Clinton, 1996* (Washington, D.C.: Government Printing Office, 1998), 2:79 (first quotation); Peter Dreier, John Mollenkopf, and Todd Swanstrom, *Place Matters: Metropolitics for the Twenty-first Century*, 2nd rev. ed. (Lawrence: University Press of Kansas, 2004), 143 (second quotation); John Kincaid, "De Facto Devolution and Urban Defunding: The Priority of Persons Over Places," *Journal of Urban Affairs* 21 (Summer 1999): 140.

7. Robert Wood and Beverly M. Klimkowsky, "HUD in the Nineties: Doubt-Ability and Do-Ability," in *The Future of National Urban Policy*, ed. Marshall Kaplan and Franklin James (Durham: Duke University Press, 1990), 253; Gelfand, *A Nation of Cities*, 389 (quotation). Neil S. Mayer notes HUD's successes as well as its failures in "HUD's First 30 Years: Big Steps Down a Longer Road," *Cityscape* 1 (September 1995), 1–28.

8. Wood and Klimkowsky, "HUD in the Nineties," 266.

9. Ibid., 261–262. Also see Emmette S. Redford and Marlan Blissett, *Organizing the Executive Branch: The Johnson Presidency* (Chicago: University of Chicago Press, 1981), chap. 2.

10. M. Carter McFarland, *Federal Government and Urban Problems: HUD: Successes, Failures, and the Fate of Our Cities* (Boulder: Westview Press, 1978), 20–21; Wood and Klimkowsky, "HUD in the Nineties," 258 (quotation).

11. Suzanne Farkas, *Urban Lobbying* (New York: New York University Press, 1971), 112 (quotation).

12. Oral History Interview with Robert C. Weaver, December 19, 1985, 30, John F. Kennedy Presidential Library, Boston; Thomas E. Cronin, *The State of the Presidency* (Boston: Little, Brown, 1980), 276.

13. David C. Schwartz, Richard C. Ferlauto, and Daniel N. Hoffman, *A New Housing Policy for America* (Philadelphia: Temple University Press, 1988), 47–51; Sidney, *Unfair Housing*, 58; Wood and Klimkowsky, "HUD in the Nineties," 266 (quotation).

14. Alice O'Connor, "Swimming against the Tide: A Brief History of Federal Policy in Poor Communities," in *Urban Problems and Community Development*, ed. Ronald F. Ferguson and William T. Dickens (Washington, D.C.: Brookings Institution Press, 1999), 77 (quotation); Christopher Howard, *The Hidden Welfare State: Tax Expenditures and Social Policy in the United States* (Princeton: Princeton University Press, 1997), 27–28; Michael Peter Smith, *City, State, and Market*, 18. Housing analyst Hilary Botein argues that the creative methods of financing middle-income housing developed by New York Governor Nelson Rockefeller in the 1960s and early 1970s presaged the federal government's increasing reliance on public-private mechanisms. See Hilary Botein, "New York State Housing Policy in Postwar New York City: The Enduring Rockefeller Legacy," *Journal of Urban History* 35 (September 2009): 833–852.

INDEX